D1244555

POLITICAL
PHILOSOPHY

POLITICAL PHILOSOPHY

Theories

Thinkers

Concepts

SEYMOUR MARTIN LIPSET
Editor

CQ PRESS

A Division of Congressional Quarterly Inc.
Washington, D.C.

CQ Press
A Division of Congressional Quarterly Inc.
1414 22nd Street, N.W.
Washington, D.C. 20037

(202) 822-1475; (800) 638-1710

www.cqpress.com

∞ The paper used in this publication meets the minimum requirements of the American National Standard for Information Sciences—Permanence of Paper for Printed Library Materials, ANSI Z39.48-1992.

Printed and bound in the United States of America

05 04 03 02 01   5 4 3 2 1

Cover designed by Yasuyo Iguchi

Library of Congress Cataloging-in-Publication Data

Political philosophy : theories, thinkers, and concepts / Seymour Martin Lipset, editor.
        p.   cm.
    Includes bibliographical references and index.
    ISBN: 1-56802-688-9 (cloth)
        1. Political science—Philosophy. I. Lipset, Seymour Martin.

JA71.P6226 2001
320'.01—dc21   2001025787

Contents

II. POLITICAL PHILOSOPHERS

III. Philosophical Concepts and Issues

Contributors

ADAMS, WALTER
Trinity University (Texas)
Laissez-faire

ANTONIO, ROBERT J.
University of Kansas
Weber, Max

BARBER, BENJAMIN R.
Rutgers University
Democracy, Justifications for
Democracy, Participatory

BARTOL, FREDERICK
Yale University
Progressivism

BAUMAN, ZYGMUNT
University of Leeds
Marxism

BEINER, RONALD
University of Toronto
Religion, Civil
Democracy, Social

BENHABIB, SEYLA
Harvard University
Theory, Critical

BERRY, JEFFREY M.
Tufts University
Interest groups

BOLLEN, KENNETH A.
University of North Carolina at Chapel Hill
Democracy, Measures of

BROCK, JAMES W.
Miami University, Ohio
Laissez-faire

BUFACCHI, VITTORIO
University College, Cork, Ireland
Justice, Theories of

CANOVAN, MARGARET
University of Keele
Republicanism
Virtue, Civic

CHAI, MAY-LEE
University of Colorado at Boulder
Confucianism

CHAI, WINBERG
University of Wyoming
Confucianism

CLARK, TERRY NICHOLS
University of Chicago
Class

CONNELL, WILLIAM J.
Rutgers University
City-states, communes, and republics

COSER, LEWIS A.
State University of New York at Stony Brook
Communism

CUNNINGHAM, FRANK
University of Toronto
Socialism

DANIELS, WILLIAM J.
Rochester Institute of Technology
King, Martin Luther, Jr.

DANNHAUSER, WERNER J.
Michigan State University
Existentialism
Nietzsche, Friedrich

DAVIES, ANN
CQ Press, Washington, D.C.
Machiavelli, Niccolò

DAVIES, TONY
Reston, Virginia
Cleisthenes, Son of Megacles

DIAMOND, LARRY
Hoover Institute
Legitimacy

DI TELLA, TORCUATO S.
University of Buenos Aires
Populism

DREWRY, GAVIN
University of London
Bagehot, Walter

DUCH, RAYMOND M.
University of Houston
Theory, Rational choice

EISENSTADT, S. N.
Hebrew University
Civil society

EKEH, PETER P.
State University of New York at Buffalo
Theory, African

ELAZAR, DANIEL J.
*Bar-Ilan and Temple Universities, Jerusalem
    Center for Public Affairs*
Federalism

EMBERLEY, PETER C.
Carleton University
Montesquieu, Charles-Louis de Secondat,
    Baron de

FORTIN, ERNEST L.
Boston College
Natural law

FOX-GENOVESE, ELIZABETH
Emory University
Feminism

GERMINO, DANTE
University of Virginia
Democracy, Critiques of

GOLDBERG, ROBERT
St. John's College
Theory, Ancient

GRIMES, ALAN P.
Michigan State University
Madison, James

GROSSMAN, JOEL B.
University of Wisconsin at Madison
Majority rule, minority rights

HAMBURGER, JOSEPH
Yale University
Burke, Edmund
Mill, John Stuart

HICKOK, EUGENE W.
Secretary of Education, Pennsylvania
Bureaucracy

HICKS, ALEXANDER M.
Emory University
State growth and intervention

HIGLEY, JOHN
University of Texas at Austin
Theory, Elite
Elites, Political

HOLMES, STEPHEN
Princeton University
Constitutionalism

HORSTMANN, STACEY
Emory University
Feminism

ISHII, YONEO
Sophia University
Buddhism

KAUTZ, STEVEN
Michigan State University
Communitarianism

KORITANSKY, JOHN C.
Hiram College
Tocqueville, Alexis de

KRAYNAK, ROBERT P.
Colgate University
Hobbes, Thomas

LAKOFF, SANFORD
University of California at San Diego
Althusius, Johannes

LAND, HILARY
University of Bristol
Wollstonecraft, Mary

LEVIN, DANIEL M.
Ripon College
Majority rule, minority rights

LIJPHART, AREND
University of California at San Diego
Democracy, Multiethnic

LINZ, JUAN J.
Yale University
Authoritarianism

Fascism
Parliamentarism and presidentialism

LIPSET, SEYMOUR MARTIN
*George Mason University and
  Stanford University*
Legitimacy

LOEWENBERG, GERHARD
University of Iowa
Legislatures and parliaments

MELZER, ARTHUR M.
Michigan State University
Rousseau, Jean-Jacques

MENSKI, WERNER
University of London
Hinduism

MERKL, PETER H.
University of California at Santa Barbara
Popular sovereignty

MEYER, ALFRED G.
University of Michigan
Leninism

MEZEY, SUSAN GLUCK
Loyola University Chicago
Democracy, Women and

MILLER, DAVID
Oxford University
Anarchy

MOUFFE, CHANTAL
University of Westminster
Citizenship

NEAL, PATRICK
University of Vermont
Theory, Postwar Anglo-American

NEWELL, WALLER R.
Carleton University
Dictatorship

NICHOLS, JAMES H., JR.
Claremont McKenna College
Pragmatism

PANGLE, THOMAS L.
University of Toronto
Spinoza, Benedict de

PARRY, GERAINT
University of Manchester
Democracy, Types of

PLATTNER, MARC F.
Journal of Democracy, *Washington, D.C.*
Human rights

QUESTER, GEORGE H.
University of Maryland
Kant, Immanuel

REMPEL, MICHAEL
University of Chicago
Class

ROSANO, MICHAEL
University of Michigan at Dearborn
Obligation

ROSE, RICHARD
University of Strathclyde
Monarchy, Constitutional

ROSE-ACKERMAN, SUSAN
Yale University
Progressivism

ROSENBLUM, NANCY L.
Brown University
Liberalism

RUDERMAN, RICHARD S.
University of North Texas
Leadership

RUESCHEMEYER, DIETRICH
Brown University
Capitalism

SAWARD, MICHAEL
The Open University
Environmentalism

SAXONHOUSE, ARLENE W.
University of Michigan
Aristotle
Cicero, Marcus Tullius
Classical Greece and Rome
Plato

SCHEUERMAN, WILLIAM E.
University of Pittsburgh
Theory, Critical

SCHMITTER, PHILIPPE C.
Stanford University
Consolidation
Corporatism
Democratization

SCHWARTZ, NANCY L.
University of Illinois at Chicago
Egalitarianism

SCIGLIANO, ROBERT
Boston College
Representation

SHELL, SUSAN M.
Boston College
Hegel, Georg Wilhelm Friedrich

SIMMONS, A. JOHN
University of Virginia
Consent

SMITH, STEVEN B.
Yale University
Theory, Twentieth century European

STEINER, DAVID M.
Vanderbilt University
Postmodernism

TAMIR, YAEL
Tel-Aviv University
Nationalism

TARCOV, NATHAN
University of Chicago
Locke, John

THERBORN, GÖRAN
Göteborg University
War and civil conflict

TIBI, BASSAM
Georg-August-Universität ze Göttingen
Fundamentalism

VARSHNEY, ASHUTOSH
University of Notre Dame
Gandhi, Mohandas Karamchand

VERNON, RICHARD
University of Western Ontario
Contractarianism

WEINBERGER, JERRY
Michigan State University
Conservatism

WOLFF, JONATHAN
University College, London
Autonomy

Preface

Political philosophy provides us with a valuable starting point on our journey to understanding the human condition. Intellectually, political philosophy is to a large extent a critical analysis of history intertwined with ideas about creating systems of government. How we think about political systems and our diverse roles within them is a reflection of our humanity. In practical terms, political philosophy, like no other analytical tool, forces us to challenge our political assumptions and goals. For example, some regard the very notion of political systems with apathy or even disdain. Others take the view that unpredictable and, on occasion, less than benign political behavior is the inevitable consequence of the interaction of individuals struggling to solve social problems. Still others strive to create an ideal community in which ideas flourish, discourse is respected, and decisions are embraced by all. Finally, some seek to create political systems in which avarice is both a means and an end. With infinite, subtle points along this continuum, one thing remains steadfast: as we consider these issues, we benefit from philosophers who, for thousands of years, have grappled with the grand questions and have studied virtually every conceivable form of government. But with thousands of years of political philosophy to mine and a vast array of ideas to consider, where realistically do we begin to address the most fundamental issues?

Political Philosophy: Theories, Thinkers, and Concepts is a collection of one hundred essays written by eminent international scholars. The essays provide an introductory analysis of ancient, modern, and contemporary philosophers and philosophies. The book is divided into three sections.

Section I explains major Western and non-Western philosophies. The forty essays in this section explore the *-isms* of political philosophy. For example, Yoneo Ishii writes about Buddhism, Dietrich Rueschemeyer about capitalism, Nancy L. Schwartz about egalitarianism, and Yael Tamir about nationalism. These essays, impressive in breadth, provide the information prerequisite to an understanding of all the major political theories.

Section II offers fundamental intellectual and biographical information about twenty-six major philosophers. Ashutosh Varshney contributes an essay about Gandhi and Nathan Tarcov one about Locke, while Arthur M. Melzer writes on Rousseau and Hilary Land on Wollstonecraft. Other essays discuss what it means to be a Hobbesian or a Machiavellian or a student of Aristotelian or Hegelian philosophy.

Section III explores philosophical ideas. Thirty-four essays define a wide range of concepts that influence political systems. Eugene W. Hickok examines bureaucracy; Chantal Mouffe, citizenship; Richard S. Ruderman, leadership; and Peter H. Merkl, popular sovereignty. Understanding these terms is essential to the study of political philosophy.

Several features of the book facilitate a better understanding of political philosophy. *See also* references are useful tools accompanying the essays. They lead readers to related essays in the book and give a more rounded perspective of topics. Each essay is supplemented with bibliographic entries that identify sources to provide researchers with greater depth and detail. Finally, a comprehensive index identifies terms and philosophers that may not otherwise be evident from the titles of individual essays.

SEYMOUR MARTIN LIPSET

I. POLITICAL PHILOSOPHIES

✦ Authoritarianism

A political corporatism system in which a leader or a small group exercises power without formal limits. Authoritarian rule does not permit two of the defining elements of democracy: free competition for political office and free participation of citizens in politics.

In authoritarian regimes, those in power are not accountable at regular intervals to an electorate or to representative bodies, although they might be responsive to certain interest groups. Some authoritarian rulers claim power for life; some are selected by the armed forces or the monarch. In authoritarian regimes, there is no freedom (or very limited freedom) to create political parties, and existing parties are usually dissolved or suspended. The regimes vary in the degree of institutionalization. Some are only temporary governments closer to the traditional concept of dictatorship as government for a crisis.

Characteristics of Authoritarian Regimes

Authoritarian regimes do not institutionalize a legal opposition, but—unlike totalitarian regimes—they do permit different forms of opposition. Some face opposition within the regime from those who have different goals—for example, the reestablishment of a monarchy. Others have an illegal, but tolerated and visible, opposition. In communist Poland the opposition of the Catholic Church and groups related to it, the illegal but visible Solidarity trade union, and the Committee for the Defense of Workers were part of political life. The existence of those various forms of opposition has made transitions to democracy less difficult and less traumatic than they might otherwise have been.

Authoritarian regimes limit the freedoms of their citizens and engage in political repression of their opponents. Often, "political" crimes are subject to military justice, which does not provide the same protection of the rights of the accused as civil courts and which can impose heavier penalties. Even when applied by civil courts, authoritarian codes of law define as criminal actions that are legal in liberal democracies: political propaganda, membership in parties, and participation in strikes. The police in authoritarian regimes have few limits on their power, and mistreatment and torture are not uncommon. Some regimes have engaged in repression that even their own legislation considers illegal—for example, "disappearances," secret detention centers, torture, and assassination.

In spite of the horrors of repression by some authoritarian regimes, however, they have not been comparable to the state terror of totalitarian regimes like the Soviet Union, particularly under Joseph Stalin, or the mass murder by the Nazis. But all authoritarian regimes violate basic human rights to varying degrees and do not recognize their citizens' political rights. Repression by authoritarian regimes has contributed to the international condemnation of their actions and to their loss of legitimacy. Democracies that succeed such regimes face a difficult legacy of official investigation of their crimes and restitution to their victims, particularly when the culprits are military officers claiming to have acted under orders or counting on the solidarity of their fellow officers.

Military Regimes

Many twentieth-century authoritarian regimes have been headed by military officers: Mustafa Kemal Atatürk in Turkey (1923–1938), Francisco Franco in Spain (1936–1975), Philippe Pétain in France (1940–1944), Juan Domingo Perón in Argentina (1946–1955, a period that includes his elected presidency), Gamal Abdel Nasser in Egypt (1956–1970), Lázaro Cárdenas in Mexico (1934–1940), Augusto Pinochet in Chile (1973–1990). But to distinguish between military and nonmilitary regimes is not adequate because the institutions and politics of military regimes themselves can be very different. Some civilian-led regimes might have more in common with some military regimes—for example, Portugal under António de Oliveira Salazar (1932–1968), Austria under Engelbert Dollfuss (1933–1934) and Kurt von Schuschnigg (1934–1938), and Brazil under Getúlio Vargas (1937–1945).

A more useful distinction is between a strictly military regime and a nonhierarchical military regime. In the first type, important decisions are made collectively by the top institutional leadership of the armed forces—the hierarchical military—with only limited participation by civilians and without the creation of a single party as a way to recruit elites. Examples are Argentina (1966–1973), Peru (1968–1980), and Uruguay from the mid-1970s to 1985. In the second type, a group of officers has also taken power, but they do not necessarily consider themselves a permanent government (even though some last a long time), nor are they likely to develop institutionally. An example here is the Greek colonels (1967–1974). Such regimes tend to end when the armed forces consider it preferable to extricate themselves from power and return to the barracks, imposing only some conditions of immunity and guarantees for their corporate interests. In the case of nonhierarchical military regimes, other officers may question the rulers' continuity in office.

Modern Authoritarian Regimes

Authoritarian rule has dominated the politics of most of the world for a large part of the twentieth century, in spite of the waves of democratization in the first two decades and in the aftermath of World War II. A number of countries (such as the United Kingdom and the Scandinavian and Benelux monarchies) underwent a slow but continuous process of democratization starting from the constitutional liberal states of the nineteenth century. But in southern and eastern Europe, the Balkans, Latin America, and Japan, that process was interrupted in the 1920s and 1930s by dictatorships and a variety of authoritarian regimes. In some countries, like Yugoslavia, the conflicts between nationalities contributed much to the turn to authoritarian regimes.

In other cases, like Iran and Turkey, nontraditional authoritarian rule was linked with efforts at social and cultural modernization. Turkey successfully made the transition to democracy in

1947. But more often the revolutionary threat of communism, ethnic and cultural fragmentation, economic difficulties, and the threat of fascism led to authoritarian rule in newly independent states and democracies, such as Poland, Latvia, Lithuania, and Estonia.

Other Nondemocratic Regimes

Distinguishing sultanistic, totalitarian, and post-totalitarian regimes from authoritarian regimes aids in understanding the complex range of nondemocratic politics. One type of rule that is sometimes considered authoritarian can also be called neopatrimonial, despotic, or sultanistic, to use a term derived from Max Weber's discussion of a type of patrimonial regime.

Sultanistic rule is motivated largely by personal goals, rather than by pursuit of a particular concept of society or defense of the interests of a class or ethnic group. The pursuit of power and wealth for themselves or their family and friends, rather than collective goals, distinguishes despots like Rafael Trujillo in the Dominican Republic (1930–1961), the Somoza dynasty in Nicaragua (1937–1979, with interruption), Jean-Claude "Baby Doc" Duvalier in Haiti (1971–1986), even Ferdinand Marcos in the Philippines (1965–1986), and—to a large extent—Mohammad Reza Pahlavi, shah of Iran (1941–1979) from dictators like Miklós Horthy in Hungary (1920–1944), Salazar in Portugal, Dollfuss and Schuschnigg in Austria, Franco in Spain, and the Brazilian military (1964–1985).

Totalitarian political systems differ from authoritarian regimes in several ways. In authoritarian regimes there is a monistic (single) but not monolithic center of power, and whatever pluralism of institutions or groups exists derives its legitimacy from that center. In totalitarian regimes there is an exclusive, autonomous, and more or less intellectually elaborate ideology identified with the ruling group or leader and the party serving the leaders. The ruling group uses this ideology as a basis for policies or manipulates it to legitimize them. The ideology goes beyond the boundaries of legitimate political action to provide some ultimate meaning, sense of historical purpose, and interpretation of social reality. Citizens' participation in and active mobilization for political and collective social tasks are encouraged, demanded, rewarded, and channeled through a single party and its secondary groups. The passive obedience and apathy characteristic of many authoritarian regimes are considered undesirable by totalitarian rulers.

Some have included in the broad category of authoritarian rule the communist regimes in Eastern Europe after Stalin, which lost or modified their totalitarian characteristics after a more or less extended period of totalitarian rule. These post-totalitarian regimes cannot be understood without reference to their totalitarian past. Such regimes are characterized by both positive changes (liberalization) and by ossification—a degeneration of the totalitarian structures and ideology after losing their "utopian" and "idealist" components. Founders of regimes did not initially intend to create post-totalitarian regimes in the way that some founders chose to set up authoritarian regimes. Instead, post-totalitarian regimes are the result of changes in totalitarian systems along a continuum, from early post-totalitarianism to mature post-totalitarianism.

In post-totalitarian regimes, there is considerably more pluralism than in totalitarian regimes. This is due to the greater autonomy of institutions, bureaucracies, and public enterprises from the party, which retains in principle its totalitarian leading function. There is also an emerging "parallel" culture in civil society. However, that pluralism is different in degree and kind from authoritarian regimes because it appears after the "flattening" of the social landscape in the preceding totalitarian period. The leadership in such regimes is still largely recruited from the party, but some leaders come from the bureaucracy and the technocratic apparatus, and political or ideological loyalty becomes less important. Leaders are often aging, and there may be a collective leadership that tends to limit the former power of a totalitarian ruler. "Socialist legality" replaces the arbitrary use of power and state terrors. There is a growing skepticism and disregard for the official ideology, whose utopian and motivating value has been lost. With that loss, the regime is less able to mobilize its cadres and organizations, and there is a growing privatization of the people.

Corporatist Regimes

Authoritarian regimes, as distinct from totalitarian regimes, generally have not had a distinctive and intellectually elaborate ideological model of how to institutionalize politics. One exception is "organic statism"—also called "state corporatism" or "organic democracy"—as contrasted with the "inorganic democracy" of political parties and representation of the citizens. Corporatism is a system of representing interest groups in which each group is authorized by the state and given the sole right to represent citizens in its category. In exchange for such right, groups must accept certain state control over the selection of leaders and the expression of political views.

Corporatists reject the individualistic assumptions of liberal democracy and seek to provide an institutional channel for the representation of the heterogeneous interests in modern or modernizing societies, while rejecting class conflict. There have been a variety of theoretical-ideological formulations of corporatism and attempts to implement them through political institutions.

The romantic-conservative idealization of the Middle Ages; the antiliberal, anticapitalist, antistatist, and antisocialist encyclicals of the Roman Catholic Church; the syndicalist current in the non-Marxist labor movement, which rejected parties and assigned to trade unions the revolutionary struggle and organization of society; even some liberal thought emphasizing the role of professional associations—all contributed to corporatist thought.

Those ideas were used in the 1920s and 1930s by the fascists, particularly in Italy under Benito Mussolini, and the authoritarians in Austria, Portugal, and Spain to create political institutions. Examples of corporatist regimes are Spain under Franco, Portugal under Salazar, Brazil under Vargas, Mexico under Cárdenas, and Argentina under Perón.

Corporative representation can disenfranchise the masses by allocating representation disproportionately to certain professions, the universities, employers, or—in the case of the Soviets—industrial workers. Elections for corporative representatives are usually organized as a multitier process from the workplace to the national level.

The assumption that such primary units share interests, rather than being internally divided, has not corresponded to reality. Nor has the related idea of "self-management" (democratic decision making, particularly in the workplace)—introduced by the dissident Communist Josip Broz Tito in Yugoslavia in the post–World War II years and adapted in Algeria, Peru, and other authoritarian regimes—ever turned into a promising new form of or road to democracy. In addition, such corporative representation cannot address major issues in society, such as religious policy, cultural conflicts, and foreign policy, as political parties can. Parties (particularly major parties) are organized to represent voters on a wide range of such issues, not on specific interests. Voters generally support them for their positions on more than one issue.

The allocation of seats in corporative legislative chambers can be made only by those in power. Authoritarian regimes therefore found corporatism a convenient form of pseudodemocracy. But since no authoritarian government has accepted the principle that it could be dismissed by a vote of no confidence in a corporative chamber, such chambers at most have had an advisory function.

Tutelary Democracies

The end of Western colonial rule in various parts of the world after World War II led to the creation of new states with democratic constitutions. After a first election, many of these became one-party states, which in turn often were overthrown by military coups that established authoritarian regimes. The regimes were initially characterized as tutelary democracies or modernizing oligarchies to highlight the continuing hope for democratization. Often inspired by the model of communist one-party rule, and strongly nationalistic, some regimes adopted an ideology labeled "African socialism" to indicate the goal of noncapitalist development. In reality, however, the single party was often a coalition of diverse groups, tribal leaders, notables, and leaders co-opted from other parties—what French-speaking Africans called *parti unifié* (unified party) rather than *parti unique* (single party). In other cases, the party had little presence beyond urban centers, without the mass membership and mobilizational characteristics of communist or fascist single parties.

A number of states in black Africa have adopted forms of highly personalized rule after a phase of single-party regimes. They range from various types of neopatrimonial or sultanistic regimes to tyrannies: Idi Amin in Uganda (1971–1979), Francisco Macías Nguema in Equatorial Guinea (1968–1979), Jean-Bédel Bokassa in the Central African Republic (1966–1979), and Sese Seko Mobutu in Zaire (1965–1997).

From Authoritarianism to Democracy

In all types of nondemocratic politics, it is important not to confuse democratization with liberalization, which entails greater legality; some freedom for voluntary associations, churches, and even trade unions; the freeing of political prisoners; greater freedom of the press; and the return of exiles. Although liberalization can facilitate democratization, democratization is often an unanticipated and unwelcome consequence rather than the intention of the rulers.

A transition to democracy requires authoritarian rulers to allow people to vote in free competitive elections and to be ready to give up power should the voters not support them. This does not necessarily mean that people identified with the former regime will be barred from competing in elections. Sometimes they win free elections, as has happened in Bulgaria, Poland, Hungary, and Lithuania in recent years.

See also Corporatism; Democracy, Critiques of; Democratization; Dictatorship; Fascism; Democracy, Types of.

JUAN J. LINZ

BIBLIOGRAPHY

Almond, Gabriel, and James S. Coleman, eds. *The Politics of Developing Areas.* Princeton: Princeton University Press, 1960.

Collier, David, ed. *The New Authoritarianism in Latin America.* Princeton: Princeton University Press, 1979.

Collier, Ruth Bevins, and David Collier. *Shaping the Political Arena*. Princeton: Princeton University Press, 1991.

Finer, S. E. *The Man on Horseback: The Role of the Military in Politics*. 2d ed. Boulder, Colo.: Westview Press; London: S. Pinter, 1988.

Hermet, G. "L'autoritarisme." In *Les régimes politiques contemporains*. Vol. 2 of *Traité de science politique*, edited by Madeleine Grawitz and Jean Leca. Paris: Presses Universitaires de France, 1985.

Huntington, Samuel P., and C. H. Moore, eds. *Authoritarian Politics in Modern Society*. New York: Basic Books, 1970.

Jackson, Robert H., and Carl G. Rosberg, Jr. *Personal Rule in Black Africa: Prince, Autocrat, Prophet, Tyrant*. Berkeley: University of California Press, 1982.

Janos, Andrew C. "The One-Party State and Social Mobilization: East Europe between the Wars." In *Authoritarian Politics in Modern Society*, edited by Samuel P. Huntington and C. H. Moore. New York: Basic Books, 1970.

Linz, Juan J. "An Authoritarian Regime: The Case of Spain." In *Mass Politics: Studies in Political Sociology*, edited by Erik Allardt and Stein Rokkan. New York: Free Press, 1970.

_____. "Totalitarian and Authoritarian Regimes." In *Micropolitical Theory*. Vol. 3 of *Handbook of Political Science*. Edited by Fred I. Greenstein and Nelson W. Polsby. Reading, Mass.: Addison-Wesley, 1975.

_____. *Totalitarian and Authoritarian Regimes*. Boulder, Colo.: Lynne Rienner, 2000.

O'Donnell, Guillermo. *Counterpoints: Selected Essays on Authoritarianism and Democratization*. Notre Dame, Ind.: University of Notre Dame Press, 1999.

_____. *Modernization and Bureaucratic Authoritarianism: Studies in South American Politics*. Berkeley: Institute of International Studies, University of California, Berkeley, 1973.

Perlmutter, Amos. *Modern Authoritarianism: A Comparative Institutional Analysis*. New Haven and London: Yale University Press, 1981.

Schmitter, Philippe C. "Still the Century of Corporatism?" In *Review of Politics* 36 (1974): 85–131.

Seton-Watson, Hugh. *Eastern Europe between the Wars, 1918–1941*. New York: Harper and Row, 1967.

✦ Buddhism

The religious system based upon the teaching of the historical Buddha, Siddhartha Gautama (c.563–c.483 b.c.). Buddhism originally developed in India but later spread over vast regions of Asia in various forms. It is an all-embracing term for a very diverse religious system. It includes the conservative Theravada Buddhism of Sri Lanka and Southeast Asia, the more liberal Mahayana Buddhism of East Asia, and the esoteric Tantric Buddhism of Tibet. Of these three the Theravada branch, which retains a portion of the original doctrine together with the early forms of its ecclesiastical institutions, is of special significance in the context of democracy.

Modern Political Influence

In its long history Theravada Buddhism has been deeply involved in the development and legitimation of political power in Sri Lanka, Burma (Myanmar), Thailand, Laos, and Cambodia. In the post–World War II history of the independent kingdoms of Laos and Cambodia, Buddhism was constitutionally made a state religion, while Sri Lanka and Burma experienced serious political crises over the legal issue of whether to grant Buddhism a privileged status as the state religion. During the early years of independence in Sri Lanka and Burma, this issue led to the assassination of political leaders and the collapse of governments.

In modern China the Chinese versions of Mahayana Buddhism—which are only one

component of the Chinese religious trio of Confucianism, Buddhism, and Daoism—seem to have
a limited role in the political arena, except perhaps
in political protest movements, like those of Vietnam when Vietnamese Buddhist monks set themselves on fire to protest the Vietnam War in the
1960s. The Mahayana Buddhist sects of Asia are
for the most part politically apathetic. One exception is the Sokagakkai, a lay Buddhist organization
of Japan that has a strong political orientation.
The Buddhism of Tibet, on the other hand, has
historically shown a strong political character; in
Tantric Buddhism a religious leader was tantamount to a political leader, as in the case of the
Dalai Lama.

In general, there has not been a close
historical relationship between Buddhism and
democratic government. Nonetheless, some
tenets of Buddhism tend to support popular constraints on authority. One such is the concept of
dhammaraja, which would constrain a king from
oppression; another is the concept of the "great
elect," which requires a monarch to keep worldly
order for the benefit of his subjects. The concept
of democracy has been called a secularized version of basic tenets of Christian theology. In
other words, the will of God is replaced in the
worldly arena by the omnipotence of the people
and legislators of a democratic polity. How does
Buddhism relate to this time-honored Western
concept of democracy?

The Buddhist Brotherhood

The original tenets of Buddhism had a strongly
elitist orientation. They were presented to disciplined monks in India to help them attain, by their
own effort, the ultimate goal of emancipation
from suffering. Buddhism presupposes neither a
god nor a savior in this spiritual quest; instead, salvation comes through self-emancipation, as is
clearly written in one of the verses of a sacred text

called the *Dhammapada:* "Only a man himself can
be the master of himself: who else from outside
could be his master?" In the present context, one
can say that this dictum clearly expresses respect
for the dignity of the individual human being, a
fundamental condition for democracy.

The social basis for the historical continuity of
Buddhism was, in its original form, a brotherhood
known as the *sangha*, a term originally referring to
an aristocratic clan-republic of northern India.
This brotherhood provided a center of spiritual
practice among Buddhist monks. Buddhism was
unique among the ancient Indian religions in that
Buddhist monks, rather than leading a wandering
life of solitary asceticism, usually joined the religious organization of the *sangha*. The *sangha* was
structured around a code of conduct called *vinaya*,
or "that which separates." The term aptly reflects
the monastic character of a religion whose core
members are "separated" in all respects from the
ordinary way of life. Members of the *sangha*
strictly followed the *vinaya*, the canonized precepts conducive to the final attainment of spiritual
emancipation, or *nirvana*.

The *sangha* in its original form was an
autonomous and democratic institution. Each
member of this self-governing body had a voice in
deciding on the group's adaptation of the *vinaya*
and was entitled to express his views on the daily
administration of the monastic community. Disputes within the *sangha* were settled according to
the *vinaya*. A set of rules for Buddhist monks,
which represents the core of the *vinaya*, lists Seven
Cases of Settlement of Litigation about Faults,
including "cancellation of litigation by the pronouncement of a majority." This practice resembles the principle of majority rule in Western
democratic decision making.

Members of the *sangha* are called *bhikkhu*, or
"one who begs for food." Traditionally, the monks
were economically unproductive and depended

for subsistence on the charity of householders. Such materially dependent communities found their most reliable supporters among Buddhist monarchs, who made vows to provide material as well as moral comfort to the monks. The relationship between the king and the *sangha*, however, was not one-sided but mutual: the king's support of the *sangha* helped to legitimize his rule. Any Buddhist king could enhance his political legitimacy by proclaiming himself a devoted "defender of the faith" and sustaining an otherwise declining community of monks.

Thailand and the Modern *Sangha*

Thailand affords the most significant example of how Buddhism has affected democratic development. The ancient *sangha* was loosely structured. Its organization had only such distinctions as senior and junior monk, fully ordained *bhikkhu* and novice, teacher and pupil. Modern communities generally are highly structured. A *sangha raja* or *sangha nayaka* ("king" or "lord" of the *sangha)* stands at the head, assisted by a council of elderly monks.

Within a decade after the constitutional revolution of 1932, the Thai *sangha* began to revise its administrative structure in imitation of the newly introduced secular democratic institutions. According to the *Sangha* Administration Act of 1941 of the kingdom of Thailand, the Thai *sangha* was reorganized upon the principle of separation of three powers, similar to the emerging constitutional form of the Thai government, which had replaced the absolute monarchy of the previous decade. The reorganized Thai *sangha* still had a *sangha raja* as its supreme head, but under him were set up the three institutions of the *Sangha* Assembly (legislative branch), the *Sangha* Cabinet (executive branch), and the *Sangha* Courts (judiciary branch). Forty-five members of the Assembly were elected propor-

tionately from among the two sects representing the Thai *sangha*. These sects were the large and traditional Mahanikai and the smaller but influential (thanks to its royal connection) Thammayut. Thus the whole administrative structure of the Thai *sangha* took on a tinge of democracy.

This democratic construct, however, was short-lived. Two decades later, during the highly centralized, despotic regime of Field Marshal Sarit Thanarat, the democratic *sangha* law was repealed. It was replaced with a law that reintroduced the traditional autocracy of the council of elders.

The Buddhist Polity

A democratic element of early Buddhism might be traced in its unique concept of an "elected king." This concept appears in some Buddhist scriptures, in which the image of an archaic king is depicted as the Mahasammata, or Great Elect, chosen by the people to maintain the worldly order. The Mahasammata was expected, according to scripture, to be angry when anger was right, to censure that which should rightly be censured, and to banish those who deserved to be banished. The Great Elect was said to receive a portion of the people's harvest for his meritorious service to the people who had elected him. A chronicle written in Pali states that some of the Sinhalese kings of Sri Lanka traced their descent from the Mahasammata.

One aspect of the traditional concept of Buddhist kingship is that a good Buddhist king must always behave as a protector of the *dhamma*, or the teachings of the historical Buddha that constitute social justice. When he is seen by his people to be properly performing his expected duty, he is praised as the *dhammaraja*, or "king of righteousness." In principle, the popular consent of his Buddhist subjects legitimizes the rule of a Buddhist king. As a corollary, it may be argued that popular consensus might even deprive a king of his claim to rule, if the king has been judged to be without *dhamma*. This can be seen in the case of King Taksin of Siam (1767–1782). Despite his admirable feat of freeing Siam from the occupation of the Burmese army, King Taksin was eventually put to death by his former comrade in war because of his cruel behavior, which was judged to be unjustifiable for a Buddhist king. One of the royal chronicles poses the question: If the king becomes dishonest and unrighteous, what do you do? The ministers' reply is that any king who behaves dishonestly should be punished as a traitor. This chronicle gives an example of popular participation in the political process of the Buddhist polity.

According to the *Dhammasattham*, or the Buddhist-influenced Law of Manu, once adopted in many parts of Southeast Asia, the ideal monarch steadfastly follows the ten kingly virtues, upholds the five common precepts (for the laity), and on holy days keeps the set of eight precepts. He lives in kindness and shows goodwill to all beings. He also upholds the four principles of justice: to assess the rightness or wrongness of any deed that is done to him, to uphold what is righteous and truthful, to acquire riches only through just means, and to maintain the prosperity of his state only through just means. In short, a Buddhist king is destined to be always under the moral pressure of his subjects. If the king is unjust, his subjects might someday take part in a mass uprising to oust him from his throne.

The traditional Buddhist concept of a political leader being obliged to follow *dhamma*, or "righteousness," seems to be a persistent theme in the political culture of modern Buddhist Southeast Asia. This is true both for a kingdom with a constitutional monarchy, such as Thailand, and for a republic, such as Burma (Myanmar), Laos, or Cambodia. Sometimes one hears how a govern-

ment of a Buddhist nation that is found to be corrupt comes under severe criticism from the populace (or the military) for its deviation from righteousness. Such logic was even followed by a Communist clandestine radio station in Thailand in the 1960s and 1970s, which accused the military regime in Bangkok of being unrighteous. The corrupt leaders, Thanom Kittikachorn and Prapas Charusathira, were eventually ousted in the wake of a student uprising in 1973.

Even democratically elected leaders are not immune to popular attack if they prove unable or unwilling to live up to the ideals of government according to righteousness. In 1991, when Chatchai Choonhavan's government in Thailand was found to be excessively corrupt, the Thai people gave tacit support to the so-called National Peacekeeping Council, which had staged a coup to overthrow the democratically elected cabinet on the pretext of its being a "parliamentary dictatorship." Similarly, the next year middle-class citizens of Bangkok revolted against the dictatorship of General Suchinda Kraprayoon, one of the leaders of the National Peacekeeping Council. The English political term *legitimacy* is usually rendered in Thai as "being in accordance with righteousness."

Buddhist Democracy

Liberty and equality are often called the twin essentials of modern democracy. These two values tend to come into conflict, however, whenever equality poses dangers to the survival of liberty. In Japan in the mid-1960s, with a view to overcoming this perennial contradiction, a novel concept of "dhammic democracy" was proposed by a leader of the Japanese Sokagakkai. Its advocates claim that only in the politico-religious ideal of *obutsu myogo*, or "the union of king and Buddha," can dhammic democracy eventually be achieved worldwide, creating a peaceful and harmonious coexistence of liberty and equality in the world.

Democracy, which was born in the West and has been nurtured in the Judeo-Hellenistic tradition of Europe, now demands universal applicability. No country in the world today can be accepted as a member of the family of nations without at least claiming to be democratic. It is therefore natural and understandable that a country with a totally different historical and cultural background should seek its own version of this Western political construct. A Buddhistic democracy would be just one among such varying versions of democracy.

Buddhism does not impose this political idea on its believers, but Buddhist doctrines and traditions do have a democratic vein. The fundamental tenet of this religion of ancient India is the dignity of each human being. The time-honored monastic tradition of Buddhism has a democratic tinge, as reflected in *sangha* autonomy. The archaic concept of the "great elect" suggests a modern application for participatory democracy. Buddhadasa Bhikkhu, a Buddhist monk and intellectual of Thailand, even goes so far as to claim the superiority of "dhammocracy" over democracy, calling the former the ultimate form of the latter. Whether a Buddhist version of democracy can help Asian countries survive and achieve further political development may depend upon the cultural tolerance of the rest of the world.

YONEO ISHII

BIBLIOGRAPHY

Aung-Thwin, Michael. *Pagan: The Origins of Modern Burma*. Honolulu: University of Hawaii Press, 1985.

Nival, Dhani. "The Old Siamese Conception of the Monarchy." In *The Siam Society Fiftieth Anniversary Commemorative Publication*. Vol. 2. Bangkok: Siam Society, 1954.

Smith, Bardwell L., ed. *Religion and Legitimation of Power in Thailand, Laos, and Burma*. Chambersburg, Pa.: Anima Books, 1978.

Tambiah, Stanley J. *World Conqueror and World Renouncer: A Study of Buddhism and Polity in Thailand against a Historical Background*. Cambridge and New York: Cambridge University Press, 1976.

Wijayaratna, Mohan. *Buddhist Monastic Life according to the Texts of the Theravada Tradition*. Translated by Claude Grangier and Steven Collins. Cambridge and New York: Cambridge University Press, 1990.

✦ Capitalism

A social system in which economic production is dominated by the owners of money, or capital, rather than by workers, landowners, political rulers, or religious leaders. Capitalism has been seen as bringing about a fundamental democratization of society and politics. Yet the specific political outcomes under capitalism have been varied and ambiguous. The precise relationship between capitalism and political democracy has long been debated.

Under capitalism, not only goods and services but also the major factors of production—capital, land, and labor—are exchanged on the market. Labor is contracted in exchange for wages in formally free agreements rather than being supplied through slavery, serfdom, or the obligations of citizenship. In capitalist systems, profit is the main criterion in economic decision making. Profit is realized in market exchanges by decentralized and more or less competitive private enterprises.

Capitalist production and exchange have proved to be a source of tremendous technical innovation and economic growth unequaled in history. At the same time, capitalism has disrupted cultural and traditional social orders and given rise to sustained conflicts between social classes. It was fostered by—and in turn fostered—the rise of the modern state. The transformations of society, culture, and politics due to capitalism have been the central theme of the classics of social science.

The State and Capitalism

The relationship between capitalism and the state is important for any analysis of capitalism. It is critical for an understanding of the interrelationships between capitalism and democracy.

A fairly high degree of separation—or, in technical terms, "structural differentiation"—between economic decision making and political rule is an essential characteristic of capitalism. It distinguishes capitalism both from earlier socioeconomic systems, such as feudalism, and from twentieth-century state socialism. Nonetheless, the rise of the modern state was closely related to the rise of capitalism.

Although state action and market functioning are often viewed as mutually exclusive opposites, a powerful state was a necessary condition for the rise of capitalism. Forceful state action was required to overcome obstacles to capitalist production and market exchange that were grounded in privilege and custom. State action also discouraged and if necessary repressed opposition from the victims of capitalist development. It gave legal shape and protection to new forms of property, contract, and enterprise organization—forms that were suitable to profit-oriented production and market exchange. This last point has been well understood since the eighteenth century, when it was formulated by the Scottish political economist Adam Smith. The new forms of economic relationships needed special protection because they often went against privileged interests, established social customs and mores, and popularly held ideas of fairness.

In turn, expanded market exchange and entrepreneurial profits made available the economic resources necessary for the rise of the modern state. Growing state revenues and large credits from merchant capitalists funded territorial conflict, expansion, and consolidation of control. They were also critical in converting the personalized, "patrimonial" state institutions of old into more impersonal and efficient "bureaucratic" structures. Only the more efficient states were capable of creating and protecting the legal infrastructure necessary for the spread of capitalist economic relations. Turning states away from military conflict and conquest and toward a peaceful role of service to the expanding capitalist economy was an important element of the self-understanding of early capitalism. This principle is illustrated in the theorem of a universal transition from military to "industrial" society, as advanced by the nineteenth-century English philosopher Herbert Spencer.

Different Forms of Capitalism

The model of competitive capitalism that has informed much of economic, social, and historical analysis does not exactly match the historical reality. Fully competitive capitalism never existed, and as the political economist Karl Polanyi persuasively argued in his book *The Great Transformation* (1944), the closest approximations to full competition lasted only a relatively short time. Karl Marx's attempt to identify inherent laws of development in capitalism turned out to be wrong in many respects. Marx was right, however, in his assumption that capitalism has a self-transforming dynamic, although this dynamic is less predictable and more dependent on different historical circumstances than he thought.

Advanced capitalist societies have typically undergone a number of changes. These include the concentration of productive property, the emergence of one or a few firms dominating an industry, collective organization of parts of the labor force, and increasing state action in the economy and society. In all capitalist countries there has been a long-term increase in politically imposed limitations on property rights, public regulation of production and market exchange, and state-provided supports for capitalist production and for the needs of the disadvantaged.

Although these trends represent broadly shared features of change in capitalism, they have varied from country to country in their speed, in their particular form, and in the ways they combined with each other. As a result capitalist societies differ substantially from each other. Relations of colonial domination and economic dependence between countries make for additional important differences. Yet even among advanced capitalist countries there are major contrasts, especially in state-sponsored social provisions. This is evident if one compares the limited welfare-state institutions in the United States with those in Europe and especially in Scandinavia. Japan presents yet another pattern.

Capitalism and Democracy: Diverse Accounts

Common wisdom, as well as much scholarly and political argument, assumes that democracy and capitalism are closely linked. In fact, they are often considered as the political and economic aspects of the same underlying socioeconomic system. Modern forms of democracy are indeed associated historically with the rise of capitalism. Furthermore, cross-national statistical research has established a significant, though by no means perfect, correlation between democracy and the level of capitalist development.

But historical association and statistical correlation alone do not yield an adequate understanding of the links between capitalism and democ-

racy. There are many exceptions to the rule, and these cast doubt on any simple conception of democracy as the political expression of capitalism. For example, there are the successes of capitalist development engineered by authoritarian regimes in East Asia; the rise of fascism and National Socialism in Europe in the 1920s and 1930s; and the Latin American authoritarian regimes of the 1960s and 1970s. Postcolonial India had democratic government while its economy was poor and for a long time was a rather imperfect example of competitive capitalism.

Analysis of the relation between capitalism and democracy requires clarification of the concept of democracy. As used here, *democracy* entails (1) regular fair and free elections with a suffrage that is not limited by class, religion, ethnicity, or region; (2) the accountability of the state executives to the elected representatives; and (3) freedom of expression and association. This is a modest definition, which fits what political scientist Robert Dahl called "polyarchy," to distinguish it from the more demanding ideal of a society in which collective decisions are equally responsive to the preferences of all citizens.

While freedom of expression and association is widely recognized as a necessary condition for the democratic process, universal suffrage and the responsibility of the state to elected representatives are on occasion neglected. For example, some scholars view mid-nineteenth-century England as a democracy, even though only about 10 percent of all men were entitled to vote. Similarly, the limited responsibility of the government to the parliament in imperial Germany from 1871 to 1918 is sometimes considered secondary to the existence of universal male suffrage and a developed party system. In the second half of the twentieth century, it appears that restrictions of democracy are more often achieved by limiting the state's accountability to elected representatives than by denying the vote to large parts of the citizenry. For example, during the 1980s the elected president of El Salvador was unable to control the army and stop its involvement in terrorizing and killing civilians.

There are several explanations for the historical association of capitalism and democracy, as well as for the statistical correlation between level of capitalist development and democracy. One view holds that there is a structural correspondence between capitalism and democracy, with strong equilibrium tendencies favoring democracy. In this view, only democracy is sufficiently flexible and complex to deal with the political issues generated by an increasingly complex capitalist economy and society. This concept relies on problematic assumptions of a close systemic integration of economy, society, and politics. And it does not explain why democracy has failed in some relatively advanced capitalist countries.

A related position sees market choice and electoral choice as parallel and mutually reinforcing mechanisms. In this view, unfettered economic freedom provides the necessary underpinning of political freedom. But this assumption makes it hard to explain how capitalist economic rationality can justify the destruction of democracy, as it did in Argentina, Brazil, and Chile in the 1960s and 1970s. This view underestimates the potential level of conflict between the economically powerful interests of the few and the politically powerful interests of the many.

Other explanations of the association of capitalism and democracy focus on social classes—on their interests, their size and place in society, and their power resources.

Both classic liberal and Marxist-Leninist theories hold that the bourgeoisie—the class of major capital owners and thus the dominant class of capitalism—is the prime promoter and supporter of democracy. Comparative historical analysis reveals a much more complex pattern. It is true that the bourgeoisie does not rival large landowners in opposition to democracy. The bourgeoisie insisted on its own inclusion in the political decision-making process, and in doing so it typically supported public debate on policy and parliamentary government. But it did not uniformly support the inclusion of the working and middle classes, especially if strong working-class organizations threatened its interests. In Latin America the bourgeoisie participated in the termination of democratic rule because it perceived such a threat.

Perhaps the oldest argument about the relationship between the structure of society and constitutional form is one that goes back to Aristotle: that democracy rests on, and is advanced by, a large and vibrant middle class. This view holds that middle-class groups tend to support a culture of moderation and tolerance. Expanding with economic prosperity, they do not present a threat to the established order, nor do they have strong vested interests against broad participation in political decisions. This is certainly a strong argument, but it tends to overlook the influence exerted on the middle classes by more powerful classes and institutions. As a consequence, the middle classes' position on democracy is particularly ambiguous in a broadly comparative picture.

A similar consideration holds for peasants and farmers. Though frequently weak in their ability to organize, they are likely to support democratic participation. But they are often closely associated with, and thus strongly influenced by, large landowners. Large landowners are the most consistent opponents of democracy if they employ a large labor force and use political means for its control. Where influence from large landowners did not shape their political orientations, farmers played a major pro-democratic role, as in Switzerland, Norway, and the North of the United States.

Marx expected that an ever growing working class would organize itself politically and would ultimately win control of capitalist society. Universal suffrage was, in his view, one of the steps toward the classless society. Arguing about a democratic future not yet known, Marx anticipated with hope a dictatorship of the proletariat, while his contemporary the French political writer Alexis de Tocqueville feared a tyranny of the majority. Marx was right in claiming that the new urban working class had far better chances of collective self-organization than peasants had had in earlier times. And the working class has almost always been a pro-democratic force. The major flaw in Marx's prediction was that the working class was less unified and far weaker than he anticipated.

Capitalism and Democracy:
The Relationship Reexamined

How, then, can we explain the historical association and the cross-national correlation between capitalism and democracy and, at the same time, account for the substantial inconsistencies and contradictions that characterize the relationship? It is no accident that so many of the theories just sketched focus on the position of social classes with regard to democratization. Promising to reduce inequality in politics, democracy is a matter of power and power sharing. A tension thus exists between democracy and a system of social and economic inequality. This insight points to two major conditions determining the chances of democracy: changes in the overall structure of social inequality and shifts in the balance of class power.

If all dimensions of inequality—income and wealth, honor and status, power and influence— are tightly linked, democracy is impossible. Democracy is possible only where political power and authority have become to some extent separate from the overall system of socioeconomic inequality. Feudalism had no place for democracy. An important prerequisite for democratic rule was established with the rise of capitalism, when political authority and economic property rights became institutionally separated. This separation, however, did not come about because of some inherent logic of capitalism but because of the power interests of new state elites and the rising bourgeoisie.

Neoliberal theories insisting on a one-to-one correspondence between economic and political freedom take this insight to the extreme. Such theories, however, are problematic even if the historical insight has contemporary relevance. The fact that the fusion of political authority and economic control in state socialism in Eastern Europe was incompatible with democracy does not mean that unfettered economic freedom and the resulting inequalities are favorable to democracy.

The tension between democracy and a system of social inequality points to another major condition for democracy: the interplay of class interests and thus the balance of class power. A shift in the balance of class power as a consequence of capitalist development best explains the association of capitalism and democracy. Capitalism weakened the power of large landlords and increased the size and the power of subordinate classes, which previously had been excluded from political participation. These were the small and medium-sized farming class, the urban middle classes, and the new urban working class. The working class stands out among the subordinate classes of history because it shares with the urban middle classes a formidable capacity for collective organization due to urbanization, concentration in factories, and dramatic improvements in communication and transportation. At the same time, the working class has proved to be—with few exceptions—the most consistently pro-democratic social class.

The class interests actually pursued in particular historical situations cannot be simply read off from the material situation and the life chances of class members. They are formulated by leaders and associations that successfully organize and speak for large numbers of class members. The interests and political orientations of a class are thus historically constructed in the very process of organization that makes the pursuit of collective interests possible.

For this reason the positions of different classes with regard to the issues of democracy are historically variable, even though there are more or less strong typical tendencies. Particularly important factors in shaping such variations are the influence of dominant classes and institutions, the degree to which self-organization protects class members from such influence, and the perceptions of threat to one group's interests from the political and economic power of other classes. As noted earlier, the influence of dominant groups is particularly important for the outlook of peasants and the urban middle class; it has far less weight in the urban working class.

The working class varied in size and strength from country to country. Nowhere was it strong enough to achieve democracy by itself. It needed allies. The availability of allies depended on how urban middle-class groups and farmers were organized and how they perceived their own interests in the broader social and political situation. Where the working class was very weak, as in much of Latin America, the push for democracy often came from the middle class, with the working class as a junior partner, provided that the relationships of middle-class groups to the working class and bourgeoisie made this likely. As noted earlier, in a few countries the major breakthrough of democratization was achieved by independent farmers and middle-class groups before the industrial working class became a decisive social force.

The success of democratization also depended significantly on the coalitions formed by the dominant classes and their perceptions of threats to their interests. For instance, if the bourgeoisie allied itself with landed interests because of its perception of a strong socialist challenge from the working class, the chances of democratization and of stable democracy were significantly weakened. Thus, in an important sense, the interrelations among classes, rather than the typical class interests, shaped constitutional outcomes.

Looking beyond the complexities of class interaction, the shift in balance of class power as a consequence of capitalist development is still the best explanation for the link between capitalism and democracy. The conflicts and contradictions of capitalism account for its connection with democracy—not an inherent structural correspondence between capitalism and democracy, the rise of the bourgeoisie, or the growth of a vibrant and tolerant middle class.

The correlation between level of capitalist development and democracy is far from perfect. One explanation for this is found in the variations in class organization and class interaction. But the deviations from the overall trend point to other factors as well. On the premise that democracy is a matter of power, three other configurations of power seem of special importance: the structure of the state and of state-society relations, the impact of international power relations, and the patterns of ethnic fragmentation and conflict. All three are historically related to capitalist development, but the relationship is complex. These factors have an effect on the chances of democracy that is independent of the level of capitalist development in a country.

The impact of state structure on democracy can be clearly seen. A state's control over a territory has to be consolidated before democratic rule is possible. Beyond that, democracy requires a complex pattern of state autonomy: a state that lacks autonomy with regard to the landed or capitalist dominant classes is incompatible with democracy. Yet a state must not be so strong and autonomous as to overpower all of society. Centralized and direct state control of the economy, as well as a strong and autonomous military, are unfavorable conditions for democracy. More subtle but still significant effects come from historical relations between state offices and landlords and from the role state churches play in the overall pattern of cultural influence and conflict.

The effect of international power relations is equally significant and must be analyzed in relation to the internal balance of class power. War affects this balance because it typically requires mass support, and in the case of defeat it discredits the dominant groups. Economic dependence on other countries and their dominant classes has been said to weaken the chances of democracy. The evidence suggests, however, that economic dependence is important only in conjunction with geopolitical relationships of dominance and dependence. In addition, the ways in which the interests of politically and economically dominant countries relate to democracy in dependent countries have varied historically.

Ethnic and cultural division and conflict can be major obstacles to democracy. Ethnic conflict may unsettle the established authority of the state as well as the minimal solidarity of the political society that is required to make majority decisions acceptable. Intense ethnic and national identification may also increase the influence of dominant groups that do not fully support democracy. Cross-national research has shown ethnic fragmentation to have a negative relationship to democracy. Quite a few culturally divided societies, however, have stable democratic politics, including Belgium, Spain, and Switzerland.

Is political culture a major factor shaping the chances of democracy? Arguments about political culture as a condition of constitutional development are often circular: the liberal culture of a country explains the survival of liberal politics. A better approach is to focus on how values and beliefs are grounded in different groups and institutions—and on how they persist or change because of this. Such an analysis largely reinforces what has been said here about the historical construction of the goals and beliefs in class-based organizations, the influence of dominant interests and defenses against it, and about the relationship of religion to the structure of the state. In this concept, political culture becomes the ensemble of beliefs and values, symbols and myths associated with diverse organizations and institutions that often are in conflict with each other.

Does Democracy Transform Capitalism?

If political democracy grew out of the conflicts and empowerment opportunities created by capitalism, did it in turn modify the structure of capitalism? Clearly, the fundamental democratization of social life, and in particular the new organizational opportunities of subordinate classes, that came about through capitalism helped to transform capitalism over time. This observation is true even where welfare-state measures and regulations of production and market exchange protecting workers and consumers were initiated by state managers and conservative political elites and perhaps opposed by working-class parties. This was the case in imperial Germany in the 1880s, where a conservative government used social policies as a political weapon against the socialist party. Yet these policies can be understood only against the background of the growing political power of subordinate classes.

Whether political democracy as such is associated with more extensive social policy programs and with the reduction of economic inequality is a more complicated question. Cross-national research has not found a clear correlation, although some results suggest that democratic rule may in the long run be associated with reductions of income differentials. The ambiguity of these research results is not astonishing. The distribution of income and wealth, as well as the state's social policies, is subject to struggles whose outcomes depend on constellations of economic and political power that vary considerably across democracies. In many countries, however, powerful unions and political parties based in the working class have achieved policies building strong welfare states and limiting the privileges of dominant classes. Democracy offers favorable conditions for the subordinate classes to use their strength to win policies that transform the system of inequality.

If history is any guide, political democracy is unlikely to transform capitalism toward similar patterns in all countries. Furthermore, the increasing globalization of capitalist production and exchange constrains political action in individual countries. Democracy will continue to make a difference, however. It is likely to create openings for egalitarian transformations of work and authority in production. It may also foster the political realization of public goods—for instance, in health, education, and the environment—where the play of private interests guided by profit yields unacceptable results.

See also Leninism; Marxism; State growth and intervention; Tocqueville, Alexis de.

DIETRICH RUESCHEMEYER

BIBLIOGRAPHY

Bollen, Kenneth A. "Political Democracy and the Timing of Development." *American Sociological Review* 44 (1979): 572–587.

Grassby, Richard. *The Idea of Capitalism before the Industrial Revolution.* Lanham, Md.: Rowman and Littlefield, 1999.

Hayek, Friedrich A. von. *The Road to Serfdom.* Chicago: University of Chicago Press, 1944; London: Routledge, 1991.

Lipset, Seymour Martin. "Some Social Requisites of Democracy." *American Political Science Review* 53 (1959): 69–105. Reprinted in *Political Man.* Expanded and updated ed. Baltimore: Johns Hopkins University Press, 1981; Aldershot: Gower, 1983.

Marx, Karl. *Capital.* 3 vols. Moscow: Foreign Languages Publishers, 1959.

Moore, Barrington, Jr. *The Social Origins of Dictatorship and Democracy.* Boston: Beacon Press, 1966.

Muller, Edward N. "Democracy, Economic Development and Income Inequality." *American Sociological Review* 53 (1988): 50–68.

Rueschemeyer, Dietrich, Evelyne Huber Stephens, and John D. Stephens. *Capitalist Development and Democracy.* Cambridge: Polity Press; Chicago: University of Chicago Press, 1993.

Schumpeter, Joseph. *Capitalism, Socialism and Democracy.* New York: Harper and Brothers, 1942.

Therborn, Göran. "The Rule of Capital and the Rise of Democracy." *New Left Review* 103 (1977): 3–41.

Weber, Max. *Economy and Society.* 2 vols. Berkeley: University of California Press, 1978.

✦ Communism

A term that originated in the mid-1830s in secret revolutionary societies, first in Paris and then elsewhere in Western Europe. *Communism* referred at times to a form of society that would be brought about through the struggles of the working class and at other times to political movements of the working class within capitalist society.

Throughout most of the nineteenth century the terms *communism* and *socialism* were often used synonymously. But toward the end of the century, Karl Marx and Friedrich Engels defined communism as the final stage of the struggle between the working class and the oppressive capitalist class. The initial victory of the working class, which Marx and Engels now called socialism, was thought still to show features of bourgeois class society and of modes and forms of human relations that were rooted in the past. On the other hand, under communism, classes would be abolished altogether and classless society would dawn as the final stage of the liberation of humankind from the enslavement and oppression that had characterized its previous history.

Marx and Engels theorized that only in classless communist society would people liberate themselves completely from the yoke of necessity and attain total freedom. Despite Marx's precise definitions, even in the latter part of the nineteenth century most Marxists and other working-class spokespersons used the terms *socialism* and *communism* interchangeably, generally with a strong preference for the former.

The early socialist circles in Russia were organized and attended largely by students and other intellectuals. One of the major problems that these early socialists faced was selecting a strategy and tactics that would link the intellectual and semi-intellectual members in these circles to the working class, about which, by and large, they knew very little.

A debate between evolutionary and revolutionary approaches to societal change led to a split in 1903 in the Russian Social Democratic Labor Party, a socialist party that had formed in 1898. The Bolsheviks (meaning "majoritarians") favored a revolutionary path led by a secretive cadre of professional revolutionaries. The Mensheviks (or "minoritarians") favored an evolutionary path.

The Mensheviks argued that Russian society was still undeveloped and that it would need a fairly long time to reach the developmental stage of, say, Germany or England. The budding labor movement, therefore, could not yet aspire to gaining power but must await the maturation of bourgeois society.

In these circumstances the Mensheviks believed that the workers and their intellectual leaders should pursue limited goals and should fight for immediate gains. It would be foolish, they argued, to talk about a proletarian revolution when Russia had not even had its bourgeois revolution. The Bolshevik wing of the party, which was opposed to waiting for the maturation of bourgeois society, was led by Vladimir Ilich Lenin.

Leninism

In 1897 the young Lenin was arrested in St. Petersburg as a main organizer of the Union of Struggle, a militant circle made up largely of young intellectuals and students. When the first mass strike of St. Petersburg workers, centered mainly in the textile industry, broke out, these young men and women found that the workers were willing to accept their help and advice in technical matters, such as the printing of handbills, but that they were not interested in the intellectuals' argument that only a large-scale political upheaval would ameliorate the miserable condition of the workers. The workers were interested mainly in immediate economic improvement or, at best, in self-improvement, and they tended to look at their sympathizers in the Union of Struggle as hopeless windbags.

After his arrest, Lenin spent three years in exile in Siberia. He then emigrated to Europe, where he discussed the issues of the day with other socialist exiles. In Europe he went through a major political and spiritual crisis. He realized that the aims of labor and of the intelligentsia did not necessarily coincide, and he came to doubt the revolutionary potential of labor. If the workers were not at least potentially revolutionary, all Russian Marxist thought resting on the idea that the development of capitalism necessarily entailed the growth of proletarian class consciousness, even if only in the long run, was in jeopardy.

Lenin proceeded to recast Marxist doctrine. He argued that the workers could never spontaneously attain class consciousness. They could, at best, attain trade union consciousness. If that was the case, the working class would become a revolutionary force only if it accepted the leadership of trained professional revolutionaries who would inculcate class consciousness in the mass of politically inert workers.

In the years that followed, Lenin built a devoted cadre of militants, first within the general socialist movement, and later in the Bolsheviks. From 1903 on, although Bolsheviks and Mensheviks cooperated at times, most of the time they fought each other for the leadership of the struggle against oppressive czardom.

When World War I broke out in 1914, Lenin and his followers believed that the defeat of the belligerents would bring about the preconditions for a revolutionary thrust forward even in backward societies such as Russia's. Lenin's Bolsheviks hence not only opposed governmental policy but worked for the military defeat of the czarist regime, while the Mensheviks clung to a policy of loyal opposition.

The czarist regime collapsed in February 1917 and was succeeded by a coalition of liberals and centrists. Not only the Mensheviks but also most of the rank-and-file Bolsheviks, as well as many of the leaders of the Bolsheviks, prepared themselves for a long period of parliamentary and trade union struggle against the new government. Therefore, when Lenin arrived from exile in Switzerland at the Finland Station in St. Petersburg in April 1917, arguing with passionate intensity that the time had come to organize a second—socialist—revolution, even some of his own comrades thought he was mad. They argued that the working class made up only a small percentage of the population of Russia, and the Bolsheviks could be counted only in the hundreds. Yet Lenin managed within a few weeks to bring his own cadre to accept his position and to make serious inroads among the cadres of the Mensheviks as well.

At the time of the November 1917 revolution, the Bolsheviks did not have the support of the bulk of the working class or of the peasants, but they had managed to build revolutionary cadres at strategic points not only in the major cities but also in small towns and in the countryside. The professional revolutionaries and semirevolutionaries conquered Alexander Kerensky's provisional government, which had succeeded the czar, and filled the commanding heights of the revolutionary state.

The Bolsheviks at first collaborated in a new government with the Socialist Revolutionaries, a largely peasant, populist party, but they soon banned all rival socialist parties. Over time, non-Leninist factions were banned from within the Bolshevik Party itself. The Leninists justified this repression by citing the need to maintain unity in the civil war that tore Russia apart for what seemed endless months and years. But in reality the repression was largely rooted in the undemocratic Bolshevik doctrine that Lenin and his coworkers had elaborated long before the outbreak of the revolution.

Elections to the Constituent Assembly, which had taken place shortly before the outbreak of the November 1917 revolution, returned 420 Socialist Revolutionaries as against only 225 Bolsheviks. Red Army troops under Bolshevik control dispersed the assembly on the first day it met, January 18, 1918, arguing that it reflected the political thought of prerevolutionary days and hence was no longer representative of the orientations of the population.

Whenever critics—including the German socialists Rosa Luxemburg and Karl Kautsky—raised their voices in protest against the suppression of all democratic opposition, the Leninist answer was always the need to close ranks around those who had the mission to safeguard the existence of the first socialist workers' state.

Russian Communism After Lenin

Lenin was a sensitive intellectual steeped in Western culture. Whenever he succeeded in suppressing critical voices, especially among some of his old Menshevik comrades in arms, he apparently felt some guilt. His successor, Joseph Stalin, was not inclined to such "bourgeois" sentiment. He murdered his opponents and those he only suspected of opposition with no qualms whatsoever. Lenin, in his prerevolutionary writings, praised participatory democracy as he imagined it to have operated in the short-lived reign of the Paris Commune of 1871. It seems likely that he believed that working-class formations after the victory of communism would do away with the powers of the state, end the long history of bureaucracy, and do away with all distinctions based on the division of labor. But none of these ideals could be pursued, Lenin believed, as long as domestic and foreign adversaries still threatened the young Soviet revolution.

Socialists and social scientists have debated for many decades whether Russian developments would have taken a different course had Lenin lived longer and had Stalin not taken power. It would seem that a post-Leninist regime under Leon Trotsky or Nikolai Bukharin might have been less draconian and more humane than

Stalin's regime turned out to be. Trotsky and Bukharin probably would not have murdered the majority of their former comrades, nor would they have endorsed a policy of extermination in the countryside. But a Soviet Union under the guidance of another Bolshevik probably would not have been different from what it turned out to be under Stalin. The isolation of the Soviet Union in a sea of basically hostile states, combined with the rule of men and women trained over years to believe that they belonged to a chosen elite that was entrusted by history to guide Russia toward a blissful future and to make the country a beacon to the unenlightened, would most likely have led to a regime only marginally less horrifying than Stalin's.

Lenin seems to have believed that one could postpone the emergence of a democratic regime to a time less stressful and dangerous than the 1920s in the Soviet Union. That idea was ultimately his major failing. One cannot turn on a democratic course of action as one turns on a faucet. The ultimate fate of the Soviet body politic was already sealed in the first few years of its existence, as Rosa Luxemburg saw with exemplary lucidity. There are exceptions to the rule that political regimes tend to follow the course in which they have been set at the beginning—but such exceptions are few.

Lenin had already broken with traditional Marxism when he set the course of his party in the direction that ultimately submitted the working class to the heavy hand of the dictatorship of the Bolshevik Party. Neither Bukharin nor Trotsky would have broken this initial deadly political mold.

The International Movement Between the World Wars

By the early 1920s it was clear to the Russian communists that the international revolution

Lenin had prophesied would not occur. This failure left the Soviet Union in a precarious position. Industrially underdeveloped, exhausted from world war and civil war, and surrounded by capitalist states, the Soviet Union sought moral and political help from its sympathizers around the world. One of the major aims of the Russian communist leaders in the post–World War I period was to create in all capitalist and colonial countries communist parties that would compete with and eventually supplant the local socialist parties. In 1919 the Russian communists created the Communist International (the Comintern), which sought to displace all existing socialist parties that were unwilling to become their instruments. They never succeeded in replacing the European socialist parties that were reconstructed after the war, but they succeeded in creating almost everywhere rival organizations subservient to the Kremlin and willing to follow every twist and strategic turn that the Russians demanded.

Throughout the 1920s and 1930s the various national communist parties that belonged to the Comintern changed their platforms, policies, and tactics at the behest of the Russian heads of the Comintern—even if those changes made no sense in the local context. The choice of strategies was made in Moscow and not in the home countries, and the shifts in the party line did not result from assessments or reassessments of the local scene but from calculations as to what political line was most advantageous for the Soviet Union. No matter how absurd were the policy guidelines that the Comintern imposed on the national parties, they invariably were followed.

The effects of Comintern vacillation on the national parties and on the European labor movement as a whole were devastating. Many old-time radicals and labor leaders with local roots and deep loyalties in the labor movements of their respective nations left the parties in disgust. As the "Stalinization" of the communist parties continued, all leaders who could still distinguish between their loyalty to the Russian dictatorship and to the working class of their own country were eliminated. A new kind of leader began to appear, the "apparatus man" (apparatchik), whose chief talent was the justification and carrying out of Moscow's orders. The professional revolutionaries of the Leninist period were, in Trotsky's phrase, "domesticated and then destroyed." Their place was taken by bureaucratic careerists whose fundamental means of judging their success in office was their standing in the eyes of Moscow.

Factional struggles broke out from time to time within the national communist parties, as in France, Italy, and the United States, but these struggles had almost nothing to do with normal political disputes. They resembled instead the jockeying for power of cliques on top of a bureaucratic structure. Rather than reflecting different assessments of the political arena at home, the factional struggles were all directed at winning the favor of the highest Russian authorities in the communist world.

In part because of vacillations in Comintern policies and in part because of philosophical disagreements that had been percolating in the communist movement since the early years of the century, the history of the European labor movement between the world wars was one of fratricide and mutual contempt. The socialist and communist parties in each European nation seldom agreed on major issues of strategy or tactics. For these reasons the European labor movement as a whole never regained the strength that it had shown before World War I. Deeply divided within itself, it went from defeat to defeat.

Some comment on the structure and function of the communist parties worldwide is in order. The basic organizational unit of the party was the cell. It was made up of not more than fifty members, often considerably fewer. The cell was connected to the next higher organizational unit by its leading cadres. The next higher organizational unit was linked through its officers to the unit above it, and so on. Because all connections were vertical, cells had no contact whatsoever with neighboring cells on their level. Furthermore, officers were "elected" by their constituency upon submission of their names by higher bureaucrats. Factions were strictly forbidden. A person who opposed party policy in any way was subject to rapid expulsion. The communists held democracy in contempt.

Given the extreme rigidity of such a structure, the only course of action open for a party member who had grown skeptical and disaffected was to leave the party. Indeed, massive fluctuation in membership was the rule in all national parties. The bureaucrats stayed on, but the rank-and-file members usually stayed only a fairly short time. Nevertheless, it would be a mistake to believe that the parties consisted only of members who would leave after a short period of disillusionment. Stalinism, though a corrupt and deadly movement, managed all the same to infuse vast numbers of members and fellow travelers with sincere devotion and readiness to sacrifice.

International Communism
After World War II

When the Soviet Union was attacked by Nazi Germany in 1941, European communists in many cases became the vanguard in their respective nations' resistance movements. Their heroic deeds became legend. Their martyrs often became the best means for the party to advertise its message and to attract a new generation of converts. The communists often provided the only message of hope for those who were disillusioned by the postwar governments.

Stalinist communists thrived whenever and wherever the traditional parties of the center or of the left failed to deliver on their electoral promises. The communists profited from the decline of those parties that had previously dominated the left. Wherever the labor movement had tasted defeat and humiliation, the typical Stalinist militant "knew" that the door to a better future was largely barred within the national borders. Only total devotion to the Soviet Union would assure a brighter tomorrow.

But when the Soviet monolith began to be shaken, when even total devotion could no longer ignore its fissures, the Western communist parties began to decline at a rapid pace. Either they became indistinguishable from social democratic parties, as in Italy, or they shrank into politically impotent sects.

Moreover, the image of the Soviet Union suffered by comparison with the welfare state that had come into existence in all Western European countries. The welfare state was far from a communist utopia, but it did diminish the sense of alienation of the working class. Although still deprived of equal access to the material goods that came as a matter of course to the members of other classes, the working class had managed to break out of the ghetto to which it had been relegated since the beginning of the Industrial Revolution. When the golden image of the Soviet Union became tarnished, and when the welfare state began to make good on at least some of its promises, the communist myth and the communist messages lost their potent appeal, and the communist movement, which for decades had seemed to be a threat to the democratic West, began to fade.

If the communist parties of Europe continue on their present course, their chances of attracting new members and voters are very small indeed. Only a revived democratic socialist movement that tempers realistic policies with a renewal of social idealism and utopian vision can hope to profit from the disillusionment of former communist party members, followers, and sympathizers.

See also Leninism; Marxism; Socialism.

LEWIS A. COSER

BIBLIOGRAPHY

Arendt, Hannah. *The Origin of Totalitarianism.* New York: Meridian, 1954.

Billington, James H. *Fire in the Minds of Men: Origins of the Revolutionary Faith.* New York: Basic Books; Aldershot: M. T. Smith, 1980.

Borkenau, Franz. *World Communism.* Ann Arbor: University of Michigan Press, 1962.

Cohen, Stephen. *Bukharin and the Bolshevik Revolution.* New York: Knopf, 1973.

Coser, Lewis A. "Death Throes of Western Communism." *Dissent* (spring 1989).

_____. "Marxist Thought in the First Quarter of the 20th Century." In *A Handful of Thistles.* New Brunswick, N.J.: Transaction, 1988.

Howe, Irving, and Lewis A. Coser. *The American Communist Party: A Critical History (1919–1957).* 2d ed. New York: Praeger, 1962.

Lenin, V. I. "One Step Forward, Two Steps Backward," and "What Is to Be Done?" In *Selected Works.* Vol. 2. New York: International Publishers, 1969.

Lichtheim, George. *A Short History of Socialism.* New York: Praeger, 1970.

Lipset, Seymour Martin. *Political Man: The Social Bases of Politics.* Expanded and updated ed. Baltimore: Johns Hopkins University Press, 1981; Aldershot: Gower, 1983.

The Passing of an Illusion: The Idea of Communism in the Twentieth Century. Translated by François Furet. Chicago: University of Chicago Press, 2000.

Pipes, Richard. *Social Democracy and the St. Petersburg Labor Movement.* Cambridge: Harvard University Press, 1968.

Schapiro, Leonard. *The Origin of the Communist Autocracy.* New York: Cambridge University Press, 1955.

Tucker, Robert. *Stalin in Power: The Revolution from Above.* New York and London: Norton, 1992.

Wilson, Edmund. *To the Finland Station.* Garden City, N.Y.: Doubleday, 1953; Harmondsworth, England: Penguin Books, 1991.

Wolfe, Bertram D. *Three Who Made a Revolution.* Boston: Beacon Press, 1955.

✦ Communitarianism

An antiliberal political theory whose advocates seek to establish a democratic politics of the common good and thereby to tame or even to supplant the prevailing liberal politics of individual rights. The communitarian movement rose to prominence in the 1980s, in the political world as well as in the academy. This revival of the idea of community has taken a remarkable variety of forms, from traditional conservative to social democratic to radical postmodernist. As a result, it is difficult to state with precision the distinctive features of a communitarian political theory.

But communitarians at least are united by a shared hostility to the pervasive individualism of contemporary liberal democratic politics. They are critics of liberal democracy founded on individual rights and partisans of more robust forms of democratic politics founded on common deliberation about the common good. Communitarians thus raise again a question that for a time had been closed by the theoretical and practical successes of liberal democracy: the nature of a just and healthy democratic polity.

Liberty, Virtue, and Equality

It is evident that there are several forms of democracy. These forms differ substantially according to the weight that each assigns to certain basic political goods—especially liberty, virtue, and equality.

First, a liberal democracy is founded on the idea that liberty (and not, say, salvation or virtue or equality) is more fundamental than all other political goods. The liberal democrat affirms, in addition, that a democratic polity is most likely to respect the rights of individuals, to secure the blessings of liberty. But because democracy itself can sometimes be a threat to liberty (what Alexis de Tocqueville called the "tyranny of the majority"), liberals are rarely unqualified partisans of democracy. Indeed, as the American Declaration of Independence makes clear, the rights of individuals might in some circumstances be made more secure through the establishment of forms of government that are only qualifiedly democratic, or not democratic at all. For this reason, more wholehearted partisans of democracy suspect that there is an anti-democratic impulse hidden at the heart of liberal philosophy. In any case, for the liberal democrat, democracy is a means to secure liberty.

Next, the foundation of a democratic republic is virtue. According to the republican argument, democracy depends on virtue to ensure good citizenship. Because the same human beings are, in a democratic republic, both rulers and subjects, as Montesquieu argues, such democratic communities cannot rely on force employed by rulers to ensure civility among the subjects. Citizens must learn to govern themselves, since there are no rulers to govern them. Democratic citizens must freely choose to serve the community, animated by patriotism or public spirit, or they will not be found to serve the community at all. According to the most formidable partisan of the democratic republic founded on virtue, Jean-Jacques Rousseau, virtue is a passionate identification with one's community, a wholehearted love of the democratic republic. Good citizens are happy to participate in the common life of the community, working for the common good even at the expense of private pursuits of happiness and somehow identifying their own happiness with the common good.

Virtue is thus utterly incompatible with liberal privacy, much less with the self-absorption that marks the ways of life of individualists today. Rousseau's democratic republic is an illiberal democracy: rights are not respected and commerce is despised, since these liberal goods invariably give rise to disharmony between public and private interest in the souls of citizens. It is also an egalitarian and homogeneous community, since inequality and diversity would undermine the love of the republic that alone makes virtue possible. The democratic republic is thus less tolerant than liberal democracy.

Finally, the foundation of pure or participatory democracy is equality. Strictly speaking, democracy is (as Aristotle says) the rule of the people, wherein each citizen has an equal share in politics and no quality distinguishes those who are fit for citizenship from those who are not. Thus the purest form of democratic argument is the argument for direct or participatory democracy: justice demands that each citizen should share equally in the goods that belong to the political community. Equality can be achieved only where the people act collectively to defend this claim (in assembly or by means of plebiscites and similar tools of direct popular action). Furthermore, egalitarian justice requires not only equality of political power but also some measure of economic equality. This form of democracy is often associated with ancient Greece; in the modern world, the cause of egalitarian democracy has been advanced primarily by social democrats.

Whether or not this democratic argument from justice succeeds, it is widely admitted that a purely democratic politics is indefensible on prudential grounds: the people are often foolish—fickle and fanatical by turns. Especially in modern societies based on mass politics and faced with problems of unprecedented complexity, partisans of democratic politics have often found it necessary to embrace various liberal and republican principles and practices designed to tame popular vices and to refine popular judgment.

The Idea of Community

The communitarian revival of the idea of community might be understood as a revival of these old republican and democratic arguments in a somewhat hybrid form: marrying the older concerns about equality and virtue yields the more or less novel idea of community. This revival comes at a time when the case for a democratic politics dedicated to securing liberty is no longer satisfying, for both political and philosophical reasons that are outlined below. For this reason, communitarianism is somewhat difficult to classify as a movement of either the right or the left: the language of community seems conservative at times and social democratic at times, depending on whether the republican (virtue) or democratic (equality) aspect of the idea of community dominates.

Communitarianism is in some sense the newest replacement for failed Marxism. Yet it lacks the moral rigor, the love of justice understood as equality, of socialism and social democracy. If communitarians are less than wholehearted in their commitment to equality, they are even more ambivalent in their praise of virtue. Thus the republicanism of today's communitarians also lacks the moral rigor of Rousseau's republicanism, which is marked by moralism, the abolition of privacy, and the unremitting self-sacrifice of citizens.

In republican moments, communitarians are tempted to excuse this or that (mild) policy of censorship, to praise "family values," or to call

for a renewal of moral education in the schools—but not, they invariably add, at the expense of toleration and the rights of individuals. In democratic moments, which are perhaps somewhat more frequent than the republican ones, communitarians are tempted to seek policies that redistribute wealth (designed to secure greater economic equality) and to call for the establishment of participatory institutions, for example, "teledemocracy" (designed to ensure a greater voice for the people in their collective capacity). But there is no question of abandoning liberal (free market) economics, much less of withdrawing from the goal of private prosperity. And there is no question of abolishing representation (as Rousseau suggested) or any of the other liberal political institutions that filter the judgment of the people and so diminish the likelihood of folly or fanaticism. In short, communitarians remain liberal democrats at bottom, in spite of the occasional immoderation of their attacks on liberal individualism. Let us turn to this more critical aspect of communitarianism, beginning with a review of the classical liberal portrait of the community.

The Liberal Community

Classical liberalism (for example, the liberalism of John Locke) is a doctrine of acquisitive individualism. It maintains that human beings are by nature solitary and selfish, not political or communal. We are not friends by nature but enemies who are driven by our most potent natural passions and needs to compete, and so to quarrel, in order to provide for our security and comfort. Thus the natural condition of human beings is a state of war, a terrible condition from which any reasonable human being seeks to escape.

Classical liberalism therefore contains an account of the nature and purpose of political community (as a means of escape from the hardships of our natural condition of war and scarcity) as well as an idea of the common good and even an account of moral and political virtue. But the liberal community is an austere one, founded only on the basis of a social contract among naturally hostile individuals, and not on the basis of any more robust common opinions about justice. For the liberal the only truly common goods are peace and the means to peace, since peace is the almost necessary condition of security in the possession of all private goods. And the liberal virtues are simply those habits of reasonable self-restraint that enable human beings to establish and to sustain such communities (Tocqueville's idea of "self-interest rightly understood").

For the classical liberal, then, community is not at all warm and cozy. The liberal community is not a home, and liberal citizens do not regard each other as lovable and trustworthy companions in a kind of extended family (or even in a common moral enterprise). Indeed, the political community is not quite natural. It has no moral authority beyond that derived from the consent of the governed, who build liberal communities in order to secure certain private goods that are naturally insecure. That is, liberal politics is a politics of fearful accommodation among natural foes who have somehow learned to transform themselves into civil friends. And so the liberal community is marked in the best case by mutual respect for individual rights (life, liberty, and the pursuit of happiness); by tolerance of a rather wide variety of ways of life and opinions (free exercise of religion); and by the moderation of parties and sects whose members refrain from seeking the community's endorsement of contentious moral, religious, and ideological opinions (no establishment of religion).

Thus liberal communities are not communities of moral opinion. There is no liberal orthodoxy regarding justice or salvation or virtue or the good life, since common deliberation about such common goods too often disturbs the peace and in any case renders private pursuits of happiness vulnerable to prejudice and authority. And the idea of a community that somehow possesses a natural moral authority independent of the consent of those individuals who establish it is always suspect for liberals, who are inclined to view partisans of such a community as romantic utopians or dangerous authoritarians. If there is no natural common good beyond peace or security, invocations of the spirit of community are either foolish or fraudulent, impossible dreams or wicked ideologies.

But this austere vision of the liberal community has proved to be unsatisfying to many critics who hope for more from community—more warmth, more justice, more nobility. We turn next to these communitarian criticisms of liberal community.

The Communitarian Critique

A variety of prominent contemporary critics of liberal individualism and the liberal democratic polity are now called communitarians (although not every so-called communitarian is eager to embrace the name). Any list of communitarian theorists would surely include the following thinkers: Benjamin Barber, Robert Bellah, Jean Bethke Elshtain, Amitai Etzioni, Mary Ann Glendon, Stanley Hauerwas, Alasdair MacIntyre, Michael Sandel, William Sullivan, and Michael Walzer. These theorists evidently disagree about many important matters, more than is common in a movement (as communitarianism is sometimes said to be). Participatory democrats, classical republicans, feminists, socialists, theologians, postmodernists, and others now raise their voices, but not altogether in unison, in praise of community. That is, they are more united in their diagnosis of the disease than in their prescriptions for a cure.

It has proved to be far easier to say why we now miss community than to say what form (democratic, republican, or something altogether new) a renewal of community might take. The communitarian criticism of liberal individualism has several dimensions. Here, we look at three arguments: political, moral, and philosophical.

According to the political argument (advanced by Barber and Walzer, among others), liberal individualism destroys citizenship and undermines civic virtue. It is incapable of providing an adequate foundation for a truly democratic community of free and equal citizens. As we have wholeheartedly embraced private life, we have also neglected to cultivate the virtues and other habits of citizenship that even a liberal community must sometimes summon. Thus we now find ourselves disempowered in face of the various impersonal modes of authority that are present in a modern bureaucratic state with a capitalist economy. What is more, we have lost the capacity to exercise even the most modest forms of self-restraint or public-spiritedness, much less to nurture old-fashioned republican virtue.

This combination of slavishness and selfishness makes possible a contemptible mode of liberal politics. We are the (happy) slaves of paternalistic elites who purchase public passivity and conformity by base appeals to selfishness—"bread and circuses" administered efficiently and rationally by hidden authorities who serve the bureaucratic state and capitalist economy. This is far from the liberal imagination of autonomous individuals capable of reasonable self-government. Only the revival of truly democratic citizenship, which teaches human beings to consider the common good and not merely their private rights and interests, can generate the civic virtues and political judgment that might enable contemporary men and women to take control of their common life once again and to throw off their new masters.

The communitarian moral critique of liberal individualism is somewhat more difficult to summarize because the communitarians are (in terms of moral psychology) a diverse lot. Nevertheless, a number of common accusations can be discerned. According to the moral argument (advanced by MacIntyre, Sandel, and Walzer, among others), prevailing liberal ways of life are morally impoverished. Thus communitarians argue not only that we are not good citizens but also that the vaunted privacy of liberal individualists is itself a fraud. In a way, this moral assault on liberal individualism is more devastating than the political criticism (at least for partisans of liberalism), since the case for liberalism rests above all on the claim that liberal polities protect a variety of dignified private ways of life from clumsy and benighted political judgment. But what if these ways of life are often contemptible? And what if the now liberated human beings who inhabit liberal communities are often miserable? Perhaps our individualism has gone too far. It has, to be sure, liberated us from tyrants and priests, as was its aim, but that same individualism has also made it more difficult for us even to imagine a genuine common life with fellow citizens, or even with family and friends.

Liberal moral psychology reduces the primitive or natural self-knowledge that makes manifest the importance of such moral attachments in a complete human life. We have learned to think of ourselves as free individuals above all, thereby forgetting that our selves are embedded in particular communities (families, religions, peoples, republics) that at least in part constitute our identities. Moreover, we have loyalties and duties toward our companions in those communities that are not acquired through our free acts as individuals. An individual who does not recognize the moral force of such attachments is shallow and pitiable. Liberation has left us lonely and helpless.

Our private ways of life are no longer marked by the proud practice of freedom but by grim dissipation, careless self-satisfaction, mindless conformity, or quiet desperation. Only a restoration of the moral authority of community can enable contemporary men and women to attribute moral meaning to their ways of life.

This moral critique of liberal individualism gives rise, finally, to a philosophical critique that is less important for present purposes than the political and moral arguments. Liberal individualism is now said to be philosophically defective insofar as it rests on an incoherent account of moral reasoning and the nature of the self. According to many communitarians (and others), the liberal quest for universal and objective principles of political right, against which one might measure the justice of the principles and practices of any particular community, is misguided. If there are any universal moral principles, they are too minimal and abstract to provide more than the framework for a moral life. Liberal philosophy is incapable of constituting communities. The proper task of philosophy therefore is poetic or creative: evocative interpretation of a shared moral horizon, not liberation from such horizons.

Against the liberal, the communitarian insists that human beings are wholly constituted by particular histories, that there is no escape from contingency (and so, no escape from community). Thus the aspiration to liberate oneself from the bonds of particularism is founded on a misguided metaphysical hope. The philosophic quest for a metaphysical comfort (that the world should be intelligible) must now give way to a communitarian quest for a certain moral comfort (that we should have a "home"). Here is the moral meaning of the new idea of philosophy: community can serve as a bulwark against the dislocating and disorienting qualities of modernity—against nihilism, meaninglessness, alienation, and the rest.

It is worth remarking that the posture of many communitarians toward liberal individualism is more ambivalent than that described here. Most such critics acknowledge that liberalism has proved to be an admirably liberating doctrine and that liberal polities have begun to reveal a notable capacity to accommodate the just claims of the formerly disadvantaged. The communitarian critique of liberalism thus lacks the radicalism of earlier antiliberal doctrines, although it is sometimes expressed in rather feverish language. As a result, some critics accuse the communitarians of taking the achievements of liberalism for granted, of forgetting that liberty is a historically precarious possession and that it may come at a high moral and political price (including the decline of virtue and the rise of inequality) that is yet worth paying. Perhaps this is the quality that most distinguishes today's communitarians: the desire to have it all, to revive virtue and to establish equality, but without diminishing the liberty achieved by the liberal democratic politics of individualism.

See also Liberalism; Locke, John; Montesquieu; Democracy, Participatory; Rousseau, Jean-Jacques; Theory, Ancient; Tocqueville, Alexis de; Virtue, Civic.

STEVEN KAUTZ

BIBLIOGRAPHY

Barber, Benjamin. *Strong Democracy: Participatory Politics for a New Age.* Berkeley: University of California Press, 1984.

Elshtain, Jean Bethke. *Public Man, Private Woman: Women in Social and Political Thought.* Princeton: Princeton University Press, 1981.

Fowler, Robert Booth. *The Dance with Community: The Contemporary Debate in American Political Thought.* Lawrence: University Press of Kansas, 1991.

Frazer, Elizabeth. *The Problems of Communitarian Politics: Unity and Conflict*. New York: Oxford University Press, 1999.

Glendon, Mary Ann. *Rights Talk*. Cambridge: Harvard University Press, 1991.

Holmes, Stephen. *The Anatomy of Antiliberalism*. Chicago: University of Chicago Press, 1993.

MacIntyre, Alasdair. *After Virtue: A Study in Moral Theory*. Notre Dame, Ind.: University of Notre Dame Press, 1981; London: Duckworth, 1982.

McWilliams, Wilson Carey. *The Idea of Fraternity in America*. Berkeley: University of California Press, 1973.

Rorty, Richard M. *Contingency, Irony, and Solidarity*. Cambridge and New York: Cambridge University Press, 1989.

Sandel, Michael J. *Liberalism and the Limits of Justice*. Cambridge and New York: Cambridge University Press, 1982.

Walzer, Michael. *Spheres of Justice: A Defense of Pluralism and Equality*. New York: Basic Books, 1983; Oxford: Blackwell, 1985.

✦ Confucianism

Chinese school of political thought founded by Confucius (c. 551–c. 479 B.C.). Although the current Chinese term for *democracy*, literally "rule of the people," was not introduced into the Chinese vocabulary until the nineteenth century, democratic principles of governance have been part of Confucianism for millennia.

Confucius spoke of the ideal of a Grand Commonwealth in which the governing elite would be elected and composed of people of talent and virtue. Since then, Chinese scholars have looked to the ideas of Confucius as the starting point for their own political reform proposals—from Mencius, in the third century B.C., who expanded on Confucius's ideas, to Kang Youwei, a nineteenth-century statesman and Confucian scholar, who advocated extreme egalitarianism, worldwide democracy, and abolition of nation-states.

In the twentieth century, discussion in China and elsewhere has centered on the nature of Confucianism and its impact on the future of China and the world. Some Sinologists in the West have dismissed Confucianism as an outmoded and negative force hindering the modernization of Asian nations. A similar stance was taken by Chinese scholars during the May Fourth Movement, an intellectual revolution that swept China in the wake of World War I. However, the current importance of Confucianism in several modern democraticizing Asian societies—particularly Taiwan, Hong Kong, and Singapore—forces the West and China to reconsider the importance of Confucianism and its compatibility with modern democratic ideals.

Confucian democratic ideals—as opposed to European ruling traditions—are embodied by the concept of the Mandate of Heaven, which portrays the emperor not only as the son of Heaven but also as the first servant of the state. Mencius expanded on this idea, stating that an emperor may rule only so long as the people's needs are met. If the emperor fails in this mission, any commoner may try to depose him and assume his role as leader. The Confucian mandate thus stands in stark contrast to the European idea of a monarch who holds divine right to the throne by birth and bloodline.

Confucius and Confucian Ideals

Confucius was born in Lu, the center of Zhou culture, and now the city of Qufu in Shandong Province. He lost his father at the age of three and was largely self-taught under the guidance of his mother. For much of his life he traveled among warring princes, seeking patronage and expounding upon his political philosophy in an effort to promote peace. Not until he was past fifty did Confucius enter government, rising to the position of minister of justice. He had to resign after only three years, however, and was once again obliged to travel from state to state seeking patronage. Throughout his life, Confucius had three goals: to serve government, to teach youth, and to record Chinese culture for posterity.

A great advocate of order and dignity, Confucius preached against the growing chaos in China, stressing the responsibilities inherent in human relationships: between ruler and subject, father and son, husband and wife, elder brother and younger brother, and friend and friend. He believed that the first step toward the transformation of a disordered world was recognition and fulfillment of each individual's proper place in society. To Confucius, the concept of individual human rights (as defined in Western democracies) was subordinate to this sense of contractual social obligation emphasizing the individual's responsibility to a greater group, such as family and nation.

Confucius believed the world would develop in three stages. The first stage would be an age of disorder; the second would be a period in which all states begin to enjoy order and peace; and the Grand Commonwealth would emerge in the third stage. Confucius thus held the Grand Commonwealth, under which a talented and virtuous elite would be elected to govern, to be the highest ideal of society. This elite was to be made up of gentlemen who had received a literary as well as a moral education that stressed truth, honor, and the promotion of just government. Breaking with tradition, Confucius held that a man was a gentleman due to his character, rather than his bloodline.

Members of the ruling elite were expected to act with the highest degree of moral responsibility as an ethical example for all people. In return,

this elite would have authoritarian powers. Confucius saw this system as the best alternative to the state of warfare then current between feudal lords and aristocratic families.

Confucius advocated *ren*—humanity or benevolence—as the highest good. He viewed the princely, or superior, man as the ideal being and the cultivation of life as the supreme duty of man. Confucius emphasized moral perfection for the individual and proper conduct based on morality for society.

Ren expresses the Confucian ideal of cultivating benevolence, developing one's faculties, sublimating one's personality, and upholding the right to education, the right to subsistence, and the right to social and political mobility without distinction according to class. *Ren* could be cultivated through filial behavior and fraternal love, which Confucius saw as the cornerstones of society. If practiced by successive dynasties, filial behavior and fraternal love would serve as the bond of social solidarity and the connection between generations. Grievances were to be resolved through a process of mutual accommodation. Under the influence of Confucianism, the Chinese state thus developed a consensual model of governance, rather than following the more legalistic and adversarial Western model.

Because *ren* applied to rulers and ruled alike, it represented a new and democratic ideal of society. Confucius was not merely idealistic, however. He also outlined three essential elements of good government that would make the practice of *ren* possible: abundance of goods, adequate armaments, and the confidence of the people. Of the three, Confucius held the greatest to be the confidence of the people, without which he said there would be no government. This theory was later expanded by Mencius into the doctrine of people's sovereignty.

Because of his desire for order in Chinese society and his disdain for the prevailing chaos of his times, Confucius also placed much emphasis on the ruler to the disadvantage of the ruled. Although Confucian doctrine was dependent on the egalitarian ideals of *ren*, as well as many other principles, many rulers in China unfortunately chose to ignore the more democratic principles and focus instead on the authoritarian aspects of Confucianism.

Disciples and Interpreters of Confucius

Mencius (c. 372–c. 289 B.C.) elaborated on Confucius's ideas about the role of the people in government in his doctrine of people's sovereignty. Born near Confucius's hometown in Shandong during a period of civil strife and political instability, Mencius studied under disciples of Confucius. Like Confucius, he traveled for most of his life, offering advice on social and political reforms to feudal lords. Also like Confucius, he failed to win royal support for his political doctrines and had to content himself with teaching and writing in his last years. Although he did not win political favor during his lifetime, Mencius later was recognized by the Chinese literati as the Second Sage—the greatest philosopher after Confucius.

According to Mencius, good government should come upward from the people instead of downward from the ruling class. The people are not only the root but also the final judge of government. A major element of this doctrine is the Confucian theory of the Mandate of Heaven, on which Mencius elaborated. Because the opinion of the people is of supreme significance in the affairs of the state, the people have the right to depose a wicked king. Mencius thus spoke favorably of the popular revolutions of the past that had ended with the overthrow of the rulers Jie and Zhou, whose autocracy and thievery from the people had caused them to lose the Mandate of Heaven.

Above all, Mencius emphasized the ruler's duty to enrich the people, arguing that virtue and peace could not come as long as hunger and cold were the order of the day. Rebellion was justified under such conditions, since the sovereign did not hold an innate right to rule. Mencius also viewed government officials as the nation's public servants, bearing the sovereign's charge to nourish the people, rather than as the private retainers of the sovereign.

The third great developer of Confucian thought was the philosopher Hsün-tzu (Xun Zi), whose life as a social and political reformer was much like that of Confucius. While the exact dates of Hsün-tzu's birth and death are not known, he is believed to have lived to witness the end of the Warring States period (402–221 B.C.), when the state of Qin conquered all its rival states and unified China for the first time (in 221 B.C.). Like Mencius, Hsün-tzu held that a contented, economically well-off populace was the basis of good government. He believed that a sovereign could win the allegiance of his people only by his noble character, not by brute force. Hsün-tzu thus conceived of the sovereign's power as derived from the general will of the people, rather than from a special commission from Heaven. Like Mencius, he supported the right of the people to revolt against the ruler who failed in four duties: nourishing, governing, employing, and protecting the people. However, whereas Mencius represents the more idealistic wing of Confucianism, Hsün-tzu was a pragmatist who emphasized social control to offset what he saw as the basic weakness of human nature.

The Chinese Imperial State

Confucianism became the predominant philosophy in China only after the imperial system was consolidated under the Qin (255–206 B.C.) and Han (205 B.C.–A.D. 220) dynasties. The first Qin emperor, a harsh Legalist monarch, took drastic measures to eradicate dangerous doctrines, burning books and burying scholars alive. Although the Han rulers disapproved of the violent methods of the Qin, they also realized the wisdom of maintaining political unity through unity of thought. Upon the recommendations of Han Confucian scholars, the Han emperor Wudi organized within the Imperial Court a board of scholars with five faculties, each specializing in one of the five Confucian classics. The board expanded from 50 TO 3,000 scholars in the second half of the first century B.C. and to 30,000 scholars in the second century A.D. At the same time, many other scholars of Confucianism were named in the outlying districts throughout China. These scholars became the backbone of China's elite.

Han emperors also established an examination system based on the five classics of Confucianism. By the first century A.D., a hundred scholars each year were said to enter government service through a process resembling modern civil service examinations, which continued throughout successive dynasties. The Confucian-based examination system helped to free common people from feudal bondage by opening up channels of economic, social, and political mobility. Through this examination system, for example, several commoners rose to the position of prime minister of China during the Han dynasty.

Although Confucian ideas did not evolve into structured democratic institutions, Confucianism did divide China into separate state and family structures, which together formed the nation-state. At the top of imperial China was the bureaucratic state, in which the Confucian scholar held exclusive political responsibility under the emperor. At the base was a kinship-centered society headed by a magistrate.

Confucianism demanded that the Chinese people demonstrate loyalty both to the state and to the family. For example, district magistrates, who often were clan elders, would not carry out absurd demands of the state that went against the welfare of the districts and their families. Thus the kinship systems existing in China throughout the dynasties provided a shield against strong-arm tactics of the imperial state.

Since the Han dynasty, China's political system has also made some provision for the distribution of powers. Although the emperor, as the source of all powers, held the exclusive right to exercise legislative, executive, and judicial powers, the powers of examination and impeachment were exercised independently by his ministers in order to ensure an efficient and honest government. For example, the imperial censors were expected to oversee and, when necessary, criticize members of the administration, including the emperor. The Chinese emperor, like the British Crown, stood above the law but was subject to the restraints of the institutions and practices of Confucian ethics and customs. Although this separation of the power of the emperor (monarch) from that of the bureaucracy suffered certain setbacks during the Ming dynasty (1368–1644), when the office of the prime minister was abolished, it nevertheless remained a basic feature of traditional Chinese government for centuries.

As time went on, the content of Confucianism went through numerous metamorphoses. Many early Confucian democratic ideas were at times deemphasized or even ignored. At other times, the idea of people's sovereignty was held up by a small group of scholars or even a single scholar, as in the case of Huang Zongxi (1609–1695). Huang criticized China's growing tendency toward despotism during the Ming dynasty and analyzed the political and economic weaknesses of seventeenth-century China in his first important work, *A Plan for the Prince.*

Huang was rare among Confucianists in attaching importance to the form or system of government rather than simply to the moral character of the ruler and his officials. Whereas Confucianists historically had ignored or been hostile to the concept of law, which they associated with the totalitarian concepts of the violent Legalists under the Qin dynasty, Huang emphasized the importance of law in preventing corruption among the ruling elite and in the civil service examination process.

Unfortunately, Huang's pleas fell on deaf ears and attracted no mass following. Under the Manchu-led Qing dynasty (1644–1911), the last dynasty before the republic, China developed along increasingly authoritarian lines into a so-called benevolent despotism. In doing so, it moved away from Confucian democratic ideals, while remaining committed to Confucian concepts of a strong leader who looked after the welfare of his people.

The Challenge of Modernization

It was not until the last years of the nineteenth century that the issue of democracy for China was raised again, this time by the last great Confucian scholar in China, Kang Youwei (1858–1927). In a series of memorials to the emperor, the last of which was written in 1898, Kang set forth a whole program of reform, including the adoption of a constitution, the creation of a parliament, and a total revision of the educational system. He convinced the emperor that these reforms were essential in order for China to survive.

In the summer of 1898 the Qing dynasty's Emperor Guangxu issued a series of reform edicts based on Kang's proposals, instituting what became known as the Hundred Days' Reform (June 11–September 20). Perhaps most significant was Kang's attempt to revitalize Confucius's concept of the Grand Commonwealth into a modern One World theory. Kang maintained that evolution toward the final one world (the third stage of evolution as envisioned by Confucius) would be a long and gradual process involving abolition of the "nine boundaries" of the contemporary world: nation, class, race, sex, family, occupation, disorder (inequality), kind (separation of people and animal), and suffering. Kang worked out a long chart of the Confucian principles of the three ages as part of his vision of uniting various nations under a universal parliament. Although a coup d'état in the royal house brought about an early end to Kang's reforms, his attempt to bring about a world government built on the concept of unity, equality, and peace must remain a great addition to the history of political thought, just as his writing remains one of the most interesting treatises on democracy with Confucian characteristics.

After the fall of the Qing dynasty and the establishment of a republic in 1911, Confucianism began to come under frequent attack. In the May Fourth Movement of 1919, student-led demonstrations led to a wide-ranging iconoclastic attack on the Confucian tradition. Many prominent reformers of the time were partisans of Western science and democracy who viewed Confucianism as a form of reactionary traditionalism. The intellectual debates of the republican era largely centered on two camps: Confucianists versus the advocates of Westernization. The movement to bring wholesale Westernization to China ended abruptly, however, with the establishment of a Communist government under Mao Zedong in 1949.

Although there has been a long tradition of hostility toward established religion and philosophy in contemporary China, Confucian tradition has been incorporated in support of communist ideology. Mao himself was fundamentally influenced by two Confucian scholars, Kang Youwei and Liang Qichao. In his writings, Mao borrowed two elements of Confucianism in particular: first, the idea that knowledge must lead to action and that action must be based on knowledge, and, second, the ideal of the commonwealth, which Mao identified with communism. As Mao strove to disassociate his ideology from China's past, however, he did not give credit to Confucianism for these concepts. Furthermore, during the violent political upheaval of the Cultural Revolution (1966–1976), the government waged a virulent anti-Confucian campaign throughout China.

Since the late 1970s China's top leader, Deng Xiaoping, and his followers have adhered to a policy of preserving what they believed to be the best of the cultural heritage of Confucianism. They made use of Confucian ethics and literature to elucidate Deng's doctrines, such as a desire for social and political order, and a sense of a new commonwealth guided by the cultivation of one's faculties and extension of one's services to the party and society. The government spent millions of dollars to repair the temples and mansions of Confucius and his descendants that were damaged by the Red Guards during the Maoist era.

China by the mid-1990s showed definite signs of a revival of Confucian studies, under the broad rubric of "socialism with Chinese characteristics." Articles on Confucianism began to reappear in Chinese newspapers during the reform movement of the 1980s and early 1990s. Confucianism is, in fact, making a theoretical comeback to provide communism with a new moral anchor. The government has sponsored many conferences and symposia linking new interpretations of Confucianism to Deng Xiaoping's policies.

Confucian Revival in East Asia

Beyond the borders of mainland China, Confucianism has developed significantly since the 1960s, as the so-called Four Tigers of the Pacific Rim—Hong Kong, Taiwan, Singapore, and South Korea—have incorporated Confucian ideas to varying degrees into the governments and social structures of their rapidly modernizing societies. The governments have combined the traditional benevolent authoritarian ruler with a democratically elected parliament and instituted a virtuous elite through a civil service examination system, creating a strong bureaucracy independent of politicians.

Interregional communication among Confucian scholars from these areas has led to lively intellectual exchanges. The New Asia College of the Chinese University in Hong Kong, founded on the principle of revitalizing the true spirit of Confucianism, has played a key role in coordinating regional efforts to promote Confucian learning and has trained a new generation of scholars in the study of various dimensions of Confucian culture.

In Taiwan, Confucianism was part of the mandatory curriculum under Chiang Kai-shek's government in conjunction with its anticommunist policy. The government in fact designated September 28 as the birthday of Confucius and made it a national holiday. Interest in Confucianism increased in the 1970s as a new generation of young scholars was encouraged to investigate the spirit of Confucianism in the modern world.

In Singapore concern over the moral and world outlook of younger Singaporeans prompted the government to introduce Confucianism into school curriculums in the 1980s. Scholars and experts on Confucianism were invited from the United States, China, and Taiwan to help the Ministry of Education develop a model curriculum. At the urging of Lee Kuan Yew, a senior leader and former prime minister, Confucian ethics was identified as among the principles forming the "national ideology" of the country in 1991.

Although Confucianism has evolved greatly over the millennia, it remains a vibrant political philosophy in modern Asian democracies. The historic Western view of Confucianism as a quasi-religious system of ethics should broaden as Western understanding and contact with Asia increases. As a political theory, Confucianism insists on the sovereignty of the people and on the government's devotion to the well-being of its people. As such, Confucianism in its ideal form is not merely sovereignty of the people but rather rule of the people, or democracy.

WINBERG CHAI AND MAY-LEE CHAI

BIBLIOGRAPHY

Chai, Chu, and Winberg Chai. *Confucianism.* Woodbury, N.Y.: Barron's, 1973.

Chai, Winberg, Carolyn Chai, and Cal Clark, eds. *Political Stability of Economic Growth: Case Studies of Taiwan, South Korea, Hong Kong and Singapore.* Dubuque, Iowa: Kendall/Hunt, 1994.

Chan, Wing-tsit. *A Source Book in Chinese Philosophy.* Princeton: Princeton University Press, 1963.

Confucius. *The Sacred Books of Confucius and Other Confucian Classics.* Edited and translated by Chu Chai and Winberg Chai. New Hyde Park, N.Y.: University Books, 1965.

Creel, H. G. *Chinese Thought from Confucius to Mao Tsetung.* Chicago: University of Chicago Press, 1953.

De Bary, William Theodore. *Asian Values and Human Rights: A Confucian Communitarian Perspective.* Cambridge: Harvard University Press, 1998.

_____. *The Liberal Tradition in China.* New York: Columbia University Press, 1983.

Fung Yu-lan. *A History of Chinese Philosophy.* 2 vols. Translated by Derk Bodde. Princeton: Princeton University Press, 1952.

Hsiung, James C., and Chung-ying Cheng, eds. *Distribution of Power and Rewards: Proceedings of the International Conference on Democracy and Social Justice East and West.* Lanham, Md.: University Press of America, 1991.

Metzger, Thomas. *Escape from Predicament: Neo-Confucianism and China's Evolving Political Culture.* New York: Columbia University Press, 1977.

Tu, Wei-ming. *Way, Learning, and Politics: Essays on the Confucian Intellectual.* Albany: State University of New York Press, 1991.

Yao, Xinzhong. *An Introduction to Confucianism.* Cambridge and New York: Cambridge University Press, 2000.

✦ Conservatism

A democratic political philosophy that favors limited government, advocates moderate change, and has doubts about the value and extent of the modern administrative and welfare state. It is common for writers on conservatism to begin by protesting that the term and the phenomenon it describes are hard to pin down or else by noting that it is contrary to the spirit of conservatism to attempt a rigorous account of its principles. Both reservations are in part correct.

First, it is difficult to define conservatism by referring to a fixed set of positions. On an array of issues—from economic policy to questions of social organization, from foreign policy to basic moral principles—conservatives will be found to differ among themselves, sometimes quite dramatically.

Second, it is true that much conservative thought rejects the idea that politics can be understood and managed by applying systems of abstract ideas to practical circumstances. This antipathy to excessive rationalism—to what is now often called social engineering—began with Edmund Burke's objections to the French Revolution. Burke, an English political philosopher and politician of the eighteenth century, believed that the French Revolution was doomed because it rested on the utopianism of the Enlightenment—on the hope that long-established orders based on religion, tradition, and aristocratic privilege could be replaced overnight by a society deduced from the abstract principles of equality and individual natural rights. Burke taught conservatives to mistrust what they take to be the lure of idealism and the utopian hopes of intellectuals. Hence to this day many conservatives resist the temptation to spin out a conservative system and object when others attribute one to them.

But it is possible to heed this objection and at the same time to identify the fundamental issues that matter to conservatives and ultimately determine their several points of view on more concrete and changeable matters. These fundamental issues are the balance between liberty and equality, the question of progress and history, and the character of democracy. Already from this brief list we can see that conservatism as we know it today is quite new. In earlier times people did not presume that there was any equality to be balanced with liberty, did not believe in progress and history, and did not think democracy was a serious possibility to be debated.

These ideas were first broached in the seventeenth century and did not burst forth until the American and French Revolutions at the end of the eighteenth century. It is telling that Burke's political positions were developed in response to these two great events, and one could say without exaggeration that his conservatism is thus paradigmatic: conservatism today almost always takes for granted that change is inevitable, that democracy is good, and that all human beings are born as moral equals. In other words, conservatism stands within, and is in large part defined by, the Enlightenment principles with which it was at first at odds.

Evolution of Conservative Thought

The term *conservatism* did not even become current until the 1830s, when it was imported from France to England and was used to designate the Tory Party as it had been defined by Burke and his followers. In France the term referred to those who, under Burke's influence, had serious doubts about the effects of the French Revolution. So one could say with some justification that the term really originated in England. But having suffered the revolution and its aftermath, European conservatives were more inclined than were the English to reject the principles of the Enlightenment altogether. Thinkers such as Joseph de Maistre and the Vicomte de Bonald in France, and Adam Müller and Klemens von Metternich in Austria, rejected wholly the ideas of republican government and the separation of church and state—and especially rejected the ideas of progress and equality. To them, such ideas ignored disastrously the divine right of kings and the natural depravity of the human race.

In England, however, the revolutionary settlement of 1688 (which resulted in the overthrow of the king, James II) involved an agreement between the Whigs, who wished to limit the king's prerogative, and moderate Tories on the basically Whiggish principle of parliamentary supremacy. English conservatism thus very early gave up the doctrine of divine right and monarchical absolutism and was therefore able to make its peace with the idea of progress and with an expanding franchise, even if it did not accept fully the Whiggish idea (derived from John Locke, the seventeenth-century English philosopher) that all legitimate government originates in a contract of free and equal individuals or the more radical utilitarianism of thinkers like Jeremy Bentham (1748–1832) and John Stuart Mill (1806–1873). Unlike most European conservatives, English politicians like Burke and Benjamin Disraeli—

who as Tory prime minister (1868 and 1874–1880) began the tradition of conservative social reform—saw conservatism as the complex of ideas, traditions, and moral dispositions that moderates inevitably change. Thus they accepted, albeit reluctantly, the most important aspect of modern times.

The same and more could be said for conservatism in America. Because the United States has no monarchical or aristocratic roots, it has never doubted fundamentally the principles of democracy, equality, and progress. As the French historian and political observer Alexis de Tocqueville pointed out in the mid-nineteenth century, the framing of the American Constitution was a conservative event that consolidated a political order embodying these revolutionary forces of the modern spirit. And so he claimed that in America there would be no really deep partisan differences. In Tocqueville's view the Americans agreed about everything fundamental, with the important disagreements appearing only in diluted quarrels about nuance and degree.

Certainly by the end of World War II, in 1945, this description could be said to apply to the whole of the Western world. The monstrous course of fascism put an end to all forms of conservatism that were opposed in principle to the modern age—that is, to secularism, equality, representative democracy, and the culture of science and technology. No conservative can be found today—at least not in a genuine democracy—who favors monarchy, aristocracy, or theocracy or who thinks that mystical nationalism is a serious or desirable alternative to the modern democratic state.

Modern Interpretations

Even in the United States, where ideological consensus runs so deep, it is possible to speak of liberals and conservatives who disagree on important matters. Surely there is a difference between twentieth-century presidents Woodrow Wilson and Franklin Delano Roosevelt, on the one hand, and Calvin Coolidge and William Graham Sumner (the famous theorist of laissez-faire, or minimal, government), on the other. So what are the principles of modern conservatism? To see them, we return to the fundamental issues mentioned earlier. To speak very broadly, the project of modernity aims to establish political and social life on three principles: (1) individuals are born free and equal, with no one warranted by nature or God to rule others without their consent; (2) the progressive conquest of nature means that poverty can be reduced to a level that makes genuine cooperation possible; (3) democracy of a limited kind—"liberal democracy"—is the particular form of government to which free and equal individuals will consent.

No one in our time denies that individuals are born free and equal and that they should be governed only by those to whom they have given their consent. But there is disagreement about the meaning of liberty and equality and the relation between them. In modern democracies the hope is that individuals will be equally free to become whatever their natural endowments and efforts will allow. No artificial barriers—including the power of government—should stand in their way. This interpretation means that individuals should be equally free to become unequal in their accomplishments. Often, however, bad luck or the stifling effects of social class get in the way of equal opportunity, and even legitimate inequalities tend to ossify into illegitimate ones, as might be said to happen when wealth and privilege are inherited rather than earned. And so in the name of equality of opportunity, it can be argued that political power should be used to restrict the liberty of some individuals for the sake of others, usually by way of redistributing income and other opportunities.

Thus, while there may be no disagreement about liberty and equality at the level of general principle, there are serious differences of opinion about which inequalities are legitimate and about how far individual liberty should be restrained in order to remedy illegitimate inequalities. On this issue, conservatives tend to judge inequalities in mature democratic societies to be legitimate and not the result of rigid, and thus unfair, advantages. They likewise think that it can do more harm than good to give government the power to remedy unfair advantages when unfair advantages do occur. In general, it could be said that conservatives favor liberty over equality—or, more precisely, that they understand equality as formal equality of opportunity and freedom as independence from political coercion.

Again, no one in our time doubts that democratic government requires what might be called the project of rationalism—the complex of ideas and practices that includes the separation of church and state, individualism and free markets, constitutionalism, and, perhaps most important, the science and technology that are essential for a rising standard of living. But there are disagreements about how completely this project can produce a fully rational society and about whether history is a force that leads inevitably to progress.

Conservatives believe in the separation of church and state. But, not expecting the complete victory of reason over the whole of life, they tend to think that no society can function well without the influence of religion and morality and that public policy must take this fact into account. They also think that the justice and efficiency of markets are diminished, not improved, by centralized and politicized planning. And they have doubts about the extent to which problems such as crime and poverty can be solved by social engineering, which uses the methods and approaches of science and technology. Conservatives tend to

doubt that history is a force that makes all innovation turn out for the better. Consequently, they usually worry more than do liberals about the consequences of what is done in the name of progress. And while in general they favor capitalism and free enterprise, a long tradition of conservative thought bemoans the way modern life corrodes old ways, coarsens manners, and levels the depths and contours of cultural life. We see this point of view in such writers and cultural critics as Jonathan Swift, Samuel Taylor Coleridge, James Fenimore Cooper, Henry Adams, T. S. Eliot, José Ortega y Gasset, and Malcolm Muggeridge, to name but a few.

Finally, in our time there is almost unanimous agreement among conservatives that democracy is a form of limited government—that it should be liberal democracy. When used in this way, the term *liberal* is not taken in its usual American sense to mean an ideological preference for big government or progressive social policy. Rather, it refers to the idea that government should derive from popular consent and have as its ultimate goal the securing of private liberty. No one today seriously thinks that modern democracies could or should be like the democracies of the ancient Greeks, which were small, homogeneous, and dedicated to the formation of the citizens' moral character and conception of the good. Preliberal forms of democracy lacked the institution of civil society, the realm of social and economic relations that exists apart from government but under its protection. In a liberal democracy, government is popular, but its purpose is to safeguard and maximize the private liberty that is exercised in civil society. In civil society, individuals are free to buy and sell, to worship as they please, to think and speak as they wish, and to pursue their own conceptions of happiness and the good life. In a liberal democracy, democratic politics is not considered a good in itself, as it was in ancient times;

rather, democracy is good because it is the only real guarantee of equal and individual liberty.

But within this broad modern agreement about democracy, there is room for disagreement about how democratic a government must be in order to accomplish its liberal purpose. Conservatives tend to mistrust attempts to bring democracy closer to the people and do not think that more democracy is always better than less. They agree with the spirit of James Madison's view, expressed in the *Federalist* No. 63. There Madison (later president of the United States, 1809–1817) said that the key to successful popular sovereignty was "the total exclusion of the people in their collective capacity" from the government. In a well-ordered democracy, only representatives of the people wield the levers of government; there is no assembly in which all the people exercise the specific functions of government.

Thus conservatives generally have doubts about populist devices—such as the initiative and referendum, the party primary, and proportional representation—intended to get around the distance imposed by the U.S. Constitution between the people and their representatives in government. They are more comfortable than are liberals and progressives with the need for secrecy in government, with the independence and vigor of executive power, and with the influence of and need for elites in politics and society. But at the same time, conservatives have doubts about the expanding power of bureaucracy and the administrative state, which liberals and progressives see as necessary engines of equality and efficiency. Conservatives are thus open to democratic "revolts" against the tendency for government to intrude into private and social life.

Partisan Identifications and Divisions

In terms of the main political parties in the older democracies, conservatism has its home in the Republican Party in the United States, the Conservative Party in the United Kingdom, the Gaullist Party (currently the Rally for the Republic) and the Union for French Democracy in France, the Christian Democratic Union in Germany (and the Christian Democratic Parties in the rest of continental Europe), the Likud bloc in Israel, the Progressive Conservatives in Canada, the National and Liberal Parties in Australia, and the National Party in New Zealand. In recent years the electorates in most democratic countries have become less well defined ideologically—in large part because they are less clearly divided by class, education, and religion—and the end of the cold war has accelerated this development.

The traditional parties of both left and right have thus lost much of their cohesion, and it is likely that new ones will appear and old ones will be defined by new concerns. Furthermore, the almost global fiscal crisis facing the modern welfare state has forced the parties of the left in a rightward direction. But whatever their new form and particular policies, conservative parties will continue to side with the interests of business. They will appeal more to rural and suburban voters than to city dwellers, and more to the better off than to the less well off, and they will resonate more comfortably with middle-class sensibilities and interests than with those of the so-called chattering classes (intellectuals, journalists, educators, and publicly employed professionals). Most important, they will confront any new problems and concerns—whether problems of the environment, ethnic and linguistic identities, regional interests, or social issues associated with mature capitalism—from the general standpoint of the conservative principles outlined previously.

It cannot be concluded, however, that all conservatives are the same, for there are important differences that have divided them and will continue to divide them. Perhaps most significant is the difference between conservatives in the tradition of Burke and those who are the heirs of what was once called radicalism—what today we would call laissez-faire libertarianism. This difference emerged as early as the mid-nineteenth century, when the Conservative Party in England was split on the issue of free trade versus tariffs that protected domestic agricultural interests. The followers of Disraeli favored protection, rural interests and traditions, and, somewhat later, paternalistic social reform from above. On the other side were those who favored free trade and took a more individualistic, business-oriented, even utilitarian view of human nature and society.

This division, which is still visible in England in the split between the more traditional, or Disraelian, conservatives and the followers of Margaret Thatcher (prime minister, 1979–1990), and in Australia in the difference between the National and Liberal Parties, can be seen in conservative parties around the globe. It is impossible to imagine Burke uttering Thatcher's now famous remark: "There is no such thing as society. There are individual men and women, and there are families."

Burke objected to revolutionary rationalism because it did not grasp the true nature of human society. According to the partisans of the French Revolution and radicals like Thomas Paine (a pamphleteer of both the American and French Revolutions and Burke's adversary), society is simply an aggregation of free and equal individuals endowed with the natural right to consent to any government that they deem necessary for their happiness and liberty. For Burke, however, the individual's right to self-government must be mediated through historically determined communities characterized by class hierarchy, established orders of hereditary property, and ancient systems of customs, moral habits, and prejudices. The people could be represented in a constitu-

tional order but certainly not directly: the representatives of the people would act for the society as a whole and would be under no binding instructions from their constituents, who need not all have the right to vote. For Burke, an abstract or theoretical doctrine of individual liberty was merely utopian—and dangerously so—if it ignored the complex moral and material articulation of society.

Traditional Conservatives and Libertarians

Although no conservative today would propose Burkeianism in all its details, the spirit of Burke is evident in contemporary conservatives who approve of privileged elites, who see religion and morality as important for society, and who doubt progressive optimism. It is on these matters that the libertarians part company with their conservative colleagues. Libertarians like Margaret Thatcher and the Austrian economist Friedrich von Hayek reject elitism and traditions of noblesse oblige. They deny that government should have any interest in morality or religion and tend to think that anything standing in the way of economic enterprise—such as tradition, nostalgia for rural life, or worry about the erosion of moral habits—is an illegitimate constraint on individual liberty. Although they think that government planning, social engineering, and income redistribution do nothing but harm, they have faith that individual free enterprise and the mechanism of the market will do nothing but good. The libertarian conservative is inclined to think that the problems of society and human life in general—war, poverty, disputes about justice, and economic instability—are caused by the dysfunctional effects of illegitimate government power. When the reach of the state is constrained to its proper limits, these problems will disappear.

Modern conservatives are divided by their degree of adherence to what we have referred to as Enlightenment rationalism. Libertarians owe more to Thomas Paine and to utilitarians such as Bentham and Mill than they do to Burke, and they believe more in progress than do their more traditional colleagues. They see the individual as a rational, free, autonomous economic actor, and they are inclined to think that there are no defects and contradictions in the human condition that right reason cannot in principle overcome. The more traditional conservative, on the other hand, thinks that human nature is crooked wood. Reason, democracy, and capitalism can bend it—but never perfectly and not without appeals to passion, belief, morality, and tradition.

The libertarian will oppose the welfare state on both moral and practical grounds. On the one hand, there is no moral obligation for resources to be transferred from the rich to the poor; on the other hand, the state's redistributive interference in the economy is the ultimate cause of the poverty that it is our supposed obligation to relieve. The more traditional conservative likewise will not see the welfare state (or the idea that the rich should be taxed at a higher proportional rate than the less well off) as a redistributive duty but may well see it as necessary for the political integration of any modern, industrialized democracy. The libertarian conservative is in principle opposed to any attempt by the state to influence the character of the citizen—whether by encouraging religion, limiting free speech, outlawing narcotics and pornography, and so on. The traditional conservative will often support such policies, believing that good character is essential for democratic liberty and that both capitalism and technological change, however necessary, can erode the social supports that such character requires.

It is important to remember that the traditional-libertarian divide is not fixed hard and fast. As one would expect in political life, the unalloyed libertarian or traditional conservative is hard to find, even though most conservatives lean more or less strongly in one or the other direction. And so it is difficult to predict specific policy preferences with precision. Thus in the United States the more libertarian conservatives may or may not be internationalists in foreign policy, and the same ambivalence is true for more traditional conservatives. In England, libertarians may be less inclined toward European integration, because they fear its domination by European socialists, and yet more inclined toward global involvement; more traditional conservatives may be more European and less global. It can also be the other way around.

Although libertarians are almost always in favor of free trade, it is less easy to predict how more traditional conservatives in Europe, the United Kingdom, and the United States will come down on this often contentious issue. In America it is hard to predict what libertarians and traditional conservatives will think about abortion rights. Some libertarians may think that such a matter is an individual decision, while others may see the fetus as an individual bearing rights to be protected by the state. Some traditionalists may see abortion as a practice that degrades good character, while others may see it as essential for limiting the spread of dependency among the poor. And in all democracies, a small minority of "far right" conservatives of both kinds will tend toward extremist politics. Thus libertarians can be inclined toward antielitist but aggressive populism, and traditionalists can be inclined toward vaguely anticapitalist populism or toward nationalism, religious fundamentalism, and xenophobia.

All conservatives were anticommunist during the cold war. But while the collapse of communism has had its unsettling effects on their self-understanding, it has not settled the fundamental issues that concern conservatives in the old democracies and even in the new ones arising around the world. Conservatives believe that as long as a government is democratic, the temptation will always exist for it to bid for votes from the various clients of the welfare state and from those producer groups—whether business or labor—who might gain from government economic policy or suffer from the dislocations and changes associated with capitalism.

And so despite their differences, and the difficulty of predicting them, today all conservatives agree in general that the modern welfare state has a dangerous tendency to grow beyond due measure and to threaten the economic well-being and expansion that is essential to democratic liberty. All likewise agree that government management of the economy must be kept to a practicable minimum, because governments are always moved more by political than by economic considerations. And all—even most libertarians—likewise oppose what they see as the relentless egalitarianism of modern life: the ever increasing tendency to leveling, mass culture, and individual dependency that often seems to threaten liberty and equality, properly understood.

Guardians Against the State

Tocqueville has given us the best account of the modern situation as seen from the conservative point of view. In *Democracy in America* (1835–1840), he explained that in the modern age no one can legitimately question the view that all human beings are endowed with equal rights to liberty and the pursuit of happiness. But equality of opportunity comes to be judged by equality of results. As equality progresses, individuals become stronger and more independent than they were in more aristocratic times. But they also become more isolated from each other and at the same time weaker in comparison to the gargantuan power of public opinion and mass taste. Similarly,

individuals who love equality become increasingly indignant at the inevitable inequalities that will always exist, even though, considered objectively, all are better off and inequalities tend to shrink.

For all these reasons there is an inevitable tendency for democratic individuals—progressively weakened and increasingly indignant—to see the centralized, administrative state as the solution to their dissatisfaction. It is no moral offense to be dependent on the state, for it is at once like no particular person and also the result of the individual's consent. The paradoxical result is an individual who will assert a right to vote but who is otherwise incapable of independent life. The danger that stalks modern democracy is not harsh tyranny imposed from without but a soft and enervating despotism that grows slowly from within.

Despite their many differences on matters both large and small, there are today no conservatives who would dissent wholly from Tocqueville's view. Virtually all are democrats. But all agree, more or less explicitly, that the task for conservatives is to prevent the dangers to democracy that spring from democracy. They may disagree about some of the means but not about the end.

See also Burke, Edmund; Laissez-faire; Liberalism; Tocqueville, Alexis de.

JERRY WEINBERGER

BIBLIOGRAPHY

Burke, Edmund. *Reflections on the Revolution in France*, with Thomas Paine's *The Rights of Man*. Garden City, N.Y.: Anchor Books, 1973.
Hayek, Friedrich A. von. *The Constitution of Liberty*. Chicago: University of Chicago Press, 1960.
Hearnshaw, F. J. C. *Conservatism in England*. London: Macmillan, 1933; New York: Fertig, 1968.
Kekes, John. *A Case For Conservatism*. Ithaca: Cornell University Press, 1998.

Kirk, Russell. *The Conservative Mind: From Burke to Eliot.* 6th ed. Chicago: Regnery/Gateway, 1978.

_____. *The Conservative Reader.* New York: Viking Penguin, 1982.

Novak, Michael. *The Spirit of Democratic Capitalism.* New York: Simon and Schuster, 1982.

Ortega y Gasset, José. *The Revolt of the Masses.* New ed. New York and London: Norton, 1964.

Rossiter, Clinton. *Conservatism in America, 1770–1945.* New York: Knopf, 1966.

Tocqueville, Alexis de. *Democracy in America.* Translated by George Lawrence. Garden City, N.Y.: Anchor Books, 1969.

Weiss, John. *Conservatism in Europe.* London: Thames and Hudson, 1977.

✦ Constitutionalism

A method of organizing government that depends on and adheres to a set of fundamental guiding principles and laws. The relation between constitutionalism and democracy, that is, between limited government and self-government, remains one of the most important but least understood subjects in political theory. Surprisingly enough, even commentators with diametrically opposite political views often agree that there is an inherent tension between these two paramount liberal values or political practices.

Progressives ask: How can political officials be responsive to the will of today's electorate if they must follow rules laid down by long-dead ancestors—rules that a majority today cannot easily change and that are interpreted by unelected judges who are institutionally insulated from public opinion? Does not constitutional democracy ask government to obey two masters: the framers and the voters? And why should the people accept

restrictions that, by a strange coincidence, turn out to serve the interests of social elites?

Conservatives reason otherwise, and come to different conclusions, but nevertheless concur that constitutional restrictions are fundamentally antidemocratic. They believe, however, that this is a good reason to celebrate constitutionalism; they cite the danger of majority tyranny and stress the need to protect individual rights against democratic excesses. Constitutionalism, as they see it, is a curb on the follies and cruelties of popular rule.

This surprising meeting of the minds between conservatives and progressives is reinforced by the dichotomy of positive and negative liberty. Having a voice in the election of those who make the laws under which we live (democracy) is not the same as being protected in our private lives from governmental bullying and interference (constitutionalism). The two aims are not merely different; it is said that they point in opposite directions.

A constitution is an antimajoritarian device, conservatives contend, because its admirable goal is the legal entrenchment of imprescriptible rights against the frivolous voting-day behavior of fleeting electoral majorities. A constitution is an antimajoritarian device, progressives reply, because its disreputable goal is the legal entrenchment of social privileges, guaranteed by property rights and freedom of contract, against the will of democratic majorities. By giving exceptional legal status to fundamental rights, both sides agree, a constitution insulates certain values against potentially dissatisfied majorities.

Any antithesis that appeals strongly, as this one does, to both sides of the political spectrum will prove enormously resilient and difficult to overturn. Nevertheless, the idea of an inherent tension between constitutionalism and democracy is empirically unconfirmed and theoretically inadequate. First, among functioning democracies in the world today, all but Great Britain, Israel, and New Zealand operate within frameworks established by written constitutions. (And there are some solemnly documented and difficult-to-change features in these systems as well.) Second, the purported contradiction between limited government and self-government depends on untenable conceptions of the two terms. Stated briefly, the contradiction assumes that the principal function of a constitution is negative (to prevent tyranny) and that the principal aim of democracy is positive (to implement the will of the majority).

If these definitions were sound, constitutionalism and democracy *would* be intrinsically at odds. But they are not sound. The primary function of a liberal constitution—as this novel political form emerged in the United States at the end of the eighteenth century—is to constitute democracy, that is, to put democracy into effect. A constitution is an instrument of government. It is a way of organizing the people for self-rule. To understand the mutually supportive relation between limited government and self-government, we need to examine, among other topics, the democracy-reinforcing role of individual rights in constitutional systems.

How to Rule the Rulers

It is crucial to distinguish between *voluntaristic democracy* and *deliberative democracy*. In the former a preexistent will is simply expressed by the people, and the people's representatives must implement it. In the latter the people's will is shaped and reshaped through an ongoing process of public disagreement and discussion. The latter conception is superior, both normatively and empirically. But for expository purposes, we begin with voluntaristic democracy and make a simplifying assumption that we will later call into question. Let us assume that all members of the democratic electorate have at the outset a per-

fectly clear understanding of their own opinions on policy questions and that a coherent electoral majority has already been formed. Under such idealized conditions, democracy is indistinguishable from majoritarianism and simply demands that the electoral majority's viewpoint be put into effect. Even such a crudely voluntaristic or non-deliberative form of self-rule, it turns out, presupposes constitutionalism of a rather sophisticated kind.

If the majority of the electorate knows perfectly well what it wants, its relation to its elected representatives can be thought of as a principal-agent relation. Decision-making power is lodged in the people, while public officials serve as the people's proxies. An elected deputy, from this perspective, can be compared with a lawyer who represents a client or an ambassador who represents a state. All principal-agent relations raise the sticky issue of how to monitor the activity of the agent, how to make sure that the agent implements the instructions of the principal and does not act secretly and deviously for private advantage, partisan ideology, or whim.

Principals have a hard time monitoring agents for the same reason that they need an agent in the first place: the time, skills, and organizational resources at their disposal do not allow them to do the job themselves. In the case of democracy, periodic elections are by far the most important technique for subordinating the actions of the agents to the wishes of their principal.

But electoral accountability alone, however indispensable, is not sufficient for this purpose. Indeed, elected officials will often succeed in cloaking their actions, whatever purposes these actions serve, with fine-sounding rhetoric about the public good. (This is the residual core of truth in the otherwise misleading commonplace that constitutionalism is essentially antidemocratic: liberal constitutions are designed to prevent public officials from illegitimately invoking the name of the people to support policies that conflict with the wishes of the public.)

In any case, even majoritarianism requires that periodic elections be supplemented by a cluster of auxiliary precautions. What all these auxiliary precautions have in common is *plural agency*. That is, constitutionalism attempts to solve the principal-agent problem not only by institutionalizing periodic elections but also by appointing multiple agents who can monitor each other. Seen in this light, the separation of powers is an innovative use of the old precept, divide and rule. By dividing the "ruling class" of agents against itself, the popular majority can enforce its wishes (at least some of the time) even against those who directly control the levers of power.

Crucial separations and mutual checks that can serve this monitoring function include divisions between executive and legislative branches in presidential systems, divisions between chambers in bicameral systems, and divisions between levels of government in federal systems. Somewhat overlapping jurisdictions laid down in the constitutional text ensure that turf-conscious elected officials will inspect with jealousy the behavior of rival officials in different branches of government. Institutional self-interest alone, without any particular commitment to the public good, will encourage mutual surveillance and whistle-blowing in case of misbehavior.

As noted, the people at large is too busy and too poorly organized to engage in full-time monitoring of its political agents. But if officials in one branch of government discern a palpable electoral advantage in disclosing the questionable actions of officials in another branch, they will alert the people to activities that ostensibly contradict the public interest and public opinion. Understood in this way, the separation of powers is a perfectly democratic arrangement.

In short, a constitution is an indispensable instrument of government, even in a purely majoritarian system. A constitution is the way the people rules itself, and it therefore includes a variety of indirect methods for monitoring and controlling the people's political agents. It is vital for constitutionalism, as a result, that the fundamental ground rules, which are meant to serve this function, cannot be changed by ordinary lawmaking procedures in an elected assembly. The British do not have such a system, for Parliament's transcendent and uncontrollable authority extends beyond ordinary legislation to the fundamental structure of government. At one point, for instance, the British Parliament unilaterally replaced triennial elections with septennial elections, continuing itself in office four years beyond the term for which its members were elected by the people. A relatively rigid constitution with fixed-calendar elections, such as the American Constitution, was designed explicitly to prevent such antidemocratic usurpations of power.

The U.S. Framers sought to establish a clear legal basis for the limited government that existed in Britain only by tradition and usage. Although it may exist in practice, limited government remains legally baseless as long as the sovereign power to change the constitution is lodged in the government itself. To provide a legal basis for limited government, the American Framers followed the ideas of the English philosopher John Locke, lodging sovereign power *outside* the government, in the people itself. Constitutionalism, in the minds of U.S. Framers James Madison and Alexander Hamilton, did not depend on rules laid down by God or fixed by custom.

Constitutionalism is self-conscious and voluntaristic, a product of enlightened popular sovereignty. Because democratic citizens have common sense, they clearly recognize the need for a variety of indirect techniques for enforcing their will on public officials.

But what about judicial review? How can we justify democratically a system in which judges insulated from public opinion can unilaterally capsize the decisions of electorally accountable politicians? If democratically elected officials always implemented the wishes of the people faithfully, there would be no democratic justification for judicial review. But because elected officials are constantly tempted to invoke the name of the people to legitimize self-interested or partisan actions, the judiciary has an important role to play in the democratic system of plural agency.

This role of the judiciary is especially important because constitutional provisions are not self-clarifying and constitutional rights are not self-specifying. Constitutions need to be interpreted on an ongoing basis, and the judiciary, which specializes in this function, makes a vital contribution to the political process by which a democratic public decides what its constitution means today. This is not necessarily an undemocratic arrangement—although it sometimes can be—because the judiciary does not have the final and unreviewable say but merely exerts influence in a system where it too can be checked by other branches. Constitutions can be amended, and, in the American case at least, the Supreme Court's appellate jurisdiction can be restricted by Congress.

To summarize: if the principal objectives of constitutionalism are, first, to prevent elected officials from escaping periodic submission to electoral competition and, second, to create a divided government in which rival officials will call public attention to actions against the public interest, then constitutionalism is obviously not undemocratic. Although undemocratic practices persist in every constitutional system, they owe more to human nature than to constitutionalism itself.

The democratic public needs a constitution to enforce its will, at least occasionally, on its officials. Constitutionalism is the method by which potentially abusive, corrupt, and negligent rulers are, to some extent, ruled by those they try to rule.

Enabling Versus Obstructionist Constitutionalism

The foregoing argument assumes the validity of the voluntaristic or majoritarian conception of democracy—that democracy is a system designed to implement the preexistent will of the majority. This is an inadequate view of democracy, but it has an important point to teach. It helps us formulate a very simple and clear refutation of the unspoken assumption, common in political theory, that a liberal constitution has essentially one function, to prevent tyranny, including majority tyranny—that is, the majoritarian violation of individual rights.

This assumption is not wrong, but it is one-sided and incomplete. The theoretical challenge is to understand all the important functions in a broader context. All existing constitutions are multifunctional. If we want to speak exclusively about the preventive functions of constitutions, we could say that liberal constitutions are designed, at a minimum, to prevent not only tyranny but also anarchy, corruption, instability, paralysis, unaccountability, unjustified secrecy, and uninformed decision making. This list brings us closer to a realistic appreciation of the many-sided contribution of constitutionalism to democracy. But why focus on preventive functions?

A distinction should be drawn between the enabling and the disabling purposes of constitutions. A one-sided emphasis on inhibiting or constraining functions is a notable defect of much constitutional theory. That constitutions are not merely prohibitory is spectacularly demonstrated by the American example. The U.S. Constitution framed at Philadelphia in 1787 was meant not simply to prevent the tyranny of the majority; it was meant also to bring a new country into being and to enable its citizens to rule themselves.

If we reconsider our expanded list of the preventive functions of democratic constitutions, we can easily tease out the positive or enabling ends. A constitution crafted to avoid paralysis and instability is meant to create stable and effective government. One noteworthy example is the constructive vote of no confidence, introduced into the 1949 constitution of the Federal Republic of Germany. Under the no-confidence procedure, the parliament cannot topple the cabinet unless it can simultaneously agree on a new candidate to replace the outgoing chancellor. Another provision meant to strengthen the executive vis-à-vis the assembly was included in the 1958 French constitution and is called the pledge of responsibility: a government bill becomes law automatically, without a parliamentary vote, unless a motion of censure is lodged and won. The French constitution also strengthens the executive by giving it considerable control over the parliamentary agenda.

These provisions are obviously sculpted not to prevent tyranny but rather to enhance cabinet stability in the face of a fragmented and rambunctious assembly and, in general, to improve the government's capacity to govern. Many constitutional provisions, including all grants of emergency power, are of this sort. They are not simply obstructionist. They also help organize the political process, distributing powers and giving them a direction, establishing a division of labor meant to foster specialization and enhance the contributions of the major political actors.

Constitutional Rights as Preconditions of Democracy

Positive constitutionalism seems an appropriate title to apply to the structure of democratic constitutions. The rules of the game—establishing, say, a presidential or a parliamentary system—do not simply throw roadblocks in front of public officials. They make political life possible in the first place. But what about the rights provisions? We do not want the right, say, to a fair trial to depend simply upon the say-so of a temporary electoral majority. Hence constitutionalism entrenches rights beyond the reach of ordinary democratic processes. But this does not necessarily mean that rights are somehow anti-democratic or should be conceived as stone-hard limits to the otherwise untrammeled will of the people. To see rights in a more positive light, we need to reevaluate the concept of democracy with which we began. Rights are an essential feature of any democratic constitution because democracy is not voluntaristic but deliberative.

Some rights arise from the needs of representative government. Voting rights, which define one of the main avenues for citizen participation in the democratic system, immediately come to mind. Legislation that unfairly restricts voting rights erodes the most essential precondition of a well-functioning democracy. Such procedural rights, therefore, should be constitutionally entrenched on strictly democratic grounds. While an electoral system is the most important guarantee of accountable government, some nonelected officials (for instance, judges) can reasonably be given custodial responsibility for the fair allocation of voting rights. Elementary knowledge of human nature suggests that no assembly benefiting from malapportionment can be expected to redesign the districting system in anything like a fair manner. Paradoxically, therefore, democracy demands that elected officials sometimes obey unelected ones. But what about other basic rights?

The key to positive constitutionalism lies in communication rights—freedom of speech, freedom of the press, and freedom of assembly.

Indeed, a persuasive argument can be made that freedom of discussion is the primary right in any democratic constitution. (This is not to denigrate freedom of religion, freedom of contract, or the right to a fair trial.) Freedom of speech and freedom of the press illustrate the truth that rights can be productive, not merely protective—in this case useful for generating intelligent and publicly acceptable solutions to collective problems—and that they are designed to protect not the lone individual but fragile channels of social communication. Such freedoms also help us rethink our two basic concepts, constitutionalism and democracy. Attention to communication rights makes it clear, for example, why we need to distinguish sharply between democracy and majoritarianism or between deliberative and voluntaristic democracy.

Majoritarianism is a purely neutral decision-making procedure, noncommittal about outcomes, compatible with any sort of decision, brilliant or barbarous, that the majority wants to make. Under majoritarianism, decisions are legitimized by their source alone, not by their content. Democracy is a slightly different system, not wholly voluntaristic but deliberative as well, and painstakingly designed to improve the chances that relatively intelligent collective decisions will be made. Put simply, democracy does not entail blind deference to what the majority happens to think today. This is the main reason why democracy cannot easily survive or flourish outside a constitutional framework.

Why should an electoral majority be constitutionally prohibited from outlawing or silencing its critics? To answer this question is to understand the difference between majoritarianism and democracy. Voting rights might be used to implement the preexistent will of the majority. Freedom of discussion, by contrast, is meant to help the people improve its thinking about public issues and to learn what it wants to do through public

debate. A democratic constitution strives to organize a people in such a way as to improve the thoughtfulness and fact-mindedness of public deliberation. Moreover, if a majority makes a decision after having engaged in an uncensored public debate, the outvoted minority will be more likely to view it as a legitimate decision, to be accepted and obeyed. For this reason, government by discussion enhances the effectiveness, not merely the intelligence, of public policy.

A Tool for the Community

Early critics of constitutionalism argued that a democratic public, rather than deferring to a "higher law" that it had created by its own discretion, would impatiently throw off that law at the first crisis. But secular democracies have produced relatively stable constitutions because constitutions are enabling, not merely disabling. They can be accepted voluntarily by a democratic people, for practical reasons, as an indispensable means for achieving widely desired aims. In the cases of freedom of speech and freedom of the press, a democratic people will accept rigid restrictions on majority discretion (for instance, the majority can never prevent its decisions from being publicly criticized) because this is the best means yet discovered for improving the quality of collective decisions, for bringing out the excellence of democracy. Freedom of speech is not based on radical skepticism but, to the contrary, on the firm belief that some policy outcomes are objectively superior to others.

There is nothing particularly strange about this arrangement, as a homely example reveals. Individuals will often want to talk things over with a friend before making a momentous decision in life, because they realize that such a back-and-forth will change the way they think about a problem and its possible solutions. They voluntarily throw themselves into a situation that will clarify their thinking and even transform their preferences. They do this because they want to discover what they really think, or what they would want if they were smart. Freedom of discussion, in political life, is publicly embraced because it promises to do something similar—to bring out and lend authority to the considered will of the people.

Representation also plays a vital role in this process. The relation between the people and its representatives cannot, ultimately, be compared with the relation between principals and agents because democratic representatives, unlike mere emissaries, help the represented discover what they really want. Voting rights are not simply a vehicle for registering a preexistent popular will; they are a method for involving citizens in a process through which the popular will is hammered out and improved by discussion.

Earlier, to explain the uses of constitutionalism under voluntaristic democracy, we described the people's attitude toward its elected officials as primarily one of distrust. There is a lot to this characterization, but it is also incomplete. We choose representatives to specialize in tasks that we need to have done but that we do not have time to do ourselves. What representatives do for us is not simply to make deals but, just as important, to concentrate on major public issues, exchange viewpoints with other deputies representing far-flung constituencies, and engage in mind-clarifying debate. Ordinary citizens need representatives to specialize in issues in order to help them find out what, as citizens, they believe and desire.

Democratic legislatures, as is well known, are also forums for striking bargains among interest groups. There is nothing particularly unsavory or sinful about such deals. The point of the deliberative theory of constitutional democracy is not to denigrate groups for acting on their interests but rather to put interest group bargaining into perspective. In fact, most groups do not have clear interests on many vital public issues, and there remains a good deal of room for the deliberative processes, for the attempt to discover the public interest on some important questions through wide-open discussion in the assembly and in the media.

Democratic citizens want to make good decisions today because, among other reasons, they realize that they will pay the costs of bad decisions tomorrow. An understandable concern for their own future leads democratic citizens to favor a system in which mistakes can be corrected. They embrace constitutionalism for this reason too: not only because it increases the probability of intelligent decision making, but also because it maximizes the opportunity for intelligent self-correction later. The present electoral majority will willingly submit to irritating criticism of its decisions by the opposition because it knows that it may want to change its mind in the future and that it needs to hear and consider, on an ongoing basis, possible reasons for doing so. Constitutional democracy, we might say, is self-correcting democracy. A liberal constitution is the way a democratic nation strives to make itself into a community that can adapt intelligently to new circumstances and continue to learn.

Democracy and Nonpolitical Rights

Not all constitutional rights arise from the needs of representative government. Freedom of religion and the right to a fair trial come to mind. But the relations between such rights and democratic politics are important and need to be explored. First of all, such rights cannot easily be defended in a nondemocratic regime, where power wielders are electorally unaccountable and media coverage is likely to be censored. Second, such rights seem to be indispensable preconditions for democratic politics. Respect for private rights creates a favorable atmosphere for peaceful electoral competition, democratic discussion, and partisan compromise. Any regime, including a majoritarian one, that respects rights will thereby enhance its legitimacy and hence its effectiveness—that is, the general public willingness to cooperate with its decisions.

The dependence of vocal and effective political opposition on the private wealth generated by a system of property rights is often mentioned in this context. To acknowledge the democratic function of property rights, it should be said, is neither to deny that such rights promote other valuable goals, such as material well-being and personal independence, nor to ignore the likelihood that accumulated riches will be used to buy political favors undemocratically.

Freedom of religion can be analyzed in the same light. Democratic citizens need to agree on freedom of religion because this right, by narrowing the range of issues over which governmental authorities can claim jurisdiction, provides an essential precondition for fruitful and cool-headed public cooperation, including democratic debate, in a multidenominational society.

But these are not the only reasons to doubt the traditional opposition between political democracy and the constitutional entrenchment of nonpolitical rights. The meaning of such rights, it should be noticed, is neither fixed unambiguously in the U.S. Constitution nor elaborated by the judiciary alone. What freedom of speech, free exercise of religion, or equal protection mean in practice is decided by intense and drawn-out political struggles, in which public debate plays an important role. Because rights, in their concrete significance and implementation, are elaborated democratically, it is not quite accurate to view them as unmovable barriers erected against the popular will.

The question of the original or ultimate source of these rights will probably never be answered unequivocally. But there is no overwhelming reason to locate this origin in divine command or immemorial custom. All we need to claim, or can justify claiming, is that a democratic public, to operate within the constraints of a liberal constitution, must have already arrived at a fairly stable consensus on basic rights, however vague and susceptible to political interpretation such a consensus remains. Such a claim sidesteps the unanswerable question of the metaphysical origin of rights and stops at the commonsensical recognition that a political culture where such rights are not widely accepted will probably be inhospitable to democracy.

The Amending Power

The essence of the so-called countermajoritarian dilemma lies in the fact that constitutional provisions are more difficult to revise than ordinary statutes. If democratic constitutions were wholly unchangeable, the countermajoritarian dilemma would be an irresoluble contradiction, an unjustifiable subordination of the present to the past and of the democratic public to unelected judges. But the rigidity of constitutions is relative, not absolute, so long as the road to constitutional amendment lies open. Judges, for instance, can be democratically overruled simply by changing the constitution they are entrusted to enforce.

Through the amending formula, the framers of a constitution share their authority over the constitutional framework with their descendants. They do this because they know that their foresight is limited. By building flexibility and adaptability into the constitution, they hope to increase the chances that it will survive and retain public support in unforeseen circumstances. Democratic citizens accept the authority of elected officials because the latter can be ousted from office in the next election. Similarly, they obey laws because they know that these laws can be changed. The legitimacy of authority in a democratic system, in other words, depends on the institutionally maintained opportunity for revision—an opportunity that can play an important role even when it is not used. The same rule applies to democratic constitutionalism.

But why will a secular and future-oriented democratic public, saddled with an imperfect constitution, accept a relatively stringent amending formula? Democratic citizens will accept a relatively rigid and imperfect constitution, first of all, because they understand that it would be a terrible waste of time and effort to be constantly haggling over the rules of the game. Procedural difficulties, by preventing hasty decisions, are meant to improve the quality of successful constitutional revisions, as well as to increase the likelihood that such fundamental changes will garner broad public support.

(Amendments are not the only way to introduce flexibility into a constitution, it should be mentioned parenthetically. One reason successor generations continue to accept a charter framed by distant ancestors is that constitutional provisions are gradually adapted to current circumstances by judicial interpretation. The judicial reinterpretation of the commerce clause is a notable example in American constitutional history. The commerce clause of Article I of the U.S. Constitution gives Congress the power to regulate interstate commerce. The provisions of the Civil Rights Act of 1964 apply to all activities in interstate commerce. The Supreme Court increased the law's effectiveness by broadly defining what is considered to be within interstate commerce. By helping adjust the meaning of the Constitution to a new society unknown to the Framers, judges sometimes serve a democratic function that supplements, rather than contradicts, the role of elected representatives. The possibility of explicit amendment, not to mention the mortality of legally irremovable judges and the subsequent appointment of their successors by democratically elected officials, lessens the chances that the judiciary will exercise this function with no regard to public opinion.)

Democratic acquiescence in an inherited constitution does not mean that citizens believe the document to be above reproach. Even if all citizens concede that the constitution needs improvement, they might not concur on the one right way to amend it. In such circumstances, they will often agree to stick with the inherited framework, not as the best possible constitution, but as the best constitution they are likely to get given the current state of political disagreement in the community. They accept the constitution not as a work of perfection but as better than, or at least as good as, any new constitution they could presumably fashion through democratic discussion and compromise.

The ordinary democratic electorate does not ratify the constitution only in exceptional or rare moments, therefore, but also by tacit consent, by continuing to act, on a daily basis, under the rules it lays down. Constitutional democracy is not the rule of the dead over the living but rather the self-rule of the living with help consciously accepted from the dead.

See also Democracy, Justifications for; Locke, John; Madison, James; Majority rule, minority rights.

STEPHEN HOLMES

BIBLIOGRAPHY

Ackerman, Bruce A. *We the People.* Cambridge, Mass., and London: Harvard University Press, 1991.

Beer, Samuel. *To Make a Nation: Rediscovery of American Federalism.* Cambridge: Belknap Press, Harvard University Press, 1993.

Friedrich, Carl. *Constitutional Government and Democracy*. Waltham, Mass.: Blaisdell, 1968.

Gordon, Scott. *Controlling the State: Constitutionalism from Ancient Athens to Today*. Cambridge: Harvard University Press, 1999.

Hamilton, Alexander, James Madison, and John Jay. *The Federalist Papers*. New York: Mentor, 1961.

Hardin, Russell. *Liberalism, Constitutionalism, and Democracy*. New York: Oxford University Press, 2000.

Hayek, Friedrich A. von. *The Constitution of Liberty*. Chicago: University of Chicago Press, 1960.

Holmes, Stephen. *Benjamin Constant and the Making of Modern Liberalism*. New Haven: Yale University Press, 1984.

_____. *Passions and Constraint: On the Theory of Liberal Democracy*. Chicago: University of Chicago Press, 1995.

Levinson, Sanford, ed. *Responding to Imperfection: The Theory and Practice of Constitutional Amendment*. Princeton: Princeton University Press, 1995.

Lijphart, Arend, ed. *Parliamentary versus Presidential Government*. Oxford: Oxford University Press, 1992.

Meiklejohn, Alexander. *Political Freedom: The Constitutional Powers of the People*. New York: Harper, 1960.

Mill, John Stuart. *Considerations on Representative Government*. Buffalo: Prometheus Books, 1991.

Sunstein, Cass. *Free Speech and the Problem of Democracy*. New York: Free Press, 1993.

_____. *The Partial Constitution*. Cambridge, Mass., and London: Harvard University Press, 1993.

✦ Contractarianism

A long and important tradition in political thought that evolved from the idea of an original contract on which political order is based. Among its exponents were Thomas Hobbes, Benedict de Spinoza, and John Locke in the seventeenth century and Jean-Jacques Rousseau and Immanuel Kant in the eighteenth. John Rawls and others continue the tradition, in modified form, today.

Contract theorists have put the tradition to varied political uses, but they share a common strategy. Each version of the theory describes a situation without government—a "state of nature," to use Rousseau's term—and then describes the conditions in which government would be introduced by general agreement. Contractarianism has been used to provide a basis for political obligation, for we are obliged to do what we have contracted to do. It has also been used as a basis for resistance or revolution, for obligation is canceled when the terms of a contract are broken. In short, the notion of a social contract has been used to define and justify the ground rules upon which politics is carried on.

Hobbes, Locke, and Rousseau

The ground rules are just, contractarians maintain, if they were agreed to or would have been agreed to (we shall return to this distinction). Contractarianism is, then, a theory of consent, and so we may expect it to have an important connection with democracy. But we must distinguish between the ongoing need for popular consent, which is part of a democratic system, and initial consent to a constitution, which contractarian theories require. It is quite possible that people might give initial consent to undemocratic systems.

Hobbes is instructive here. Because people are approximately similar in their capacities, he argued, there is no natural basis for order: all may reasonably hope to get what they want by relying on their strength and wit. So order must be artificial, the product of agreement. But how can the agreement be enforced? Hobbes imagines a special kind of agreement that immediately creates its own enforcement mechanism. All agree to lay down their right to live by their own strength and wit, on condition that one person, "the sovereign," retains this right. The sovereign, or ruler, is thus empowered to do whatever is necessary to preserve his own office; and because the value of his office will increase with the tranquillity and prosperity of his society, he will have a direct personal interest in exercising this absolute power prudently. Hobbes does not rule out democracy: the sovereign could in principle be one person (as he preferred) or a group or an assembly. But the legitimacy of Hobbes's system does not depend on the renewal of popular consent; the initial act of consent is binding and forbids resistance to government.

Locke, however, developed a theory in which ongoing consent was given considerable importance. Like Hobbes, he maintained that the natural state would be one of equality, a state in which no one would owe obedience to any other person. Unlike Hobbes, he maintained that even in such a state, people would seek to follow and to enforce a set of rules because they would grasp that the equality of human beings entails principles of mutual respect ("natural law"). They would actively try to ensure that they and their neighbors were treated respectfully by others and would protect their own and their neighbors' lives and property. But they would see that the private enforcement of natural law is inefficient and uneven and that a public agency would do it better. So they would unanimously agree to form a "civil society," a social group that has undertaken to obey a single political authority.

By majority decision the society would entrust the power of enforcing natural law to some person or group. In any case, Locke believed, there would have to be a means to raise revenue, and so there would have to be an elected assembly at which property owners, through their representatives, would give their consent to taxation.

Moreover, whoever has been entrusted with the power to govern must maintain the support of a majority of the people, who retain the right to revoke the trust for sufficiently serious cause. Both of these provisions (no taxation without representation and the right of revolution) have been important in the American democratic tradition. It must be noted, however, that the extent of Locke's notion of "the people" has long been a matter of debate.

With Jean-Jacques Rousseau we arrive at a contractarian theory imbued with a democratic spirit. In Rousseau's hands the tradition becomes an instrument of radical social and political critique. In *Discourse on the Origins of Inequality* (1775) Rousseau maintains that existing society could owe its origins only to a duplicitous social contract in which the rich tricked the poor into perpetuating inequality. In the state of nature we all have something to lose, said the rich, so let us create law and government to confirm us in our possessions. And the poor agreed, forgetting that some had much more to lose than others.

But in *The Social Contract* (1762), Rousseau describes a quite different contract, one that would produce a legitimate political order. It resembles Hobbes's contract in creating an absolute power: here, however, the absolute power is to be held by the people themselves. All surrender their rights to the society as a whole, on two conditions. First, the society will establish equality of right—that is, no one will enjoy any right that is not universally enjoyed. Second, the criterion of all subsequent legislation will be the "general will"—that is, public decisions will be made in the light of the general interest, not on the basis of what some coalition of special interests happens to want. This looks very much like a theory of democracy, in which "the people" is sovereign, and the shared interests of the people take precedence over any partial interests. As it happens, however, Rousseau did not describe his theory as democratic. He reserved the term *democracy* to describe a system in which the people not only make but also execute the laws—a system that he considered utopian.

Criticisms

Over the years contractarian theories have attracted many criticisms. One of these is the obvious objection that with a few exceptions there *was* no social contract. Coercion and custom, or some blend of the two, explain how societies have come to be. Another objection is that even if there had been a social contract, it is not clear why it should be binding. Those who made it would be bound by it, but why should we? Hobbes and Locke respond in roughly similar ways to these objections. Hobbes maintains that submission to those in power is equivalent to adopting a social contract, for in both cases people are preferring obedience to insecurity. Locke has a notoriously difficult doctrine of "tacit consent," according to which any enjoyment of the amenities of a society amounts to agreeing to obey its laws. As for Rousseau, the critique does not apply, for neither of his two discussions involves the claim that some past event has led to a present obligation.

But contractarianism can take another escape route here. Instead of claiming that a social contract or some substitute for it has actually taken place, the contract can become a purely hypothetical device, a thought experiment. If there were no government, why and on what terms would we agree to create one? In thinking about this, we may settle upon a general reason for government's existence, and a list of things that governments must and must not do, if they are to be worth having. We can then measure the system of government that we do have against the one that we would have chosen.

This method is a powerful way of criticizing political institutions. But it poses two problems. First, although people are certainly bound by agreements that they did make, they are not bound by ones that they would have made, however rational and sensible. If you had asked me yesterday for five dollars, I would have agreed. But that does not mean that you can come to me today and say that I owe you five dollars because I would have agreed if you had asked me yesterday. Your demand stands on its own merits, and the fact that I would have agreed yesterday means nothing. This difficulty leads directly to the second problem. When we make use of a hypothetical agreement, we are appealing to a set of background principles that we think people would have used in making an agreement—principles such as fairness or human equality or the importance of freedom. But why should we not just appeal directly to those principles and say that a political system is legitimate if it is fair or equal or free?

John Rawls

This question certainly applies to the most important current contractarian theory, that of John Rawls, as elucidated in *A Theory of Justice* (1971). Among Rawls's most striking ideas is a thought experiment that he terms "the original position." Suppose that we face the task of agreeing on a set of basic political principles for a society, but that none of us knows what position we would occupy in it: we are under "a veil of ignorance." Rawls suggests that we would arrive at three ideas. First, we would want to ensure that, wherever we ended up in the society, we would enjoy some basic liberties. Second, we would want to ensure that, whatever talents we ended up having, opportunities to exercise them would be open to us. Third, we would be particularly anxious about the condition of those who would have the least advantaged position, where, after all, we might end up ourselves. It would not make sense for us to prohibit any inequality at all, because some inequalities may indirectly benefit everyone, by providing incentives. But we would want to say that there should be only as much inequality as was necessary to improve the well-being of the least advantaged.

Rawls's device is a way of drawing out the implications of a basic sense of moral equality. It prevents us from making any privileged claim on the basis of some attribute or talent that we happen to have, by denying us knowledge of our attributes and talents and requiring us to adopt principles that we would agree to live by whatever our attributes and talents happened to be. But why not just appeal to the idea of moral equality? What does the device of a hypothetical agreement add? This is a much-discussed issue. In Rawls's defense, we may say that an important part of the idea of moral equality is that each person should believe that the principles that he or she favors should be open to every other person: that what is to be politically enforced must be given a fully public justification. Rawls's contractarianism attempts to meet this condition, by seeking a justification that anyone, in given circumstances, would agree to.

Rawls's theory has also been criticized. To a theorist of radical individualism such as Robert Nozick, Rawls implausibly detaches individuals from their talents: if talents do not belong to those who possess them, who do they belong to? To deny people the rewards that their talents earn is a form of exploitation. To a communitarian theorist such as Michael Sandel, Rawls implausibly detaches individuals from their socially produced beliefs: given that I believe something profoundly, what does it matter what I would hold if I did not know what I believed?

In these disputes the democrat will side with Rawls. If we believe that a society's political arrangements must be acceptable to all its members, and if we believe that acceptance must be a matter of critical acceptance, or public justifiability, we will see Rawls's contractarianism as a major asset to democratic theory.

See also Consent; Hobbes, Thomas; Kant, Immanuel; Locke, John; Natural law; Rousseau, Jean-Jacques; Spinoza, Benedict de.

RICHARD VERNON

BIBLIOGRAPHY

Dworkin, Ronald. "The Original Position." In *Reading Rawls*, edited by Norman Daniels. Oxford: Blackwell, 1975.
Hobbes, Thomas. *Leviathan*. New York: Collier, 1962.
Lessnoff, Michael. *Social Contract*. London: Macmillan, 1982.
Locke, John. *Second Treatise of Government*. Cambridge: Cambridge University Press, 1960.
Nozick, Robert. *Anarchy, State and Utopia*. New York: Oxford University Press, 1974.
Rawls, John. *A Theory of Justice*. Cambridge: Harvard University Press, Belknap Press, 1971; Oxford: Oxford University Press, 1973.
Riley, Patrick. *Will and Political Legitimacy*. Cambridge and London: Harvard University Press, 1982.
Rousseau, Jean-Jacques. *The Social Contract*. Harmondsworth, England: Penguin Books, 1968.
Sandel, Michael. *Liberalism and the Limits of Justice*. Cambridge and New York: Cambridge University Press, 1982.

✦ Corporatism

One of several possible arrangements through which organized interests can mediate between their members—individuals, families, firms, communities, and groups—and various entities, especially agencies of the state or government. Central to this process is the role of associations, permanently established and staffed, which specialize in and seek to identify, advance, and defend interests by influencing and contesting public policies. Unlike political parties—the other principal intermediaries in modern polities—these organizations neither present candidates for electoral approval nor accept direct responsibility for forming governments.

Corporatism, either as a practice in political life or as a concept in political theory, has always been politically controversial. It has been heralded as a novel and promising way of ensuring harmony between conflicting social classes. It also has been condemned as a reactionary and antidemocratic formula for suppressing the demands of autonomous associations and movements.

After the collapse of fascism in Italy, National Socialism in Germany, and various other authoritarian regimes that flourished in Europe between the end of the First World War and the end of the Second World War (1919–1945)—all of which claimed to be practicing some form of corporatism—the concept more or less disappeared from the lexicon of respectable political discourse. The exceptions were in Francisco Franco's Spain and António de Oliveira Salazar's Portugal, where the practice was left anachronistically on display until both countries "transited" to democracy in the mid-1970s.

At almost the same time, scholars from several countries and academic disciplines revived the concept to describe certain features of the politics of advanced democratic polities that did not seem adequately accounted for by pluralism, the dominant model that had been applied to state-society relations. Austria, Finland, Norway, and Sweden were especially singled out as "neocorporatist"

countries in which this type of interest politics was prevalent. Important traces of neocorporatist practice in the making of macroeconomic policy have been observed in Australia, Belgium, Denmark, the Federal Republic of Germany, the Netherlands, and even in postauthoritarian Portugal and Spain. Great Britain and Italy attempted similar arrangements in the 1960s and 1970s without success. Elsewhere, for example, in France, Canada, and the United States, neocorporatism seems confined to specific sectors or regions.

Once the authoritarian-fascist-statist variety of corporatism had been virtually extinguished—first by the wave of democratizations that came after World War II and later by the wave that began in 1974—it became increasingly clear that small European countries with well-organized interest associations and highly vulnerable, internationalized economies were most successful in practicing the more bottom-up or societal version of neocorporatism. The tendency was all the more marked if these countries also had strong social democratic parties, stable electoral preferences, relative cultural or linguistic unity, and neutral foreign policies. Indeed, those that had the most difficulty sustaining such social pacts had weaker social democracies, more volatile electorates, and deep divisions over military and security issues—for example, Denmark and the Netherlands. Belgium's relative lack of success can be traced to its split into rival linguistic groups.

Protracted neocorporatism at the national or macroeconomic level has been convincingly linked to certain desirable outcomes: less unruliness of the citizenry, lower strike rates, more balanced budgets, greater fiscal effectiveness, lower rates of inflation, less unemployment, less instability at the level of political elites, and less tendency to exploit the "political business cycle"—all of which suggests that countries scoring high on neocorporatism have been more governable. This does not, however, make them more democratic.

Since its rediscovery in the mid-1970s, corporatism has borne the burden of its past association with fascism and other forms of authoritarian rule. To describe a polity or practice as corporatist was practically synonymous with accusing it of being undemocratic. Moreover, certain of corporatism's enduring features seemed to confirm this suspicion: organizations replaced people as the principal participants in political life; specialized professional representatives gained at the expense of generally interested citizens; privileged (if not exclusive) access was accorded to particular associations; monopolies were recognized and even extolled at the expense of overlapping and competing intermediaries; organizational hierarchies reaching up to very comprehensive national associations diminished the autonomy of more local and specialized organizations.

As inquiry into corporatism expanded, however, judgment about its effect on democracy shifted. For one thing, many of the countries that are manifestly corporatist are also obviously democratic in the sense that they protect the full range of civic freedoms, define citizenship in the broadest fashion, hold regular competitive elections of uncertain outcome, hold political authorities accountable for their actions, and pursue public policies that seem responsive to popular demands. Some corporatist countries, especially those in Scandinavia, have been in the vanguard of experimentation with such advanced democratic measures as worker participation in management, open disclosure of policy processes, ombudsman arrangements for hearing citizen complaints, public financing of political parties, and even profit-sharing arrangements with workers to extend popular ownership of the economy.

In addition, it soon became apparent that corporatist arrangements have a substantial effect on the conditions under which competing interests can participate in the influence process. Although the spontaneous, voluntaristic, and episodic relations of pluralism seem freer in principle, in practice they produce greater inequality of access to those in power. Privileged groups with smaller numbers, concentrated resources, and more compact location have a natural advantage over larger, dispersed groups such as workers and consumers. Corporatism tends to even out the distribution of resources across more comprehensively organized categories and to guarantee at least a formal parity of access to the making of decisions. Moreover, the direct incorporation of associations into subsequent implementation processes may ensure greater responsiveness to group needs than is possible through the arm's-length relationship that separates the public and the private realms under pluralism.

Evaluations of the impact of corporatism on democracy depend very much on which qualities of democracy one chooses to stress. Seen from the perspective of encouraging the participation of individuals in the decisions that collectively affect them and of ensuring that all public authorities accord equal access to all citizens' demands, corporatist arrangements have a negative effect. If one asks whether those in power can be held effectively accountable for their actions and whether those actions are likely to be responsive to citizen needs, corporatism is bound to be judged more positively. The effect of corporatism on the central mechanism of democracy—competitiveness—is more ambiguous. On the one hand, corporatism diminishes competitiveness by eliminating the struggle between rival associations for membership and access. On the other hand, it enhances competitiveness by encouraging rival conceptions of common interest to express themselves within the same association.

Most of today's democracies are being transformed by the practice of modern corporatism. Organizations are becoming citizens alongside, if not in the place of, individuals. Accountability and responsiveness are increasing, but at the expense of participation and access. Competitiveness is less interorganizational and more intraorganizational. Although the pace is uneven, the acceptance is unequal, and the outcome by no means unequivocal, democracy is becoming more "interested," more "organized," and more "indirect."

See also Authoritarianism; Fascism; Democracy, Multiethnic.

PHILIPPE C. SCHMITTER

BIBLIOGRAPHY

Berger, Suzanne, ed. *Organizing Interests in Western Europe: Pluralism, Corporatism, and the Transformation of Politics.* Cambridge and New York: Cambridge University Press, 1981.

Cawson, Alan. *Corporatism and Political Theory.* Oxford and New York: Blackwell, 1986.

Lehmbruch, Gerhard, and Philippe C. Schmitter, eds. *Patterns of Corporatist Policy-Making.* Beverly Hills, Calif., and London: Sage Publications, 1982.

Schmitter, Philippe C. "Democratic Theory and Neo-Corporatist Practice." *Social Research* 50 (winter 1983): 885–928.

———. "Interest Intermediation and Regime Governability in Contemporary Western Europe and North America." In *Organizing Interests in Western Europe,* edited by Suzanne Berger. Cambridge and New York: Cambridge University Press, 1981.

Schmitter, Philippe C., and Gerhard Lehmbruch, eds. *Trends toward Corporatist Intermediation.* Beverly Hills, Calif., and London: Sage Publications, 1979.

Williamson, Peter J. *Varieties of Corporatism: A Conceptual Discussion.* New York: Macmillan, 1985.

✦ Dictatorship

A form of rule associated in the twentieth century with totalitarian and authoritarian political systems. The term is of ancient Roman origin. Roman dictatorship was a function of constitutional government, akin to the emergency or war powers provisions of some modern democratic constitutions. These constitutions provide that, with the consent of the legislature, a president or prime minister may suspend civil liberties or due process for a brief period, to protect the authority of the elected government from violence or insurrection.

In its specifically contemporary meaning, the concept of dictatorship was revived in light of the breakdown of constitutional or traditional governments in Europe and Russia in the aftermath of World War I. In the twentieth century the term *dictatorship* has been applied to two sorts of nondemocratic rule, the totalitarian and the authoritarian. The former, typified by Nazism in Germany under Adolf Hitler and Stalinism in the Soviet Union under Joseph Stalin, pursued millenarian objectives—that is, these dictatorships sought to create what they considered an ideal society through revolutionary means. The latter has been typified by the less radical, nonmillenarian fascism of Benito Mussolini in Italy and Francisco Franco in Spain and by a number of "patrimonial" rulers, such as Anastasio Somoza in Nicaragua, Ferdinand Marcos in the Philippines, and Idi Amin in Uganda.

Totalitarian and Nontotalitarian Dictatorships

There is a fundamental difference between, on the one hand, totalitarian dictatorship and, on the other, ancient dictatorship, rule by emergency or war powers, and authoritarian dictatorship. Totalitarian dictators have assumed power not to curb revolutionary activity but to extend and radicalize it. Hence Hitler's accession to power in Germany in the 1930s was sometimes called the "legal revolution," while Stalin's rule in Russia during these years has been called the "revolution from above." Although dictatorship originally meant (and sometimes in its authoritarian variant still means) a more or less temporary suspension of constitutional government, totalitarian dictatorship is a catalyst for the transformation of human nature called for by totalitarian ideologies.

In the twentieth century, therefore, the phenomenon of dictatorship has been impossible to understand fully unless it is studied in conjunction with the phenomenon of totalitarianism. At the same time, we cannot fathom totalitarianism apart from the extraordinary ambition of dictators like Hitler and Stalin, Mao Zedong in China, or, more recently, Pol Pot and the Khmer Rouge in Cambodia.

Accordingly, contemporary dictatorship can to some extent be analyzed in terms of the classical typologies of tyranny set forth by Plato, Aristotle, and Xenophon in the fourth and fifth centuries B.C. In the classical typologies, tyranny is the product of an overweening ambition to master and exploit others. This is particularly the case when we are speaking of dictatorial rule over authoritarian or other nontotalitarian political systems. Here, where the ruler is not committed mainly to an ideological imperative, but is instead desirous of ruling a country as if it were his own property and the property of his family or clients, we encounter a modern variant of the tyrannies discussed in Book 9 of Plato's *Republic* and Book 5 of Aristotle's *Politics*. Similarly, Xenophon, in the *Hiero* and the *Education of Cyrus*, depicts the tyrant as a ruler who characteristically merges government authority with his personal, patrimonial authority over his own household. In the twentieth century, Franco and António de Oliveira Salazar of Portugal are sometimes offered as examples of this kind of patrimonial ruler—dictatorial but nontotalitarian. In both the ancient and modern cases, the ambition to possess the state as one's property can coexist with varying degrees of administrative talent and an avowed aim to preserve stability.

Tyrannical Ambition and Totalitarian Ideology

Students of politics in the liberal democracies need to be alive to the phenomenon of tyrannical ambition as the basis for one-party or one-person rule. Our traditions of peaceable democratic self-government can lull us into believing that it is universally true of human nature that people prefer consensus, consent, and compromise to belligerence and domination. In fact, democratic self-government is the outcome of a long and painstaking civic education and economic evolution whose influence so far has been paramount only in a limited number of countries in Europe and North America. Important as it is to understand the classical typology of tyranny and the tyrannical psychology, however, it would be a mistake to conclude that the ideology of totalitarian rulers is only of secondary importance compared with their ambition for power.

Under totalitarianism, dictator and ideology are mutually reinforcing dimensions of a single system. The ideology is crucial for summoning forth the personal qualities of fanatical willpower and aggressiveness that characterize the leaders' psychologies. What distinguishes modern dictators like Hitler or Stalin from a traditional tyrant like Hiero I of Syracuse in the fifth century B.C. is not just the existence of modern military and communications technology, important as this factor is. The fundamental element that distinguishes these totalitarian dictators from traditional tyrants is the project of social transformation that solicits and justifies the meticulous and methodical terror inflicted by these leaders. Their discipline, commitment, and consistency set them apart from the more sporadic and capricious greed and violence of traditional patrimonial tyrants (both in the past and in our own era).

The totalitarian "great leader" (depicted by the regime's propaganda as all-knowing and all-powerful) and totalitarian ideology have been made for each other. Neither can attain full development without the other. Totalitarian ideologies call for the eradication of "bourgeois" traits so that the individual can be reconciled with the classless or racially pure community. In the case of Stalinism, the allegedly bourgeois qualities of greed and corruption were externalized as an object for destruction in the mythical "rich peasant" used to justify forced collectivization and genocidal famines created by the state. In the case of Nazism, Jews were used for a similar purpose. As Konrad Heiden suggested in his study of dictatorship, *Der Fuehrer*, the Nazis drew on their own feelings of displacement, anxiety, and injured self-esteem and projected them upon Jews as the cause of their sufferings. By overcoming Jews, Nazism claimed, Germany could overcome all the evils of liberal and capitalist modernity and usher in a millenarian "world blessing."

Totalitarian ideology calls for the forcible eradication of all sources of alienation in modern life. In practice, this requires the destruction of every tie that relates individuals to one another—family, property, religion, custom, regional loyalties— and, when these are vanquished, the purging of each individual's inner thoughts and doubts. As G. W. F. Hegel foresaw in his brilliant analysis of the Terror of 1793 during the French Revolution, the goal of authentic revolutionary politics (as opposed to liberal or social democratic demands for concrete reform or widened opportunity) is the creation of an entirely abstract individual—a

bondless individual who, lacking the substantive independence that comes from loyalty to and support from the real communities of tradition, clan, and faith, can be integrated into the equally abstract, contentless racial or classless "community" submerged in loyalty to the leader.

Thus, as we learn from the Russian writer Aleksandr Solzhenitsyn, the Gulag Archipelago of Stalinist slave labor camps was not merely a source of cheap labor but was the prototype of the "new Soviet man" itself. Because this project is limitless in principle—stripping people of all private ties and thoughts is an endless task—the totalitarian ideology requires a leader whose austere fanaticism and millenarian sense of purpose enable him to set in motion the program of terror necessary to create this abstract community of abstract subjects.

The Totalitarian Appeal

The appeal of totalitarian dictators like Hitler and Stalin to their followers is not fully intelligible apart from the followers' commitment to these ideologies. This is evidenced by the particularly intense loyalty these two dictators evoked (respectively) in the SS, Hitler's secret police, and the KGB, the Soviet security police, the "cream" of the armed bohemians (to use Konrad Heiden's apt phrase) who translated the ideological blueprints into murderous reality. All independent-minded observers of these dictators who saw them close up found them to be coarse and undistinguished, lacking the urbanity and education that have sometimes mitigated the assessment of traditional tyrants and usurpers such as Julius Caesar (100–44 B.C.). Their followers' adulation for Hitler and Stalin (to the extent that it was not merely coerced) can be accounted for only by their ability to tap the primordial hatreds and resentments required to energize the ideologies and achieve their goals of pure community.

To arrive at a fuller account of the phenomenon of dictatorship, then, we need to think through the interactions between the personality type of the dictator and the inner dynamic of their ideologies. The key to understanding totalitarian dictatorship does not lie in the literal "doctrines" of Nazism, Stalinism, or the Khmer Rouge. Hitler and Stalin could be dismissive of their parties' formal doctrines and people who believed in them in a literal-minded way. Neither allowed a tenet of his party's ideology, however apparently sacred, to stand in the way of enhancing his power or extending its revolutionary scope to transform human nature and society. Hence, as soon as Stalin had secured his dictatorship by acting as the steward of V. I. Lenin's relatively moderate New Economic Policy, he returned to the "hard left" policies of rapid collectivization and industrialization that had characterized the opening years of Bolshevik rule. The scope and radicalism of those policies favored the concentration of power in his hands. Hitler ruthlessly suppressed his old party comrades in 1934 during his purge of the private Nazi militia ("the night of the long knives"). His intent was to earn the trust of the German army and thus more quickly procure the instrument he needed to pursue the ideological war against the "Jewish commissars."

The point, then, is not to see totalitarian dictators as applying the ideologies chapter and verse. Instead, the ideologies can be seen as shifting variant strategies and forms of rhetoric enabling the dictator to carry out the core mission. The core mission is the mobilization of mass hatred and resentment, generalized by being directed at a mythical class or racial enemy. Hence hatred is taken out of the sphere of subpolitical society, where such animosities normally dwell, and is endowed with the trappings of a disinterested political mission. Whereas traditional tyrants are often voluptuaries—brutal but inconsistent—the totalitarian project calls for an idealist of destruction—the gloomy pedant, ex-seminarian, or café intellectual who dons a "plain field tunic."

The methods of extermination called forth by such a project may be banal (to recall Hannah Arendt's formulation about the Holocaust) in the sense of being technologically highly efficient and well organized. But the goal for which such dispassionate efficiency is mobilized is anything but banal—it is, in fact, passionate hatred.

The Future

Some believe that, with the apparent triumph of liberal democracy, it will be less important in the future either to understand dictatorship as a matter of political analysis or to identify and condemn tyranny as a moral aberration. In the light of human history to date, however, it would seem more prudent to conclude that the danger of tyranny is bound together with political life and our hopes for a just and well-ordered political community. In the future we still will need to recollect and reflect on previous sources of tyranny in order to have a basis for identifying new threats to human liberty and constitutional government when they arise.

Some forms of contemporary dictatorship, like Nazism and Stalinism with their plans for reconstructing human nature, appear to have passed from the scene. But numerous old-fashioned tyrannies of the sort based on revenge, greed, and plunder still exist in our world, as they have since ancient times. Sometimes these dictatorships based on vengeance or greed adopt features of the totalitarian project of methodical extermination. The recent horrors of "ethnic cleansing" in the former Yugoslavia and in Rwanda remind us that, although full-blown totalitarian dictatorships like Nazism and Stalinism appear to have passed from the historical scene, the violence and social strife from which such dictatorships arise are still prevalent in the world.

See also Communism; Fascism.

WALLER R. NEWELL

BIBLIOGRAPHY

Arendt, Hannah. *Eichmann in Jerusalem: A Report on the Banality of Evil.* New York: Viking, 1974.

Conquest, Robert. *The Great Terror.* Toronto: Macmillan, 1969.

Hegel, G. W. F. *Phenomenology of Spirit.* Translated by A. V. Miller. Oxford: Oxford University Press, 1979.

Heiden, Konrad. *Der Fuehrer: Hitler's Rise to Power.* Translated by Ralph Manheim. Boston: Houghton Mifflin, 1944.

Leites, Nathan. *A Study of Bolshevism.* Glencoe, Ill.: Free Press, 1953.

Rauschning, Hermann. *The Revolution of Nihilism: A Warning to the West.* New York: Alliance Book Corp., 1939.

Solzhenitsyn, Aleksandr. *The Gulag Archipelago.* 3 vols. Translated by Thomas P. Whitney and Harry Willetts. New York: Harper and Row; London: HarperCollins, 1974–1978.

Strauss, Leo. *On Tyranny.* Ithaca, N.Y.: Cornell University Press, 1968.

✦ Egalitarianism

The belief that all people are of equal worth and should be treated equally in society. The passion for equality is at the heart of democracy. It encompasses the struggle against inequalities in social, political, and economic conditions. Egalitarianism in its broadest form advances the idea that all people have equal moral worth because of an essential human nature. In a political sense, egalitarianism declares the equal dignity of all citizens in a democratic polity. Even though democratic republics structure certain political inequalities into their constitutional design, and even though civil society is prone to the growth of economic inequality, the law as it applies to citizens in their daily rights and responsibilities is egalitarian.

Aristotle characterized democrats as people who are equal in some respects, wanting to be equal in all. For democrats, free birth—rather than high birth or wealth or intellectual virtue—constitutes a valid claim to political office, to participation in ruling and being ruled. To this arithmetic equality, in which every person counts for one, Aristotle contrasted proportionate equality, in which different persons receive rights and privileges differently, according to what is their due. What is one's due may depend on one's contribution to the whole. Karl Marx acknowledged the Aristotelian distinction. In his analysis of capitalism, Marx criticized the arithmetic equality characteristic of the modern market, in which any individual's labor is bought and sold as if comparable to any other's. Hoping for a more egalitarian society under communism, Marx spoke of proportionate equality: "From each according to his ability, to each according to his needs."

Political Inequalities and Elites

Historically, equality of condition—or a general leveling of social and property distinctions—increases with the advent of democracy, although it tends to be at its height in the early stages of a new society. In feudal societies, inequalities of political status and power, based on landed wealth, existed between lords, vassals, and serfs. Struggles against feudalism made an early democratic claim to civil and political rights based on the acquisition of property by free individuals. More egalitarian movements then challenged property holding as the basis of rights and appealed to service and participation in society. After the English Civil War of the 1640s, in the debates on extending the right to vote, army spokesmen appealed to the Englishman's birthright and his service as a soldier. The French raising of a citizen army, after the French Revolution in the 1790s, heralded the coming of mass democracy, since people of all ranks were mobilized by the state. Equal rights are awarded based on membership in the political life of a nation.

Mass democracy thus involves a certain relativism with regard to what constitutes the basis of equal citizenship. Different qualities can be valued in different people, each and all contributing to the whole. Even those who do not currently contribute to national production, such as the unemployed, are granted civic equality. Ancient democratic theory regarded the contribution of farmers and mechanics as necessary to the polity but of less worth than that of warriors, statesmen, and philosophers because the artisans were considered less rational than these other groups. In contrast, modern democratic theory counts as equal the value of all kinds of contributions, whether manual or mental. Modern communist theory reverses the ancient hierarchy and exalts workers and artisans above the propertied and leisure classes, although it would not offend against democratic standards by disenfranchising individuals. Rather, it attempts to transform them into workers by removing their special privileges.

Democracies are egalitarian in challenging traditional elites' political power based on family, tribe, ethnicity, status, or inherited wealth. Yet in both communist and capitalist countries that aspire to be democratic, new political elites arise. They control or gain access to crucial political resources such as the state bureaucracy and the mass media. In this sense, democracy involves a certain elitism. Mass political democracy has been described as involving a competition among elites

for power. The degree to which the political elites are open to recruiting new members from the mass and the degree to which citizens are able to select among significantly different leaders in regular and open elections are indicators of the relatively democratic nature of large representative democracies.

Economic Inequalities and Democracy

As industrialization develops, with its increased technical and social division of labor, relative deprivation may increase even where the overall standard of living improves. The great reform and revolutionary movements of nineteenth-century Europe challenged the new economic inequalities. In some countries, the working-class movement organized socially before gaining political rights; in other countries, the reverse was true. As T. H. Marshall has pointed out, over several centuries the sphere of expected equalities generally broadened. Democratic citizens came to demand equality of civil rights (such as freedom of speech and the right to own property), then political rights (such as the right to vote and hold office), and finally social rights (for example, public education and social security). Citizenship as a relation of membership entails a certain minimum equality of treatment, even if not equality of results.

Various studies have tried to establish a connection between political democracy and socioeconomic equality in developing countries. Democratic governments, it is argued, foster greater distributional equality than do other governments as they undergo economic development. Democracies, like all governments, must establish legitimacy, and their political base requires attention to the less-well-off members of the society, especially as these citizens organize into interest groups, unions, and political parties.

Some political analysts maintain that democracies promote economic development less well than do bureaucratic-authoritarian governments. It is argued that democracies foster internal political conflict and government policies that are short-term and vacillating. Thus democracies, through their inaction, preserve an equality of resources that economic development tends to destroy. Authoritarian governments are said to promote development because they can make hard decisions to restrain consumption, enforce savings and investment, allocate resources, control labor markets, and replace imports of consumer goods with intermediate and capital goods useful for industrialization. Yet, although authoritarian governments can make these decisions, they cannot enforce them without civil upheaval.

Finally, some argue that in authoritarian societies the government can act on behalf of the disadvantaged. Political power in democratic nations, however, often simply parallels economic power, and the economically disadvantaged thus cannot adequately protect and advance their relative position. Also at issue is the question of whether certain levels of economic development and socioeconomic equality are necessary prerequisites to democracy. A rich variety of empirical studies of the past few decades have not conclusively answered these questions.

Equality of Opportunity

In liberal democracies, equality of rights tends to mean equality of opportunity. It does not necessarily mean equal outcomes as it does in socialist egalitarianism. Persons coming under equal protection of the law gain equal access to the opportunities offered by civil and political society—the equal chance to participate and compete. Equal protection of the law is interpreted by the courts to forbid discrimination based on race, religion, or national origin. If it is found that certain groups have been systematically excluded from or disadvantaged in an arena, the law may mandate a policy of affirmative action to try to rectify historic inequalities. To restore or create equality, private and public institutions making decisions about inclusion are allowed to introduce, as one factor among others such as merit, the categories that previously were prejudicial. Race, gender, and national origin of certain designated minorities are such categories. Policies that distinguish inequitably among persons based on group classifications are valid only if they serve a compelling state objective and are clearly tailored to that purpose.

Gender is a controversial category: the extent to which women and men are different and the degree to which this difference is relevant for social policy are being contested in many countries. Contested issues include volunteer and compulsory overtime work, occupational health and safety, parental leave, pension benefits, and equal pay for work of comparable worth. Beyond issues of gender, other categories being debated are sexual preference, disability, age, resident and illegal alien status, illegitimacy of birth, and wealth. In all these cases, the question for politics, law, and judicial interpretation is, what is the relevant standard for equality? In what respects do people have to be similar in order to be treated the same, and in what respects should the law respect their differences in order to treat them with proportionate equality?

The developments toward equal protection of the law have not followed a straight line. In the United States, for example, the right to vote did not grant the same weight to each person's vote until the 1960s. Previously, populous urban areas often elected the same number of representatives as did sparsely populated rural areas. Countries such as the United Kingdom still allow a certain inequality in the size of single-member voting districts; thus an individual vote in one district does not have equal weight to a vote in another district. Other examples of equality before the law concern citizenship involving shared responsibilities as well as rights. Compulsory jury duty preserves equality of service, as does universal conscription. It might be argued that moving from universal military service to armed forces recruited by monetary and other incentives is a retreat from equality.

Equality of Spirit

On what grounds do large societies legislate equality? Beyond the nature of the law itself, how can one know that one's compatriots, who are often strangers, possess similar selves or souls? Considering the soul in its classical three-part division—reason, spirit, and appetite—we may see different emphases in different eras.

In Western political thought, the earliest moral argument for universal equality stressed the reasoning and willing parts of the soul. Human reason can recognize general principles about human purposes or ends in natural law. The Stoics in ancient Greece argued that every person can be educated into reasoned deliberation to determine these ends and willed action to achieve them. (Plato, in contrast, had suggested a more sophisticated reasoning power generally found only in the philosophers.) In the seventeenth century John Locke said that Christianity democratizes the natural law, making it equally accessible to all people. Thomas Hobbes, leery of religion's role in fomenting civil war, had tried to give equality a secular grounding, turning to the appetitive part of the soul, its fears and desire for security. Civil society involves a relativism regarding people's hopes, but it is based on their similar fears and roughly equal power to hurt each other in the hypothetical state of nature. Jean-Jacques Rousseau mounted a devastating critique of people's equal ability to reason, not only in the state of nature but in civil society

where language is corrupt and unreason can masquerade as wisdom. He focused on the third, spirited, part of the soul (albeit his modern rendition of it). Rousseau based his egalitarianism on will: equal participation in the general will, equal mastery of one's private will. In their equal capacity for action and limited reasoning, and in their similarity of appetites, persons are assumed to be the same.

Egalitarianism demands that people be treated equally. The question again is whether this means arithmetic equality (as if people are the same) or proportionate equality (as if they are different). In the past few decades, many democratic movements—for racial awareness, feminist consciousness, ethnic and linguistic self-determination, regional recognition, and local autonomy—have stressed that citizens of the nation-state are diverse in their heritages and sensibilities.

If people are unlike one another, how can they be equal? If we understand the third part of the soul not as will but as spirit, this perception allows for equality amidst difference. Christianity advanced the idea that people are alike in spirit; brothers and sisters under the Lord, they all aspire to further union with the deity. On this earth the ideal of fraternity recognizes differences among the brothers and sisters, while hope and love unite them. But egalitarianism is less universal and more political than this, situated within particular communities each with its own metaphors and history. We are not all one family; beliefs in different gods separate us. The Hebrew Bible acknowledged equality across difference, yet within political boundaries: "You shall not oppress a stranger; you know the heart of a stranger, for you were strangers in the land of Egypt."

Citizens in large modern states remain strangers to each other. Equal under the law, they do not have the first-hand knowledge of each other's characters that can occur in smaller democracies. Yet all people—from their own knowledge of past oppression—can have empathy for the suffering of others and respect their struggle for dignity. This equality of heart provides a basis, however partial and incomplete, for the equality of respect accorded to the different life experiences of fellow citizens in contemporary democracies.

See also Theory, elite; Hobbes, Thomas; Rousseau, Jean-Jacques; Theory, Ancient.

NANCY L. SCHWARTZ

BIBLIOGRAPHY

Aristotle. *Politics.* Translated by Ernest Barker. Oxford: Oxford University Press, 1946.

McWilliams, Wilson Carey. *The Idea of Fraternity in America.* Berkeley: University of California Press, 1973.

Marshall, T. H. "Citizenship and Social Class." In *Class, Citizenship and Social Class.* Chicago: University of Chicago Press, 1965.

Marx, Karl. "Critique of the Gotha Program" and excerpts from *Capital*, Vol. I. In *The Marx-Engels Reader*, 2d ed. Edited by Robert C. Tucker. New York: Norton, 1978; London: Norton, 1980.

———. "On Equality as the Moral Basis of Community." In *The Moral Foundations of the American Republic*, edited by Robert Horwitz. Charlottesville: University Press of Virginia, 1977.

Sirowy, Larry, and Alex Inkeles. "The Effects of Democracy on Economic Growth and Inequality: A Review." In *On Measuring Democracy: Its Consequences and Concomitants*, edited by Alex Inkeles. New Brunswick, N.J.: Transaction, 1991.

Tocqueville, Alexis de. *Democracy in America.* Vols. I and II. Edited by Phillips Bradley from translations by Henry Reeve and Francis Bowen. New York: Random House, 1990.

Tribe, Laurence H. "Model VI—The Model of Equal Protection." In *American Constitutional Law.* 2d ed. Mineola, N.Y.: Foundation Press, 1988.

✦ Environmentalism

A political ideology that stresses the need to maintain or enhance the quality of the natural and man-made environment. The environmentalist movement has spawned political parties in several Western democracies. Most environmentalist political parties have adopted the title "green." The term ecologism is sometimes used as a synonym, although some commentators regard the latter as a more radical version of environmentalism.

Various aspects of the impact of environmentalism on the practice and the theory of democracy are explored in this article: the spectrum of views that environmentalism contains; the electoral and policy effects of green parties and pressure groups in Western democracies; the logical relationship between the ideals of democracy and environmentalism; and the environmental critique of other prominent democratic political ideologies, in particular socialism and liberalism.

The Spectrum of Environmentalism

Environmentalism encompasses many different shades of opinion. Nevertheless, some key environmentalist values can be identified. The influential 1983 Program of the German Green Party gives four basic principles of environmentalism: (1) the ecological, based on the perceived need for political and economic systems that protect the stability of ecosystems; (2) the social, including commitments to social justice, self-determination, and the quality of life; (3) grassroots democracy, incorporating calls for decentralization and direct democracy; and (4) nonviolence, derived from the notion that "human goals cannot be achieved by inhumane means." Further, globalism (rather than nationalism or isolationism) and a concern about the long-term impact of past and present actions are often put forward as guiding principles of environmentalism.

In recent years the principle of *sustainability*—sometimes *sustainable development*—has come to occupy a central place in environmentalist thinking and policy proposals. The influential United Nations World Commission on Environment and Development report, *Our Common Future* (1987), defines sustainable development as "development that meets the needs of the present generation without compromising the ability of future generations to meet their own needs." Clearly, the concept of sustainability is open to many interpretations, from relatively small adjustments in current economic policies and technological developments to a more radical overhaul of political and economic institutions.

A common distinction is made within environmentalism between shallow and deep ecology, or between light greens and dark greens. Broadly speaking, light greens pursue reform strategies through the existing institutions of Western democracies, whereas dark greens express a greater distrust of existing forms of democratic organization, often regarding liberal representative democracy in its current form as being deeply implicated in environmental degradation.

To a considerable degree, this distinction arises from different ethical assumptions about human beings and their roles within (and relationships to) the natural environment. Human-centered (or anthropocentric) approaches to environmentalism stress the conservation and preservation of natural resources because the latter are useful to humans, providing, in the words of Warwick Fox (in *Towards a Transpersonal Ecology*, 1990), an "early

warning system," a laboratory for scientific study, a useful stockpile of genetic diversity, a recreation resource, and a source of aesthetic pleasure, spiritual inspiration, and psychological health. More radical, or ecocentric (earth-centered), approaches assert that sentience, life, and naturally self-renewing processes have value in themselves, quite apart from whatever instrumental value they may have for humans.

Electoral and Policy Impact

Environmental pressure groups such as Friends of the Earth and Greenpeace sprang up in the early 1970s to address such issues as pollution, irreversible resource depletion, overpopulation, and nuclear power. These groups have gained large memberships and a high profile in the day-to-day politics of several Western democracies. Their internationalist and explicitly ethical outlook has set them apart from more traditional labor, business, and professional interest groups. Indeed, it is sometimes asserted that a new class, concerned with the quality of life rather than material gain, has formed the bedrock of support for environmentalism.

The major electoral breakthrough for green political parties was the election of Green Party candidates to the lower house of the West German national parliament, the Bundestag, in 1983. The German Green Party remains the most prominent of the world's environmentalist parties; in terms of principles, policy, and organization it has been a significant influence on green parties in other countries. Although greens have nowhere participated in national government, they have participated in government at the state level in two federal democracies: Germany (in the Land, or state, of Hesse) and Australia (in the state of Tasmania). In other European countries, notably Britain, France, the Netherlands, Belgium, and Italy, green parties now have an established place in electoral politics (though their electoral performances were uneven throughout the late 1980s and the early 1990s).

The 1989 elections to the European Parliament were an electoral high point for green parties; the previously little-known British and French parties, for example, gained 14.9 percent and 10.6 percent of the national vote, respectively. Such successes may reflect many factors, including the fact that European economies were in a comparatively healthy state and voters felt able to look beyond immediate economic concerns. It is worth noting, however, that the late 1980s witnessed a rapid growth in worldwide awareness of environmental issues, not least because of the media prominence of problems such as the Chernobyl nuclear accident in the Soviet Union, global warming, acid rain, and the depletion of the earth's protective ozone layer.

Electoral success for green parties depends to a considerable degree upon the nature of electoral systems. Britain's "first past the post" elections, for example, afford little opportunity for smaller parties to enter Parliament, whereas proportional representation systems such as Germany's enhance such opportunities. The two-party stranglehold on electoral politics in the United States has led environmentalists to focus on pressure group activities rather than to form a green party.

In the face of considerable political and scientific pressure, governments in some Western democracies have adopted quite comprehensive environmental policy plans covering such areas as pollution control, health, transport, agriculture, and the urban environment. Notable examples are the Dutch national environmental policy plan of 1989, the Canadian "Green Plan," and the British government's policy paper, "Our Common Inheritance." Further, supranational bodies have played an increasingly crucial role in developing comprehensive environmental policies—appropriately

enough, since problems such as ozone depletion and global warming by their very nature cannot be addressed effectively by national governments acting alone.

Environmental policy has been a core concern of the European Community (now the European Union) since the mid-1980s, and the United Nations Conference on Environment and Development at Rio de Janeiro in 1992 (the "Earth Summit"), the world's largest gathering of heads of government, resulted in agreements of varying strength on climate change, biodiversity, deforestation, aid, and sustainable development. Forging international agreements on the environment has been no easy matter, however: the Earth Summit brought to the surface simmering arguments between the rich north and the poorer states of the south over which countries were the worst environmental offenders and which should make the greater economic sacrifice in the name of environmental protection.

Environmentalism and Democracy

As the German Green Party's program suggests, environmentalists promote a distinctive vision of democracy. Most visions of green democracy are variants on a model of direct democracy in a small and often rural community, characterized by self-reliance and labor-intensive production. One influential expression of this model is bioregionalism, which, according to Kirkpatrick Sale (in *Dwellers in the Land*, 1985), holds that human communities should be organized according to features of the natural world— clearly a doctrine that would have major implications for the future of the nation-state as we know it. These ideals of direct democracy and decentralization have found practical expression in the organization of green parties, notably in the early years of the German Green Party, when "grassroots democracy" in the formulation of policy and the rotation of members of the parliament (with an eye to preventing the emergence of an elite leadership) were basic axioms of party organization and structure.

Depending on which particular environmental account of democracy is being considered, within this broad composite model one can find traces of anarchist thinking, communalism, romanticism, feminism, and even aspects of ancient Athenian democracy. The goal of building ecologically and economically sustainable political communities, however, renders the environmentalist model of democracy more than a mere amalgam of older views.

Advocacy of direct democracy has created some tensions within environmentalist ideology. If instituting direct democracy means that public policies will reflect the wishes of citizens more closely, then a direct democrat must surely feel constrained by the expression of the popular will through elections and referendums. What if the citizenry does not wish to have green outcomes reflected in public policy? In such a case, presumably something has to give—either some environmentalist goals must be diluted or abandoned, according to the popular will, or the commitment to direct democracy must itself be softened. Because of this tension, environmentalism has presented a broad target for those who see it as an antiliberal, and ultimately an antidemocratic, doctrine.

Some support for this view was provided by an early wave of survivalist environmental literature from the late 1960s and early 1970s. Writers such as Garrett Hardin, in his influential article "The Tragedy of the Commons" (first published in 1968), and Robert Heilbroner, in *An Inquiry into the Human Prospect* (1974), argued that the depth of the ecological crisis called for drastic, and in some cases authoritarian, measures. In the most extreme versions of this "eco-doom" literature,

human beings were seen as being innately destructive if allowed to do more or less as they pleased; coercion (in Hardin's words, "mutual coercion mutually agreed upon") was the only realistic answer.

Since then the strengthening and deepening of democratic practice has become a central and founding principle of environmentalism. As Robyn Eckersley has put it (in *Environmentalism and Political Theory*, 1992), the "survivalist" approach gave way to a stress on "emancipation" in the 1980s. Environmentalism sees a close link between the deepening of democracy and the achievement of environmental protection and environmental justice. In other words, democracy is regarded as part of the solution, not part of the problem.

Environmentalism is critical of both liberalism and socialism for their attachment to comparatively unconstrained industrial expansion and ecologically destructive forms of economic growth. As Robert Goodin has argued (in *Green Political Theory*, 1992), greens see value as residing primarily in natural processes—like the creation of an ecosystem—rather than in labor inputs or market value. Elements of both liberal and socialist thinking have, however, been adopted and adapted by environmentalists. For example, greens adhere closely to the progressive social policies of the left, while seeking to extend the liberal concept of rights to animals and even species and ecosystems. Central tenets of newer political ideologies, notably feminism, have also been incorporated into environmentalist thinking.

Future Challenges

From a democratic perspective, environmentalism faces major challenges in the next century. How can a world of competing nation-states be encouraged to act in principled concert? Can electoral support, and the shift in cultural values that it requires, be consolidated and extended? In the realm of ideas, can the liberal notion of rights effectively be extended to include a range of ecological rights?

However environmentalism responds to these and other challenges, it is clear that it has added a new and probably lasting dimension to politics in the liberal democracies of the West. In some states it has played a role in altering the calculus of electoral politics. Although environmentalism is not an ideology free from internal tensions, its impact on more venerable ways of thinking about the obligations of democratic states and citizens has been clear, considerable, and rapid.

See also Anarchy; Feminism; Liberalism; Socialism.

MICHAEL SAWARD

BIBLIOGRAPHY

Dobson, Andrew. *Green Political Thought: An Introduction.* London: Unwin Hyman, 1990.

———, and Paul Lucardie, eds. *The Politics of Nature: Explorations in Green Political Theory.* London and New York: Routledge, 1993.

Doherty, Brian. "The Fundi-Realo Controversy: An Analysis of Four European Green Parties." *Environmental Politics* 1 (spring 1992): 95–120.

Eckersley, Robyn. *Environmentalism and Political Theory: Toward an Ecocentric Approach.* Albany: State University of New York Press; London: UCL Press, 1992.

Goodin, Robert E. *Green Political Theory.* Cambridge: Polity Press, 1992.

Jamieson, Dale, ed. *A Companion to Environmental Philosophy.* Malden, Mass.: Blackwell, 2001.

Paehlke, Robert E. *Environmentalism and the Future of Progressive Politics.* New Haven and London: Yale University Press, 1989.

Young, Stephen C. "The Different Dimensions of Green Politics." *Environmental Politics* 1 (spring 1992): 9–44.

✦ Existentialism

A philosophy that concentrates on the individual's search for authenticity and meaning in a hostile or indifferent world. Existentialism is difficult to describe or define, in part because it is as much a pervasive philosophical persuasion or mood as a philosophical movement. Its stance toward democracy is thus difficult to determine; it is above all one of ambivalence.

Historical Development

The German thinker F. M. Heinemann first used the term *Existenzphilosophie* in 1929. Following World War II it gained prominence among the victorious Allies who found no clear meaning in their victory over the defeated fascist powers. Its history antedates these developments, however. One can find antecedents to existentialism in the Old Testament in Job's intransigence in the face of the sufferings inflicted on him by a mysterious God; in the brooding depiction of human fate by the Greek tragedians in the fifth century B.C.; in Jean-Jacques Rousseau's insistence, in the eighteenth century, on the essential solitude of human beings; and in the whole corpus of Western poetry.

The more recent history of existentialism is relatively clear, but it raises a whole cluster of questions. Existentialism can be seen as the fusion of the philosophy of Søren Kierkegaard (1813–1855), the Danish religious thinker, and Friedrich Nietzsche (1844–1900), modernity's most audacious atheist. These two thinkers shared a conviction of the insufficiency of reason for understanding the deepest problems and a preference for the individual over collectivities. Yet existentialism has always been split as to the question of God.

Its exponents include pious figures like Gabrielle Marcel (1889–1973), the French author of much devotional literature, and Franz Rosenzweig (1886–1929), the German Jew whose "new thinking" helped to spawn postmodernism. Yet Jean-Paul Sartre (1905–1980), the French philosopher whose links to existentialism are even more prominent, repeatedly emphasizes existentialism's core belief that God does not exist and that even if he did it would make no difference. One can somewhat dissolve this tension by realizing that for religious existentialists the existence of God indeed makes very little difference in this world, a vale of tears, except to provide an escape from it by a leap of faith that transcends rational analysis.

The philosopher who fused the thought of Nietzsche and Kierkegaard into an enigmatic whole is Martin Heidegger (1889–1976). Heidegger's philosophy is an analysis of human dread, angst. It is justly considered to be the heart of existentialism, but that raises yet further problems. Two difficulties deserve particular mention. First, Heidegger rejected the label of existentialism, as did other prominent existentialists, including Karl Jaspers (1883–1969). Indeed the only prominent thinker who never objected to the designation of "existentialist" at some time or other is Albert Camus (1913–1960), who usually is relegated to the second rank in regard to the profundity of his philosophy.

Heidegger's indisputable link to fascism poses a second problem. He joined the Nazi Party in 1933 and retained his membership for the duration of Germany's Third Reich. Moreover, his emphasis on resoluteness involved a rejection of all political moderation, and his brooding on blood, soil, and rootedness was bound to lend support to the irrationalism one associates with fascism. If one considers Heidegger's philosophy alone, one bends in the direction of understanding existentialism as a straightforward antidemocratic system of thought. One must, however, balance Heidegger's close ties to the right with Sartre's close ties to the left. (Sartre frequently defended the policies of the Soviet Union.) One must also bear in mind Camus's intrepid allegiance to a policy in which human beings avoid being either victims or executioners.

It thus seems that existentialism is difficult to situate because it is compatible with all other political and moral positions. It is in part a ceaseless elaboration of Nietzsche's dictum that God is dead, but Christian and Jewish existentialists abound. It is the very antithesis of Marxism, stressing subjectivity whereas Marxists emphasize objectivity; identifying optimism with shallowness, whereas Marxists hold that humanity sets itself only such tasks as it can solve; focusing on the solitary individual instead of classes and collectivities; and stressing freedom instead of determinism.

The Existentialist Response to Democracy

Existentialism's compatibility with the politics of both the extreme right and the extreme left can be connected with its aversion to any present situation in which it finds itself. It prominently involves a nostalgia for an imagined or real wholeness in the past, which is why existentialist literature comes to sight as a kind of late romanticism. It also yearns for a future that will overcome the fragmentation of the present time. The contemporary situation it castigates is likely to be liberal democracy.

Existentialism has always exerted the strongest hold on the life of the mind in Western Europe and America, the strongholds of democracy. The sentiments it has cultivated—including nostalgia for the past and yearning for the future—may not be honored by typical democrats, but they will most likely be tolerated. One should remember that Heidegger's master work, *Being and Time* (1927), was first published in democratic Weimar, Germany.

Typical democrats may well hold the existentialist's view of the world in contempt, but they will think that one's worldview is one's own business. Liberal democracies honor a distinction between the private and the public, and existentialism, with its clear preference for the private over the public, needs such tolerance to thrive. Authoritarian and totalitarian countries of both the left and the right, by contrast, are likely to condemn existentialists as antisocial decadents or even degenerates.

Existentialists are not famous for showing gratitude for the hospitality, or at least toleration, democracies grant them. They are more likely to respond to liberal democracy with indifference and disdain. One notices the indifference when one searches in vain for existentialist treatises on what can be considered the nitty-gritty prerequisites of democracies: voting, parties, constitutions, courts, public administration, and so forth. One can find an existentialist sociology or psychology, but an existentialist political science does not exist.

What is more, economic considerations are always crucial to liberal democracies, whereas existentialism says next to nothing about economics. Karl Marx, John Stuart Mill, Adam Smith, and even Rousseau wrote on economics, but it borders on the unthinkable that Heidegger, Nietzsche, or Kierkegaard would write an economic treatise. And those existentialists who profess closeness to Marx deal with topics like alien-ation rather than surplus value. Existentialism is simply indifferent to the allocations of scarce resources or the way human beings work to make a living. The crises that concern it are spiritual rather than material.

It is not, however, indifferent to the fact that liberal democracies are likely to center on economic concerns. Democracies are almost always commercial republics; at least no democracy fails to be critically concerned with alleviating poverty and furthering prosperity. At this point, existentialist indifference yields to disdain. One can look at this matter in another way. Democracies, being incurably middle class, at least at the present time, are linked to bourgeois life. Existentialists on both ends of the political spectrum agree in their denunciation of the center as bourgeois.

Identifying, and perhaps overidentifying, liberal democracy with bourgeois democracy, existentialism charges it with a number of grave shortcomings. It accuses liberal democracy of devoting itself almost exclusively to the further-ance of economic prosperity, to making self-preservation not only its highest but almost its exclusive goal. The making of money triumphs over all other concerns, producing a nation of shopkeepers.

Such a nation, to be sure, refuses to see itself for what it is, cultivating an all-pervasive hypocrisy. In liberal democracies one disguises one's vices by paying empty tribute to virtue. Thus one praises the family as a central institution, but sexual promiscuity abounds. One speaks of lofty goals, even while becoming blind to higher values. Liberal democracy, according to the accusations of existentialism, fosters a listless and common-place life in which people no longer believe in anything strongly enough to be willing to die for it. Bourgeois life is a life of quiet or noisy desperation, of empty pursuits in ugly suburbs, of infi-nite pettiness and stultifying tediousness.

Existentialists tend to agree with the classical notion that regimes foster certain types of human beings in the sense that Socrates in Plato's *Republic* can speak of "democratic man." To existentialists, the democratic type is increasingly oblivious to all that is noble. The bourgeois personality is anything but autonomous; indeed, bourgeois individuals can be understood as those who always think of themselves while in company and of others while alone.

One can judge the kinds of personalities cultivated by various regimes according to the virtues they honor in theory and practice. The bourgeois type no longer covets honor, taking a dim view of courage, especially the bravery of soldiers: democracies prefer butter to guns. The virtues that are praised center on such bourgeois traits as frugality, thrift, and a kind of moderation that existentialists find impossible to distinguish from mediocrity. Following Nietzsche, existentialism connects virtue with squandering and with living dangerously.

The principles of liberty and equality that liberal democracy extols contribute to a lowering of standards. Liberty amounts to a kind of license in which citizens do what they like, and what they like to do is to indulge in their petty pleasures. Equality degenerates into the distrust of higher forms of life by lower forms of life, into resentment of all that even hints of human greatness.

The existentialist critique of bourgeois life does not limit itself to a rejection of the ignoble or even seamy aspects of democratic regimes. It ridicules not only the practice of liberal democracy but its theory as well. It rejects the notion that one can base democracy on objective principles. As an antecedent of postmodernism, existentialism represents an early version of antifoundationalism in the United States. Democracy seeks to justify itself by an appeal to what the American Declaration of Independence of 1776 calls "self-evident truths," permanent realities that can be discovered by the human mind. According to existentialism, such truths do not exist; what human beings call truth is not what they discover but what they construct or create. Modern democracy has sometimes been criticized for abandoning the tenets of classical political philosophy, but existentialism emphasizes, and rejects, its continued adherence to those tenets. It views democratic theory as a futile appeal to a discredited essentialism—the belief in a permanent human nature.

That existentialists have a point in this characterization can be seen in the language of the Declaration of Independence as well as the basic documents of other democracies, such as the French Declaration of the Rights of Man and of the Citizen (1791). Democratic theory abounds with such references as "the laws of Nature and of Nature's God," and democratic rhetoric imprints the very core of citizens with such views. According to existentialism, however, human beings have no permanent nature but rather a history that fashions and molds them. Existentialism finds the appeal to God equally problematic for reasons already suggested: either God does not exist or he offers no visible guidance for human or political affairs.

Because existentialism rejects any appeal to transcendent standards, it also rejects the democratic espousal of natural rights. In the democracy of the United States, and either explicitly or implicitly in other modern democracies, human beings are entitled to a certain amount of consideration because—in the language of the Declaration of Independence—they are "endowed by their Creator with certain unalienable rights." Existentialism must regard such a pronouncement as either a noble lie or a futile delusion: human beings cannot have such rights because nothing or nobody exists to endow them with rights. At best, human beings have needs, longings, and drives. They may also possess reason, but rationality is not what is deepest in them.

From this point of view, it makes no sense to declare that all are created equal for that statement is demonstrably false: human beings are unequal in strength, in mental capabilities, and in many other respects. Once humans stop counting on a God who is father to all human beings, equality becomes a wish rather than a fact.

Similarly, the notions of life, liberty, and the pursuit of happiness lose the aura with which democratic theory surrounds them. Because existentialism rejects the idea of a beneficent nature and a providential God, it must doubt that human beings are entitled to life. Following the thought of John Locke, the seventeenth-century English philosopher, democracy considers the desire for self-preservation to be basic. But following Nietzsche, existentialism holds that those who are alive need not desire life, and those who are not alive are unable to wish for it. Instead, existentialism sees life as the will to power, which in its milder forms becomes the desire for self-expression.

Liberty, too, is an ambiguous goal for existentialism, which does, to be sure, think in terms of the dreadful freedom of human beings as they face life without being pointed by nature or by God to any preordained ends. Yet existentialism is agnostic on the issue of whether human beings really have free will or whether liberty is merely an illusion accompanying the will in action. In either case, liberty cannot be the freedom to do what one ought to do: it cannot rise above the freedom to do what one likes.

Finally, in its generally baleful view of things, existentialism refuses to think in terms of a right to the pursuit of happiness. Or at least it understands such a pursuit to be futile, for human beings were not made to be happy, and the universe is far too hostile or at least indifferent to have the slightest concern for their welfare.

The existentialist critique of democracy also extends to the democratic propensity to develop governments of laws rather than of human beings. It regards laws as designed for universal applicability, which is to say that laws must cater to the meanest human capacities. Existentialism regards anything that is universally applicable as detrimental to the cultivation of human greatness.

The diagnosis of existentialism, then, is that democracy is a deficient system of government, working against any possible elevation of humanity, and that citizens under such a regime are neither happy nor good. Existentialism thinks in terms of an all-encompassing crisis of the present time and of democracy as a leading symptom of that crisis.

Nihilism

If one agrees to such a diagnosis, one is naturally led to ask about the suggestions of existentialism in regard to a cure for current ills. Even the most sympathetic students of existentialism, however, are likely to conclude that it offers no comprehensive solutions for the problems it expounds. Traditionally, one has turned to religion as a bulwark against the spiritual sickness of one's time, but, as has already been stated, a leading strand of existentialism subscribes to the dictum that "God is dead"; even religious existentialists do not put much stock in organized religion. They think in terms of the individual's quest for faith and do not find in religious institutions a cure for what ails humanity.

The pronouncement that God is dead implies that religion has lost its capacity to act as a binding force for society and points to the nihilism that existentialism finds rampant in modern life. God's death suggests the demise of all transcendent standards by which human life might be understood and rationally arranged. Nihilism holds that all the highest goods human beings have cherished are now exposed as arbitrary.

Existentialism in no way invented nihilism. Since the beginning of the nineteenth century, nihilists were considered godless creatures who reasoned that since there is no God, everything is permitted, with all morality exposed as merely convention. The term gained currency largely because of the graphic depiction of nihilists in the Russian novels of Ivan Turgenev (*Fathers and Sons*, 1862) and Fyodor Mikhailovich Dostoyevsky (*The Possessed*, 1871; *The Brothers Karamazov*, 1880). Existentialism provides an analysis of the nihilist's way of looking at the world, a worldview according to which the highest values are exposed as unsupported by reality.

Two fundamentally different responses to the devaluation of the highest values are possible. One can become a passive nihilist and react to a chaotic universe by devoting oneself to self-gratification, or one can strike out against a meaningless world in a kind of absurdist protest. The latter response takes into account the fact that there is no longer any reason to strive for one thing rather than another, but there is the conviction that it is better to will nothingness than to cease willing. Neither response bodes well for democracy. Passive nihilists lack all civic virtues; active nihilists resort to gratuitous acts of destruction.

Existentialism does more than articulate the mood of despair that is nihilism. It insists that the mood is based on accurate perceptions of reality, for humanity's striving for goodness, truth, and beauty really does lack all cosmic support. Existentialism does, to be sure, attempt to move beyond a description of humankind's abysmal condition, but its positive teachings have not attained widespread acceptance. That is in part because they are shrouded in paradox and obscurity, as is the case with Nietzsche's doctrine of the eternal return of the same, which counsels a stance of acceptance and even gratitude for the world as it is, and in part because no specific moral advice issues from an existential analysis. Thus existentialists extol commitment but have little to say about the goals to which one ought to commit oneself.

Existentialism then appears as a profound dissection of the ills of democracy without much to say about a cure, since it doubts that there is a cure. One must, however, add that most existentialists are far from being either bomb throwers or craven hedonists. They are more likely to be bemused but loyal citizens. A conviction of the absurdity of the human lot is compatible with adherence to the fundamental decencies of human life.

See also Nietzsche, Friedrich; Postmodernism.

WERNER J. DANNHAUSER

BIBLIOGRAPHY

Barrett, William E. *Irrational Man*. New York: Anchor Doubleday, 1962.

Dictionary of Existentialism. Edited by Haim Gordon. Westport, Conn.: Greenwood, 1999.

Kaufmann, Walter, ed. *Existentialism from Dostoevsky to Sartre*. New York: Meridian, 1956.

Langiulli, Nino, ed. *The Existentialist Tradition*. New York: Anchor Doubleday, 1971.

Löwith, Karl. *Nature, History, and Existentialism*. Evanston, Ill.: Northwestern University Press, 1966.

Rosen, Stanley. *Nihilism: A Philosophical Essay*. New Haven and London: Yale University Press, 1969.

✦ Fascism

A generic term used to characterize a type of ideology and the nationalist and authoritarian movements and regimes that governed in Europe in the years between the two world wars and until the defeat of Germany in 1945. Fascism as a movement was founded by Benito Mussolini in Italy in 1919. Fascist movements subsequently appeared in many countries with varying degrees of success. The most important of these was the National Socialist German Workers Party, or Nazi Party, which arose in Austria and Germany and was led by Adolf Hitler.

The term *fascist* in common usage has become a term of opprobrium. It has been applied to violent antiliberal actions by extremist groups—even the radical student groups in the 1960s and leftist nationalist terrorists—and to many ultraconservative, antiliberal groups and parties—particularly those that are also nationalist or antiforeign. Communists even labeled the social democratic parties "social fascist," arguing that a democratic polity like West Germany's with its capitalist development was preparing for the return of fascism. But to label such political groups and movements fascist does not explain the success of fascism in the first half of the twentieth century.

After World War I, when the defeat and disintegration of the three continental empires (Germany, Austro-Hungary, and czarist Russia) seemed to have made the world safe for democracy, two antidemocratic movements—Leninist Bolshevism (communism) and Italian fascism—appeared on the European scene. Communism would be the more important and successful, but fascist ideology and movements would threaten and destroy democracy in the interwar years. There can be no doubt about the affinity between Hitler's movement and Italian fascism, which ultimately led to the Axis domination of Europe in World War II.

Foundations of Fascism

There is considerable debate about the exact definition of the fascist phenomenon—why fascist movements emerge, why they succeed or fail, and which parties and regimes outside Italy and Germany should be considered fascist. But a certain consensus is emerging.

Generally speaking, fascism had roots in nineteenth-century critiques of liberal democracy, parliamentarism, socialism, and conservative authoritarianism and in philosophical currents such as irrationalism, social Darwinism, and radical romantic ethnic nationalism. As a latecomer competing for political space with other parties, fascism defined itself by what it opposed: liberalism, communism, internationalism, conservatism, and clericalism. And it was antiproletarian more than antisocialist. Fascism considered Marxism and the advocacy of the class struggle a threat to national integration.

The extreme nationalism of fascism is reflected in a deep-seated hostility to all organizations, movements, and groups that can be considered international in character. Examples include communism and socialism, international finance capitalism, the Roman Catholic Church, Freemasonry, the League of Nations (the antecedent of the United Nations), pacifism, and the Jews.

Ideologically, fascism exalted violence, struggle, sacrifice, the heroic deed, and the cult of those who had died for the cause. It was characterized by an extreme nationalist sentiment and the restructuring of the relationship of the nation with other powers. Coincident with its priority of politics over economics, it sought to create a regulated national economy that would subordinate classes to politics. It rejected traditional authority and status structures, although sometimes, as in Italy, compromise was necessary. It favored separation of church and state, thus excluding clerical influences—even though some fascist movements (like the Romanian Iron Guard) incorporated religion as part of the national tradition.

Fascists tried to create a new culture and a "new man," sometimes with futurist ideas and sometimes looking backward to a primitive or medieval past. Fascist innovations in political style included symbols like the black shirts of the Italian fascists and the brown shirts of the German Nazis; they developed particular rituals and a language and style of their own. Fascists assigned a positive value to masculinity and youth, as expressed in party militias and youth organizations. The distinctive style and rhetoric and hatreds and hopes of fascism attracted a generation of Europeans, particularly the young.

In fact, fascism was a youthful movement when it began. In 1933 its leaders—Mussolini, Hitler, Oswald Mosley (the British fascist leader), Jacques Doriot (founder of the French fascist party), Corneliu Zelea Codreanu (the Romanian fascist leader), José Antonio Primo de Rivera (founder of the fascist Falange in Spain), and Léon Degrelle (the Belgian fascist leader)—all were in their thirties or early forties. The established politicians they confronted were much older.

Fascism included a mythical concept of rebirth, of a new start for a society in crisis, of victory over decay. It promised to replace gerontocracy, mediocrity, and weakness with youth, heroism, and national greatness; to banish anarchy and decadence; and to bring about order and health. It was populist in intent and rhetoric, yet elitist in practice.

Fascism and Democracy

Fascists were clearly opposed to what they called "demo-bourgeois" institutions and values, like the liberal parliamentary state and institutions of the state of law (the *Rechtsstaat)*, but they would not have admitted to being antidemocratic. In fact, they (like the communists) argued that they offered an opportunity to achieve true democracy by establishing a direct relationship between the people and the leaders without the intervention of political parties and interest groups. They favored a plebiscitarian concept of direct democracy, in which the people would say yes or no to the decisions of the leaders without any debate.

Fascist democracy was to be achieved by an emotional identification of the people with the leaders, by acclaiming those leaders in mass rallies, and by voting for one slate of candidates proposed by the party. The party was to appeal to all people, without distinguishing them by class, interests, or religious attitudes—characteristics the fascists saw as dividing the nation. Initially, fascist leaders were to be elected, but soon the leader was vested with charismatic authority. The cult of personality of the *Duce* in Italy and the *Führer* in Germany acquired an almost religious tone.

Fascist parties could claim to be democratic because they were based on mass participation with large numbers of active members. Fascists contrasted this level of participation with the infrequent political activity of most citizens, whose only activity was to vote and attend a few party meetings. Members of fascist parties participated in constant rallies and marches, bought uniforms to identify themselves with the party, contributed money to the party, and organized against their opponents in "punitive" expeditions. The activism gave members—particularly the young, students, and demobilized officers and soldiers—a sense of participation that contrasted with normal politics. Participation in an essentially antidemocratic movement thus often seemed to be a form of democratic participation.

Fascists perceived their movement as democratic for another reason: leadership positions were open to all party members without regard to social status or prestige in societies that had rigid status and class distinctions. Young people and those with no established social positions might find themselves directing (and demeaning) people who otherwise might be considered their social betters. The appeal to youth also subverted society's traditional hierarchy. Egalitarianism was reflected in the use of the term *comrade* as well as informal forms of address among party members. Furthermore, the nationalist ideology broke down the class barrier by speaking of the "proletarian nation," transferring the class conflict within the society to a conflict between the weaker, less developed, defeated nations and the victorious "pluto-democracies" (Britain, France, and the United States). A sense of common interest among all members of the nation, regardless of class, was thus created.

However, by any definition of democracy prevalent today—that is, democracy based on respect for pluralism in the society, the freedom of individuals to make their own choices, the existence of civil and political liberties, and respect for the rights of minorities—fascism was profoundly antidemocratic. The exaltation of violence as a means to gain and retain power is incompatible with the possibility of peaceful change in government. Charismatic leadership and one-party monopoly of political power are incompatible with democratic leaders' accountability and limits on time in office. The exclusionary concept of citizenship, and more particularly the racism and anti-Semitism of the Nazis, are the opposite of the ideal of inclusionary citizenship that is held by democracies.

Italian Fascists and German Nazis

Fascism came to power in Italy in 1922 when Mussolini became prime minister. He ruled as a dictator from 1925 until 1943. Mussolini had been a socialist party leader during World War I, when he broke with the socialists and became a nationalist who favored Italian intervention in the war. He gathered a following of veterans, intellectuals, students, and members of trade unions and created a party that fought leftists in the streets.

Later, his party was strongly supported by landowners and wealthy farmers who opposed the demands of socialist farm unions and tenants.

In the 1920s democratic forces in Italy were divided between those who had favored and those who had opposed intervention in World War I, between communists and socialists, and between Christian Democrats and anticlerical liberals. The split in the ranks of the democrats enabled Mussolini to come to power with the support of a large part of the traditional right.

In spite of the conflicts in Italy, Mussolini succeeded in stopping disorder (which had been created largely by fascist violence) and in promoting public works and economic development. His superb oratorical and organizational skills and his orchestration of public support generated much admiration abroad. In many countries, groups calling themselves "fascist" appeared on the political scene.

Fascist parties succeeded in coming to power on their own only in Italy, Germany, and—briefly—Romania. The fascist parties failed to gain majority electoral support before they seized power. Only in Italy, Germany, Romania, Belgium, and Hungary did they ever receive more than 10 percent of the vote.

Even the Nazis in Germany failed to win a majority. Their best results came in the half-free election of March 1933 when Hitler was already in power. In that election the Nazis managed to obtain 43.9 percent of the vote and 44.5 percent of the seats in the parliament. Only the support of the Conservatives, who had received 8 percent of the vote, gave the antidemocratic right 52 percent of the vote in that election. The strength of the Nazis and the communists in the parliament in 1932 made any democratic majority impossible. This fact and their fear of the left led many conservatives to look for an accommodation with Hitler and made it possible for the aging president, Paul von Hindenburg, to appoint Hitler as chancellor in 1933. The Conservatives were mistaken in their belief that power would moderate Hitler and that they would be able to control him.

Although there were similarities between Italian fascists and German Nazis, there were also fundamental differences. Hitler's ideology was founded on race, whereas Mussolini's was based on nationalism in a political and cultural sense. With Nazism's elements of extreme social Darwinism and pseudoscientific racist and biological theories, anti-Semitism became a central theme, although there is some doubt about how much this contributed to its mass appeal. Anti-Semitism was not part of the program of other fascist movements, although under German influence or as a result of traditional anti-Semitism in their societies many other fascists did hold anti-Semitic views.

Another difference between Italian fascists and German Nazis was that Italy generally continued to follow formal law and to include some elements of pluralism, both characteristics of authoritarian states. Nazi Germany, by contrast, was a totalitarian regime that came close to destroying the social pluralism of its society and to controlling most institutions. The role of the leader was much more important under Hitler than under Mussolini. Certainly, there is no comparison between the situation in Italy and the repression and terror in Germany.

Fascism's Rise and Fall

The domination of Europe by Germany and Italy during World War II allowed fascists to gain complete or partial power in other countries, as in France under Marshal Philippe Pétain, hero of the First World War. In some authoritarian regimes, fascists participated in a ruling coalition, as in the Falange in Francisco Franco's Spain. Franco came to power in Spain in 1939 after a three-year civil war in which he had been aided by Germany and Italy. His movement, however, was a coalition of fascists and clerical right-wing conservatives and monarchists.

Fascism was basically a European phenomenon, although there were fascist parties on other continents, the most important among them in Brazil. However, fascists influenced other parties competing for the same vote, such as authoritarian conservatives and some Christian parties, as in Austria and Spain. In many countries, particularly in France but also in England, a number of intellectuals and writers became fascists or expressed their admiration for fascism (to mention just one, the American poet Ezra Pound). Without reference to the complex intellectual currents in Europe at the end of the nineteenth century and the first four decades of the twentieth, it is impossible to understand the success of fascism.

Fascist parties could not succeed in countries where democrats of the left and right united against them, nor in countries where authoritarian regimes decided to outlaw or persecute them, such as Portugal, Brazil, Japan, Estonia, and Latvia. But it was the horror of Nazi atrocities that finally removed all legitimacy from fascism, even though other fascist parties were not responsible for crimes on that scale.

See also Democracy, Critiques of.

JUAN J. LINZ

BIBLIOGRAPHY

Bracher, Karl Dietrich. *The German Dictatorship*. New York: Praeger, 1970.

De Felice, Renzo. *Interpretations of Fascism*. Translated by Brenda Huff Everett. Cambridge: Harvard University Press, 1977.

_____. *Mussolini el fascista: la conquiste del potere, 1921–1925*. Turin: Einaudi, 1966.

Gregor, James. *The Ideology of Fascism: The Rationale of Totalitarianism*. New York: Free Press, 1969.

_____. *Interpretations of Fascism*. Morristown, N.J.: General Learning Press, 1974.

Griffin, Roger. *The Nature of Fascism*. London: Pinter, 1991.

Hamilton, Alastair. *The Appeal of Fascism: A Study of Intellectuals and Fascism, 1919–1945*. New York: Avon, 1971.

Hamilton, Richard F. *Who Voted for Hitler?* Princeton: Princeton University Press, 1982.

Laqueur, Walter, ed. *Fascism: A Reader's Guide*. Berkeley: University of California Press; Aldershot: Wildwood House, 1977.

Larsen, Stein Ugelvik, Bernt Hagtvet, and Jan Petter Myklebust, eds. *Who Were the Fascists? Social Roots of European Fascism*. Bergen: Universitets Forlaget, 1980.

Linz, Juan J. "Notes toward a Comparative Study of Fascism in Sociological Historical Perspective." In *Fascism: A Reader's Guide*, edited by Walter Laqueur. Berkeley: University of California Press; Aldershot: Wildwood House, 1977.

Lyttelton, Adrian. *The Seizure of Power: Fascism in Italy, 1919–1929*. New York: Scribner's, 1973.

Mosse, George L. *The Crisis of German Ideology: Intellectual Origins of the Third Reich*. New York: Grosset and Dunlop, 1964.

_____. *The Fascist Revolution. Toward a General Theory of Fascism*. New York: Howard Fertig, 1999.

Nolte, Ernst. *Three Faces of Fascism: Action Française, Italian Fascism, and National Socialism*. New York: Mentor, 1969.

Payne, Stanley G. *Fascism: Comparison and Definition*. Madison: University of Wisconsin Press, 1980.

✦ Federalism

A form of political association and organization that unites separate polities within a more comprehensive political system, allowing each polity to maintain its own fundamental political integrity. Federalism can be understood as constitutionalized power sharing through systems that combine self-rule and shared rule. In federal systems, basic policies are made and implemented through negotiation so that all the members share in making and executing decisions. The political principles animating federal systems emphasize the importance of bargaining and negotiated coordination among several power centers; they also stress the virtues of dispersed power centers as a means of safeguarding individual and local liberties.

To use a biological analogy, we can consider federalism to be a genus of which there are several species. Modern *federation*, the best known of the various species, is a national union in which a constitution is the supreme law of the land but in which authority and power are divided and shared by a general government and constituent governments. It was invented by the Founders of the United States who drafted the Constitution of 1787. Until then the accepted definition of federalism was what today we call *confederation*, a situation in which two or more polities come together to establish a limited-purpose general government that functions through the constituent states. The constituent states are the primary political communities and retain ultimate sovereignty within the polity.

Today federalism is one of the most widespread forms of political organization. In 1993 at least nineteen countries were organized as federal systems, and at least twenty-one others utilized federal principles to incorporate a measure of constitutionalized decentralization into their systems of government. In addition, there are three supranational confederations and twenty-three associated states, federacies, and condominiums. An *associated state* is nominally sovereign but is constitutionally tied to or dependent on another state for certain purposes; for example, Monaco is an associated state of France. *Federacies* are arrangements in which a smaller state is constitutionally linked to a larger one (the federate power) in an asymmetrical manner; Jersey has such an arrangement with the United Kingdom. *Condominiums* are states that are jointly controlled by two or more other states; for example, France and Spain have sovereign authority over Andorra.

Conceived in the broadest sense, federalism looks to the linkage of people and polities in lasting yet limited union by mutual consent, without the sacrifice of their respective integrities. Federalism must be considered a "mother" form of democracy like parliamentary democracy or direct democracy.

Fundamental Principles of Federalism

Federal systems are based on six fundamental principles. They are noncentralized; they are predisposed toward democracy; they have established a system of checks and balances; they operate through a process of open bargaining; they have a written constitution; and they have constitutionally determined the fixed units of power within the polity.

Noncentralization. The first principle of federalism is noncentralization. The political framework has no single center but rather multiple centers linked by a shared fundamental law and communications network. Federalism reflects a matrix model of organization: a number of separate but equal states (the constituent states) are encompassed by a set of framing institutions (the federal government) and are further divided internally into even smaller cells (local governments). Each cell is an arena of government—larger or smaller, not higher or lower. The cells have different power "loadings" for different tasks; the whole functions as a cybernetic system. Federal-

ism stands in opposition to a hierarchical pyramid in which power and authority are concentrated in or gravitate toward an apex, with all other power centers seen as "levels" subordinated to the apex. By the same token, federalism does not have a power center and a periphery, whereby elites are formed by or gravitate to the center.

Democracy. Federal systems are strongly predisposed toward democracy. Some would even argue that to be truly federal a system must be democratic, since it must involve public and constitutional choice in every arena. Federal democracy is built on a somewhat different set of premises than democracy based on the two other models of the polity: Westminster democracy and consociational democracy. In the Westminster model (based on the British system) the parliament is supreme, and the government exercises power as long as it is supported by a parliamentary majority. A consociational democracy is one that has deep ethnic, linguistic, or religious divisions and that makes special arrangements to accommodate the needs of various groups. Belgium and Switzerland are examples of consociational democracies in pluralist societies.

Checks and balances. Federal democracy rests on a system of checks and balances. The polity must be constructed in such a way that every institution is checked and balanced by other institutions that have their own constitutionally based authority and that are sufficiently autonomous to sustain themselves politically and socially. In the words of *Federalist* No. 51, written by James Madison in support of the new American Constitution, "ambition must be made to counteract ambition."

Open bargaining. Federalism must allow for bargaining. Bargaining must take place among institutions and their representatives, and it must be done openly as a legitimate part of the federal political process. In fact, bargaining takes place in every system, even in the most centralized or hierarchical ones, by the very nature of human relationships. Federalism, however, is the only political system that makes bargaining an integral and required part of the process, subject only to the requirement that it be open and accessible. A major part of the politics of federal systems is to maintain the openness of bargaining both in terms of the bargaining itself and in terms of access to the bargaining table.

Constitutionalism. The complexities of making noncentralization, checks and balances, and bargaining work in federalist systems—not to mention managing authority and powers shared among the constituent polities and the overarching one—are a powerful impetus for developing clear-cut, mutually agreed upon fundamental rules embodied in written constitutions. A written constitution is needed to bring the federal system into existence and to give all parties to it a common understanding of the system they have erected or joined. Over time, these constitutions come to include both the written document, or documents, and accepted interpretations, most frequently provided by a supreme or constitutional court.

Fixed units. The demarcations of the polity in federal systems must be fixed constitutionally. The divisions can be either territorial, consociational, or both. Although in theory the constituent units of a federal system can be nonterritorial, in fact the areal, or regional, division of power is most common and most successful.

Historical Bases

The first recorded federal system was that of the ancient Israelite tribes more than 3,200 years ago. It is a matter of historical dispute whether this system was analogous to a federation or a confederation under today's definitions. It is described in the Bible as having a common constitution, the Torah of Moses (the first five books of the Bible). It was also noncentralized, with most powers resting with the individual tribes. This federal system lasted nearly 700 years with various modifications (such as the introduction of kingship). There have been many other tribal "confederations," including the Bedouin tribes of Africa and the Middle East and the Native American confederacies in North America, but the Israelite federation was, in all likelihood, the first to have a detailed written constitution or a written history.

The leagues of Hellenic city-states 2,400 years ago in what is today Greece proper and in Asia Minor were by today's definition confederations. That is to say, ultimate authority and sovereignty were lodged with the constituent units, while the confederated leagues pursued only those common purposes for which they were formed. Both the Israelite and Greek federal systems were designed to combine what were essentially democracies to gain certain benefits of scale, usually in the realm of defense. Both disappeared when they were conquered by larger imperial aggressors. In the case of the Greeks, first Alexander the Great and then Rome were the conquerors.

The Roman Republic, at least formally, established yet a third form of federal system some 2,400 years ago, a system now called *federacy*. Rome became the federate power, and weaker cities were attached to it as federal partners, preserving their local autonomy and not in return gaining the full political rights of Roman citizens. During its imperial period, Rome in theory preserved some of the forms of federalism, but in actuality it became a centralized empire.

The next wave of federal developments, which came in medieval Europe, were associated with democratic republicanism. Where cities developed, as in northern Italy and Germany, leagues of cities were established as loose confederations. These confederations survived as long as it was in the interests of their rulers for them to do so. In the more remote and rural areas of the continent, small republics confined to a particular mountain valley or coastal swamp came together first in nonfederal and then in federal arrangements. The modern Swiss Confederation has its roots in the Helvetic confederation *(Coniuratio)* of 1291. This league of cantons in the mountains of central Europe was transformed into a modern federation in 1848. In 1991, still a federal system, it celebrated the seven hundredth anniversary of its founding.

The provinces of the Netherlands, on the coastal swamps of the North Sea, had substantial local autonomy under the Holy Roman Empire (considered by some to have been a federal arrangement) and later under Hapsburg rule. The Netherlands became an independent confederation in the late sixteenth century after revolting against Spain, whose king had become the hereditary Holy Roman Emperor. The United Provinces of the Netherlands survived until they were conquered by Napoleon in the early nineteenth century.

In the sixteenth century, much of the political thought of Reformed Protestantism (which later became identified with the doctrinal tradition of John Calvin) was founded on the same biblical principles of covenant that underlay the federalism of ancient Israel. A covenant is a morally informed agreement or pact based upon voluntary consent and mutual oaths or promises, witnessed by higher authority, between independent peoples or parties. It provides for joint action to achieve defined ends under conditions of mutual respect and obligation that protect the integrity of all the parties. Building on covenant ideas, Reformed Protestantism developed a federal theology (so named explicitly) to explain the relationship between people and God. Reformed Protestant theologians and political philosophers applied that

theology to the relationship between human rulers and the ruled. They denounced tyranny as a violation of God's ordinances and authorized the people under their legitimate leaders to take decisive action to remove tyrants. In the process, Reformed theologians had to begin to articulate a political theory of federalism. This was developed in full-blown fashion by Johannes Althusius in his *Politica Methodice Digesta* (1603), the first comprehensive published theory of federalism.

Modern Federalism

The prototypes of modern federalism were the British settlements in North America in the seventeenth century, especially those in New England. They often were founded on the federal theories of Reformed Protestantism.

In the eighteenth century the theory of confederation was presented in secularized form by the French political philosophers Montesquieu and Jean-Jacques Rousseau. Montesquieu's works inspired the invention of both modern confederation and federation by the Founders of the United States. The American Founders' principal theoretical work was *The Federalist*, a collection of explicative essays written by James Madison, Alexander Hamilton, and John Jay that advocated for the adoption of the Constitution of 1787. These writers, who called themselves Federalists, labeled opponents of the Constitution, who preferred a reformed confederation, Antifederalists. These terms ultimately became more or less universally accepted.

Federal theory in the United States has, since 1788, unfolded almost exclusively in relation to the American situation. In the early to mid-nineteenth century such figures as John C. Calhoun of South Carolina, the leading American advocate of the states' right to secede from the Union, argued a confederalist position. President Abraham Lincoln, on the other hand, argued for national supremacy and led the country through the Civil War (1861–1865) to preserve the Union.

Meanwhile, in nineteenth-century Europe, four schools of federal theory arose. One, exemplified by the work of the French political theorist Alexis de Tocqueville, tried to understand the successes and weaknesses of the American experience. The second school was concerned principally with the possibilities and problems of federalism in the Germanic countries. A third group, anchored in the French tradition, advocated for a broader federal theory that sought to rebuild the world along more cooperative lines: the utopian goal was to end the various political conflicts that emerged in society during the nineteenth century. A fourth group, which arose within the British Empire, presented theories of imperial federalism to achieve the more limited goal of transforming the empire into a worldwide federal system.

Indeed, many of the new federations of the nineteenth century, such as Canada and later Australia, drew on the British tradition, albeit in more limited ways. Latin American federalism, influenced by U.S. ideas, was unique in explicitly linking federalism and liberalism in a single democratic package.

The events of the twentieth century led to new federal efforts. In Western Europe federation was rejected after World War II in favor of new forms of confederation through the Common Market, the predecessor of the European Union. Spain and Belgium were transformed into federations, while Germany built a new democratic federation, ultimately reunifying East and West Germany in 1990. The Indian subcontinent produced two centralized federations (India and Pakistan), as did Africa (Nigeria and Ethiopia).

Federative and confederative arrangements are widely used outside the governmental realm to unify or integrate religious, labor, commercial, and cultural organizations. Federative organization is particularly common in the Calvinist and Reformed churches, ranging from the fully federal Presbyterians to the loosely confederated Baptists. Labor unions and business groups frequently are functional federations. Liberal democracy, with its emphasis on pluralism, is highly conducive to such arrangements.

How Modern Federalism Works

The very terminology of federalism is characterized by a revealing ambiguity. The verb *federalize* is used to describe both the unification of separate states into a federal polity and the permanent diffusion of authority and power within a nation between general and constituent governments. In this ambiguity lies the essence of the federal principle: the perpetuation of both union and noncentralization.

Federalism is more than simply a structural arrangement; it is a special mode of political and social behavior as well, involving a commitment to partnership and active cooperation on the part of individuals and institutions that at the same time take pride in preserving their own integrity.

In modern democratic theory the argument between federalists and pluralists has frequently revolved around the respective values of areal and functional diffusions of power. Proponents of the federal system based on areal division argue that the deficiencies of territorial democracy are greatly outweighed by the advantages of a guaranteed power base for each group in the political system. Furthermore, they claim, no other system devised for sharing power has proved able to cope with the complexities and changes of a dynamic age.

The basic principles of federalism can be grouped according to their primary impact on the systems they serve: the federal union, noncentralization, and the federal principle.

Maintaining union. Modern federations generally provide direct lines of communication between the citizenry and all the governments that serve them (for example, local, regional, and national). The people usually elect representatives to all the governments, which administer programs that directly serve individual citizens. The existence of these direct lines of communication is one of the features distinguishing federations from leagues or confederations. Federation is usually based on a sense of common nationality binding the constituent polities and people together.

In some countries this sense of nationality has been inherited, as in Germany, while in Argentina, Australia, and the United States it had to be at least partly invented. Canada and Switzerland have had to evolve this sense of nationality in order to hold together strongly divergent groups. Yugoslavia failed to do so. In the more recently formed federations of India, Malaysia, and Nigeria, the future of federalism is endangered by the absence of such a common sense of nationhood.

Geographic necessity has played a part in promoting and maintaining union within federal systems. The Mississippi valley in the United States, the Alps in Switzerland, the island character of the Australian continent, and the mountains and jungles surrounding Brazil have all been influences promoting unity; so have the pressures for Canadian union arising from that country's situation on the border of the United States and the pressures on the German states generated by their neighbors to the east and west. In this connection the necessity for a common defense against common enemies has stimulated federal union in the first place and acted to maintain it. In contemporary confederations, economic needs have replaced defense as primary, but they bring less far-reaching union.

Maintaining noncentralization. The constituent polities in a federal system must be fairly equal in population and wealth or else somehow their inequalities must be balanced geographically or numerically (for example, the United States has large states and small states in all sections of the country). In Canada the ethnic differences between the two largest and richest provinces (Ontario and Quebec) have prevented them from combining against the others. Swiss federalism has been supported by the existence of groups of cantons of different sizes and religious and linguistic backgrounds. Similar distributions exist in every other successful federal system.

A major reason for the failure of federal systems has often been a lack of balance among the constituent polities. In the German federal empire of the late nineteenth century, Prussia was so dominant that the other states had little opportunity to provide national leadership or even a reasonably strong alternative to the policy of the king and government.

Successful federal systems have also typically had fixed internal boundaries. Boundary changes may occur, but such changes are made only with the consent of the polities involved and are avoided except in extreme situations. The United States divided Virginia during its Civil War, Canada enlarged the boundaries of its provinces during its founding period, and Switzerland has divided cantons. But these changes have been exceptions rather than the rule, and in every case the formal consent of the constituent polities was given. Even in Latin America state boundaries have tended to remain relatively secure.

In a few very important cases, noncentralization is given support through the constitutionally guaranteed existence of different systems of law in the constituent polities. In the United States each state's legal system stems directly, and to a certain extent uniquely, from English law (except in one case, Louisiana, where the legal system is derived from French law), while federal law occupies only an interstitial position binding the systems of the fifty states together. The resulting mixture of laws keeps the administration of justice substantially noncentralized even in federal courts. In Canada the existence of common-law and civil-law systems side by side has contributed to French Canadian cultural survival. Noncentralized legal systems are a particularly Anglo-American device, based on traditional common law. Federal systems more often than not provide for modification of national legal codes by the constituent governments to meet special local needs, as in Switzerland.

The point has often been made that in a truly federal system the constituent polities must have substantial influence over the formal or informal constitution-amending process. Since constitutional changes are often made without formal constitutional amendment, the position of the constituent polities must be such that serious changes in the political order can be made only by the decision of dispersed majorities that reflect the agreement of people throughout the various polities. Federal theorists have argued that this provision is important for popular government as well as for federalism.

The principle of noncentralization is also strengthened by giving the constituent polities guaranteed representation in the national legislature. For example, each state of the United States has two seats in the Senate (the upper house) and a number of seats in the House of Representatives (the lower house) based on each state's population. Often the constituent polities also are given a guaranteed role in the national political process. In the United States this is done through the electoral college. The role of the states is guaranteed in the written constitutions of the United States and Switzerland. In other systems, such as those of Canada and countries of Latin America, the constituent polities have acquired certain powers of participation, and these have become part of the unwritten constitution.

Perhaps the most important single element in the maintenance of federal noncentralization is the existence of a noncentralized party system. Noncentralized parties initially develop out of the constitutional arrangements of the federal compact, but once they have come into existence they tend to be self-perpetuating and to function as decentralizing forces in their own right. The United States and Canada provide examples of the forms that a noncentralized party system may take. In the two-party system of the United States (where the Democratic and Republican Parties are dominant), the parties are actually coalitions of the state parties (which may in turn be dominated by specific local party organizations). They function as national units only for the presidential elections every four years or for purposes of organizing the national Congress. Party financing and decision making are dispersed either among the state organizations or among widely divergent nationwide factions.

In Canada, on the other hand, the parliamentary form of government requires party responsibility, which means that considerably more national party cohesiveness must be maintained in order to gain and hold power. The need for strong party discipline means that after elections a polity can speak with one voice. The parties are organized along regional or provincial lines, each provincial organization being more or less autonomous. The one or two parties that function on a nationwide basis are subject to great shifts in popular support from one election to another. At the same time, individual provinces are frequently dominated by parties that send only a few representatives to the national legislature. The party victorious in national elections is likely to be the one best able to expand its provincial electoral basis temporarily to national proportions.

Federal polities with less developed party systems frequently gain some of the same decentralizing effects through what the Latin Americans call *caudillismo*, in which power is diffused among strong local leaders operating in the constituent polities. Caudillistic noncentralization apparently exists also in Nigeria and Malaysia.

Ultimately, however, noncentralization is maintained through respect for the federal principle. Such respect requires recognition by the decision-making publics that the preservation of the constituent polities is as important as the preservation of the union as a whole. The Canadian confederation was formed not only to unite the British North American colonies but also to give Ontario and Quebec, which are divided by culture and language, autonomous political systems. Similarly, a guiding purpose in the evolution of the Swiss Confederation has been to preserve the independence of the cantons both from outside encroachment and from revolutionary centralism. A good case can be made that similar motivations also played a part in the founding of most other federal systems.

Maintaining the federal principle. Several of the devices commonly found in federal systems serve to maintain the federal principle itself. Two of these are of particular importance.

First, the maintenance of federalism requires that the general government and the constituent polities each have substantially complete governing institutions of their own, with the right to modify those institutions unilaterally within limits set by the federalist compact. Separate legislative and administrative institutions are both necessary. This requirement of separation does not mean that all governmental activities must be carried out by separate institutions in each arena. The agencies of one government may serve as agents of the other by mutual agreement. But each government must have enough of its own institutions to function in the areas of its authority and to cooperate freely with the other's counterpart agencies.

Second, the contractual sharing of public responsibilities by all governments in the system appears to be a central characteristic of federalism. Sharing, broadly conceived, includes common involvement in policy making, financing, and administration. Sharing may be formal or informal. The contract is used as a legal device to enable governments to engage in joint action while remaining independent entities. Even where there is no formal arrangement, the spirit of federalism tends to infuse a sense of contractual obligation.

Successful Federal Systems

Over the years, there is likely to be continued tension in any federal system between the federal government and the constituent polities, with different balances between them at different times. This tension is an integral part of the federal relationship. The questions of intergovernmental relations that it produces are perennially a matter of public concern, because they are reflected in virtually every political issue that arises. This is particularly true of those issues that affect the very fabric of society. The race question in the United States, for example, is a problem of federal-state relations, as is the cultural question in Canada and the linguistic question in India.

The more noncentralized a federal system is, the more likely it is to rely upon collegiality as a means of decision making. In a collegial system all the constituent units are represented more or less equally in a common decision-making body. This sense of collegiality is particularly true of confederations—as in the case of the Commission and the Council of Ministers that exercise policy and administrative control over the European Union—but it is also true of federations like Canada, where the First Ministers Conference and its parallels play a major role in governance.

The successful operation of federal systems requires a particular kind of political environment, one that is conducive to popular government and that has the requisite traditions of political cooperation and self-restraint. Beyond this, federal systems operate best in societies in which the fundamental interests are homogeneous enough to allow a great deal of latitude to the constituent governments and to permit reliance on voluntary collaboration.

The use of force to maintain domestic order is even more inimical to the successful maintenance of federal patterns of government than to other forms of popular government. Federal systems are most successful in societies that have the human resources to fill many public offices competently and the material resources to afford to do so as part of the price of liberty.

See also Constitutionalism; Democracy, Multiethnic.

DANIEL J. ELAZAR

BIBLIOGRAPHY

Beer, Samuel H. *To Make a Nation: The Rediscovery of American Federalism*. Cambridge, Mass., and London: Harvard University Press, Belknap Press, 1993.

Bosco, Andrea, ed. *The Federal Idea: The History of Federalism from the Enlightenment to 1945*. Vol. 1. London: Lothian Foundation, 1992.

Burgess, Michael, and Alain-G. Gaignon, eds. *Comparative Federalism and Federation: Competing Traditions and Future Directions*. Toronto: University of Toronto Press, 1993.

de Villiers, Bertus, ed. *Evaluating Federal Systems*. Boston: M. Nijhoff, 1995.

Duchacek, Ivo D. *Comparative Federalism: The Territorial Dimensions of Politics*. New York: Holt, Rinehart and Winston, 1970.

Duff, Andrew, John Prinder, and Roy Pryce. *Maastricht and Beyond: Building the European Union*. New York and London: Routledge, 1994.

Elazar, Daniel J. *American Federalism: A View from the States*. 3d ed. New York: Harper and Row, 1984.

_____. *Exploring Federalism*. Tuscaloosa: University of Alabama Press, 1987.

Frenkel, Max. *Federal Theory*. Canberra: Center for Research in Federal Financial Relations, Australian National University, 1986.

Grodzins, Morton. *The American System: A New View of Government in the United States*. Chicago: Rand McNally, 1966.

Watts, Ronald. *New Federations: Experiments in the Commonwealth*. Oxford: Clarendon Press, 1966.

✦ Feminism

A movement that arose with modern democracy and usually has been taken to mean the extension to women of the political and legal rights that democracies guaranteed to men—hence, the term *equal rights feminism*. As women gained equal rights, many feminists discovered that those rights did not guarantee full social and economic equality. Thus in the postmodern world, feminism, like democracy, has lost a single uncontested definition, and the term means different things to different people.

The word *feminism* was coined in France in the 1880s by Hubertine Auclert, the founder of the first French women's suffrage society. The term caught on in England and the United States about the turn of the century, but many women who would later be classified as feminists shunned the term at the time, and many others who are today considered feminists did not refer to themselves as such. During the twentieth century, especially after the 1960s and the emergence of second-wave feminism, the use of *feminist* to describe those who supported the improvement of women's position in society became much more common. Yet many women (and men) who steadfastly support "women's issues" no less steadfastly proclaim that they are not feminists.

To complicate matters further, even those who call themselves feminists frequently differ over priorities and tactics, with the result that there has been a proliferation of feminisms. Many feminists would insist that the term *feminist* resists any single definition. In a general way, however, feminism has stood for the active promotion of women's rights, notably the right to vote, but increasingly the right to enjoy equality with men in all spheres of life.

The Origins of Feminism

Feminism, understood as a movement to defend—and theories to justify—women's rights as individuals, took shape within the Western European and American liberal and democratic political traditions, from which it borrowed heavily and which it has, in turn, expanded.

Today, varieties of feminism, especially movements to improve women's standing, are proliferating throughout the world. Non-Western feminists, notably in Islamic countries, frequently view Western feminism as yet another form of imperialism, and they insist upon their right to define what the women of their society want and need. These various feminisms command attention and respect, but the core of feminist thought remains closely tied to Western ideas of individualism, individual freedom, and democracy. This article, accordingly, will focus on Western feminism, albeit with the recognition that in the foreseeable future the challenge of non-Western feminism may be expected to gain in importance.

The relationship of feminist theory to democracy lies in feminism's basic commitment to women's full political rights: citizenship, whatever that means at any particular moment, must be extended to women on an equal basis with men. Whenever the scope and significance of citizenship for men changes, feminists extend the discourses on these changes to women. This tendency has prevailed from the eighteenth-century democratic revolutions to the flourishing of postmodernist thought in recent years. Whenever the meaning of citizenship is discussed, debated, or reinterpreted, feminists relate those discussions to women.

The Enlightenment philosophy of individualism, as espoused by the English philosopher John Locke and the French philosopher Jean-Jacques Rousseau, provided the intellectual underpinnings for governments arising from the eighteenth-century revolutions. This radical new philosophy argued that legitimate authority could be derived only from the consent of the governed. Men of the North American British colonies and men of France during the reign of Louis XVI overthrew governments that did not meet these qualifications, and they sought to establish governments that did. As the philosophical cornerstones of their new governments, American revolutionaries drafted the Declaration of Independence (1776), and French revolutionaries drafted the Declaration of the Rights of Man and of the Citizen (1789). In these documents the future leaders of the United States and France established the modern definition of democracy as a government formed by the consent of virtuous citizens. Their definition of citizens, however, included only white men who owned property. Individualism did not apply to women.

A few women on both sides of the Atlantic understood the revolutionary nature of the political discussions of the time. Advocates for women long before the word *feminism* was uttered, they made the first arguments for women to be included as citizens in modern democracy. As American colonists were writing the Declaration of Independence in 1776, Abigail Adams wrote to her husband, John Adams, one of the drafters and a future president, entreating him to "remember the ladies" in the "new code of laws." French revolutionary Olympe de Gouges wrote the *Declaration of the Rights of Woman and the Female Citizen* in 1790 as an argument that the rights that were being granted to masses of men should be extended to women as well. Mary Wollstonecraft, a radical British writer, wrote *A Vindication of the Rights of Woman* in 1792 in response to the writings of Rousseau and the events of the French Revolution. All these women emphasized the rights and responsibilities of women as individuals, but their pleas fell on deaf ears.

In 1848, at the invitation of American abolitionists Elizabeth Cady Stanton and Lucretia Mott, a group of reformers gathered in Seneca Falls, New York, to discuss the condition and rights of women. The convention endorsed the Seneca Falls Declaration of Sentiments and Resolutions, a document that Stanton drafted. Closely modeled on the American Declaration of Independence, it demanded the inclusion of women as citizens on the same basis as men. By using the Declaration of Independence as their model, these women demonstrated their belief that they too were individuals and had unalienable rights that men could no longer usurp. Their demands included not only suffrage but also opportunities for education and rights of property ownership, which they regarded as integral aspects of citizenship.

After the American Civil War (1861–1865), the Fourteenth (1868) and Fifteenth (1870) Amendments to the U.S. Constitution guaranteed citizenship and voting rights for former male slaves, but not for women. Some members of the women's rights movement responded by supporting Congress as it amended the Constitution and by acknowledging that this would be the "Negro's hour," with the understanding that they would continue to push for women's rights. Other women, however, felt betrayed and campaigned against the amendments on the grounds that no more men should be made citizens until white women had achieved this status. The women's movement in the United States remained divided until the eve of the twentieth century.

Feminist impulses in European democracies in the nineteenth century arose not only with the expansion of the electorate but also with the rise of working-class movements, both of which demanded expansion of citizenship. Both bourgeois and working-class women in England and France began to recognize that they should be granted citizenship on the same basis as men.

Women of the bourgeoisie enjoyed the privilege of inherited wealth, and they and the men of their families were free of the burdens of salaried jobs. They understood and accepted that rights to full citizenship in their countries were predicated on property ownership. Consequently, they sought to open the door to citizenship for women of their class by advocating both women's property laws and an improvement in education opportunities.

In 1851 Harriet Taylor Mill, wife of English philosopher and economist John Stuart Mill, wrote *On the Enfranchisement of Women*, in which she proposed improvement in women's education and changes in legal and political traditions that had subordinated women. Following her death in 1858, John Stuart Mill wrote *The Subjection of Women* (1869) based on her ideas. In it, he compared women to slaves and proposed granting women all the rights of citizenship that men of that time enjoyed.

Unlike Wollstonecraft, the Mills had an audience for their arguments. In the 1860s a group of middle-class women led by British education reformer Barbara Leigh-Smith Bodichon organized the Married Women's Property Committee, and another group of bourgeois women formed the London National Society for Woman's Suffrage.

Working-class women who participated in or witnessed the rise of the Chartist movement in England, which sought to obtain political rights for working-class men, and of socialism, which advocated social revolution, began to demand that women be included in these movements on equal footing with men. As they worked for the political and economic rights of men, some women recognized that they could benefit from the same or similar rights. In England, Anne Knight and other Chartist women formed the Female Political Association, the first political society to demand women's suffrage.

Working-class movements in France also inspired working-class sentiment. In the 1830s and 1840s, such women as Jeanne Deroin and Flora Tristan, feminists and labor activists, argued that an assembly of men could not adequately represent the interests of all people. As socialism caught on in the late nineteenth century, some socialist women, including Hubertine Auclert, expanded the socialist message to include demands for women's suffrage and legal equality for both sexes.

These women had limited success in getting their countries' political leaders to listen to them. They also faced strong opposition both from the men of their organizations and from bourgeois women who neither understood their economic situations nor advocated the economic reforms that socialist women believed necessary to improve the lot of all women.

The Fight for Full Citizenship

In democratic countries during the late nineteenth and early twentieth centuries, economic changes created within both the middle class and the working class an audience receptive to the ideas of feminism. The rise of industrial society, which began in England in the eighteenth century, eventually took hold in other democracies in the nineteenth century. Like the political system of democracy, the economic system of industrial capitalism was predicated on individualism. Women's roles within this system separated them from the men of their class as well as from women of other classes. Yet the industrial system provided women of various classes with the rhetoric and experience they would use to turn feminism into a movement.

Industrialization precipitated the rise of a new salaried middle class, consisting of professional and white-collar workers who lacked the inherited wealth of the bourgeoisie. Men and women of this class operated within "separate spheres." Men represented their families in the public sphere. They maintained financial security by going to work and protected their families' interests in relation to the state by participating in politics. Women maintained the private or domestic sphere by providing a comfortable home for their families and upholding moral and religious values. Their central responsibility was to prepare their sons for their role in the republic. The association of women with the private sphere resulted in a vision of women as more moral than men, an idea that has strongly influenced some feminist arguments down to the present day.

Most middle-class women embraced their role as the keepers of morality in society. Yet the progress of industrialization and urbanization, which resulted in the need for adequate sewers and street lighting, controls on the purity of purchased food, and campaigns against such social problems as alcoholism and prostitution, forced women to recognize that they could no longer maintain the health and moral integrity of their families by remaining within the private sphere of home and church. Their determination to clean up society led them into the public sphere.

Some women continued to believe that they could achieve this goal through moral suasion, remaining outside formal politics. Others insisted that in order to protect their families and neighborhoods, women needed to gain the rights of full citizenship. Because men and women were different and had different roles within society, they argued, men would never fully understand women's needs and could not be expected to meet these needs in politics. Consequently, it was woman's difference that made it essential for women to become equal citizens.

This growing commitment to equal political rights for women characterized the late-nineteenth and early twentieth-century middle-class and bourgeois women's movements throughout industrializing democracies, although France and Germany developed less vigorous women's movements than Great Britain and the United States. The British and American women's movements focused primarily on women's suffrage, but in some cases they also focused on equal property ownership and child custody rights.

In the United States the two dominant women's suffrage organizations merged in 1890 to form the National American Woman Suffrage Association. The association fought for votes for women on both the state and national levels for the next thirty years. Initially a fringe movement, it grew into a mainstream movement that had the widespread support of middle-class women throughout the country. Similarly, the women's rights movement in England united in 1897 to form the National Union of Women's Suffrage Societies. The women's suffrage movement in both England and the United States benefited from the political stability of these two countries and the ideology of separate spheres, which had created a common identity for women. Women, the suffrage advocates believed, shared common goals that frequently differed from the economic goals of men.

While the bourgeois feminist movements in the United States and Europe demanded women's inclusion in existing political and economic structures, working-class women, especially in Europe, tended to ally with working-class men in demanding basic changes in the economic and political systems of their nations. Women needed more than equal rights with men to improve their lives, these women argued; they also needed improved economic opportunities for themselves as well as for the men of their class. Socialist feminists believed that the status of women in relation to men of all classes had to be improved. They supported all standard feminist demands, including the right to vote, access to equal educational opportunities, entrance into the professions, the right to divorce, and the right for all women to own property. Yet socialist feminists had to struggle not only against the resistance of socialist men to feminism but also against the inability of bourgeois women to understand the plight of working-class women.

Despite significant differences between bourgeois and socialist feminists, they agreed that it was in their best interests as women (and sometimes they also believed that it was in the best interests of society as a whole) for women to enjoy the full benefits of citizenship. As World War I and World War II divided European nations and split apart socialist parties, most women remained loyal to their own countries. For their patriotism, they were rewarded with full citizenship. The United States, England, and Germany enfranchised women after World War I; the women of France won the vote after World War II.

At this point, most Western women had gained the status of equal political citizenship that they had been seeking, and feminism as a strong political movement fell dormant. Some women, however, kept its ideals alive in seeking to protect and expand the voting rights they had just achieved.

Introduction of the Equal Rights Amendment

Although enfranchisement was central to the feminist movement of the nineteenth century, some women believed that suffrage was not enough. They argued that women would not be full and equal citizens until they had formally won equal rights. In the United States, Alice Paul, a veteran leader of the women's suffrage movement, and other radical suffragists mobilized the National Woman's Party to campaign for an equal rights amendment (ERA) to the Constitution, which would simply declare, "Equality of rights under the law shall not be denied or abridged by the United States or by any State on account of sex." They believed women had to be protected constitutionally from encroachment on their rights. Otherwise, women would forever be disadvantaged legally, and their right to vote would have little meaning. The amendment was introduced in Congress in 1923.

Paul and her group, however, failed to convince others that equal rights served women's interests. The director of the powerful National Consumers' League, Florence Kelley, a reformer interested in protecting working women and children, voted along with other board members to oppose the ERA because they believed working women required special protection. Other reform organizations and labor unions opposed it for the same reason. This opposition signaled a tension between those who wanted women to have absolute equality with men and those who wanted to retain some protection for women's special needs arising from their differences from men, notably their ability to bear children.

This tension between equality and difference had always existed within feminist thought, but once women had received the vote, it began to gain a visibility and importance that would persist throughout the twentieth century. Unlike Kelley, Paul and her associates represented mainly affluent women who sought to compete equally with men, notably in government and the professions.

Postwar Developments

The Great Depression, which began in 1929, and other difficulties of the years between the two world wars led to a lull in feminist activism. Immediately after World War II, the attention of women—and men—in the United States and Europe focused primarily on restoring a world in which men could support non–wage earning wives and children—what many still regarded as "normalcy."

In this climate, the publication of French writer and philosopher Simone de Beauvoir's *Second Sex* (1949), in which she argued that women's subordinate status was based not only on politics but also on deep-rooted social and cultural traditions, had little or no immediate impact. Yet following World War II, most European countries were developing or consolidating some version of the welfare state, which usually provided women with a variety of benefits and protections for their work as mothers. In many nations, notably predominantly Roman Catholic countries such as France, Italy, and Spain, women still did not have easy access to divorce or contraception, much less abortion, and in no European country did women easily rise to top positions in business, the professions, or politics. But, in general, ordinary women could count on significant support in combining participation in the labor force with family life.

During the same period, Eastern European socialist countries, following the lead of the Soviet Union, also provided women with a broad range of citizenship rights and public policies to support motherhood. Although they retained primary responsibility for housekeeping, shopping, and child care—domestic work that American sociologist Arlie Hochschild has called the "second shift"—most women in socialist countries participated fully in the labor market and frequently had fairly easy access to divorce, contraception, and abortion. Indeed, socialist countries offered women greater formal equality with men than did any Western democracy.

Still, in no country did formal equality or even enlightened social policies guarantee women substantive equality with men. Women remained extremely rare in the most lucrative occupations and the higher levels of political leadership. But socialist countries and, in some measure, Western welfare states did take women's issues seriously, at least in encouraging and supporting motherhood under conditions in which large numbers of women worked for wages. These pronatal policies help to explain why feminism did not enjoy a significant following in Europe during the postwar years. In the United States, which did not provide similar supports for working mothers, postwar prosperity helped to discourage development of a vigorous feminism.

The Revival of Feminism

In the 1960s, however, everything began to change. In 1963 American journalist and middle-class housewife Betty Friedan published *The Feminine Mystique*. This book served as a call to action for middle-class American women whose mothers had lived out the suburban domestic dream of the 1940s and 1950s. These women had an excellent college education but no outlet for their talents. Calling their unease and restlessness "the problem that has no name," Friedan passionately defended women's right to develop their talents in rewarding work. The feminist movement that rapidly developed owed much to Friedan, but it also was decisively informed by the larger social radicalism manifested in the civil rights, student, and antiwar movements that exploded during the decade.

Although it was not clear at the time, by the late 1960s and early 1970s Americans were in the throes of a dual economic and sexual revolution that was reshaping women's relation to society and expectations for themselves. A series of government measures began to expand rights and opportunities for all women. Foremost among those measures was Title VII of the Civil Rights Act, enacted in 1964, which prohibited job discrimination on the basis of sex, race, color, religion, or national origin.

In 1966 a group of women, including Friedan, launched the National Organization for Women (NOW), and in 1970 NOW launched a new campaign to secure ratification of the ERA. Between 1972 and 1982 the battle to ratify the amendment raged, provoking widespread public discussion about feminism and women's role in American society. Although the movement for ratification ultimately failed narrowly, it helped to make feminism a recognized presence in national life.

Meanwhile, even people who did not agree with many feminist positions began to take women's issues seriously. By the early 1970s married women could (still sometimes with difficulty) get credit in their own names. Thanks to no-fault divorce, they could more easily break free from unsatisfactory marriages. Discrimination in employment or education had become illegal, and affirmative action in admissions, hiring, and promotion had begun to expand women's educational and employment opportunities.

The Second Wave

For most American feminists, however, the centerpiece of this new phase of feminist activity, which was called second-wave feminism to distinguish it from the campaign for women's suffrage, was the 1973 Supreme Court decision in *Roe v. Wade*. The *Roe* decision, which legalized abortion, signaled the first signs of a new feminist agenda that would gain strength throughout the next two decades: it shifted the focus from politics and work to sexuality.

Feminists, to be sure, did not draw that distinction. Indeed most insisted that sexual freedom and autonomy were preconditions to women's equal participation in other realms. Increasingly, during the next two decades, as specific provisions of the *Roe* decision were challenged and limited, feminists would refer to a woman's right to choose to have an abortion as a fundamental right, analogous to those granted by the Bill of Rights. But as some feminists later would concede, the successive struggles over abortion tended to distract attention from other issues and widen the gap again between feminism and a simple concern for women's issues.

Second-wave feminism was never exclusively an American movement, although it had more political presence and public impact in the United States than elsewhere. Various European countries produced their own second-wave feminist movements of varying size and significance. The French case is especially interesting, because the most visible strand in French feminism took a primarily academic and literary form, focusing on women's secondary status in culture and on psychoanalysis. French feminism acquired considerable prestige in intellectual circles in the United States and Great Britain, but it had little direct influence on changes in women's political and economic status.

The most important effect of second-wave feminism lay in its growing presence throughout the world. The United Nations targeted 1975–1985 as the Decade for Women, and a succession of international conferences fostered a comparative perspective on women's status and needs throughout the world.

This cross-cultural attention to women's concerns has underscored the extent to which feminism has been a Western European and, perhaps, above all an American phenomenon. In general, women in the non-Western world suffer infinitely heavier burdens and disadvantages than women in Western nations, and they frequently have a fierce commitment to the improvement of women's situation. But they also are preeminently conscious of the ways in which Western feminism has grown out of a culture that is not their own. Many feel considerable tension between their desire to improve women's situation and their loyalty to their own culture. Many women want to work for improvement in their own ways and define their own priorities.

Often they see close links between Western feminism and Western economic and cultural imperialism. These responses demonstrate how closely Western feminism has been tied to the distinctive political and economic development of the West, notably democracy and industrial capitalism.

The Global Perspective

The economic and sexual revolution that has, since the 1960s, pushed women into independence and individualism in the Western world also is influencing the situation of women throughout the globe. Feminism has earned its prominent place in public discussions because of its efforts to improve women's situation, notably their competitive position relative to men. As feminists in the United States have succeeded in securing formal equality of opportunity and citizenship for women, they have discovered that substantive equality continues to elude them. Thus they have increasingly turned their attention to issues of sexuality and culture.

Contemporary feminism is ever more likely to focus on rape, wife abuse, incest, sexual harassment, acquaintance rape, sexual preference, and related issues. At the same time, distinct groups of feminists focus on a variety of specific issues: religion, ecology, and lesbian separatism. This proliferation of feminisms suggests that notwithstanding the importance of women's issues to many people, there is little agreement about what those issues require.

It is abundantly clear that throughout the world, economic developments are radically transforming women's traditional relations to society. Feminism first emerged in response to the earliest manifestations of these changes, notably the great revolutions of the eighteenth century. Developments of our time suggest that that era may be drawing to a close, or at least that it is being radically transformed by a postindustrial, global economy. If feminism has, above all, embodied women's aspirations to a full place in the individualism fostered by industrial capitalism and democracy, it may not easily survive if that individualism disappears. Thus, although women's issues are becoming increasingly important throughout the world, feminism's continuing ability to encompass and express them may be less certain.

See also Locke, John; Mill, John Stuart; Rousseau, Jean-Jacques; Wollstonecraft, Mary; Democracy, Women and.

ELIZABETH FOX-GENOVESE AND
STACEY HORSTMANN

BIBLIOGRAPHY

Ahmed, Leila. *Women and Gender in Islam: Historical Roots of a Modern Debate*. New Haven and London: Yale University Press, 1992.

Elshtain, Jean Bethke. *Public Man, Private Woman: Women in Social and Political Thought*. Princeton: Princeton University Press, 1981.

Fox-Genovese, Elizabeth. *Feminism without Illusions: A Critique of Individualism*. Chapel Hill: University of North Carolina Press, 1991.

Friedan, Betty. *The Feminine Mystique*. New York: Dell, 1963.

Mansbridge, Jane. *Why We Lost the ERA*. Chicago: University of Chicago Press, 1986.

Rendall, Jane. *The Origins of Modern Feminism: Women in Britain, France, and the United States, 1780–1860*. New York: Schocken Books, 1984.

Rossi, Alice S., ed. *The Feminist Papers: From Adams to de Beauvoir*. New York: Columbia University Press, 1973.

✦ Fundamentalism

A political ideology that is based on the politicization of religion with the goal of establishing God's rule over the secular order. A global phenomenon, fundamentalism can be observed in a variety of the world's religions—among them, Christianity, Hinduism, Islam, Judaism, and Sikhism.

Because fundamentalists reject not only secular values but also international morality, local fundamentalist cultures dispute the universal validity of such Western principles as democracy and universal human rights. They also reject pluralism and the tolerance that flows from it. Thus fundamentalism clearly runs counter to democracy and its underlying values. The rise of funda-mentalism worldwide seems to be the hallmark of an age in which conflicts between civilizations are beginning to replace political and economic con-flicts between nation-states.

Although fundamentalism is equally affected by modernity and directed against it, most reli-gious fundamentalists view their approach as an alternative to the modern culture, on which democracy is based. In contrast to democracy—a secular political expression of global civiliza-tion—fundamentalism is an expression of local cultures and their politicized religious and cul-tural beliefs. The invoked religious ideology becomes the vehicle for the articulation of sociopolitical, economic, and cultural demands. Fundamentalists' conflict with modern democ-racy takes shape in their emphasis on the group rather than the individual. Most important, they draw a clear line between the believers, their "we-group," and the groups of the others, the infidels, who are declared to be the enemy. Thus funda-mentalists reject democratic conflict resolution. They perceive themselves to be the defenders of God and God's rule.

Is fundamentalism, as some observers contend, the most recent variety of totalitarianism? Studies of the ideology and practice of politicized reli-gious fundamentalism—be it related to Chris-tianity, Hinduism, Islam, or Sikhism—have revealed that it does come into conflict with democracy, since fundamentalists do not believe in pluralism and consequently deny rights and freedom to other communities as well as to those in their own community who do not share their commitments. Because fundamentalism is itself a global phenomenon, some scholars foresee a new global cold war between fundamentalists, with their ideology of God's rule, and the secular democratic state.

Fundamentalism and the Nation-State

The fact that modern democracy is specifically a democracy of the nation-state points to one basis of the conflict between fundamentalism and democracy. Islamic fundamentalists not only reject democracy as an imported system but also dismiss the nation-state as a means employed by the West, the enemy of Islam, to divide the com-munity of all Muslims into numerous entities, allegedly to facilitate Western dominance over the Islamic religion. In the lands of Islam the nation-state was not an indigenous phenomenon. It was imposed from the outside after the caliphate (the rulership of Islam) was abolished by Mustafa Kemal Atatürk in 1924, and it was a product of the expansion of the international system of nation-states. For this reason, modern democracy, as associated with the secular nation-state, is not found in Islamic or other non-Western countries. In fact, the Middle Eastern nation-states, like most nation-states in Asia and Africa, are nominal states (states with formal sovereignty but no real statehood).

Because many of these nominal nation-states, such as Algeria, have failed to cope with urgent developmental tasks, crises have arisen in which fundamentalism has become an expression of a revolt against the West and the modern demo-cratic nation-state. Although fundamentalists in Russia, southeastern Europe (followers of Slavic Orthodoxy), and the West (American Protestants) also reject secularity and therefore some aspects of democracy, the conflict between the secular state and ethnic-religious fundamentalism is centered largely in non-Western countries.

The Case of Islamic Fundamentalism

In most countries, fundamentalists belong to the political opposition, protesting against exist-ing democratic secular regimes. In the Islamic case, however, the fundamentalist goal of establishing God's rule, presented as the platform for political action, is often considered an alternative not just to one regime but to the whole democratic and secular nation-state. This concept of God's rule is also found in some non-Islamic fundamentalist movements.

Some Western scholars do not share the assessment that the ideology of fundamentalism runs counter to any effort at democratization. They view the negative attitude of Islamic fundamentalists toward democracy as a defense of Islam against the West rather than a wholesale rejection of democracy. Thus they recommend that Western policymakers accept the notion of the Islamization of democracy based on God's law. To be sure, political events do not support the alleged compatibility of fundamentalist Islam and democracy. In June 1992, for example, the Islamic Egyptian writer Faraz Foda was killed by Islamic fundamentalists for advocating secular democracy. A year later the prominent sheik Mohammed al-Ghazali ruled in the highest court in Egypt that in Islam no penalty exists for the Muslim who kills an apostate (a person found guilty of abandoning his or her faith). Advocating secular democracy and suspending God's law are, according to this Islamic legal opinion, apostasy. Thus the argument that fundamentalists thrive on a non-Western type of democracy is a flawed interpretation based on a lack of intimate knowledge of fundamentalism. Comparable undemocratic patterns are found in Hindu and Sikh fundamentalism.

The weak institutional basis of the nominal nation-states in the Middle East and the prevailing undemocratic political culture, which is susceptible to fundamentalist totalitarianism, create great obstacles to democratization. In Asia and Africa, too, the fundamentalist revolt against the artificial secular nation-states does not promise any type of democracy. The authoritative writings

on democratization argue that economic development is the basis for democracy. Indeed, economic growth has contributed to a third wave of democratization worldwide—but not in the world of Islam. In most Islamic states rapid economic development, social dislocation, and sociocultural crisis have not given rise to democracy but rather to fundamentalism.

In Jordan and Egypt, two Middle Eastern states with considerable records of democratic achievements, Islamic fundamentalism is the current mainstream opposition. Both Jordan and Egypt have elected, not appointed, parliaments. In Jordan fundamentalists make up one-third of the parliament. In Egypt the three legal fundamentalist parties boycotted the November 1990 elections and are not represented in the current parliament. In an earlier Egyptian parliament, however, Islamic fundamentalists formed a considerable faction. In Algeria a democratically elected fundamentalist government might have assumed power had the army not intervened.

Two questions may be raised in regard to fundamentalism and the prospects of democratization in the world of Islam as it exists at the turn of the century. First, given that fundamentalism currently represents mainstream public choice in the world of Islam, would democratization lead to the empowerment of Islamic fundamentalists? Such a possibility applies to Jordan and Algeria. Tunisia may follow, as well as Syria and possibly a destabilized Egypt. Iraq is open to becoming an Islamic republic along Iranian lines in the post–Saddam Hussein era. Second, given that Islamic fundamentalists regard democratic political pluralism as divisive to the Islamic community and alien to an Islamic unifying culture, would keeping such fundamentalists out of the process of power sharing be detrimental to democratization? In other words, are efforts at democratization in countries such as Egypt less democratic because the fundamentalists are not represented in the parliament?

It is clear that the seizure of power by fundamentalists does not promise democratization. In Iran and Sudan, states governed by fundamentalists, there is no evidence of democratization. Fundamentalists in the Kuwaiti parliament have introduced all kinds of bans, including a ban on female suffrage. Ironically, some undemocratic non-Western governments pay lip service to democratization in order to deny substantive power to fundamentalists. In countries like Syria and Tunisia threatening references to fundamentalism allow the rulers to keep efforts at democratization extremely limited.

Without democratization in the world of Islam, particularly in the Arab Middle East where its political-cultural core lies, there likely will be neither peace nor stability. The path toward democracy, however, is rocky and entails high risks. Paradoxically, democratization may empower fundamentalism, which is essentially antithetical to democracy. Most fundamentalists refuse to accept and practice pluralism even among themselves; they argue that there is one homogeneous religious community without any division, whether the community be Islamic, Hindu, Sikh, or Serbian Orthodox. If fundamentalists come to power, they deny individual rights and pluralism and thus refuse democratic power sharing.

It is important to note that fundamentalism is not just an attitude; it also reflects political and economic conditions. Most of the fundamentalists in Egypt, Sudan, Tunisia, and Morocco are young students or jobless graduates. They believe that an Islamic system of government will solve their economic problems. If these problems could be solved by secular governments, fundamentalism might lose its appeal. Coming to terms with economic problems, then, is one way to combat fundamentalism. This is not, however, a realistic prospect in the near future. On the contrary, economic malaise is more pronounced than ever in Africa and the Middle East.

Views of the Future

Some observers argue that it is too simple to conclude that because fundamentalists do not have democratic values, they may bring about an undemocratic outcome if allowed to participate in elections. The professed ideology of groups does not necessarily predict the way they will act once they hold political power. These observers argue that even groups that do not profess democracy can be socialized into the system. If elites are astute enough, they can divide these groups, co-opting some into the system and leaving others behind.

As for the values fundamentalists hold and how these values relate to democracy, these observers concede that certain values really are antithetical to the establishment of democracy. But they draw attention to the specific values held by fundamentalists as they are related to local religious cultures such as Islam or Hinduism. Although it is true that fundamentalists are populists and base their ideology on local cultures, some observers confuse the populism of fundamentalists with democratization.

One might ask, will the Islamic solution being developed by the fundamentalists as an alternative to Western democracy lead to an "Islamization" of democracy? In this case the argument of cultural relativism that underpins the reference to local cultures does not hold, for Muslim fundamentalists are not cultural relativists but religious neo-absolutists. They contest the democratic concept of secular democracy and individual human rights as entitlements of the individual on a universal level. They do not believe in human freedom. Their basic view is that sovereignty belongs to God and that those who claim this right for

themselves in the name of secular democracy con-
travene the basic authority of the Creator and the
Ruler of the universe. Thus the political ideology
of Islamic fundamentalists is based on the politicization of an uncompromising theocentrism. It
leaves no room for individual freedom and human
self-determination. Other brands of fundamentalism are similar.

Democracy cannot be achieved by a movement that subscribes to such an undemocratic
ideology. Democratization and the ideology of
religious fundamentalism—be it Islamic, Jewish,
Christian, Hindu, or Sikh—are incompatible.
Fundamentalists in power—as is the case in Iran
and Sudan—have not contributed to democratization. When fundamentalists pay lip service to
democracy, it is only a tactical means of seizing
power to establish the rule of God. The
employed formula—"God's rule"—has different
meanings in Islamic, Hindu, Jewish, Christian
(Protestant, Catholic, or Orthodox), and other
varieties of fundamentalism. Nevertheless, all of
these kinds of fundamentalism have in common
their opposition to democracy as a secular and
pluralistic order.

See also Hinduism.

BASSAM TIBI

BIBLIOGRAPHY

Choueiri, Youssef. *Islamic Fundamentalism.* Boston:
Twayne; London: Pinter, 1990.
Esposito, John L. *The Islamic Threat: Myth or Reality?*
New York: Oxford University Press, 1992.
Huntington, Samuel P. *The Third Wave: Democratiza-
tion in the Late Twentieth Century.* Norman: Univer-
sity of Oklahoma Press, 1991.
Juergensmeyer, Mark. *The New Cold War? Religious
Nationalism Confronts the Secular State.* Berkeley:
University of California Press, 1993.
Lawrence, Bruce W. *Defenders of God: The Fundamen-
talist Revolt against the Modern Age.* San Francisco:
Harper and Row, 1989; London: I. B. Tauris, 1990.
Marty, Martin, and Scott Appleby, eds. *Fundamentalisms
Observed.* Chicago: University of Chicago Press,
1991.
Tibi, Bassam. *The Challenge of Fundamentalism: Politi-
cal Islam and the New World Disorder.* Berkeley: Uni-
versity of California Press, 1998.
_____. *Islam and the Cultural Accommodation of Social
Change.* Boulder, Colo.: Westview Press, 1991.
_____. "The Simultaneity of the Unsimultaneous: Old
Tribes and Imposed Nation States in the Modern
Middle East." In *Tribes and State Formation in the
Middle East*, edited by Philip S. Khoury and Joseph
Kostiner. Berkeley: University of California Press,
1990; London: I. B. Tauris, 1991.
_____. "The Worldview of Sunni Arab Fundamental-
ists: Attitudes toward Modern Science and Tech-
nology." In *Fundamentalisms and Society*, edited by
Martin Marty and Scott Appleby. Chicago: Univer-
sity of Chicago Press, 1993.
Watt, Montgomery W. *Islamic Fundamentalism and
Modernity.* London: Routledge, 1988.

✦ Hinduism

A social system and set of religious beliefs
found primarily in India and Nepal. Hinduism is
not based on belief in any one doctrine or god and
is, in effect, a group of religions centered on the
concept of universal order, of which everything is
an integral part. Thus it involves a continuous balancing of competing interests and concentration
on the individual's duties within a complex universal worldview.

Hinduism is more closely linked to the idea of
democracy than is commonly thought. Within
Hinduism, ruler and ruled, producer and cus-

tomer, husband and wife are not simple binary oppositions but are engaged in complex relationships of give and take, based on morality as much as on power, on rights as well as on duties. The system, idealistic as it is, certainly does not preclude abuses of power. In the Hindu context, however, a higher awareness or consciousness appears to provide a balancing check that can easily be overlooked, in particular if one focuses only on one theory or aspect.

The assumption that Hindu tradition does not allow for democracy and that Hinduism, as a caste-ridden, authoritarian, male-dominated philosophical tradition, is inherently undemocratic stands challenged by the somewhat baffling evidence of modern India's functioning democracy. The enigma of India's democracy may be better understood by a closer look behind the secular and socialist labels of modern India and an analysis of relevant aspects of Hinduism as a traditional conceptual system that emphasizes duties rather than rights and demands diversity rather than uniformity.

Of course, modern India is not a Hindu state; the only Hindu kingdom in the world today is Nepal. So it could be argued that India's democratic success has nothing to do with Hinduism and is due to a successful adoption of Western models. American writers, among others, have declared Indian traditions "displaced" by the modern system. That explanation, however, is manifestly too simple and too Eurocentric to be convincing. What is portrayed as secular and modern in India is still very Hindu at its base, and the way in which Indian democracy has functioned can be distinguished from Western models for this reason.

Basic Concepts

Hinduism is centered on the concepts of *rita* (macrocosmic order) and, more prominently, *dharma* (microcosmic order), every individual's duty to act appropriately at any given time. It envisages a created, total order that simply exists and cannot be explained. Crucially, the existence of this ordered universe is not seen as dependent on any one centrally defined god. In effect, Hindus have agreed to disagree on who is in charge of this order and have chosen the most democratic way of ascertaining what is ultimately right and wrong by relying on every individual's conscience and sense of self-control as a source of *dharma*. Of course, this approach is diametrically opposed to models in which leaders of any kind claim to determine systematically what people should do.

Even if the world is motivated by greed and lust for power, as Hindu cultural texts constantly emphasize, the ultimate concerns of the whole system are supposed to prevail over any private interest. The systemic need to balance power structures and the requirement to avoid anarchy and the abuse of power (frequently illustrated as "rule of the fish," in which the big fish devour the small ones without control) demand a complex system of checks and balances as the conceptual core of Hindu democracy. The right of every individual to be heard and counted is, however, subordinated to everyone's duty to bow to a higher order.

For all human relationships this view implies at once not only the inferiority of individual preferences in view of higher concerns and an emphasis on duties rather than rights but also the recognition of different statuses based on age, gender, and position in the caste system (to name only the most obvious aspects). In the political sphere it means that even the most powerful ruler has duties and that the welfare of subjects must be a matter of concern for those who rule. Hindu tradition does not appear to have developed a theoretical model of formal universal elections, but there is plenty of evidence that popular acclaim is an important element of the ruler's mandate to rule (*kshatra*), which is linked to the term for the traditional rulers' caste (*kshatriya*). As in Confucian China, the authority to govern in ancient India could be withdrawn if the ruler proved inefficient or was seen to work against *dharma*. Thus it can be a meritorious action to oppose an immoral or despotic ruler. Various forms of protest and formal political opposition are legitimized in this way.

According to Hindu theory, those in power have a dual obligation: to protect their realm against outside aggression and to promote *dharmic* order within it. Hindu rulers should fulfill this duty not by prescribing in detail what their subjects should do but by making existing orders work well, enabling others to fulfill their respective *dharma*. Thus order is not imposed from above by the state but exists independent from it and is regenerated from below as an aggregate of myriad small ordered universes. This view leads almost inevitably to the concept of a minimalist state, mainly concerned with protection against external aggression and with the deterrent power of punishment. This notion signifies that the ruler should interfere as little as possible in the personal affairs of citizens. For example, the state should respect personal laws, which tend to remain based on religious, local, caste, and family traditions.

Constitutionalism and Equality in India

According to its powerful constitution of 1950, India is a secular and, since 1976, socialist federal republic. The use of such labels hides the fact that Hindu values remain operative in modern India's democracy. India combines parliamentary democracy with explicit recognition of inequality. Equality before the law is constitutionally guaranteed and is practiced, when it comes to voting, in a system of universal adult suffrage for the lower house (*Lok Sabha*). But provision is also made for differential treatment of certain categories of people.

Thus a number of historically disadvantaged groups—most prominently various "backward communities" but also women and children—have been given preferential treatment through policies of positive discrimination.

India's development strategies appear to imply that the country's aim is never going to be total equality of all citizens but a rebalanced inequality, based on Hindu conceptualizations of individual duties and differential statuses. Thus modern India operates within an apparently Western structure but functions by combining Western and indigenous principles. The Indian constitution puts the state under a firm obligation to safeguard various human rights but does not demand absolute equality because of the need to take account of diversity and pluralism in modern India. It also places all citizens under a set of fundamental duties, including the duties to promote harmony and the spirit of common brotherhood, to protect the environment, and to have compassion for living creatures.

Indian democracy, then, is a complex system of checks and balances designed to ensure a harmonious whole based on many component parts. That this system operates, in practice, to the advantage of economically and socially privileged individuals and groups is certainly not peculiar to India, nor germane to Hindu concepts alone. Explicit recognition of inequalities in status and the need to balance them is found in many non-Western cultures.

The constitution is said to represent the collective will of the people of India. It forms a code of conduct for the state that is above any one government. The fact that it has been taken so seriously and has been interpreted so creatively over the years demonstrates the entrenchment of Indian democracy. Its operation shows that it is not a foreign implant but a hybrid Indian frame of reference that must be studied on its own terms.

The surprise of political scientists about India's democratic success story is born largely of ignorance about basic Hindu (and sometimes Muslim) concepts, manifested as evolving composite value systems underpinning the way in which modern India functions. The entrenched position of the constitution indicates that even a distinctly Hindu force like the Bharatiya Janata Party (Indian People's Party) is unlikely actually to harm Indian democracy. It would change the rhetoric, not the substance. In fact, swift public realization that politicians in Hindu garb are no less corruptible than secular leaders has brought a quick end to hopes of Hindu fundamentalist ascendancy in India.

It is now widely agreed that modern India is only nominally secular and socialist. Behind these expedient labels, combined with latent anticolonial reactions, powerful forces of democratization continue to operate, but they operate on the basis of Hindu or indigenous principles without slavishly copying Western models. The latter are widely seen as discredited by the colonial experience and pervasive racism against Indians abroad.

Concepts of the State and of Democracy

Generally, writing on the Indian state has underrated the informal cultural sphere and "invisible" Hindu concepts and has overstated the importance of visible political structures. Political scientists have faced problems identifying "the state," let alone democracy, in ancient India. In a colonial context, it suited some researchers to claim that traditional India had a mass of unscrupulous petty rulers, no viable political order, and certainly no democracy, while others idealized ancient Indian rulers as divine kings. Several pioneering Indian studies, influenced by earlier pronouncements of Western scholars, who tended to be linguists, sought to demonstrate that ancient India had fully developed political structures equivalent to those in the West, including early forms of democracy. Such assertions served the agenda of anticolonialism rather than that of scholarship. The religious dimensions of the Indian state were quite deliberately overstated. The same process also worked for Indian law; the role of cultural texts as sources of state law was exaggerated. What was lost—or, rather, never developed—was an interdisciplinary view of Hindu political institutions. This deficiency has led to the current misconceptions.

For example, following the 1905 discovery of ancient India's major handbook on political science, the *Arthashastra*, studies emphasized the assumption that the dominant concept in this field is *artha*, the acquisition of secular merit—that is, wealth and power. Within the Hindu conceptual framework, however, *artha* always remains subservient to the core concept of *dharma*. Thus even the most powerful of rulers cannot be an "absolute" ruler; a despot who ignores the supremacy of *dharma* is a failed role model. The Hindu ruler, the *raja*, whether he likes it or not, remains a servant of *dharma*, accountable to the overriding concerns of an ordered universe. In effect, he serves his subjects, as the elaborated concept of the ruler's duties (*rajadharma*) clearly shows. Failing to see this clearly, most writers on Indian politics have taken refuge in institutional technicalities and are misinformed about the basic nature of the Indian polity.

The most obvious recent example of such lack of understanding was the assessment of Prime Minister Indira Gandhi's imposition of a state of emergency for eighteen months in 1975–1977. It appeared that the emergency was declared because of strikes and growing unrest. Superficially, it brought a formal suspension of the democratic structures. But, in fact, only belatedly realized, Gandhi—acting as a kind of benevolent dictator—also used the emergency to introduce into the Indian polity more effective forms of democratic control.

To understand this, one needs to study the important Forty-second Amendment to the Indian constitution, added in 1976. Among other things it introduced several directive principles based on the explicit recognition that the existing political and legal framework did not do enough to secure equal justice and adequate access to legal remedies. These new provisions have served as a basis for the development of India's powerful human rights jurisprudence and, in particular, have improved the accountability of "the state" to its citizens. Far from destroying Indian democracy, Prime Minister Gandhi's emergency invigorated it, not only through the shock therapy of eliciting opposition to her autocratic rule but by providing firmer conceptual and structural foundations for modern Indian democracy and a new duty-based Hindu jurisprudence.

Traditionally, academic analysis has concentrated on the Oriental despot, the *raja*. This view results in a romantic oversimplification, caused by the traditional focus in research on leader figures (which is itself undemocratic) and the mystique of Oriental splendor. It is misleading to take *raja* to mean only "king." The same label may be applied to leaders who have the mandate to govern only so long as they enjoy popular acclaim. This appears to have been measured in two ways.

First, usually at the local level, it was determined by collective or representative agreement that a particular leader's claim to rule was in the interest of *dharma*. In the second place— although this system did not ensure protection against usurpers—historical studies have shown that political structures in India depended to a large extent on hierarchically ordered networks of political dependency, from the level of villages and towns to local and regional rulers. Rarely did these networks constitute a unified subcontinental system. Since the position of any one ruler in

this system depended not only on power and patronage but also on popular acclaim arising from heads of families, local groupings, and assemblies, one can argue that such a system of legitimizing political rule is just as democratic as a formal electoral system. At least it is a variant form.

Institutions that look familiar to the West may turn out to be more complex than they first appear. The realities of Hindu politics must be studied within the framework of basic Hindu concepts, which have shown a remarkable resilience in overseas Indian settlements as well as in India proper. Studies on Indian state formation have apparently focused unduly on caste. This focus on caste undervalues the fact that anyone could become a leader, thus acquiring the functional characteristics, if not the status, of a *kshatriya*, a member of the rulers' caste.

Democracy in Modern India

In modern India universal suffrage has had important effects through the power of numbers. Politicians expressing concern for the disadvantaged run the risk of raising unrealistic expectations and have to balance this "welfare approach" with concerns of the establishment. The growth of the Indian middle classes presents a danger that the latter may prevail at the expense of the poor— a familiar problem in Western democracies.

Hindu concepts, by not requiring subjugation of all diversities into one uniform pattern, have helped to keep modern India together. In terms of democracy, it is not a problem that well over 100 million people in India today are Muslims rather than Hindu (of a population of almost 900 million). It may be difficult for some Muslims to live under Hindu domination, and their dissatisfaction can be exploited for internal politics, as has happened in Kashmir. Other minorities have raised objections against centralized Hindu rule. For example, violence has broken out in northwestern

India, where Sikh separatists want to establish Khalistan as an independent homeland.

Again, it has not been sufficiently well understood that minority discontent in India relates, in large measure, to resistance against uniform, centralizing forces. Thus the Sikhs are in effect protesting against being classed as Hindus, while many Muslims find it difficult to reconcile their Islamic identity with being treated as secular Indians. In a complex federal setup that differs significantly from the experience of the United States and seems closer to the German progression from a multitude of small, medieval states to a federal republic, modern India faces new forms of ancient "*dharma* dilemmas," situations in which outwardly incompatible elements have to be accommodated.

By constantly balancing complex diversities at every level, modern India's political system recreates the old patterns of ordering, while many politicians find it expedient to use modern, secular, and democratic rhetoric. To study India's democracy today one must therefore learn to "see" its indigenous elements, which are largely, though not exclusively, of Hindu origin.

The best recent example is India's concept of public interest litigation. Both foreign and Indian writers have interpreted this as "social action litigation," a variant of American adjudication techniques focused on group litigation and concerns of the underprivileged. Indian public interest litigation, however, has gone much beyond the formal and conceptual limits of foreign models and relies heavily—without saying it in so many words—on Hindu concepts of public accountability. It is, in other words, a Hindu democratization technique, tilting the balance in favor of the disadvantaged, without claiming to secure absolutely equal rights for them.

In the process, established procedural barriers have been removed in order to improve access to courts, and letter petitions have been explicitly encouraged by the higher judiciary—mainly by some activist judges relying on a combination of socialist, human rights, and Hindu rhetoric. Some judges found their conscience pricked by reports of human rights violations and abuse of power and have acted of their own accord. Such judicial activism has not remained rhetoric. The focus on implementation can itself be seen as evidence of the democratization of the legal system.

Of course, such strategies have their limits. They cannot feed millions of impoverished Indians. But public interest litigation has significantly affected the balance of power between rulers and ruled and is part of India's modern "democracy with Hindu characteristics," in which the right to be heard has ancient precedents. Pakistan has developed a remarkably similar form of litigation that relies on Islamic rhetoric about democratic values and is also much more than a tool for the implementation of Western-style concepts of human rights.

The countries of South Asia are deeply involved in a reappraisal of the traditional concepts that strengthen democratic principles, supporting the argument that Hindu culture and Hinduism are not inherently undemocratic. It may be difficult to comprehend this, but the evidence is there.

See also Democracy, Types of.

WERNER MENSKI

BIBLIOGRAPHY

Altekar, A. S. *State and Government in Ancient India.* 3d ed. Delhi: Motilal Banarsidass, 1977.

Day, Terence P. *The Conception of Punishment in Early Indian Literature.* Waterloo: Wilfrid Laurier University Press, 1982.

Derrett, J. Duncan M. *Religion, Law, and the State in India.* London: Faber and Faber; New York: Free Press, 1968.

Dirks, Nicholas B. *The Hollow Crown: Ethnohistory of an Indian Kingdom.* Cambridge and New York: Cambridge University Press, 1987.

Galanter, Marc. *Law and Society in Modern India.* Delhi and New York: Oxford University Press, 1989.

Kane, Pandurang Vaman. *History of Dharmashastra.* Vol. 3. 2d ed. Poona: Bhandarkar Oriental Research Institute, 1968–1977.

Kurien, C. T. *Growth and Justice: Aspects of India's Development Experience.* Madras and New York: Oxford University Press, 1992.

Rama Jois, M. *Seeds of Modern Public Law in Ancient Indian Jurisprudence.* Lucknow: Eastern Book Company, 1990.

Scharfe, Hartmut. *The State in Indian Tradition.* Leiden: E. J. Brill, 1989.

Sharma, J. P. *Republics in Ancient India.* Leiden: E. J. Brill, 1968.

✦ Laissez-faire

An economic theory that is based on a peremptory rejection of government interference with economic affairs and a faith in unrestricted private decision making as an instrument for promoting the public welfare. The origin of the term *laissez faire* is generally credited to an eighteenth-century French trademark inspector, Vincent de Gournay. Exasperated with government trade regulations, he reportedly exclaimed, *"Laissez faire! Laissez passer!"* ("Let [them] do [as they please]! Let [them] pass!"), calling for noninterference in enterprise and trade.

The Eighteenth and Nineteenth Centuries

Following the lead of François Quesnay and Anne-Robert-Jacques Turgot (who were members of the eighteenth-century French school of economics known as the physiocrats), the clas-

sical economists of the British liberal school made laissez-faire the centerpiece of their attack on state mercantilist economic policy. In his landmark treatise, *The Wealth of Nations* (1776), for example, the Scottish economist Adam Smith expounded what he called the natural economic system wherein self-interest, the private pursuit of profits, and individual freedom to trade would be guided—as if by an "invisible hand"—to promote the social welfare. The system would compel individuals to utilize their resources in accordance with consumers' wants and to strive to do so in ever more efficient and technologically superior ways. These socially beneficial outcomes would be the result, Smith argued, not of altruistic motives but of the narrow-minded pursuit of individual self-interest. As he put it, it is not from the benevolence of the butcher, the brewer, or the baker that we obtain our dinner but from their efforts to provide what others desire and what, therefore, is profitable for them to produce.

Although Smith identified some major deficiencies in private enterprise as a system of economic organization, and although he explicitly assigned certain responsibilities to government, his advocacy of private enterprise has served for more than two centuries as an ideological justification for opposing government economic policies as "dangerous" and "unnatural."

Social Darwinism, or economic Darwinism, as articulated in mid-nineteenth century England by Herbert Spencer (*The Man versus the State,* 1884) and in late nineteenth century America by William Graham Sumner (whose views were posthumously collected in *The Challenge of Facts and Other Essays,* 1914) reinforced and buttressed the doctrine of laissez-faire. (Actually, Spencer's work preceded, and to some degree shaped, Darwin's conjectures about the evolution of animal species.) According to this view, the press of the economic environment, coupled with unrestrained competition among individuals for income, forces the development of socially beneficial talents and aptitudes. Life rewards those who succeed in proving themselves to be most fit in these regards, while punishing those who are less fit.

Spencer and Sumner, for example, argued that government programs to protect the poor—to provide food, shelter, and education for them—only worsened their lot by depriving them of the energy and incentive to improve their economic condition. Similarly, Spencer contended that government should not in any way regulate the sale of lethal quack medicines, on the grounds that the fatal decisions made by some would encourage more intelligent decision making by everyone else and that the misfortune of one would serve as a powerful lesson for thousands of others. In general, according to this school, any government cure is far worse than the disease itself: government interference in economic matters violates natural social laws, weakens the strong, dulls initiative, and saps a society's economic vitality.

Twentieth-Century Thought

A later version of laissez-faire thinking emerged during the 1930s and became known as the Austrian school of economics, named in honor of its progenitors, Friedrich von Hayek and Ludwig von Mises. Economic systems, they argued, are fraught with uncertainty and subject to continual change in unpredictable and unanticipated ways. Only private individuals possess both the incentives and the abilities to obtain, interpret, and act expeditiously upon information concerning the nature and significance of these unforeseeable changes. Although the state could in theory duplicate the performance of the private marketplace in a static world, the information and decision-making requirements in the dynamic

environment of the real world preclude government from acting in a fashion capable of promoting the public welfare.

More recently, the laissez-faire doctrine has been supported by the public choice school of economic analysis. This view, which emerged during the 1960s, applies economic theory to question the very foundations of democracy. It concludes that, in practice, the democratic political process suffers from inherent flaws. As a result virtually all government economic policies—no matter how well intentioned—are likely to fail. The political process is defective, it claims, because voters in a democracy are "rationally ignorant": they recognize that their individual vote cannot alter the outcome of elections and that the personal cost to them of informing themselves about issues and candidates far outweighs any benefits they might personally derive from casting an informed vote. Moreover, the political process is believed to yield questionable results because it typically is manipulated by special-interest groups in order to produce benefits for themselves at society's expense. Finally, government officials are considered prone to pursuing their personal self-interest. Self-interest induces them to exacerbate the problems they are ostensibly responsible for resolving, in order to secure their personal employment and enhance their income. Therefore, according to the public choice theorists, although private enterprise may generate social problems, government cures are, once again, worse than the disease.

Finally, the Chicago school of economics, which reached its apogee of influence during the 1980s, represents a latter-day reincarnation of nineteenth-century social Darwinism and a repository for all these various strains of laissez-faire thinking. Like Spencer and Sumner a century earlier, the Chicago school's most forceful advocate, Milton Friedman, has long condemned govern-

no

ment welfare programs for the poor, reasoning that welfare programs weaken incentives to work and save and that they produce a permanent underclass bereft of motivation and self-reliance. Like Spencer, he has opposed consumer protection legislation, arguing that the private marketplace will protect consumers better than government agencies can do. If a consumer is sold rotten meat by one grocer, Friedman says, the consumer can switch to another store. The market will force the first shop to improve the quality of its meat or go out of business.

Criticisms of Laissez-faire

The laissez-faire doctrine has not escaped virulent criticism. Some have attacked it as nothing more than a naïve rationalization—a simplistic faith that "whatever is, is right," an excuse for egregious inequalities, a shield for domination by unregulated and uncontrolled private power blocs. Adam Smith's invisible hand may be a powerful force for compelling socially desirable decision making, they say, but only so long as markets are protected from subversion by private cartels and monopolies. But laissez-faire slogans developed by Smith to destroy monopoly may, ironically, become monopoly's bulwark when used to oppose government actions that would preserve, restore, or promote the competition Smith advocated.

Others argue that the doctrine is self-contradictory. On the one hand, it demands that government refrain from interfering with "private" economic affairs. On the other hand, it ignores the fact that the capacity of individuals to engage in such activities hinges on the "interference" of the state in myriad ways—specification of legal title to property, provision of courts to enforce and adjudicate commercial contracts, statutory provision of the advantages of the corporate form of organization, and so forth.

Moreover, as John Kenneth Galbraith and others contend, a more active economic role for government may have enabled the market system to endure, by softening the harshest edges of unregulated capitalism. Darwinian survival of the fittest, they say, is fundamentally inappropriate when applied to human affairs, because all human advances—from scientific agriculture to high-technology medical care—stem at bottom from deliberate efforts to interfere with the "natural" environment.

Most generally, as the economist John Bates Clark pointed out in *The Control of Trusts* (1912), championing survival of the fittest begs the critical question, fittest to do what? Survival in the prize-fighting ring, he observed, means fitness for pugilism but not necessarily for bricklaying. Only with the right kind of rules can the right kind of fitness emerge. Determining these rules, and harnessing self-interest to best serve the common good, is the central economic challenge in a free society.

See also Capitalism; State growth and intervention.

WALTER ADAMS AND JAMES W. BROCK

BIBLIOGRAPHY

Adams, Walter E., and James W. Brock. *Antitrust Economics on Trial: A Dialogue on the New Laissez-Faire.* Princeton: Princeton University Press, 1991.

Friedman, Milton, and Rose Friedman. *Free to Choose.* New York: Avon Books, 1980.

Galbraith, John Kenneth. *The New Industrial State.* Boston: Houghton Mifflin, 1967; Harmondsworth: Penguin Books, 1991.

Hayek, Friedrich von. *The Counter-Revolution of Science: Studies in the Abuse of Reason.* Glencoe, Ill.: Free Press, 1952.

Hofstadter, Richard. *Social Darwinism in American Thought*. Boston: Beacon Press, 1955.

Lippmann, Walter. *The Good Society*. Boston: Little, Brown, 1937.

Smith, Adam. *An Inquiry into the Nature and Causes of the Wealth of Nations*. 2 vols. Oxford and New York: Oxford University Press, 1979.

✦ Leninism

The aims, policies, and organization of the Bolshevik faction of the Russian Marxist party as formulated by the Russian revolutionary Vladimir Ilich Lenin (1870–1924). Bolshevism represented one attempt to apply Marxist ideas and programs in czarist Russia; the Bolsheviks brushed aside the notion that Marxism might not be applicable in Russia.

In the nineteenth century Friedrich Engels and Karl Marx had argued, in effect, that genuine political democracy presupposes economic equality. Marxism accepted that the material preconditions for such a community—that is, an economy of abundance—had been created by capitalism, but only in Western Europe. Czarist Russia differed from Western Europe in several important ways: economic development, social structure, level of education, and other indicators of modernity. Although constitutional government and citizens' participation in public life were the rule in Western Europe, in Russia the czars and their bureaucrats still ruled without any constitutional checks on their powers. Disregarding these differences, some Russian radicals turned to Marxism and founded the Russian Social-Democratic Workers Party in 1898.

Bolshevism originated in 1903 in a dispute over the organization and membership criteria of the Russian Social-Democratic Workers Party. The faction developed its broader views and programs and, ultimately, its identity as a separate party in the years between 1905 and 1911. At that time it had a dual identity and two leaders. On the one hand, the Bolshevik Party was an underground workers' movement within Russia led by A. A. Bogdanov. On the other hand, it was a small circle of Bolsheviks living in Central European exile and led by Lenin.

The ideas of these two leaders increasingly diverged, and they fought over the right to define Bolshevism, lead the party, train its cadre, and dispose of its funds. Bogdanov (whose real name was Malinovsky) was the son of a school teacher, trained as a physician, scientist, and philosopher. His compassion for the poor turned him toward revolutionary activity. Lenin (whose real name was Ulyanov) was the son of a high-ranking czarist official of noble rank. Lenin was a lawyer. He had turned toward radicalism when his older brother was hanged for having conspired to assassinate the czar.

Believing that the workers would not rebel against their exploitation, Lenin wanted a highly disciplined party of professional revolutionaries drawn from the educated classes, who would act as the general staff of the revolution. In contrast, Bogdanov placed his faith in the working class and in a workers' intelligentsia. Lenin's aim was to overthrow the power of money in a political revolution, while Bogdanov argued that such an event would have to be complemented by a cultural revolution—that is, by changing people's attitudes and styles of behavior. Bogdanov believed that the Bolsheviks would have to create a distinct workers' culture as well as to mobilize the masses politically.

Leninism took as its model the radical leaders of the French revolutions of 1789 and 1848, who believed that the seizure of power by an enlightened vanguard would effect revolutionary change. Lenin insisted on the thoroughly bureaucratic organization of such a revolutionary party. Bogdanovism took its cue from radical theorists who believed that revolutions needed to begin from the grass roots, not in the actions of any leadership. In this case, Bogdanov believed, the revolution had to spring from the spontaneous action of militant labor unions. Thus the preferred revolutionary strategy of Bogdanovism was the general strike.

Bogdanov wanted to incorporate some aspects of religion into the Bolshevik movement. He sought to mobilize Russia's so-called Old Believers. The Old Believers were a fundamentalist sect that had split from the Russian Orthodox Church in the seventeenth century and ever since had been persecuted by the authorities. Lenin, however, defended a dogmatic atheism.

Lenin insisted on adherence to the dialectical materialism preached by the theorists of "orthodox" Marxism, such as Karl Kautsky and Georgy Plekhanov. Bogdanov wished to integrate into Marxist philosophy the new theories of modern physics, especially those of Ernst Mach. His vision of the future was colored by the seemingly unlimited possibilities of advanced technology.

By 1909 Lenin had managed to discredit Bogdanov and his associates and to gain control of the Bolshevik faction, including its treasury. From then on Leninism and Bolshevism were one.

Leninist Revolutionary Strategy

Leninist strategy foresaw two revolutions for Russia: a "bourgeois" revolution that would remove Russia's precapitalist vestiges, and a "proletarian" revolution that would bring about the dictatorship of the Bolshevik Party, which claimed to represent the proletariat. The first revolution would introduce "capitalism American style." This meant some sort of Jeffersonian democracy, also called the revolutionary-democratic dictatorship of workers and peasants.

To bring about the first revolution, Lenin sought to mobilize not only Russia's industrial workers but also the peasants and the national minorities. The peasants, who made up most of the population, resented the oppressive financial burdens they had to carry and the privileges of the nobility with their vast land holdings. The non-Russians, numbering in the millions, felt persecuted and threatened by the dominant Russian nation. In 1917 Leninist propaganda added to these potential allies the war-weary troops who had been poorly led during World War I and had suffered tremendous hardships. Grassroots democracy in the new regime was to be exercised by councils formed in villages, factories, and troop units; the Russian word for these action councils is *soviet*.

Lenin expected that a Russian revolution would spark a worldwide chain reaction of proletarian revolutions, which would ensure the success of the Russian one. He believed that the outcome of these revolutions would be a genuine democratic community in which the burdens and benefits of citizenship would be shared equally. People would learn to be cooperative and productive without the incentive of profit. Coercive institutions and political elites would gradually become superfluous. The remaining administrative tasks could then be rotated among all citizens.

Lenin believed that his views and activities were well in tune with democratic ideas. But his conception of democracy was substantive rather than procedural. Procedural democracy is a method of mitigating conflict through institutions that afford all citizens structured and limited participation in the discussion of issues and the choice of representatives. Its goal is to arrive at compromise solutions that all can accept. Substantive democracy means rule by, and policies benefiting, the masses of the poor. This is the definition of democracy that was generally accepted before the nineteenth century. From this viewpoint, mitigating conflict through compromise would be undemocratic. Thus substantive democracy is identical with the dictatorship of the proletariat or with government by soviets.

The substantive theory of democracy also contains the notion that the worth of any society is judged by its treatment of those at the bottom. Lenin included workers, peasants, and national minorities among the exploited. More globally, his writings point toward a theory of capitalism in which entire nations can be placed under class categories. For example, in his book on imperialism Lenin suggested that the affluent nations of Europe and North America were playing the role of a ruling class, while their colonies, as well as the underdeveloped nations of Asia, Africa, and Latin America, had become the global proletariat. The overthrow of imperialism thus became part of his program for a worldwide proletarian revolution.

World War I was disastrous for Russia. Heavy military losses and painful defeats, economic dislocation and grave civil disorders (including bread riots), continued corruption, and inefficiency in high places put the Russian people in a rebellious mood. In early 1917 the first riots occurred in the capital city. The system promptly collapsed; the czar abdicated, and nobody wanted to occupy the empty throne. The Leninists hailed the fall of czarism as the expected bourgeois revolution. At Lenin's urging, the Bolshevik Party almost immediately began planning to lead the next phase—the proletarian revolution. Eight months after the czar's abdication it seized power. What explains this success?

After more than three years of war, Russia was exhausted, its people starving, its economy ruined. The end of czarism aroused expectations for the solution of many burning problems. Russians wanted a democratic constitution, equitable land reform, an end to hunger, and lasting peace. A growing number of voters wanted these goals achieved at once, but political leaders argued that such weighty issues needed to be discussed at length. The Bolsheviks stoked the fires of discontent, and only Lenin's party chimed in with answers to the utopian demands of the masses. As a result the Leninists had significant popular support when they seized power.

The Leninist Theory of Governance

The expected worldwide chain reaction of proletarian revolutions did not occur. Moreover, the membership and clientele of the Bolshevik Party were unprepared for the tasks of governing a country ruined by previous misgovernment, by war and civil war. From the beginning, rule by the party was crisis management. In the last few years of his life, Lenin established some guidelines for ruling, which one might call the Leninist principles of governance.

First, Leninists wish to govern a strong unified state not weakened by any checks and balances. The citizens' organizations, the soviets, combine legislative and executive functions. But the soviets are to be controlled by the single party that claims to represent the working class; all other parties are to be outlawed.

Second, in all its functions the ruling party is to adhere to the rules of "democratic centralism." This formula is designed to combine democratic and bureaucratic principles. Lenin held that under democratic centralism, pending issues could be debated freely by the party membership. Once a decision was made, members had to accept it without further questioning. In practice, however,

Leninist political culture—especially when linked with a ban on the formation of factions—discouraged and eventually outlawed all free discussion.

Third, a Leninist definition of citizenship stresses duties instead of rights and the interests of the collective rather than those of individuals. It boldly favors people from the lower classes while discriminating against those who previously had enjoyed wealth, education, or social status. Some of this discrimination takes the form of "revolutionary justice," allowing security forces to punish alleged class enemies, whether or not they have committed any crimes.

Fourth, the principal task of the Leninist state, once it is secure from enemies inside and outside its borders, is to promote modernization. This means introducing technology and the skills associated with it—what Lenin called "learning from capitalism." Equally important, modernization implies the difficult task of resocializing the Russian peasantry and other "backward" elements of society by making them unlearn their traditional habits and outlooks. Lenin defined this as a cultural revolution.

Finally, in world affairs, Leninism is committed to two tasks: promoting the spread of the anticapitalist and anti-imperialist revolution throughout the world and securing the continued existence of the Soviet state by cementing fruitful relations with "capitalist" states. In fact, these two tasks were incompatible. By pursuing both tasks at the same time, the Russian Leninist state ultimately failed in both.

After Lenin's death the Bolshevik Party was deeply divided over the policies to be derived from these principles of Leninism. The aspiring leaders all sought to justify their views by reference to Lenin; the term *Leninism* was coined at this time. The disputes over Lenin's intellectual heritage suggest that the totalitarian excesses of his successor, Joseph Stalin, were one possible result of the spirit of Leninism, but not necessarily the only one.

The conflict within the party concerned the best method of modernizing the Soviet Union, since modernization was seen as the precondition for socialism. Advocates of gradual, relatively painless methods clashed with those who recommended drastic methods. In the end, the radical group won, and under their leader, Joseph Stalin (whose real name was Dzhugashvili), managed a crash program of industrialization that modernized the Soviet Union and helped it win over a very strong enemy in World War II. The success, however, came at the cost of transforming the country into a totalitarian dictatorship. Under Stalin, Leninism turned into a reactionary ideology justifying every hardship and sacrifice that the party was imposing on the people.

See also Communism; Marxism.

ALFRED G. MEYER

BIBLIOGRAPHY

Daniels, Robert V. *The Conscience of the Revolution: Communist Opposition in Soviet Russia.* Cambridge: Harvard University Press, 1960.

Haimson, Leopold H. *The Russian Marxists and the Origins of Bolshevism.* Cambridge: Harvard University Press, 1955.

Meyer, Alfred G. *Leninism.* Boulder, Colo.: Westview Press, 1986.

Service, Robert. *Lenin: A Biography.* Cambridge: Harvard University Press, 2000.

Sochor, Zenovia A. *Revolution and Culture: The Bogdanov-Lenin Controversy.* Ithaca, N.Y.: Cornell University Press, 1988.

Williams, Robert C. *The Other Bolsheviks: Lenin and His Critics, 1904–1914.* Bloomington: Indiana University Press, 1986.

✦ Liberalism

A theory of limited government aimed at securing personal liberty. Toward this end, the chief concern of liberalism is opposing political absolutism and arbitrariness. To guard against political absolutism, liberal government is limited in its purposes and the scope of its legitimate powers. To guard against arbitrariness, it treats individuals according to known, settled laws, impartially applied. Its defining institutions are constitutionalism and the separation of powers, including an independent judiciary; the rule of law; a system of political representation; and enforceable civil rights to secure the liberties of individuals and minority groups.

Although it sometimes is confused with a particular social structure (bourgeois society), economic organization (free market economy), epistemological stance (skepticism), or philosophy of the person (moral autonomy), liberalism is first of all a theory of government with personal liberty as its goal.

Specific rights guarantee liberty and protect against official abuse. These fundamental rights should be secured to all adult citizens without regard to race, class, sex, or social or cultural affiliation: freedom of religion, freedom of speech and association, freedom to own property, and freedom to travel. Particularly important are the rights associated with due process of law. Among these rights are habeas corpus, which protects individuals against arbitrary imprisonment or detention; freedom from unwarranted search and seizure; and protections for the accused in criminal matters, such as trial by jury.

In addition to these civil rights, essential political rights include the right to vote and to run for public office. This list is not exhaustive.

Limited Government and Guarantees of Liberty

Various mechanisms have been devised to limit government. Institutional design, through which power is divided between elements of government, is one mechanism. The French philosopher Montesquieu (1689–1755) and the American statesman James Madison (1751–1836), who was influenced by Montesquieu's thought, are the principal theorists of constitutionalism and the separation of powers. The elements of government—the chambers of the legislature in bicameral systems, the executive, the judiciary, and federalist arrangements—are designed to divide authority and check one another. Montesquieu reflected on the British tradition of unwritten constitution in his *Spirit of the Laws* (1748). In this account, the branches of government correspond not only to separate governmental functions but also to separate social estates—the king, the aristocracy, and the common people. The constitutional ideal was a balance among them. In the 1780s, in *The Federalist Papers*, Madison developed the modern idea that popular conventions draw up written constitutions and that all branches and levels of government, including the executive office and senate, represent the people generally. Both Montesquieu and Madison thought that liberty should not have to depend on enlightened statesmanship or strenuous civic virtue. Institutions could limit government if they were designed to balance opposite and rival interests and to make ambition counteract ambition.

Another safeguard for civil liberties and limited government is a pluralist civil society with a wide range of religious, economic, cultural, and ideological groups. The political justification for individuals to be free to amass private property and form economic associations is that this freedom disperses power and provides material and social resources for resisting official injustice. The political justification for freedom of association for voluntary groups organized around a virtually unlimited array of noneconomic interests and opinions is the same: associations are sources of resistance against absolutism and arbitrariness. If pluralist groups are brought into the framework of government through a system of representation, Madison argued, they check one another and prevent the formation of a permanent, potentially tyrannical majority. Liberalism and pluralism are mutually reinforcing. Pluralism helps guard against tyranny, and civil liberty encourages the formation of secondary associations and a diverse civil society.

A third security for civil liberties is an attitude of mistrust toward government. John Locke (1632–1704) warned in *The Second Treatise of Government* (1689) that governors are potential lions who will use power cruelly and arbitrarily to advance their sinister interests. Institutional mechanisms and social pluralism only protect against abuse of power if citizens are vigilant; if they care about the liberty of others, not just their own; and if the disposition to resist oppression is sufficiently widespread. Popular vigilance and mistrust are made effective by publicity and a free press, which writers as different as the German philosopher Immanuel Kant (1724–1804) and the British utilitarian Jeremy Bentham (1748–1832) saw as the key to liberty. Government must be open to public inspection, policy must be publicly justified, and public criticism must be permitted.

Limited government does not mean weak government incapable of collective action, however. Political authority must be strong enough to eliminate inherited privileges, entrenched hierarchies, and private coercion. Government must be able to enforce equal civil liberties against opposition from many quarters: a feudal nobility, traditions of caste and exclusion, large concentrations of landed wealth, powerful business corporations,

and dominant cultural or racial groups who would deny rights to minorities.

Finally, limited government does not mean inactive government. It is neither logically nor historically tied to libertarianism, which advocates a minimal state restricted to maintaining order and defense against external aggression. Nor is liberalism tied to a laissez-faire doctrine in economic affairs. Liberal government is compatible with economic orders that regulate production, exchange, and the conditions of labor in different ways and to different extents. Various kinds and degrees of free enterprise and public ownership are found in liberal governments. Some are expansive welfare states, while others are mixed systems that combine capitalist economic freedoms and inequalities with welfare state egalitarian policies.

Changing Concerns

Liberalism approaches questions of social justice and active government out of concern for liberty. If all citizens are to exercise their rights in practice, redistribution of social resources and opportunities may be necessary. State-provided legal representation, for example, is necessary to make due process of law as effective for the poor as for those who can afford private counsel. Policies of "affirmative action" in hiring may be necessary to ensure equal opportunity in employment for members of groups that historically have suffered systematic discrimination. Liberals disagree about the social conditions and degree of equality necessary for realizing full liberties for all citizens and debate these questions of social justice as ardently among themselves as with their ideological opponents. But the outlines of liberal social justice are clear. Although liberty does not necessarily have priority over other goods, such as social justice, particular liberties do have priority. Expansion of public purposes and growth of government cannot violate basic civil rights (such as the freedom to choose one's occupation) or eclipse certain guaranteed spheres of personal liberty (such as the decision whether and whom to marry).

The content of rights and the boundary between public and private is always shifting. Religious practice was the first activity designated private and protected from government interference and control, and churches were the first institution to benefit from the principle of autonomy for the internal life and the governance of private associations. As the free exercise of religion indicates, personal liberty is not restricted to the inner citadel of thought and belief but extends to conduct. The critical question for liberalism is, What areas of life are legitimate objects of political control and what are sacrosanct?

Today, feminists are among those recasting the divide between the public and the private. The practice of restricting women to the domestic sphere and denying them rights to hold property, to sue in court, to conduct business, to sit on juries, and to vote made them vulnerable to exploitation and domination, as the British philosopher John Stuart Mill (1806–1873) described in *The Subjection of Women* (1869). Once considered private and beyond the reach of government, the justice of family arrangements and the rights of individual family members against one another have become appropriate subjects of legislative reform. At the same time, feminists understand reproductive decisions to be irretrievably private and beyond the reach of criminal law. Where the line between public and private is drawn is a matter of changing principles, technology, and experience.

Opposition to liberalism comes from Marxism and other varieties of socialism, authoritarianism, fascism, totalitarianism, racism, social Darwinism, antiliberal nationalism, imperialism, and mili-

tarism. It also comes from some forms of democracy. Throughout the course of its three-hundred-year history, liberalism has been the exception, even in Western Europe and North America. The United States was a liberal state in name only until civil and political rights were extended to African Americans and to women. French and German liberalism has had a precarious existence in the twentieth century. The effectiveness of the Soviet empire in Central and Eastern Europe, and powerful challenges to liberalism's emergence in newly independent states, both former colonial and former Soviet countries, should dispel any notion of steady liberalization. Even in stable, liberal democracies, individuals continue to be excluded from rights and opportunities on the basis of gender, race, or cultural affiliation. And opposition to liberalism from ideological tendencies such as racism and sexism remains strong.

Tension Between Liberalism and Democracy

There is a difference between the democratic question "Who governs?" and the liberal question "What are the limits of government?" Direct self-government and a duty to participate in public affairs are not defining characteristics of liberalism. In fact, liberalism is in tension with many forms of democracy, as became evident when the liberal French Revolution of 1789 was transformed into the Terror of the democratic revolution of 1793. The French thinker Benjamin Constant de Rebecque (1767–1830) observed that it makes no difference whether individual liberty is crushed by despotism or by popular sovereignty. Unconstrained majoritarianism is only one form of democratic tyranny. Neither democracy modeled after the "general will" of the philosopher Jean-Jacques Rousseau (1712–1778) nor deliberative ideals aimed at consensus and a single idea of the common good are committed to or protect minority rights. They put self-government in the service of some higher ideal—public order, economic progress, equality, or a particular vision of the good life, which takes priority over basic liberties. Both Mill in *On Liberty* (1859) and Alexis de Tocqueville in *Democracy in America* (1835–1840) warned about the tyranny of the majority, which does not recognize limits on the power that can legitimately be exercised over individuals. Mill and Tocqueville also warned that even apart from laws, democratic society tends to exercise a tyranny of opinion that demands conformity and inhibits individuality and independence. Thus a disposition to tolerate diversity is at the heart of liberalism.

Despite the potential for conflict, liberalism today accepts a marriage of convenience with democracy and sees some form of representative government as essential. Temporary, elected representatives are necessary to counterbalance executive power, to ensure that social interests are not ignored or trespassed, and to hold officials accountable. The American revolutionary demand for "no taxation without representation" has not stopped at fiscal matters. The idea that everyone has interests and opinions to advance and defend through political representation has led to the extension of political rights to previously excluded groups. The expectation is that new political groups and social movements will bring ever changing notions of interests, needs, and values into public arenas. Unlike many forms of democracy, liberal democracy does not imagine that well-devised systems of representation and deliberative procedures can harmonize interests or produce moral consensus. Rather, the hope is that within an agreed-upon procedural framework conflicts can normally be negotiated, many interests can be accommodated, and a modicum of agreement can be reached on the basic requirements of social justice.

Majoritarianism and the utopian hope for consensus on a common good are not the only sources of tension between democracy and liberalism. Liberalism and democracy are in conflict wherever a particular cultural, religious, or racial identity is made key to the enjoyment of rights of citizenship and of effective political participation. Constitutionalism and rights are purely formal and fail to secure the liberties of individuals and minorities where the purpose of democratic self-government is the preservation and promotion of the culture, values, and historical goals of a particular national group. Democracy is not liberal if the dominant ethnic, religious, or racial group's interest defines the rights and liberties of others in a multinational society. Indeed, where the justification for democracy is self-government by and for a nationally defined people, nothing is more common than minorities suffering exclusion, legal discrimination, and in the worst cases exile, torture, or massacre.

Liberal democratic citizenship is a legal category, not a social or cultural one. It encompasses all native-born adults or long-time residents who want naturalization. In the United States, for example, the guarantee of equal protection of the law is supposed to ensure that offices and occupations are open to individuals without regard to race, religion, sex, or national origin. The liberal promise is that rights and benefits are secure, whether individuals are members of one group or of none. People of mixed ethnic or cultural backgrounds and individuals who resist being identified with a particular group are not at a disadvantage in the public distribution of social goods, and political participation is not tied to social identification.

At the same time, liberal democracy may encourage political recognition and representation for powerless minority groups when the object is to remedy systematic discrimination and to eliminate caste. Liberalism invites the formation of voluntary associations dedicated to preserving the cultural identity of groups. It may allow a degree of cultural autonomy in order to sustain fragile communities. The Amish in the United States, for example, are exempted from the general obligation to send their children to school until the age of sixteen. Aboriginal tribes in many places are afforded autonomy. The difficulty for liberalism is to strike a balance between freedom for groups and voluntary associations, on the one side, and excessive autonomy for subcommunities uncommitted to a political society of equal rights and liberties, on the other.

Evolution of the Liberal Tradition

Liberalism has taken a different course in Britain, France, Italy, Germany, and the United States. It arose in different political conditions, and different social groups (barons, merchants, and landowners) were its initial advocates and enemies. In some places its first task was to limit absolute authority; in others it was to strengthen government against powerful private groups in order to ensure equality before the law. The history of liberalism's shift in the direction of democracy differs from country to country, as does the extent to which democracy, when it arose, was liberal. Doctrinally, too, liberalism has national variations, depending on whether its principal theorists were jurists and historians (as in France) or philosophers (as in England). Despite political vicissitudes and national variations in the theoretical underpinnings of limited government, we can still speak of a liberal tradition and survey briefly some of its historical highlights.

The rise of liberalism occurred in post–Reformation Europe in the seventeenth century. Religious persecution and wars of faith provided the impetus to one of the first limits on government. Public officials were prohibited from enforcing religious practices on nonbelievers and from dictating matters of faith. Locke's *Letter on Tolera-*

tion (1690), although it did not make the argument for separation of church and state familiar from the U.S. Constitution, argued for toleration of dissenters from official orthodoxy. A policy of religious liberty is not liberal if it is a pragmatic tool of government for maintaining public order, however, or if it is the work of one dissenting sect winning the privilege of religious liberty for itself while permitting the repression of rival faiths.

Principled toleration, Locke argued, rests on the inviolability of conscience in matters of faith. It follows that people are justified in religious dissent from the state church and in political dissent from government if government trespasses on this liberty. The original connection between conscience and liberal freedoms lies here. Principled toleration is part of the broader idea that the legitimate purposes of public authority are limited and stop short of favoring or enforcing a particular religious faith or philosophy of the good life. Religious nonconformism is part of the broader idea that peace and liberty are compatible with social and moral diversity.

In its origin, liberalism was a revolutionary doctrine that provided a theory of legitimate resistance to absolute and arbitrary rule. John Locke's *Second Treatise of Government* is the classic statement, echoed in the American Declaration of Independence of 1776. When governors exercise force without right, they put themselves in a state of war with the people. Invoking a violation of the social contract or of universal natural rights, or simply the experience of a long train of abuses, people have a right to resist tyranny. Like liberal government, liberal revolution is limited. Its object is to remove arbitrary and corrupt rulers and restore a government that will secure liberties; it is political, not social, revolution. The revolutionary import of liberalism remains powerful today.

A recurrent strain of utopianism in liberal thought dates from the Enlightenment of the late eighteenth century. The French philosopher the Marquis de Condorcet (1743–1794) wrote that liberalism weakened the hold of political authority and with it other authorities such as the church and tradition. By liberating human reason from superstition and dogma, it made infinite perfectibility possible. In the same spirit, the American revolutionary Thomas Paine (1737–1809) believed that liberal democracy provided freedom for continual experiments in happiness. Paine looked forward to a progressive revolution in every generation.

From its inception, a defining element of liberalism was the right of private property. This idea does not reflect the view that possessive individualism characterizes liberals or that acquisitiveness and competitiveness are moral virtues. Instead, private property was thought to serve political purposes. It was a source of independence and of resistance to political authority. Thinkers of the Scottish Enlightenment, among them David Hume (1711–1776) and Adam Smith (1723–1790), saw private property as a support for liberal practices and institutions. The habits of rule following, contracting, and regularity associated with manufacture and trade were conducive to legalism and civil peace. Measured calculations of economic interests were thought to counterbalance more disturbing passions, such as the aristocratic pursuit of honor or military glory. Montesquieu argued that trade promotes tolerance by requiring people to deal with one another fairly and impersonally, regardless of religious or other differences. Kant went a step further: he predicted that, because war is intolerably disruptive of commerce and the legal order on which it rests, a peaceful cosmopolitan order would arise among liberal states.

The classic economic doctrine of laissez-faire, familiar from Adam Smith's seminal work *The Wealth of Nations* (1776), was directed against feudal or customary obstacles to the free flow of labor and capital and toward freedom of contract. Among those obstacles were local tariffs, royal monopolies and privileges, the guild structure of occupations, the restriction of certain occupations to particular castes, and legal restraints on inheritance and the sale of land. Laissez-faire was a program of legal reform aimed at overcoming these impediments to economic liberty. Its proponents did not anticipate the regulation of property or labor conditions by democratic governments or taxation for the purposes of social welfare. In the twentieth century, in reaction to modern government regulation of the economy, neoclassic liberals such as the Austrian economist Friedrich von Hayek (1899–1992) called regulation the road to serfdom, and "libertarian" liberals made a nearly absolute right of private ownership and control the premier liberty.

For the most part, however, since the late nineteenth century, liberal thinkers and governments have recognized powerful nongovernmental obstacles to freedom. Civil and political liberties can be effectively diminished if people are forced by economic necessity to accept any conditions others impose in return for having basic needs met. Endorsing ideas shared by socialists, liberals argued that true freedom of contract requires measures to counterbalance the inequality of contracting parties, such as legislative protection for wages and working conditions and the legalization of trade unionism. Increasingly the question for liberalism has been, in what conditions do liberties have equal worth to citizens, and what is the responsibility of government for creating those conditions?

Justifications

There are three main philosophic and political justifications for liberalism: self-protection, natural rights, and moral autonomy. Each has a long history, and each draws attention to a particular facet of liberalism's preoccupation with personal liberty.

The first justification is the right of self-protection. The experience of unlimited power, torture, and war by governments against their own citizens has been sufficiently common to demonstrate the benefits of liberal institutions as a defense of the relatively powerless against public officials. Fear is a universal reaction to absolutism and arbitrariness. One justification of liberalism is based on the recognition that fear is paralyzing, it makes every endeavor impossible, and it is incompatible with human dignity. The universal disposition to avoid fear is the moral force behind limiting government, enforcing rights, and guarding against extralegal, arbitrary, unnecessary uses of public power. This justification focuses on what is to be avoided by enforcing rights and limiting government. It highlights self-protection and "negative liberty"—that is, freedom from government regulation and control.

A second justification of liberalism is the doctrine of natural rights, which says that people are governed by natural laws and endowed with natural rights discoverable by reason. Rights may be divinely given or reflect the secular moral order of the universe and human nature—for example, rights of self-preservation and self-defense and imperatives against needless cruelty. In either case, natural laws and rights point to a basis for the moral equality of individuals outside custom and convention. They establish universal standards for judging political arrangements. Natural rights direct us to preserve our lives, liberty, and property and to punish transgressors. They recommend consent to political authority in order to enforce rights effectively and impartially. Natural laws instruct us in our obligations, such as keeping promises, but they also set limits to the oblig-

ations we can assume. Consent is not unconditional but is regulated by natural law, and natural rights are inalienable. Natural law prohibits consent to slavery or to absolute authority, for example. In short, natural laws describe a moral order that government should guarantee to all, and natural rights prescribe legitimate grounds of resistance when governments violate this order. This justification highlights liberalism's revolutionary potential and the moral basis of equal liberties.

A third justification of liberalism rests on a particular philosophic notion of the individual as morally autonomous. Moral autonomy comes into play when individuals are independent of authority, determining for themselves which obligations are binding and making their own choices about happiness and the good life. Because liberalism limits authority and guarantees a sphere of personal liberty, it is the most favorable political condition for pursuing and even conceiving various ends. As Mill argued in *On Liberty*, moral autonomy is exercised where there is pluralism and liberty to choose among values and ways of life. Liberalism, however, is more than just a background condition for the exercise of moral capacities. Its institutions have an educational character and impose a positive obligation to respect the moral dignity and rights of others. In romantic justifications of liberalism, the notion of men and women as essentially morally autonomous is replaced by a focus on individual self-expression. The conditions for developing each individual's unique personality form the basis of Wilhelm von Humboldt's romantic defense of liberalism.

No justification of liberalism translates directly into a specific account of the limits of government or the boundary between public and private life. Each can be used to support diverse notions of social justice and prescriptions for government activism or restraint. But together they provide an overlapping consensus for constitutionalism, the rule of law, universal civil and political rights, and tolerance of diversity, as securities for liberty.

See also Conservatism; Constitutionalism; Locke, John; Montesquieu; Pragmatism; Rousseau, Jean-Jacques; Laissez-faire; Theory, Postwar Anglo-American; Theory, Twentieth Century European; Tocqueville, Alexis de.

NANCY L. ROSENBLUM

BIBLIOGRAPHY

Berlin, Isaiah. "Two Concepts of Liberty." In *Four Essays on Liberty.* Oxford: Oxford University Press, 1969.

De Ruggiero, Guido. *The History of European Liberalism.* Translated by R. C. Collingwood. Oxford: Oxford University Press, 1927.

Fowler, Robert Booth. *Enduring Liberalism: American Political Thought since the 1960s.* Lawrence: University Press of Kansas, 1999.

Hirschman, Albert O. *The Passions and the Interests.* Princeton: Princeton University Press, 1977.

Kymlicka, Will. *Contemporary Political Philosophy: An Introduction.* Oxford: Oxford University Press, 1991.

Locke, John. *A Letter Concerning Toleration* and *Two Treatises of Government.* Edited by Peter Laslett. Cambridge: Cambridge University Press, 1967.

Merquior, J. G. *Liberalism Old and New.* Boston: Twayne, 1991.

Shklar, Judith. "The Liberalism of Fear." In *Liberalism and the Moral Life,* edited by Nancy L. Rosenblum. Cambridge: Harvard University Press, 1989.

✦ Marxism

A body of thought on economics, politics, and society created by Karl Marx (1818–1883) and Friedrich Engels (1820–1895). Neither Marx nor Engels left a cohesive critique or description of democracy from the Marxist perspective. Their written comments on democracy dealt not with how it could be used to constrain and tame the power of the state, but rather with how a society could use it to realize certain material goals. Marx and Engels never clearly separated the idea of the rule of the people from the prospect of achieving a just and equal society through the abolition of class division. What counted for Marx and Engels was what was to be achieved (social welfare and just distribution of resources), not how that goal was to be achieved and preserved (the political procedure used). At no time did Marx or Engels consider the possibility that political procedures themselves might divert society from promoting the values "guaranteed" from class relations.

The Derivative Nature of Democracy in Marxist Theory

This curious neglect was caused in part by the structure of the Marxist theory of society. In this theory the state and politics in general were given no autonomous role to play; they were part of the "superstructure" that serves and is fully determined by the economic "base." Politics, therefore, is secondary and derivative, and the state is not considered to be an independent agency with its own impact on the shape and character of the society. The existing state, based on capitalist economics, was seen as an instrument in the hands of the exploiters, and it would be naïve to consider the possibility of the people ruling as long as the ownership structure remained unchanged.

The future communist society, on the other hand (which, Marx and Engels believed, was bound to result from the overthrow of the exploiters), would implement the rule of the people by the very fact of doing away with exploitation. Therefore, communist society would have no need for separate political institutions and elaborate, specialized instruments of state coercion. (This view was subsequently described as the Marxist theory of the "withering away of the state.") In any case it seemed redundant to consider democracy as a certain type of government and a certain code of political behavior—indeed, to think of it as an issue in its own right.

Marx addressed the question of the form that the self-government of emancipated producers might take only once, in an enthusiastic description of the political practices spontaneously improvised under the auspices of the short-lived Paris Commune in 1871, when workers rebelled against the government. Even in this case, however, the institutions invented by the *communards* were seen by Marx as temporary political means to promote the revolution. In an 1875 letter to German social democratic leader August Bebel on the party program, Engels demanded that there should be no more talk about the state, since the state as such ceases to exist as soon as true freedom arrives. Having reduced the state to an outgrowth of economic relations (and one emerging only from a certain type of economic relations, soon to be left behind), Marx and Engels saw no reason to dissect the effects of various procedures a state might use.

To be sure, this Marxist neglect of democracy had other causes beyond the structure of Marxist theory. Marx and Engels did not live long enough to witness the introduction of universal voting rights. While they were developing their political theory, the workers (whose exploiters were to be overturned by the communist revolution, which would do away with their misery) remained disenfranchised and for all practical purposes had no part in the body politic. The existing state did indeed look like the exclusive domain of the propertied classes—and in their calling it a "dictatorship of bourgeoisie," Marx and Engels were in tune with many progressive liberal thinkers of the time. Whatever democratic procedures were observed, they certainly did not include the lower classes, and it was hard to see how existing democratic practices could guarantee attention to the grievances of the dispossessed or offer fair representation of their interests. From the point of view of the disenfranchised, there was little to distinguish between "democracy" as it was practiced and the dictatorship of the rich and powerful.

The Expansion of Voting Rights and Marxist Revisionism

Radical change occurred at the end of the nineteenth century when voting rights were extended to include most of the working class. Just as the opponents of universal voting rights feared and warned, this expansion drastically altered the stakes of the political game. The sheer numbers of the newly enfranchised working-class voters meant that democratic mechanisms of government would force the questions of just distribution of wealth and influence onto the political agenda. In practical terms, that meant the creation and development of the welfare state—a state that uses political instruments to intervene in the economically determined distribution of wealth and one that guarantees basic necessities for those members of society incapable of securing them through their own individual efforts.

This change prompted enhanced interest in the daily workings of the state on the part of the political movements based on the Marxist theory and program, especially since unionized labor, the chief supporter of these movements, was unwilling to wait for the improvement of its lot until society and the state were thoroughly overhauled along Marxist lines. The forms of government could no longer be neglected by Marxists and related movements. Active involvement in politics, made possible by democratic procedure, seemed to promise visible and immediate social gains. Attempts to rethink the vision of the state as irredeemably an instrument of the exploiting classes—and as such beyond salvation—were soon undertaken. Initiated among German Marxists by Eduard Bernstein, these attempts at first encountered keen and angry resistance from orthodox Marxists as revisionist heresy, yet they soon became the practice, and eventually the official program, of the organized political movement inspired by Marxism.

Marx himself saw the passage from an exploitative capitalist society to a just socialist society as catastrophic. The revolution of the impoverished proletariat would abolish the system of private ownership, already—in Marx's view—hopelessly entangled in its own internal contradictions and nearing collapse, and would replace the state, the instrument of exploitation, with some association of free producers, the form of which would be determined by the newly emancipated people themselves. But this idea of catastrophic change gave way to an evolutionary perspective, with the old society of competing enterprises gradually becoming a regulated economy.

This was a fateful change. The traditional disdainful neglect of Marxists for the capitalist state as such, and their resulting refusal to evaluate the different ways in which that state's business was conducted, had to give way to an acute theoretical and practical interest in the existing state, in order to speed up and smooth the gradual socialist transformation of society. By the time of World War I (1914–1918), the sometimes vicious struggle in Western Europe between revisionist and orthodox tendencies had ended in favor of the former, and it had become clear that social democrats, the heirs to Marxism, should engage in practical politics as a party. This would enable them to strive to shorten working hours; protect workers against the most blatant and outrageous

forms of exploitation; protect and enhance workers' bargaining power, to change the balance between profits and wages in their favor; and make sure the state provided a comprehensive network of insurance for unemployment, disability, illness, and other causes of poverty. In other words, social democrats would press for the creation of the welfare state, fight existing class inequality, and promote justice. Such an understanding of the role of the state forced Marxist-inspired political movements to become ardent and militant supporters of representative democracy, on which they now relied to protect the interests of the laboring majority.

The Failure of Evolutionary Marxism

By and large, there was little difference between the social democrats and other, non-Marxist theorists of the early twentieth century in what they thought the procedural aspects of representative democracy should be. However, Marxist analysts were particularly concerned by the lack of increased support for the socialist transformation of society. Their writings on democracy asked why democratic procedures alone had failed to secure the results predicted by Marxist theory and tended to explain the malfunctioning of democratic mechanisms by the active or passive resistance of capitalist interests. Hence, they emphasized the limits set on democracy by the economic and cultural domination of capitalists. The increasingly evident inability of democracy to produce a socialist transformation prompted orthodox Marxist writers (particularly the German Social Democrats) to seek causes in mainly economic factors—in the friction between formal equality of political rights and the lack of real power caused by class relations institutionalized by a capitalist economy.

But an increasing number of Western Marxists from the 1920s on stressed the role of ideological and cultural factors. Leaders of these theorists included György Lukács in Hungary and Antonio Gramsci in Italy. Lukács coined the concept of false consciousness to explain why workers did not vote so as to produce a socialist transformation of society: individual workers were too involved in their daily struggle for survival in a society biased against the workers' true long-term interests. Influenced by Gaetano Mosca, among others, Gramsci explained the power of the present class society over the minds of the oppressed by the cultural hegemony of the exploiting classes. It was the cultural folklore that prevented workers from even imagining an alternative to present reality.

Lukács's and Gramsci's insights were elaborated on by Louis Althusser, who was to have enormous influence on the thinking of Western Marxists in the 1960s and 1970s. Althusser argued that most of the institutions of capitalist society were designed to prevent workers from moving beyond the experience of deprivation to the desire for socialist change, brought about through democratic choice.

Still other Western Marxists remained suspicious of democratic procedures, as long as they were associated with the exploitative capitalist economy. According to this view, it would be foolish and unforgivable to invest the hopes of the impoverished and the exploited in parliamentary democracy, which would never go further toward improving the conditions of the oppressed than was absolutely necessary to stave off the immediate danger of rebellion. These theorists believed that the proletariat should seek freedom from capitalist domination through other means. Workers' involvement in collective, extraparliamentary, political actions would do the most to show the oppressed the nature of their oppression, to open the eyes of the masses to the true shape of social divisions and conflicts.

At the beginning of the twentieth century this view was upheld most conspicuously by the leaders of French syndicalism, a movement that preached direct action in the forms of a general strike or terrorism. Both general strikes and terrorism were seen as powerful means of simultaneously implementing socialist goals and educating the masses in socialist ideas. The syndicalists dismissed parliamentary democracy as a conspiracy to keep the capitalists in power.

The idea of the general strike figured prominently in Polish-German theorist Rosa Luxemburg's views of the socialist revolution, which she advanced in opposition to Vladimir Ilich Lenin's idea of revolution as the work of a small group of professional revolutionaries. However, Luxemburg's emphasis on the general strike did not stem from a concern with the limited revolutionary potential of parliamentary democracy. Rather, it stemmed from her premonition—later to be proved correct—that without the active involvement of the working class as a whole in the revolution allegedly accomplished in its name and for its sake, the resulting postrevolutionary regime could be only another form of dictatorship—over the proletariat, rather than of the proletariat.

Eventually, Western Marxists came to share the view that democratic procedures and freedoms were necessary to allow for unhampered socialist propaganda and the possibility of gaining popular support for the socialist transformation. But they believed that these procedures and freedoms alone were not sufficient, and certainly not a guarantee that the socialist society would ever be achieved. Democracy, in this view, was either a mixed blessing (the thought vividly expressed in Herbert Marcuse's memorable phrase of "repressive tolerance"), blocking the radical critique of existing society and the consideration of alternatives while ostensibly allowing and promoting them; or at best it was merely a formal condition of class struggle, with the results to be decided by factors located outside the political process. Whichever was the case, procedural democracy was seen as an instrument rather than the purpose of political struggle, and the theorists always distinguished between procedural and substantive democracy (the latter being seen as possible only after the abolition of capitalism).

The evolution of Marxist views on the role and significance of political democracy should be set against the background of Marxists' continued conviction that politics has no autonomy and is bound to play second fiddle to the maintenance or transformation of economic relations. But as electoral rights expanded in the West, Marxist-inspired movements increasingly participated in the daily life of democracy. This was not the case in Eastern Europe, which did not import democratic forms of government—unlike other modern inventions—from the West, and where democratic traditions were nonexistent or fragile.

Marxism in Russia

Czarist Russia, in particular, remained a police state into the twentieth century, with only rudimentary forms of political democracy and strictly limited electoral rights, shaped with a view toward protecting the advantages of the propertied classes. Russian political institutions came nowhere near the goal of majority rule. Moreover, the indispensable preconditions of democratic politics—such as habeas corpus and human rights in general—were systematically violated, and there was no well-developed and widely accepted liberal theory to promote them. In this context the incipient Marxist movements in Russia led a precarious existence, even when the movements were legally constituted. No wonder that Russian disciples of Marx believed that the possibility of social or economic change through democratic procedures was infinitely remote and not worthy

of serious—or at any rate immediate—consideration.

Russian Marxists were divided on the best way to achieve change, however. The Mensheviks proposed to wait until capitalism developed and generated both a majority in favor of socialism and the democratic instruments necessary for the realization of that majority will. On the other hand, the Bolsheviks, of whom Lenin was by far the most energetic and important figure, concluded that world capitalism had already become irreversibly imperialist and that therefore it was too late for a democratic bourgeois state to develop. Thus the democratic road to socialism, however plausible it might be in the West, was not possible in economically backward and politically underdeveloped Russia. There was no point in waiting for the state to become democratic, since politics simply reflected economic forces and interests, and a monopolistic capitalist economy, as in Russia, would neither create nor tolerate a democratic government. The only way to implement socialist goals was to have an elite group of professional revolutionaries use the various grievances of the population to mobilize the people and to show them that the socialist transformation of society was in their long-term interests.

Western options, so Lenin insisted, were not open to Russian socialists or to Marxists in other countries that were economically underdeveloped when they entered the monopolistic-imperialist stage of capitalism. In Russia the exploiting classes had to be dislodged from power by force, so that a new political elite, determined to bring about a Marxist future and capable of repelling the adversaries who sought to retain capitalism, could use the state to promote full economic development. Only once, in 1917, did Lenin try to explain how that government, destined to overthrow and replace czarist rule and to promote socialism, would be organized and conducted.

Lenin addressed this question in his unfinished book *The State and Revolution*, an extended, impassioned commentary on Marx's resounding endorsement of the 1871 experiments of the *communards* of Paris. In the book, Lenin described direct democracy, implemented through arming the people (that is, through the cancellation of the state monopoly of coercion) and characterized by rota (succession of officeholders), recall of the members of parliament by the voters, and remuneration of the members relative to the manual worker's wage. To Lenin, the "general will" (that is, the will one can deduce from an analysis of the proletariat's historical interests and mission) would be identical to the spontaneously expressed will of the masses, once they were free to express their opinions and to act on them.

In fact, Lenin's lofty goal of direct rule could not and did not stand up to the realities of postrevolutionary Russia. The almost total destruction of economic life brought about by the prolonged civil war between communist and anticommunist forces from 1918 to 1921 and the dissipation of Russia's small modern working class meant that the ruling Communist Party had to create virtually from scratch the class whose interests, purportedly, it took power to promote. The theoretically conceived "general will" proved to be jarringly at odds with the actual desires of virtually all classes of the population, and it was evident that true majority rule would not push postrevolutionary Russia toward socialism.

In addition, reconstructing ruined industries required an expert administration and stern labor discipline. By 1920 Leon Trotsky, then Lenin's first lieutenant and spokesman, openly declared the need to "militarize" labor, to reeducate the workers in order to increase productivity. The state was to hold power, and expert opinion would be preferred to the opinion of the working class.

Lenin also believed that democracy must always be subordinated to revolutionary interest.

With ruthless determination, Joseph Stalin implemented Lenin's and Trotsky's ideas. The Communist Party had become virtually identical to the state and acted as the sole employer and the distributor of all scarce goods. Accordingly, politics turned into the administration of economic production. This role allegedly demanded, but at any rate justified, the suppression of interests characterized by the government as "sectional" and "short-term." No opinion different from that of the rulers and planners could be expressed freely.

The extinction of democratic rights and procedures in the Soviet Union necessarily led to a police state of unprecedented ruthlessness and to a degree of oppression rarely matched in history. Alongside the Nazi regime in Germany, the Stalinist state is the most conspicuous embodiment of the antidemocratic, totalitarian tendency of modern times. Nonetheless, Soviet Marxists depicted their society as the fullest embodiment of the democratic idea. Following Marx, they saw the proper role of the socialist state as doing what its essential being dictated, regardless of what the proletariat thought should be done.

Neither Marx nor Lenin ever acknowledged that variety of opinion or diversity of political standpoint within the working class was necessary or desirable. Both believed that if freed from oppression and faced with its historical mission, the working class could only speak with one voice. What mattered, therefore, was not so much that all opinions be expressed and defended but that the government act on the true voice of the working class, even if that voice was not expressed by the class itself. The interests of the working class could be determined through knowledge of the relentless laws of history, described in Marxist theory. Soviet Marxists identified democracy with action on that knowledge, regardless of the suppression of individual and group rights and freedoms that accompanied it.

The important point is that suppression of human rights in the Soviet Union, the nation that best exemplified a Marxist state, did not generate much democratic freedom nor equality or justice.

See also Capitalism; Class; Communism; Leninism; Socialism; Theory, Twentieth Century European.

ZYGMUNT BAUMAN

BIBLIOGRAPHY

Arendt, Hannah. *On Revolution.* New York: Viking, 1963.

Beilharz, Peter. *Labour's Utopias: Bolshevism, Fabianism, Social Democracy.* London: Routledge, 1992.

Harding, Neil. "The Marxist-Leninist Detour." In *Democracy, the Unfinished Journey*, edited by John Dunn. New York and Oxford: Oxford University Press, 1992.

Lenin, V. I. *Collected Works.* Moscow: Foreign Languages Publishing House, 1960–1970; London: Lawrence and Wishart, 1970.

Marx, Karl, and Friedrich Engels. *Collected Works.* New York: International Publishers, 1975.

Offe, Claus. *Der Tunnel am Ende des Lichts: Erkundungen der politische Transformation im neuen Osten.* Frankfurt: Campus Verlag, 1994.

Polan, A. J. *Lenin and the End of Politics.* Berkeley: University of California Press, 1984.

Trotsky, Leon. *Terrorism and Communism.* Ann Arbor: University of Michigan Press, 1961.

Weber, Max. "Socialism." In *Political Writings.* Edited by Peter Lassman and Ronald Speirs. Cambridge: Cambridge University Press, 1994.

Wheen, Francis. *Karl Marx: A Life.* New York: Norton, 2000.

✦ Nationalism

A political doctrine that regards the nation as the primary object of loyalty and advances a cultural, social, political, and moral point of view in which nations play a central role. Semantically, the term *nationalism* comes from the Latin word *natio*, which is derived from the verb *nasci*—"to be born." The term came to be used to define a group of individuals born in the same area. In medieval universities, for example, communities of students coming from particular regions were defined as *nations*.

There is a debate as to when the term acquired political significance. Some argue that as early as the beginning of the sixteenth century the term *nation* was applied to the population of a particular state, thus becoming synonymous with the term *people*. Others trace this development to the American and French Revolutions. It is widely accepted, however, that by the end of the eighteenth century the term *nation* referred to a sovereign people or, alternatively, to the government of a sovereign state.

The tendency to identify *nation* with *state* resulted from a shift in the type of legitimacy sought and claimed by political institutions. In his philosophical writings, Jean-Jacques Rousseau (1712–1778) rejected the legitimacy of divinely or historically appointed rulers in favor of a new source of legitimacy—popular sovereignty. This ideal, which lies at the heart of democratic theory, turned into a nationalist one as the body of citizens came to be identified with the nation. The doctrine of self-rule was thus bound up with the ideal of national self-determination. It therefore became widely accepted that sovereignty resides essentially in the nation. The state, previously identified with the ruler, came to be seen as the institutional representation of the nation's will. The nation thus became the symbol of fellowship among all members of the political framework as well as the tie between the ruled and the ruler. Hence a new political norm was established that fostered the belief that the legitimating principle of politics and state making is nationalism.

This norm found its best expression in the nation-state, which evolved in the nineteenth century. The nation-state was supposed to allow for the development of the most stable and advanced form of democratic life. National homogeneity was to lead to internal harmony and solidarity as well as to patriotic feelings and readiness to defend the state from external threats.

How deep is the link between nationalist and democratic ideals? Some argue that democracy and nationalism are inherently linked because they share two basic tenets: the belief that members of the various social-economic classes are political equals and that sovereignty lies with the people. This claim is, however, somewhat misleading. The equality that membership in a nation accords is not necessarily a democratic one. Nationhood may grant individuals a feeling of belonging and a certain sense of mutuality, but it does not necessarily imply either political equality or democratic structures. The kind of equality that nationalism grants fellow nationals is not necessarily political but communal. If nationalism was necessary for the development of democracy, it was not because it justified political equality but because it gave a rationale for the division of the world into distinct political units in which democratic principles could be implemented. The belief in liberal democratic values may be fundamental to the culture of some nations—to the English, American, and French national cultures, for example—yet these values are not nationalist values in that they are not inherent to the national way of thinking. Nationalist movements have indeed been invariably populist in outlook, and their emergence, in a modern sense, has been tied

to the political baptism of the lower classes. They often have been characterized by attempts of the middle classes and intellectual leadership to induct members of the lower classes into political life and to channel popular energies into support for new states. Nonetheless, many of these movements were hostile to democracy and entertained totalitarian, fascist, and racist ideologies.

The growing rift between contemporary nationalist movements and democratic ideals does not indicate that these movements are illiberal and undemocratic by nature; rather, it follows a change in political circumstances that has not been met by appropriate theoretical and political developments. The identification between the citizens of a state and members of a nation has been frustrated as new states inhabited by more than one nation have been established, massive waves of immigration have taken place, and groups previously excluded from the political process have been included.

At the end of the twentieth century, hardly any state is homogeneous from a national point of view. Yet the idea that the nation is the only valid source of state legitimacy is still widely accepted. Consequently, every group of individuals who consider themselves a nation wants to establish their own independent state—a desire that leads to separatist and secessionist policies. Existing governments are also pressured to prove that they represent a nation rather than a mere gathering of individuals. Nation-states are therefore interested in homogenizing their population: they intervene in their population's language, interpretation of history, myths and symbols, or—to put it more broadly—in their culture. Modern nation-states thus are agents for cultural, linguistic, and sometimes religious unification. Their attempts to build a nation lead to the oppression of national minorities and, in extreme cases, to ethnic cleansing and genocide.

In a world of nationally heterogeneous states, nationalism and democracy can coexist only if the nationalist ideal is moderated and reshaped. This calls for a redefinition of the terms *state* and *nation* that will draw a sharp distinction between the two, with the former seen as a political organization and the latter as a cultural group that shares a common history, tradition, language, sometimes religion, and national consciousness. This conceptual redefinition will imply that the democratic ideal of self-rule, seen as the right of individuals to participate in decision-making processes, and the nationalist ideal of national self-determination, seen as a desire to retain an active and lively national life, should not be used synonymously. Divorcing the nationalist ideal from the demand for independent statehood and acknowledging the multinational nature of most states might allow nationalism to retain its alliance with democratic ideals and play a role in a world in which the need for cross-national cooperation on a variety of economic, ecological, and strategic questions cannot be ignored.

See also Fascism; Locke, John; Majority rule, minority rights; Popular sovereignty; Rousseau, Jean-Jacques.

YAEL TAMIR

BIBLIOGRAPHY

Anderson, Benedict R. *Imagined Communities: Reflections on the Origin and Spread of Nationalism.* London and New York: Verso, 1983.

Barry, Brian M. "Self-Government Revisited." In *Democracy and Power: Essays in Political Theory,* edited by Brian M. Barry. Oxford: Clarendon Press; New York: Oxford University Press, 1991.

Bauer, Otto. *The Question of Nationalities and Social Democracy.* Edited by Ephraim J. Nimni. Translated by Joseph O'Donnell. Minneapolis: University of Minnesota Press, 2000.

Gellner, Ernest. *Nations and Nationalism.* Oxford: Blackwell; Ithaca, N.Y.: Cornell University Press, 1983.

Greenfeld, Liah. *Nationalism: Five Roads to Modernity.* Cambridge, Mass., and London: Harvard University Press, 1992.

Smith, Anthony D. *National Identity.* Las Vegas: University of Nevada Press, 1991.

_____. *Theories of Nationalism.* 2d ed. London: Duckworth; New York: Holmes and Meier, 1983.

Tamir, Yael. "The Enigma of Nationalism." *World Politics* 47 (spring 1995): 418–440.

_____. *Liberal Nationalism.* Princeton: Princeton University Press, 1993.

✦ Natural law

A two-thousand-year-old ethical, political, and legal theory that, in its later forms, supplied the philosophical foundations of modern liberal democracy. The term *natural law* is often loosely applied to any theory that adheres to objective standards of morality. In its proper sense it designates a moral law that exists by nature and is known by nature to be binding on everyone. Thus defined, natural law is distinguished from civil law, whose statutes are enacted and enforced by some human legislator, and from divine law, which is communicated through sacred scriptures. Natural law is also distinguished from Immanuel Kant's moral law, which presents itself as a law of reason rather than a law of nature.

Natural law was for centuries the cornerstone of Western ethical and political thought. It inspired some of the most famous documents of modern liberalism, including the American Declaration of Independence (1776) and the various versions of the French Declaration of the Rights of Man and the Citizen (1789, 1793, 1795). Today it is for the most part an object of historical study rather than a source of authoritative moral judgment. Although efforts to revive it have not been lacking, nothing indicates that it is about to regain the prominence it once occupied in the Western tradition. Even the Roman Catholic Church, where until recently it continued to hold sway, now appeals less and less frequently to natural law in its official documents.

The doctrine of natural law that informs modern constitutions is the dynamic and reformist doctrine of the seventeenth- and eighteenth-century Enlightenment. The original theory of natural law was considerably more conservative than that of the Enlightenment. The theory emerged by way of transformation of Plato's and Aristotle's teaching of natural right. Its most conspicuous departure from the classical teaching is that it not only points to what is intrinsically right or wrong but commands the performance of the one and the avoidance of the other under threat of sanction.

Classical and Medieval Background

Modern scholars usually attribute the invention of natural law to the Stoic philosophers. There is no solid evidence, however, that the old Stoics ever used the term *natural law*. Stoicism nevertheless furnished one of the fundamental premises of that theory: the notion of a providential god who guarantees the moral consistency of the universe by ensuring that the just are rewarded and the wicked punished, if not in this life at least in the next. The mode and severity of the punishments in question are not specified by the natural law itself. They are left to be determined by the civil law and may vary according to circumstances. Capital punishment, for example, is neither imposed nor forbidden by natural law.

The earliest extant accounts of natural law are found in the *Republic* and *Laws* of the Roman statesman and philosopher Marcus Tullius Cicero (106–43 B.C.). In the *Republic* the jurist Laelius,

one of the dialogue's main characters, uses natural law to defend the justice of Rome's conquest of the civilized world. It is doubtful whether Cicero, a critic of the Stoic notion of divine providence, personally subscribed to Laelius's theory. Cicero seems to have endorsed it less as a true doctrine than as a rhetorical tool with which to curb the excesses of Roman imperialism.

From Cicero, the natural law was absorbed into the Roman legal tradition, and soon thereafter it became a standard feature of the theological tradition of the Christian West. St. Augustine (354–430 A.D.) invoked it to defend his own just-war theory (*Contra Faustum*) and also to absolve God of the blame that he would have incurred for the sins of his creatures had he left them invincibly ignorant of the basic principles of moral behavior. For Augustine, compliance with the natural law, which requires the subordination of the lower to the higher both within the individual and in society at large, is synonymous with the whole of human perfection.

The premodern doctrine of natural law achieved its classic formulation in the works of Thomas Aquinas (1225–1274). Thomas distinguishes between the primary principles of the natural law, which are immutable, and its secondary principles, which are subject to change. The primary principles are said to be self-evident and form the object of a special virtue that the Christian tradition called *synderesis*, the storehouse of the most general principles of the moral order. These principles are intimated to human beings through the natural inclinations by which they are directed to the most general ends of human existence, the highest of which are the knowledge of the truth and life in society. Nowhere are we given an exhaustive list of these principles, although Thomas does say that the moral law of the Old Testament, which is summed up in the Ten Commandments, belongs to the natural law.

Thomas's teaching met with much resistance on the part of later medieval philosophers and theologians. Marsilius of Padua (c.1280–c.1343) rejected it on the Aristotelian ground that human reason alone is unable to prove that God is a legislator. Duns Scotus (1266?–1308) and William of Ockham (c.1285–1349?) objected to it, asserting that by binding God to its precepts natural law conflicted with the biblical notions of divine freedom and omnipotence. Accordingly, Scotus reduced the natural law to a single negative precept, the one that prohibits the hatred of God. Ockham went even further, asserting that God could command us to hate him if he so desired.

The sixteenth and seventeenth centuries witnessed a return to the Thomist teaching, spearheaded by a number of influential commentators among whom Francisco de Vitoria and Francisco Suárez stand out, along with Hugo Grotius. The motivation for this revival was furnished by the wars of religion that were ravaging Europe and by the cruelties inflicted on the American Indians by the Spanish conquistadors. The rules of just warfare were spelled out in ever greater detail, and the old Roman notion of the "law of nations" was transformed into what became known as international law.

Modern Theory

A milestone in the development of modern democratic theory was the appearance of the natural law teachings propounded by the seventeenth-century founders of modern liberalism, especially the teachings of Thomas Hobbes and John Locke. Breaking decisively with tradition, Hobbes and Locke sought to establish political thought on a new, more solid foundation. Human beings no longer were said to be political and social by nature. They were seen as solitary individuals who once existed in a prepolitical "state of nature" and were actuated, not by a desire for some preexisting end in the attainment of which they achieved their perfection, but by a premoral passion, the desire for self-preservation, from which the "right" of self-preservation arises. In the thinking of Hobbes and Locke, individual rights, conferred by nature, replace duties as the primordial moral phenomenon. Civil society is not something natural and desirable for its own sake. It comes into being by way of a contract made by human beings who enter freely into it for no reason other than to escape the dangers that threaten them in the state of nature. As for the natural law, it has nothing to do with the self-evident principles of which the medieval philosophers spoke, but it is identified with the sum of the conclusions that human reason arrives at by a process of deduction from the right of self-preservation. In the *Leviathan* (1651), Hobbes lists nineteen such principles, all of them calculated to ensure the individual's security and physical well-being.

Unlike the old doctrine of natural law, which was not essentially egalitarian and whose compatibility with any decent regime, whether democratic or aristocratic, was never doubted, the new doctrine held that there was but one just and legitimate regime—that is, liberal democracy or popular sovereignty—in the name of which authoritarian or nondemocratic regimes could rightfully be overthrown (as in fact they were in America and France during the last quarter of the eighteenth century).

The last and the most radical of the modern theorists of natural law was Jean-Jacques Rousseau, who criticized the Hobbesian and Lockean schemes for fostering a bourgeois mentality that undermines civic virtue and therewith the freedom and equality for the protection of which civil society was established. The solution to the problem, Rousseau thought, lay in forming small societies in which all citizens would participate on an equal basis in accordance with the principle of "one man, one vote."

The Demise of Natural Law

Rousseau argued that neither Hobbes nor Locke had found the true state of nature for the simple reason that they took as their standard a human nature that was already corrupted by society. Rousseau's search led him backward in time to a stage that antedates not only the formation of civil society but the emergence of rationality and, indeed, of humanity itself. But if the state of nature is not a properly human state, one fails to see how it could serve as a reliable guide to human behavior. The critical next step was taken by Immanuel Kant, who abandoned nature as the touchstone of the moral rightness of human actions and replaced it with the categorical imperative, or the laws of universal reason.

Further challenges to natural law came from two of the most powerful intellectual forces of modern times, historicism, or historical relativism, and social science positivism. Historicism originated as a reaction against the atrocities spawned by the French Revolution. It tried to forestall the possibility of such revolutions in the future by rejecting the notion of a permanently valid natural or higher law to which a direct appeal could be made from existing civil laws. Social science positivism denies scientific status to any proposition that is not empirically verifiable and relegates all principles of natural law—none of which is subject to this kind of empirical verification—to the subjective realm of "value judgments."

This is not to say that the idea of natural law has simply vanished from our midst. The Neo-Thomist movement of the nineteenth and twentieth centuries did much to keep its memory alive, even though the literature that it produced is more notable for its abundance than for its originality. Some scholars, such as R. W. and A. J. Carlyle and Edward S. Corwin, have argued that the tradition of natural law continued unbroken from its inception in pre-Christian antiquity to the end of the eighteenth century. Jacques Maritain and John Finnis have since offered revised versions of both the medieval doctrine of natural law and the initially antithetical doctrine of modern rights in a valiant attempt to reconcile the two streams of thought, though with limited effect. Rightly or wrongly, most contemporary thinkers remain suspicious of natural law, finding it either too vague to be of any real use, too inflexible for the proper conduct of the affairs of state, or potentially subversive.

Yet experience has shown that dispensing with natural law altogether is not an easy matter: without it one is deprived of a valuable moral argument against the blatantly unjust laws under which people often are made to live. Some Germans resorted to natural law in the 1940s to justify their resistance to the Nazi regime and the assassination attempt on Hitler's life. After the war the same argument was pressed into service at the trials of Nazi war criminals at Nuremberg, the legality of which could not be established on the basis of existing national and international laws. Martin Luther King, Jr., referred to natural law in his famous letter from the Birmingham City Jail, citing Thomas Aquinas in support of the view that a human law not rooted in eternal and natural law is an unjust law. Similar problems arise when a country, either alone or with the help of others, intervenes in the domestic affairs of another country to prevent crimes against humanity. Finally, a serious question arises as to whether judges, in upholding or striking down civil laws, can consistently avoid being drawn into some kind of reasoning based implicitly on natural law.

See also Aristotle; Contractarianism; Hobbes, Thomas; Human Rights; Kant, Immanuel; King,

Martin Luther, Jr.; Liberalism; Locke, John; Obligation; Plato; Rousseau, Jean-Jacques.

ERNEST L. FORTIN

BIBLIOGRAPHY

Carlyle, A. J., and R. W. *A History of Mediaeval Political Theory in the West.* 6 vols. 2d ed. New York: Barnes and Noble, 1950.

Corwin, Edward S. *The "Higher Law" Background of American Constitutional Law.* Ithaca, N.Y.: Cornell University Press, 1955.

Crowe, Michael B. *The Changing Profile of the Natural Law.* The Hague: M. Nijhoff, 1977.

George, Robert P. *In Defense of Natural Law.* New York: Oxford University Press, 2001.

Jaffa, Harry V. *Thomism and Aristotelianism: A Study of the Commentary by Thomas Aquinas on the Nicomachean Ethics.* Chicago: University of Chicago Press, 1952.

Maritain, Jacques. *The Rights of Man and Natural Law.* New York: Scribner's, 1943.

Nussbaum, Arthur. *A Concise History of the Law of Nations.* New York: Macmillan, 1954.

Sigmund, Paul E. *Natural Law in Political Thought.* Cambridge, Mass.: Winthrop, 1971.

Strauss, Leo. "Natural Law." In *International Encyclopedia of the Social Sciences.* New York: Macmillan, 1968.

✦ Parliamentarism and presidentialism

Parliamentarism and presidentialism are the two dominant forms of democratic governmental systems. In presidential systems the head of government (called the president) and the legislature (often called the Congress) are elected for terms of office prescribed by the constitution. Except under exceptional circumstances the Congress cannot force the president to resign, although it can remove him or her by the highly unusual process of impeachment. In most presidential systems the president cannot dissolve Congress. In parliamentary systems, on the contrary, the head of government (who may be called prime minister, premier, chancellor, president of the government, or—in Ireland—*taoiseach)* can be dismissed from office by a vote of no confidence in the legislature. Normally, the prime minister can also dissolve the legislature and call for new elections. Presidentialism is based on a stricter separation of powers, whereas parliamentarism, although distinguishing between the powers of the executive and legislature, is based on cooperation between the two branches of government.

A basic characteristic of presidentialism is that the president is popularly elected, either directly or through an electoral college, which is elected for that sole purpose. In parliamentary systems the people elect only their own representatives—the members of parliament—who in turn select the head of the government.

In parliamentary systems there is a distinction between the head of state, who represents the nation symbolically, and the chief executive, or prime minister, who governs. The head of state, who can be a monarch or a president of the republic, is generally not popularly elected and has no power to govern, although he or she exercises some influence, offers advice, and often acts as a moderator by working with political leaders to craft an agreement or, occasionally, trying to influence public opinion. Japan, Spain, the United Kingdom, the countries of Scandinavia, and the Benelux countries are parliamentary monarchies. Among the parliamentary republics are Hungary, Italy, the Czech Republic, the Federal Republic of

Germany, and the French Third and Fourth Republics.

Terms of Office for Presidents and Prime Ministers

In many presidential systems, presidents cannot be reelected at all, or they cannot be reelected for more than a certain number of terms or without a period of time elapsing after the end of the first term. In parliamentary systems the prime minister can stay in office as long as his or her party, or the coalition supporting the government, has a majority in the parliament.

One disadvantage of the presidential system is that a successful and competent politician who has the trust of the people often cannot continue in office. A "lame duck" president, who cannot run again, has limited power. A former president is not likely to be the leader of his or her party in the Congress and may not be able to use the experience and knowledge acquired in office. Another problem is that an incompetent president has to finish his or her term unless there are grounds for impeachment; such a president is often unable to govern effectively. Similarly, if a president faces a hostile Congress, the president may be unable to govern, however competent or popular he or she is. Unlike a prime minister, a president cannot dissolve the legislature and call for new elections.

In parliamentary systems the legislators can dismiss the prime minister through a vote of no confidence. The disadvantage, however, is that the parliament can be too powerful and replace prime ministers too often. In multiparty systems or cases with little party discipline, coalitions of parties can realign themselves continuously, causing many changes in leadership in a short time. This has been the situation in the Third and Fourth Republics of France and in Italy.

Some modern constitutions, like those of Germany and Spain, have introduced mechanisms to ensure government stability. In Germany, for example, electoral laws establish a threshold of representation to keep small, often extremist parties out of the parliament. Or the parliament may be allowed to vote no confidence only by electing a successor to the current prime minister.

Other Members of the Executive Branch

Many presidential systems have a vice president. Sometimes the vice president and the president are elected separately. If they are elected separately, they may be of different parties and the vice president may try to undermine the president. Normally, however, they are elected on the same ticket, with the president playing a large role in choosing a vice presidential running mate. This practice may result in a vice president who would not have been chosen on the basis of qualifications. For example, María Estela (Isabel) Martínez de Perón, the wife of Juan Domingo Perón, succeeded him to the presidency of Argentina in July 1974. Or it may result in a vice president who is selected mainly to balance the ticket in one way or another—perhaps geographically or in terms of political appeal to the voters. An example is Boris Yeltsin's selection of Aleksandr Rutskoi as his running mate in 1993. In the fall of 1993 Rutskoi, together with Ruslan Khasbulatov, president of the legislature, led a revolt against Yeltsin.

The automatic succession of the vice president to the presidency if the president is unable to complete the term of office can therefore bring to the highest office someone who never could have won election independently, as happened in Brazil in the cases of both José Sarney in 1985 and Itamar Franco in 1990. In parliamentary systems the death or resignation of a prime minister does not necessarily involve discontinuity or even new elections. The ruling party or coalition can simply elect a new prime minister, as happened when

John Major replaced Margaret Thatcher in the United Kingdom in 1991.

The cabinet, which helps the president or prime minister govern, is much more independent in a parliamentary system than in a presidential system. In a parliamentary system the prime minister is merely one among equals. Many cabinet members will serve under more than one prime minister, since they are likely to be important leaders in their party and members of parliament with experience in preparing legislation. In a presidential system, on the other hand, the president usually has considerable freedom to appoint members of the cabinet. This means that few cabinet members will have served another president, and they may lack experience in government.

Choosing a President or Prime Minister

In presidential systems, many voters focus on the personalities of the presidential candidates more than on their parties and programs. It is possible for someone who has never held any elective office, or only a local office, to win a substantial number of votes for president (like Ross Perot in the United States in 1992 and Stanislaw Tyminski in Poland in 1990). If such a candidate is elected (as was Alberto Fujimori in Peru in 1990), he or she is likely to come into office without the support of any party in the legislature and may be unable to govern effectively. In parliamentary systems, on the other hand, a politician who wants to become prime minister must build support within a party or coalition of parties, which will share the responsibility of governing.

Unsuccessful candidates for the presidency may leave politics, and their parties may be left largely leaderless. In parliamentary systems, however, defeated candidates become the leaders of the opposition.

An elected prime minister knows he or she has the support only of those who voted for the governing party or coalition of parties and of the members of parliament who supported his or her candidacy. An elected president, by contrast, represents all the people, even if he or she may not have obtained a majority of the votes cast. Bolivia is an exception here. When no presidential candidate receives an absolute majority of the popular vote, the legislature decides between the two front-runners.

Governing

In a parliamentary system, only the parliament has democratic legitimacy, and it supports the prime minister or withdraws that support by a vote of no confidence. In a presidential system the president and the legislature both have democratic legitimacy, and it is not possible to say which more accurately represents the will of the people. If they conflict, the only solution is to turn to the judicial power—the constitutional or supreme court. In Latin America, where the judicial power does not always enjoy high prestige, such conflicts have often been resolved by the armed forces. The armed forces sometimes support the president and close the legislature, sometimes dismiss both the president and the legislature and install an interim government, or sometimes assume dictatorial power for a long period of time.

The separation of powers in the United States is designed to weaken the power of presidents. If a president has only minority support in Congress, his or her power to implement policies can be severely limited. This inability to implement policies can be an important source of frustration among voters and a cause of political instability.

On the other hand, the greater independence of Congress means that many special or regional interests are better represented than in a parliamentary system, since members of Congress can vote against their party and president to win favor with constituents. In parliamentary systems, party discipline is enforced to support governments, thus weakening the "representative" function and causing voters to feel ignored. This problem may be magnified in cases where no party has a majority and the government relies on a coalition of parties.

Other Forms of Democratic Institutions

Although presidentialism and parliamentarism are the dominant forms of democratic government, a few other forms can be mentioned. In some systems, voters elect more than one person to executive office. In Crete between 1960 and 1963 a Greek Cypriot was president and a Turkish Cypriot was vice president. In Uruguay from 1952 to 1967 a nine-member body called the *Colegiado* governed. There are also executives elected by the legislature who have a fixed term of office and thus cannot be dismissed by a vote of no confidence; examples are the president of Lebanon and the seven-member Swiss Federal Council.

Another form of government has been called dual-executive, premier-presidential, or semipresidential. In this type of system there is both a popularly elected president and a prime minister selected and supported by a majority in the legislature. The president assumes a major role in foreign affairs and defense, while the prime minister deals with other matters. In this system the president may belong to one party and the prime minister to another, as happened in France between 1986 and 1988 and again from 1993 to 1995, with socialist President François Mitterrand and conservative prime ministers Jacques Chirac and Edouard Balladur. This arrangement is called *cohabitation*. Some argue that when the two offices are held by the same party, the system is like presidentialism, whereas if the two offices represent different parties, it is more like parliamentarism. In either case the system requires considerable flexibility on the part of both leaders.

The semipresidential system was originally introduced in Germany in 1918, but it began to fail as the parties abdicated their responsibility to govern and let the president use emergency powers—a situation that led to the Nazis' rise to power. Other semipresidential regimes—such as those in Austria, Finland, France, Greece, Iceland, and Ireland—were more successful. It is perhaps no accident that a number of these regimes were founded in moments of national crisis and that quite a few of the first presidents were military men (like Carl Gustav Mannerheim in Finland, Charles de Gaulle in France, and António Ramalho Eanes in Portugal).

There is considerable debate about which type of government is more stable. Some argue that presidential and parliamentary systems are equally stable, while others say that presidential systems have a greater risk of instability. Research on the question is only beginning, though a recent study reveals a better performance by parliamentary systems. It will be interesting to see how successful presidential or semipresidential systems are in the successor states of the Soviet Union.

See also Legislatures and parliaments.

JUAN J. LINZ

BIBLIOGRAPHY

Beyme, Klaus von. *Die parlamentarischen Regierungssysteme in Europa.* Munich: R. Piper, 1970.

Cronin, T. E. *The State of the Presidency.* Boston: Little, Brown, 1980.

Duverger, Maurice, ed. *Les regimes semi-presidentiels.* Paris: Presses Universitaires de France, 1986.

Jennings, Ivor. *Cabinet Government.* 3d ed. Cambridge: Cambridge University Press, 1959.

Linz, Juan J., and Arturo Valenzuela, eds. *The Failure of Presidential Democracy: Comparative Perspectives.* Vol. 1. Baltimore: Johns Hopkins University Press, 1994.

Mainwaring, Scott. "Presidentialism in Latin America." *Latin American Research Review* 25 (1990): 157–179.

Neustadt, Richard. *Presidential Power: The Politics of Leadership.* New York: Wiley, 1960.

The Postcommunist Presidency. Special issue of *East European Constitutional Review* 2–3 (fall 1993–winter 1994).

Riggs, Fred W. "The Survival of Presidentialism in America: Para-constitutional Practices." *International Political Science Review* 9 (October 1988): 247–278.

Rose, Richard, and Ezra N. Suleiman, eds. *Presidents and Prime Ministers.* Washington, D.C.: American Enterprise Institute, 1980.

Shugart, Matthew Soberg, and John M. Carey. *Presidents and Assemblies: Constitutional Design and Electoral Dynamics.* Cambridge: Cambridge University Press, 1992.

Verney, Douglas V. *The Analysis of Political Systems.* London: Routledge and Kegan Paul, 1979.

✦ Populism

A political movement that emphasizes the interests, cultural traits, and spontaneous feelings of the common people, as opposed to those of a privileged elite. For legitimation, populist movements often appeal to the majority will directly—through mass gatherings, referendums, or other forms of popular democracy—without much concern for checks and balances or the rights of minorities.

The Nineteenth-Century Origins

The term *populism* was first used in Russia in the 1870s to refer to the beliefs of a heterogeneous group of thinkers and political activists, called *narodniki*, who rejected the use of foreign ideologies in the struggle for democracy or socialism. Most of them believed that capitalism was not necessarily a progressive stage of development and that a better social system could be built on the basis of national popular traditions and institutions, such as the village landowning community.

Aleksandr Herzen (1812–1870) pioneered most of these ideas, which clashed with the Marxist tenet that a revolution in a backward country had to be capitalist because no historical stages of development could be skipped. A later generation incorporated elements of anarchism as interpreted by Mikhail Bakunin (1814–1876). Bakunin valued the spontaneity of the masses, including the large socially uprooted population in Russia, over the meticulous and deadening organizational skills of the Germanic social democrats.

In a completely different context, the term *populism* was also applied to a political movement that thrived in the United States at the end of the nineteenth century. American populism had many anti-capitalist components, though its doctrines did not converge with those of socialism. Its leaders espoused traditional values, and many held authoritarian views, including elements of anti-Semitism and white supremacy.

The U.S. populist movement had no single, towering national leader; rather, it relied on local organizers, many of whom had little formal education, to undertake necessary tasks and provide its intellectual orientation through an independent press. The movement was based on the support of farmers and small-town businesspeople. It flourished at a time when the growth of capitalism was hurting producers who could not compete with modern industry.

Farmers in particular resented their indebtedness to merchants and bankers. They also disliked the high cost of rail transport, which they blamed on monopoly operation. To act on their views, the farmers organized a widespread movement.

They formed cooperatives, engaged in intensive educational efforts, and developed a partisan press.

In 1892 a People's Party was formed, supporting looser money and credit policies. It also proposed state or municipal ownership of major transport, communications, and other utilities. In 1896, after much internal debate, the party supported William Jennings Bryan for president. Bryan was a Democrat who had renovated his party by breaking with the more conservative orientation of President Grover Cleveland. Bryan accepted part of the Populists' program, especially in matters relating to free silver coinage, but he did not go along with the more radical points of the new party's platform.

Activists resisted the decision to become involved in traditional politics. Electoral defeat followed, and the Populist movement began to deteriorate, becoming internally divided. By the end of the nineteenth century both the movement's political program and the farmer cooperative organization that had backed it were moribund. In several states, Populist traits persisted for decades after the movement's demise, most notably in Louisiana under Huey Long's authoritarian reign as governor in the late 1920s and early 1930s.

One possible development of the basic populist mentality was the adoption of socialist values. This is what happened in Canada in the second quarter of the twentieth century, with the growth of the Cooperative Commonwealth Federation. Similar populist inspiration can be traced in the more conservative Social Credit Party, a strong element in the Canadian province of Alberta, and in other political groups formed in Quebec.

Populism in Developing Nations

Today, the term *populism* generally refers to a third kind of political phenomenon, common in Latin America and, in a different form, in Asia and Africa. In this sense it refers to political parties that are not socialist but are based on the support of the common people and are hostile to the dominant classes. On closer inspection, these parties are seen to be based on a constituency that has little experience of associating for civic purposes—in sharp contrast to the basis of American populism.

Because populist movements in developing countries are not based on autonomous self-organization, they need some other way of holding supporters together. That social cement is the presence of an undisputed leader, who establishes a charismatic relationship with followers. Such movements have two additional requirements. First, the mass of common people must be socially mobilized, that is, cut off from traditional loyalties and prepared to accept new types of leadership. Second, the leaders must emerge from the upper or middle layers of society, but they must be at odds with the majority of their own class of origin. Situations that may produce this effect are a traditional aristocracy menaced by upstart moneyed sectors, a clergy swept aside by modernization processes, industrialists in dire need of protection against foreign competition, military personnel whose economic position does not equal their potential power, high school or college graduates with few job opportunities, or ethnic elites deprived of recognition by a racist ruling class.

Depending on how the first and second requirements are combined, four different kinds of populist parties may emerge: multiclass integrative parties, middle-class populist parties, working-class populist parties, or social revolutionary parties.

Multiclass integrative parties. Multiclass integrative parties include a large portion of the bourgeoisie and the middle class. They are likely to emerge when there has been a nationwide confrontation against a closed oligarchical regime, as in Mexico, or against foreign domination, as in India. The corresponding parties, the Mexican Institutional Revolutionary Party and the Indian Congress Party, have been capable of mustering widespread popular support, though controlling their followers through state-dominated mass organizations. Typically, small parties at the right and left complete the political system, without much capacity to compete for power. In the long run, as economic development takes place and new entrepreneurial and bureaucratic groups are consolidated, the multiclass integrative party tends to grow more conservative and eventually to become divided.

A variation of this kind of movement is a military national popular regime, which occurred in Egypt under Gamal Abdel Nasser, who came to power in the 1950s. This situation is typical of developing Asian and African countries, where the military replaces the nonexistent bourgeoisie. The military creates a bureaucracy, which often branches off into private enterprise. In Asia and Africa both religion and ethnicity separate the local upper classes from the foreign dominant powers, helping to recruit leaders into this type of anti–status quo political movement. But long exercise of power may blunt the movement's cutting edge and create the conditions for the emergence of an alternative form of military regime or a fundamentalist theocracy. Such conditions gave rise to the Iranian revolution, which in 1979 established Shi'ite Islam as the official state religion.

Middle-class populist parties. In countries torn by internal class divisions, if a multiclass integrative party has not taken hold, a populist movement must be based on the experience of the middle class. Most likely, it will recruit support from among the less well-off provincial members of

that class, as well as unemployed or underemployed intellectuals and college graduates. This is the case of Peru's Aprista Party, which combined a tightly organized middle-class component and a popular component united to its leader, Víctor Raúl Haya de la Torre (1895–1980), by a strong political religion. Venezuela's Democratic Action, Costa Rica's National Liberation Party, and Bolivia's Nationalist Revolutionary Movement are other cases of parties formed according to this pattern.

Generally, these parties receive little support from the bourgeoisie and from the better-off members of the middle class. As a result, there is ample room for a more conservative party, or parties, capable of winning elections. The conditions for a democratic alternation in power are thus more likely to develop in this situation than when a multiclass integrative party rules the scene. As the party system settles down within a democratic format, and economic growth and modernization continue, the populist character of these parties tends to diminish, particularly after the death of their founder. Their organization becomes stronger, new leaders emerge in a more routine fashion, and they may move toward another form of party.

Working-class populist parties. The best example of a working-class populist party is Argentina's Peronist movement. Argentina has a relatively high level of urban and educational development and a strong working class that easily becomes a significant actor in politics. In such a milieu a populist movement cannot hope to include both the majority of the working class and large numbers of the middle or upper classes. Strategic minorities of the middle and upper classes, and of the military, however, can be an integral part of this kind of party. After the death of its leader, Juan Domingo Perón (1895–1974), Peronism became, like the Aprista Party in Peru, a more moderate movement than it had been originally. It lacks strong support among the upper and middle classes, leaving an opening for a centrist or conservative party. A conservative party, however, has not yet proved its ability to win a sizable vote in Argentina.

Brazilian Varguism is often considered a populist movement, comparable to Peronism. In fact, the two are quite different. Brazil has a much lower level of urban and educational development than does Argentina. Its populist movement was an alliance of two parties, the Social Democrático and the Trabalhista Brasileiro (Brazilian Labor Party), set up in 1945 by Getúlio Vargas (1883–1954). The alliance resembled a multiclass integrative coalition, along the lines of the Mexican Institutional Revolutionary Party. The Trabalhista Brasileiro branch of Varguism evolved toward a working-class populist party, especially under João Goulart's presidency (1961–1964), but it has not been able to gain more than a small slice of the electorate. It has lost most of its union support to a leftist party, the Partido dos Trabalhadores (Workers' Party).

Social revolutionary parties. Social revolutionary parties are found in developing countries, such as Cuba, Central American countries, Caribbean nations, and some parts of South America. Their strategic component is a determined elite, recruited from parts of the middle class experiencing severe occupational tensions. Under a highly repressive regime, an explosion is likely to occur, if and when the dictatorship faces a crisis. These parties usually have a Marxist-Leninist ideology, so it might seem wrong to classify them as populist. But the charismatic relationship between these parties' leaders and the mass of followers is typical of populist movements. The organizational structure of social revolutionary parties is generally solid, with strong control from the top. After decades of exercise of power they tend to become multiclass integrative parties, including postrevolutionary classes.

Historical and Comparative Evidence

Since the early nineteenth century, forms of populism have often appeared in Latin America. Many have been conservative movements, notably the regime led by Juan Manuel de Rosas (1793–1877) in Argentina or the more radical but short-lived one initiated by José Gervasio Artigas (1764–1850) in Uruguay.

Another well-studied forerunner of populism is the political movement built by Louis Napoleon (1808–1873), who staged a coup in France in 1851 and was confirmed by a massive vote. His case is often seen as an early example of plebiscitary democracy, making a direct appeal to voter support without regard for due legal process and checks and balances. His regime, however, is better seen as a combination of authoritarianism and mass consensus, that is, popular Caesarism. He built his following in opposition to the traditional conservatives and liberals as well as the socialist left. To describe the process by which Louis Napoleon obtained such overwhelming support, Karl Marx coined the term *Bonapartism*. Marx argued that Bonapartism could develop when there was a peculiar equilibrium between classes, thus allowing an apparently non–class-determined political leader to appear as an arbiter of conflicting interests. Marx saw Bonapartism as a temporary phenomenon, coinciding with the final crisis of capitalism, when classical conservative or liberal-conservative parties could no longer obtain the support of a large part of the electorate.

A later generation of Marxist scholars, especially the Austro-Marxists of the period between World Wars I and II, such as Otto Bauer (1881–1938) and Karl Renner (1870–1950), explored the issue of national self-determination.

They were concerned about the lack of internationalist revolutionary spirit among the working class. They saw that with increasing democratization, nationalism, which had been restricted to bourgeois parties, would also take hold of popular parties. As democratization grew, the mass of the population would be freer to assert themselves. Until that time internationalism had been a trait of working-class parties because such parties represented only a minority of their class and deferred to the intelligentsia. Nationalism might occur under the banner of social democracy, but it could also express itself in populist, or "national popular," movements.

Fascism and Nazism have sometimes been seen as having a populist component. Nazism can be described as an extremist movement of the center, with enemies on both sides. Its main foe, however, has been the trade union–organized left. The term *populism* as used today refers to political movements born of confrontation with conservative elements, even though the populist groups may eventually come to terms with their opponents or even form alliances with them.

The spread of populism in developing countries is sometimes attributed to their lack of civic traditions and to cultural traits that emphasize individual leaders. It has also been seen as the result of military dominance, because in many cases the leader of a populist party comes from the armed forces.

Without denying these facts, a sociological analysis of the underlying causes of populism must consider other aspects of the social structure. It should also explain the absence of populism in some developing countries. According to Gino Germani, a founder of this type of study in Latin America, populism results mainly from social mobilization. Social mobilization is a process by which large masses of the population, affected by internal migration or improved mass communication, break with their traditional loyalties and become available for new involvements. Since the masses have had little experience with voluntary associations, they are likely to follow some highly visible national leader, preferably one who wears the trappings of the dominant classes but sets himself against the elite. The leader emerges as the result of social tensions, which set some members of the upper classes against the majority conservative opinion of their peers.

Populism must not be confused with other types of popular parties, which rely largely on autonomous organization by workers and intellectuals. Examples of such parties are the social democrats and reborn communists of the developed world. In Latin America, Chile's socialist and communist parties approach this pattern, and so do the Uruguayan Broad Front and the Brazilian Workers' Party.

The Democratic Party in the United States provides a model of a popular party that is neither populist nor social democratic, has strong trade union support, and holds wide appeal across classes. In Latin America some populist movements are evolving in that direction after the death of their leaders; they are dropping their mobilizational and charismatic features. Examples of such movements are Venezuela's Democratic Action and Argentina's Peronism.

Populism has a paradoxical aspect. It is usually authoritarian and antimodern, thus representing a threat to democracy. Yet it often provides the working class or the peasantry with their only available political channel. In such cases it becomes a necessary element in building a democratic polity.

See also Anarchy; Authoritarianism; Leadership; Majority rule, minority rights; Democracy, Social.

TORCUATO S. DI TELLA

BIBLIOGRAPHY

Bottomore, Tom, and Patrick Goode, eds. *Austro-Marxism*. Oxford: Clarendon Press, 1978.

Collier, Ruth Berins, and David Collier. *Shaping the Political Arena: Critical Junctures, the Labor Movement, and Regime Dynamics in Latin America*. Princeton: Princeton University Press, 1991.

Di Tella, Torcuato S. *Latin American Politics: A Theoretical Framework*. Austin: University of Texas Press, 1990.

Germani, Gino. *Authoritarianism, Fascism, and National Populism*. New Brunswick, N.J.: Transaction, 1978.

Goodwyn, Lawrence. *Democratic Promise: The Populist Moment in America*. New York: Oxford University Press, 1976.

Ionescu, Ghita, and Ernest Gellner, eds. *Populism: Its Meanings and National Characteristics*. London: Weidenfeld and Nicolson, 1969.

Venturi, Franco. *Roots of Revolution: A History of the Populist and Socialist Movements in Nineteenth-Century Russia*. London: Weidenfeld and Nicolson, 1960.

Zeldin, Theodor. *The Political System of Napoleon III*. London: St. Martin's, 1958.

✦ Postmodernism

A philosophical, cultural, and political movement marked by aversion to absolute truths, fixed meanings, and the authority of Western reason. The term *postmodernism* is a general label applied to a broad range of ideas encompassing academia, politics, and the arts that developed in reaction to modernism. Postmodernism's skepticism in regard to absolute truth has made it a natural ally of democratic thinking.

Modernism itself was a broad-based movement in which linguistic philosophers, anthropologists, architects, and composers sought to define meaning and truth by means of fixed rules of interpretation. The term *postmodernism* achieved widespread recognition as a movement only in the 1980s, when it began to be used by those thinkers who questioned the very possibility of finding such rules or lawlike scientific principles. Postmodern philosophers, literary critics, anthropologists, and psychologists, often under the name "deconstructionists," have followed the French philosopher and literary critic Jacques Derrida in teasing out linguistic tensions that simultaneously make possible and undermine fixed meanings.

Derrida's best-known example traces Western philosophy's preference for speech over writing (because writers are not there to explain their words). Since Plato, philosophers have viewed speech as a transparent conveyor of meaning and thus a necessary component of rationality. But, according to Derrida, the concept of transparency (or the immediate ability to understand) can convey its "meaning" only if the listener already understands the degree to which transparency is not opacity. In other words, the meaning of "transparency" must always already have within it its difference from the word "opacity." But, if so, then "transparency" cannot simply be transparent. In order for speech to be transparent, it must (and yet cannot) harbor "opacity," or writing. All language, Derrida argues, is constituted by this essential instability: presence could not be presence without already subsuming the concept of absence, soul could not be soul without body, enlightenment without madness, democratic freedom without pathological repressiveness. Western thought has celebrated the first term in each of these pairs, without realizing that each term must depend impossibly on the second.

Academics on both sides of the Atlantic have further developed Derrida's ideas. Jean-François Lyotard, the French philosopher and social theorist, noted that postmodernists treat with skepticism all grand theories that claim to have discovered Truth or the nature of Reason or the Good. In particular, Lyotard denied that there is a unique solution to the problem of political justice. In his view, even democratic efforts to forge consensus through free discussion illegitimately constrict other language games that might not aim at consensus at all. In the United States, Richard Rorty has echoed Lyotard's views but with a somewhat liberal political twist. Because no one view on politics, religion, or aesthetics holds the Truth, the only remaining policy is to keep public conversation going without excluding anyone from speaking.

Linking postmodernism to open conversation appeals to many educators and has particular appeal to some feminists. In the United States, and to a lesser degree in Western Europe, postmodernists have questioned the traditional list of great books, which in their view sustains a particular concept of Western reason. Their efforts have contributed to the controversial movement for "political correctness"—an effort to ensure that minorities are treated with respect by those with power. Feminists contend that politics, even so-called democratic politics, tends to represent a conversation of white males with one another, excluding what Carol Gilligan, an American scholar of education and psychology, has termed the "female voice." More radical postmodern feminists have tried to undermine the very notion of an essential male or female voice. Following Jacques Lacan (1901–1981), the French psychoanalyst, they stress the dynamic quality of all identities. They look to a politics beyond the division of women and men, as Derrida looks for the play of meaning beyond the traditional binary pairs of subject and object or truth and falsity.

The influence of postmodernism has spread beyond universities and politics. In art and music and especially in architecture, it refers to a genre in which a deliberate effort is made to disrupt the conventional, to break up any uniformities, to celebrate the dynamic and even the chaotic over the systematic or the ordered. In the work of artists such as Robert Rauschenberg, musicians such as John Cage, and architects such as Philip Johnson, one finds multiple themes superimposed upon one another, absence (or silence) juxtaposed with presence, and an ironic, almost playful, mixing of styles and periods.

The postmodern rejection of traditional truths in philosophy, literature, politics, and ethics has stimulated a strong counterreaction from people convinced that postmodernism promotes indiscriminate relativism. In the view of these critics, democracy's vitality depends on certain habits of discipline and responsibility that postmodern views threaten to undermine. These critics are unlikely to be moved by a thinker such as the Italian philosopher Gianni Vatimo, who seeks "an accomplished nihilism" as the source of new values. Instead, critics point out that postmodernism offers no coherent set of political ideas, limited by its suspicion of fixed programs.

Finally, detractors can point out that, at least in its philosophical forms, postmodernism begins with Martin Heidegger (1889–1976). Heidegger tried to undo the entire tradition of Western philosophy, suggesting that we need to rethink the nature of existence itself. He made a crucial distinction between Being and beings—the things that actually appear in our world. Heidegger argued that the occurrence of any being (humans included) owes an absolute debt to that which is absent, that which opens the possibility for those beings to exist, namely Being itself. Supporters find in Heidegger a thinking as profound as that of Plato. But critics note that Heidegger's questioning of traditional metaphysics failed to prevent his membership in and sometime support for the Nazi Party of Germany in the 1930s.

See also Theory, critical; Existentialism; Feminism.

DAVID M. STEINER

BIBLIOGRAPHY

Benhabib, Seyla, and Drucilla Cornell, eds. *Feminism as Critique.* Minneapolis: University of Minnesota Press, 1991.

Derrida, Jacques. *Dissemination.* Translated by Barbara Johnson. Chicago: University of Chicago Press; London: Athlone, 1981.

Harvey, David. *The Condition of Postmodernity.* Oxford and Cambridge, Mass.: Blackwell, 1989.

Heidegger, Martin. *Being and Time.* Translated by John Macquarrie and Edward Robinson. New York: Harper and Row, 1962.

Lyotard, Jean-François. *The Postmodern Condition: A Report on Knowledge.* Translated by Geoff Bennington and Brian Massumi. Manchester: Manchester University Press, 1992.

Rorty, Richard. *Philosophy and the Mirror of Nature.* Princeton: Princeton University Press, 1979; Oxford: Blackwell, 1981.

✦ Pragmatism

An American philosophy or philosophical method that claims that the meaning of ideas is found in their consequences. Unlike other philosophical methods, pragmatism avoids the search for the ultimate or highest reality, for eternal truth, and for the all-comprehensive system of knowledge. Instead, it tests the truth of concepts and theories by examining their consequences.

The term *pragmatism* also is used to denote a style of action that gets results by adapting to circumstances or by doing whatever it takes without too much concern about fixed rules or principles. The most famous exponents of pragmatism as a philosophy were Charles S. Peirce (1839–1914), William James (1842–1910), and John Dewey (1859–1952).

Because it developed and evolved over time, pragmatism is difficult to define. For example, Peirce chose at a certain point in the evolution of pragmatism to indicate his disagreement with James's position by renaming himself a pragmaticist instead of a pragmatist. The most widely influential, brief descriptions of pragmatism come from James's essay *Pragmatism: A New Name for Some Old Ways of Thinking.* The pragmatic method, according to James, tries "to interpret each notion by tracing its respective practical consequences. What difference would it practically make to anyone if this notion rather than that notion were true?" From a pragmatic perspective, then, ideas are true if they work—that is, if the ideas join various parts of people's experience together in a way that satisfies them. Thus an idea's truth is not a timeless attribute but something that happens to an idea. The idea becomes true when it proves itself—when results and events show it to be helpful, useful, or satisfying in giving people guidance or orientation in their experience.

In the first chapter of the second volume of *Democracy in America* (published in 1835–1840), French political observer Alexis de Tocqueville gives his now-famous characterization of Americans' philosophical method. This method, according to his analysis, grows out of the basic equality of Americans' social condition and the consequent tendency for each to rely on his or her individual intellectual efforts rather than to accept the direction of supposedly higher intellectual, moral, or political authorities. Americans, he wrote, tend to free themselves from intellectual systems, from habits, from class opinion, and even, to some extent, from national prejudices. They do not simply let tradition guide them but take it as one among many pieces of information and eagerly seek improvements over traditional ways. They try to achieve results without being overly concerned about the means employed, and they downplay the importance of forms or formalities in favor of the substance of things or the bottom line. In this way Tocqueville sketched, half a century before it emerged, the striking features of pragmatism, the first distinctively American philosophy. Pragmatism was often described in the first half of the twentieth century as *the* American way of thinking.

John Dewey

Any examination of the implications of pragmatism for democracy is probably best centered on the thought of philosopher and educator John Dewey, who developed a pragmatic political teaching. His political thought came most clearly to light when he engaged politically the thought of the American Founders and contemporary practices in American democracy.

Dewey, on the one hand, endorsed and admired several important traits of the American Founders. They were progressive, democratic, and liberal. They aimed at increasing the opportunities for the American people to develop their capacities freely. And they were innovators and experimenters, eager to develop a new science of politics that would expand liberty and increase human well-being in the emerging circumstances of their times.

On the other hand, Dewey rejected fundamental principles as enunciated and elaborated by the Founders. Their concept of the human individual as naturally endowed with certain unalienable rights, their thinking on natural rights and natural law, their crucial teachings that legitimate government must be instituted by a compact or

social contract and that the primary purpose of government is to secure individuals' rights—all these basic convictions were described by Dewey as useful and progressive at the time they were prescribed but not later. The deepest difference between the Founders and Dewey, then, was that the Founders believed they had uncovered certain decisive truths about human nature and had derived from them some important true consequences for the foundations of a good society. Dewey, by contrast, denied that any such permanently true insights into human nature, the human individual, and the foundation of legitimate government were available to them (or to people today).

Dewey's position stemmed from his acceptance and application of Darwinian evolutionary science, which questions whether there is any definite human nature that one can know, and Hegelian historical philosophy, which teaches that the human world and all its ideas, institutions, and practices change fundamentally in the course of history. Accordingly, what is good or true politically, even on the level of the most fundamental principle, is different in different historical epochs. German philosopher G. W. F. Hegel believed that he had understood history through grasping its movement toward a final synthesis. Dewey rejected any such conception of a final outcome. He kept a notion of progress—but an open-ended one. Accordingly, Dewey could praise the ideas of, say, Founder Thomas Jefferson as good and progressive in 1776, while holding that these same ideas in the twentieth century obstructed further progress or even served as reactionary slogans.

The crucial area of economics or political economy, which often drew Dewey's attention, illustrates his pragmatist approach to democratic politics in contrast to the Founders' constitutionalism. According to Dewey, the eighteenth-century ideas of individual personal and property rights and the insistence on securing these rights against encroachment by political power were good for the time and circumstances of America's first decades. But later, given the rise of large industrial corporations, for example, the defense of individual liberties and property rights against abuses of political power no longer addressed the people's real needs. Individuals were no longer the decisive economic actors; they were weak and ineffective in the face of these massive new concentrations of economic power. Thus just as the abuse of political power may have been the crucial danger requiring vigilance in the 1780s, in the twentieth century the dangers of unchecked private economic power likewise required sustained attention.

Pragmatism in the Twenty-first Century

What, then, might pragmatism prescribe for the political economy of democracy in the twenty-first century? There is no simple answer because pragmatism seems to call for a series of experiments that test the various ways of handling problems (and seizing opportunities) as they arise in conjunction with new developments in production, ownership, organization, and the like. Dewey believed that greater social control of economic forces was needed in order to bring about a more equitable distribution of the goods that society produced, counteract the imbalance of power between weak individuals and strong corporations, and remedy such ills as inhumane working conditions.

Greater social control of the economy, however, should not be limited to goals that are ordinarily thought of as merely economic. For example, Dewey hoped that pragmatic approaches to society's problems could improve everyone's participation in the expanding possibilities of culture. The pragmatic endeavor to improve the educa-

tion of all in a democratic society, in fact, was the unifying theme in Dewey's philosophy of democracy. Indeed, democracy's highest purpose is to provide the best possible education for its citizens. Correlatively, genuine democracy, as distinguished from a mass society variously manipulated by propagandists and exploiters in positions of political and economic leadership, depends on the education of citizens. Today, education is even more important than at the time of America's founding because the social and economic lives of Americans have become more complex and more difficult to understand on the basis of ordinary life experience than in the past.

With its claim that the nature of man or the limits of human potentiality cannot be determined, pragmatism cannot understand education in its traditional sense as that which guides its students toward attaining the perfection of human nature. How then does pragmatism understand the goal of education? Dewey suggested that education does not aim at an end but is itself the end. Good education is that which makes further education possible; growth is for the sake of further growth. Indeed, the best education is a life-long process. The appeal of this position lies in its depiction of human well-being as consisting of activities that develop a person, sustained throughout a whole life. But the problem with this position is that it may not leave one equipped with any clear way of distinguishing healthy growth from malignancies or other changes for the worse.

According to Dewey, a democratic education should model itself on experimental natural science. Democracy needs the pragmatic methods of science if it is to deal successfully with its problems and to meet new challenges. The practical efficacy of science, engineering, and technology is reflected in their demonstrated power. That power, however, can be used for bad ends, such as domination, as well as for good ones, such as the improvement of democratic society. Accordingly, science needs to be guided by democratic moral values. And, in fact, scientific researchers and politicians who have a genuinely democratic character show certain moral traits: honesty, fair-mindedness, open communication, willingness to innovate and experiment, and devotion to progress.

Pragmatism insists—almost on principle—that people remain open to revisions of and challenges to their fundamental economic, political, and moral concepts. For democracy, the strengths of pragmatism lie in its promotion of innovation and adaptability and its opposition to thoughtless rigidity and easygoing complacency. But costs tend to accompany these benefits. The pragmatic spirit makes it difficult to enjoy the benefits of venerable tradition and assured stability. James Madison, himself a great constitutional innovator, nonetheless recognized that even the wisest and freest governments might not possess enough stability without the veneration that only the passage of time can bestow (*Federalist* No. 49). Pragmatism leaves everything up for grabs and displays an eagerness to experiment with social engineering untrammeled by limits that were accepted in the past. If, as the French philosopher Montesquieu wrote, the political liberty of a citizen is the tranquillity of mind that arises from each person's opinion of his security, one must wonder whether pragmatism does not conflict to some extent with the notion of political liberty.

The ambiguous significance of pragmatism for political life is revealed in the ways pragmatism is both praised and blamed. When a politician or diplomat is praised for being pragmatic, he or she is compared favorably to people who are absolutist, rigidly doctrinaire, ideological, or "true believers." Someone pragmatic can adapt flexibly to changing circumstances. But political discourse also suggests that pragmatic adaptability can be carried too far—as when a politician is accused of "unprincipled pragmatism." When he was charged with being unprincipled, U.S. senator Everett Dirksen retorted that he was a man of principle and that one of his main principles was his flexibility. In the same way, French president Charles de Gaulle was often attacked and often defended for his pragmatism. These complexities of political judgment on pragmatic flexibility testify to the fact that the political action most admired requires both principle and prudence.

After World War II pragmatism as a philosophy lost prominence and vitality in American intellectual life. Within the academic discipline of philosophy, linguistic analysis moved to the forefront and pragmatism declined. More recently, however, pragmatism has regained philosophical respectability in the wake of postmodernist arguments that most earlier philosophy was caught up in an allegedly impossible search for the ultimate eternal reality or for permanent foundational principles. The writings of Richard Rorty are noteworthy for seeking to restore Dewey's philosophy to its former importance. Rorty shares Dewey's democratic commitments, but in line with the postmodernist view he discards Dewey's faith in science and scientific method. Thus pruned of its connection with science, pragmatism might still aid democracy by criticizing the claims of antidemocratic movements. But such a weakened pragmatism seems unlikely to offer much positive guidance for democratic institutions and policies.

See also Postmodernism; Tocqueville, Alexis de.

JAMES H. NICHOLS, JR.

BIBLIOGRAPHY

Dewey, John. *Democracy and Education.* New York: Macmillan, 1916.

_____. *Freedom and Culture*. New York: Putnam's, 1979.

_____. *Individualism Old and New*. New York: Minton, Balch, 1930.

_____. *Liberalism and Social Action*. New York: Putnam's, 1935.

James, William. *Pragmatism and Other Essays*. New York: Washington Square Press, 1963.

_____. *The Varieties of Religious Experience*. New York: Modern Library, 1936.

Nichols, James H., Jr. "Pragmatism and the U.S. Constitution." In *Confronting the Constitution: The Challenge to Locke, Montesquieu, Jefferson, and the Federalists from Utilitarianism, Historicism, Marxism, Freudianism, Pragmatism, Existentialism*, edited by Allan Bloom. Washington, D.C.: American Enterprise Institute Press, 1990.

Rescher, Nicholas. *Realistic Pragmatism: An Introduction to Pragmatic Philosophy*. Albany: State University of New York Press, 2000.

Rorty, Richard. *Consequences of Pragmatism: Essays, 1972–1980*. Minneapolis: University of Minnesota Press, 1982.

✦ Progressivism

A wide-ranging series of efforts to make democratic political systems the basis for a more just, efficient, and cohesive socioeconomic order. The Progressive movement, which dominated U.S. politics between 1900 and 1920, was one manifestation of progressivism. The causes and concerns that fostered the Progressive movement remain a potent source of reform impulses at the end of the twentieth century.

Progressivism is a distinctive reform spirit expressed in activism at all levels of government in the United States and throughout much of American society and culture. Amidst intense political, social, and intellectual ferment, early-twentieth-century progressivism helped lay the foundations for the modern American regulatory and social welfare state and is generally considered the precursor of contemporary American liberalism.

Progressive Politics

Progressivism grew out of the political crisis that intensified during the 1890s as U.S. political institutions struggled to adjust to the closing of the western frontier, the rise of large-scale industry, the growth of cities, massive new waves of immigration, and rapid technological change. It assumed its most characteristic forms about the turn of the century as growing discontent with the effects of these developments—discontent first dramatized by the agrarian Populist movement of the 1880s and early 1890s—galvanized middle- and upper-class activists who were confronting more specifically urban and industrial problems. Over the next twenty years indignation at commercial abuses, symbolized by business monopolies, and at government corruption, epitomized by boss-led political machines, generated an array of reforms that have been closely identified with progressivism ever since.

Progressivism's origins lay in the cities, where activists and reform-oriented mayors sought honest and efficient administration of urban affairs and campaigned for improved streets, lighting, water, and parks; firmer regulation of gas, electric, and public transit services and rates; and stricter housing, sanitation, and workplace standards. Many localities instituted nonpartisan city-manager governments as means to these ends; a few pressed for direct public ownership of selected utilities and for comprehensive programs of urban beautification and planning.

Meanwhile Progressives in numerous statehouses promoted electoral reforms, such as the

Australian, or secret, ballot and curbs on campaign-related corruption. They worked to expand state regulatory powers through new public utility, railroad, and corporation commissions; labor laws to benefit women and children; and new provisions for employers' liability and workers' compensation for industrial accidents. But state-level Progressives were best known as champions of such innovations as the primary election, initiative, referendum, and recall—mechanisms that allowed citizens to nominate candidates directly, put policy questions to a general vote, pass judgment on legislative proposals, and call special elections to vote politicians out of office.

The presidency of Theodore Roosevelt (1901–1909) brought progressivism to national government. A growing contingent of Progressives in Congress helped pass laws to expand the federal regulation of interstate commerce and monopolistic business practices. Roosevelt's 1912 independent Progressive Party campaign for a third presidential term pressed his "new nationalist" argument that strong government regulation could harness the industrial efficiency of the trusts in the national interest. Roosevelt lost to Woodrow Wilson, whose own version of progressivism called for a "new freedom" through more limited government intervention to oppose the formation of commercial trusts. Yet, during his first term (1913–1917), Wilson pursued a reform agenda comparable to Roosevelt's, extending federal commerce regulation through the Federal Trade Commission, creating the Federal Reserve system of national banking regulation, and levying the first peacetime federal income tax.

Efforts to make public authority both more accountable and stronger also involved new techniques for its acquisition and exercise. Progressives at all levels relied on executive leadership as a way around obstructionist courts and inefficient and corrupt legislatures. Roosevelt and Wilson redefined the role of the presidency and greatly increased its powers through their initiatives, administrative innovations, and personal styles. Reformers also strove to place larger areas of government activity in the hands of independent commissions staffed by, or heavily reliant upon, nonpartisan experts in specific policy fields. Along with the rest of the expanding public sphere, these new commissions felt the influence of increasingly powerful private interest organizations. The rapid proliferation of business and professional groups, of single-issue citizens' campaigns, and of federations of interest groups was a central feature of the Progressive Era. Roosevelt's attempt to unite Progressives under a single party banner proved short-lived, and although Wilson's presidency saw the Democratic Party replace the Republicans as the party of reform, interest group politics was beginning to eclipse party politics.

The Progressive Ethos

Pervading all this diverse reform activity was a distinctive spirit or ethos which John Whiteclay Chambers has aptly described as a blend of Protestant evangelical fervor, a faith in scientific inquiry, and a belief in the power of organization. Nothing captured this spirit better than the urban settlement-house movement, which became one of the earliest vehicles for Progressive causes. The same groups that worked to provide some of the nation's worst slums with civic amenities, educational opportunities, and a sense of community also surveyed urban social conditions and investigated the causes and effects of poverty. In the process, they created institutional outlets for growing numbers of men and women willing to make the spiritual and material salvation of the masses a full-time occupation.

Over time, analogous energies drove large-scale, official attempts to regulate social and economic life and found expression in distinctive ways of talking about socioeconomic problems and their solutions. In his seminal essay, "In Search of Progressivism," Daniel Rodgers argues that three themes linked otherwise disparate participants in Progressive reform. These were hostility toward monopolies and special privilege, belief in social cohesion and individual interdependence, and faith in social efficiency and engineering. It was through these themes that Progressives defined and conveyed their varied discontents, aspirations, and activist enthusiasms.

At the peak of the Progressive Era, between 1905 and 1915, elements of this ethos infiltrated virtually all walks of American life. Progressive jurisprudence called for the interpretation and enforcement of law to reflect concrete social realities and democratic consensus rather than abstract logic or reasoning from precedent. Preachers of a new "social gospel" awakened organized religion to the needs of the working and poorer classes and to the crusade for a more ethical industrial order. Progressive educators sought to make schooling compulsory, comprehensive, and better organized as well as to transform learning from rote absorption to creative preparation for practical life and democratic citizenship. A new journalism pursued "muckraking" investigations into political corruption, business abuses, and social vices in the name of informing the citizenry and invigorating public debate. Art and literature strove for greater realism and naturalism in attacking old taboos and depicting new conditions. Business sought both higher profits and better labor relations through "scientific management" aimed at efficiency in production. Organized labor built on its increasingly secure legal position by seeking reform through political activity. Finally, professional academic disciplines spawned new fields of specialization in sociology, economics, political science, and history, many of which were geared to reform advocacy and public service.

Indeed, nowhere was the ferment more intense than in the realm of ideas. Progressivism made important innovations in political, economic, and social thought. New theories elaborated on the central Progressive conviction that human conduct and development were determined by the surrounding environment rather than by innate character. At the same time, reformers pressed the equally vital Progressive claim that human beings could alter their environment through conscious collective effort. An important corollary of both beliefs was the historicist argument that the principles and practices adhered to by one generation could prove wholly inappropriate for another living in changed conditions. A further corollary was that society could progress only by abandoning fixed axioms and learning from experience and experiment.

All these themes converged in the philosophy of pragmatism as articulated by John Dewey, a leading Progressive who insisted that both society and individuals advanced best through the collective participation of all in the continuing experiment of democratic governance. Similar themes ran through what many consider the most important presentation of Progressive political theory, Herbert Croly's *The Promise of American Life* (1909), which argued that the active use of national power for domestic reform did not subvert American democratic traditions but represented their highest fulfillment. All this reasoning challenged deeply rooted American antipathies toward active government and countered the individualistic, anti-interventionist ideologies that dominated the nineteenth century. But it by no means produced agreement on any single doctrine or program of social reform.

Competing Interpretations, Continuing Dilemmas

Many of the conceptual innovations central to Progressive thought borrowed heavily from European intellectual trends. Many Progressives drew on European social science and European social policies in setting an American agenda for reform. This borrowing, along with the emergence in turn-of-the-century Great Britain of a self-styled Progressive alliance of labor, nonsocialist liberals, and revisionist socialists has led some to identify American progressivism with a broader transatlantic effort to reconcile capitalism and socialism. But American Progressives drew at least as deeply on American liberal, republican, popular-democratic, and religious traditions in addressing uniquely American problems of political development. And, despite their occasional collectivistic and antibusiness rhetoric, American Progressives rarely questioned the basic structure of capitalism as vigorously as did their European counterparts. On the contrary, the point at which expansion of the public sphere implied extending democracy to social and economic as well as political life marked the site of American progressivism's deepest ambivalence.

Indeed, many American Progressives consciously tried to avoid any hint of socialism through timely reform and occasional repression. They were, if not hostile to organized labor, "neutral" toward labor and management at a time when management was clearly in command. As many commentators have noted, major elements of the business community not only benefited from efforts to regulate competition and set commercial standards but actually championed the reform agenda and turned it to their advantage. The most strenuous "corporate liberalism" interpretations depict progressivism as a movement to reconstruct American society in the name of corporate interests, according to corporate capitalist values, and around the business corporation as model for virtually all social and political institutions. Although it is misleading to overlook the hostility many Progressives felt toward the influence of business or to attribute reform solely to business interests, progressivism clearly helped legitimize a corporate presence in the American polity that continues to vex American democrats.

Perhaps the most compelling interpretations of progressivism focus on its general organizational imperative and the contradictions that resulted from the almost religious fervor of many Progressives. Progressives believed both that a democratic society could consciously control its destiny and that honest and competent exercise of that control would elicit the support of an enlightened democracy. But when such support proved equivocal and democratic processes seemed to hinder rather than advance the rule of reason, a strong current of elitism surfaced to contradict Progressives' democratic rhetoric. Moreover, the evolution of Progressive reform revealed differences among Progressive elites themselves over the purposes of collective action. Several commentators have emphasized the tension between progressivism's pursuit of social justice and its yearning for social control, and they have noted the often deeply complicated relationship Progressives saw between the two goals. Others have pointed to conflicts within the Progressive outlook between a desire to restore and preserve traditional values and a determination to embrace and master modernity and change.

Traces of the tensions between social justice and social control are visible in many Progressives' ambivalence toward the increasing pluralism of American society and their hesitancy to take up the claims of disenfranchised and minority groups. Many women were prominent reformers, and feminist crusades for women's suffrage and other rights became central to the Progressive agenda. Progressive women, however, divided over whether reform should aim mainly at social and economic equality between the sexes or at extending women's distinctive nurturing and protective roles to new areas of social life.

Male, or female, Progressives rarely challenged prevalent racial stereotypes and sometimes embellished them with new theories of race discrimination. Southern Progressives improved opportunities for white citizens while aggressively and systematically disenfranchising and segregating African Americans.

Throughout the country, meanwhile, new waves of immigrants represented, with African Americans, "problems" to be addressed. It was sometimes difficult to separate honest assaults on urban machine "corruption" from nativist attacks on the new ethnic arrivals whom those machines often served or to differentiate the humane aspects of the push to "Americanize" immigrants through education from the less noble instincts behind immigration quotas and policies of exclusion.

Progressivism's recognition that true democracy might require an expanded public sphere occasionally pointed in the direction of a paternalistic state. The conflicting impulses behind progressivism are evident in the constitutional changes the Progressives helped bring about: amendments that gave women the vote, that provided for direct election of U.S. senators, that facilitated new social policies by permitting a federal income tax, and that strictly prohibited the sale or consumption of alcoholic drink.

The terms on which President Wilson led the United States into World War I in 1917 were likewise emblematic of such conflicting impulses. Wilson and other Progressives who loathed militarism nevertheless celebrated conscious, organized intervention to "make the world safe for democracy." World War I and the surge of

nationalism and reaction it ushered in also put an end, for the moment, to sustained reflection on the tensions at the core of Progressive thought. When some elements of the earlier progressivism reemerged during the 1930s in President Franklin D. Roosevelt's New Deal, they brought with them the unresolved dilemmas that are a major part of the Progressive legacy.

Progressivism Today

The tensions between expertise, social justice, and democratic control remain within progressivism today, but they have taken new forms since the end of World War II. Progressivism developed before the invention of modern welfare economics and the creation of policy analysis. Yet its ideas are reflected in present-day justifications for activist government derived from economics.

In addition to the inefficiencies of monopoly, modern progressives point to the presence of spillover effects, such as air and water pollution, and to the public's limited access to information about risks and product characteristics. They are also concerned with disparities in the distribution of income and wealth and with inequities in the way such basic goods as education are provided. These failures of the market justify government action to improve the efficiency and fairness of society.

Many modern scholars and political commentators cast a critical eye on some of the policy initiatives of the Progressive Era and the New Deal. They argue that regulation is unnecessary for such potentially competitive industries as airlines and trucking. While the deregulatory mantle is sometimes appropriated by the libertarian right, responsible arguments for deregulation are as much in the progressive tradition as the social regulation of the 1970s expanding the federal role in controlling environmental pollution and protecting the health and safety of workers and consumers. In both cases, the aim is to ground government intervention in sound economic principles. Along these lines, many progressives join with libertarians in supporting free trade and arguing against market restrictions that lack an efficiency rationale.

Progressivism accepts as given an economic system based on private property and capitalist production. It does not, however, make a fetish of either institution. Thus private property rights can be rearranged to improve the fairness or efficiency of the system, and private capitalist firms can be required to pay the costs of the damage they impose on society. The existing distribution of entitlements has no special legitimacy in progressive thought.

But if the government does intervene, it should do so in a cost-effective way. Thus one aspect of modern progressive thought is the design of efficient public programs—a process that requires both expert knowledge and regulatory techniques that minimize the amount of expertise needed. Programs should be designed to economize on information as well as to allocate resources efficiently. For example, economists recommend the use of pricing systems to regulate environmental harms and to allocate scarce government resources, such as rights to use the airwaves or to graze cattle on public land. For redistributive programs, they favor monetary subsidies rather than in-kind benefits. Such programs limit the information needed concerning regulated firms, ranchers, and the poor. Nonetheless, expertise can never be entirely avoided. The state must fix the price or determine the quantity. It must set eligibility standards for subsidies and monitor compliance. Marketlike strategies cannot entirely overcome the market failure that justified the public program in the first place. Progressives recognize the

value of marketlike incentives without assuming that they will eliminate the need for bureaucratic expertise and judgment.

A final strand in postwar progressive thought concerns the political system itself. The public choice movement in the social sciences, as expressed in the work of James M. Buchanan, Gordon Tullock, and others, has posed a challenge. By pointing out that politicians, bureaucrats, and experts may have interests opposed to those of citizens, these mostly conservative scholars argue that government will not invariably further the public interest. To them, the best solution is limited government.

Progressives are too sensitive to the failures of private organizations and the market to accept this conclusion. Yet they have had to respond to this negative view of government. One response has been a revived interest in ideology and professionalism as checks on raw self-interest. The second response is a heightened concern for procedures. If even experts can be self-interested, one cannot rely on unconstrained delegation to resolve the technical problems of a regulatory law. Bureaucratic procedures must be accountable to the public. If we cannot assume the good will of political and bureaucratic actors, we can, at least, seek procedures that minimize the conflict between self-interest and public values even when the market cannot function.

Although economics has set the stage for modern progressivism, it is insufficient to resolve the political dilemmas facing the modern regulatory welfare state. Progressivism in the late twentieth century needs the insights of political science and philosophy as well as economics. It is still engaged in the search for a balance between competence and democratic legitimacy.

FREDERICK BARTOL AND
SUSAN ROSE-ACKERMAN

BIBLIOGRAPHY

Buenker, John D., and Edward R. Kantowicz, eds. *Historical Dictionary of the Progressive Era, 1890–1920.* Westport, Conn., and London: Greenwood, 1988.

Chambers, John Whiteclay, II. *The Tyranny of Change: America in the Progressive Era, 1900–1917.* New York: St. Martin's, 1980.

Crunden, Robert. *Ministers of Reform: The Progressives' Achievement in American Civilization, 1889–1920.* Urbana: University of Illinois Press, 1984.

Gould, Lewis L., ed. *The Progressive Era.* Syracuse, N.Y.: Syracuse University Press, 1974.

Kloppenberg, James. *Uncertain Victory: Social Democracy and Progressivism in European and American Thought, 1870–1920.* New York: Oxford University Press, 1986.

Levine, Peter. *The New Progressive Era: Toward a Fair and Deliberative Democracy.* Lanham, Md.: Rowman and Littlefield, 2000.

Link, Arthur S., and Richard L. McCormick. *Progressivism.* Arlington Heights, Ill.: Harlan Davidson, 1983.

Rodgers, Daniel. "In Search of Progressivism." *American History* 10 (December 1982): 113–131.

Rose-Ackerman, Susan. *Rethinking the Progressive Agenda: The Reform of the American Regulatory State.* New York: Free Press, 1992.

Sklar, Martin. *The Corporate Reconstruction of American Capitalism, 1890–1916.* Cambridge: Cambridge University Press, 1988.

Wiebe, Robert H. *The Search for Order, 1870–1920.* New York: Hill and Wang, 1967.

✦ Religion, Civil

Civil religion is a theme in the history of political thought that concerns the political utility of religion. Religion, from this view, is seen as supplying an essential basis for civic ties and obligations.

Going back to Plato's *Laws* in the fourth century B.C., political philosophers have been concerned with the function served by religion in helping to secure political order. In the sixteenth century, Niccolò Machiavelli, in important respects the founder of modern political philosophy, acknowledged the problem of the political function of religion in his *Discourses on Livy*, in which he discusses the political advantages of Roman paganism relative to Christianity. Notwithstanding the process of secularization that has been characteristic of modernity and the secularism of modern thought, this issue has been an important one in modern democratic theory as well, notably in the writings of Jean-Jacques Rousseau and Alexis de Tocqueville.

Rousseau

Contemporary liberal democracies generally are committed, either in practice or by constitutional doctrine, to a separation of church and state. Rousseau, one of the first great theorists of democracy, concluded his political masterpiece, the *Social Contract* (1762), with an argument to the effect that republican politics must strive to unify temporal and religious authority. It may help to shed light on the relationship between religion and democracy to review Rousseau's analysis of the problem of a civil religion.

Rousseau concludes the *Social Contract* with a stunning notion: no state has ever been constituted without religion serving as its base. This statement occurs in the context of a penetrating analysis that lays out an exhaustive survey of religious-political possibilities. Rousseau sets forth two main alternatives: the first, which he calls *natural divine right*, is strictly otherworldly in its focus and finds its purest embodiment in the Christianity of the Gospels. The second, which Rousseau refers to as *civil*, or *positive*, *divine right*, embraces a variety of more worldly theocratic regimes. These divide basically into two types: local pagan religions like that of ancient Rome and more universalistic, and therefore potentially imperialistic, theocracies such as Islam and Judaism. All national religions will appear parochial relative to the universalism of Christianity, but as the contrast of Judaism and Islam with paganism shows, this parochialism can have either a (relatively) tolerant or an aggressive cast.

Rousseau also presents a third possibility, *mixed right*, which divides authority between church and state. In practice, this hybrid type of religion means that the priests are tempted to usurp temporal authority for themselves and to this extent undercut the established authority of the state. Rousseau calls it the religion of the priest, and like Thomas Hobbes denies to this worldly-otherworldly religion any moral claim whatsoever on the ground that sovereignty as such cannot be divided. The most blatant target of this polemic is Catholicism, but Rousseau concedes that the dividing of sovereignties is latent in Christianity in general.

Rousseau's statement that no state has ever been founded that is not based on religion rules out the possibility of a sound politics in the absence of a civil religion. A religion that is neither strictly worldly nor strictly otherworldly (namely Catholicism) is vehemently rejected. A religion that is strictly otherworldly (non-Catholic versions of the Christianity of the Gospels) is religiously true but, at best, is politically useless. It fails to make available the civil religion that Rousseau insists is politically indispensable. Rousseau goes to great lengths to show that attempts to reconcile Christianity with the requirements of politics are hopeless. It makes no sense to speak of a Christian republic: the two words are mutually exclusive. This belief might suggest that Rousseau, as a partisan of republican politics, would be forced to embrace some species of theocracy, either of the pluralistic, pagan variety or of the imperialistic, monotheistic variety.

Although Rousseau voices sympathy for Roman religious practices, and declares that the views of Muhammad, the founder of Islam, were sound, he ultimately repudiates theocracy as an option. Theocracies breed intolerance, and intolerance is morally unacceptable. In this respect, Christian universalism embodies a moral truth that must be retained. All good politics is parochial, and a religion that encourages this parochialism, rather than helping us to transcend it (as true Christianity does), would diminish our humanity. So, although Rousseau accepts and restates the analysis of the antipolitical character of Christianity presented in Machiavelli's *Discourses on Livy*, he is too sensitive to the perils of neopagan politics to be able to follow Machiavelli in the latter's unqualified desire for a return to some kind of paganism (or some other radical alternative to Christianity). As Rousseau points out, the Crusades show what results when Christianity is turned in a pagan direction, and the Crusades were an abomination.

But even if we could conceive of a civil religion that was not subject to this criticism—that is, some kind of morally and politically attractive theocracy—Rousseau says that we would be seeking a possibility that is no longer attainable. Christianity has definitively superseded all other religions. So we are left with the two unhappy alternatives of a morally true religion that is in its essence subversive of politics and a sound civil religion that is morally unattractive and historically an anachronism.

The standard reading of the *Social Contract* is that Rousseau does offer a civil religion. This comes in the closing paragraphs of the penultimate chapter of the book, in which Rousseau seems to try to combine the idea of a civic cult, in at least a minimalist version, with a strong emphasis on the ideal of tolerance found in John Locke. But it remains puzzling how any civil religion, if it is to be robust enough to satisfy Rousseau's political requirements, can be rendered compatible with the moral imperative of tolerance. Moreover, it is hard to see how such a civil religion can succeed in eluding the powerful Rousseauian arguments reviewed above. It would have to be at the same time as particularistic as Machiavelli's political vision and as tolerant as Locke's, a feat that seems to be squaring the circle.

One presumes that in urging the adoption of a civil religion Rousseau had in mind a "real" religion, one that could shape the motivations of citizens, thus fostering good citizenship and helping to consolidate the foundations of the state. But what he offers is a diluted, "phantom" religion, an Enlightenment-style religion of tolerance, one might say, in which liberal or negative tenets prevail over those that might positively build republican citizenship. In Rousseau's embracing of this thin quasi religion, it is as if he has bid farewell to his republican ideal, with the hearty parochialism and potential illiberalism that it implies. He fails to explain how the liberalized and anemic religion that he conjures up can possibly satisfy the need for a robust political religion hailed through most of his argument. Thus, in typical fashion, Rousseauian politics ends with a paradox rather than a proposal.

We can summarize Rousseau's analysis of religious possibilities in the *Social Contract* as follows: Rousseau rejects politics without a civil religion. He accepts "pure" Christianity morally but rejects it politically. He forcefully rejects corrupted Christianity, which contests the sovereign's claim to undivided political authority. (The chief example

is Catholicism, but Rousseau refers also to Shinto and Tibetan Buddhism.) He rejects monotheistic theocracy, which is either conquering and proselytizing (the warrior religion of the Quran) or simply conquering or genocidal (the warrior religion of the Old Testament). And he rejects as historically anachronistic a benign theocracy such as Roman paganism, despite his evident sympathy for this kind of national religion.

One is left somewhat baffled as to the basis upon which Rousseau thinks any politically useful religion can be sustained. He has rejected vigorously any possible compatibility between Christianity and sound republican politics while dismissing all the obvious alternatives to Christianity.

Tocqueville and a Modern Civil Religion

To locate a workable civil religion for modern democratic societies, we might turn to Tocqueville, a thinker deeply immersed in Rousseauian thought. Like Rousseau, Tocqueville highlights the function of religion in fostering attachment to the laws and institutions of the political community and in providing a pillar of decent republicanism. Indeed, various contemporary theorists (Robert Bellah, William Galston, Wilson Carey McWilliams, and Thomas Pangle, to name a few) have been inspired by Tocqueville to see the attractions of an American civil religion of just this kind.

Tocqueville tries to show, in the face of Rousseau's challenge, that Christianity, and even Catholicism, can meet the test of political utility applied to religion at the end of the *Social Contract*. Yet only in a very qualified sense does Tocqueville share in the enterprise of civil religion as Rousseau defines it. For Tocqueville places religion firmly within the sphere of what liberals tend to call *civil society*, as opposed to the realm of the state. And, like Locke, he strongly supports the strict separation of church and state, a principle that Hobbes and Rousseau severely criticized. Tocqueville tries to show, in response to Rousseau, that one can have a political religion that is both Christian and moderately this worldly, both tolerant in spirit and politically useful in securing the required ethos of a democratic state. To this modest Tocquevillean vision of a civil religion, Rousseau no doubt would reply that it offers a much watered down version of Christianity in the service of a much watered down version of republicanism.

It is perhaps easy to assume that we live in a radically secularized age in which religion and politics inhabit mutually exclusive spheres of life. Indeed, the very question of the relationship between religion and politics seems anachronistic in a world in which religion has been thoroughly privatized by Protestant Christianity in alliance with political liberalism. Yet perhaps the question has been brought to life with the contemporary vitality of political Islam asserting, once again, the possibility of a theocratic regime. If liberal democracies with their secularized politics are to address the claims of this renewed theocratic politics, they may have to avail themselves of that whole dimension of theorizing made available in Rousseau's acute analysis of the various civil religions, with their advantageous and destructive contributions to political life.

See also Communitarianism; Hobbes, Thomas; Locke, John; Machiavelli, Niccolò; Republicanism; Rousseau, Jean-Jacques; Tocqueville, Alexis de; Virtue, Civic.

RONALD BEINER

BIBLIOGRAPHY

Bellah, Robert N. "Civil Religion in America." *Daedalus* 96 (winter 1967): 1–21.

Hobbes, Thomas. "Philosophical Rudiments concerning Government and Society." In *Man and Citizen*, edited by Bernard Gert. Garden City, N.Y.: Anchor Books, 1972, chaps. 15–18.

Kolakowski, Leszek. "Politics and the Devil." In *Modernity on Endless Trial*, edited by Leszek Kolakowski. Chicago: University of Chicago Press, 1990, chap. 15.

Locke, John. *A Letter concerning Toleration*. Edited by James H. Tully. Indianapolis: Hackett, 1983.

Löwith, Karl. *Meaning in History*. Chicago: University of Chicago Press, 1949.

Machiavelli, Niccolò. *The Discourses*. Edited with an introduction by Bernard Crick; translated by Leslie J. Walker. Harmondsworth: Penguin Books, 1970; New York: Modern Library, 1950. Book 1, chaps. 11–15.

Rousseau, Jean-Jacques. *On the Social Contract*. Edited by Roger D. Masters; translated by Judith R. Masters. New York: St. Martin's, 1978. Book 2, chap. 7; Book 4, chap. 8.

Tocqueville, Alexis de. *Democracy in America*. Edited by J. P. Mayer; translated by George Lawrence. Garden City, N.Y.: Anchor, 1969.

✦ Republicanism

A tradition of thought concerned with the celebration and preservation of free states that originated in ancient Greece and Rome. Republicanism was revived in the city-states of medieval Italy and influenced the founding of modern republics in America and Europe. Although overshadowed by the rise of liberalism as the dominant Western ideology, it has recently been revived as part of a critique of modern democratic politics that attacks liberal individualism and appeals to older notions of citizenship.

Classical Republican Theory

The original meaning of republicanism depended upon a contrast with monarchy. Republics were free states in the sense that they were run by citizens who were not subject to arbitrary power. Instead of being a king's personal possession, government was in principle the common business *(res publica)* of the citizens. Although the word *republic* is Roman in origin, the principle was established earlier in the Greek city-state, or *polis*, where a variety of elaborate institutions diffused power so that, as Aristotle observed, citizens could rule and be ruled in turn. If such a state was to remain free in a world of despots and tyrants, its citizens had to be prepared to defend it and to participate in its government.

Classical republican theory, drawing upon the experience first of the small city-states of Greece and then of the expansionist Roman Republic, had two connected aspects: first, the celebration of free states and, second, discussion of how they could best be preserved in a world where they were always exceptions and always threatened with tyranny as a result of internal divisions or external conquest. In the fourth century B.C., Aristotle maintained in his *Politics* that life in a *polis* is a necessary condition of human fulfillment. On the whole, however, the achievements celebrated in republican literature were military glory and heroism, reflecting the fact that ancient republics were above all warrior bands whose freedom from conquest and tyranny depended upon their military prowess.

In such circumstances it was out of the question that citizenship, which entailed military and governmental responsibilities, could be extended to the entire population. Even where (as in Athens) the state was considered to be democratic, the *demos*, or people, did not include women, slaves, or resident aliens. Democracy in the sense of inclusiveness was a lower priority within republican thought than the qualities that enabled free states to flourish and persist. Liberty was inseparable from courage, patriotism, and public spirit, and republican heroes were praised for their willingness to sacrifice their private interests for the common good.

Republican thinkers were preoccupied with the question of how freedom could be preserved. Alongside emphasis on the virtue of the citizens went interest in the social and institutional structure of successful republics. Aristotle, surveying the experience of 158 examples of the Greek *polis*, identified the division of wealth among citizens as an important source of strife, with cities liable to predatory rule either by oppressive oligarchs or by confiscating democrats. Lasting harmony seemed to him most likely where a large middle class of independent landowners flourished and where the extremes of oligarchy and democracy were avoided. Speculations about the virtues of constitutional mixed regimes were popularized by the Greek writer Polybius, reflecting in the second century B.C. upon the success of the Roman Republic. Instability, according to Polybius, was the natural condition of city-states, with forms of government changing into one another in an endless cycle. Rome had been able to break out of this cycle because its constitution contained monarchical, aristocratic, and democratic elements. In this view, Rome owed its greatness to the complexity of its political system as well as to the virtue of its citizen-soldiers.

The Middle Ages and Renaissance

In the twelfth century A.D., after a thousand years dominated by the presence or memory of the Roman Empire (during which time the dominant political ideal had come to be Christian monarchy), republicanism came to life again in the city-states of northern Italy. Like the ancient cities, they diffused power among their citizens, developing elaborate institutional devices such as multiple councils and executive officers elected for short terms. Again like the ancient cities, they were democratic in the sense that a large proportion of citizens at some time or other held public responsibility, but they were undemocratic in that citizenship was never extended even to the whole adult male population. Drawing on Roman writers such as Sallust and Cicero, their spokesmen celebrated the greatness of free states, stressing the need for concord among the citizens, fostered by impartial justice.

By the late Middle Ages, however, the Italian city-republics were increasingly under threat from tyrants at home and powerful new monarchies abroad. The Florentine humanists, who drew heavily on classical learning, found themselves in a situation similar to that of many ancient republican thinkers, trying to explain the eclipse of republican freedom and to provide prescriptions for preserving free states. Like their predecessors, they stressed both the moral qualities of citizens and the ingenuity of constitutions. One notably long-lived and stable republic was Venice, whose success many republicans attributed to her institutional balance: the three-part system of a leader (doge), Senate, and Council was interpreted as a classic mixture of monarchical, aristocratic, and democratic elements.

Although Renaissance republicanism was in many ways a revival of classical themes, a note of novelty was injected in the early sixteenth century by Niccolò Machiavelli, whose Discourses on Livy became an influential source of republican ideas for the next two centuries. Concentrating on the Roman example of military glory achieved by a free state, Machiavelli asserted the need for public-spirited citizens to be prepared to fight in defense of their city. He also advanced more controversial ideas: that the struggles between Rome's patricians and plebeians had contributed to the city's greatness, that republican citizens needed a civic religion considerably fiercer and more secular than Christianity to motivate them, and that republics (and especially the leaders who founded or revived republics) must be prepared to suspend justice and morality when politically necessary.

Beginnings of Modern Republican Thought

After the end of the Florentine republic in 1520, the republican ideal of a free state of patriotic citizen-warriors lived on as an alternative tradition of political thinking alongside mainstream monarchism. One of Machiavelli's most influential followers was James Harrington, whose republican utopia The Commonwealth of Oceana, published in 1656 after the English Civil War, adapted classical principles to contemporary English conditions. Armed freeholders, in possession of enough land to secure their independence, were cast as the citizen-warriors of classical tradition, and Harrington devised elaborate institutions to secure the diffusion and rotation of power among them. Although Oceana was intended as the blueprint for a new republic to replace the much-disputed unwritten English constitution, it had become by the early eighteenth century the source of a convenient vocabulary in terms of which that constitution could be defended against developments that were seen as a threat to freedom.

In the eyes of publicists who claimed to represent the "country" against the corrupting influence of the king's court, England was itself a kind of republic, its parliamentary monarchy standing for the traditional mixed constitution, and the freeholding electors of the shires for classical citizens. From this point of view, freedom was increasingly under threat from the monarchy, which had established a standing army instead of relying for defense upon a citizen militia. These critics, seeing in financial speculations and venal politicians the luxury and corruption that proverbially destroyed republics, looked to the virtuous freeholders to safeguard freedom by regaining control of Parliament.

One of the major issues of eighteenth-century political thinking was the extent to which this antique vocabulary of classical republicanism could still be applied in what was seen by some as an age of progress and improvement. Montesquieu's *Spirit of the Laws* (1748), which describes virtuous republics in traditional terms, nevertheless locates political liberty elsewhere, in the mixed constitution of the English parliamentary monarchy, presiding over a nonvirtuous commercial society. In his *Social Contract* (1762), Jean-Jacques Rousseau revived the classical ideal, complete with mythical lawgiver, direct participation in government, civil religion, and heroically patriotic Spartan citizens, but he made clear that this ideal was unattainable in decadent modern times. His followers among the French revolutionaries tried nevertheless to revive the militaristic heroes of ancient republicanism, but elsewhere a new kind of liberal republicanism was emerging, one much less heroic and more businesslike in tone. At the opposite extreme from Rousseau, Jeremy Bentham and his followers understood a republic simply as the most efficient solution to the problem of government. Taking for granted that both rulers and subjects will be selfish, they placed no reliance on public spirit, concentrating instead on devising means whereby power holders could be made responsible to those whose interests they represented.

The American Experience and the New Republicanism

The Founders of the United States occupied a space somewhere between Rousseau's classical idealism and Bentham's cynical modernism. Although both the authors and the opponents of the U.S. Constitution were aware of the classical emphasis on a united body of citizens leading independent and frugal lives, and feared the possible corrupting effects of size and riches, James Madison argued in *Federalist* No. 10 (1787–1788) that a large, federal, representative republic was an improvement on the small, intensely communal

states favored by classical nostalgia because it would allow self-interested factions to cancel one another out. Similarly, the elaborate checks and balances built into the system could turn self-interest to the common good rather than relying on an improbable degree of public spirit. At the time, the Constitution was subjected to a great deal of criticism based on republican traditions. To critics accustomed to a suspicion of executive power that traditionally had expressed itself in duplication of authority or in rapid rotation in office, the position of the president seemed little short of monarchy.

Although republicanism remained throughout the nineteenth century a cause to be fought for against monarchical government, it showed less and less of its classical ancestry. The difference between classical republicanism and modern liberal republicanism was spelled out in 1819 by the French political thinker Benjamin Constant de Rebecque. In his time, Constant observed, liberty was an individual matter, enjoyed in private and in peace, whereas in the ancient republics liberty meant collective public activity, largely concerned with war. Constant saw clear evidence of progress in the difference between the two.

This new republicanism became increasingly associated with democracy in the sense that the rights of citizenship were claimed for wider and wider sections of the population. Classical republicanism had always been democratic in the sense that power was in the hands of citizens rather than in those of a monarch. Citizenship, however, normally had meant membership in one of several different orders with different rights and had always been a privilege carrying with it specific duties. As this condition ceased to be the case, political thinkers, led by Alexis de Tocqueville, began to worry whether public spirit (even of the minimal kind required to maintain freedom in a modern republic) was compatible with the historic trend toward democracy in the sense of a society without hereditary ranks. Tocqueville feared that in a democratic society individuals would tend to become isolated, impotent, and indifferent to public affairs, thus allowing tyrants to establish themselves. In America in the 1830s, however, although worried by signs of a "tyranny of the majority," Tocqueville observed a level of participation in political parties and voluntary organizations of all kinds that bore witness to the active citizenship needed to sustain a free state.

Tocqueville's concerns have been revived in recent decades by political thinkers (from Hannah Arendt to contemporary communitarians) who have once again adapted the themes of classical republicanism to new circumstances. Faced with societies in which politics can be portrayed as a matter of bidding for the votes of indifferent and atomized masses, critics of modernity have reasserted an ideal of active citizenship and public spirit. As a revival of classical republicanism, this reappearance is highly selective: contemporary republicans do not seek to resurrect the Spartan warrior, to reinstate slavery, or to deprive women of citizenship, and their stress usually is on the satisfaction to be got from participating in public affairs—an Aristotelian theme, but one that can be given a modern, individualistic slant. Meanwhile, as faith in inevitable progress toward freedom for all humanity falters, another aspect of classical republicanism is beginning to look topical: inquiry into the conditions in which political liberty can be instituted and preserved.

See also Aristotle; City-states, communes, and republics; Classical Greece and Rome; Machiavelli, Niccolò; Montesquieu; Rousseau, Jean-Jacques; Theory, Ancient; Tocqueville, Alexis de; Virtue, Civic.

MARGARET CANOVAN

BIBLIOGRAPHY

Aristotle. *The Politics*. Edited by Stephen Everson. Cambridge and New York: Cambridge University Press, 1988.

Hamilton, Alexander, James Madison, and John Jay. *The Federalist*. Edited by M. Beloff. Oxford and New York: Blackwell, 1987.

Harrington, James. *The Commonwealth of Oceana, and A System of Politics*. Edited by J. G. A. Pocock. Cambridge: Cambridge University Press, 1992.

Machiavelli, Niccolò. *The Discourses*. Edited by Bernard Crick; translated by Leslie J. Walker. Harmondsworth: Penguin Books, 1970.

Montesquieu, Charles-Louis de Secondat, Baron de. *The Spirit of the Laws*. Translated and edited by A. M. Cohler, B. C. Miller, and H. S. Stone. Cambridge and New York: Cambridge University Press, 1989.

Pocock, J. G. A. *The Machiavellian Moment: Florentine Political Thought and the Atlantic Republican Tradition*. Princeton: Princeton University Press, 1975.

Rahe, Paul A. *Republics Ancient and Modern: Classical Republicanism and the American Revolution*. Chapel Hill: University of North Carolina Press, 1992.

Rousseau, Jean-Jacques. *The Social Contract, with Geneva Manuscript and Political Economy*. Edited by R. D. Masters. New York: St. Martin's, 1978.

✦ Socialism

An alternative to capitalist profit-driven and competitive economies, in which such measures as constraints on economic inequalities and control of labor or capital markets are undertaken in order to achieve substantial social equality and cooperation. During the nineteenth and early twentieth centuries, socialism was considered linked with democracy in the broad sense of self-government both by theorists and in the popular consciousness. From the mid-twentieth century through the collapse of communist regimes beginning in 1989, however, socialism and democracy came to be generally considered antithetical. The chief causes of this shift were the autocratic behavior of socialist states and the resilient combination of liberal-democratic political institutions with capitalist economies in the wealthier countries.

These developments create a problem for contemporary socialists. Like their predecessors, socialists in the 1990s believe that the vicissitudes of a capitalist market and the ability of private owners to dispose of profits and to manage labor perpetuate inequalities of wealth and power. These inequalities in turn at least impede and at worst render impossible an otherwise attainable level of democracy. Accordingly, socialists who resist the view that a socialist alternative to capitalism is doomed to be even less friendly to democracy are divided. Some claim that liberalizing reforms—such as those attempted by Alexander Dubcek in Czechoslovakia in the 1960s or by Mikhail Gorbachev in the Soviet Union in the 1980s—could in principle have succeeded. Others argue that the socialism in such countries was not of the right sort or was not socialism at all.

Contemporary socialists also disagree about several other important issues: whether capitalism can be reformed or must be replaced; whether the chief constraint on democracy is located in a division between capitalist owners and propertyless workers, in an anti-cooperative competitive market, or in unequal distribution of goods; and what alternative forms of production or principles of distribution are to be preferred. The answers to these questions involve such fundamental issues as how to define socialism and democracy themselves. These debates, like the unfulfilled democratic promises of socialism that prompted them, have historical roots, well summarized by G. D. H. Cole and Leszek Kolakowski in their histories of socialism and Marxism.

The Early Nineteenth Century

Socialism was named in the early nineteenth century by followers of the French social theorist Claude-Henri Saint-Simon and the British social reformer Robert Owen. Both men advocated education of workers and capitalists alike to achieve reforms leading to a society in which people would cooperatively produce and equitably distribute goods. Other early socialists had somewhat different visions of social reform. Louis Blanc advocated what today is called a welfare state. Blanc was less speculative and utopian than Saint-Simon and Owen. But Charles Fourier projected a radical change of societies to "phalanxes" in which the constraints of a division of labor and of mores such as monogamy had been overcome. Pierre-Joseph Proudhon, who coined the phrase "property is theft," favored industrial democracy and "mutualist" federations of manufacturing and agricultural communities.

These early socialists shared a belief in the power of education and experimental communities to win converts from all classes who would work toward these goals. This belief distinguished them from other socialists of the time, such as Louis-Auguste Blanqui. The Blanquists were inspired by the French agitator François-Noël Babeuf. He and his followers saw the French Revolution as a forerunner of a more radically egalitarian revolution. The Blanquists in turn participated in militant and insurrectional activities that led in 1871 to the short-lived Paris Commune, when workers occupied part of that city. Blanqui saw revolution as essentially a working-class affair. Like Babeuf before him, he thought that revolutionary conspirators would initially be obliged to employ dictatorial methods.

These were by no means the only socialist tendencies in the early nineteenth century. In France, Etienne Cabet saw in early Christianity examples of egalitarian and communal societies. In England in 1838–1839 a campaign for passage of a bill called the People's Charter sparked a working-class movement, the Chartists. This group demanded universal manhood suffrage and democratic parliamentary reform. The views of Owen and the Chartists also merged with English utilitarianism, which sometimes took on a socialist flavor, especially in the work of John Stuart Mill. The seeds of most later socialist trends, organizational disputes, and debates about the relation of socialism to democracy can be found in these early socialist thinkers and movements.

The Late Nineteenth and Early Twentieth Centuries

In the late nineteenth and early twentieth centuries, socialist parties and coalitions formed in nearly all countries of Europe. Each of these groups included a wide variety of orientations toward socialism and toward democracy. This was especially true of the two main international organizations: the International Workingman's Association (First International), founded in London in 1864, and the Second International, founded in Paris in 1889. Of the many positions that emerged in the complex politics of these organizations, three broad streams bearing on the relation of socialism to democracy can be identified: reformist, Marxist-revolutionary, and anarchist.

The reformist stream was the forerunner of later twentieth-century social democracy. (The term is historically confusing, since the nineteenth-century revolutionaries also called their parties social democratic.) The Marxist stream yielded revolutionary political organizations—mainly communist parties—and also influenced generations of independent socialists and move-ments. The more militant anarchist trend gave rise to relatively few organizations of anarchists and to the ideas of a variety of radicals.

The differences between the reformist and the Marxist-revolutionary streams began to clarify at a conference held in Gotha, Germany, in 1875, when Germany's two socialist parties merged to form the Socialist Workers' Party. The reformist group was the former Social Democratic Party. Its members were called Lassalleans after Ferdinand Lassalle, who, though deceased by that time, had been an influential founder of this group. Lassalleans favored parliamentary activity to achieve democratic political and egalitarian economic reforms and workers' cooperatives. Against them stood August Bebel and Wilhelm Liebknecht, leaders of the former Social-Democratic Workers Party, together with Karl Marx and Friedrich Engels. Although they were not completely opposed to reform activity, this group looked primarily to political organization of the industrial working class to achieve radical transformation of existing political and economic structures, eventually producing a conflict-free, collectivist society.

Similar differences emerged in France between the Socialist Party of France, whose dominant figure was the revolutionary Blanquist, Jules Guesde, and the French Socialist Party, which followed the reformist thinking of Jean Jaurès.

In Russia, V. I. Lenin polemicized against those whom he called "legalists," notably Peter Struve, for trying to achieve social change by strictly parliamentary and legal means. Like its Western European counterparts, the Russian Social Democratic Party was divided into wings. After a party congress in 1902 the members of these wings were called Bolsheviks and Mensheviks (respectively, those who were in the majority and in the minority of a crucial vote). Lenin and the Bolsheviks pushed for largely extraparliamentary activity and minimal cooperation with nonsocialist anticzarists. The Mensheviks charged the Bolsheviks with Blanquism; Lenin retorted by associating his critics with the views of Louis Blanc.

The First International was founded in London because of the presence there of exiled revolutionaries, like Marx. The main line of British socialist thinking, however, was more in the tradition of Robert Owen. The playwright George Bernard Shaw, Sidney Webb, and Beatrice Webb campaigned for educational reform and economic welfare achieved by parliamentary means. In 1883–1884 some British socialists founded the Fabian Society with this aim. The group took its name from the Roman general Fabius Cunctator, who was known for military tactics that avoided direct confrontation. Democracy for the Fabians meant electoral politics and parliamentary government, and they came increasingly to be affiliated with Britain's Labour Party.

On the Continent, socialistic ideas were popularized by the French writer Victor Hugo, as they were in Britain by writers such as Shaw and William Morris. In Germany, Eduard Bernstein, whom some regard as the theoretical founder of social democracy, championed the Fabian views in his debates with Marxists in the Second International.

Before and just after World War I, influential Austrian and German liberal socialists were concerning themselves with parliamentary and legal reform. One of these, Hugo Preuss, drafted the constitution of the German Weimar Republic. British socialist G. D. H. Cole shared Preuss's liberal values, but thought that these would be best served if national associations of manual and professional workers coordinated industry in the service of the public good. Cole led the movement called *guild socialism* to promote this end and founded the National Guilds League in 1915.

The furthest removed from the Fabians and other reformers were the anarchists. Notable anarchists included the Russians Pyotr Kropotkin (a prince who renounced his title) and Mikhail Bakunin (also an aristocrat) and the Italian Enrico Malatesta. Like the Marxist revolutionaries, anarchists were attracted to radical critiques of existing society in the style of the Blanquists. Although the Marxists wished to temper the Blanquist refusal to work within the existing system, the anarchists rejected any accommodations to the status quo. As to their goals, they were influenced by Proudhon and thought of socialism as self-managed communities. This made socialism and democracy identical in their eyes, since in these communities people governed themselves cooperatively and directly.

Formal institutions of the state are unnecessary in self-governed societies and actually form a major obstacle to their attainment. Although a loose association of anarchists, informally called the Black International, was founded in 1881, anarchists extended their critique of institutions to political parties. Contrary to the popular image of anarchism, they also opposed organized conspiratorial groups of the sort Babeuf and Blanqui thought necessary. In this and in their Proudhonist emphasis on communities of workers, the anarchists resembled the syndicalist movements of France, Italy, and Spain. The chief advocate of syndicalism, Georges Sorel, believed that spontaneous uprisings of workers, as in general strikes, would bring into existence mutualist societies of the sort Proudhon favored. Syndicalism came to be known as anarcho-syndicalism.

Socialist ideas were less sharply defined and socialist organizations less prominent in North America than in Europe, though populism and Jeffersonian democracy to some extent shared the socialists' antipathy to capitalist inequalities of power and wealth and favored local self-government. More explicitly socialistic were members of the social gospel movement, who advocated equality and democracy on Christian grounds. The chief exponents of these views were the German exile Walter Rauchenbusch in the United States and James Shaver Woodsworth in Canada. Eugene Debs drew on various strands of populist, Jeffersonian, and egalitarian thought to participate in founding the Socialist Party (called the Social Democratic Party of America at its founding in 1897). Although Debs was not a member of the social gospel movement, both he and Norman Thomas, who later headed the Socialist Party, shared its secular values and were influenced by it.

Attempts were made in North America to put into practice the visions of some of the early socialists—Saint-Simon, Owen, Fourier, Cabet—by constructing utopian communities. Since there were few of these experiments, and they were short lived, they had little effect on popular thinking. Workers' and farmers' cooperatives, designed on lines recommended by Proudhon, met with more success. Canada's Cooperative Commonwealth Federation (forerunner of its current social democratic New Democratic Party) was founded on the basis of such cooperatives; its first leader was the social gospelist Woodsworth. In the United States populism proved fertile ground for anarcho-syndicalist movements, which found their most colorful leader in William "Big Bill" Haywood. A militant miner, Haywood was a prominent leader in both the Socialist Party and the International Workers of the World (called the Wobblies). He and other populists came into conflict with Marxist-inspired workers' movements, such as the Socialist Labor Party of Daniel De Leon.

Dictatorship of the Proletariat

Controversies over the relationship between reform and revolution in the late nineteenth and early twentieth centuries largely concerned strategies for achieving socialism. They also involved some far-reaching differences about the nature of socialism and democracy. Until the debates of the First and Second Internationals, it was assumed that socialism had to do with social cooperation and equality, but socialists differed over the meaning of these concepts. For Saint-Simon a cooperativist society maintained social hierarchies based on merit. People should make contributions appropriate to their abilities while being rewarded according to their contribution to society. Blanc advocated distribution in accord with people's needs. Fourier wished to overcome divisions of labor, so that each person would be able to perform a variety of tasks.

Marx and Engels complicated this debate. In their writings they divided communism into two stages. The first of these, which they called socialism, would prepare society's economy and culture for the higher stage of communism proper. Saint-Simon's principle of distribution in accord with work was to prevail under socialism. Under communism the more thoroughgoing egalitarian principle of distribution by need would be achieved. In addition, the division of labor would be overcome, and people would acquire completely cooperative values. Another Marxist intervention was to have profound effects on later socialist practice related to democracy. At the meeting of German socialists in Gotha, Marx and Engels took issue with the central place the Lassalleans accorded equality. They insisted instead that the first stage of communism should be regarded exclusively in revolutionary working-class terms.

Basing their argument on economic and historical theory, they claimed that socialist revolutions, whether achieved by electoral means (as they thought possible in England, Holland, and the United States) or by armed insurrection, had to be undertaken by the industrial working class, or proletariat. Having achieved state power, this class would deploy state means, including force and the threat of force, to achieve a transition to full communism. All previous states had maintained armies, police, and other institutions of coercion, and to this extent they were dictatorial. The working-class state would differ from them because the "dictatorship of the proletariat," as Marx and Engels called it, would act in the interests of the majority working class. Socialism, then, should be identified with the dictatorship of the proletariat.

Later debates about this notion threw into sharp relief the major differences among reform, Marxist-revolutionary, and anarchist strains of socialist theory and practice. Rather than suggesting a bridge between pre- and postcommunist societies, as the Marxists intended, the idea highlighted the difference between Marxists and the reformists, who saw socialism as the extension of existing economic and democratic gains attainable within reformed political structures. Anarchists shared the Marxist vision of higher communism, but they saw institutions of state coercion as the main impediment to such a future. Thus they regarded a revolutionary workers' state as a contradiction in terms.

Marx and Engels thought that socialist revolutions would begin in the industrialized countries and would then spread within a few decades to the entire world. When it appeared that this would not happen, but that there was a real possibility of socialist revolution in economically backward Russia, the Marxist debate over the dictatorship of the proletariat intensified. To Lenin, the dictatorship of the proletariat really meant the dictatorship of a political organization, the Bolsheviks, claiming to represent the proletariat. He accordingly devoted much attention to questions of party composition and organization.

Lenin's focus on revolutionary political organization sharpened his differences with the Mensheviks, who concluded from the adverse circumstances of Russia that the only realistic course was patience and reform in alliance with the bourgeoisie. It also brought him into conflict with other Marxist revolutionaries, such as Rosa Luxemburg and Karl Kautsky. Luxemburg, though a strong critic of reformists like Bernstein, also criticized Lenin. She feared that the dictatorship of the Bolsheviks would replace working-class revolutionary activity and become oppressively antidemocratic. Kautsky, known as a leading defender of Marxist orthodoxy, charged Lenin with being out of accord with Marxism. He observed that Marx and Engels had modeled the dictatorship of the proletariat after the Paris Commune, which included political parties and liberal freedoms and in any case was intended to be of short duration.

Lenin responded to these criticisms that the dictatorship of the proletariat—regarded as the political hegemony of the Bolsheviks, if necessary in a single-party state—was itself a form of democracy, superior to other forms. He further asserted that one should never talk of democracy without asking whose class interests are served by institutions called democratic. These views constituted a departure from previous socialist thinking about democracy. The socialist tradition had included elitist (Saint-Simon) and dictatorial (Blanqui) strains, but these were seen as necessary constraints on democracy and not as exercises in democracy. At the same time, Lenin introduced an instrumental concept of democracy; he saw democracy as a means to the goal of socialist revolution rather than as a goal of socialism.

A Dark Interlude

The Russian Revolution was seen for several decades as a triumph of popular self-determination. But its democratic credentials disappeared as the grossly oppressive nature of its government, especially in the 1930s and 1940s under Joseph

Stalin, began coming to light. In this period and beyond, the worst fears of Lenin's critics were realized. Blatant state oppression was excused as necessary for a revolutionary cause more important than democracy; at the same time it was rationalized as identical with a higher form of democracy.

These problems did not attend social democracy, though it languished somewhat before and during World War II. In this period those who might have pursued specifically socialist politics either involved themselves in governments limited to welfare measures, such as the New Deal in the United States, or else became embroiled in constraining political coalitions, like the socialist-led government of Léon Blum in France. After World War II both reformist and revolutionary socialists found it difficult to develop theories or engage in socialist politics because of cold war repression.

Within the communist movement during this time, two events stand out as potentially innovative from a democratic point of view: the revolution in China, based on its large peasant majority, and an attempt in Yugoslavia to combine workers' self-managed enterprises with a noncapitalist market. Viewed as democratic experiments, these are inconclusive, since both were subject to autocratic Communist Party policies similar to those of the Soviet Union. China in addition suffered the brutal and anti-intellectual Cultural Revolution.

From the 1960s Onward

In the late twentieth century, established socialist theory and practice has twice been surprised by democratic upheavals. First, there was the explosion of extraparliamentary democratic activity in the 1960s, giving rise to the civil rights, women's, students', and national liberation movements. Second, there was the collapse of commu-

nist governments in the name of democracy in the Soviet Union and Eastern Europe. The Eastern European collapse, dramatically marked by the fall of the Berlin Wall in 1989, was explicitly anti-socialist, at least as socialism had been known in the affected countries.

The student-led demonstrations and university occupations in France, the United States, and nearly every other developed country beginning in 1968 included anticapitalist and sometimes anarchist rhetoric and demands. Still, most participants in what were called the new left movements viewed them as generally liberating rather than as specifically socialist.

Socialists of the old schools awakened to new democratic possibilities, and socialists born of the democratic movements soon accommodated themselves to these events. Humanist socialists, such as the English historian E. P. Thompson, criticized a previous socialist emphasis on impersonal economic and historical forces. In a similar spirit, authors of the new left revived early writings of Marx, in which he had discussed personal alienation.

The civil rights movement led socialists to reevaluate traditional disparagements of civil liberties. Some socialists, notably the Canadian political theorist C. B. Macpherson, developed more balanced appraisals of liberal democracy. The women's liberation movement gave rise to a school of Marxist feminists who retrieved interpretations of the oppression of women by Engels, Bebel, and other early socialists as expressions of class struggle. In reaction against this class reductionism a variety of non-Marxist socialist feminist writers sought alternative explanations.

Very few socialists in the earlier twentieth century had addressed the question of national self-determination. With the exception of largely pragmatic discussions by Lenin, only Max Adler, Bruno Bauer, and other members of an Austrian school of thought called Austro-Marxism had treated this subject in any depth. National liberation movements in the developing world led socialists to return to this earlier work and to develop new approaches to the relationships among nationalism, socialism, and democracy.

In the post–cold war period a variety of approaches called democratic socialist emerged to challenge both Marxism and social democracy. After the Russian Revolution the Second International coalition of revolutionaries and reformists had largely broken down. Communism on a world scale came under strict Soviet control—first in the Comintern, or Third International, established by Lenin in 1919 and then under the Cominform imposed by Stalin in 1947. Although the Cominform was dissolved in 1956, because of discontent on the part of Yugoslav and other communists with Soviet domination, its member parties continued to rationalize authoritarianism as a special form of democracy.

The Second International continued to exist as a forum for exchange of opinion among social democratic parties. However, its socialist wing, represented by leaders such as Willy Brandt in Germany and Olof Palme in Sweden, continued to weaken until by the mid-1980s social democratic politics was content to accommodate to capitalism. Democratic socialism thus emerged as an effort to find a "third way" between communist authoritarianism and social democratic capitalist accommodation.

For the most part, democratic socialist views found organizational expression within specific social movements instead of political parties. One exception was the Green Party in Germany, which included socialist planks in an ecological platform. Another was the Democratic Socialists of America, a coalition of leftist groups founded by Michael Harrington and others in 1983. This party has attempted to define a leftist social democratic position that had been elusive in U.S. politics.

On a grander scale were the efforts in the 1970s and early 1980s of people in the democratic wings of communist parties to break ranks with the Soviet approach to democracy. These efforts succeeded, at least for a time, in Italy, Spain, France, England, and Japan. Labeled *Eurocommunism* by the press, this movement was strongest and most consistently anti-Leninist under the leadership of Enrico Berlinguer in Italy. Like many other democratic socialists, the Eurocommunists drew on the work of Antonio Gramsci, a founder of the Italian Communist Party. Gramsci was unique among thinkers of the Second International in wishing to combine radical, revolutionary values with a reformist view about continuity between capitalism and socialism regarding democratic advances. Similarly, he adhered to a Marxist belief in the necessity of a revolutionary party, while sharing the anarchist emphasis on independent popular democratic struggles.

Some of the Eurocommunist parties, such as the one in France, reverted to more traditional Marxism. Others changed their names and adopted policies even further removed from Marxism. All these parties, along with non-Marxist socialist and social democratic organizations, suffered from the collapses of communist governments that began in 1989. In public consciousness the idea of socialism generally was tainted by communist autocracy, inefficiency, and corruption. Contemporary democratic socialists have thus devoted attention to explaining the fall of these regimes and have also begun to develop alternative concepts of socialism and its relation to democracy.

These efforts have been marked by pluralism in three senses. First, there has been a rapprochement between socialism and the theory called pluralist by political scientists in the 1950s, which focused on conflicts among interest groups. Socialist forerunners of these political scientists, such as the Russian legalists, Preuss, and Joseph Schumpeter, had been in the minority of socialist thought. Most socialists had defended a notion of democracy as popular sovereignty against pluralist concepts of conflict management and competition. Many democratic socialists now share the idea that democracy must accommodate conflict, while the leading U.S. pluralist, Robert Dahl, has adopted socialism.

Pluralism in a second sense refers to the toleration of people with life goals different from one's own. Nearly all democratic socialists now try to fit into their theories traditional, liberal democratic respect for different people's differing values. This attitude is in keeping with suspicion of the class reductionism and paternalism associated with the notion of the dictatorship of the proletariat, and it departs from an earlier socialist view that saw homogeneity of values as a necessary prerequisite for a cooperative, socialist society.

Finally, democratic socialist theory itself draws on a large diversity of theoretical perspectives. For example, some democratic socialists propose ethical views in the rationalist tradition of the eighteenth-century Enlightenment, while others favor anti-Enlightenment, postmodernist theory. The failure of communist command economies has sparked work by democratic socialists on market socialism, and some even borrow from traditionally procapitalist economic models. Both individualistic and communitarian approaches to democracy are used. Religious views, such as those of the liberation theologians in South America and elsewhere, supplement predominantly secular socialist thought. Many democratic socialists incorporate feminist or ecological ideas into their theories.

In a pluralist spirit, democratic socialists are for the most part open to yet more alternative perspectives. Moreover, the collapse of communism calls for imaginative thinking by socialists. For both these reasons, democratic socialist ideas will likely continue to proliferate. It remains to be seen, however, whether a viable third way between authoritarian socialism and capitalism can be found.

See also Anarchy; Capitalism; Communism; Leninism; Marxism; Democracy, Social.

FRANK CUNNINGHAM

BIBLIOGRAPHY

Bobbio, Norberto. *The Future of Democracy.* Minneapolis: University of Minnesota Press, 1987.

Cole, G. D. H. *A History of Socialist Thought.* London: Macmillan, 1965.

Cunningham, Frank. *Democratic Theory and Socialism.* Cambridge and New York: Cambridge University Press, 1987.

Gould, Carol C. *Rethinking Democracy: Freedom and Social Cooperation in Politics, Economy, and Society.* Cambridge and New York: Cambridge University Press, 1988.

Habermas, Jürgen. *Legitimation Crisis.* Boston: Beacon Press, 1973.

Kolakowski, Leszek. *Main Currents of Marxism: Its Rise, Growth, and Dissolution.* 3 vols. Oxford and New York: Oxford University Press, 1981.

Laclau, Ernesto, and Chantal Mouffe. *Hegemony and Socialist Strategy: Towards a Radical Democratic Politics.* London: Verso; New York: Routledge Chapman and Hall, 1985.

Lipset, Seymour M., and Gary Wolfe Marks. *It Didn't Happen Here: Why Socialism Failed in the United States.* Norton, 2000.

Roemer, John E. *A Future for Socialism.* Cambridge: Harvard University Press; London, Verso, 1994.

Schweickart, David. *Against Capitalism.* Cambridge and New York: Cambridge University Press, 1994.

Young, Iris Marion. *Justice and the Politics of Difference.* Princeton: Princeton University Press, 1990.

✦ Theory, African

African democratic theory is an aspect of African political thought that shows ambivalence toward the role of democracy in the management of African public affairs. The attention of theorists to democratic modes in Africa has sometimes been indirect, as it was in the political arrangements of precolonial Africa. In many other instances, democratic issues have been addressed more directly, as has been the case during the colonial and postcolonial periods.

Precolonial Indigenous Societies

The parentage of modern African studies can be traced to colonial social anthropology. Scholars in that field studied the principles of government in Africa's indigenous societies in order to facilitate the administration of European colonies established in the last quarter of the nineteenth century. The most famous formulation of these principles was provided by Meyer Fortes and E. E. Evans-Pritchard in their distinction between hierarchically organized societies, which were ruled by chiefly aristocratic orders, and egalitarian societies, which were governed by more democratic processes (*African Political Systems,* 1940).

The more egalitarian societies were based on kinship lineages that organized their fluid politics on the basis of situational alliances. The modern construction of democratic thought in Africa has grown largely from this egalitarian version of indigenous politics—a kind of precursor of democracy, or protodemocracy, which respected and protected the role of individuals in traditional politics—and has been opposed to the principle of aristocratic governance.

The most illustrious example of protodemocratic governance in indigenous Africa is the Igbo political system in southeastern Nigeria. Igbo public affairs were managed on the basis of open discussions involving all adult male members of the community in a democratic forum. Social anthropologists paid considerable attention to the politics of egalitarian and protodemocratic societies exemplified by the Igbo system. Such other indigenous groups as the Tiv in northern Nigeria, the Nuer in Sudan, and the Tallensi in Ghana provided the model of what social anthropologists labeled *segmentary lineage systems;* in these groups, politics was organized on the basis of varying kinship alliances. Although these stateless societies lacked the aristocratic hierarchies of kingdoms, they were able to govern themselves effectively. Their unit of political action was the kin group to which the individual was firmly tied—in place of a formal state.

Although the egalitarian systems had an apparent relationship to democratic means of governance, some traditional aristocratic societies also had features that could foster democratic behaviors. For instance, many traditional states in Africa excelled in creating the kinds of constitutional formations on which liberal democracy thrives. Succession in most indigenous states was regulated by custom and constitutional usage. Furthermore, many traditional states practiced constitutional restraint. For example, the Fanti confederacy, a collection of traditional Akan states situated in modern Ghana, was formed in 1867 as a constitutional arrangement to stop warfare among neighboring states and to promote cohesion.

Unfortunately, in the wider sphere of precolonial African geopolitics, the simpler stateless societies fell victims to the ambitions of more powerful neighboring kingdoms. This was especially the case during the era of the slave trade in Africa, when aristocratic societies exploited weaker ones that were based on popular and democratic modes of governance.

The Slave Trade

The slave trade sharpened the distinction between aristocratic societies and stateless societies in Africa. The democratic principle was threatened by the Arab slave trade (c. 950–1850) and the European slave trade (1480–1850). These were enforced by state organizations, and most kin-based stateless societies in Africa suffered disproportionately. There is ample evidence that the internal protodemocratic organization of stateless societies deteriorated during the slave trade. For example, the Igbo institution of *osu* forbade the bestowal of citizenship status and privileges on kinless persons. That principle led to the utter degradation of kinless persons in a society suffused with kinship, and it palpably diminished the potential for the development of democratic processes in Igboland.

The problems of the slave trade brought to the fore of African politics the antagonism between democratic advocacy and practice and aristocratic privilege. The community of ex-slave "recaptives" of Sierra Leone advocated and practiced democratic self-governance for a short while in the latter half of the nineteenth century. The organization of this community was conceived by the leadership of the descendants of those whom British abolitionist expeditions had recaptured from slave-running ships in the Atlantic and resettled in Sierra Leone. The community's leader, James Africanus Horton, a direct descendant of an Igbo recaptive, designed a mode of self-government that was based on British democratic institutions but fully run by Africans. This system of self-government was practiced briefly in Horton's own political base on McCarthy Island in Sierra Leone. In contrast,

native African aristocrats preferred to retain traditional African aristocratic institutions as a definition of African independence.

Democracy's Misfortunes in Africa

European contact with Africa from the end of the eighteenth century onward coincided with the growth and expansion of democratic institutions and traditions in Western Europe. Indeed, the four French communes of Saint-Louis in Senegal, including its African residents, were part of the original experimentation with democracy following the French Revolution (1789) and the revolution of 1848. By 1848 the residents of Saint-Louis were holding local elections, involving both the French and the Africans, to run their own affairs. At one point a Creole Senegalese was elected mayor of Saint-Louis. African leaders in this era—including especially the influential Edward Wilmot Blyden, a statesman based in Liberia who was of Caribbean origin and descended from former Igbo slaves—encouraged the expansion of European contact with Africa because they were convinced that Africa would benefit from the burgeoning democratic impulse in Europe.

Subsequent European expansion and imperialism in Africa actually had the opposite result. The colonizers nullified democratic self-rule among the Sierra Leonean recaptives; they severely limited, for Senegalese, the democratic benefits from the republicanism of the revolution of 1848; and they disenfranchised Africans in the Cape Colony of South Africa. Indeed, European imperialism not only limited the democratic potential inherent in indigenous African institutions but also denied Europe's African colonies any potential benefits from the growing democratic movement inside imperial European nations.

The three dominant models of European colonial rule in Africa were intrinsically antidemocratic. These were indirect rule, assimilation, and separatist doctrine. The British doctrine of indirect rule grew out of negotiations in the early part of the twentieth century between the Fulani aristocracy, the old conquerors of Hausaland in modern northern Nigeria, and the British, the region's new conquerors. Forerunners of the practice can be traced to English rule in Ireland and British rule in India.

From its outset indirect rule involved layers of hierarchy based on chiefs and discouraged democratic practices, even those inherent in traditional rulership. Indirect rule imposed new aristocratic orders on egalitarian societies. For example, British colonial rulers created a new rank of warrant chiefs among the egalitarian Igbo by issuing warrants or certificates of authority to men who previously exercised no special political powers. Indirect rule also curtailed the traditional checks and balances that had restrained rulers from arbitrary and despotic rule in traditional states.

In French colonies the doctrine and practice of assimilation set criteria for Africans to become French citizens, thus devaluing the political worth of ordinary individuals, the overwhelming majority, in the colonies. This practice was a major breach and reversal of the democratic principles of the French Revolution.

Various separatist doctrines and devices informed colonial rule in European settler colonies—ranging from Kenya, Rhodesia, and the Portuguese colonies to South Africa with its system of apartheid. These practices represented open denials of democratic self-rule for Africans.

Colonialism's attack on democratic prospects in Africa had two devastating results. First, colonialism devalued Africa's political cultures, placing them beneath Europe's and implying that they were not capable of organizing democratic self-government. Second, the colonial state treated the individual as a subject rather than as a citizen. Consequently, Africans were alienated from the colonial state and found their political forums in kinship enclaves, which thus became politicized. Kinship systems expanded enormously under colonialism, and the public realm became fragmented. Such fragmentation is hardly hospitable to democracy, which thrives best when citizens operate within a single public realm that they value and nourish.

Anticolonialism

Anticolonialism arose from the ranks and works of pan-Africanism, the movement begun by Africans residing in the United States and the Caribbean at the beginning of the twentieth century. Its primary purpose was to improve the political and social situation of Africa and Africans. Pan-African advocates of the nineteenth and early twentieth centuries were confident that European colonialism would be beneficial for Africans largely because they believed that the introduction of European political institutions would lead to liberal democratic rule in Africa. This was clearly their expectation at the time of the First Pan-African Congress, which was held in London in 1900 and was largely organized and directed by W. E. B. Du Bois, the African American intellectual. Du Bois and the congress wanted European colonialism to prepare Africans for democratic rule, primarily through education.

Pan-African nationalism quickly turned against colonialism when these expectations foundered, leading Du Bois, forty-five years after the First Pan-African Congress, to characterize colonialism as the antithesis of democracy and freedom. Anticolonialism turned European imperialism on its head, charging it with tyranny and subversion of democracy. A series of native African nationalists—beginning with Nnamdi Azikiwe from

Nigeria and including Kwame Nkrumah (Ghana), Mbonu Ojike (Nigeria), and many others, who were educated in the United States and Europe— challenged European imperialism for its antidemocratic character.

Anticolonialism's conception of democracy was, however, remarkably different from contemporary European usage. Whereas European democracy emphasized the unique individual's rights, democracy-professing anticolonialism attacked imperialism for devaluing African cultures and for allowing aliens to rule indigenous African peoples. While democratic freedom meant the achievement of positive rights for the ordinary European, for the African nationalist democracy had a negative meaning of gaining the right not to be ruled by foreigners. Accordingly, individuals never much mattered in the anticolonialist concept of democracy. Whereas domestic tyranny was the enemy of democracy in European politics, Pan-African anticolonialists preached that democracy would be achieved if Africans rid themselves of foreign tyranny. This lack of attention to the needs of the individual, and the emphasis on collective rights of Africans, colored the meaning of democracy in colonial Africa. That limited concept now haunts African politics, for foreign tyrannies have departed and internal tyrants have replaced alien colonial rulers.

Evolution of Democratic Institutions

African independence movements had two parts whose distinction from each other will help to clarify the construction of democratic institutions in Africa. There was, first, a period of anticolonialism marked by unmitigated antagonism between the European imperialists and their main critics, African nationalists. This period was followed in some countries by decolonization, a period of negotiation and cooperation between the colonizers and their African challengers in arrangements for terminating colonial rule. The relationship between anticolonialism and decolonization is paramount in assessing the potential for democracy in any African nation.

Anticolonialism was widespread in twentieth-century Africa and can be identified in every region of Subsaharan Africa. In West Africa it took the form of elitist confrontation with colonialism, sometimes in fierce rhetoric, for which Azikiwe and Nkrumah were particularly famous. It also involved civil disobedience by trade unions and student organizations. In West Africa such actions were punished by the colonizers and resulted in court trials for many nationalists, earning jail terms for some, like Nkrumah in Ghana and Anthony Enahoro in Nigeria.

In East Africa in the 1950s the Mau Mau war was waged against white settlers in the Kenyan highlands. The British countered in heavy reprisals, court trials, and imprisonment of many nationalists, including Jomo Kenyatta, who eventually became Kenya's first prime minister. The Kenyan experience was to be repeated in other British settler territories in Rhodesia and South Africa. Anticolonialism was particularly bloody in the Portuguese colonies because of Portugal's absolutist definition of its colonies as Outer Portugal. Varying degrees of anticolonialism can be traced in other colonial experiences—in the Belgian Congo (Zaire) and in the French colonies in West and Central Africa.

Although all colonial regimes and regions experienced anticolonialism, not all of them had organized programs of decolonization. The need to grant independence to its African colonies was first recognized by Great Britain following World War II. The pattern of negotiations with British colonies had been established in India, which was granted independence in 1947.

In general, British colonies went through the routine of decolonization in two stages. First, there was an attempt in each case to reconcile the aspirations and claims of the nationalists with the objectives of the British government in granting self-rule. The nationalists who fostered anticolonialism had demonized the imperialists as enemies; conversely, the colonizers had portrayed nationalists as dangerous and irresponsible. Decolonization afforded each side the opportunity to reevaluate the opponent's positions.

Second, decolonization included various attempts to reconcile competing proposals for governmental arrangements by vested interests in the colonies. This reconciliation process was particularly important in dealing with the rift between anticolonial nationalists and the chieftains who collaborated with colonial rulers and who tended to reject the call by the anticolonial nationalists for full-blown democracy.

In Ghana, there were attempts to reconcile Nkrumah's expansive political ambitions with the more conservative opposition to his call for wholesale democracy involving all regions of Ghana in one undifferentiated forum. In Nigeria, Azikiwe's notion of a common platform for all voters had to be reconciled with the views of Obafemi Awolowo and Ahmadu Bello. Awolowo was the leader of the powerful Yoruba, whose idea of a "people's republic" was a confederation of small ethnic states (the "people" in Awolowo's people's republic referred to cultural groupings, not to individuals). Bello represented the Fulani aristocracy, which was fighting for a restoration of its nineteenth-century empire in northern Nigeria. In Zimbabwe, compromises had to be forged not only between the African nationalists and the white settlers but also between two major factions among the nationalists.

Above all else, decolonization was a period of constitution making, embodying compromises between competing viewpoints. Under the British sphere, decolonization was partially a process of building governmental structures that were for the most part patterned on British parliamentary democracy.

Other European colonial powers did not fare as well as the British in negotiating decolonization for their African colonies. After a period of denying the need to do so, the French began a regime of decolonization following the general referendum in France's African colonies in 1958. Guinea, under Ahmed Sékou Touré's guidance, was allowed to opt for immediate independence, while all other French colonies chose gradual weaning toward independence in 1960. Decolonization in the French colonies included copying French ideals of democracy.

In contrast, there was little opportunity for decolonization in colonies ruled by Belgium and Portugal. Zaire, Rwanda, and Burundi were plunged into immediate independence from Belgium, without any period of measured decolonization. The Portuguese colonies of Angola, Mozambique, and Guinea-Bissau went through treacherous wars of liberation in order to gain their independence from Portugal, without the opportunity of negotiation under the aegis of decolonization.

In general, African nations that had marked transitions from periods of anticolonialism to regimes of decolonization have had fewer problems with the management of the institutions of parliamentary democracy than have those nations that never experienced a weaning transition from anticolonialism to decolonization. The political disasters in all the former Belgian and Portuguese colonies may well have multiple causes—but the inability of opponents in these nations to compromise may ultimately be traced to their lack of preparation under a regime of decolonization. Democracy thrives in a political culture of tolerance such as was cultivated by regimes of decolonization. On the other hand, democracy does poorly in circumstances of intolerance such as the absolutism that anticolonialism fomented. The weaning from anticolonialism to decolonization was an act of institutional political socialization that may have fostered the ability to run democratic regimes and to revive them when they are imperiled.

The Cold War Period

Whatever its inherent benefits, decolonization was of short duration and in most instances represented a hurried attempt to reverse the dictatorship of imperialism by replacing the institutions of colonial rule with new democratic structures. The democracies that followed colonialism faltered badly, in most instances yielding to military dictatorships, personal rule, or one-party state dictatorships. It is entirely possible that the failures of these democracies were the natural consequence of Africa's harsh history of tyranny under colonial rule and that the democratic pretensions of decolonization could not overtake an entrenched political culture of dictatorship.

Even so, the international environment of the 1960s through the mid-1980s was inhospitable for emerging democracies. During this cold war era the Western democracies were willing to support dictatorships in African countries in exchange for their promise to take sides with the West against the menace of Soviet communism. As a consequence, democratic stirrings in Africa did not receive wholesale support from established Western democracies, and, more remarkably, dictatorship gained specious respectability as an acceptable alternative to democracy.

Aristide Zolberg's *Creating Political Order* (1966) captures the views of postcolonial African leaders who monopolized power on the claim that their first responsibility was to create political order and improve the prestige and economic health of their nations. Touré of Guinea,

Nkrumah of Ghana, Kenneth Kaunda of Zambia, and many other monopolizers of power in African nations were sophisticated men of letters, who read what Western social scientists wrote about them. They followed and encouraged "charismatic legitimation theory," which argued that the apparent dictatorship of charismatic rulers would eventually pay dividends for their nations. Various dictators embraced this version of the principle of developmental dictatorship, which contended that rapid escape from economic backwardness required a period of dictatorship.

The rationalization of dictatorship attained its intellectual peak in the theory of one-party state democracy in Tanzania under the benign guidance of Julius Nyerere, Tanzania's first president. The goal of one-party state democracy was the people's sovereignty and strong government. Missing from this ideology was any reference to the needs of the unique individual, the concern of liberal democracy. Clearly, the theory of one-party state democracy inherited the collectivistic strands of anticolonial nationalist thought.

One-party state democracy sought to enforce communal consensus and to avoid the dissension that seemed to be the nemesis of liberal democracy. In pursuing these goals, its protagonists have frequently misstated and exaggerated the degree of consensus in the traditional African societies they sometimes claimed as their model. In reality, one-party state democracy—as much in capitalist Kenya as in socialist Tanzania—was closer to the command politics in the Soviet Union than to traditional African politics. Not unexpectedly, the appeal and legitimacy of this form of government waned with the end of the cold war.

Prospects in the Multiethnic States

Despite the barriers to democracy in postcolonial Africa, especially during the cold war, the basis for democratic governance has not been eradicated. Richard Sklar, who has provided a major analysis of democracy in Africa, maintains that democracy's infrastructure is not absent from Africa's social and cultural institutions. Although three of Africa's smallest and relatively uncomplicated nations—Mauritania, Gambia, and Botswana—have usually provided examples of surviving democracies, the lasting elements of democracy are more apparent in less homogeneous countries. The cost of managing dictatorship in multiethnic nations is very high, and trends toward the compromises of democracies may be encouraged by these nations' own political momentum. That is why Nigeria's and South Africa's political experiences may contain seeds of democracy that will survive as lasting examples for other African nations.

From 1976 to 1979 Nigerians sought to overcome their political divisions through constitutional engineering. The principal problems that faced Nigeria's constitution makers were two. First, Nigerians owed their loyalties primarily to their ethnic groups, starving the greater nation of badly needed support. Second, ethnic groups competed to obtain common public goods for their own exclusive benefit; stronger groups were able to monopolize power. The solution was to organize a constitution in which access to power required winning support from more than one's own ethnic or subethnic constituency and in which common benefits and public goods had to be distributed on the basis of the federal attributes of the nation or its subunits. This was what the constitution makers branded *federal character*. Its inept administration by a corrupt regime turned out to be unsatisfactory, but most Nigerians believe the principle of federal character was sound.

Although establishing democracy was not the announced purpose of Nigeria's 1979 constitution, the consequences of the constitution were clearly democratic. As a democratic document, however, it was marked by a characteristic endemic to African democratic thought. It made individuals, and their needs, the instrument of public policy rather than its goal. The aim of the constitution was to strengthen the state by redirecting individuals' loyalties and also to protect all ethnic groups. Western liberal democracy sees the individual as the end of politics, whereas African political thought since the era of the slave trade has consistently belittled the worth of the individual, subsuming the person's essence under some kinship grouping. Although individuals do have value within their own ethnic groups, they count for little in the wider national arena. The worth of the individual is a strand of liberal democratic thought that has not taken root in Africa.

Ironically, in light of the country's dismal record, South Africa's political experience may supply such liberal elements to African political thought. David Horowitz, in *A Democratic South Africa?* (1991), has suggested that the Nigerian constitutional experience could be helpful to South Africa by leading it to design a constitutional system that compels contestants for power to look beyond their ethnic base. But South Africa has a different political tradition from Nigeria's, one that is liable to enrich Africa's political thought further. The liberal tradition of respecting the individual's worth and dignity is strong in those fragments of South Africa (Afrikaners, the English, and the Jews) that have been included in the state—although the same regard has not been extended to the African masses who were until recently outside the South African apartheid state. In neighboring Zimbabwe the settlers' political culture is being blended with that of the indigenous people. Similarly, one imagines that the South African state will accord the same respect to its indigenous African citizens as to those already privileged to be South African citizens; in so doing, it will increase the notional worth of the ideal citizen by focusing on the unique individual's needs and on individual human dignity as the goal of public policy.

Prospects for the Second Liberation

Democracy has fared poorly in Africa since colonial times. The hopes for a democratic order in postcolonial Africa have largely been unfulfilled. However, given favorable new international circumstances since the end of the cold war, and disgust with dictatorship in domestic affairs, prospects for renewed engagement with democracy in African nations appear good. Unfortunately, Samuel Huntington's conclusions in *The Third Wave* (1991), which accords economic prosperity a large share in the emergence of democracy, are not wholly encouraging with respect to Africa's chances. There is clamor among informed Africans, scholars, and politicians, as well as foreign scholars of African politics, for renewed commitment to democracy, a call labeled in the late 1980s and 1990s the *second liberation*. The diagnosis of democracy's ills—and hopes for cure through the second liberation—varies widely.

The first credible African voices calling for second liberation democracy tied it to popular struggles. In *Popular Struggles for Democracy in Africa* (1987), the Kenyan political scientist Peter Anyang' Nyong'o and his African coauthors saw popular struggles against dictatorship as the means to democracy. The control of the state is at issue here, and this view permits the establishment of participatory one-party state democracy. Indeed, much of the blame for Africa's undemocratic circumstances has been laid to states' inefficiency in the hands of corrupt and inept tyrants.

Other scholars, such as Michael Bratton, see the absence of the institutions of civil society as the cause of Africa's problems with democracy, sometimes implying that such institutions could be alternatives to the state. The ultimate quest of the second liberation movement is to "liberate" the African masses. Questions remain about what structures and processes the masses should be liberated from. The diversity of viewpoints on the second liberation is troubling to African democratic theory and suggests the need to specify the elements of that theory, since in this area familiarity with Western notions of democracy often imposes false categories on African political thought.

There are three constructs whose interrelationship provides the context for African democratic theory. These are the state, kinship, and the individual.

Derived from the colonial state, the modern African state is the civil arm of African nations. Although the African state may look like the Western state, on which it was originally modeled, its functions and its relationships with society and the individual are radically different from the familiar pattern of the Western state. The elements of the state have not been fully aligned with those of society because the African state's origins are outside indigenous African societies. Moreover, the individual has largely been alienated from the state—a relationship that persists from colonialism and one that postcolonial states have not corrected.

Kinship, broadly conceived to include ethnic groups and other categories of assumed blood relationships, is the most potent representation of society in Africa. From the slave trade era through colonialism and into our times, kinship has acquired an extraordinary significance in African public affairs. It provides an alternative public forum to the state's civic public. For their political actions, many Africans have come to rely on kinship's primordial publics, political forums limited to those bonded by the same moral ties of assumed blood relationships. Whereas the state has largely had difficult relationships with the individual, primordial publics have managed individuals' welfare. Many Africans live outside the purview of the state and rely on kinship groupings for their security. But the price that Africa pays for this arrangement is that the public realm is severely fragmented along the fault lines of kinship groupings.

For the individual, the second liberation can mean only two types of freedom. First, individuals need negative freedom from kinship groupings. But that freedom will become a possibility only if the state provides the essential personal security for which individuals now rely on their kinship networks. Second, the individual can enjoy positive freedom only by gaining legal, political, and social rights in the state's civic public realm. Only when individuals gain the freedom to exercise their rights in the civic public domain can Africans expect to participate fully in democratic freedoms.

The romantic views of those advocating civil society as a replacement for the state to the contrary, the second liberation calls for the state's strengthening into a responsible organization, not its weakening.

See also Civil society; Democracy, Multiethnic.

PETER P. EKEH

BIBLIOGRAPHY

Diamond, Larry, Juan J. Linz, and Seymour Lipset, eds. *Democracy in Developing Countries: Africa.* Boulder, Colo.: Lynne Rienner; London: Adamantine Press, 1988.

Du Bois, W. E. B. *Color and Democracy: Colonies and Peace.* Millwood, N.Y.: Kraus-Thomson, 1945.

Ekeh, Peter P. "Colonialism and the Two Publics in Africa: A Theoretical Statement." *Comparative Studies in Society and History* 17 (1975): 91–112.

_____, and Eghosa E. Osaghae, eds. *Federal Character and Federalism in Nigeria.* Ibadan, Nigeria: Heinemann, 1989.

Eribor, Festus, Oyeleye Oyediran, Mulatu Wubneh, and Leo Zonn, eds. *Window on Africa: Democratization and Media Exposure.* Greenville, N.C.: Center for International Programs, East Carolina University, 1993.

Jennings, Ivor. *Democracy in Africa.* Cambridge: Cambridge University Press, 1963.

Nyong'o, Peter Anyang', ed. *Popular Struggles for Democracy in Africa.* Atlantic Highlands, N.J., and London: Zed Books, 1987.

Padmore, George, ed. *History of the Pan-African Congress.* London: Hammersmith Bookshop, 1963.

Sklar, Richard L. "Democracy in Africa." In *Political Domination in Africa*, edited by Patrick Chabal. Cambridge: Cambridge University Press, 1986.

Wiseman, John A. *Democracy in Black Africa: Survival and Revival.* New York: Paragon House, 1990.

✦ Theory, Ancient

Ancient democratic theory is the study of democracy in Greek and Roman antiquity by such thinkers as Thucydides, Socrates, Plato, Xenophon, Aristotle, and Cicero. Ancient theory may seem to be of merely historical interest, with no more to teach us about modern democracy than ancient architecture has to teach us about skyscrapers. After all, what we mean by democracy was unknown to the ancients: a political system of representation governing a huge, often continental, and heterogeneous country under a written constitution that protects the equal natural rights of all citizens. As reflection on this description of modern democracy would show, not only has democracy changed fundamentally, so too has political science. Natural rights, for example, were a discovery or invention of early modern political science.

Moreover, democratic theory as we know it did not exist in ancient times. Contemporary democratic theory is dedicated to the study and advocacy of various types of democracy. It classifies those types, articulates their principles, investigates how each works, and takes for granted that one type or another is the just and good political order. By contrast, the ancient study of democracy forms part of another study—the study of or inquiry into what the ancients called the *best regime.* The ancients did not take for granted that any type of democracy was the just and good political order. Indeed, they were deeply critical of democracy. Aristotle went so far as to classify democracy among the deviant political orders or regimes.

But perhaps it is just this feature of ancient democratic theory, or ancient political science, that has something of value to teach us. Ancient political science achieved a critical distance from democracy not likely to be encountered in modern democratic theory. Although the ancients understood something different by democracy from what modern readers of their thought understand, this difference is not so great a difficulty as it first appears. All democracies have something in common: the rule of the people. That rule may be direct or indirect, but in either case the ultimate authority in a democracy is the people. Ancient political science was concerned with understanding whether and in what sense the people ought to have that authority.

The Method of the Ancients

Greek and Roman thinkers approached the study and teaching of politics with much the same concerns as ordinary citizens, and they used much the same vocabulary to articulate those concerns. They began by taking political partisans and statesmen at their word. If, for instance, the partisans of democracy claimed that they deserved to rule because they were as free by birth as the wealthy, the ancients did not immediately look beyond this claim to some ulterior motive, such as economic self-interest, alleged to be more fundamental than the concern for justice. Rather, they investigated what it would mean to deserve to rule and whether free birth or any other quality could confer such an entitlement. Nor did the ancients return to an alleged state of nature to see how a political community might legitimately come into existence. The question of what makes a political community with its particular political order legitimate or just was answered instead by examining the various claims about legitimacy or justice together with due reflection on human needs and on the requirements of political community.

Ancient political science thus approached political life as it was lived. Thucydides helps us to examine the justice and goodness of democracy by presenting both the actions of the Athenians and the speeches by which they defended them during the Peloponnesian War between Athens and Sparta in the fifth century b.c.. Because this account would give only part of the story, however, Thucydides invites us to compare the Athenians' actions and speeches with those of the Spartans, who lived under an oligarchy (which means "rule of the few"), and of the other participants in the war. Aristotle approaches the question of who should rule as a political dispute that arises typically after a democratic revolution. The democrats assert that democracy alone is just because it exists not through domination but for the common good. The oligarchs claim to deserve to rule because of their wealth, while the democrats claim to deserve an equal share in ruling because they are equal to the wealthy in freedom. This method of beginning from ordinary political opinions, from politics as it manifests itself in both ordinary and extraordinary times, compels thoughtful readers to think through and evaluate those opinions for themselves.

The most famous praise of Athenian democracy is found in Thucydides' *Peloponnesian War*. That praise comes not from Thucydides, however, but from Pericles, the Athenian statesman and general whose name is attached to a period of spectacular artistic, political, and imperialist achievement. In his funeral oration for the first Athenian soldiers killed in the Peloponnesian War, Pericles declares that Athens is worthy of the greatest admiration and love. According to Pericles, the Athenians combine extraordinary liberty with the stern discipline needed to fight wars. Moreover, the individual can devote himself to public affairs while developing himself to the fullest as a human being. Above all, Athens rules a marvelous empire that testifies to its power to do good and evil alike.

Thucydides does not endorse this praise; rather, he turns immediately to describe the plague that devastated Athens. He thus invites us to rethink Pericles' assessment of the Athenians in light of what was revealed about their nature by the selfishness and brutality that surfaced under the havoc of the plague. In addition, elsewhere in his work Thucydides praises Sparta for obtaining good laws earlier than any other city and for being moderate in prosperity. Athens, Thucydides makes clear, was never moderate but always restlessly bold. During the peace that marked the end of the war with Sparta (or, as it turned out, the end of the first half of that war), the Athenian people undertook and then, fearing for their own rule, rashly bungled the conquest of remote Sicily. Moreover, a careful reading of Pericles' funeral oration points to certain limits of the Athenians that Pericles praises. For example, a man who minds his own business, not meddling or joining in the affairs of the city, is counted a good-for-nothing. Judging from this, we might say that democratic Athens was remarkably successful at turning out citizens dedicated to democratic Athens. But the ancient political scientists doubted that a dedicated citizen was identical to a good human being.

It should be noted here that Socrates, the founder of political philosophy, was put to death by democratic Athens for impiety and corrupting the young, that is, for undermining the traditional authorities of the democracy—the people and the gods. It was Socrates who developed the method of proceeding from ordinary opinions about morality and politics, through contradictions in those opinions, to what he claimed were noncontradictory truths about morality and politics. In more than thirty dialogues Plato shows Socrates conversing with Athenian citizens and statesmen as well as foreigners. In most of the dialogues Socrates brings to light contradictions in his interlocutors' opinions, some of which are the authoritative opinions of democratic Athens. From the beginning, then, there was a tension between democracy, on the one hand, and the study of democracy, on the other. That tension reveals an important limit of democracy.

The Question of the Best Regime

The study of democracy was, as we have said, part of the inquiry into the best regime. To understand that inquiry, we must first consider what was meant by a regime. The ancients spoke of regimes where we speak of forms of government. Democracy was looked upon as much more than just a form of government; like every other kind of regime, democracy was looked upon as a political order—an order of the whole city or political community in which one particular group ruled. The word *politeia* (regime) denoted both the political order and the ruling group or class. *(Politeia* may also be translated as "constitution," but it never means a written document.) So important was the regime as a theme of ancient political science that the title of Plato's most famous political dialogue, the *Republic*, is in Greek the *Regime*, and every book of Aristotle's *Politics* after the first one is explicitly about the regime.

Ancient political science focused on the regime because the ancients considered the regime the most important fact of political life. According to the ancients, a city's regime decisively shapes the lives of its citizens. Every regime imparts to those who live under it a specific notion of justice—that is, of what human beings owe to one another—and each regime holds up one thing as most honorable and therefore most worthy of being pursued. In oligarchy, for instance, wealth is honored above all else, while in democracy, freedom or equality is most honored. The character of a city or country changes according to the kind of regime that governs it.

The influence of the regime on the lives of citizens is much more pervasive than is implied in the terms "form of government" and "the democratic process." Because of the pervasive influence of the regime, Aristotle speaks of the regime as the way of life of the city. In light of the ancient view, the principle of legitimacy articulated by early modern thinkers such as Thomas Hobbes and John Locke and most widely accepted today—the consent of the governed—necessarily leads to a regime that is fundamentally democratic; the actual form of government comes to be of secondary importance. The closest modern approximation to the ancient analysis of democracy as the way of life of a country was supplied by Alexis de Tocqueville's *Democracy in America* (1835–1840).

Because the ancient Greek cities did not have substantial middle classes, they were divided into two main factions: the wealthy and the poor. As a result, democracy and oligarchy were the two kinds of regime most frequently found. In democracy, the people ruled; in oligarchy, a much smaller number of citizens (typically the wealthy) ruled in their own right and were not answerable to the rest. Each kind of regime or ruling class could defend its rule by appealing to some notion of justice. According to oligarchic justice, the wealthy deserve to rule because of their special economic contribution to the city; according to democratic justice, the poor deserve to share in rule as much as the wealthy because they are equally free by birth.

In mediating between the claims of the wealthy and those of the poor, the ancients were compelled to ask whether the democratic or the oligarchic view of justice and of what is most honorable in life was true; they were compelled to ask what the best regime was. Even this question had a direct connection to politics. When political life breaks down—in times of revolution, for instance—political partisans are forced to make arguments for their political preferences. All such arguments implicitly invoke notions of the best regime. A defense of democracy for Athens must argue that democracy is superior to any alternative. It must argue that democracy is just and good or that democracy is a necessary step in the right direction. To make these arguments, it must have recourse to what is just and good simply or by nature.

The argument for democracy seems at first to be stronger than arguments against it. Whereas other regimes exclude some from full citizenship, democracy excludes no one. Democracy is the one regime that is inclusive; it alone serves the common good. To this view, the ancients responded as follows. Although no one is excluded from citizenship in a democracy, inclusion does not mean that the concerns of every citizen are given equal weight. Democracy (which means "people power") is the rule of the people (*demos*), of the majority. In a democracy the concerns of the common people predominate. For that reason the ancients viewed democracy as a partisan political order, a political order in which one part of the community rules over the rest. The claim that democracy is the just and good regime cannot rest on the unfounded assertion that democracy is the rule of all. Moreover, in the eyes of the ancients the fact that the largest class in a democracy rules does not automatically make democracy more just than other possibilities.

That democracy is not in and of itself a just and good political order was also recognized in recent times by thoughtful men sympathetic to democracy. James Madison and Tocqueville, for example, saw the potential for various forms of majority tyranny inherent in popular governments. What, after all, is to prevent a pure democracy from acting tyrannically? Do the people necessarily rule for the good of all or the common good? A complete answer to that question would require an investigation, such as Aristotle undertook in the *Politics*, into the character of "the common good" and its relation to the comprehensive good of individuals. If there were not a common good between rulers and ruled, all regimes or ruling classes would exercise rule with a view to their own good; all political orders, democracy included, would be essentially despotic. Plato presents the Sophist Thrasymachus challenging Socrates with precisely this position in the *Republic*. And in the *Memorabilia*, Xenophon, the other great student of Socrates, presents the young Alcibiades, companion of Socrates and future Athenian statesman, arguing this position against his guardian, Pericles. Leaving aside the difficult question of the content and character of the common good, however, it was at least the contention of the ancients that not every people could be trusted with political power. A given people might, for example, attempt to seize and redis-

tribute the property of the wealthy out of resentment, plunging the city into civil war. And, of course, the wealthy as such were no more trustworthy than the common people.

Furthermore, the fact that the people met in assembly to conduct the business of the city meant that those individuals with the greatest rhetorical gifts became the de facto leaders of the people. Hence the danger always existed that the people would fall under the sway of mere demagogues (literally, "popular leaders") tapping into various forms of resentment. It was only by chance that Pericles, who would not stoop to flattering the people, was the most gifted Athenian speaker of his day. It was also by chance that Cleon, "the most violent of the citizens," was a few years later the most gifted Athenian speaker. Under the influence of Cleon, an indignant Athenian people came close to executing all the adult males and enslaving the women and children of Mytilene, an island city that Cleon had accused of grave injustice for revolting against imperial Athens. The Athenians were saved from error on this occasion by the all but miraculous intervention of an even more gifted speaker, Diodotus, from and about whom we never hear another word.

We find in the third book of Aristotle's *Politics* the most complete working out and assessment of the claims to deserve to rule advanced by the well-off and by the multitude. Those competing claims are based on different principles: according to the well-off, the political community exists above all to protect and to increase wealth; according to the multitude, its primary purpose is to protect freedom. Each group claims that its contribution to the city is the decisive one. This fact enabled Aristotle to assess these claims in part by investigating the purpose of the political community. Here Aristotle, like the ancients generally, disagrees with the characteristic modern answer—that the political community or country exists to protect life, liberty, and property. Although the country's purpose might include such protection, it cannot be limited to this goal. Aristotle pointed out that every country must claim that obedience to its laws is good for the citizens, but the laws necessarily place limits on liberty as well as on the acquisition of property. Then, too, every country has a regime, and every regime teaches the citizens to hold a particular view of justice and to honor a particular way of life. Moreover, every country teaches the overwhelming importance of being just and may demand the sacrifice of some of its citizens in war, the "supreme sacrifice." In light of these observations the highest purpose of the country seems to be the nobility or virtue of its citizens. Those with virtue, or political virtue, should have a larger share in ruling because they contribute more to this purpose than do either the wealthy or the multitude.

But contribution to the country is not the only criterion for assessing the claims of political partisans to deserve to rule. Because the ruling class exercises enormous power, its members ought to possess extraordinary character and judgment. Furthermore, they ought to possess the knowledge relevant to making sound domestic and foreign policy. In view of these considerations the claim that wealth or freedom entitles a class of citizens to rule appears defective. If the people do not collectively possess the judgment and character required to rule well, placing the ultimate authority in their hands entails certain risks. Moreover, even if the people are well intentioned and not uneducated, a democratic regime reflects their concerns, not those of extraordinary individuals. Hence ancient thinkers feared that even a moderate democracy would not do enough to lead its citizens toward the best way of life and might even be a hindrance in this regard. In the language of Aristotle the virtue of the good man and that of the dedicated citizen can be the same only in the best regime.

For all these reasons the ancients thought the best regime would be one in which the best men ruled. By the best they meant something akin to what Thomas Jefferson meant when he wrote to John Adams of the "natural aristoi." The ancients were less certain, however, that the natural aristoi, described by Jefferson as possessing "virtue and wisdom" or "virtue and talents," could be discerned and elected by the people and that the natural aristoi would or should wish to rule chiefly with a view to the good of the common man. Be that as it may, according to the ancients, not only would those who are best rule most competently, but a regime in which those who are best occupy the place of honor would also be the most likely to lead capable citizens toward virtue and wisdom.

Moreover, this regime treats outstanding individuals with the appropriate respect for their capacities. Democracy, by contrast, constrains outstanding individuals by subjecting them to laws created by people whose judgment and character are inferior to their own. Those laws are shaped by the people, whether intentionally or inadvertently, with a view to their own good. For the people cannot help but view the common good in terms of what they believe to be good for themselves, any more than the merely wealthy can. The people, for instance, aim first and foremost at preserving their own rule, even at the expense of other goods they may desire; hence ancient democracies from time to time ostracized those of exceptional political talent.

Democracy does not treat excellent human beings appropriately or justly, according to the ancient thinkers, and it discourages their development in the first place. Democracy constrains excellence through the combination of its defining principles, freedom and equality. By honoring freedom above all, it downplays the importance of the uses to which freedom is put. By presupposing equality for political purposes, it tends to deny the existence of meaningful inequalities. For if all are presumed equal regarding so demanding and honorable a task as exercising authority for a whole country, any inequalities that persist must be of no more than secondary importance. Moreover, if any qualities are acknowledged as "virtue and talents," those qualities will be ones that dispose and enable an individual to satisfy the wishes of the people; hence individuals with potential for extraordinary accomplishments will tend to become ministers to the people's needs and desires.

Because what the ancient political scientists meant by genuine human virtue or excellence is exceedingly rare, they thought the best regime would be the rule of, at most, a few men. Indeed, it would be fortunate if even one such person were to be found in a given time and place. In part for that reason, the ancients investigated monarchy and the conditions that favored it. So we find Plato or Socrates experimenting in speech with the possibility of a philosopher-king; Xenophon holding up Cyrus the Great, the founder of the Persian empire more than a century earlier, as a model ruler of human beings; and Aristotle maintaining that the best regime is the absolute monarchy of the man of outstanding virtue. Only the rule of such individuals, unhampered even by law, which in circumstances that are always particular must be inferior to the judgment of the wise ruler, could be thought to satisfy all the requirements of a just and good regime. The certainty that such outstanding virtue does not even exist appeared to the ancients as no more than a prejudice instilled by democratic regimes.

Moderate Democracy and the Mixed Regime

Ancient political scientists were more than skeptical that genuine human virtue could ever be the principle of an actual political order. For one thing, genuine virtue arises only in very civilized times, the same times in which the majority—all those who do not possess that virtue—refuse to be ruled as children or worse. Because of the obstacles to such rule, including the opposition of the people, the best practicable political order would have to be based on something other than human virtue. Consequently, the argument for monarchy, or for aristocracy in the precise sense, has the character not of a practical political proposal but of an articulation of the nature of politics, as Cicero explained in his *Republic*. Only after one has answered the question of the best regime can one accurately assess the quality of actual regimes.

The ancient political scientists were not idealists. They did not advocate aristocratic revolutions, nor did they think that all regimes other than the best regime were unjust. The best possible regime might be a certain kind of aristocracy that falls short of rule by the truly best, an aristocracy in which gentlemen rule with a view above all to the noble or beautiful use of leisure—what today we loosely would call culture. Although the appreciation of culture differs considerably from what the ancients found to be the best life—that is, the life of the mind, or philosophy—it at least reminds us of that life and points to it as the culmination of culture.

The conjunction of conditions necessary for this aristocracy cannot be brought about by human effort, however, and is most unlikely to come about by chance. These conditions include human beings of just the right nature; a location easy to defend; land suitable for farming, mining, and pasturing; a population and territory small enough for every citizen to be familiar with the qualities of every other citizen; a carefully controlled plan for procreation; and, in a pretechnological age, a docile slave population fit to do the work of the city and also fit for eventual emancipation.

The ancients thought that an aristocratic republic devoted to culture, though not impossible, was beyond the reach of the vast majority of cities. Hence, to the question of the best regime, the ancients characteristically gave a second answer: the best regime is not aristocracy but a mixture of elements from two or more regimes—democracy, oligarchy, aristocracy, and kingship. The reason is not that the mixed regime promotes human excellence or treats outstanding individuals appropriately but that it achieves a stability that other regimes do not. To that extent it permits the cultivation of human excellence. A mixed regime might even make something like excellence one basis for election to ruling offices.

Most likely, a mixed regime will combine elements of democracy and oligarchy alone. By giving to this form of the mixed regime the name *polity*, the same word that means regime, Aristotle implies that the rule of the poor together with the well-off is most appropriately spoken of as a regime. If a regime is a stable arrangement of the city with respect to the ruling offices, that regime which incorporates both the rich and the poor and thus forestalls factional strife is perhaps especially deserving of the name. This regime is characterized by a combination of oligarchic and democratic arrangements or by arrangements that are midway between the two. For example, it is democratic to have ruling officials chosen by lot with no property qualification, while to have officials elected, and elected from among those with at least a certain amount of property, is oligarchic.

In polity, then, the officials might be elected rather than chosen by lot but elected from among all the citizens without regard to property. Another arrangement of a polity might be to ensure the attendance of both the well-off and the poor at courts and assemblies by paying the poor so that they can afford to attend while fining the well-off if they do not attend.

In the best case, the well-off will be of good birth, educated, and decent or fair. A mixed regime in which the well-off have these traits might for all practical purposes be called aristocracy. True aristocracy, as distinct from the aristocracy the ancients experimented with in thought, comes down to a mixture of oligarchy and democracy in which the well-off are men of some refinement who are concerned with administering the laws fairly.

Even the mixed regime, however, was thought to lie beyond the reach of most cities. The reasoning appears to have been as follows. In every city the real power is likely to lie either with the well-off or with the poor; neither will have a clear incentive to compromise with the other, a difficulty often exacerbated by the fact that each class views the regime as the prize for victory in factional struggle. Indeed, even the kind of democracy or oligarchy a city has is beyond the means of any human being to control. In a democracy, for instance, the farmers might make up the majority, or the majority might consist of the urban working class; the character of the democracy will vary accordingly. Moreover, the distribution of power between rich and poor in a given city has little to do with choice.

In Athens, for example, the strength of the poor grew after the naval victory over the Persians at Salamis in 480 B.C. Because of their importance to the navy in manning the ships, and because of the importance of the navy to the defense of Athens, concessions had to be made to the poor. Athens thus came to be more democratic at that time as a result of military necessity, not of legislation. Either a city's regime cannot be legislated, or the scope for such legislation is much narrower than one might wish. The laws do not establish the regime but reflect it; that is, they reflect the character of the class that holds power.

Because this version of the best regime could not be legislated but depended largely on the distribution of power, the ancients turned to a more modest version—the regime based on a large middle class. A middle class that outnumbered the well-off and the poor and had interests in common with each would stand as a sort of umpire between the two. Thus the stability of the middle-class regime would not depend on the justice or benevolence of any class. The middle class would have neither the arrogance and contempt characteristic of the wealthy nor the humility and envy characteristic of the needy; the middle-class regime would be characterized more than other regimes by civic friendship or fraternity. Aristotle goes so far as to call the regime based on the middle class the best regime and to imply that it is the standard by which actual regimes should be judged. The realization of such a regime became the undertaking of early modern political science.

In antiquity, however, the emergence of the middle-class regime was seen to depend more on fortune than on legislation. As mentioned earlier, ancient cities tended to have small middle classes. To the ancients it appeared that the best possible regime for a given city was likely to be some form of oligarchy or democracy. For that reason, the ancients were not averse to giving advice on making modest improvements to these inferior or "deviant" regimes and even on preserving them. In their view, revolutions were more likely to lead to something worse than to something better, and, in any case, the best regime they could conceive of had been shown to be impossible. But by gradually uncovering the virtues of the middle-class regime, beginning with the investigation into the best regime, the ancients supplied legislators and good citizens with the theoretical considerations needed for improving or preserving their own regimes.

Both oligarchies and democracies could be improved by using legislation to add to the ranks of the middle class. This means, of course, that the middle-class regime, a second form of polity, is not so different from either oligarchy or democracy. In fact, it bears a close resemblance to the moderate forms of both. Aristotle initially characterizes polity as the correct, or good, form of the rule of the multitude, whereas he gives the name democracy to the bad, or deviant, form. One way to achieve a polity, understood now as the middle-class regime, would be to institute a property qualification for full participation in political life. The best amount for qualifying would be that which is required to purchase and maintain heavy arms needed for serving in the infantry or cavalry. In other words, the ability to serve in the armed forces of the city would be the prerequisite for full citizenship, for sharing in all the rights and duties of the citizen. This requirement would give the polity an oligarchic cast but would justify it on the ground of contribution to the city's defense. It would incidentally ensure that those participating in the regime would have more force at their disposal than those not participating, a necessary component of stability.

The best practicable regime differs little from a moderate democracy. The ancients thought the best form of democracy was that in which the people governed least; the best democracy existed in less civilized times, when the mass of the people were farmers. The reason for this opinion was not that the ancients discerned special virtues in an agrarian people but that an agrarian people living in the country had little access to the instruments of government. Such a people would be content to allow wealthy citizens, who had the leisure to engage in politics, to govern the city—according to the established laws—as long as the people retained the right to elect them and to review their performance. The power of the people to elect and review would help to keep the well-to-do officials decent. Aristotle calls this arrangement "most beneficial in regimes." As the artisans and laborers become more numerous, however, and as the urban population grows, the rule of law and the balance between the well-off and the poor erodes. The poverty of an urban populace eventually opens the way to extreme democracy, in which not the law but the assembly of the people reigns supreme, and the well-off are at the mercy of the multitude and the demagogues who lead them.

The Best Way of Life

Because in middle-class regimes the common people remain the ultimate authority, these regimes are exposed to the most serious objections raised earlier to the rule of the people; they cannot be simply just. But the fact that the ancients could speak of some form of democracy as the best regime reveals another side of their view of democracy. In Plato's *Republic*, in the middle of a sharp critique of democracy, Socrates tacitly compares democracy with the golden age of the heroes in the poet Hesiod's account of the world. Only when speaking of democracy does he mention even in passing the presence of philosophy. And Aristotle calls democracy the mildest and the least bad of the bad regimes—that is, of those regimes that are "bad" by the standard of genuine aristocracy—as well as the most stable and lasting.

It is worth recalling that Socrates, Plato, and Aristotle all lived and taught in Athens and that Thucydides begins his work by identifying himself as an Athenian. Because the freedom to live as one likes is one defining principle of the regime, democracy tends to ignore or implicitly denies the possibility that one way of life is best. At the same time, it accidentally makes room for those rare individuals who, not succumbing to the influence of democracy, use that freedom to investigate the truth about the city and about the whole within which the city exists.

As the death of Socrates shows, however, freedom to live as one likes has strict limits.

Democracy frowns upon those who question the goodness of making that freedom the principle of a regime, and who question the goodness of majority rule and hence the existence of gods who sanction that rule. The ancients thought that of the two ways of life that attracted serious individuals, the philosophic and the political, the philosophic way of life was superior. They thought that a truly good human being, though he might serve as a teacher of statesmen, would not wish to be a practicing statesman himself. Even the philosopher-king of Plato's *Republic* would have to be pushed into ruling in the best regime, which was still based on a lie, however noble.

The ancients thought that ignorance regarding human affairs, especially justice, and the divine was the most shameful condition for an individual to be in. The study of the justice and goodness of democracy, and the ancient political science of which that study was an important part, was strictly subordinate to the pursuit of knowledge of the whole, or philosophy in the original sense.

See also Aristotle; Cicero; Class; Classical Greece and Rome; Communitarianism; Hobbes, Thomas; Leadership; Locke, John; Madison, James; Majority rule, minority rights; Montesquieu; Democracy, Participatory; Plato; Religion, Civil; Rousseau, Jean-Jacques; Tocqueville, Alexis de; Virtue, Civic.

ROBERT GOLDBERG

BIBLIOGRAPHY

Aristotle. *The Athenian Constitution.* Translated by H. Rackham. Cambridge: Harvard University Press, 1971.

_____. *Nicomachean Ethics.* Translated by Martin Ostwald. New York: Macmillan, 1962.

_____. *The Politics.* Translated by Carnes Lord. Chicago: University of Chicago Press, 1984.

Cicero. *The Republic.* Translated by Clinton Walker Keyes. Cambridge: Harvard University Press, 1977.

Plato. "The Apology of Socrates and Crito." In *Four Texts on Socrates.* Translated by Thomas G. West and Grace Starry West. Ithaca, N.Y.: Cornell University Press, 1984.

_____. *The Laws of Plato.* Translated by Thomas L. Pangle. New York: Basic Books, 1980.

_____. *The Republic.* Translated by Allan Bloom. New York: Basic Books, 1968.

Strauss, Leo. *The City and Man.* Chicago: University of Chicago Press, 1977.

_____, and Joseph Cropsey. *History of Political Philosophy.* 3d ed. Chicago: University of Chicago Press, 1987.

Thucydides. *The Peloponnesian War.* Translated by Thomas Hobbes. Chicago: University of Chicago Press, 1989.

Tocqueville, Alexis de. *Democracy in America.* Edited by J. P. Mayer. Translated by George Lawrence. Garden City, N.Y.: Anchor/Doubleday, 1969.

Xenophon. "Constitution of the Athenians." In *Scripta Minora.* Translated by G. W. Bowersock. Cambridge: Harvard University Press, 1971.

_____. *Cyropaedia.* Translated by Walter Miller. Cambridge: Harvard University Press, 1968.

_____. *Memorabilia.* Translated by E. C. Marchant. Cambridge: Harvard University Press, 1968.

✦ Theory, Critical

A mode of neo-Marxist radical social analysis that emerged during the crisis-ridden final years of the German Weimar Republic, which lasted from 1919 to 1939. The ideas of critical theory came out of the Institute for Social Research, which was founded in Frankfurt, Germany, in 1924.

The institute was an interdisciplinary research organization that brought together philosophers, sociologists, economists, political scientists, and psychologists. After Adolf Hitler's rise to power, members of the "Frankfurt school" went first to Geneva, Switzerland (in February 1933), and then to New York City (in 1935).

The Authoritarian State

Totalitarian movements scored several political victories in Europe in the 1930s, with Italy and Germany coming under fascist governments and the Soviet Union falling under Joseph Stalin's unchallenged control. Max Horkheimer (1895–1973), who was director of the institute, and the neo-Marxist intellectuals grouped around him tried to explain the apparent capitulation of previously radical social movements in the face of European fascism and particularly Nazism. The political traumas of this period, and particularly the collapse of liberal democracy in Germany, encouraged the institute's members to break with pivotal components of orthodox Marxist theory.

Most important, Horkheimer encouraged his colleagues to question the economistic character of traditional Marxism's explanations of collective actions and thus to emphasize the influence of what earlier Marxists had relegated to the so-called superstructure (politics, law, culture, and ideology). This new radical social analysis, which would be called "critical theory," continued to criticize capitalist-bourgeois society in the name of a better, as yet unrealized social order.

The institute's members developed a groundbreaking analysis of how ongoing changes in political and legal institutions, family life, and culture contributed to the growth of authoritarianism. Franz L. Neumann (1900–1953) and Otto Kirchheimer (1905–1965) chronicled the breakdown of traditional liberal legal protections in the Weimar Republic and analyzed the fragility of liberal democratic representative institutions in the face of advancing fascism. In their view, Nazism was the most extreme case of a global trend toward dictatorship, which was facilitated by the demise of crucial political and legal mechanisms that had mediated, though with limited success, between the rights of individuals and the interests of large capitalist cartels and corporations.

Horkheimer and Erich Fromm (1900–1980) led the way in synthesizing Sigmund Freud's theory of psychoanalysis and Marxism. Scholars at the institute argued that the disintegration of the traditional patriarchal family tended to produce personality types vulnerable to mass-based political and social coercion. Dominant, economically independent patriarchal fathers—and the resultant psychological struggles that Freud had associated with the concept of the Oedipus complex—helped to produce (male) offspring capable of some degree of personal autonomy. The fascist experience had shown that the decline of the patriarchal family seemed to make children more open to potentially harmful mechanisms for socialization outside the family.

Horkheimer, Leo Löwenthal (1900–1993), and Theodor Adorno (1903–1969) continued this line of research into the causes of prejudice and the development of authoritarian personality traits after fleeing Germany. The results of this research were published in 1950, in collaboration with other social scientists, as *The Authoritarian Personality*.

Adorno, Löwenthal, Walter Benjamin (1895–1940), and Herbert Marcuse (1898–1979) argued that new forms of mass culture (radio, film, even sports) represented a more thorough subordination of cultural activities to the pressures of capitalism than had occurred in previous periods in the development of bourgeois culture. Benjamin countered the most pessimistic features of his colleagues' argument by focusing on what he considered to be some of the potentially positive aspects of "art in the age of mechanical reproduc-

tion." In particular, he suggested that popular media such as film could produce a shock effect that might be mobilized for politically progressive purposes. Nonetheless, the dominant position within the institute was that the capitalist "culture industry" tended to trivialize and even dismantle the most valuable accomplishments of modern culture. Even more disturbingly, the culture industry's ascent contributed to cultural illiteracy and hence conveniently buttressed authoritarian trends. In a 1938 essay on popular music, Adorno went so far as to claim that contemporary society was undergoing a "regression in listening" and increasingly was unable to communicate.

Many of the writings of members of the institute from this period (1937–1945) take on melancholic overtones. Typically, they draw a contrast between the achievements of an earlier phase of bourgeois civilization and contemporary trends, which allegedly suggest the decay of the most progressive bourgeois ideals and institutions. Neumann and Kirchheimer repeatedly compared the progressive features of the traditional liberal rule of law—such as respect for individual rights and fair and equal treatment before the law—with the obvious horrors of fascist law. In addition, they were concerned about the far less terrifying but worrisome dangers posed by the proliferation of discretionary legal standards in welfare-state democracies, which were developed through the power of administrative bodies and often without legislative debate and decision.

Despite Horkheimer's critique of traditional Marxism as giving undue significance to economic factors, the institute's overall theory during this period is dominated by a set of underlying economic assumptions—formulated most clearly by Friedrich Pollock (1894–1970). According to Pollock, modern societies undergo a transition from competitive capitalism (characterized by a large number of relatively independent entrepreneurs and minimal state intervention) to a system of monopoly capitalism (characterized by growing state activity in the economy, the disappearance of the independent entrepreneur, and the rise of cartels and monopolies). The institute's creative inroads into areas traditionally passed over by Marxism ultimately can be interpreted as attempts to explain how these larger economic trends are accompanied by political, legal, cultural, intellectual, and psychological developments.

Divergent Paths

By 1941 the institute's members were engaged in a fierce debate concerning precisely those economic trends that had played such an important background role in their thinking during the 1930s. Neumann and Kirchheimer continued to insist on the analytical superiority of the concept of monopoly capitalism for explaining these trends, whereas Horkheimer and Pollock were more interested in shifts in contemporary capitalism (in particular, the growth of state planning). Horkheimer and Pollock argued that monopoly capitalism was being supplanted by a system of state capitalism in which traditional economic mechanisms were replaced by political mechanisms capable of warding off many of capitalism's economic shortcomings. Capitalism had liberated itself from the endemic economic crises described by earlier Marxists. Social actors formerly considered subversive, such as the industrial working class, were being integrated into the political and economic status quo to a greater extent than had been anticipated even by the institute's own somber analysis just a few years earlier.

The state capitalist model inspired an increasingly pessimistic mode of theorizing. Adorno and Horkheimer outlined a philosophical position that, at least implicitly, conceived fascism to be the pivotal experience of Western modernity and a logical consequence of subterranean trends within

it. As the fascist experience allegedly demonstrates, Western rationality was destined to destroy itself. A far-reaching critique of the fundamentals of Western reason, with some similarities to contemporary postmodernist theory, took center stage for Adorno and Horkheimer.

Marcuse, who remained more loyal to traditional Marxism than did his colleagues, struggled to avoid the political paralysis often evident in the later work of Horkheimer and Adorno. He continued to hope that oppositional and subversive social movements would emerge. His writings after World War II, however, were similarly influenced by the concept of "total administration," a term first used by Adorno. The ideas of "one dimensionality" and "total administration" meant that the capitalist-bureaucratic welfare state overruns all aspects of social existence, eliminating all efforts at, and hopes of, radical social transformation.

Neumann and Kirchheimer, by contrast, pursued an innovative alternative version of postwar critical theory. Both argued that the state capitalist model exaggerated the capacities of contemporary political and economic institutions to control social life and to solve economic crises. Their postwar writings (in political sociology as well as in political and legal theory) exhibit a far more subtle understanding of the contradictory and conflict-ridden nature of contemporary welfare state democracies than was formulated by Horkheimer, Adorno, or Marcuse. Neumann's and Kirchheimer's refusal to succumb to the theory of "total integration" clearly heightened their sense of the importance of precisely those institutional mechanisms, such as the rule of law, that play a pivotal role in counteracting inequalities in power in contemporary society—by regulating and curbing the power of corporations through antitrust legislation and by defending individuals' civil and economic rights.

Habermas and the Reconstruction of Critical Theory

Jürgen Habermas is the most prolific and the most complex of any theorist in the Frankfurt school tradition. A professor of philosophy at the J. W. Goethe University in Frankfurt until his retirement in 1994, he has made significant contributions to moral, social, political, and legal theory as well as actively participating in postwar public debates in Germany. Despite clear differences separating Habermas's version of critical theory from that of first-generation critical theorists, the underlying thrust of his work builds upon that of his predecessors.

In the spirit of continuing the institute's work of the 1930s, Habermas vigorously advocates an interdisciplinary approach that combines philosophical theory with empirical social research. In the process, he has engaged in critical debate with a wide variety of divergent theoretical traditions, ranging from hermeneutics, represented by Hans-Georg Gadamer, to the systems-theory approach, as represented by Niklas Luhmann, and the "power knowledge" approach of Michel Foucault.

Furthermore, Habermas has more rigorously acknowledged the achievements of liberal democracy than did his predecessors at the Institute for Social Research. As early as 1962, his *Structural Transformation of the Public Sphere* aspired to revive the "utopian core" of the bourgeois political traditions—in the simplest terms, an ideal of opinion and consensus formation on public issues through processes of genuinely free and uncoerced communication among participants. While critical theory in the 1930s similarly appealed to the more radical aspirations of the European Enlightenment of the eighteenth century, Habermas has gone further, insisting that these ideals, like freedom, equality, and civic engagement, must be defined through a rigorous moral and political theory.

In synthesizing the views of the German philosophers G. W. F. Hegel and Immanuel Kant, Habermas has developed a moral and political theory called "discourse ethics." Discourse ethics attempts to lay bare the normative presuppositions of democratic legitimacy—namely, the participation of all affected by a norm in a process of free and equal public deliberation regarding the validity of that norm. In a 1993 work, *Faktizität und Geltung* (English translation, *Facticity and Validity*, 1995), Habermas theorizes that the institutional correlate of a discursive concept of political legitimacy would be a multiple, decentered, and free public sphere, situated in civil society.

In the process of retrieving and restating the legacy of Western modernity in science and politics, Habermas has not only distanced himself from the radical critique of Western rationality once advanced by his own teachers (Horkheimer and Adorno), but he has also responded to what he considers the one-sided dismissal of Western modernity and rationalism advanced by theorists such as Jacques Derrida and Jean-François Lyotard.

Since 1989, and with the collapse of authoritarian communism, Habermas's ideas of the public sphere, discourse ethics, and civil society have become influential for those reconstructing democracy in Eastern Europe and the former Soviet Union. As these societies struggle to establish democracy, it becomes increasingly clear that democracy not only refers to a representative system of free elections and a multiparty system but also that it requires a free public sphere of debate and contention as well as the formation among citizens of free associations and organizations that can influence public life. Habermas's theories of discourse ethics, free public sphere, and democratic legitimacy provide inspirations for such efforts.

See also Fascism; Marxism; Postmodernism.

SEYLA BENHABIB AND
WILLIAM E. SCHEUERMAN

BIBLIOGRAPHY

Arato, Andrew, and Eike Gebhardt, eds. *The Frankfurt School Reader*. New York: Continuum, 1982.

Habermas, Jürgen. *The Philosophical Discourse of Modernity*. Cambridge: MIT Press, 1987.

_____. *The Structural Transformation of the Public Sphere*. Cambridge: MIT Press, 1989.

_____. *The Theory of Communicative Action*. Vols. 1 and 2. Boston: Beacon Press, 1987.

Horkheimer, Max. *Between Philosophy and Social Sciences: Selected Early Writings*. Cambridge: MIT Press, 1993.

_____, and Theodor Adorno. *Dialectic of Enlightenment*. New York: Continuum, 1972.

Marcuse, Herbert. *One-Dimensional Man*. Boston: Beacon Press, 1964.

Neumann, Franz L., and Otto Kirchheimer. *The Rule of Law under Siege: Selected Essays of Franz L. Neumann and Otto Kirchheimer*. Los Angeles: University of California Press, 1995.

✦ Theory, Elite

An approach to political explanation that addresses three principal issues: the inevitability of elites, the effect of elites on political regimes, and the interdependence between elites and mass publics in politics. Elites are the principal decision makers in a society's largest or otherwise most pivotal political, governmental, economic, military, professional, communications, and cultural organizations and movements.

Elite theory is identified with the Italian triumvirate Gaetano Mosca (1858–1941), Vilfredo Pareto (1848–1923), and Robert Michels (1876–1936). Michels was a German scholar who migrated to Italy in 1907 to take a position at the University of Turin, where Mosca was then teaching. Mosca emphasized the dominance of small minorities over large majorities in political matters. Pareto stressed the proficiency of some individuals in using force or persuasion to gain the upper hand in politics. And Michels noted the strong tendency of mass political parties to spawn self-perpetuating oligarchies. They labeled any body of thought that ignores the inevitability of elites, such as Marxism, strictly utopian.

Mosca and Pareto developed general theories, based on the rise and fall of different kinds of elites, to explain the variant forms of political regimes throughout history. They made no claim, however, that political regimes are reducible to elites alone. Unless elites are replenished by able new members, they tend to become ineffective; therefore, the extent of circulation between mass and elite categories is decisive for the maintenance or downfall of regimes. Likewise, although elites routinely use legitimizing myths and ideologies to mobilize and govern a general populace, people possess interests and propensities to which elites must in some degree conform. Elites always need mass support, and to get it they must use rhetoric and programs that resonate with people's interests, values, hopes, and superstitions.

During the middle decades of the twentieth century, elite theory was largely eclipsed by the struggles between democratic, fascist, and socialist doctrines. Some theorists, such as James Burnham and Karl Renner, attempted to bridge the gap between elite theory and Marxism. But the bold theories put forth by the Italians were not greatly refined, and no new theory using elites as its main explanatory concept gained notice.

Elite theory evolved in piecemeal fashion, and several of its tenets are now widely employed. Harold Lasswell, ignoring Pareto's equation of elite with "the best," used the term simply to designate those with the most power in any institutionalized sector of society—politics, business, the military, religion, and so on. Thinking of elites as the incumbents of powerful or authoritative posi-

tions in all kinds of organizations and institutions has become standard practice. The danger is that this view deprives the elite concept of special meaning and amounts to a truism. The concept must also refer to groups of powerful persons with distinctive structures and dynamics or, if one wishes to retain Pareto's evaluative usage, groups whose talents and skills are most apt for rulership.

Current elite theory holds that a basic consolidation of elites is vital for some kinds of political regimes. Theorists usually distinguish two patterns: enforced consolidation, imposed by a sharply centralized party or movement that requires adherence to its ideology and program as a qualification for elite positions, and voluntary consolidation, stemming from a willingness to share power on the basis of substantial agreement by elites about political game rules. Enforced elite consolidation is seen as the basis of rigidly authoritarian or totalitarian regimes; voluntary consolidation is regarded as essential for democratic regimes. The origins and persistence of each pattern are the subject of much research.

In democratic elite theory, or democratic elitism—there is no agreed-upon label—tenets of elite theory and democratic theory are fused. Democracy is conceived as the peaceful, restrained competition of elites for popular support in free and fair elections that are open to the participation of all or most citizens. Seeking to win this competition, elites offer and promise to establish programs that respond to the conflicting interests of voters. Democratic elite theory places much emphasis on the decision-making reciprocities and tacit understandings among elites that restrain their competition so that conflicts within electorates are not exploited and inflamed beyond manageable limits.

One influential variant of the theory holds that democracy in culturally fragmented societies requires "consociational" decision making according to the principle of proportionality among elites leading the cultural fragments. Arend Lijphart cites Belgium, Malaysia, the Netherlands, and Switzerland as prominent examples. Another important variant contends that, whether or not societies are culturally fragmented, democracy often involves "corporatist" bargaining and decision making among elites heading up monopolistic functional interests such as organized business, organized labor, and the state bureaucracy. Philippe Schmitter and others have studied Austria, Germany, Norway, and Sweden from this position.

Common to all variants of democratic elite theory is the idea that stable democracy depends on institutionalizing a particular mode of elite behavior that avoids perceptions of politics as warfare. But this elite-centered conception of democracy raises controversial issues. For example, the importance attributed by elite theorists to power networks and tacit understandings that deliver satisfactory payoffs and protections to elites implies, ironically enough, that populist reforms that might shatter these networks and understandings undermine democracy. Some elite theorists, going further, worry that the contemporary tendency to elevate democracy to the status of an ultimate value overlooks its requirements for elites, ignores the rarity with which those requirements are met, and assumes blithely that a pure, unfettered democracy could somehow avoid the difficulties that elite theory addresses.

See also Elites, Political.

JOHN HIGLEY

BIBLIOGRAPHY

Dahl, Robert A. *Polyarchy: Participation and Opposition.* New Haven and London: Yale University Press, 1971.

Etzioni-Halevy, Eva. *The Elite Connection: Problems and Potential of Western Democracy.* Cambridge: Polity Press, 1993.

Field, G. Lowell, and John Higley. *Elitism.* London: Routledge and Kegan Paul, 1980.

Lijphart, Arend. *Democracy in Plural Societies: A Comparative Exploration.* New Haven: Yale University Press, 1977.

Michels, Robert. *Political Parties: A Sociological Study of the Oligarchical Tendencies of Modern Democracy.* Translated by Eden and Cedar Paul. London: Jarrold, 1915; New York: Collier, 1962.

Mosca, Gaetano. *The Ruling Class.* Translated by Hannah D. Kahn. Edited by A. Livingston. New York: McGraw-Hill, 1939.

Pareto, Vilfredo. *The Mind and Society: A Treatise on General Sociology.* Edited by A. Livingston. New York: Harcourt, Brace, 1935.

Sartori, Giovanni. *Theory of Democracy Revisited, Part 1: The Contemporary Debate.* Chatham, N.J.: Chatham House, 1987.

✦ Theory, Postwar Anglo-American

Postwar Anglo-American democratic theory is the systematic inquiry into the conditions, institutions, purposes, and meaning of democratic political practices since World War II. The practice of this inquiry is distinctive in two respects. First, it has taken place within societies where democracy was nearly universally taken to be a good thing and wherein the way of life was widely understood to be democratic. Second, democratic theory in these societies has been, for better or worse, largely the preserve of professional academics rather than political actors or public intellectuals.

The development of democratic theory in the twentieth century is closely bound up with the rise of social science as a profession practiced on a massive scale in Anglo-American universities. Scholarly arguments concerning the criteria identifying democratic governments often became at the same time arguments concerning the criteria of theory itself, encompassing concepts of evidence, validity, and scientific objectivity. This commingling of issues of political theory with issues of the philosophy of science at times generated confusion and more than a little mutual miscomprehension among those involved in the debates. Still, incredible vitality and intellectual energy resulted from this development. Within the discipline of political science, no issue in the twentieth century attracted so many of the best minds and spurred them to such heights of intellectual endeavor and achievement.

Another factor contributing to the vibrancy of democratic theory has been its close and relatively evident connection with the turbulent political history of the twentieth century. The encounter with totalitarianism in the first half of the century and the continuing fragmentation of traditional sources of moral, political, and social authority in the latter half are reflected in many of the themes discussed by democratic theorists. These discussions have attracted greater attention in the culture at large than is usually the case with the works of academics. In turn, this practical relevance has served as a spur to innovation in the academy.

Finally, it is not surprising upon reflection that in long-standing and relatively successful democratic regimes, the topic of democracy should be a perennial and primary concern of intellectual, and indeed civic, life. A people who would rule themselves will have a great deal to talk about, including how to go about ruling themselves. There are as many democratic theories as there are possibilities in that regard.

It is impossible to state an agreed-on set of propositions or axioms that might be taken to define democratic theory. The term *democracy* itself admits of no canonical definition beyond the abstract "rule by the people." But what constitutes a "people"? How is "rule" to be known when it exists, and how is it to be distinguished from "coercion" and "force"? The questions multiply endlessly. There is not a single definition of democracy that has not been rejected by some student of the subject.

To proceed, then, we will do best to avoid any attempt to define once and for all the domain and concerns of democratic theory. Instead, let us examine what those conventionally referred to as "democratic theorists" have chosen to discuss. We shall first look at this from a historical point of view, describing the primary types of democratic theory that emerged in the course of the twentieth century. We shall conclude by adopting a more analytical point of view, examining briefly three problems that have been of interest to democratic theorists throughout the century.

Revisionist and Classical Theory

In the years between 1945 (at the end of World War II) and 1970 there developed a distinctive way of understanding democracy that came to be called the "revisionist" theory of democracy. Among the works best exemplifying this view were Joseph Schumpeter's *Capitalism, Socialism, and Democracy* (1942), Robert Dahl's *Preface to Democratic Theory* (1956), and Seymour Martin Lipset's *Political Man* (1960). The revisionists understood themselves to be revising a "classical" theory of democracy, which was seen to be deeply flawed in a number of respects. The classical theory comprised three major points, which the revisionists criticized.

First, the classical theory supposed a relatively high degree of rationality and political knowledge on the part of democratic citizens. In its popular version the classical theory is personified in the image of the New England town meeting as a par-

ticipatory expression of the essential good sense and knowledge of the common person. The revisionists, however, pointed out that this image was largely a myth. As evidence, they cited the results of the first large-scale studies of public opinion carried out on the basis of systematic polling in accordance with the standards of scientific method. Study after study demonstrated that citizens were far less aware of, and knowledgeable about, political issues and affairs than the classical theory would have led one to expect.

Moreover, and even more unsettling, a series of empirical studies showed that at least at the level of opinion, ordinary citizens were decidedly less attached to the ideals of democratic tolerance and respect for different views than were political elites. These studies thus were taken to suggest that democracy was not so much threatened, as had traditionally been thought, by the usurpation of power by elites as it was by the incapacities of its citizens. The recent memory of the mass basis of fascism in Germany and Italy only served to buttress this view.

Second, critics faulted the classical theory for failing to distinguish systematically between normative speculation and empirical scientific inquiry. Revisionist democratic theory was closely tied to the behavioralist movement in Anglo-American social science. This movement attempted to model the social sciences on the natural sciences, especially with regard to method. In this view, "theory" was understood to denote a systematic set of empirically testable propositions aimed at predicting the behavior of operationally defined variables, as opposed to a more traditional and less scientific understanding that theory in politics was to be concerned with issues of values and morality. The behaviorists tended to dismiss normative theory as hopelessly subjective and unscientific, an impediment to the progress of objective and value-free social scientific inquiry.

This behaviorist attitude is manifest in many of the works of revisionist democratic theory. The revisionists understood themselves to be scientific realists, testing and often debunking the more grandiose speculative claims of classical theorists, who were portrayed as unsophisticated amateurs. The classical theorists had been concerned with the normative question of how democracy ought to work; the revisionists were concerned with the scientific question of how it actually worked.

A third criticism often made by revisionists was the classical theory's alleged failure to account for the need for leadership in democratic politics. The classical theory saw democracy as primarily the collective work of citizens and valued widespread participation in politics. It tended, perhaps unwittingly, to downplay the significance of the role of leadership in the organizations of democracy because the greater that significance, the less democratic the practices would seem. The revisionists, especially and most sharply Schumpeter, criticized what they portrayed as squeamishness regarding the unavoidable fact of leadership, and hence inequalities of actual power, on the part of classical theorists.

Faced with overwhelming evidence that the citizens of the Anglo-American polities were far less interested in, knowledgeable about, and capable of effectively dealing with the highly complex issues of modern politics than had been supposed, students of democracy could make one of two moves. One response was to take the evidence as suggesting that the political systems of the Anglo-American polities in the mid-twentieth century were in fact simply not very democratic. By making this move, they would maintain the classical theory's criteria of democracy but jettison the postulate that the regimes most proud of referring to themselves as "democratic" were in fact that. Christian Bay (in *Strategies of Political Emancipation*, 1981) expounded such a view, suggesting that

democracy was such a fine idea it was a shame no nations were willing to try it out.

Proponents of the revisionist theory made the other move. They revised the criteria of "democracy" so as to render the idea consistent with the observed realities in the Anglo-American polities. The battle between adherents of these differing responses to the first wave of modern empirical social science was immediate, hostile, and longstanding. Indeed, it can fairly be said to continue, though in a somewhat muted fashion, to this day.

Main Elements of Revisionist Theory

The revisionist theory of democracy acknowledged the failings of citizens and found a compensation for each of them elsewhere in the system. Did citizens lack the skill and experience necessary to rule successfully? The revisionist theory expected less; citizens were not literally to rule themselves but were to choose their rulers through exercising the vote in competitive elections. Were citizens less intensely active in political affairs than the civics textbooks advocated, participating only sporadically in relatively undemanding activities? This very lack of involvement was said to provide the slack necessary within the system to allow political leaders to manage policy efficiently. Were citizens less attached to norms of civil tolerance than were elites, and hence more open to the destructive appeals of demagogues and charismatic, but undemocratic, leaders? All the more reason to recognize that apathy on the part of such citizens could be seen as a functional component of a healthy democratic system, rather than a detraction from it.

Were political organizations, especially parties, organized internally along hierarchical rather than democratic lines? Did the parties shape more than respond to the issue preferences of ordinary citizens? Perhaps. But again the revisionists pointed to the systemic functions served by such arrangements. A democratic system as a whole, it was argued, need not be democratic all the way down throughout every internal subsystem. Indeed, balance could be achieved only if this was not the case. Moreover, given the degree to which individual political attitudes were discovered to be derived from emotional and symbolic sources rather than from cognitive bases of information, the role of parties and elites in providing guidance to civic energy seemed not only beneficial but absolutely necessary.

Aside from recognizing and affirming a much more significant role for political elites in a democracy, the revisionist theory also highlighted the importance of groups, rather than individuals, as a basic component of a viable democratic polity. David Truman and Robert Dahl were among the most eloquent and insightful analysts in this respect. Modifying Schumpeter's point that democracy was better understood as a method for choosing rulers than as a method of direct rule, Dahl emphasized the importance to democracy of a pluralism of groups within society. In Schumpeter's view the democratic method required only that there be more than one elite (party) competing for the votes of the electorate in order to ensure governmental accountability.

Dahl's view of democracy was not so minimalist. The range and diversity of interest groups at the level of civil society was seen to be as important a factor as elite competition. A system composed only of political elites controlling the state, on the one hand, and, on the other, a relatively unorganized and quiescent body of citizens was dangerously unbalanced. A diversity of interest groups seeking to advance their respective claims in the political arena would serve as a buffering level between the other two strata, functioning both to protect and to advance individual interests more efficiently than individuals could and also to provide a watch and check upon the responsive-

ness of governors. From a systemic point of view, the existence of a multiplicity of groups also compensated for the lack of competency on the part of individual citizens.

Reaction to Revisionism: Participatory Theory

Just as revisionist theory developed through a critique of classical democratic theory, so another theory, which we can label "participatory," developed out of the critical response to revisionism. The critics of revisionist theory did not, by and large, challenge the descriptive adequacy of the theory. It was agreed that the facts were pretty much as the revisionists related them. The challenge was over what exactly should be made of those facts and how they should be properly understood.

The critics of revisionism advanced four major claims. First, they argued that the notion of a classical democratic theory was something of a straw man created by the revisionists, implying greater homogeneity among prerevisionist theorists than had actually existed. Although there is some basis for this complaint, it is largely misguided. Obviously, no two theorists agreed upon everything, but there was a recognizable thrust to prerevisionist theory that was, broadly speaking, quite optimistic about the potential and capacity of ordinary citizens if only they were provided with sufficient opportunity for exercising democratic rights of participation. The writings of John Dewey in America (*The Public and Its Problems*, 1927) and A. D. Lindsay in England (*The Essentials of Democracy*, 1935) are characteristic.

A second frequently made criticism was that the revisionist theory had abandoned the aspirational elements of democratic values, transforming the idea of democracy from a vision that looked forward to, in John Stuart Mill's famous words, "the improvement of mankind," to a "mere" procedural mechanism. Critics complained that the revisionist view of human nature and human capabilities was unduly static and pessimistic. C. B. Macpherson (*Democratic Theory*, 1973; *The Life and Times of Liberal Democracy*, 1977) argued that the observed political failings of citizens in the Anglo-American regimes were a consequence of too little institutional opportunity and incentive to develop the powers of citizenship, rather than any intrinsic or necessary limit rooted in human nature. The idea was that citizens would develop the powers of citizenship if more avenues of meaningful democratic participation were opened to them so that they might actually learn by doing. The revisionists were seen as being committed to blocking this development, insofar as their thought suggested that democracy was not something that needed to be built and achieved but rather was what citizens of "democratic" countries were already doing, apparently rather well.

This point led to a third criticism, in many ways the most biting (and contentious), for it directly challenged the scientific self-image of the revisionists. The critics' claim was that revisionist theory was not so much a scientific theory dispassionately derived from facts as it was an ideological defense of the political status quo. The implication was that the academics articulating the revisionist theory were not the objective and neutral observers of political reality they claimed or aspired to be but in effect were the intellectual servants of the dominant political powers.

Thus the debate over democracy between the revisionists and their critics became entangled not only with the debate in Anglo-American social science generally over the possibility of scientific objectivity and the relationship between truth and power but also with the political conflicts of the period between, roughly, 1955 and 1975. These conflicts were intense and divisive, especially the conflict at the level of public opinion in the United States over American military involvement in Southeast Asia. Academics were as much a part of that conflict as were the students they taught, and the debates between revisionists and their more radical critics during this period bear the traces of those political conflicts.

The fourth criticism was that the pluralism of groups and the consequent dispersal of power envisioned in the revisionist portrait of the Anglo-American regimes was more apparent than real. Although most critics granted that these regimes were not characterized by the concentration of power generally found in the communist world, they nevertheless denied that power was dispersed enough to constitute the degree of egalitarianism required by democracy. Critics charged that the needs and interests of large-scale corporations were systematically privileged over those of other interest groups and that hierarchy rather than pluralism characterized the political process.

The difference between the two positions was exemplified in two works that became classics: Robert Dahl's *Who Governs?* (1961) and C. Wright Mills's *The Power Elite* (1956). An entire generation of graduate students would cut their political science teeth on the analysis of these two works and the perspectives they embodied.

Dahl and other pluralists argued that, while groups were not equal in their power and resources, the inequalities were not cumulative. Different groups were seen to have advantages in different issue areas, the competition between them serving to prevent the development of a monopoly on political power by any single elite or group. The political system provided opportunities for participation sufficient to ensure that no significant interests were blocked from success in the political process. Mills saw something different when he looked at the American political system. He claimed that the political conflict highlighted by the pluralists described only the "middle levels" of power. Above this, he argued, was a cohesive and interlocking "power elite" comprising economic, political, and military leaders at the apex of their institutional hierarchies.

The criticisms of the revisionist theory went hand in hand with the development of an alternative, participatory theory of democracy. Participatory theory aimed at criticizing and contributing to the transformation of Anglo-American political reality rather than scientifically describing it; in many ways the new theory harked back to the moral and developmental themes of classical theory. Prominent examples were Carole Pateman's *Participation and Democratic Theory* (1970) and Benjamin Barber's *Strong Democracy* (1984).

Drawing on the critical points just discussed, participatory theorists advocated the extension of democratic procedures of decision making to what had conventionally been understood as "nonpolitical" spheres of collective life. Employer-employee relations in the workplace were deemed especially significant in this respect. Theorists argued that it was unrealistic to expect citizens to develop the civic competencies necessary to rule themselves actively so long as most of their experience with decision making and authority occurred within the unequal and authoritarian context of the workplace structured on owner-employee lines. The democratization of industry and the workplace thus became the focal point of the practical reforms advocated by participatory theorists.

Of course, calls for increasing the power and control of workers over economic decision making directly challenge the traditional rights and prerogatives attaching to the ownership of property and capital in the capitalist market economies of the Anglo-American world. Such calls have been strenuously, and thus far successfully, resisted. Advocates of participatory theory often

take this result to testify to the ability of corporate power to thwart mass demands for more democracy, but it is not at all evident that the demand for democratization attributed to "the people" by participation theorists is really there. Defenders of the status quo argue that the absence of widespread mass demand for the dismantling of capitalist property relations and for greater worker ownership and control of the economy is testimony not to corporate power but to the common sense of the worker, who appreciates the economic efficiency and productivity of capitalist economic relations.

Participatory democrats have tended to be critical of the elements of individualism and the consequent emphasis on the rights of individuals (rather than the good of the community) prevalent in Anglo-American political culture. They are more committed to a populist concept of democracy than to a liberal one—that is, they are more committed to a politics aimed at giving expression to a majority or "popular" will said to characterize the political community as a whole than to a politics aimed at the more mundane purpose of securing individual freedom, including the freedom to avoid the public realm.

On the whole, participatory theorists have taken a relatively optimistic view of human nature, seeing the cure for democracy to be more democracy. This view conforms with the idea that democratic participation is an educational process through which citizens will develop ever greater levels of interest and rationality.

More conservatively inclined theorists see the participatory idea of democracy as dangerous insofar as it aims at politicizing more and more areas of social life. The conservative sees this tendency as the unwarranted intrusion of the public realm into the private—a process the ultimate end of which is totalitarianism, the penetration of political concerns and categories into every aspect of human life. Critics of participatory theory have also tended to hold a somewhat more pessimistic (they would say "realistic") view of human nature, one that counsels citizens to be wary of political power and its inevitable abuses. This counsel is applied to democratic politics as well as to other forms, and it is argued that the participatory theorists fail to appreciate the dangers arising from politicization.

The Crisis of Democracy: Overload and Legitimation

From 1975 onward the rancor of the debate between the revisionists and the participatory democrats tended to decline. This is not to say that much agreement on the political issues dividing them was reached. Rather, the conflict over behavioralism and issues of the scientific status of the social sciences simply lessened to a great degree. A "live and let live" mentality with regard to these issues became more prevalent. Stripped of the entanglement with issues of science and method, however, the conflict between the two perspectives continues today; the basic differences are the same even though some of the labels, catchwords, and names have changed.

Beginning in the mid-1970s and throughout the 1980s a major concern of scholars was the so-called crisis of democracy. Adherents of one view maintained that an "overload of demand" severely threatened the stability of the Anglo-American governments. More and more demands were being placed on the system by increasingly aggressive and self-interested groups, especially those trying to increase their access to a greater range of entitlements provided by the welfare state—that is, the poor. These thinkers argued that too much democracy was dangerous. Because traditional cultural norms of deference and restraint that had checked the level of demand in the past had broken down, and because the world

economy had changed in ways that severely restricted the capacity of the Anglo-American economies to grow at the rate they had maintained in the post–World War II era, the state, it was argued, could not effectively meet the demands being placed on it by the populace. The democratic electoral process only exacerbated this condition, because, in order to be elected, politicians had to promise more to a demanding electorate than they could possibly deliver. These promises then encouraged even greater levels of demand in turn.

The solution for this vicious circle resulting in "demand overload" was seen to lie in the direction of a more frankly authoritarian mode of firm and decisive leadership, especially in the executive branch of government. Such leadership would be willing to say "no" rather than capitulate to the various interests charged with creating the problem. Representative examples of this view are Samuel Brittain's "The Economic Contradictions of Democracy" (*British Journal of Political Science*, 1975), and *Democracy in Deficit: The Political Legacy of Lord Keynes* (1977), by Nobel Prize–winning economist James Buchanan and R. E. Wagner.

A very different view was taken by another group of thinkers who saw a "crisis of legitimacy" of the democratic state. They were greatly influenced by the work of the important German social thinker Jürgen Habermas, especially his *Legitimation Crisis* (1976). Leading Anglo-American exemplars of this view are James O'Connor's *The Fiscal Crisis of the State* (1973) and John Keane's *Public Life and Late Capitalism* (1984).

These thinkers attributed the inability of the contemporary state to manage economic policy in a way sufficient to achieve the levels of growth and productivity necessary to meet mass demands for goods to the state's inability to escape the controlling thumb of corporate capital. Thus, whereas the more conservative "overload" view blames the public and its demands for the crisis of democracy, the more radical "legitimation crisis" view places the blame on the system of capitalism, which requires that the interests of capital take priority over public interests. The leftist view claimed to detect a growing popular dissatisfaction with the state that was potentially the source of widespread dissatisfaction with the capitalist economy within which it was embedded. From this view arose the idea of a crisis in the degree to which the state could legitimate itself to its citizens as being genuinely democratic. Although it is certainly true that dissatisfaction with the state and alienation from public life are ever increasing in Anglo-American regimes of the late twentieth century, it is not the case that capitalist economic relations are widely and consciously seen as the cause of these phenomena.

The contrast between the overload and legitimation views of the alleged crisis of democracy is reminiscent of that between the revisionist and the participatory democratic theorists. Like the revisionists, the overload theorists fear greater mass participation in politics and see it as a destabilizing force threatening efficient policy making and administration. Like the participatory theory of democracy, the legitimation crisis view sees democracy as stunted and inhibited by the power of economic elites, and it looks forward to the dismantling of this power through the democratization of society and the politicization of citizens. Each side yearns for what the other fears.

The rhetoric of crisis applied to the Anglo-American regimes came to seem inappropriate, and fell out of use, with the fall of Eastern European communism in the late 1980s. In the last decade of the century a great new wave of interest in democratic theory and democracy arose throughout many parts of the world that had been under authoritarian rule and were attempting a transition to democracy—especially in South America and Eastern Europe.

This renewed vigor and interest in democracy in other parts of the world came at a time when the Anglo-American systems increasingly seemed to be exhausted with the demands of democracy. Civic alienation and cynicism continued to plague the health of the Anglo-American systems, and democratic theory continued to oscillate between what John Dunn calls the "dismally ideological" voice of the latest version of revisionist theory and the "blatantly utopian" voice of the latest version of participatory theory. If the democratic theory of the twenty-first century is to be helpful in alleviating these difficulties and reinvigorating Anglo-American democracy, the inspiration will likely come, ironically, from political energies, inventions, and discoveries in polities that, throughout much of the twentieth century, were considered by most Anglo-American thinkers to be incapable of practicing democracy.

Having completed the historical overview, we can conclude by examining three topics that perennially attract the attention of democratic theorists. These are the relation between political equality and social inequality, the nature of representation, and the justifiability of civil disobedience.

Political Equality and Social Inequality

At the least, political equality entails the equal legal status of all adult citizens within the democratic regime: all are equal as persons before the law, and each is possessed of the same set of political rights, permissions, and duties. There can be no second-class citizenship in a democracy. Yet to say these words is merely to specify the formal and legal requirements of political equality; the question of the degree to which political equality is compromised by the existence of inequalities in the social, economic, and familial spheres of collective life has been hotly debated throughout the twentieth century.

Democratic theorists have adopted a variety of positions in regard to the relationship between political status and the inequalities in wealth and power arising from economic class differences. At one (leftist) extreme are those Marxist socialists who maintain that democracy rightly understood is necessarily incompatible with a capitalist economy; true democracy requires a socialist economy comprising the public ownership of productive resources and a radically egalitarian (re)distribution of income shares. The underlying premise is that one's economic class identity is of such great significance that it tends to determine one's actual political status. Economic class division between those who own capital and those who do not is held to undermine and subvert the rhetoric of democratic political equality, revealing it to be a sham.

At the other (rightist) extreme are those libertarians who maintain a sharp conceptual division between the various spheres of collective life and who thus argue that formal or legal equality is itself a sufficient condition of political equality. Indeed, these thinkers argue that reformist state policies aimed at decreasing the amount of inequality in nonpolitical spheres of life so as to contribute to the realization of equal citizenship in the public sphere result in exactly the opposite. The libertarian claim is that such policies destroy political equality in the pursuit of social equality.

Of course, the great majority of democratic thinkers who address this issue take a position somewhere between these extremes. Defenders of the capitalist welfare state, ranging from American Republicans to European social democrats, disagree about the amount of redistribution of wealth to be undertaken by the state, but nevertheless they accept in principle some conceptual and practical connection between political status

and economic class. Thus, for example, it is nearly universally accepted that children should have access to publicly funded education without regard to their parents' ability to pay. The premise here is that one cannot meaningfully be described as an equal citizen if one is illiterate and unable to understand the rudiments of political affairs.

Obviously, however, there is abundant room for debate and reasonable disagreement even among those who accept the general idea of a connection between political and economic status. This is not least because there is no singular or "correct" definition of political status. Whether an aspect of a person's identity or status is political or nonpolitical is dependent on the historically contingent definitions of "political" that the community has created over time. These definitions change and shift, expanding and contracting as a result of the practice of politics. An excellent account of this process of the development of "shared understandings" and its relationship to democracy is that of Michael Walzer in *Spheres of Justice* (1983).

Economic status is not the only form of social inequality that raises serious questions about the meaning of political equality. Race, especially in the United States, has since the beginning of the regime been the dimension of "social" status that has made a lie of the proudest boasts of the realization of political equality. With the development of feminist consciousness and theorizing, gender, once conceived as a quintessentially private and nonpolitical dimension of identity, has increasingly come to be seen as highly salient to the meaning of political equality. Indeed, much of the most interesting contemporary democratic theory is being formulated by young thinkers looking at race and gender, rather than economic class, as factors bearing on democracy and political equality. Examples would include Anne Phillips (*Engendering Democracy*, 1991) and Derrick Bell (*And We*

Are Not Saved: The Elusive Quest for Racial Justice, 1987).

The Nature of Representation

What is the proper task of the legislator in representative democracy? The "passive" view of representation maintains that the legislator should, in principle and to the degree possible, aim at literally "re-presenting" the preferences of those for whom he or she stands. In this view the legislator is a channel for passing information, necessary only as a concession to the constraints of time and space that make it impossible for all citizens to "present" their own views.

In an "active" view of representation, the representative bears a much greater responsibility and consequently is charged with more tasks than is the passive legislator. The representative is to lead and educate the people he or she represents, not simply respond to their demands. Leadership requires that the representative exercise his or her own judgment about what is wise and prudent policy, even should this judgment diverge from the expressed preference of the majority of those represented. In that case the educative function of representation requires that the representative engage in the process of shaping constituents' opinion in the direction of the policy choices that the representative thinks are wise and prudent.

Participatory democrats tend to be hostile to representation generally, and especially hostile to the active view of representation, which is seen as paternalistic, manipulative, and elitist. Revisionist democrats tend to take the opposite view, seeing in active representation a counterweight to the inadequacies of the ordinary citizen.

Civil Disobedience

The question of the justifiability of civil disobedience arises in the context of any political regime, but it is especially acute in democracy.

Democracy more than any other regime is built on the political competency of the ordinary citizen. The systematic development of this competency means that the regime has an investment in positively encouraging citizens to understand themselves as a source of valid political claims who need offer no apology for exercising their voices in the public realm. Consequently, the limits to such activity, which are essential from the point of view of the order and stability of the regime as a whole, are always controversial and subject to challenge by citizens.

The democratic regime's primary claim on the obedience of its citizens, even when some particular citizens disagree with the substance of the policy pursued by the regime, derives from an appeal to the fairness of the democratic procedure of majority rule among political equals. Insofar as the process can correctly be said to have been a fair one, citizens, including those whose preferred policy or candidate lost, nevertheless are expected to obey. To refuse to do so is to claim an individual veto power inconsistent with the recognition of oneself as a political equal with one's civic peers. Hence civil disobedience would seem to be unjustifiable in terms of democracy.

Matters are not quite this simple, however. First, although it is true that fairness as modeled through a democratic procedure is considered a good thing, it is certainly not the only good thing, and it can and does conflict with other goods. Many claims to justifiable civil disobedience make appeal to some wider notion of justice or right, which is taken to limit and trump democratic procedure when the two conflict. While it would be foolish to say that such claims are valid simply as claims, it would be equally foolish to jump to the opposite conclusion and deny out of hand the justifiability of any such claim. Ultimately, such justification must depend upon the truth, whatever it is, in regard to ultimate right. Defenders of democratic procedure may be tempted at this point to claim that such procedures allow us to avoid having to inquire into and render judgment on such contentious and disputable matters. This claim is shortsighted, however, for democratic procedure is not itself self-justifying, and the chain of reasons by which a defense of democratic procedure is given will lead back to these very same perplexing matters.

Second, it is possible to argue plausibly in support of justifiable civil disobedience even within the confines set by the values of democracy itself. Indeed, it is ordinarily thought that one important factor distinguishing civil disobedience from mere crime or lawlessness on the one hand and revolutionary action on the other is that the aim of civil disobedience is to strengthen and improve, not destroy, the system of civil law disobeyed by bringing to public light and consciousness some defect within it in need of reform. The actor thus disobeys the law for the sake of the law itself, giving practical expression to this commitment by accepting the penalties that attach to the "crime."

Civil disobedience in a democracy could thus be understood as action in the service of democracy itself. Indeed, this is precisely the sort of public justification that has been given in many cases of civil disobedience in the Anglo-American regimes in the twentieth century. For example, one justification given of the various acts of civil disobedience carried out by civil rights activists in the American South in the 1960s was that these actions were necessary to goad and provoke Americans to change their blatantly undemocratic behaviors with regard to race so as to live up to their own professed democratic commitment to the political equality of all persons.

See also Capitalism; Class; Communitarianism; Elites, Political; Representation.

PATRICK NEAL

BIBLIOGRAPHY

Arblaster, Anthony. *Democracy.* Minneapolis: University of Minnesota Press, 1987; Ballmoor: Open University Press, 1994.

Bay, Christian. *Strategies of Political Emancipation.* Notre Dame, Ind.: University of Notre Dame Press, 1981.

Dahl, Robert. *Democracy and Its Critics.* New Haven and London: Yale University Press, 1989.

_____. *A Preface to Democratic Theory.* Chicago: University of Chicago Press, 1956.

Duncan, Graeme, ed. *Democratic Theory and Practice.* Cambridge: Cambridge University Press, 1983.

Green, Philip, ed. *Democracy: Key Concepts in Critical Theory.* Atlantic Highlands, N.J.: Humanities Press, 1993.

Held, David. *Models of Democracy.* Cambridge: Polity Press, 1986; Stanford, Calif.: Stanford University Press, 1987.

Levine, Andrew. *Liberal Democracy: A Critique of Its Theory.* New York: Columbia University Press, 1981.

Lipset, Seymour Martin. *Political Man.* New York: Doubleday, 1960.

Macpherson, C. B. *The Life and Times of Liberal Democracy.* Oxford and New York: Oxford University Press, 1977.

Pateman, Carole. *Participation and Democratic Theory.* Cambridge: Cambridge University Press, 1970.

Pennock, J. Roland. *Democratic Political Theory.* Princeton: Princeton University Press, 1979.

Plamenatz, John. *Democracy and Illusion.* New York: Longman, 1973.

Sartori, Giovanni. *The Theory of Democracy Revisited.* 2 vols. Chatham, N.J.: Chatham House, 1987.

Schumpeter, Joseph A. *Capitalism, Socialism, and Democracy.* New York: Harper and Row, 1942.

Stankiewicz, W. J. *Approaches to Democracy.* New York: St. Martin's, 1980.

✦ Theory, Rational choice

A theoretical system that assumes that political actors (individuals, states, groups, and so forth) have goals and that they will adopt effective and efficient means for achieving these goals. Rational choice theory is deductive: from basic premises about purposive goal-oriented behavior we can deduce explanations for political events, such as the functioning of democracy.

Game theory, often employed by rational choice theorists, models the behavior of political actors engaged in cooperative or conflictive interactions. In game theories, political actors are assumed to be aware that their fates are affected by what other actors do, they adjust their behavior to take this interdependence into consideration, and they recognize that other political actors are also sensitive to this interdependence. An example is a game of chicken. You understand that if you opt to continue on a head-on course, your rewards are very much determined by what your opponent decides to do. Of course, your opponent is engaged in exactly the same kind of reasoning.

Rational choice theory has contributed to our understanding of democracy by addressing three questions: Why do governments exist? Why do societies adopt democratic institutions? And what political outcomes occur in democratic settings?

Rationality and Government

Rational choice theory characterizes government as a solution to the problem of collective action within a society. The general problem of collective action is that individuals have every incentive not to cooperate in the provision of collective goods but rather, in the term used by Mancur Olson, to "free ride." If other citizens contribute to the provision of a collective good (for example, by paying a "tax"), an individual might be tempted to cheat on the assumption that her noncompliance would have a negligible effect on the provision of the collective good.

The flaw in this analysis, of course, is that all rational citizens will engage in a similar reasoning. Hence no individual citizen will be willing to contribute to the provision of the collective good if he expects others to free ride. If you expect others to cheat, your best strategy is to cheat as well, even if society as a whole would be better off if everyone cooperated by paying the tax. Thus, without some external enforcement of cooperation, individuals will not cooperate and pay the tax. Government, then, is an external solution to the problem of collective action. A monarchical or totalitarian government, for example, can enforce cooperation by imposing severe costs for free riding. Alternatively, societies can adopt democratic solutions to the problem of collective action.

The Choice of Democracy

Why do some societies develop democratic institutions to enforce cooperative behavior in place of monarchies or authoritarian structures? According to Olson, democracy emerges in those unique historical circumstances when two conditions are met: when a dictator is overthrown, and the conspirators are a heterogeneous group with no single leader or dominating party. If no one faction can suppress the others or segregate itself into a separate country, the choice for all the factions is either to engage in pointless conflict or to agree on a way of coexisting.

Hence the development of representative institutions is predicted in those circumstances where small groups of actors (for example, the nobility of seventeenth-century England) with relatively equal resources (for example, land) expect to interact with each other well into the future. This expectation makes these political actors more inclined to agree to representative institutions in which they can resolve conflicts over issues of collective concern (such as defense or protection of private property). This rather unique set of circumstances, which characterized England after the Glorious Revolution of 1689, when James II was overthrown and William and Mary were invited to assume the throne, provides an explanation for the country's early development of democratic institutions.

Rational choice models also attempt to explain why democratization fails. One school of inquiry employs rational choice models to explain the successful (or unsuccessful) transition from authoritarianism to democracy. The focus of this inquiry is on the major groups and parties involved in negotiating the transition. For example, using game theory one can treat the major factions negotiating the transition as actors in a two-person game. The cooperative agreements possible in the transition depend upon the coalitions into which the various factions are inclined to enter. Adam Przeworski points out that the struggle for democracy involves conflict both between the authoritarian regime and its opponents and among the allies who are vying for a favorable position once democracy has been established. He divides the opponents of authoritarianism into moderate and radical factions. The supporters of authoritarianism are divided into reformers and hard-liners. Depending upon how these factions coalesce, the transition to democracy will be successful, troubled, or a failure. For example, if moderates within the opposition bloc and reformers within the authoritarian bloc are too suspicious of each other to cooperate, the transition to democracy will likely fail.

At issue here are the types of political structures and procedures that these factions agree upon. The initial rules of the political game that are agreed upon in these new democracies will not be neutral with respect to election outcomes and leg-

islative policy decisions. For example, certain electoral laws can favor one faction over another. In Spain's transition to democracy in the 1970s after Francisco Franco relinquished power, conservative-rural parties were initially favored by electoral laws that set a minimum number of representatives that could be elected from the country's multi-member constituencies. Hard-liners had more of an influence on initial legislation than they would have had if there had been strict proportionality between constituency size and number of representatives elected to the national parliament.

Although new democratic institutions are not neutral, they must be designed so that, at a minimum, they make all major political factions comfortable with the prospect of losing power. Democracies fail when certain important political factions fear that if they lose the contest for political power they will have little chance to regain power in subsequent elections. For these factions the benefits of revising the rules of the political game are relatively high.

Collective Decisions Under Democratic Rules

Rational choice theory suggests that although individuals are able to rank their preferred outcomes from most favored to least favored, society is unable to deal with these individual rankings in any coherent fashion. When citizens' preferences are translated into collective decisions under democratic rules, the outcomes are not stable or coherent.

Lack of stability, or coherence, in voting is often illustrated by the voters' paradox. As an example, take the 1994 U.S. presidential election. Assume there are three voters. Voter 1 prefers George Bush to Ross Perot and ranks Bill Clinton last. Voter 2 ranks Clinton over Bush and Bush over Perot. Finally, voter 3 prefers Perot to Clinton and Clinton to Bush. When Bush is pitted against

Perot, the coalition of voters 1 and 2 results in a victory for Bush. A contest between Perot and Clinton results in a Perot victory. If majority rule generated coherent outcomes, we would expect Bush to beat Clinton in a two-person contest. Paradoxically, Bush defeats Perot, Perot defeats Clinton, and Clinton defeats Bush. Although individuals are able to rank their preferences from best to worst, groups are unable to do so.

In certain circumstances, voting outcomes are coherent. The median voter theorem predicts that candidates in a majority rule contest will adopt policy positions closest to the position of the median voter. (The median voter is the voter who falls right in the middle of all voters aligned on a single policy continuum.) This theorem supports the notion that the ideal point of the median voter represents the equilibrium outcome under majority rule.

Consider the ideal points of the same three voters arrayed on a single dimension, with voter 1 on the left, voter 2 in the middle, and voter 3 on the right. In a two-candidate election between Bush and Clinton, both candidates would adopt issue positions that converge to the ideal point of the median voter 2 because that voter can form a coalition with voter 1 to defeat alternatives to the right or with voter 3 to defeat alternatives to the left. Hence the ideal point of voter 2 is the equilibrium outcome; it cannot be defeated.

But we can only be sure that majority rule generates coherent outcomes when there is only one issue dimension. When there is more than one dimension, an individual who is the median voter on one dimension is not necessarily the median voter on the other dimension(s). Thus, with majority rule, in a multidimensional issue space a coalition can win on one issue and be outvoted on another. There is, as was the case with the voters' paradox, no stable outcome; we cannot predict which coalition of voters will form and whether it will last for any length of time.

These insights into democratic voting mechanisms suggest that voting results become "incoherent" when more than two candidates are running or when more than one issue dimension is being considered. Believing that democratic outcomes are not as chaotic as these findings might suggest, rational choice theorists have refined these early models. In particular, they argue that the institutional setting in which voting takes place can reduce instability, or the degree to which outcomes can cycle.

For example, formal and informal procedures in a legislature can promote more coherent outcomes by reducing the number of choices voted upon or by reducing the issue dimensions. The use of specialized legislative committees makes outcomes more stable because votes on one issue dimension are separated from those on other dimensions. An agriculture committee, for example, will consider legislation that typically can be evaluated in terms of one single issue dimension (such as relative support or opposition to agriculture subsidies).

Rational choice theory has made two major contributions to our understanding of democracy. First, democracy is essentially a set of institutions designed to allow citizens to make choices. Rational choice theory has generated elegant and powerful explanations, many of them surprising, for the outcomes we can expect from these democratic procedures. Second, the emergence of democracy is the result of bargains struck among various political actors.

Once again rational choice theory, particularly game theory, offers nonobvious, if not counterintuitive, explanations for why these actors choose democratic forms of government and for why these democratic institutions either succeed or fail.

RAYMOND M. DUCH

BIBLIOGRAPHY

Black, Duncan. *The Theory of Committees and Elections.* Cambridge: Cambridge University Press, 1958.

Downs, Anthony. *An Economic Theory of Democracy.* New York: Harper and Row, 1957.

North, Douglass C. *Institutions, Institutional Change, and Economic Performance.* Cambridge and New York: Cambridge University Press, 1990.

Olson, Mancur. "Dictatorship, Democracy, and Development." *American Political Science Review* 87 (September 1993): 567–576.

_____. *Logic of Collective Action.* Cambridge, Mass., and London: Harvard University Press, 1965.

Przeworski, Adam. *Democracy and the Market: Political and Economic Reforms in Eastern Europe and Latin America.* Cambridge and New York: Cambridge University Press, 1991.

Riker, William. *Liberalism against Populism.* San Francisco: W. H. Freeman, 1982.

Shepsle, Kenneth A., and Barry Weingast. "Structure Induced Equilibrium and Legislative Choice." *Public Choice* 37 (1981): 503–520.

✦ Theory, Twentieth century European

Twentieth-century European democratic theory incorporates the diverse range of continental thinking on the possibility of democracy. The renaissance of democracy in Europe today is an event of immense practical as well as theoretical importance. Democratic or constitutional government originally found its home in modern Europe in England, Holland, Italy, and France, but in the twentieth century these achievements often have been eclipsed by misfortune. The Continent has endured two world wars, the Holocaust, and until the early 1990s the division between the West and the Soviet-dominated East.

Moreover, Europe was the home of the earliest expressions of democratic thought and sentiment in the writings of Benedict de Spinoza, the Baron de Montesquieu, Jean-Jacques Rousseau, and Alexis de Tocqueville. But, despite some rare exceptions, these considerable achievements have often been overlooked by equally powerful critics of democracy.

Critics of Democracy

The critics of democracy have stemmed primarily from two opposing camps. Karl Marx set forth the left-wing attack on democracy. In an essay titled "On the Jewish Question" (1843), he identified the achievements of democracy in France and North America with the emergence of capitalistic economies. Marx's attack on democracy stems from a radicalization of Rousseau's famous statement in his *Discourse on the Origins of Inequality* (1755), which attributed the foundation of civil society to the enclosure of private property. Rousseau was not a communist, but it would be difficult to find a more heartfelt denunciation of the evils attending the creation of property and the establishment of social classes. Representative or, as the Marxists later called it, bourgeois democracy, was taken to be no more than a mask for protecting the property interests of the newly enfranchised middle class.

The right-wing attack on democracy goes back to the assault by Joseph-Marie de Maistre (1753–1821) on the French Revolution, but its more powerful and plausible critics were Friedrich Nietzsche (1844–1900) and Martin Heidegger (1889–1976) in Germany and José Ortega y Gasset (1883–1955) in Spain. These critics saw democracy as part and parcel of the emergence of a new phenomenon: mass society. This term was understood not simply as a numerical or quantitative category but as a new egalitarian social order, which brought with it the destruction of the network of corporate ties, guilds, churches, and landed estates that had functioned as the bedrock of premodern, traditional society. Democracy was often linked to the brutalization and uglification of life that went hand in hand with the new industrial order.

In many respects, the attacks on democracy from the right and the left were not as far apart as they often appeared. For example, Max Horkheimer (1895–1973) and Theodor Adorno (1903–1969), founders of the Frankfurt school of Marxism, took great delight in reviling what they called "the culture industry" for cheapening European art and literature through television, the cinema, and other instruments of the mass media.

The left- and right-wing attacks on democracy have declined, even if they have not disappeared altogether. After World War II the rightist assault went into eclipse because of its political associations with the defeated fascist regimes in Italy and Germany. In the wake of the emergence of the Soviet Union as a world power in the 1950s, however, the Marxist critique continued to gain power and influence even in the noncommunist West. Even though so-called Western Marxists usually repudiated the despotic features of the Soviet model, they sought to keep Marxism alive as a "critical theory" of culture and society. This endeavor often involved considerable feats of intellectual gymnastics in which Marxist theory was combined with other doctrines culled from a variety of philosophic quarters. Thus at various times in the twentieth century Marxism sought to align itself with existentialism (Jean-Paul Sartre), phenomenology (Maurice Merleau-Ponty), Freudianism (Herbert Marcuse), and structuralism (Louis Althusser). These attempts at intellectual synthesis proved exceedingly thin, and

with the collapse of the Soviet Union in 1991 there was no longer any reason to retain the pretense. The result has been the greatest resurgence of democratic theory in continental Europe since the French Revolution.

Procedural Theory of Democracy

Arguably, the most important work of democratic theory in the twentieth century was written by an Austrian economist. Joseph Schumpeter's *Capitalism, Socialism, and Democracy*, published in the United States in 1942, developed what became known as the procedural theory of democracy. This theory has had greater resonance in the United States and Great Britain than on the European continent, but the central European origins of the work are unmistakable. Schumpeter's defense of the method of democracy was developed in explicit opposition to the totalitarian experiment in "people's democracy" then under way in Soviet Russia, not to mention the rise of populist demagogues—Adolf Hitler and Benito Mussolini—in Germany and Italy.

Schumpeter's definition of democracy was based on a rejection of what he regarded as the two cardinal tenets of the classical theory of democracy. The first was the belief in "the common good," which could be determined by a rational electorate working in concert. The second was the belief in the "will of the people," which, like the common good, Schumpeter regarded as artificially manufactured or created by political leaders. In place of the classical theory, Schumpeter offered his own account of democracy as a method for arriving at collective decisions by means of a competitive struggle for people's votes. This purely functional definition, intentionally stripped of all abstract notions such as human rights or the utilitarian goal of "the greatest happiness for the greatest number," was thought to have the advantage of reducing democracy to its bare essentials: electoral politics, pure and simple. Schumpeter's contribution was to see democracy along the lines of a market in which political parties, like firms, compete with one another for votes.

Schumpeter's definition of democracy has been vastly influential and has inspired the work of theorists such as Maurice Duverger in France and Robert Dahl, Anthony Downs, and Mancur Olson in the United States. Like any influential work, however, *Capitalism, Socialism, and Democracy* has also met with severe criticism. In the first place, Schumpeter's identification of democracy with electoral politics seemed overly austere and indifferent to the whole range of democratic values without which competitive elections would be meaningless. Competitive elections, while necessary, are not a sufficient criterion to establish democracy, which must equally be concerned with political participation, deliberation, and the formation of a democratic character among citizens.

Second, Schumpeter's concept of democracy has been widely criticized as economistic and reductionist. Not surprisingly, it has gained its widest adherence among students of "public choice" and the "logic" of collective action, who view politicians as entrepreneurs and voters as consumers in the marketplace of politics. His analogy between electoral politics and the marketplace was either blind or indifferent to the very real differences in political power and resources mobilized by different groups. Furthermore, without introducing philosophically contestable notions such as "fair" or "free" to describe elections, Schumpeter had no grounds for asserting that Hitler, who gained power through popular election, was not a democrat.

Return of the Political

Schumpeterian democracy has become virtually the norm in all Western European countries and the states of North America, but the matter has not rested there. In opposition to the procedural theory of democracy, a new group of theorists drawing on the tradition of classical republicanism extending from Niccolò Machiavelli to Alexis de Tocqueville to Hannah Arendt has attempted to revive such traditional concerns as freedom, rights, equality, and deliberation as central to democracy. Recent European democratic theorists have been concerned not only with securing procedural goods, such as fair elections and party competition, but substantive goods, such as citizen participation, social justice, and the affirmation of distinct cultural and collective identities. To be sure, these themes have been developed unevenly by different writers representing diverse political experiences and unique national contexts. But rather than examining these themes for their internal tensions and inconsistencies, we will treat them here as parts of a single family seeking to adapt democratic theory to the realities of a postcommunist world.

A first step in the direction of a renewal of democratic theory has been undertaken by Claude Lefort. An early associate of Merleau-Ponty's and coeditor of the journal *Socialisme ou Barbarie*, Lefort has written widely on bureaucracy, ideology, and totalitarianism and has published a defense of democratic theory entitled *Democracy and Political Theory* (1988). Under the guise of "rehabilitating" the political, Lefort has sought to establish political experience as something autonomous, distinct from sociological phenomena such as class or economic development.

Lefort plays on an ambiguity in the French language that distinguishes between the terms *le politique* (the political) and *la politique* (politics or policy). Politics or policy refers to a specific set of procedures or activities susceptible to observation and testing that can be studied alongside other empirical phenomena (for example, economics and society). The political, however, refers not to actual distributions of power or resources but to the principles that generate society or, more accurately, different forms of society. An investigation into the political, then, must take the form of a search for the "regime" and its "shaping" of human coexistence and relations of power. It is the specific historical shape or form of power that constitutes the regime and that provides the basic unit of political analysis.

Following Leo Strauss, Lefort maintains that the concept of the regime is worth maintaining only if it refers to more than the formal structure of power. It must also take into account those traditions and beliefs that testify to a set of implicit norms determining notions of just and unjust, good and evil, noble and ignoble. The concept of the regime refers to the existence of something like a political culture that defines the shared values of a people or its way of life.

Lefort's distinctive claim is that modern democracy represents a new kind of regime unprecedented in history. Every previous regime has been based on a particular identification of power with the representation of truth. In medieval Europe, for instance, all power was thought to emanate from the monarch who was both a political agent and the representative of God. In twentieth-century totalitarian societies, all power is said to emanate from the political party, which is both representative of "the people" and the ultimate guardian of the knowledge of the laws of history and society. The modern democratic polity is unique because it breaks from all these previous attempts to identify power with a localized political space and has instead constituted a new form of sovereignty as "an empty place."

Lefort's idea is that in modern democracies power belongs simultaneously to no one and to everyone. It is characterized precisely by the breaking up of the old standards of certainty that defined traditional politics. Democratic regimes have instituted a sense of uncertainty regarding the uses of power, law, and the representation of truth. Rather than regarding this new configuration of power as dangerous or destabilizing, however, Lefort sees in it exciting new possibilities for the future. At the least, modern democracy prevents any person or group of persons from monopolizing power and thus claiming a lock on the truth. More positively, democracies have instituted a new skepticism about the uses of power. Implicit in the social practices of democracy and the periodic contestations or redistributions of power is the belief that no one has the definitive answers to the problems of society and that all attempts to restore the previous landmarks of certainty can only result in totalitarian thought control. Lefort's paradoxical formulas for democracy are "power belongs to no one" and "those who exercise power do not possess it."

In Lefort's view, what makes democracy distinctive is that it not only welcomes but preserves indeterminacy at its core. It is not so much a new constitution of authority but a continuous, albeit controlled, challenge to all authority. What Lefort does not indicate, unfortunately, are the means by which the periodic challenges to power are controlled. What is it that prevents a democratic contest for power from degenerating into a Hobbesian struggle to the death? Lefort's pleasing picture of democracy thus presupposes what it needs to establish, namely, people who are already committed to democratic norms and procedures. Instead of considering the conditions that help to create and preserve democratic indeterminacy, Lefort invites us to consider the possibility that democracy is no longer a regime bounded by law but rather is founded on an ongoing debate about what the role of law should be, about the very boundaries of the legitimate and the illegitimate.

Rule of Law

The problems of democracy raised by Lefort have been addressed with equal seriousness by his Italian contemporary, Norberto Bobbio. Like Lefort a former Marxist, Bobbio has since come to stress the need for an independent legal framework capable of preserving the fundamental rights of individuals. His works, such as *Liberalism and Democracy* and *The Future of Democracy*, have shown great indebtedness to the works of Schumpeter, Dahl, and Giovanni Sartori. Unlike Lefort, who sees democracy as an empty place full of open-ended possibilities, Bobbio regards it first and foremost as a set of procedural rules for arriving at collective decisions.

The advantage of this procedural definition of democracy, Bobbio contends, is that it fits closely with the predominantly individualistic character of modernity. Rejecting organic models of society that have a discomfiting relation to fascism (which in the past have been used to subordinate individual rights and liberties to some theoretical "general will"), Bobbio maintains that democracy is best understood in Schumpeterian terms as a form of representative government in which competitive political parties are authorized to act as intermediaries between individual actors and the government.

Bobbio's model is, then, a defense of representative government as opposed to leftist appeals for direct or participatory democracy. In historical terms he takes the defense of "modern liberty" made by the French politician and writer Benjamin Constant de Rebecque (1767–1830) against Rousseau's and the French Revolution's appeal to the absolute power of the general will. Bobbio is not insensitive to the shortcomings of existing democratic norms and procedures. In the past the problem of democracy was confined to such issues as extending the franchise, removing obstacles to voting, and holding representatives publicly accountable. These tasks, he acknowledges, have been more or less accomplished, but the surface of the problem has only been scratched. The question for democrats is not the old one of who can vote, but what people may vote for. The process of democratization has not even begun to penetrate the twin pillars of contemporary autocracy: big business and the bureaucracy. The task for future democratic leaders will be to extend democratic procedures outside the political arena, narrowly conceived, to wider areas of civil society.

To his credit, Bobbio is as aware as anyone of the pitfalls of extending democracy to the range of private and semiprivate institutions that populate modern society. He traces with considerable skill the sometimes uneasy historical alliance between liberalism and democracy. The democratic movement (which historically has enlisted the aid of socialism) has defined itself by the demand for greater equality and collective participation in all walks of life, chiefly including the workplace, while liberalism has demanded recognition of individual rights against the state, principally meaning economic liberties. Rejecting radical egalitarianism, Bobbio has defended the historical achievements of liberalism as an effective bulwark against the autocratic state. At the same time, he worries whether liberalism has the internal resources adequate to deal with the problems of inequality and social justice. Bobbio does not give a formula for how much democratization of society is either possible or desirable. Rather his procedural definition of the term leaves it open for people to decide for themselves how far to extend the democratic mandate.

The one norm on which Bobbio insists is strict adherence to the rule of law. As a former Marxist, he is all too aware of how easy it is to denounce law as an instrument of class interests and to oppose to it the rule of charismatic leaders claiming to speak for the interests of the people as a whole. But, he admits, law remains the best defense of democracy and liberty. Considering the classic question framed by Aristotle in the *Politics* whether the rule of law is to be preferred to the arbitrary rule of either the few or the many, Bobbio leaves no doubt as to the superiority of the former. Democracy is nothing other than the rule of law, and what is law but a set of rules for the peaceful resolution of conflict? The task of a democratic government today is to instill a rigorous respect for the rule of law. Without this it will become indistinguishable from the various autocracies that have haunted the chronicles of human history.

Recovery of Human Rights

The conflict between liberal and democratic values that Bobbio traces with great historical skill has been treated with even greater philosophical cogency by Luc Ferry and Alain Renaut. Because they belong to a younger generation of democratic theorists, their ideas were relatively untouched by the epic struggles between communism and fascism in which the thought of Lefort and Bobbio developed. Although deeply skeptical of Marxism, they have concentrated their attention on a critique of the French philosophy of the 1960s and the postmodern critique of Western metaphysics and its characteristic forms of rationality. In place of these postmodernist assaults, which were inspired by Heidegger and Michel Foucault (1926–1984), Ferry and Renaut have defended an interpretation of rights understood as powers and freedoms.

In an Anglo-American context, this last statement would come as no particular surprise, but in the overheated debates of contemporary French thought it stakes out a highly contested terrain. In their three-volume *Political Philosophy*, Ferry and Renaut have responded to the various "antihumanisms" that have come to populate the Euro-

pean scene. The most important of these derives from Heidegger's critique of democracy as inseparable from the technological urge to dominate and control the earth.

According to Heidegger, democracy is one vast, technological feeding frenzy erected upon a philosophy of the "subject" as the omnipotent and arrogant "lord of Being." In their various works, Ferry and Renaut have sought to rehabilitate the autonomy and dignity of the moral agent from the Heideggerian and Foucauldian assaults of the postmoderns. Drawing on the insights of the German philosophers Immanuel Kant (1724–1804) and Johann Gottlieb Fichte (1762–1814), they treat the individual as a moral agent open to an undetermined and in principle undefinable future. The meaning of their self-proclaimed juridical humanism is that human beings lack any determinate essence beyond a capacity for free agency. It is this capacity that surpasses in value all other historical, social, or national markers of identity.

Although Ferry and Renaut have defended the idea of the free individual as the most enduring legacy of modernity, they cannot help but note that the idea of democracy has suffered from the outset from a fundamental ambiguity in its understanding of rights. Drawing on the work of the American political theorist Hannah Arendt (1906– 1975), they trace this ambiguity back to its origins in the American and French Revolutions, respectively. The American Revolution is identified with the liberal concept of rights as permissions that individuals exercise on their own behalf and that serve as a bulwark against the intrusive incursions of state power. The French Revolution by contrast developed a democratic concept of rights as entitlements, which are not to be entrusted to individuals as such but are the property of the state to implement for the improvement of the collective welfare.

This distinction between rights as permissions and rights as entitlements has helped to define the shape of democracy over the past two centuries. The balance has slowly shifted from fundamentals—such as life, liberty, and the pursuit of happiness—to encompass an enlarged package of social, cultural, and economic rights to such entitlements as universal health care, paid vacation and leave time, and the right to work.

Ferry and Renaut recognize that both the liberal and the democratic traditions of rights contain flaws. If the democratic (and later socialist) concept of rights as entitlements is allowed to go unchecked, it may expand indefinitely the power of the state over civil society. But the liberal concept of rights as permissions seems unable to address adequately the needs of social justice and ways to correct inequality. The solution they offer to this alleged contradiction is an idea that is neither strictly liberal nor strictly democratic. The "republican idea" centers on the rights of political participation exercised through the vote. Rights of participation are not just permissions to vote for representatives who will then be held publicly accountable; they also provide citizens with an opportunity to form political judgment, exercise responsibility, and establish new bonds of collective solidarity among themselves. Political participation is a means not only to satisfy private, nonpolitical goals but also to ensure a more fully developed, more fully human, life.

Democracy and Civil Association

Where the new European democratic theorists have often gone beyond the older Schumpeterian concept of democracy is in their concern with the problems of citizenship in multiethnic, increasingly pluralistic societies. With the collapse of communism, where these issues were systematically repressed or denied, Eastern European theorists like Václav Havel, Adam Michnik, and Georg Konrad have turned their attention to the phenomenon of "civil society" as an alternative to the state. Originally used by John Locke and the leading members of the Scottish Enlightenment, the term entered the European political lexicon through G. W. F. Hegel's *Philosophy of Right* (1821). For Hegel, civil society referred to a web of semiautonomous associations, independent of the state, that bound citizens together in matters of common concern. Today the term has been rehabilitated to indicate the domain of uncoerced cultural, religious, and economic associations that can fill the void left by the demise of the Leninist state.

The concept of civil society has been used by democratic theorists in at least two ways. The first grew out of dissident movements in countries such as Czechoslovakia, Hungary, and Poland. These movements saw civil society as an alternative to the coercive state apparatus. Their strategy was essentially antipolitical; they regarded politics and the state as irredeemably hostile to freedom and urged citizens to join with others in sharing a life organized around nonpolitical goals. Today, however, the term has been used less as an alternative to politics than as a means of widening and enhancing the sphere of citizen participation within the framework of parliamentary systems. For thinkers like Jürgen Habermas and Claus Offe, democratic institutions require an attitude of democracy that only the institutions of civil society can provide.

The most important aspects of the civil society argument stem from the effort to sustain and promote a democratic culture and new forms of democratic citizenship. Sometimes this argument is stated in terms of reestablishing an atmosphere of trust as a fundamental precondition for a stable democratic regime, in contrast to the overwhelming environment of fear and servility imposed by the Leninist state. Citizens must be able to trust one another as well as their representatives if democracy is to prove viable. At other times, civil society is charged with reestablishing the basic norm of civility, or the mutual recognition of the worth and dignity of every individual. Unless citizens recognize one another as worthy of basic esteem and respect, democracy will not flourish. Finally, it is alleged that civil society is the very means by which democratic society can be legitimized. Civil society crucially includes the institutions of public debate through which opinion is formed. In the absence of the older means of legitimizing power, public opinion takes on an enhanced role in shaping the character of democracy and the citizens who will inhabit it.

Civil society is related to the phenomenon of political education or culture mentioned earlier. Political theorists as different as Habermas and Hans-Georg Gadamer have interpreted civil society as tied not to the pursuit of power but to the open recognition of differences and the need for a nonmanipulative kind of communication. Habermas's version of a democratic society is one in which collective decisions are arrived at through a process of argument and debate, not distorted by disparities of power. Civil society is thus conceived, somewhat idealistically, along the lines of the ancient Greek and modern German concepts of education, both of which convey a model of a liberally cultivated person.

For many of the theorists of civil society, democracy represents something like a condition of difference within a shared identity. Democracy is based upon certain common values, such as respect for the uniqueness and freedom of the individual, a market economy, and the rule of law. At the same time, the principles of a democratic culture must serve to foster an awareness of human diversity (cultural, linguistic, religious) and educate citizens toward a tolerance of and respect for these differences. Civil society today is, then, ultimately an educational institution whose goal is toleration of diversity. Democratic toleration is not simply a concession to the brute fact of difference and the frailty of human judgment. It grows out of an awareness of the deep-rooted pluralism of human association. This recognition of the multifold character of the human condition offers the best hope of promoting a democratic culture in Europe today.

Resurgence of Democratic Theory

The reemergence of democratic theory in Europe is one of the most hopeful signs on the political horizon today. Many of the debates and concerns touched upon here mirror or even reproduce arguments that have long been familiar to the Anglo-American world. But these concerns are often enriched by a language and vocabulary shaped by distinct political experiences and intellectual traditions. European democratic theorists are more likely to draw inspiration from Hegel than from Mill, from Fichte than from the writers of the *Federalist*, from Spinoza than from Locke. American political theorists who confront this renascent European democracy with an open mind and willingness to learn may well find their own understandings enlarged by the experience.

It would be foolishly optimistic to believe that the resurgence of democratic theory will be sufficient to guarantee the success of many of the new experiments in democratic rule and constitution making now abounding in Eastern Europe and the former Soviet Union. As the breakdown of Yugoslavia has demonstrated all too graphically, talk of equal rights and citizenship are fragile entities when confronted with ancient ethnic and religious hatreds. Furthermore, the survival of democratic institutions, especially in Germany, in the post–World War II years has been in large part sustained by the cold war and the artificial division of Europe by the iron curtain. Whether the future of democracy will flourish in new, radically altered conditions remains a troubling question with which political theorists will have to grapple.

See also Civil society; Class; Kant, Immanuel; Marxism; Montesquieu; Nietzsche, Friedrich; Rousseau, Jean-Jacques; Tocqueville, Alexis de.

STEVEN B. SMITH

BIBLIOGRAPHY

Arendt, Hannah. *On Revolution.* New York: Viking, 1963.

Bobbio, Norberto. *The Future of Democracy: A Defence of the Rules of the Game.* Translated by Roger Griffin. Oxford: Polity Press, 1987.

_____. *Liberalism and Democracy.* Translated by Martin Ryle and Kate Soper. London: Verso, 1990.

Ferry, Luc, and Alain Renaut. *The French Philosophy of the Sixties: An Essay on Anti-Humanism.* Translated by Mary Cattani. Amherst: University of Massachusetts Press, 1990.

_____. *From the Rights of Man to the Republican Idea.* Vol. 3 of *Political Philosophy.* Translated by Franklin Philip. Chicago: University of Chicago Press, 1992.

Gadamer, Hans-Georg. "The Diversity of Europe: Inheritance and Future." In *Hans-Georg Gadamer on Education, Poetry, and History.* Edited by Lawrence Schmidt and Monica Reuss. Albany: State University of New York Press, 1992.

Habermas, Jürgen. "Justice and Solidarity: On the Discussion Concerning State 6." In *Hermeneutics and Critical Theory in Ethics and Politics.* Edited by Michael Kelly. Cambridge: MIT Press, 1990.

Havel, Václav. *The Power of the Powerless: Citizens against the State in Central-Eastern Europe.* Edited by John Keane. London: Hutchinson, 1985.

Lefort, Claude. *Democracy and Political Theory.* Translated by David Macey. Minneapolis: University of Minnesota Press, 1988.

_____. *The Political Forms of Modern Society: Bureaucracy, Democracy, Totalitarianism.* Edited by John Thompson. Cambridge: Polity Press, 1986.

Schumpeter, Joseph. *Capitalism, Socialism, and Democracy.* New York: Harper and Row, 1942, 1962.

Seligman, Adam. *The Idea of Civil Society.* New York: Free Press, 1992.

II. POLITICAL PHILOSOPHERS

✦ Althusius, Johannes

German Calvinist political theorist who was a noted antiroyalist, a champion of federalism, and the originator of the theory of consociationalism. Born in Westphalia and educated in Basel and Geneva in civil and ecclesiastical law, Althusius (1557–1638) taught in Herborn and became rector of an academy at Heidelberg. In 1604 he was invited by the city council of Emden, in East Friesland, to become its syndic, a post that combined the functions of city attorney, advocate, and diplomatic negotiator. Because of its intense Calvinism and influence over the Dutch Reformed Church, Emden was known as the Geneva of the North. The inhabitants of Emden, who nominally were within the jurisdiction of the German empire, yearned for the independence that had been won by other northern German cities and looked to their Dutch neighbors and coreligionists for help in attaining it.

Althusius was chosen to manage the city's difficult political maneuvering because of his *Politica Methodice Digesta* (Politics Methodically Set Forth) (1603), which summarized Calvinist and antiroyalist political thought. He later was made a member of the council of church elders. His influence on religious and political thinking in Emden has been compared with that of John Calvin in Geneva.

Althusius's theory of society resembles that of other Calvinist writers but is unique in important respects. Although steeped in scriptural references, it is much more naturalistic than other Calvinist accounts. And although it is couched in the language of emerging theories of social contract, and embodies the then-radical view that authority requires the consent of the governed, it is pluralistic rather than individualistic and aimed at conciliation rather than at justification of resistance.

Althusius's naturalism followed the Aristotelian tradition, according to which people are naturally gregarious and the aim of society is harmonious association, rather than the individualistic and mechanistic view that would emerge later in the century in Thomas Hobbes's *Leviathan* (1651). Hobbes, who conceived of the human being as a moving mechanical apparatus, would characterize the state of nature as one of isolation, fear, and antagonism. Althusius, however, defined politics as "the art of associating men for the purpose of establishing, cultivating, and conserving social life among them." Society is a symbiotic association of communities on successive levels. The family is the natural association; the collegium in its various forms (mainly the guild and corporation) is the artificial, or civil, association.

From this beginning, Althusius constructed what he called a consociational model of society, one with a federal political structure based on a succession of free unions, from village to town to province to kingdom (or state) to empire. In effect, Althusius replaced the hierarchical structure of feudalism (built on the principle of subordination) with a cooperative federation of associations. In this reformed model, authority and power are distributed among constituent groups that are roughly equal in status. The whole is knit together by shared morality (based on the Ten Commandments) and common interests. Aware of the distinction between confederation and federation, Althusius allowed for both, depending on the actual degree of integration, while insisting that in either case the political system should be understood as an association of associations or a community of communities.

Althusius's federalism contrasts sharply with the early and far more influential defense of absolutism by the French political theorist Jean Bodin in his *Six Books of the Commonwealth* (1576). Although Bodin accommodated the notion that sovereignty can be located in a legislature, his refusal to recognize the feasibility of a mixed constitution best suited the claims of absolute monarchs and ruled out any effort to divide sovereignty, including the idea of federalism. Althusius's thinking, while indebted to Bodin's scholarship, reflected a concern with preserving the benefits of medieval constitutionalism, with its limitation of the power of royalty and the nobility and its functional devolution of authority among the estates, the church, the guilds, and the corporations.

Mindful of medieval experience, especially that of the leagues of German cities, and of federal practice in Switzerland and the United Nether-lands, Althusius proposed that the social contract should be understood as a mutual exchange of promises among lesser associations to create a larger association. The larger body would not dissolve these lesser associations but would include them as integral constituents. In a deliberate departure from Bodin's central thesis, Althusius assigned sovereignty not to a ruler or ruling group but to the symbiotic process by which the entire body politic engages in self-government on the various levels.

As absolutism became the norm in much of Europe, Althusius's theories came to seem anachronistic and unrealistic. Bodin's defense of sovereignty was restated, without the religious underpinnings and customary limitations, in the starkly survivalist logic of Hobbes. Those who criticized absolutism did so in the name of popular sovereignty or individual rights and saw group autonomy as inimical to both. Althusius had argued not for the rights of the isolated individual or the "general will" of an entire society but for the rights of all social groupings, emphasizing the natural bonding of the individual to the group.

In recent times, Althusius's stock has risen, as scholars have called attention to his contributions to the development of democratic theory. In shaping his concept of the constitutional state, they have pointed out, he sought to prevent the new secular authority from becoming so powerful as to deprive all lesser associations of any standing. As the theorist who introduced the consociational model of society and politics, Althusius can rightly be considered a forerunner of the many later advocates of federalism, pluralism, and other forms of power sharing, including especially the theorists of consociational or consensual democracy.

See also Consent; Contractarianism; Federalism; Hobbes, Thomas.

SANFORD LAKOFF

BIBLIOGRAPHY

Althusius, Johannes. *"Politica methodice digeste" of Johannes Althusius.* Edited by Carl Joachim Friedrich. Cambridge: Harvard University Press, 1932.

———. *Politics* [abridged]. Translated and edited with an introduction by Frederick S. Carney. Foreword by Daniel J. Elazar. Indianapolis: Liberty Classics, 1994.

Figgis, J. N. *Political Thought from Gerson to Grotius: 1414–1625.* New York: Harper and Row, 1960.

von Gierke, Otto. *The Development of Political Theory.* Translated by Bernard Freyd. New York: Howard Fertig, 1966.

✦ Aristotle

Greek philosopher who offered the first theoretical analysis of democracy. Aristotle (384–322 B.C.) was the son of the court physician of Philip of Macedon (father of Alexander the Great). He studied in Athens with Plato. After Plato's death, he traveled extensively in Asia Minor, returning briefly to Macedonia to tutor the young Alexander. Back in Athens, he founded the Lyceum. When the Athenians charged him with impiety, he fled the city, supposedly claiming with reference to the execution of Socrates in 399 B.C. that he did not want the Athenians to sin twice against philosophy.

Aristotle's study of the Greek city-state, the *polis*, presents a theory of politics that emphasizes the relationship between participation and democracy. His *Politics* analyzes the human who is "by nature a political animal." Whoever does not live in the *polis* is either a beast or a god. Humans alone possess speech, which enables them to debate the advantageous and the harmful, the just and the unjust. Only in the setting of the *polis*—and particularly in the assembly—can humans engage in such debates. To be human, one must live in a community in which one exercises the powers of one's speech, debating the collective choices that a community must make. Aristotle defines the citizen as one who shares in the decisions of the community and its offices and takes turns ruling and being ruled. Citizenship appears possible only in a regime in which "the many" participate.

Aristotle categorizes regimes according to the numbers in authority (one, a few, or "the many") and whether those in authority rule in the interest of the whole or in their own interest (good or bad regimes). He calls a regime in which the many rule for the interest of the whole a *polity*, the generic term for all regimes; he calls a regime in which the many rule for their own interest a *democracy*. Although this classification of regimes focuses on the numbers of individuals in positions of authority, Aristotle argues that the many will always be poor and only a few will be rich. Thus democracies will be the rule of the poor.

Aristotle finds most regimes to be either democratic or oligarchic (ruled by a few). Because each type has limitations, he proposes as the best practical regime one that combines the qualities of both—namely the participation of a large number of individuals but not so large a number as to create instability or allow the poor to participate. He also calls this mixed regime *polity*. No regime can be a pure form; all practical regimes mix aspects found in each of the pure forms, such as monarchy or democracy.

See also Classical Greece and Rome; Theory, Ancient.

Arlene W. Saxonhouse

✦ Bacon, Francis

English philosopher, essayist, courtier, jurist, and statesman. Bacon (1561–1626) was the first to suggest that technology—the application of natural science to practical uses—is essential for the development and endurance of democracy. Bacon's proposition was novel in the early seventeenth century and became widely accepted only after the French Revolution. It was antithetical to the position of the ancient Greeks and to the long tradition of political thought and practice influenced by Aristotle.

The Greeks thought unbridled technical innovation was incompatible with the requirements of political liberty because such innovation flatters the human love of power and novelty and hence threatens the political order that it underpins. They also rejected the concept of human nature at the root of the modern view of technology: the idea that human needs are infinite.

According to Aristotle the end of political life is moral virtue, not endless material acquisition, which even if it were possible would distort the soul and constitute a false happiness. For Aristotle, one who believed that life is fulfilled by material acquisition would care more for riches than for freedom, more for fleeting pleasure than for genuine contentment and virtue. True human happiness requires the ability to rise above the material needs that assail us.

Aristotle thought such freedom from needs possible in rare circumstances and individuals, and he used this possibility—the gentleman—as the standard for measuring the moral worth of the various political regimes. Thus aristocracy is better than democracy because an aristocracy produces and is ruled by such virtuous men. A democracy that inclines in an aristocratic direction is better than a more egalitarian one. And in any good regime, excessive wealth should be

avoided, and those engaged in the mechanical arts should not be considered citizens.

But Bacon argued that the ancient view was based on a false understanding of nature and a consequent failure to understand how far science could go in forcing nature to satisfy our desires. The ancients rejected the idea of our infinite neediness because in their view it would lead inevitably to dissatisfaction and despair. In Bacon's view the ancients came to this conclusion because they woefully underestimated the practical powers of the human mind and did not understand the real possibilities of technology.

According to Bacon, the Greek intellectual legacy was a crippling burden to be jettisoned as soon as possible. In a world rent by religious strife, it would be far better to replace the war of sect against sect by the war of all humanity against nature than to preach vain lessons about moral virtue. Moreover, a proper understanding of natural science—one that focused on the material causes of things rather than on theological speculation and metaphysical abstractions—would help solve one of the most intractable of political problems: the difference between the talented and energetic few and the slower, less talented many. In the world Bacon envisioned, the most exacting and exciting activity would be the conquest of nature, to which the gifted and ambitious would be attracted. But, in this case, the results of unfettered ambition—technological progress—would redound to the benefit of all.

Bacon's views on the nature of human needs and his belief that technology was a positive force in meeting human needs influenced all the great theorists of modern politics—including Thomas Hobbes and John Locke, the American revolutionaries, the Framers of the American Constitution and their Antifederalist opponents, the classical economists such as Adam Smith, and the great theorist of communism, Karl Marx. They all

agreed about the character of human desire: people seek power in order to get more power; the end of government is not to produce rare virtue but to facilitate ever growing prosperity; happiness, whatever it is, must take account of the fact that human wants become needs and multiply as fast as we are able to satisfy them.

Experience has proved Bacon and his followers to be correct at least in this regard: modern democracy is indeed dependent on technological progress. No one now thinks that prosperity is dangerous to democracy. On the contrary, both in theory and in practice we know that democracy is threatened by a stagnant or declining economy and that economic growth depends on scientific technology. When economic decline threatens, the social consensus—based on the shared hope for material improvement—is fragmented: the rich and the less well off mistrust each other, the old fear the young, the powerful look hungrily at the weak, and the fearful look to a tyrannical savior.

See also Hobbes, Thomas; Locke, John.

BIBLIOGRAPHY

Bacon, Francis. *New Atlantis and Great Instauration.* Rev. ed. Edited by Jerry Weinberger. Arlington Heights, Ill.: Harlan Davidson, 1989.

Caton, Hiram. *The Politics of Progress: The Origins and Development of the Commercial Republic, 1600–1835.* Gainesville: University of Florida Press, 1988.

Ellul, Jacques. *The Technological Society.* Translated by John Wilkinson. New York: Knopf, 1964.

Melzer, Arthur, Jerry Weinberger, and M. Richard Zinman, eds. *Technology in the Western Political Tradition.* Ithaca, N.Y.: Cornell University Press, 1993.

✦ Bagehot, Walter

English economist, journalist, and essayist. Bagehot (1826–1877) covered a wide range of subjects in his writings, including parliamentary representation and democracy. Chief among his contributions was his recognition and analysis of the distinction between, and interdependence of, the "dignified" (or ceremonial) and the "efficient" (or practical) characteristics of government.

Bagehot graduated with first-class honors in mathematics from University College, London, in 1846. He also qualified as a lawyer but never practiced. After working in his family's banking firm in Somerset, he succeeded his father-in-law as editor of the *Economist* in 1860. Editing, combined with a continuing interest in the family bank, remained his main occupation until his death.

On several occasions Bagehot tried and failed to enter Parliament as a Liberal. He became a close confidant of ministers, particularly on matters of economic and financial policy. Reputedly, British statesman William E. Gladstone, who served as prime minister four times between 1868 and 1894, once referred to him as "a kind of spare Chancellor of the Exchequer."

Bagehot's extensive political and constitutional writings were influenced by the works of, among others, political philosophers Jeremy Bentham and John Stuart Mill, historian Alexis de Tocqueville, and anthropologist Henry Maine. Sharing the alarm of many middle-class Victorians about being swamped by the votes of the uneducated masses, Bagehot wrote in a skeptical vein about the movement for working-class enfranchisement. Following passage of the 1867 Reform Act extending the franchise, however, he argued that the new electorate should be fitted for their new responsibilities through improved living conditions and by education. In *Principles of Political Economy* (1848), he had

written that "the only effective security against the rule of an ignorant, miserable, and vicious democracy, is to take care that the democracy shall be educated, and comfortable, and moral."

Bagehot's best-known work, *The English Constitution*, was first published in book form in 1867. The Reform Act, passed that same year, heralded the rise of a mass, disciplined party system, which was destined to render some important parts of his analysis out of date. The enduring importance of the book, however, lies in its imaginative departure from obsolete constitutional doctrine about the separation of powers and the role of the monarch, inherited from, among others, philosophers John Locke and Baron de Montesquieu and legal writer William Blackstone. As Alastair Buchan noted (in *The Spare Chancellor*, 1959), Bagehot had for some years been impressed by the contrast between the omnipotence that the rural inhabitants of Somerset attributed to the Crown and the nobility and the reality as he saw it each week in London. Buchan pointed out that Bagehot's purpose was to look at the realities of power as they existed in 1867.

Bagehot began *The English Constitution* by observing that the importance that traditionally had been attached to the separation of powers, on the one hand, and to checks and balances, on the other, had overlooked the crucial distinction between the "dignified" and the "efficient" elements of government. For many centuries past, but no longer, those elements had united in one person, the monarch. The dignified parts—the pomp and ceremony surrounding the monarch and lords—appealed to people's deference to the "theatrical show of society," Bagehot wrote. He observed that the real rulers "are secreted in second-class carriages; no one cares for them or asks about them, but they are obeyed implicitly and unconsciously by reason of the splendor of those who eclipsed and preceded them."

In Bagehot's view the efficient secret of the English Constitution lay in the cabinet, which he described as "a combining committee—a *hyphen* which joins, a *buckle* which fastens, the legislative part of the State to the executive part of the State." In contrast to the separate legislative, executive, and judicial branches derived from the U.S. Constitution—with which Bagehot drew mostly unfavorable comparisons throughout the book— the cabinet embodied a fusion rather than a separation of legislative and executive powers.

Bagehot's analysis was a brilliantly original snapshot of the English Constitution as it had come to operate in 1867. The simple but effective dichotomy between "dignified" and "efficient" aspects of government remains a valuable example. The rise of mass political parties, however, quickly overtook his depiction of the House of Commons as the place where "ministries are made and unmade." (He had in fact conceded that the House of Commons embodied a dignified as well as an efficient role, a view that is even more appropriate today.) In his introduction to a 1963 edition of *The English Constitution*, English politician and political theorist Richard Crossman observed that Bagehot had not even a premonition about the nature of the modern political party—in part because he had never visited the United States, where parties already were firmly established.

Among Bagehot's writings are literary criticism and biography as well as politics, economics, and anthropology. His collected works run to fifteen volumes. After *The English Constitution*, he embarked upon *Physics and Politics* (1872), which was an attempt to apply evolutionary theories to political development.

Bagehot is not in the first rank of democratic theorists. Nor is he one of the great pioneers of social science: his views about popular deference and political naïveté were based upon a mixture of

bourgeois prejudice and amateur psychology rather than upon systematic empirical investigation. But he was an astute, eloquent, and versatile political commentator who exerted considerable influence on his contemporaries, and his constitutional analysis throws valuable light upon the operation of representative government in an important formative era of modern British government.

See also Legislatures and parliaments; Montesquieu.

GAVIN DREWRY

BIBLIOGRAPHY

Bagehot, Walter. *The Collected Works of Walter Bagehot.* Edited by Norman St. John-Stevas. 15 vols. Cambridge: Harvard University Press, 1965–1986.

_____. *The English Constitution.* Introduction by R. H. S. Crossman. London: Collins, 1963.

_____. *The English Constitution.* Edited by Paul Smith. Cambridge and New York: Cambridge University Press, 2001.

Buchan, Alastair. *The Spare Chancellor.* London: Chatto and Windus, 1959.

St. John-Stevas, Norman. *Walter Bagehot.* London: Eyre and Spottiswoode, 1959.

Stephen, Leslie, and Sidney Lee, eds. *The Dictionary of National Biography.* Supp 1. *From Earliest Times to 1900.* Oxford and New York: Oxford University Press, 1953.

✦ Bentham, Jeremy

English reformer, author, and philosopher. Bentham (1748–1832) was one of the creators and most important proponents of utilitarian theory—the ethical theory holding that actions and policies should be approved of if they maximize happiness—and a strong advocate of democracy. Bentham's slogan about the doctrine of utility promoting "the greatest happiness of the greatest number" has a democratic ring. Although he and most of his disciples promoted democracy, there is no necessary or logical connection between utilitarianism and democracy. Some notable utilitarians, for example, John Austin and James Fitzjames Stephen, were opposed to democracy.

Bentham approved of democracy because it counteracted the tendency of all governments to be corrupt. According to his analysis, those who exercised power would, if they had an opportunity, use it for personal gain. Their interest was separate from that of the people and was therefore sinister. Because one could not rely on the honesty or sense of justice of those who held public office, the only way to prevent them from exploiting their opportunity to serve themselves instead of the people was to establish democracy. Democracy would give a political voice to the people, whose interest, by virtue of encompassing the entire populace, was whole and universal.

To promote the universal interest, the electoral institutions of democracy were required. Universal suffrage would allow the voice of the people to be reflected in the legislature; frequent elections would subject the conduct of representatives to popular scrutiny; and the secret ballot would make it likely that the votes cast were a true reflection of the people's interest. Bentham called the institution of these procedures "democratic ascendancy." In his analysis he distinguished between interests that were separate, corrupt, and sinister and the interest of the people, which was universal and democratic. This utilitarian rationale for democracy rested on the claim that democracy is an effective obstacle to corrupt government and not on any claim of justice or natural right. As a utilitarian, Bentham was concerned with happiness more than with justice.

Bentham's understanding of democracy was adopted and disseminated by many of his disciples, most notably by James Mill and a prominent group of intellectuals and politicians known as the philosophic radicals. Among them was John Stuart Mill, who subsequently made important revisions in Bentham's theory, becoming one of the most important nineteenth-century theorists of democracy.

The character of democracy, as Bentham understood it, was determined by other features of the utilitarian theory of government, all of which made his concept of democracy majoritarian but left it without checks or obstacles to the unrestrained exercise of power. One feature of utilitarian theory was opposition to the very idea of constitutional limitations; such a notion was incompatible with the utilitarian view that sovereignty was indivisible and incapable of legal limitation. Thus for utilitarians it was illegitimate to claim that limits on sovereign power could be derived from extralegal notions of morality or tradition. Bentham thought it absurd and an abuse of language to talk about government exceeding its authority or going beyond its right. He believed that utilitarianism could be linked to a science of legislation that would become the source of laws maximizing happiness, therefore making it unnecessary to place constitutional limitations on legislators.

In light of the utilitarians' opposition to constitutional limitations, it is not surprising that Bentham and most of his disciples, while admiring American democracy, criticized the American institutions that were established as constitutional limitations. These included federalism, separation of powers, judicial review, and the establishment of the Senate as a second chamber.

Another feature of the utilitarian theory of government that promoted unchecked democracy was its denial that there were human rights other than those created by a sovereign power. Utilitarians rejected the language of natural, inalienable, and universal rights. The belief that such rights were the basis of valid claims was rejected by Bentham as fictional and as originating in false views about laws of nature. Bentham called natural rights "nonsense on stilts," saying they were invented by poets and dealers in moral and intellectual poisons. He criticized both American and French references to the rights of man during their respective revolutions.

The language of rights was objectionable for another reason. Rights, Bentham said, were proclaimed in "terrorist language"; they led to anarchy and chaos. When he encountered the passage in the U.S. Declaration of Independence asserting that all men are created equal and are endowed with certain unalienable rights, Bentham decided that the Americans had reached an extreme of fanaticism. Consequently, these features of the utilitarian theory of government allowed the exercise of power without limitations, thus raising the specter of democratic despotism.

See also Mill, John Stuart.

BIBLIOGRAPHY

Bentham, Jeremy. *An Introduction to the Principles of Morals and Legislation*, edited by J. H. Burns and H. L. A. Hart. London: Athlone Press, 1970.
_____. *Plan of Parliamentary Reform*. Vol. 3 of *The Works of Jeremy Bentham*, edited by John Bowring. Edinburgh: William Tait, 1843.
Hamburger, Joseph. "Utilitarianism and the Constitution." In *Confronting the Constitution*, edited by Allan Bloom. Washington, D.C.: AEI Press, 1990.

Long, Douglas G. *Bentham on Liberty: Jeremy Bentham's Idea of Liberty in Relation to His Utilitarianism.* Toronto: University of Toronto Press, 1977.

Stephen, Leslie. *The English Utilitarians.* 3 vols. New York: A. M. Kelley, 1968; Bristol: Thoemmes Press, 1991.

✦ Burke, Edmund

British Whig politician and pamphleteer. Burke (1729–1797) was trained in the law but never practiced. After a brief career in literary journalism, he spent more than three decades in the House of Commons, where he was one of its leading orators.

Although Burke addressed contemporary issues in most of his writings and produced no formal treatise of political philosophy, he discussed all aspects of politics, including democracy, in his many pamphlets and speeches. Burke is well known for his defense of the American colonists in their dispute with the British government; for his belief that parliamentary representatives ought to form judgments in light of the broadest considerations of public policy and not by reflecting the local interests and wishes of their constituents; for his criticism of despotic British rule in India; for his condemnation of the oppressive penalties imposed on Catholics in Ireland; and above all for his critical analysis of the ideas and conduct of the French revolutionaries in *Reflections on the Revolution in France* (1790) and other works. His critique of the French Revolution defined debate about the revolution and provoked a considerable response from pamphleteers; among them was Thomas Paine's *Rights of Man* (1791).

Burke was deeply skeptical about democracy. He was not absolutely opposed to it, acknowledging that in some circumstances it might be necessary, even desirable. But he could not foresee what those circumstances might be, and he strongly believed they did not exist in his own time. Assessing the educational and economic conditions of eighteenth-century England, he concluded that democratic government would be not only inept but oppressive.

Burke's opposition to democracy, first of all, was based on his assumption that the qualifications for governing were not likely to be found within the general populace. Governing required knowledge and intelligence; moreover, those who made laws had to foresee their consequences. Foresight required prudence, which Burke called the first of political virtues. In addition to educated intelligence, prudence required experience and wisdom. All these qualities were more likely to be found among the privileged than among the common people. This antiegalitarian assumption did not prevent Burke from recognizing that many among the privileged did not possess these qualities. Although he was aware that occasionally a person in humble circumstances did possess them, he was convinced that among the common people such persons were rare.

Burke's opposition to democracy was also based on his belief that the common people had predatory and angry passions that would readily be aroused and vented if the people gained power. Normally such passions were moderated, for one of the functions of government was to restrain and discourage them. In a democratic government, however, the incentive to perform this moderating function would be removed. Moreover, the antiauthoritarian impulses unleashed in a democracy would lead to the undermining of tradition and religion, which, Burke argued, should supplement government by restraining popular passions and upholding authority. Once such controls were lifted, the result would be fraud, violence, rapine, and confiscation.

Burke offered a third argument against democracy: it had a tendency to tyrannize minorities. Democratic power—whether exercised by the people themselves or by demagogues acting in their name—could be as arbitrary and intolerant as any other power. Thus, Burke argued, the majority in a democracy was capable of inflicting on minorities greater oppressions with greater cruelty than would occur even under a tyrannical monarch. This tendency to oppress minorities was aggravated by a certain "fearless" character in democratic majorities, for they sensed that as holders of sovereign power and as makers of positive law they were above punishment. Burke therefore emphasized that democratic majorities must not be allowed to believe that their will was the standard of right and wrong. The wishes and decisions of the populace, in other words, should be subject to an independent and higher moral law. The risk that a majority might seek arbitrary power was increased by its inclination to follow the lead of ambitious, selfish demagogues. Burke's fear of majorities was similar to James Madison's concern about majority factions and anticipated Alexis de Tocqueville's warning about the tyranny of the majority.

Although Burke had little opportunity to observe democracy directly, he based his views and assumptions about it largely on the writings of ancient philosophers, including Plato and Aristotle. He used these ideas in his analysis of the French Revolution, which was the occasion for his most notable work, *Reflections on the Revolution in France*. Burke regarded the Revolution as egalitarian and democratic: it used the rhetoric of the universal rights of man, made claims in behalf of those previously excluded from participating in government, and sought to overthrow many established institutions. Early in the Revolution, however, before its main features unfolded, Burke predicted that although it affected to be a pure democracy it would soon turn into a "mischievous and ignoble oligarchy." He complained that the revolutionaries were guided by abstract theories, including the egalitarian claim of the rights of man. He also noted the revolutionaries' wish to reduce everyone to the same level; their policy of destroying monarchy, aristocracy, and church in order to achieve this goal; and their efforts to undermine religious belief and traditional morality. This course, he argued, removed obstacles to despotic power and opened the door to rule by ambitious leaders who would claim to speak in the name of the people. Having made this analysis, he called the revolutionary government "a despotic democracy" and forecast an increasingly despotic outcome to the democratic revolution. This prediction was proved correct.

For all Burke's opposition to democracy in his time, he would probably approve of democracy today, at least as it has emerged in constitutional regimes that protect individual liberty, practice the rule of law, and provide constitutional protections against arbitrary rule and despotism. He would particularly approve of those democracies that allow the perpetuation of moral and religious traditions, which, he believed, also serve as obstacles to despotism. Because the prospect today for preventing despotism is greatest in constitutional democracies, we can be confident that Burke, were he alive now, would be among their most vigorous defenders.

See also Democracy, Critiques of.

JOSEPH HAMBURGER

BIBLIOGRAPHY

Burke, Edmund. *Burke's Politics: Selected Writings and Speeches of Edmund Burke on Reform, Revolution, and War.* Edited by Ross Hoffman and Paul Levack. New York: Knopf, 1949.

_____. *On Empire, Liberty and Reform: Speeches and Letters*. Edited by David Bromwich. New Haven: Yale University Press, 2000.

_____. *Reflections on the Revolution in France and on the Proceedings in Certain Societies in London Relative to That Event*. Edited by Conor Cruise O'Brien. Harmondsworth, England: Penguin Books, 1982.

Canavan, Francis P. *The Political Reason of Edmund Burke*. Durham, N.C.: Duke University Press, 1960.

Cone, Carl B. *Burke and the Nature of Politics*. 2 vols. Lexington: University of Kentucky Press, 1957, 1964.

Freeman, Michael. *Edmund Burke and the Critique of Political Radicalism*. Oxford: Blackwell; Chicago: University of Chicago Press, 1980.

Mansfield, Harvey C., Jr. *Statesmanship and Party Government*. Chicago: University of Chicago Press, 1965.

✦ Cicero, Marcus Tullius

Statesman, orator, and writer during the late Roman Republic. Cicero (106–43 B.C.) overcame the traditional boundaries that reserved high political office to patricians. In 63 B.C. he became the first nonaristocrat in thirty years to attain the highest political office in the Roman Republic, the office of consul. While consul, he successfully defended Rome from conspiracy, but he may have acted illegally by condemning the conspirators to death. This action limited his subsequent involvement in politics, though after Julius Caesar was assassinated in 44 B.C., Cicero eloquently warned against Mark Antony's designs on the republic. When Antony came to power, he arranged for Cicero's assassination.

While removed from active public life, Cicero drew on Plato's primary political works to write his own *De republica* and *De legibis* (on laws).

Cicero did not favor a widespread democratic regime. In *De republica*, he asks which is the best form of government (monarchy, aristocracy, or oligarchy) and praises the liberty characteristic of the regime in which no power is greater than the people. He distinguishes between regimes in which the people choose their leaders and those, like Athens, where the people themselves hold political office. He praises the former. In aristocracies and in kingships the people will be ruled by the "better" or more virtuous and will benefit when their concerns are addressed by those most capable of attending to their interests.

Of the three regimes, Cicero favors the kingship of the most virtuous man, but he argues against any pure regime. Instead, a mixed regime provides security against the injustice of one man, the arrogance of the few, and, quoting from Plato's *Republic*, the unbridled power of the many found in democracies. The best model for the stable mixed regime appears in the Roman Republic of the second century B.C.

In *De legibus*, Cicero tries to balance tendencies toward both democracy and aristocracy by proposing laws that would moderate the excesses of too much power among the people. Although eager to retain the institutions that gave Rome its democratic aspects, Cicero worried about democracy's potential for corruption and disorder. The virtuous are by nature obliged to provide leadership for the state, which will benefit by accepting their rule.

See also Classical Greece and Rome.

ARLENE W. SAXONHOUSE

BIBLIOGRAPHY

Cicero. *On the Commonwealth and on the Laws*. Edited and translated by James E. G. Zetzel. Cambridge and New York: Cambridge University Press, 2000.

✦ Cleisthenes, Son of Megacles

Greek statesman and political reformer who molded ancient Athenian democracy into its final form. Cleisthenes (c. 570–c. 508 B.C.) set up democratic institutions that endured through Athens's golden age of the fifth century B.C. and survived as long as the political independence of the city itself.

Cleisthenes was a leading member of the ancient family of the Alcmaeonids, who were influential in Athenian politics from the seventh through the fifth centuries B.C. In Cleisthenes' time, Athens was evolving from an agrarian community with a government dominated by local aristocrats into a more prosperous city-state with extensive overseas commercial interests. Public life was in continual civil strife, much of it based on rivalries between traditional clans and between people from different parts of the surrounding territory. Political reform was clearly needed.

Solon, celebrated for codifying the city's laws, began the transition from aristocracy to democracy with his reforms of 594 B.C. About 570 the process was interrupted by Peisistratus, who established a dictatorship that passed after his death to his son Hippias. Cleisthenes and the Alcmaeonids were generally opposed to Peisistratus and his family. Most of this time the Alcmaeonids were in exile, but in 510 they persuaded Sparta, a rival city-state, to send an army to return them to Athens and eject Hippias.

After the fall of Hippias, Cleisthenes was given the task of setting up a new form of government. He modified Athenian government in two important ways. He opened full citizenship to many people who previously had been excluded. And his restructured government, which reduced the influence of local magnates and ancient clan structures, encouraged all citizens to view themselves as part of a larger Athenian state.

He abolished the four traditional tribes into which the citizens of Athens had been grouped and created ten new ones. Each new tribe consisted of the men living in different neighborhoods, or demes, carefully selected from across Athens's territory. No one region dominated any tribe. This reorganization was successful because, although the new tribes discouraged regional factions by being built from neighborhoods scattered across Athens and its territory, the neighborhoods themselves were natural and traditional units of population.

Cleisthenes also created an executive Council that was chosen from the ten tribes, first by election, later by lot. The Council prepared business for an Assembly of all adult male citizens. The Assembly ultimately voted on all matters of state.

A long-term benefit of Cleisthenes' reforms was that they spread the experience of governing widely among the ordinary citizens of Athens. In practice, any interested citizen could serve on the Council. Much of Athens's day-to-day government was handled by subcommittees of the Council. All Council members rotated through these subcommittees for short periods, and ordinary citizens could thus acquire high-level government experience that usually is reserved for professional politicians and civil servants.

After Cleisthenes, Athenian democracy grew strong because every citizen felt that he could become involved and make a difference.

TONY DAVIES

BIBLIOGRAPHY

Forrest, William George Grieve. *The Emergence of Greek Democracy, 800–400 B.C.* London: Weidenfeld and Nicolson, 1966; New York: McGraw-Hill, 1979.

Hignett, Charles. *A History of the Athenian Constitution to the End of the Fifth Century B.C.* Oxford : Clarendon Press, 1970.

✦ Gandhi, Mohandas Karamchand

A leading practitioner of civil disobedience and the father of India as a nation. Gandhi (1869–1948) was born into a Hindu business caste at Porbandar in Gujarat, India. His childhood was religious but unstriking. After studying law in England he went in 1893 to South Africa, where as a young lawyer he became involved in politics and nonviolent civil disobedience. He returned to India in 1915 and took up the cause of Indian freedom from British rule, for which he worked for the rest of his life. He was assassinated in 1948.

During his student days in England, confronted with an alien environment, Gandhi was forced to reflect on questions about his identity, culture, and religion. He read a great deal about other religions. Until he left India, Rama, an important figure in the Hindu pantheon who was viewed by many as an embodiment of moral excellence, was the greatest religious influence in his life. As a result of his further readings, Gandhi was influenced by Jesus. He found the Sermon on the Mount especially moving. Subsequently, the works of Leo Tolstoy, Henry David Thoreau, and John Ruskin would also impress him.

Gandhi's early experiences in South Africa were transformative. Like India, South Africa was a British colony. Many Indians had been taken there as indentured laborers, and the laws were racially discriminatory. Gandhi was thrown off a first-class railway compartment and kicked off a footpath because he was not white. In each case, he refused to respond violently. From a quiet religious man, he gradually became a political activist, organizing the Indian community in Natal, launching collective acts of civil disobedience, and forcing the British to withdraw several racial laws. In the process, Gandhi developed a remarkable reputation for his philosophy and technique of struggle, called *satyagraha* (truthful and nonviolent struggle). He also came to be known as a *mahatma* (great soul).

Civil Disobedience

A few years after his return to India in 1915, Gandhi began to apply the principles he had practiced with the small Indian community in South Africa on a much larger scale. A campaign for inclusion of the masses in the nationalist movement against British rule was Gandhi's first significant political success. The Indian National Congress (also called the Congress Party) was leading the nationalist movement, but it was headed by politicians who distrusted the masses and wished to engage in constitutional negotiations with the British for self-rule. Arguing that unless the masses supported the leaders the British would not concede self-rule, Gandhi wrested the leadership of the Congress Party from the "moderates." He persuaded the party to use the tactic of civil disobedience. The emphasis would be on the use of indigenous language and symbols to mobilize the masses, most of whom were in no position to understand the rhetoric and language of the anglicized elite of the Congress Party.

The first civil disobedience movement was launched in 1920. Gandhi called off the movement in 1923, when a nonviolent march degenerated into the killing of a score of police officers. Earlier, Hindu-Muslim riots had broken out in several parts of India. India, concluded Gandhi, needed greater education in nonviolence. The second civil disobedience movement in the early 1930s turned out to be more effective. It shook the British, as millions disobeyed British laws, suffered blows, and went to jail.

Gandhi saw politics and religion as inextricably linked to each other. His charisma was based on an exemplary display of ethical behavior and on a remarkable capacity to endure personal suffering in pursuit of what he called truth and nonviolence.

He influenced a whole generation of Indians (and many people from other countries), turning what was essentially an English-speaking, urban middle-class struggle against the British into a mass movement for Indian independence between 1919 and 1947. Civil disobedience was practiced on a vaster scale, and for a longer period, than at any other time in history.

Violence, Gandhi argued, was not the way to deal with British rule in India. The superior military force of the colonial power could always overwhelm violent acts of defiance, whereas colonial rule would not last for long if the rulers used force against a people who, while protesting, did not react violently. By making the use of violence morally disgusting, principled nonviolence would produce helplessness in the ruler. The British thus were not to be killed; they were to be politically defeated. Nonviolent resistance to unjust laws—civil disobedience—would subdue the British and build a strong Indian nation.

As it turned out, although anti-British violence was minimal in India's struggle for independence, Gandhi could not eliminate violence from India. Fighting between Hindus and Muslims accompanied the nationalist movement. Ultimately, not one but two nations—India and Pakistan—were born. On the whole, however, that the nationalist movement remained nonviolent was an extraordinary achievement. Historically and comparatively speaking, most national independence struggles began with violence or eventually turned violent.

Religious Ideas and Implications for Democracy

Politics was central to Gandhi's life, but it was for him a moral pursuit and an expression of his deeper religious and ethical beliefs. It is hard to comprehend his politics without understanding his key religious ideas. His insistence on nonviolence, for example, stemmed from the nondualistic tradition of Hinduism, which teaches the fundamental unity of the divine and the created. If all human beings are children of God, nobody, Gandhi argued, can be killed. He maintained that because human beings have innate goodness, they can be persuaded to realize their true self. If one has the moral courage to suffer for the sake of truth, even a mighty adversary, he believed, can be converted. His emphasis was on moral and psychological transformation. Nonviolent mass mobilization in politics was a means to that end. It would restore India's pride and strength, build a national community, and enhance the moral standards of the nation so built.

These beliefs had implications for democracy. Gandhi's emphasis on the moral transformation of society meant that he did not like a definition of democracy that stressed institutions and processes, ignoring the ends they served. He believed, with Thoreau, that the best government was that which governed least. This position led to the idea of "village republics," which would manage their own affairs fully and depend only minimally on the central government. People who led moral lives would require little governmental direction. Gandhi preferred direct democracy, which is possible at the village level, to indirect representative democracy.

Still, his emphasis on nonviolent resistance left a positive legacy for India's representative democracy. After Gandhi, nonviolent protests and mass mobilizations acquired such legitimacy that in the first twenty years of Indian democracy most political parties used them as a way to oppose the government of the day. Ironically for Gandhians but fortunately for the more pragmatic politicians of independent India, the legitimacy of nonviolent means and the abhorrence with which political violence was viewed also implied that governments could use coercion to crush parties or movements that used violence in politics. That, in effect, made it easier for the government to deal with violent protests.

Gandhi's success in building a nation also had a positive influence on India's democratic life. There has to be a political unit within which a democratic system can take root. One of Gandhi's principal aims was to build an Indian nation out of an old, disparate civilization. Through mass involvement in the nationalist movement against a common adversary, Gandhi and his colleagues turned India's diverse ethnic, political, and linguistic groups into a nation. Democracy in independent India was a distinct beneficiary of Gandhi's nation building.

A serious failure marred Gandhi's extraordinary political life, however. He was unable to convince the Muslim upper and middle classes that an independent India would represent their interests. Being a religious Hindu, he argued, did not mean being anti-Muslim: piety and religious tolerance could go together. The Muslim League did not agree. It led the movement for a partition of India on Hindu-Muslim lines. Gandhi had Muslim followers, including many who were deeply religious. Muslim politicians, however, triumphed over them in winning the loyalties of the Muslim middle class. Of the 100 million Muslims in India in 1947, 65 million became citizens of Pakistan. The rest stayed in India. The emergence of Pakistan was accompanied by horrendous Hindu-Muslim riots.

Arguing that Gandhi was too soft toward the Muslims, that he was "feminizing" the "Hindu nation" by celebrating nonviolence, compassion, and suffering, a Hindu fanatic killed Gandhi a few months after India achieved independence. In his defense, the assassin would later argue that he shot Gandhi in order to save the nation from weakening further and to restore national strength. Meanwhile, millions gathered, including many from abroad, for Gandhi's funeral—to offer their final respects to a monumental life.

See also Hinduism; King, Martin Luther Jr.

ASHUTOSH VARSHNEY

BIBLIOGRAPHY

Brown, Judith. *Gandhi: Prisoner of Hope.* New Haven and London: Yale University Press, 1992.

Dalton, Dennis. *Mahatma Gandhi: Nonviolent Power in Action.* New York: Columbia University Press, 1993.

Gandhi, Mohandas Karamchand. *The Essential Writings of Mahatma Gandhi.* Edited by Raghavan Iyer. Delhi: Oxford University Press, 1991.

Nandy, Ashis. "The Final Encounter: The Politics of the Assassination of Gandhi." In *At the Edge of Psychology.* Delhi: Oxford University Press, 1980.

Nehru, Jawaharlal. *Nehru on Gandhi.* New York: John Day, 1948.

Parekh, Bhikhu. *Gandhi.* New York: Oxford University Press, 2001.

_____. *Gandhi's Political Philosophy.* Notre Dame, Ind.: University of Notre Dame Press; Basingstoke: Macmillan, 1989.

Rudolph, Lloyd, and Susanne Rudolph. *Gandhi: The Traditional Roots of Charisma.* Chicago: University of Chicago Press, 1983.

✦ Hegel, Georg Wilhelm Friedrich

German philosopher of the early nineteenth century. Hegel (1770–1831) is best known for his philosophy of history and for a comprehensive system of thought that touches on all major branches of knowledge. His political significance is a function of both the power of his own doctrines and the influence of his students and followers (preeminently Karl Marx), who interpreted and transformed them.

Born in Stuttgart, Hegel studied theology at the University of Tübingen, where he met Friedrich Wilhelm Joseph von Schelling. The two collaborated for several years though they later broke apart. Hegel's important early works include an 1802 essay on natural right and positive law and the famous *Phenomenology of Mind* (1806), which many scholars consider his greatest work. He published the first edition of his *Science of Logic* between 1812 and 1816. He was appointed to the University of Berlin in 1818, from which post he published, among other works, the *Philosophy of Right* and an expanded version of the *Encyclopedia of Philosophical Sciences in Outline*.

Hegel supported a modified constitutional monarchy, with significant liberal elements. He argued that a state organization of this sort (effectively realized or about to be, he claimed, in the Prussia of his day) was rational in the sense of satisfying human beings' basic material and spiritual requirements. His theory of the state thus constitutes an essential link in his general argument about the progressive direction of history and its culmination in the present as the objective realization of human freedom.

Hegel's followers split between those (such as Karl Rosenkranz and Johann Erdmann) who favored a more conservative reading of his politics and those (such as Ludwig Feurbach and Marx) who stressed what they claimed to be its revolutionary implications.

SUSAN M. SHELL

BIBLIOGRAPHY

Patten, Alan. *Hegel's Idea of Freedom*. New York: Oxford University Press, 1999.
Pinkard, Terry. *Hegel: A Biography*. Cambridge and New York: Cambridge University Press, 2000.

✦ Hobbes, Thomas

English philosopher and author of the political treatise *Leviathan*, published in 1651. Hobbes (1588–1679) is widely recognized, along with his contemporaries Francis Bacon, Galilei Galileo, Benedict de Spinoza, and René Descartes, as one of the founders of modern science and modern politics. But his contribution to the theory of democracy is disputed and remains a controversial subject today.

The reason for the controversy is that Hobbes's political science includes some features that are highly undemocratic and others that are fundamental to modern democracy. On the one side, Hobbes argued that absolute sovereignty and arbitrary power are necessary to prevent civil war. He favored a strong unified state—which he compared to the Leviathan, a mythical monster in the Old Testament Book of Job—and specifically defended absolute monarchy while castigating the republics of ancient Greece and Rome for their instability and for causing bloodshed in the name of their ideals.

On the other side, Hobbes originated many principles that later were incorporated into the traditions of liberal democracy, such as the theories of the state of nature and the social contract, the notion of individual natural rights (especially the right of self-preservation), the theory of representation, and a broad cultural argument for the materialism of bourgeois civilization and the enlightenment of the common people. Probably the best label for Hobbes's political theory is "enlightened despotism," a term that immediately indicates why modern democrats are ambivalent about Hobbes.

The Historical Problem of Civil War

To understand what led Hobbes to advocate views that seem offensive or extreme to many people today, one must recognize the fundamental political problem that motivated his thinking: the fear of civil war. Many scholars assume that Hobbes's views were simply a consequence of his times and personal temperament—the reaction of an admittedly timid man to the chaos brought on by the major event of his life, the English Civil War (1642–1660). Although one cannot deny the influence of personal experience, Hobbes clearly demonstrated in his historical writings that his thoughts transcended his times. He had studied the history of civilization from the days of ancient Egypt and Israel to the classical republics of Greece and Rome to the feudal monarchies of Christian Europe and uncovered a common flaw in all traditional forms of authority—namely, their dependence on disputable opinions and doctrines. Hobbes's political science therefore had a rational beginning point rather than a purely personal one. Beginning with a historical analysis of civilization, Hobbes explained why every society hitherto had been prone to degenerate into civil war.

Hobbes argued that every civilized society emerged from barbarism when it attained sufficient leisure to cultivate the arts and sciences and to refine the intellect. As a result, the domination of primitive societies by military chiefs and tribal patriarchs gave way to the authority of wisdom and learning possessed by priests, philosophers, and scholars. Instead of using coercive power, the learned authorities of civilized societies use opinions and doctrines—divine law, natural law, and customary law—to rule over others. Civilization therefore seems an advance over barbarism because the rule of force is replaced by the rule of opinion.

But Hobbes did not think this development makes civilization a more felicitous condition than barbarism, for the intellectual authorities who preside over civilization are quarrelsome and destructive. By disdaining the use of force and attempting to rule simply by controlling opinions, they separate might from right and create a division of sovereignty between temporal and spiritual powers. At the same time, they quarrel among themselves about whose doctrines are authoritative. Their claims of superiority, however, rest on nothing more than appeals to authority, in the form of privileged knowledge about intangible higher powers. Thus their disagreements over doctrines cannot be settled by arguments alone. Each party gathers its followers and resorts to violence, making doctrinal warfare the plague of civilization.

This was true, Hobbes argued, in ancient Israel, when the prophet Moses claimed to be the sole spokesman for God and was challenged by Aaron and Korah, as well as in the later period of kingship, when self-appointed prophets criticized royal rule. It was true in the time of Socrates, when dialectical philosophers disturbed the Greek city-states with disputes about natural justice. It was also true in the Middle Ages, when Scholastic disputation over the metaphysical abstractions of Aristotle and Thomas Aquinas rocked the universities, and in Hobbes's own time, when the doctrines of the Protestant Reformation and democratic Levellers led to the sectarian violence of the English Civil War. In fact, Hobbes explained the entire English Civil War between King Charles I and Parliament as a war over doctrines, the inevitable result of doctrinal disputes that were built into Western civilization. His general conclusion was that the very activity of civilization—its cultivation of the arts and sciences and its reverence for the wisdom of intellectual authorities—is the cause of its own destruction.

Changing History Through the Enlightenment

Because Hobbes viewed doctrinal conflict as the historical problem of civilization, he faced an unusual dilemma in designing a solution. Would not any doctrine he proposed simply create another conflict? Could the very science and philosophy developed in Western civilization be used to promote lasting civil peace rather than doctrinal warfare? In attempting to answer these questions, Hobbes never seriously entertained the possibility, as did Jean-Jacques Rousseau and the later romantics, of returning to a more naïve, prescientific era. He rejected this option as undesirable because he recognized that primitive men were killers too, although he conceded that they were less cruel than civilized intellectuals. Hobbes also rejected a return to primitive life because he thought it unnecessary: a new kind of science could be developed that would establish indisputable knowledge for the first time in civil history. Hobbes described this new kind of science metaphorically as bringing light to the kingdom of darkness; it later became known as the science of enlightenment, or simply the Enlightenment.

For Hobbes, the Enlightenment aimed to make a radical break with the habits of thought that had prevailed in every civil society until the seventeenth century. The most stubborn habit was the tendency to trust in the wisdom of authorities—in the inspired words of priests and prophets, in the learning of philosophers and wise men, in the traditions of ancestors, in the jurisprudence of legal scholars, and in the ideas of anyone with expert knowledge. Hobbes believed that such trust was responsible for much of the bloodshed and irrationality of civilization and must be replaced with a radically new attitude: the questioning of all intellectual authorities and the determination to teach all individuals to think for themselves. These two simple notions—distrust of authorities and thinking for oneself—were the driving force of Hobbes's science of enlightenment.

Hobbes was aware that his new science faced formidable obstacles. The tendency to trust in the superior wisdom of authorities is rooted in certain passions that are so powerful and universal that they seem ineradicable. One is the fear of invisible powers: the fear of demons, ghosts, and other supernatural beings that haunt the imagination. Such fear causes the ignorant masses to surrender their minds to religious authorities. But the problem of blind faith is not confined to the masses; the authorities themselves are too trusting to act rationally. They are driven by the passion of vanity, or vainglory, which causes them to believe that they are specially favored by superhuman powers. Their characteristic illusions are the belief that God speaks to certain men in inspired language and that those with special abilities to reason are naturally superior—beliefs that support the notion of a divine or natural title to rule and that encourage private citizens to rebel against the established laws. Such beliefs have been especially influential in the Western world, where the Aristotelian-Scholastic tradition predominates.

Hobbes sought to overthrow the traditional way of thinking with a science of enlightenment that operated on two levels, psychological and metaphysical. The psychological level attacked the passion of vanity with an opposing passion, the fear of death. Lessons in the dangers of vain philosophy were combined with metaphysical arguments about the ultimate nature of reality: that bodies in motion are the only reality and mechanical causation explains all phenomena of nature. Explanations that relied on immaterial causes, such as occult qualities or miracles, were rejected as superstitions and delusions. The only safe course is to abandon the grandiose conception of man as a spiritual being (possessing a soul, free will, and an incorporeal mind) and to adopt the Hobbesian view of man as a machine, a creature of mechanistic passions who responds to external stimuli with reflexive appetites and aversions.

Hobbes added to these lessons in humility by showing that the ultimate consequence of misguided beliefs is the collapse of civilization. This warning was made in his famous teaching about the state of nature. Although many scholars claim that the state of nature is merely a logical hypothesis, Hobbes did not simply invent it; rather, he derived it from historical knowledge and the premises of his science of enlightenment.

Hobbes's concept of the state of nature depicted mankind's natural condition as a war of all against all in which every trace of common authority has been abolished, every convenience of civilization is destroyed, every individual is exposed to continual fear and danger of violent death, and "the life of man is solitary, poor, nasty, brutish, and short." This condition is natural in the sense that it is a description of primitive life as well as the fate of every preexisting civilized society. It reflects the historical experience of anarchy and warfare brought about by the universal passions for security, power, and glory.

On a more theoretical level Hobbes intended to refute the Aristotelian-Scholastic claim that man is by nature a social and political animal. In a stark image, he showed that man is by nature antisocial and that rulers are not natural or divinely ordained. The only thing that can be considered natural is the passion of fear or the desire for self-preservation. This is the ultimate lesson of Hobbes's science of enlightenment: individuals are left naked and alone in the world, without God or nature to provide for their needs. Everything of benefit—civilization, government, law, property, science and technology, even words for good and evil—must be made by an effort of the human will in the interest of self-preservation.

Hobbes's Political Science

Hobbes's political science focused on the logical steps of moving from the premises of the state of nature to the construction of an artificial society. The primary assumption of the state of nature is that government does not exist by nature or by divine ordination; it must be created from the wills of isolated individuals. Hobbes outlined the steps in nineteen rational precepts, which he called laws of nature. The guiding idea of these precepts is that the natural right of self-preservation is the only justifiable moral claim and that transferring the means of self-preservation to a common power is the most rational course of action.

The common power is the sovereign, a person or body with undisputed coercive power and final authority in all matters. The sovereign can be created in two ways, both of which are legitimate but not necessarily equally effective. The first is by natural force—the action of a conqueror or tribal patriarch (a warlord, a clan leader, a military chief) who simply overpowers everyone else and makes them submit in return for a cessation of hostilities and, hence, preservation. Hobbes called this method *commonwealth by acquisition* and noted that it is the way most of the nations of the world were created (including England, a hereditary monarchy established by conquest in 1066). The problem with conquest is that it lacks a doctrine of right to justify it in the eyes of the people.

Hobbes therefore proposed a second way, *commonwealth by institution*, which means creating a sovereign by consent or by contract—a voluntary submission of all people to a third party who alone possesses coercive power and acts as the arbiter of disputes. By this act of submission, the people authorize the sovereign to represent their wills. But the sense of mutual obligation is limited because the sovereign is not accountable to the people, and the people are not bound to obey if the sovereign is not powerful enough to protect them. For Hobbes, the social contract implied popular consent, but it entailed only conditional obligations.

The sovereign, whether created by force or by consent, has absolute and arbitrary power. Hobbes insisted that the will of the sovereign is law and cannot be disputed as unjust because there is no higher authority on earth to judge its actions. The sovereign unites the temporal and spiritual realms under a single head and possesses formidable powers—including the use of all means to maintain civil peace; the right to determine what doctrines are fit to be taught publicly; the power of war and peace; the power of rewarding and punishing (by settled laws if possible, by arbitrary will if necessary); and the power to resolve religious disputes and to determine the rules for public worship. Against these powers, no subject may rebel, although every individual retains the inalienable right to self-preservation and hence a personal right of resistance to anyone who threatens his life.

Because the powers of rulers inhere in sovereignty as such, the choice of which form of government is best—monarchy, aristocracy, or democracy—is a secondary matter. The decisive criterion is prudential: the best government is the one most able to preserve civil peace by virtue of its strength and efficiency. Following this guideline, Hobbes recommended absolute monarchy and condemned democratic or republican forms of government. The crucial factor in Hobbes's evaluation of regimes was the nature of the deliberative process: whether it encourages the rational passion of fear or the irrational passion of vainglory.

In monarchies, deliberation is private; it takes place between the king and a few trusted counselors where there is no need for vain posturing or displays of rhetoric. Because caution, even fear and doubts, can be expressed, rational discussion of policy is possible. By contrast, deliberation in democratic or republican governments occurs in public assemblies where political rhetoric is used to sway public opinion and contests of oratory are the featured spectacles. In public assemblies the passion of vainglory drives each speaker to outdo the others with extravagant claims, causing factionalism, extremism, and instability. Hobbes therefore viewed democracy as nothing more than an "aristocracy of orators." He referred to the republics of the ancient world as the Greek and Roman anarchies that inspired many bloody revolutions, including that of Parliament in the English Civil War. For these reasons Hobbes believed that democracy should not be glorified by being linked with the exalted names of liberty and justice but condemned for fostering anarchy and rebellion.

In judging regimes solely by the criterion of stability, Hobbes took the momentous step of abolishing the distinction between just and unjust regimes. He flaunted this pronouncement by declaring that tyranny is nothing more than a misliked monarchy. His only concession to those fearful of tyranny was to counsel sovereigns to be enlightened in exercising their power. If they ignored his advice, he reminded his readers of the fundamental lesson of historical experience and the state of nature: any government is better than no government.

The Controversial Legacy

Hobbes is controversial because he defended absolute monarchy and condemned democracy. But his political science is based on a theoretical doctrine that has important democratic implications because it is modern, secular, and rational—a product of the scientific enlightenment.

Scholars who emphasize Hobbes's political absolutism and extremism put him in the antidemocratic tradition; they see him as a precursor of modern totalitarianism and the "new Leviathan" states of the twentieth century. Other scholars argue that Hobbes's undemocratic political views can be downplayed because they are not logically required by his scientific doctrine, which is not only enlightened but essentially democratic. They contend that Hobbes's science promotes a critical attitude toward traditional authorities, even among the common people; that it establishes the state of nature and the social contract as the foundations of government, thus implying popular sovereignty; that it treats the state as a secular institution whose purpose is limited to preserving civil peace and protecting the natural right of self-preservation; and that it opens a private sphere of limited freedom for economic activity and the pursuit of material comforts. In this view Hobbes is the philosophical founder of bourgeois liberalism.

Scholars who see Hobbes as a founder of liberalism can also point to his influence on John Locke and Rousseau. Both philosophers adopted the radical teaching of Hobbes's state-of-nature doctrine: government is not natural or divinely ordained and must be created artificially by a social contract or the consent of the people. Locke's modification was in softening Hobbes's teaching about the dangers of anarchy and in making government accountable to the people for the protection of property rights. Rousseau further softened Hobbes's state-of-nature teaching and developed a more democratic but no less absolutist version of the social contract. Hobbes thus may be seen as the philosopher who first stated the bold and sometimes harsh premises of liberalism, the leading democratic theory of the modern age.

See also Contractarianism; Locke, John; Obligation; Rousseau, Jean-Jacques; Spinoza, Benedict de.

ROBERT P. KRAYNAK

BIBLIOGRAPHY

Baumgold, Deborah. *Hobbes's Political Theory*. Cambridge and New York: Cambridge University Press, 1988.

Collingwood, R. G. *The New Leviathan*. Oxford: Clarendon Press, 1942.

Eisenach, Eldon. *The Two Worlds of Liberalism: Religion and Politics in Hobbes, Locke, and Mill*. Chicago: University of Chicago Press, 1981.

Johnston, David. *The Rhetoric of "Leviathan": Thomas Hobbes and the Politics of Cultural Transformation*. Princeton: Princeton University Press, 1989.

Kraynak, Robert P. *History and Modernity in the Thought of Thomas Hobbes*. Ithaca, N.Y.: Cornell University Press, 1990.

Macpherson, C. B. *The Political Theory of Possessive Individualism*. Oxford: Oxford University Press, 1964.

Martinich, Aloysius. *Hobbes: A Biography*. Cambridge and New York: Cambridge University Press, 2001.

Strauss, Leo. *The Political Philosophy of Hobbes*. Chicago: University of Chicago Press, 1936.

Warrender, Howard. *The Political Philosophy of Hobbes: His Theory of Obligation*. Oxford: Clarendon Press, 1957.

✦ Hume, David

Scottish philosopher and historian. Hume (1711–1776) was a leading figure of the Scottish Enlightenment, a period of remarkable intellectual achievement by a disparate group of eighteenth-century Scottish thinkers that included Adam Smith, Francis Hutcheson, Adam Ferguson, and Thomas Reid. Hume contributed to the theoretical foundations of democracy by tipping the balance toward the moderns in the contest between ancient and modern understandings of human nature and the purpose of political life. His contributions to contract theory and political economy may be understood in part as a reaction to the intellectual achievement of the main thinkers of the Enlightenment of the seventeenth century.

Hume's Critique of Contract Theory

Hume was the first to discern danger lurking in the rationalism of his seventeenth-century predecessors. The political science of both Thomas Hobbes and John Locke was built on their intellectual construction of a state of nature, intended to reveal the "natural condition" of humankind. From this teaching, people were to derive political guidance, specifically for understanding the civil order as the result of a social contract. The social contract, in turn, was presented as the only legitimate foundation for a political order because such a contract requires the consent of the members of the political community. Hume believed such theories were dangerously abstract: they had no historical basis and could serve only to delegitimize otherwise successful and even exemplary political institutions.

Hume regarded the British constitutional order as the most perfect system of liberty ever found compatible with government. The British system involved a complex and fragile balance of forces and moreover was the gradual result of a long historical evolution. It could not be traced to any legitimating contract. Hume believed "original contract" theory, as he called it, was an abstraction with dangerous practical implications. He noted the development of what he called parties from principle (especially abstract speculative principle), which, he suggested, pose an unprecedented political danger because they lead to ferocious and intractable factional conflict. Hume thus anticipated the dangerous political consequences of abstract rationalism, or what we would today call ideological politics, such as emerged in the French Revolution some years after his death. Hume's emphasis on the evolution of political institutions and practices, and the necessarily fragile nature of a decent civil order, were antecedents of the more famous observations of Edmund Burke near the end of the eighteenth century.

Political Economy

The thinkers of the Scottish Enlightenment are celebrated perhaps most of all for their contributions to political economy. With some justice they are often regarded as the founders of this discipline. The seminal work was Hume's *Political Discourses* (1752).

Trade, as Hume noted, had never been considered a matter of state before the seventeenth century. The explanation is partly to be found in the deep prejudice against commerce and trade that had been characteristic of men of honor and ambition since the republics of antiquity. The ancient republics were fiercely independent communities; their citizens regarded political matters to be of the highest importance. Trade and commerce were handled by resident aliens and were regarded with contempt.

The political thinkers of the seventeenth century, however, proposed to lower the goals of political life: the justification of a commonwealth should be security and prosperity for individuals, not virtue or empire. Hume's first essay confronts this issue directly by asking whether the ancient or the modern approach is a better guarantee of the greatness of a state or sovereign. Hume argues convincingly that the modern emphasis on free individuals seeking their own prosperity is superior because this emphasis accords with human nature. The inclinations for individual security and prosperity are much more powerful and universal than is the fierce patriotism of the republics of antiquity. Knowledge, industry, and sociability coincide with the spread of commerce and civility. The progress of the arts and sciences is naturally accompanied by political institutions that foster humanity and justice.

Although there is no necessary connection between Hume's political economy and political democracy as such, the relation to liberal individualism is obvious and undeniable. Insofar as democracy depends on respect for the judgment of the common people (including the principle that individuals are the best judges of their own interests), we can trace a connection to the Scots' explanation of how a complex economic order results naturally and spontaneously from the decisions of individuals seeking only to improve their circumstances.

Hume's Influence on the American Republic

Eighteenth-century America, like Europe, witnessed a debate between the principles of ancient republicanism (virtue, public spirit, and the suppression of commerce or trade) and those of modern commercial society, in which the greatness of the state or sovereign is linked to a flourishing economy of free individuals pursuing their private interests. The Scottish Enlightenment contributed substantially to the eventual victory of the latter view. James Madison's argument in *Federalist* No. 10 follows Hume's view in suggesting that an extended republic offers a remedy for the furious factional conflict which throughout history had been the bane of the republican form of government. Alexander Hamilton was a powerful advocate and spokesman in behalf of the principles of commerce and economic development, which were championed by Scottish thinkers against the agrarian republicanism favored in other quarters.

Even Thomas Jefferson, who much later attempted to get Hume's *History of England* banished from the library at the University of Virginia because he believed it showed Tory sympathies, seems to have taken the Scots seriously. Certainly Jefferson was proud of his role in eliminating the laws of entail, which preserved aristocracy. Perhaps more than any other single political measure, the elimination of such inheritance laws cleared the field for the growth of rambunctious commercial impulses, as Alexis de Tocqueville later observed.

See also Burke, Edmund; Hobbes, Thomas; Locke, John; Madison, James; Tocqueville, Alexis de.

BIBLIOGRAPHY

Campbell, R. H., and Andrew S. Skinner, eds. *The Origins and Nature of the Scottish Enlightenment*. Edinburgh: John Donald Publishers, 1982.

Graham, Henry Grey. *Scottish Men of Letters*. New York: Garland Publishing, 1983.

Hume, David. *Essays: Moral, Political, and Literary*. Edited by Eugene Miller. Indianapolis: Liberty Classics, 1985.

Livingston, Donald W. *Hume's Philosophy of Common Life*. Chicago: University of Chicago Press, 1984.

Mossner, Ernest Campbell. *The Life of David Hume*. 2d ed. Oxford: Clarendon Press, 1980.

✦ Kant, Immanuel

Eminent and influential German philosopher. The son of a poor saddle maker, Kant (1724–1804) studied at the University of Königsberg, where he became a professor and remained the rest of his life. He is rightly regarded as a major German advocate of democracy, at a time when democratic ideas were still revolutionary in Prussia, which was governed largely by the principles of hereditary monarchy and feudal privilege. In particular, he is regarded as a positive example of the kind of thinking that might have taken hold in Germany rather than the ideas of the imperial state and Nazism.

Many of Kant's writings were directed to philosophers and thus are not easily accessible.

The one work that was most clearly intended for the general reader, and which was widely read and translated, is *Perpetual Peace* (1795). This work, which eloquently argues for democracy in domestic government, sees democratic government as the way to avoid international war. By rooting the prospects for international peace in such a domestic shift toward political self-rule, Kant got past the criticisms of naïveté directed at earlier proposals for the elimination of war. He argued that the tendency of states to be power-minded rather than peace-minded would cease when they were governed by their own people rather than by hereditary rulers. The processes of democracy would require openness rather than secrecy. Democracy would produce rational decision making that would serve the true interests of the majority of the people. Secrecy sets the stage for international intrigues, power politics, and wars, but wars never serve the real interests of the people.

One of the continuing questions posed by Kant's arguments is whether political processes that work well for domestic government can work as well for international relations. Relations among states tend to be anarchic. An advocate of world government overcomes this difficulty by eliminating the anarchy and by eliminating international dealings, as all sovereignty is combined. But Kant did not endorse this solution. He favored retaining the idea of separate nation-states, with these states perhaps eventually coming to be governed democratically. He envisaged openness rather than secrecy and peaceful rather than violent settlement of disputes working among such states.

Rather than advocating world government, Kant proposed a league of free states, all maintaining separate sovereignties but settling their disagreements without recourse to violence. Separate sovereignties would preserve the variety of cultures and allow a set of choices for individuals. Anticipating the ideas, and some of the paradoxes, of the League of Nations and the United Nations, Kant was committed to democratic rule within separate nations, large and small, rather than in one democratic worldwide entity in which every individual's vote would count the same.

If only because many states might remain under autocratic rule, and thus continue to be power-minded and expansion-minded, Kant did not argue that peace was easy or inevitable. He argued, however, that war would be almost impossible among self-governing states. His proposal for a league was addressed to guarding such states, collectively, against the attacks of nondemocratic powers.

Kant's optimism about the interrelationship between a good solution in domestic affairs and a good outcome in international affairs was echoed later in the writings of the Italian patriot Giuseppe Mazzini (1805–1872) and in the thinking of the American president Woodrow Wilson (1856–1924). Indeed, such a belief might be regarded as implicitly present in virtually all of Western liberal thinking (and in Marxist thinking) about politics: a belief that good things go together and that what solves domestic problems solves international problems as well.

Admirers of Kant's reasoning today note that it is indeed difficult to find an example of a war fought between two political democracies. Anyone carrying forward an enthusiasm for such a linkage between political democracy and peace could, like Kant, attribute this connection to a variety of factors. Democracies presumably are more likely to find each other's governments morally legitimate and will be less likely to perceive an ideological reason to intervene in each other's affairs. Democracies are governed by checks and balances, and they require openness of decisions, both of which preclude some aspects of militarism and preparation for war. Finally, governments by consent of the governed will reflect the aversion to war and killing that most humans feel.

This reasoning parallels the classic Marxist-Leninist belief that wars would never be fought between socialist states. Marxists and liberals have agreed that good domestic arrangements lead to the good international outcome of peace; they have disagreed, of course, as to what a good domestic political and social arrangement would be. Skeptics respond to liberals (and to Marxists as well) that good things do not necessarily go together and that an absence of war between democracies may reflect only how few democracies have developed over the years. Democratic government has not yet had a fair chance to get into a war with its own kind.

Democracy, however, seems to be replacing communist rule in some areas of the former Soviet Union. And it has replaced military juntas in many countries in Latin America and Africa. Political scientists are again asking whether Kant's optimism will finally get a fair test.

GEORGE H. QUESTER

BIBLIOGRAPHY

Doyle, Michael J. "Kant, Liberal Legacies and Foreign Policy." *Philosophy and Public Affairs* 12 (summer/fall 1983): 205–235, 323–353.

Flikschuh, Katrin. *Kant and Modern Political Philosophy.* Cambridge and New York: Cambridge University Press, 2000.

Gallie, J. B. *Philosophers of Peace and War.* New York: Cambridge University Press, 1978.

Hinsley, F. H. *Power and the Pursuit of Peace.* New York: Cambridge University Press, 1967.

Kant, Immanuel. *Kant's Political Writings.* 2d ed. Edited by Hans Reiss and translated by H. B. Nisbet. Cambridge and New York: Cambridge University Press, 1991.

Kuehn, Manfred. *Kant: A Biography.* Cambridge and New York: Cambridge University Press, 2001.

Saner, Hans. *Kant's Political Thought: Its Origin and Development.* Translated by E. B. Ashton. Chicago: University of Chicago Press, 1973.

Waltz, Kenneth. *Man, the State, and War.* New York: Columbia University Press, 1965.

✦ King, Martin Luther, Jr.

African American theologian who played a pivotal role in changing the course of race relations in the United States. King (1929–1968) was the son of the minister of Ebenezer Baptist Church, one of the largest and most prestigious Baptist churches in Atlanta, Georgia. The family's social position gave them some protection from the pervasive and rigid segregation and racism of the time. A gifted student who entered college at age fifteen, King initially rejected the idea of becoming a minister but later changed his mind. He graduated at the top of his class from Crozer Theological Seminary. In 1954 he became minister of the Dexter Avenue Baptist Church in Montgomery, Alabama.

King's views on social issues, including democracy, were cast in a religious perspective. For thirteen years of public life, he made the policy of passive resistance (begun by Mohandas Gandhi) the basis of his efforts to provide visibility and moral direction to the civil rights movement. King saw the evils of racism, discrimination, political inequality, and economic injustice as significant deviations from the democratic ideal of governmental authority derived from the people and as obstacles to effective participation and equality among all citizens.

King's public life, from December 1, 1955, to April 4, 1968, spanned some of the tensest years of race relations in the twentieth century. Segregation was a way of life in the American South, and King saw indignities heaped upon African Americans by public authorities and private individuals. To King, these conditions demanded action; clearly, a political struggle was in order. His work challenged the customary relations between whites and African Americans. The changes sought by blacks such as King not only disturbed the relative social positions of the races but also revised the practice of democracy to extend political rights and social privileges to African Americans.

The now well known event that brought King national visibility seemed insignificant at the time. Rosa Parks, a tailor's assistant in a department store, violated the seating regulations for Negroes on a Montgomery city bus. She was arrested on December 1, 1955, when she refused to comply with segregationist law and move to the black section at the back of the bus. King led the Montgomery bus boycott that followed and achieved national prominence when he directed a stream of protests against segregated public facilities across the South.

King felt that many educated blacks were complacent and indifferent to the civil rights struggle, while many uneducated blacks were passive. Both groups feared economic reprisals and suffered from a lack of self-respect. Many leaders in the black community were not respected because they were thought to have been chosen by the white community. Those officials who did not emerge from the ranks of blacks were stigmatized.

King felt that, under pressure, the white community would withdraw its support for segregation. He believed that by appealing to their conscience, he could make the great majority of white Americans recognize the difference between democracy and the practice of segregation. He wanted to establish strong ties between whites and blacks who had common problems and a common belief in a democratic order.

The approach King advocated was nonviolent resistance, one of the most potent weapons available to oppressed peoples in their quest for social justice. Not based on hate, and essentially forgiving, passive resistance is direct action that channels anger at injustice into a loving and creative search for a resolution. After the Montgomery bus boycott, King's thoughts and actions ultimately had repercussions throughout the world. He is closely identified with the founding of the Southern Christian Leadership Conference in 1957; massive protests in Birmingham, Alabama; the March on Washington, D.C., in 1963; and marches for voting rights in Selma, Alabama, in 1964. For his efforts to achieve international brotherhood, King received the Nobel Peace Prize in 1964.

King later worked against the Vietnam War. He saw that the war diverted government resources and attention from the civil rights movement and that it led to new injustices. The pace of government enforcement of school desegregation was slow, the government was reluctant to move against other racist practices, and African Americans were being conscripted for front-line combat duty in numbers double that of their percentage of the population.

With the passage of time, the impatience of African Americans grew and the resistance of whites stiffened. King urged mass civil disobedience as the next step after nonviolent resistance—though he did not live to see that step taken.

In 1968 he announced a Poor People's Campaign to focus on the plight of the poor, a major component of which was to have been a march on Washington, D.C. Before this campaign he went to Memphis, Tennessee, in support of a strike by sanitation workers. He hoped to discourage threats of violence and to give nonviolent protest a chance. In Memphis on the evening of April 4, 1968, King was shot and killed by James Earl Ray as he stood on his motel room balcony. He was thirty-nine years old.

King's effectiveness as a key actor in the American civil rights movement is beyond question. In 1983 the U.S. Congress designated his birthday, January 15, a federal holiday in honor of his contributions to American society and democratic government.

See also Gandhi, Mohandas Karamchand.

WILLIAM J. DANIELS

BIBLIOGRAPHY

Bishop, Jim. *The Days of Martin Luther King, Jr.* New York: Putnam's, 1971.

King, Martin Luther, Jr. *Stride toward Freedom: The Montgomery Story.* New York: Harper and Row, 1958.

_____. *Where Do We Go from Here? Chaos or Community?* New York: Harper and Row, 1967.

_____. *Why We Can't Wait.* New York: Harper and Row, 1964.

Lewis, David L. *King: A Critical Biography.* New York: Praeger, 1970.

Miller, William Robert. *Martin Luther King, Jr.: His Life, Martyrdom, and Meaning for the World.* New York: Weybright and Talley, 1968.

✦ Locke, John

English philosopher whose writings helped lay the foundations of modern liberal democracy. Locke (1632–1704) studied, taught, and practiced medicine at Oxford University from 1652 until 1667. He then became secretary to the Whig leader Anthony Ashley Cooper (later Lord Shaftesbury), who had him appointed secretary to the Board of Trade and sent him on a diplomatic mission. He was expelled from Oxford for his anti-Royalist politics and fled to Holland in 1683, returning to England in 1689.

Whether Locke advocated a democratic form of government remains controversial, though he did develop many of the principles of liberalism that were influential in the history of democratic theory. These fundamental principles included the natural liberty and equality of human beings; individuals' rights to life, liberty, and property; government by consent; limited government; religious toleration; the rule of law; the separation of powers; the supremacy of society over government; and the right of revolution.

Locke's most important work of political theory was the *Two Treatises of Government*, published in 1689 to vindicate the Whig revolution of 1688, in which the English Parliament replaced James II with William and Mary and reasserted its own constitutional role (though most of the book was written earlier). In the *First Treatise* Locke refuted the theory of the divine right of kings as advanced by Sir Robert Filmer (1588–1653). This theory was widely invoked in Locke's time by the Tory advocates of royal power. Locke rejected Filmer's derivation of political principles from obscure scriptural passages, his assumption that a particular form of government and even particular rulers were divinely ordained, and his acceptance of the patriarchal family as the model for politics. Locke thus cleared the ground for his own *Second Treatise*, which derived political principles from human reason, relegated forms of government and rulers to human choice, and considered family and politics as separate spheres of human activity.

The State of Nature and the Idea of Consent

Locke's fundamental hypothesis in the *Second Treatise* is what he called the *state of nature:* the natural condition of all human beings as one of freedom and equality. By nature human beings are constrained only by their own reason (the dictates of which Locke called the *law of nature)*, not by the will of any other human being. This hypothesis contrasts sharply with the theory of divine right, which asserts that God subordinates some human beings to others, as well as with Aristotle's claim that natural inequalities subordinate some human beings to others.

Locke argued that in a state of nature, prior to government, individuals could acquire property through their own labor without help from God or a human sovereign. Others would be obligated by the law of nature to respect private property. Individuals could give away, exchange, sell, or accumulate property. Locke's justification for such natural economic rights was that human labor produced almost all value, with nature providing only the raw materials, which he deemed almost worthless, and that accordingly private appropriation and accumulation did not lessen but increased the amount left for others. In *Several Papers Relating to Money, Interest, and Trade* (1696), Locke argued against government limitation of interest rates and currency depreciation, contending that civil laws cannot successfully thwart the laws of value or supply and demand resulting from the actions of individuals. These claims have led to Locke's being considered one of the originators of the spirit of capitalism. His theories laid the groundwork of modern political economy as developed by Adam Smith in *Wealth of Nations* (1776).

Men and women in a state of nature could form families through voluntary conjugal contracts. It was the duty of parents to preserve, nourish, and educate their children until the children reached the age of reason. Locke's account of these natural relations, which gives the economic and familial spheres a kind of priority to and independence of government, also helps to clarify the distinctive features of political power. Unlike economic and familial power, political power includes power over life and death. But political power does not belong to its owners as a kind of property to be used or sold for their benefit, nor does it consist in paternalistic education of irrational individuals by rational ones.

In the state of nature individuals enjoy and defend rights not only to their lives (as in Thomas Hobbes's account) but also to their liberty and property. Liberty is the basic fence protecting life; any threat to one's liberty, any attempt to place one individual under another's arbitrary power, may be resisted as an attack on one's life. No one can reasonably consent to slavery, a condition that may be worse than death, though slavery may be the penalty imposed on those who have violated the law of nature. In the state of nature it is each individual's right to execute the law of nature by all penalties including death. Because, in the state of nature, every least difference is apt to end in war, and war once begun tends to continue, the enjoyment of natural rights to life, liberty, and property is uncertain. Thus it is reasonable for individuals to leave the state of nature and establish civil society.

Because adult human beings are by nature free and equal without any natural subordination of one to another, all rightful political power exists only by consent. Locke's view contradicts any justification derived from conquest as well as the classical conviction that superiority in wisdom or virtue carries with it a right to rule. By consenting to membership in a society, individuals give up entirely the right possessed in a state of nature to punish others. But the liberty they enjoyed there is surrendered only as far as is necessary to preserve themselves and the other members of society.

The tacit consent indicated merely by being within the territory of a government and enjoying the protection of its laws obliges people to obey those laws; however, the consent that makes them permanent members of a civil society and that renders its government rightful must be the express consent of living individuals (not long-dead ancestors), such as that expressed in freely taken oaths of allegiance by adults. (Locke would regard as nonsensical pledges of allegiance by children not yet of the age of consent.) Governments that do not enjoy the consent of the governed are not entitled to obedience.

The Limited End and Power of Government

As Locke conceived of individuals as possessing rights to life, liberty, and property in a state of nature, so he regarded the end of government as the protection of the lives, liberties, and properties of all members of society as far as possible. (Locke sometimes called the end of government the preservation of "property," referring to these three rights collectively, because each is conceived of as property, something that individuals cannot rightfully be deprived of without their consent.) Governments may deprive individuals of life, liberty, or property only as required by that end, and they may protect individuals only from force or fraud by others, not from their own negligence or prodigality. This limited end of government, which is the heart of modern liberalism, contrasts sharply with classical and medieval conceptions of the end of government as the improvement or salvation of souls, the punishment of vice or sin, the propagation of the truth, or the glorification of God.

This limitation and contrast are especially important in Locke's *Letter concerning Toleration* (1689), in which he argued that the civil power is confined solely to the care and advancement of civil goods (such as life, liberty, health and freedom from pain and possession of property) and that it neither can nor ought to be extended to the salvation of souls. Locke concluded that government should tolerate all religious opinions and practices except those that interfere with the civil rights of others or the preservation of civil society or that reject the duty of such toleration. Although few denominations might have met that test in Locke's time, through *The Reasonableness of Christianity* (1695) he contributed immensely to the modern liberalization of religion, which allows it to meet those conditions for toleration.

In the *Second Treatise* Locke tried to limit not only the end of government but also its power. Government cannot possess absolute arbitrary power over the lives and property of the people. This limitation of power is a corollary of the limitation of end: a power given only for the end of preserving life, liberty, and property cannot be used to destroy, enslave, or impoverish its subjects. Locke also stated this limitation in the traditional terms of the priority of the public good and natural law over civil law. But, in the new understanding of liberal individualism, he took the public good and natural law to mean the preservation of society and the good of every particular member of society as far as by common rules it can be provided for. Government cannot rule by decree without officially published laws and authorized judges: rule of law distinguishes civil society from a state of nature in which the law of nature is unwritten and unrecognized by human beings swayed by passion and interest.

Government likewise cannot take any part of an individual's property without consent, which Locke equates with the consent of the majority or their representatives. Locke also treats this limitation as a direct consequence of the definition of the end of government as the preservation of property. It is this limitation that inspired the American revolutionary slogan "no taxation without representation." Finally, rulers cannot transfer power as if it were their own property to hands other than those designated by the people.

Forms of Government

One of the most democratic elements of Locke's political theory is that once individuals have consented to government, political power belongs to the people acting by majority decision, constituting what Locke calls a perfect democracy, unless or until they establish another form of government. Even in a form of government other than a direct democracy, political power therefore should ultimately be derived from democratic action. The people, or society acting through the majority, are prior and superior to the government or state. Locke, however, avoided saying that the people are sovereign: the limitations he set on the end and power of government were meant to limit even the people and to counter any doctrine of sovereignty understood as absolute arbitrary power.

Locke's principles of government by consent with limited end and power and ultimate popular supremacy laid the ground for liberal constitutionalism. The people by majority decision establish the form of government by a voluntary grant, which Locke calls the *original constitution*. Because this constitution is the original and supreme act of the society, antecedent to all other laws, and because it depends wholly on the people, no inferior power can alter it. Thus Locke establishes the basis of the position that a constitution is paramount over ordinary laws: it is prior to them, it is what authorizes the legislature to make them, and it is the act of the people themselves rather than the act of the legislature (a position argued in its classic form by Alexander Hamilton in 1788 in *Federalist* No. 78). Locke was a constitutionalist rather than a populist. Once the people have delegated their authority through the constitution to the authorities it constitutes, they do not resume that authority as long as that constitution and government last. Locke was not, however, a doctrinaire constitutionalist; he recognized that the

uncertainty of human affairs may prevent the framers of a government from settling important questions and compel them to entrust such matters to the prudence of later governors. He also recognized that the people may be irrationally averse to amending even the acknowledged defects of the original constitution, so much more powerful is custom than reason.

Unlike Plato and Aristotle, Locke was concerned less with sketching a best form of government than with delineating the origin and extent of government and thereby distinguishing rightful governments that subjects are obligated to obey from illegitimate ones they are entitled to resist. Indeed, his claim that the majority may exercise legislative power themselves as a perfect democracy, put it into the hands of a few men and their heirs or successors as an oligarchy, give it to one man as a monarchy, or create a mixed form of government, as they think good, suggests almost an indifference to forms of government, the central subject matter of classical political philosophy. Allowing the majority to establish the form of government they think good might seem both more democratic and less democratic than insisting that they establish a democracy and regarding any other form of government as illegitimate.

But Locke allowed the majority less latitude in choosing a form of government than first appears. First of all, he ruled out absolute monarchy as inconsistent with civil society and therefore not a form of civil government. For civil society implies the possibility of appeal, in a dispute between any two persons, to common laws and recognized judges. By uniting all legislative and executive power in one man, absolute monarchy leaves him still in the state of nature in regard to those under his dominion. Second, Locke's stipulation that government may not take property without the consent of the majority or their representatives effectively requires every form of government to include one democratic branch for purposes of taxation (as the English mixed constitution was supposed to do with its king, lords, and commons). Indeed the breadth with which Locke sometimes used the term *property* and the wording of other passages in the *Second Treatise* suggest that the consent of a representative body may be required not only for taxation but for all legislation. Thus, although Locke did not insist on an unmixed government composed entirely of democratic elements, he did require that the government established by the majority in the original constitution must include at least one representative democratic component.

The Structure of Government

Whatever the form of government, Locke argued that the same persons should not control both the legislative and the executive powers. It is too great a temptation for human beings apt to grasp at power to enable the persons charged with making laws to exempt themselves from their execution. Legislators who are themselves subject to the laws are compelled to make laws that serve the public good. The legislative power is the supreme power because the power that can give laws to another must be superior to the power that merely executes those laws. Legislative supremacy appears to be a corollary of the rule of law: if individuals are to be free from absolute arbitrary power, they should be subject only to general laws and those commands necessary to enforce them.

In addition to the legislative and executive powers familiar from later versions of the theory of the separation of powers, Locke discussed what he called the *federative power*—the power over war and peace, leagues and alliances, and all transactions with persons and communities outside the commonwealth. This power is an extension of the power possessed by every individual in the state of nature. Locke acknowledged that the executive and the federative powers are almost always united in the same hands because both require control over the armed force of the society. He insisted, however, that they are really distinct. Although the executive power is subordinate to the legislative power, the federative power is much less capable of being directed by laws and so necessarily must be left to the prudence of those who wield it. General laws cannot direct in advance the actions of foreign powers as they can those of subjects; foreign policy must instead flexibly take account of other countries' varying actions, designs, and interests.

Foreign policy is not the only area in which Locke qualified legislative supremacy. Where the executive shares in the legislative power (as the English monarch formerly did and the American president does in a qualified way through the veto), Locke conceded that the executive may also be called supreme. More generally, Locke argued that because it is impossible to foresee all accidents and necessities, the good of the society requires that many decisions must be left to the discretion of the executive, both where the law is silent and sometimes even against the law. This doctrine of executive prerogative seems to contradict not only legislative supremacy but the rule of law itself. Locke, however, believed that the people may judge whether the exercise of such prerogative tends toward their good. If necessary, they can limit executive prerogative through laws passed by the legislature. Because prerogative exists only for the people's good, and indeed is nothing but what the people allow and acquiesce in, such limitations are not encroachments on a power belonging inherently to the executive.

Revolution and Education for Liberty

Although Locke considered the legislative power to be supreme within any form of government, it is a fiduciary power given by the people as a trust to be employed for their good and is forfeited when used contrary to that trust. The people retain the supreme power to remove or alter the legislative power. This supremacy of the people or society over the government or state is expressed in the election of representative legislative bodies and ultimately in the right of revolution. Transgression of its limits dissolves a government and the obligation of its subjects to obey it. Political power reverts to the society acting through its majority, which must act to remove the offending rulers and establish a new government before society dissolves under the pressure of tyranny.

Balancing this sense of vigilance and urgency in the exercise of the right of revolution is the people's obligation to be sure the violated right is worth the cost of vindicating it. They may well tolerate great mistakes, and even many wrong and harmful laws, and overlook the oppression of one or even a few unfortunate individuals. But if acts of oppression extend to the majority or to a few individuals in such a way that the precedent and consequences threaten all, if a long train of abuses and the general course of things manifest a design against liberty, resistance becomes a moral necessity. This justification of resistance was echoed by Thomas Jefferson in the American Declaration of Independence of 1776.

Although, according to the *Second Treatise*, the end of government is limited to the protection of rights rather than the cultivation of virtue, Locke in other works was concerned with the education of human beings in the virtues required for liberty, an endeavor with which later theories of the democratic personality should be compared. In *An Essay concerning Human Understanding* (1690) he argued against the doctrine of innate ideas, which he regarded as a justification for subservience to prejudice, superstition, and intellectual tyranny. He encouraged readers to question the opinions others would impose on them by authority and to refrain from imposing their own opinions on others by authority. Drawing on his own experience as a tutor, he showed in *Some Thoughts concerning Education* (1693) how children could be educated in the virtues necessary in a free society: respect for the rights of others, civility, liberality, humanity, self-denial, industry, thrift, courage, and truthfulness. These virtues were to be inculcated not through coercion but through appeals to our love of liberty, our pride in human rationality, and our sense of what is suitable to the dignity and excellence of a rational creature.

See also Capitalism; Consent; Constitutionalism; Hobbes, Thomas; Leadership; Montesquieu; Natural law; Spinoza, Benedict de.

NATHAN TARCOV

BIBLIOGRAPHY

Dunn, John. *The Political Thought of John Locke: An Historical Account of the Argument of the "Two Treatises of Government."* Cambridge and New York: Cambridge University Press, 1969.

Grant, Ruth W. *John Locke's Liberalism.* Chicago: University of Chicago Press, 1987.

Harris, Ian. *The Mind of John Locke: A Study of Political Theory in Its Intellectual Setting.* Cambridge and New York: Cambridge University Press, 1998.

Jolley, Nicholas. *Locke: His Philosophical Thought.* New York: Oxford University Press, 1999.

Kendall, Willmoore. *John Locke and the Doctrine of Majority Rule.* Urbana: University of Illinois Press, 1965.

Pangle, Thomas L. *The Spirit of Modern Republicanism: The Moral Vision of the American Founders and the Philosophy of Locke.* Chicago: University of Chicago Press, 1988.

Tarcov, Nathan. *Locke's Education for Liberty.* Chicago: University of Chicago Press, 1984.

Vaughan, Karen Iversen. *John Locke: Economist and Social Scientist*. Chicago: University of Chicago Press, 1980.

✦ Machiavelli, Niccolò

Florentine bureaucrat, writer, and political theorist. Machiavelli (1469–1527), the son of a lawyer, served the Florentine Republic in several important administrative and diplomatic capacities, including leading missions to France, Germany, and other Italian city-states. He was exiled by the Medici, the ruling family of Florence, when they were restored to power in 1512 after being expelled in 1494. He spent his remaining years in retirement writing at his estate just outside Florence.

Machiavelli's most famous work, *The Prince*, is a handbook on how an aspiring dictator might gain and retain power. Among other things, Machiavelli supported the use of deceit and craftiness in the interest of political expediency. In the *Discourses on Livy*, he widened the discussion to other kinds of regimes, beginning with those described in the writings of the ancient political philosophers: monarchy, aristocracy, and democracy. He argued for a free, well-ordered republic.

In the *Discourses*, Machiavelli looked back to the Roman Republic as his ideal. Rome's greatness was based on the *virtù* (which means strength and ability as much as civic virtue) of its citizens. According to Machiavelli, the tribunes of the people (elected officials responsible for protecting the interests of the Roman people against those of the nobility) were essential to the success of the republic. An equilibrium between the aristocratic Senate and the common people made the republic strong and stable. Machiavelli warned that the formidable power of the people must be taken into account.

The supreme political realist, Machiavelli separated questions of religion and morality from politics. His primary concern was the survival of the state. He considered a republican government superior to a state ruled by a prince—when the people have sufficient *virtù*—because a republic is more stable. A successful republic, however, must have a mechanism for turning to an autocratic ruler in times of emergency.

Although he was no democrat, Machiavelli believed that the people must have a share in power for a state to maintain political stability. Finally, he argued, it would be difficult for an autocrat to overthrow an effective republican government.

See also Classical Greece and Rome; Democracy, Critiques of; Leadership; Republicanism; Virtue, Civic.

ANN DAVIES

BIBLIOGRAPHY

Viroli, Maurizio. *Niccolo's Smile: A Biography of Machiavelli*. Translated from the Italian by Anthony Shugaar. New York: Farrar, Straus and Giroux, 2000.

✦ Madison, James

A founder of the American political system and fourth president of the United States. Born at Port Conway, Virginia, Madison (1751–1836) was taught by a private tutor until he entered the College of New Jersey (now Princeton University). In 1776 he was elected to the convention that declared Virginia's independence from Great Britain and that drafted both the first state constitution and the first state bill of rights. He was elected to the General Assembly under the new state constitution. He served in the Continental Congress as a delegate from Virginia from 1780 to 1783.

In 1784 he was again elected to the Virginia General Assembly, where, the following year, he drafted the *Memorial and Remonstrance*, which helped bring to passage Thomas Jefferson's historic Bill for Religious Liberty. In 1786 Madison was the delegate from Virginia to the Annapolis Convention, which called for a constitutional convention to revise the Articles of Confederation (the original framework for the federal union).

It was as a delegate from Virginia to the Constitutional Convention meeting in Philadelphia in 1787, and as a defender of the Constitution drafted there, that Madison established his reputation as a preeminent political theorist and practical politician. He brought to the convention the benefits not only of his years of study of political systems but also of his experience in a variety of public offices. To these must be added his desire for a firm, national political union and his acknowledged zeal for a republican form of government. Madison kept careful notes on what was said and done that spring and summer in Philadelphia; these notes have been the primary source for scholarship on the Constitution of the United States.

When the new constitution was sent to the states for ratification, the vote on the issue was expected to be close in several of the states, particularly in New York and Virginia. Alexander Hamilton asked Madison to join John Jay and himself in writing a series of articles for the New York newspapers to support ratification. Eighty-five articles, known as *The Federalist*, were written. Of these Madison wrote twenty-nine, including two of those most frequently cited, Nos. 10 and 51.

In framing a government, Madison wrote in *Federalist* No. 51, it was necessary to ensure not only that the government controlled the governed but that it controlled itself. A system of elected representatives would help keep the government responsive to the citizenry; but such a system would not prevent the majority from tyrannizing the minority. Society was composed of separate interests and different classes. Wherever the interests of the majority were united, the interests of the minority would be insecure. In the federal republic, society would be composed of such a numerous variety of interests that it would be difficult to unite them in a tyrannical majority. In the same way that a multiplicity of sects protects religious rights, a diversity of interests would protect minorities from the usurpations of a majority.

A further precaution, Madison noted, was in the structure of the government. The separation of powers into different branches of government, each possessed of the constitutional means to protect itself from the encroachment of others, would check any moves toward a concentration of power in any office. Moreover, the ambitions of officeholders in each department would serve as a check on any dangerous enlargement of powers advanced by another department.

Among the objections of those opposed to the new constitution was the claim that republican government could survive only in a small state. In *Federalist* No. 10, Madison turned the argument around. A large federal republic, he asserted, could better resist the turbulence of factionalism than a small republic, for the greater the area encompassed by the republic, the greater would be the number of diverse interests encompassed in it. So many interests would be present that it would be difficult to find a majority united in a purpose that might endanger a minority. He believed also that the quality of representatives would improve in a large state, where there would be more potential candidates to choose from.

When Madison was writing *The Federalist*, he did not believe that a bill of rights was needed in the Constitution. He changed his mind, however, when he listened to the objections of the Antifederalists. As a delegate to the Virginia ratifying convention, he promised that if the Constitution was ratified he would prepare a bill of rights for Congress to propose as amendments. Elected to the House of Representatives in the first Congress, he prepared the amendments now known as the Bill of Rights.

Before Madison was forty years old he had helped to create the Virginia constitution (1776), the Virginia bill of rights (1776), the Virginia statute for religious liberty (1786), the Constitution of the United States (1787), and the first ten amendments to that Constitution (1789). He had been elected to the legislatures of both Virginia (1776–1777, 1784–1786) and the United States (1789–1797).

Madison retired from Congress in 1797 expecting to return to private life. But he was soon drawn back into politics. The Alien and Sedition Acts, passed by Congress in 1798, prompted him to draft the Virginia Resolution, companion to Jefferson's Kentucky Resolution, which called on the states to consider whether Congress had enacted unconstitutional legislation. Many states' rights politicians saw these resolutions as support for nullification of congressional acts by states that thought them to be unconstitutional.

From 1801 until his election as president in 1808 Madison served as Jefferson's secretary of state. As president (1809–1817) he was concerned mainly with international affairs, searching for a safe course for the nation amid the international turmoil caused by the Napoleonic Wars. His pol-icy of embargo and nonintercourse failed to check the hostile acts toward the United States of either Great Britain or France, and in 1812 he declared war against Britain. Before a treaty of peace was signed in 1814, the British had entered Washington and burned the White House.

In 1829 Madison came out of retirement again to participate in Virginia's constitutional convention. He made his most enduring contribution to democracy, however, in the early years, when he was one of the Founders of the American political system. He was the last survivor of those who had attended the Philadelphia Convention.

See also Majority rule, minority rights.

ALAN P. GRIMES

BIBLIOGRAPHY

Brant, Irving. *James Madison*. 6 vols. Indianapolis: Bobbs-Merrill, 1961.

Burns, Edward. *James Madison, Philosopher of the Constitution*. New Brunswick, N.J.: Rutgers University Press, 1938. Reprint, New York: Octagon Books, 1968.

Ketcham, Ralph L. *James Madison: A Biography*. New York: Macmillan, 1989.

McCoy, Drew R. *The Last of the Fathers: James Madison and the Republican Legacy*. Cambridge and New York: Cambridge University Press, 1989.

Miller, William Lee. *The Business of May Next: James Madison and the Founding*. Charlottesville: University Press of Virginia, 1992.

Morgan, Robert J. *James Madison on the Constitution and the Bill of Rights*. Westport, Conn., and London: Greenwood, 1988.

Rosen, Gary. *American Compact: James Madison and the Problem of Founding*. Lawrence: University Press of Kansas, 1999.

Rutland, Robert A. *James Madison, the Founding Father*. New York: Macmillan, 1987.

Sheldon, Garrett Ward. *The Political Philosophy of James Madison*. Baltimore: Johns Hopkins University Press, 2000.

✦ Mill, John Stuart

English philosopher, economist, and political theorist. Mill (1806–1873) wrote frequently about democracy, and as a journalist and member of Parliament sought to promote democratic change over a period of five decades. He is widely recognized as a leading nineteenth-century spokesman for Anglo-American liberalism and remains one of the most important theorists of democracy in this political tradition.

Mill's initial views on democracy were adopted from those of the utilitarian legal philosopher Jeremy Bentham (1748–1832) and his father, James Mill (1773–1836), who was Bentham's leading disciple. At first Mill believed that universal suffrage, frequent elections, and the secret ballot would secure democracy. Agreeing with Bentham and his father, he recommended these devices as the democratic remedy for bad and corrupt government. Defective government was traced to a tendency among all who held public office to seek personal gain and pursue what Bentham called their sinister, or separate, interest. Mill followed Bentham in assuming that the sinister interest of the few would be countered by the universal interest of the entire populace and that corruption thus would be eliminated. In this perspective, democracy was useful, but it was not justified on the ground of natural rights or as being closer to a republican ideal than other forms of government or as promoting individualism and liberty.

After proselytizing in behalf of the utilitarian view for a decade, Mill developed doubts about it, influenced by the Saint-Simonians, who advocated a technocratic and socialist organization of society, and by the legal philosopher John Austin. Although he continued to approve of the creation of obstacles to corruption, Mill questioned whether democratically elected representatives had the special knowledge and highly developed intellectual capacities necessary for devising effective policies and making good laws. He likened politics to medicine. Patients know they have a problem, but they cannot devise the remedy. After consulting a physician, patients can decide whether to accept the recommendation of the medical experts, but they should not substitute their own remedy for that of the physician. Comparably, in politics, the democratic populace, exercising its sovereign power, can decide whether to adopt the policies recommended by political experts, but the people should not presume to diagnose problems or devise remedies. These responsibilities should be the function of the specially trained and qualified—the small group of truly knowledgeable persons Mill called the "instructed few."

The clearest analysis of the tension between the claims of the numerical majority and those of the best qualified intellectually is found in Mill's final statement on these matters. In *Considerations on Representative Government* (1861), Mill argued that democratically elected assemblies, because of the mediocre intellectual abilities of the representatives and of the public who elected them, are unfit to govern and legislate. He also warned that a democratically elected assembly would be responsive to the interests of a single class, thus creating class legislation. Yet, for all his criticism of the numerical majority, Mill remained convinced that popular control of government is essential. Therefore, wishing to combine representation of the majority, which would provide for popular control, with the knowledge and intelligence that would provide for skilled legislation and administration, he advocated that government draw in both the few and the many. Government was to be directed by the experienced and trained few while also being democratic.

In *Considerations on Representative Government*, Mill laid out the specific means required to bring about this combination. He proposed a commission of legislation, whose members were to be recruited from the intellectual elite; the commission's purpose was to devise laws but not to enact them. Because the commission's proposals were subject to approval by the democratically elected assembly, popular control was provided for. The same combination was to be promoted by universal suffrage, with extra votes for the well educated—a scheme Mill called "plural voting." He also proposed open voting (abandoning his earlier defense of the secret ballot), in order to subject voters to the social pressures arising from the fact that their votes were being scrutinized by their intellectual superiors. Most important to Mill, he recommended a plan of proportional representation in order to supplement majority representation with assured representation for minorities. He was enthusiastic about this device, considering it a way to give representation to the minority of those educated persons who formed the intellectual elite.

Mill was so convinced of the necessity of providing representation for knowledge and intelligence as well as for the numerical majority that he distinguished between true and false democracy. The true kind—he also called it "the pure idea of democracy"—included representation of the intellectual elite, and because it was government by this minority as well as by the majority, he regarded it as genuinely egalitarian. In contrast, the false kind was government of the whole people by a "mere majority." This form, moreover, was a government of privilege, not one of equality, for knowledge and intelligence, swamped by the majority, was denied a voice. False democracy was exemplified by government in the United States, where, Mill believed, the numerical majority ruled despotically.

Mill was uneasy about democratic majorities for another reason: their intolerance of those who do not comply with conventional norms of belief and conduct—that is, those with individuality. Such intolerance constitutes an infringement of individual liberty, a theme that occupied Mill in *On Liberty* (1859). He characterized the majority as a collective mediocrity consisting of persons who are passive, imitative, and slavish followers of custom. Using Alexis de Tocqueville's famous phrase "tyranny of the majority," he protested against attempts to impose conventional majoritarian tastes and norms of conduct on those with individuality.

Although an antimajoritarian theme runs through most of Mill's mature writings, his continued belief in the egalitarian ideal was evident in *The Subjection of Women* (1869). In this work he argued against claims that men are intellectually superior and deserving of patriarchal authority. His belief that majoritarian democracy should be tempered by provision for intellectually enlightened leadership has influenced much twentieth-century debate about democracy.

See also Representation; Tocqueville, Alexis de.
JOSEPH HAMBURGER

BIBLIOGRAPHY

Anschutz, R. P. *The Philosophy of J. S. Mill.* Oxford: Oxford University Press, 1953.
Burns, J. H. "J. S. Mill and Democracy, 1829–61." In *Mill: A Collection of Critical Essays*, edited by J. B. Schneewind. Garden City, N.Y.: Anchor Books, 1968.

Hamburger, Joseph. *John Stuart Mill on Liberty and Control*. Princeton: Princeton University Press, 1999.

Mill and the Moral Character of Liberalism. Edited by Eldon J. Eisenach. University Park: Pennsylvania State University Press, 1999.

Robson, John M. *The Improvement of Mankind: The Social and Political Thought of John Stuart Mill*. Toronto: University of Toronto Press, 1968.

Stephen, Leslie. *John Stuart Mill*. Vol. 3 of *The English Utilitarians*. London: Duckworth, 1900.

✦ Montesquieu, Charles-Louis de Secondat, Baron de

French political theorist who formulated the idea of separation of powers. Charles-Louis de Secondat, baron de La Brède et de Montesquieu (1689–1755), was educated in the law at the University of Bordeaux. After inheriting his uncle's estate in 1716, he had sufficient wealth and leisure to study Roman law and pursue research in the natural sciences. He traveled extensively in Europe and spent time in England before settling down to serious writing.

Montesquieu's paramount work is *The Spirit of the Laws* (1748). Like his seventeenth-century predecessors Thomas Hobbes and John Locke, Montesquieu was dissatisfied with the ineffectiveness of a classical political science centered on the idea of a perfect regime. Examining various political arrangements and historical conditions from the perspective of modern science, he recommended principles that would ensure greater justice than those of previous regimes.

The Spirit of the Laws made three important arguments. First, Montesquieu replaced the classic taxonomy of regimes—monarchy, aristocracy, and democracy—with his own classification—republic (democratic or aristocratic), monarchy, and despotism. Each regime has a fundamental principle: virtue, honor, and fear, respectively. A prudent legislator will rule in such a way as to maintain and strengthen the regime's distinctive principle. The principle will determine whether certain tools of governance are appropriate. In a republic, for example, where the principle is virtue, censorship is necessary because attention must be paid to the practices subverting virtue. In monarchies, though, where honor acts as an omnipresent censor, there is no need for additional censors.

Montesquieu's second major argument was that moderate governments should divide governing authority among three branches: executive, legislative, and judicial. Only when each of these powers is held by independent bodies, each exercising authority in its own area of competence, and preferably each representing a different social group, can liberty thrive. The idea of separating powers also allowed for a diversity of classes. The great, Montesquieu argued, by virtue of their honor, wealth, or birth, should have the power to check the enterprises of the people as the people should have the power to check the great. Equally important for the balance of power are intermediary institutions—the church, local and provincial parliaments and courts, professional associations and guilds—as well as political parties. Freedom of expression promotes a healthy plurality that also serves to check power. The balance of power ensures security as well as liberty. For example, the effect of mutual correction and moderation separate states can have on one another will play a major role in ensuring their collective security.

Finally, Montesquieu argued that laws alone do not determine how individuals act or whether legislation will be successful. In each society a general spirit is operating. This inner logic of human conduct is formed by religion, laws, customs, manners, economics, and geography and climate. Effective rulers must understand the causes that form national character. The general spirit is one more variable rulers must account for in attempting to foster freedom and security. It requires that they exercise a Machiavellian prudence, sometimes adapting to the general spirit, other times resisting that spirit. Religion, for example, must be judiciously deployed by rulers for its political effects.

Montesquieu also considered which regime was best able to ensure the security and freedom of its members and the possibility for free self-government. Monarchy, he believed, was best suited to modern Europe and most capable of governing human passions. Moreover, it granted individuals the most freedom. Yet the honor system in a monarchy, insofar as it is based on preferment and social distinction, is unstable, for it is subject to the irregularity of capricious pride. In addition, in a monarchy political participation and self-rule are not open to all citizens. Democracy satisfies the need for the people to hold sovereign power in making law, and its citizens are the least corruptible. But, unless tempered, the spirit of equality will grow beyond the desire of equal protection before the law to the people's demand for a right to manage all political offices. Liberty can degenerate to license. The best choice is a mixed government, in which some guide and command, but the people have the power to choose and recall them.

English society, to Montesquieu, was a model of a mixed government. It effectively converted private interest to public good and ensured peace and natural humanity; in short, it was a modern commercial republic. Montesquieu praised the English system because he saw it as an alternative to the virtuous republics of antiquity, whose ideals he considered to be a threat to security and freedom. English commercial society and its monarch were constrained by a balance of powers. Humanity and tolerance prevented the harshness associated with regimes based on virtue. The moderation of the English system inclined people to think of the common good. Montesquieu saw the dangers of a society based on selfish passions from which avarice and ambition could easily grow. But the strength of the English system was that its institutions were the most effective in guaranteeing political liberty and civic virtue because they moderated the most powerful passions of the people. Social and political plurality were used to preserve liberty.

Moreover, in England education was used to moderate private desire and to produce love of country and of the law. Montesquieu believed that the political virtue education fostered could evolve only if the regime could prevent excesses of equality and inequality. Sumptuary laws regulating luxury, as well as controls on property accumulation and the judicious use of taxation, were necessary to prevent the corruption of morals. Only if these conditions were met would the spirit of commerce produce frugality, tranquility, and self-rule. The English commercial republic would be a regime in which people would experience freedom as security from fear.

Montesquieu sharply distinguished between a state based on security and a despotism based on fear. In a despotism, people's lives are like those of beasts. Life under despotism is one of isolation, timidity, fear of violence, blind obedience, ignorance, suspicion, and lack of spirit. Montesquieu also warned that the predominance of these characteristics, as well as excess equality, can tip a free, self-governing society toward despotism. The moderate regime Montesquieu favored had some potent tendencies inclining toward its corruption: a mediocrity of talents, the prevalence of destabilizing passions, unrelenting mobility, and inconstancy. But he still preferred it to virtuous republics whose ardor was usually irascible, and he believed its weaknesses could be counteracted by prudent rulers.

Montesquieu's work has particular significance for liberal democracies, providing lessons that were not lost on the American Founders and Alexis de Tocqueville. More than anything, Montesquieu taught the need for moderation, especially in regimes where the people are self-governing.

See also Nationalism; Virtue, Civic.

PETER C. EMBERLEY

BIBLIOGRAPHY

Althusser, Louis. *Politics and History: Montesquieu, Rousseau, Hegel, and Marx.* Translated by Ben Brewster. London: NLB, 1972.

Cohler, Anne M. *Montesquieu's Comparative Politics and the Spirit of American Constitutionalism.* Lawrence: University Press of Kansas, 1988.

Destutt de Tracy, Antoine-Louise-Claude, Comte. *Commentary and Review of Montesquieu's Spirit of the Laws.* Translated by Thomas Jefferson. Philadelphia: Burt Franklin, 1969.

Durkheim, Emile. *Montesquieu and Rousseau: Forerunners of Sociology.* Ann Arbor: University of Michigan Press, 1965.

Hulliung, Mark. *Montesquieu and the Old Regime.* Berkeley: University of California Press, 1976.

Montesquieu's Science of Politics: Essays on the Spirit of Laws. Edited by David W. Carrithers et al. Lanham, Md.: Rowman and Littlefield, 2001.

Pangle, Thomas L. *Montesquieu's Philosophy of Liberalism: A Commentary on The Spirit of the Laws.* Chicago: University of Chicago Press, 1973.

Richter, Melvin. *The Political Theory of Montesquieu.* Cambridge: Cambridge University Press, 1977.

Waddicor, Mark. *Montesquieu and the Philosophy of Natural Law.* The Hague: M. Nijhoff, 1970.

✦ Nietzsche, Friedrich

German philosopher of aristocratic radicalism and advocate of militant atheism. Descended from a family of Lutheran pastors, Nietzsche (1844–1900) was educated at the University of Leipzig and in 1869 became a professor of classical philology at Basel, Switzerland. After resigning in 1876, he wrote in sickly solitude until a nervous breakdown in 1889 ended his career as a writer and thinker.

Nietzsche's work can be divided into three phases. In his youth, as a romantic disciple of Richard Wagner, he fought for a revival of German culture and, inspired by the pagan poetry of the Greeks, wrote such books as *The Birth of Tragedy* (1872). A middle period of disillusioned positivism was expressed in *Human, All Too Human* (1878–1879) and similar works. And the mature Nietzsche produced *Thus Spoke Zarathustra* (1883–1885) and the works following it.

The hero of *Thus Spoke Zarathustra* utters Nietzsche's most famous sentence, the basis and core of all his philosophical labors: "God is dead." By this statement, Nietzsche means primarily that belief in the Christian God has lost its efficacy and thus has plunged humanity into an all-encompassing crisis. Ultimately he means that all transcendent and objective standards by which human beings have taken their bearings have crumbled to reveal a chaotic world of meaninglessness.

Nietzsche finds signs of that loss of meaning wherever he looks. Hitherto human beings have been constituted by their reverence, their aspirations; now all yearnings are revealed as arbitrary, all preferences and longings as capricious in a world deprived of meaning and standards—whether one calls them God or nature or goodness—and human beings confront an abyss.

They can react in various ways. They may take refuge in the petty pursuit of comfortable self-preservation. Nietzsche calls such people, whose lives lack all poetry and grandeur, "last men." They may lash out against a world that is indifferent at best and malignant at worst by becoming nihilists, seeking the destruction of all they encounter. Or they may seek to reinterpret the catastrophic death of God as the discovery of human creativity, a new realm of possibility in which human beings create their own meaning, believing themselves to be liberated from ordinary responsibilities and morality. They will attain a cosmic innocence of becoming, ridding themselves of the resentment that has plagued humanity throughout history by affirming as necessary and good all that exists. Nietzsche refers to these creatures as "supermen." They will be a synthesis and a surpassing of the highest human types of the past: poets, philosophers, rulers, saints.

Nietzsche constructs a new philosophical doctrine to buttress his analysis of the crisis of his and our time, a teaching to explain the world's flux and humanity's way of overcoming it. He calls that doctrine "the will to power": human beings are motivated by a ceaseless desire to overcome and possess, a desire that at its peak can become self-overcoming. Human beings are not fundamentally characterized by their rationality but by their instinctive yearning for domination. Nietzsche seeks to understand all reality as will to power, positing the world as energy rather than as matter, a vast field of conflicting wills.

According to Nietzsche, the doctrine of the will to power explains how beasts overcame their beastliness to become human, even as it explains how human beings can overcome their humanity to become supermen. He struggles to resolve the difficulties of his own teachings: Is his doctrine of the will to power the result of his own will power

or is it true? If everything can and will be overcome, will not a humanity no longer faced by challenges decline into last men? Can one overcome the past? His final and most enigmatic teaching of the eternal return of the same describes a world in which the future will become a past that human beings can will.

Nietzsche's influence is pervasive in the twentieth century, but the implications of his thought for politics in general and for democracy in particular remain ambiguous, above all because of the tensions in his thought. One strand of his philosophy is apolitical: Nietzsche celebrates the creative individual for whom society is at best a necessary evil. He counsels superior people to flee into solitude. At the same time, he conceives of the superman as the molder of the human future, a legislator on the grandest scale. He praises war for its energizing effects and writes vaguely but enthusiastically of a great politics of the future that will undo the legacy of the petty politics afflicting the present.

At rare intervals Nietzsche comments benignly on democracy, mostly because it counterbalances the corruptions of authoritarian regimes. More often, however, his attitudes range from contemptuous indifference to vehement hostility. He frequently holds democracy responsible for the mediocrity that softens modern life and the egalitarianism that endangers human greatness. He faults it for being little but a prelude to communism, for being the decadent inheritor of a Christian morality that can no longer function, for inculcating people with softness at a time when they need to be hard, and for denying the imperatives of human cruelty. Nietzsche tends to equate democratic rule with the rule of the last men.

Such views necessarily raise the problem of Nietzsche's influence on and responsibility for fascism. He was not a conservative in any conventional sense because he thought a return of any kind to former times impossible. Instead, he dreamed of a new planetary nobility. His image of the radical individuals fit to preside over human regeneration is that of a genuine nobility gifted with artistic productivity and moral sensitivity. It thus bears no resemblance to the reality of Adolf Hitler. Nevertheless, Nietzsche is responsible for making extremism seem more desirable than moderation, for deriding rationality, and for mocking the common decencies. Moreover, his general aversion to Western civilization played into the hands of a feeling in Germany that it was not properly part of the West.

See also Authoritarianism; Democracy, Critiques of; Fascism.

WERNER J. DANNHAUSER

BIBLIOGRAPHY

Detwiler, Bruce. *Nietzsche and the Politics of Aristocratic Radicalism.* Chicago: University of Chicago Press, 1990.

Hales, Steven D., and Rex Welshon. *Nietzsche's Perspectivisim.* Urbana: University of Illinois Press, 2000.

Jaspers, Karl. *Nietzsche: An Introduction to the Understanding of His Philosophy.* Translated by Charles F. Wallraft and Frederick J. Schmitz. Tucson: University of Arizona Press, 1965.

Kaufmann, Walter. *Nietzsche: Philosopher, Psychologist, Antichrist.* Princeton: Princeton University Press, 1974.

Löwith, Karl. *From Hegel to Nietzsche.* Translated by David Green. Garden City, N.Y.: Anchor Books, 1956.

Schaberg, William H. *The Nietzsche Canon: A Publication History and Bibliography.* Chicago: University of Chicago Press, 2001.

Warren, Mark. *Nietzsche and Political Thought.* Cambridge: MIT Press, 1988.

✦ Plato

Greek philosopher whose thirty-five dialogues provide the foundation for much of Western philosophy. Born into the Athenian aristocracy, Plato (427–347 B.C.) was expected to pursue a political career. Instead, he withdrew from politics to write his dialogues and founded, about 385 B.C., the Academy, a center for education for young men from all over Greece.

Plato's dialogues often demonstrate a hostility to the Athenian democracy that executed his teacher, Socrates, in 399 B.C. Plato portrays democracy as dependent on the changeable opinions of the many, rather than on the certain knowledge of the philosopher who through the study of dialectic has seen what Plato calls the "forms," the true and unchanging nature of things. In a famous parable from the *Republic*, Plato has Socrates compare the city to a ship whose owner, a large but slightly deaf man, is controlled by those who know nothing about piloting the ship. The "true pilot" who understands the seasons and knows the stars is called a stargazer and is considered useless. Also in the *Republic* Socrates describes how democracy corrupts the young, who see and are influenced by the echoing praise and blame conferred by the assemblies of the many.

In the categories of regimes developed in the *Republic*, Socrates places democracy as the second worst regime, right before tyranny. He caricatures democracy, portraying it as a regime of license and equality where all can do as they wish and no distinctions are made between slaves and freemen, between men and women. It is, however, the only regime in which it would be possible to find a philosopher like Socrates.

In the *Statesman*, Plato presents democracy as the best of the lawless regimes. Because democracy is able to do nothing great, whether good or bad, it causes the least harm if it is without restraint; if orderly, it is the worst, while monarchy is the best when "yoked" by good rules. In Plato's final work, the *Laws*, an Athenian stranger in conversation with a Spartan and Cretan offers a constitution for what he calls a "second best" regime. Its laws incorporate elements of Athenian democracy but always with an emphasis on moderation and limitations.

See also Classical Greece and Rome; Theory, Ancient.

ARLENE W. SAXONHOUSE

BIBLIOGRAPHY

Monoson, S. Sara. *Plato's Democratic Entanglements*. Princeton: Princeton University Press, 2000.

✦ Rousseau, Jean-Jacques

Geneva-born French philosopher, critic of modern philosophy and politics, and proponent of both extreme individualism and extreme collectivism. Rousseau (1712–1778) ran away from home at age sixteen and spent his youth wandering among various employments and cities of southern Europe before settling in Paris. The publication of his *First Discourse* (1750) made him an overnight sensation; twelve years later the publication of *Emile*, with its attack on revelation, led to his expulsion from France. He spent much of his remaining years fleeing persecution, real and imagined.

The philosophical and political revolution known as the Enlightenment had plenty of enemies, but Rousseau was its first defector. In criticizing it from within, using its own principles against itself, Rousseau inaugurated the "radical tradition" of Western political philosophy. He began the tendency, reproduced in every generation after him, to denounce modern humanity as fundamentally unhealthy, to blame its ills not on human nature or original sin but on the character of modern society, and to seek a solution through a still more radical application of the new ideas and principles that had given rise to that society.

Rousseau was both heir and opponent of the political ideas of Thomas Hobbes and John Locke. He shared their realist and activist orientation toward politics, their empiricist theory of knowledge, their egoistic psychology, their rights-based individualism, and their contract theory of the state. But he argued that these principles fostered a society of restless, materialistic individuals who were enslaved to their rulers, in conflict with each other, and divided within their own souls. By interpreting and applying these principles more intransigently, Rousseau turned them squarely against their first authors and derived a radical (and seemingly self-contradictory) set of prescriptions that pointed simultaneously toward a highly collectivized, militantly patriotic, and rigidly democratic republic and toward a hyper-individualistic life of withdrawal from society and communion with nature and one's inner self.

To understand the inner logic of this complex Rousseauian rebellion, we shall begin with the central idea of Rousseau's philosophic system: the natural goodness of man.

The Argument for Natural Goodness

Human beings are wicked and unhappy, Rousseau maintains, but this condition is wholly the work of society. By nature, people are good, both for themselves and for others. They are good for themselves because they are at one with themselves and self-sufficient; they are good for others because they have no natural desire to harm others and lack the artificial passions, needs, and prejudices that now put their interests in conflict with others. Moreover, although altruism and morality are not natural, compassion is, and compassion leads people to avoid inflicting needless harm on others.

Rousseau argues for the doctrine of natural goodness in his *Discourse on the Origins of Inequality* (1755), in which he implicitly attacks the church's doctrine of original sin and explicitly confronts Hobbes's teaching on the state of nature. Hobbes had argued that human beings are selfish, asocial individuals, that their natural condition is a brutal state of war, and that absolute monarchy is the only form of government strong enough to create peace and order. Rousseau responds that precisely on the Hobbesian premise of human asociality, the state of nature and its inhabitant, "natural man," must have been good and not bad. He reasons that if one subtracts from man's present character all that could have been acquired only in society, what remains is a simple, self-sufficient creature, devoid of language, reason, foresight, and vanity, and thus lacking all the passions and social relations that, in Hobbes's account, produce enmity and war.

In support of his doctrine, Rousseau also appealed to the evidence of solitary introspection, which seemed to reveal that humans are fundamentally peaceful and contented creatures who take an elemental joy in the mere sentiment of their existence. What seems to have confirmed Rousseau in his belief in human goodness, however, was his new understanding of the origin of human evil. Only by systematically explaining existent human evil—which Rousseau considered to be great—in terms of the effects of society, could he free nature of all blame.

Rousseau's general argument runs as follows. If we accept the modern premise of human asociality, we must explore more fully than heretofore

the possibility that all human evil is simply a derangement caused by the unnatural environment—civil society—into which human beings have evolved. Human asociality means that by nature we do not love or care for others and that we do not need them. We are naturally solitary and self-sufficient: that is why we are good. But society, by bringing us together and stimulating the development of our faculties and artificial desires, makes us need others without making us love them. This social condition of mutual selfish need is the true source of all the evil we do to others and to ourselves.

Society makes us need others by stimulating the development of three characteristics: foresight, which fills us with new cares and worries; imagination, which teaches us new hopes and pleasures; and vanity, which makes us obsessed with our rank and merit in the eyes of others. To provide for these new needs, humans eventually develop a system to divide up various tasks; this division of labor, by making all individuals into "specialists" who live by exchange, deals the final blow to natural self-sufficiency and institutionalizes mutual dependence. All subsequent "progress" of society only further heightens our faculties, our needs, and thus our interdependence.

Mutual dependence might not be a bad thing if human beings were naturally social and so inclined to love and help one another. But Rousseau is exploring the assumption that people are naturally selfish; and society only intensifies this egoism. Consequently, this social condition of mutual dependence, in which self-concerned individuals find themselves other-dependent, is unnatural and self-contradictory. Rousseau believes that in this fundamental "contradiction of the social system" he has discovered the true, social source of human evil, the historical cause that destroyed the natural goodness of human beings, making them exploitative toward others and divided against themselves.

Society makes people exploitative because the needy selfishness it fosters makes them need others more while loving them less. All are driven to use others, knowing that others are likewise driven to use them. In such an environment, people are forced by their self-interest to be enemies. This condition often compels individuals to make mutually beneficial agreements. But it also compels them to wish to avoid delivering on their part of the agreement. It is to this end that the strong devote all their strength and the weak all their ruses. In short, society is a community of secret enemies: it is formed and held together by each individual's need to use the others. It thus systematically forces everyone to be deceitful and exploitative.

At the same time, society makes individuals bad for themselves. Social men are all actors and hypocrites; they are divided against themselves by the contradiction between their intense self-concern and the obsession with others that this very selfishness necessitates. As other-directed egoists, they spend their lives serving and manipulating others precisely because they care only about themselves.

In sum, civil society produces and builds upon mutual selfish dependence and, in so doing, compels people to falsify and divide themselves in a constant effort to manipulate and exploit others. Because this structural contradiction in society explains all the evil we now observe in human beings, it is unnecessary to suppose them evil by nature. Impelled by this evidence and his other inferences, Rousseau concluded that man was naturally good.

Rousseau's Two Solutions

Rousseau's analysis of the problem of human evil has revolutionary implications for its solution.

Generally, by arguing that all evil arises from the effects of society, Rousseau transforms the problem into a social or historical issue, whereas before it had seemed a natural or divine one. This change raised radical and potentially totalitarian hopes—albeit less in Rousseau than in thinkers who followed him—that through political action one might transform the human condition itself.

More specifically, by tracing evil to the contradictory social condition of mutual dependence, Rousseau's analysis points rigorously to two diametrically opposite solutions. The contradiction of selfish other-directedness can be resolved either by making individuals wholly self-concerned and self-dependent or wholly other-concerned and other-directed. People must be either totally separated or totally united, but they must never depend upon others while caring only for themselves. Thus Rousseau's search for solutions branches into two opposite ideals: extreme collectivism and extreme individualism.

The Collectivist Solution

The collectivist solution is the subject of Rousseau's political writings, especially the *Social Contract* and the *Discourse on Political Economy*. Its overall strategy is to eliminate the phenomenon of selfish dependence by eliminating human selfishness, at least to the extent possible. To this end, Rousseau makes a variety of proposals designed to rework our malleable human nature, to transform naturally selfish individuals into patriotic citizens who love and live for the community. These proposals include smallness of size of the political unit (akin to the Greek city-state), relative equality and homogeneity of the population, an agrarian economic base, public education that cultivates virtue and patriotism more than talents, strict republican morals, patriotic public festivals, a civil religion, and censorship of the arts and sciences.

These institutions—both in their moralizing intention and in their invasive effect—involve a clear break with the "limited government" of liberal political theory. Indeed, they are consciously modeled on the practice of the ancient republics, especially Sparta and Rome. Yet Rousseau's return to ancient practice, combined as it is with modern theories of the radical asociality and malleability of human nature, constitutes something new and portentous. It is not altogether unfair to say that, in his conception of the state as an instrument for overcoming human nature, Rousseau planted the first seeds of modern totalitarianism.

Still, Rousseau, a fierce opponent of every form of oppression, was fully aware of the dangers posed by a state powerful and meddlesome enough to accomplish the crucial task of transforming men into citizens. To counteract this danger, he proposed to maximize the power of the citizenry over the state by placing the sovereign power in the hands of what he called the "general will." The meaning of this most famous Rousseauian institution is notoriously obscure. It can best be approached by taking up Rousseau's formal doctrine of the state from the beginning.

Because human beings are by nature asocial and arational, the state does not exist by nature and there are no natural titles to rule. For essentially the same reasons, there are no natural rules of justice or natural law. In making the latter claim, Rousseau brings to completion a crucial and fateful tendency of early modern thought: he liberates politics and morality from nature, indeed from all higher or transcendent standards.

Given the absence of natural rule and natural law, and given the state of war that prevails in their absence in the final stage of the state of nature, human beings are compelled to create the state through the conclusion of a social contract. The ruling power thus created must be "sovereign" in the strict sense: it freely creates the rules of morality, without reference to any higher or external standard. It makes things just, by commanding them, or unjust, by forbidding them.

But how can it be safe to create so free and awesome a power, and where should it be lodged? Rousseau argues that, paradoxically, the sovereign freedom of this power is the key to its safety. Liberated from the need to do justice to our natural inequality and individual uniqueness, the social contract is free to impose an artificial equality and conventional equivalence. In so doing, it makes the state a homogeneous unity that can be ruled through general laws, which, coming from all, apply identically to each. These laws are the expression of the general will: the will of the whole community regarding the community as a whole.

Consider, for example, a state of five individuals. If one rules, it is a monarchy; if two, an aristocracy; if three or more, a democracy. Each of these traditional forms of government involves the rule of a part over the whole and thus easily can become tyrannical. But if the five agree to be governed by general rules on which all vote and that apply equally to each, there is no longer the rule of a part—of some over others—but of all over each: the general will. This will, although it may be mistaken regarding what is good, cannot be tyrannical or ill intentioned because no one wishes to harm himself or herself. The general will, then, should be made sovereign.

To this end, Rousseau proposes that the laws be made by an assembly of the people in which all have the right to vote. But he knows that factions in the assembly can easily prevent the general will from being expressed and that supplemental institutions, tailored to local needs and conditions, must be added to ensure the right outcome. These supplemental institutions include the requirement of more than a simple majority for passing laws, the proper management of subpolitical groups (clans, parties, interest groups), the artful apportionment of votes among the different segments of the population, and, above all, the creation of a virtuous, or patriotic, citizenry.

Because extraordinary wisdom would be required to arrange all these elements properly, Rousseau suggests that the main body of the laws must be drafted by a great legislator and then ratified by the people. Furthermore, he argues that the executive power, which enforces the laws made by the sovereign general will, ideally should be placed in the hands of an elective aristocracy. This executive, he implies, should attempt indirectly to lead and improve the people, much as the legislator does at the beginning. In these ways, Rousseau tempers the extreme egalitarianism of his primary principles and, without granting special rights to virtue or wisdom, grants them a special role in the state.

A healthy political order, in Rousseau's view, is extremely rare and difficult, to be found only a few times in ancient history and scarcely at all since. In the modern world, he believed, the predominance of large nation-states, the rise of materialistic individualism, and the combination of atheism and universalistic religion (Christianity) had all but destroyed the possibility of genuine republican morals. Accordingly, Rousseau was a historical pessimist with few hopes for the political improvement of the large monarchies of Europe, notwithstanding the revolutionary role that his writings would play shortly after his death.

Ultimately, his political writings illustrate the tragic tensions and contradictions that beset all political life as such: the conflict between the need for transformative political power and the inevitable abuse of that power, or between the need for freedom and equality and the need for superior wisdom or virtue. These inevitable shortcomings of the collectivist solution encouraged Rousseau to turn to the individualist solution.

The Individualist Solution

If human beings cannot be wholly united, they must be wholly separated, to avoid the corrupting effects of selfish dependence. Obviously, this solution is not practicable for the vast majority but works only for the rare, gifted individual—the solitary philosopher or artist—as exemplified by Rousseau himself. Indeed, this way of life is elaborated primarily in Rousseau's autobiographical writings: the *Confessions; Rousseau, Judge of Jean-Jacques;* and, above all, the *Reveries of a Solitary Walker.* These works describe how Rousseau, by dint of philosophic genius and extraordinary strength of soul, freed himself from the false needs and hopes that arise in society and enslave us to it. He withdrew from society to live in natural freedom, unity, and goodness as did natural man, immersing his soul in the sweet and simple plenitude of the "sentiment of existence." But his faculties, artificially extended in society, also took him beyond natural man. He expanded his existence over the communities of kindred spirits painted for him in reveries by his highly developed artistic imagination, and he contemplated and identified with the spectacle of nature.

In *Emile,* his treatise on education, Rousseau presents a more accessible and egalitarian, if also less perfect, form of the individualistic solution by showing how the ordinary individual, without superior qualities of mind or character, might remain relatively healthy and happy even within society if reared from birth with the proper method. Emile is brought up in total spontaneity and freedom, without ever being submitted to the overt will or command of another human being. Thus his natural independence and self-directedness is preserved. But all along, his tutor, by manipulating the physical environment, supervises and controls Emile's every experience. The tutor uses this power to fabricate for Emile a limited sociality that makes him genuinely care for others, and so refrain from using them, while still leaving him whole within himself. For this purpose, the tutor makes primary use of two natural but highly malleable impulses: compassion and sex.

As Emile matures, the tutor teaches him to read hearts and to see the weakness and suffering that people hide behind their masks of respectability and cheerfulness. So, when the age of vanity, envy, and competition arrives, Emile, seeing and responding to the inner man, will feel only a generous compassion. At the same time, the tutor endeavors to delay, purify, and elevate Emile's sexual desires, sublimating them into love. Emile will become a romantic lover and then a bourgeois family man, possessing a moral idealism composed in equal parts of lofty erotic longings and solid patriarchal interests. This complex idealism will culminate in a love of God. Thus, living with his family in rustic retreat, Emile will be protected by relative isolation, compassion, love, and religion from all tendency to selfish other-dependence, the social source of human evil.

Ultimately, Rousseau's individualist writings, like his political ones, illustrate the intractability of the problem more than they provide a practicable solution. In civilized society the healthy individual, it seems, must either be a philosopher or be raised by one. Still, through this side of his teaching, Rousseau became the ideologist of such institutions of modern individualism as romanticism, bohemian intellectualism, the sentimental and child-centered family, the cult of compassion, and the pursuit of authentic selfhood through introspection and self-disclosure.

See also Communitarianism; Hobbes, Thomas; Montesquieu; Natural law; Religion, Civil; Spinoza, Benedict de; Tocqueville, Alexis de.

ARTHUR M. MELZER

BIBLIOGRAPHY

Cooper, Laurence D. *Rousseau, Nature, and the Problem of the Good Life*. University Park: Pennsylvania State University Press, 1999.

Gildin, Hilail. *Rousseau's Social Contract: The Design of the Argument*. Chicago: University of Chicago Press, 1983.

Kelley, Christopher. *Rousseau's Exemplary Life: The Confessions as Political Philosophy*. Ithaca, N.Y.: Cornell University Press, 1987.

Masters, Roger D. *The Political Philosophy of Rousseau*. Princeton: Princeton University Press, 1968.

Melzer, Arthur M. *The Natural Goodness of Man: On the System of Rousseau's Thought*. Chicago: University of Chicago Press, 1990.

Rousseau, Jean-Jacques. *Discourse on the Origin of Inequality*. New York: Oxford University Press, 2000.

Shklar, Judith N. *Men and Citizens: A Study of Rousseau's Social Theory*. Cambridge: Cambridge University Press, 1969.

Starobinski, Jean. *Jean-Jacques Rousseau: Transparency and Obstruction*. Translated by Arthur Goldhammer. Chicago: University of Chicago Press, 1988.

✦ Spinoza, Benedict de

First theorist of liberal democracy. Baruch ("Benedict" in Latin) Spinoza (1632–1677) was born in Amsterdam, to parents who had fled the Inquisition in Spain and Portugal. He was educated in rabbinical schools and taught the trade of lens grinding, by which he supported himself after his excommunication from Jewish society in 1656.

Spinoza formulated the idea that the best government is one in which ultimate authority rests with the majority, who govern a society where all may think as they wish and say what they think.

He was the first theorist to articulate a fundamental harmony between democracy and science, devoted to unfettered rational inquiry.

Before Spinoza, philosophic and political freedom were at odds. Both historical experience and theoretical reflection argued that healthy self-government depended on severe communal civic virtue and therefore on a legally enforced code of shared morals and beliefs. Particularly important were beliefs in divinities who enforce justice with rewards and punishments. As a result, a profound tension persisted between the closed character of republicanism at its best and the life of the inquisitive mind, which was seen as humanity's highest, if rarest, calling.

Classical political philosophy was keenly aware that democracy, because it entails rule by the unleisured poor, tends to let citizens live as they please, preoccupied with making a living and therefore careless of moral education and the common good. This democratic tendency to license, however favorable in the short run to freedom of thought (and hence philosophy), was seen as a grave long-run deficiency. Only if democracy were "mixed" with less permissive oligarchic, aristocratic, and monarchic constitutional elements was it likely to produce serious-minded youth, potentially alive to philosophy's disturbing challenge, and sober, educated statesmen and citizens who could oppose the drift toward mob rule, demagoguery, and class warfare. Left to itself, democracy tended to vibrate between moral laxity and periodic reactions of popular religious fanaticism. Such outbursts of popular religious fervor had been a principal factor in the trial and execution of Socrates in Athens in 399 B.C. and in persecutions of Aristotle and other philosophers, not only in other Greek city-states but in Roman, medieval, and modern republics as well.

Like his classical predecessors, Spinoza believed that the highest and most fulfilling human existence was the philosophic life. He recognized that misguided religious piety poses the gravest political threat (and most unsettling intellectual challenge) to philosophy and science. But he advocated disposing of the threat by advancing a new, scientific basis for religion and government. To enlighten both elites and masses, he devoted the greater part of his chief work of political philosophy, *The Theologico-Political Treatise* (1670), to a critical examination of the Bible. In the process, he founded the modern study of biblical textual criticism.

Spinoza claimed to demonstrate that the Scriptures, read literally and in the light of empirical reasoning, reveal themselves to be a record of intellectually primitive but highly imaginative attempts by leaders to instill obedience in the superstitious masses that composed prescientific tribal cultures. The core teaching to which obedience was sought was a simple notion of justice and charity that corresponds roughly to what reason teaches is the true ethics. There is thus nothing expressly taught in Scripture that cannot be seen as agreeing with science and philosophy, which have an independent and largely superior access to the nature of all things, including God and morality. Any attribution of the truly miraculous, or supernatural, to biblical theology is the result of misreadings that mistake the original context and character of prophecy.

The second part of the *Theologico-Political Treatise* outlines the new, scientific principles of justice. The doctrine is derived, with significant modifications, from Spinoza's great contemporary, Thomas Hobbes. The starting point is the undeniable necessity, and hence the inalienable "natural right," of every being (and therefore of every human being) to preserve itself in a competitive world. For humans, preservation means not only physical security but also rational self-governance to whatever degree is possible. The reasonable basis of political society is in the contract individuals make with one another to provide for their mutual preservation. Thus they transfer their natural rights to a "sovereign" government that will have the collective force to ensure that individuals abide by the laws that promote the general welfare. Justice is nothing more and nothing less than strict fidelity to this contract.

The sovereign power can be placed in the hands of one (monarchy), a few (aristocracy), or the majority of the people (democracy). Democracy—and more particularly liberal democracy, which can allow a diverse populace to live in harmony—is the most natural and reasonable form of government. Its consensual character, grounded in free debate among conflicting points of view, promotes prudent policy making, while best preserving the original, natural equality and self-governing liberty implicit in the contract. Liberal democracy consequently is least likely to depart from the original purpose of government or to become oppressive. Because it is least likely to lose its legitimacy in the eyes of the multitude, it is the most stable form of government. What is more, liberal democracy can allow freedom for philosophy and in the process promote true virtue.

Although democracy does require some civic virtue, or patriotic and charitable transcendence of self-interest, that virtue can be grounded in the citizen's attachment to "liberal" virtue, or the sense of dignity afforded by loyalty to a free society. In a free society individuals are given a voice in public policy, and left free to think and speak as they wish, as long as they behave with justice and charity. Because most human beings, however, are neither very reasonable nor sufficiently attached to rational and liberal dignity, virtue continues to need the sanction of belief in a God who rewards and punishes. But true piety ought to be understood as rooted in uncoerced assent of the mind. Hence government, while supporting religion, should also support religious toleration. It ought not to police the thought or words of citizens but to judge everyone pious as long as their beliefs engender behavior that conforms to the rules of justice.

In his *Political Treatise* (1677), Spinoza examined the best version of each of the three forms of government. He died before writing the section on democracy. Scattered remarks suggest that he would have advocated a federation of commercial republics, centered on the urban entrepreneurial middle class.

Through his theory of a contractual democracy animated by a virtue centered on freedom and supported by a civil religion, Spinoza profoundly influenced Jean-Jacques Rousseau. Spinoza's synthesis of Hobbes's notion of individual natural rights and the older classical notion of virtue as the "highest good" inspired the German idealists from Immanuel Kant to G. W. F. Hegel and Karl Marx. His biblical criticism is the foundation of all modern liberal theology. But nearly all those who followed in his wake were forced to soften and mitigate his ruthlessly unsentimental vision of human psychology.

See also Hobbes, Thomas; Liberalism; Rousseau, Jean-Jacques; Theory, Ancient; Virtue, Civic.

THOMAS L. PANGLE

BIBLIOGRAPHY

Powell, Elmer. *Spinoza and Religion.* Boston: Chapman and Grimes, 1941.

Spinoza, Benedict de. *The Collected Works of Spinoza.* Edited and translated by Edwin Curley. Vol. 1 [others forthcoming]. Princeton: Princeton University Press, 1985.

_____. *The Correspondence of Spinoza.* Edited by Abraham Wolf. London: Dial Press, 1928.

_____. *The Political Works of Spinoza*. Edited and translated by A. G. Wernham. Oxford: Oxford University Press, 1965.

Strauss, Leo. "How to Study Spinoza's Theologico-Political Treatise." In *Persecution and the Art of Writing*. Glencoe, Ill.: Free Press, 1952.

✦ Tocqueville, Alexis de

French statesman, political thinker, and historian. Tocqueville (1805–1859) was born in Paris to a distinguished aristocratic family. As a youth, he witnessed the fall of Napoleon Bonaparte and the recovery of his family's estates and at least a portion of the status they had before the French Revolution.

These events, however, did not cause Tocqueville to hope for anything like a restoration of the pre-revolutionary regime. Through study and thought, he had concluded that the fundamental idea of democracy, that of liberty as everyone's birthright, had revealed itself so clearly to humanity in general that it could no longer be resisted. He therefore took an oath of allegiance to the liberal monarchy of Louis-Philippe when it displaced the Bourbon monarchy in 1830. Taking the oath was in effect a declaration of independence from his aristocratic lineage. Henceforth Tocqueville would devote his life of writing and public service to the legitimization and improvement of democracy.

Public Career and Writings

Tocqueville's legacy consists almost entirely of two books: *Democracy in America* (1835–1840), which he wrote at the beginning of his public life, and *The Old Regime and the French Revolution* (1856), written in his final years. In the intervening years, Tocqueville devoted himself to a career in politics. He served his constituents of Volognes as a member of the Chamber of Deputies from 1839 until the end of the Second Republic in 1851. To his frustration, however, his influence as a statesman never matched his fame as an author. He labored valiantly to preserve the republic, participating in the drafting of a new constitution in 1848. Near the end of his career, he was appointed by the president, Louis Napoleon, to be minister of foreign affairs. He held this office for only five months, however, because his opposition to Louis Napoleon's ambitions of dictatorship became clear. When Tocqueville protested the coup d'état that ended the republic, he had to retire from public service.

During the last two years of his political career, Tocqueville wrote some *Recollections*—his memoirs of the events of 1848 and their aftermath. These observations, like much of his work, were not intended for publication. Had Tocqueville lived longer, some of the material in his *Souvenirs* might have found its way into his projected work on *The European Revolution*. He was able to complete only part of this ambitious project: *The Old Regime and the French Revolution*.

In *The Old Regime and the French Revolution*, Tocqueville presented his account of the causes of the French Revolution, an account still influential among historians of the period. He showed how the decadence and political ineptitude of the French aristocracy ultimately provoked the violence of 1789. Tocqueville also began to trace the gradual emergence of the idea—or perhaps it should be called the feeling—that is at the core of modern democracy and is responsible for its overwhelming power and grandeur—namely, the equal right of all human beings at birth to liberty.

By returning to this inspiring core of the French Revolution and of democracy, Tocqueville intended to overcome what he viewed as the sadly farcical politics of the mid-nineteenth century.

His best hope for this book, as for all of his writings, was that it might begin to generate a level of statesmanship equal to the brightest prospects of democracy—but which there is no guarantee that democracy will produce. *The Old Regime* contains an implicit call for modern democratic statesmanship to provide social and political forms through which the democratic idea can be manifested in a healthy, active way. But there is little or nothing in *The Old Regime* that shows just what that might mean.

Tocqueville left no clearer or fuller prescriptions for democratic statesmanship than those in the book of his early years, *Democracy in America*. Despite the many reasons that American democracy could not, according to Tocqueville, stand as a model for Europe, *Democracy in America* came closest to providing some positive direction for European legislators. The book remains Tocqueville's masterpiece.

The Question of Equality

The two volumes of *Democracy in America* complement one another in the presentation of what Tocqueville intended as a "new political science for a world quite new." By this he meant at least that the new world is a democratic one; a system of government that depends upon the authority of any natural elect—anyone superior by nature or labeled as chosen by God—is no longer possible. Political science will have to be guided by the fact that equality and the passion for equality are the dominant facts of political life. But what equality? An informing new political science is needed, Tocqueville maintained, because *equality* is an ambiguous term; the love of equality can take either a noble form or a debased form.

At its worst the love of equality is merely jealousy, hostile to any kind of individual distinction. In Volume One of *Democracy in America*, Tocqueville shows how this base passion gives to the democratic majority its own propensity to tyranny. It is as if the majority were a being with a soul that insisted on administering every aspect of human life, embarrassed by the success of anything not brought about by its own will. The most likely, and very noxious, consequence of this tyranny is an excess of political and especially administrative centralization that robs individuals of any necessity or even opportunity for self-reliance.

In Volume Two, Tocqueville further shows how the love of equality tends to break down all forms of human association subordinate to the democratic community as a whole. Because a person's belonging to a family or a voluntary association, or even a friendship, might provide the psychological support as well as the ground for resisting the democratic majority's authority, the democratic majority tends to suppress these things or tolerate them only in a truncated form. The result is an atomization of civil society. Individuals are denied almost any emotional connection with anything outside themselves, imprisoned, as it were, within their own personal opinions and their own immediate self-interest.

Tocqueville calls this phenomenon *individualism*. By this he does not mean the independence and strength of soul that the word has come to connote as a result of John Stuart Mill's usage in his later work *On Liberty* (1859). What Tocqueville means is almost the opposite of that. By individualism, he means the isolation, and hence the weakening, of the individual. Ultimately, Tocqueville fears that democratic individuals will offer no resistance to the absolute tyranny of a single person; they may even welcome tyranny so long as the tyrant promises to protect the condition of social equality. Short of that, however, Tocqueville is also concerned about the danger of a softer tyranny, of public opinion, among democratic citizens who are so weakened by individualism that they cannot really think or even feel for themselves.

The antidote to these horrors is the healthy or noble love of equality—a love of the political and moral equality among self-legislating human beings that Tocqueville almost certainly learned from the writings of the eighteenth-century philosopher Jean-Jacques Rousseau. Tocqueville's debt to Rousseau is indicated most clearly in the second chapter of Volume One of *Democracy in America*, which he says contains the "germ" of everything that follows. Here Tocqueville gives his description of the New England Puritan communities, where the real spirit of American democracy was implanted long before there was an American nation.

The outstanding, even startling, fact about the New England communities is that no aspect of life was held private, beyond the community's concern. The Puritans had come to America to establish a "city on a hill," to be governed directly by the laws of the Old Testament. In their zeal for their idea, they imposed upon themselves a code of civil legislation that often contained terrible penalties for what Tocqueville considers relatively light offenses.

The fact that Tocqueville declares the Puritans "free" shows how far he is from thinking of freedom as the limited license of, say, John Stuart Mill. Rather, the liberty to which we have equal right at birth means active involvement in our own self-government. Fundamentally, the definitive democratic passion is a sort of instinct for the general will. And Tocqueville's "new science of politics" has the aim of showing how this principle can act.

Local Autonomy and Voluntary Associations

Throughout the remainder of *Democracy in America*, Tocqueville seeks to explain how the Americans are able to keep alive anything of the spirit of those Puritan towns. It is intriguing because, obviously, the conditions that made the political experiment of the Puritans possible no longer existed. The active involvement in public life by all citizens of those New England towns was possible in part because of their small size and relative isolation. But the existence of such small entities is itself a violation of the forces tending toward democratic civilization, guided as those forces are by the growing perception of the commonality among human beings. The democratic world is a world of great nations, perhaps even empires. How, then, can a degree of local autonomy be maintained that allows people a direct active involvement in public life when the local jurisdictions are not politically independent?

Tocqueville's description of how Americans find an answer to this question is richly detailed, in a way that accounts for much of the early prestige of the book. Part of the answer lies in the American scheme of complex government and administrative decentralization. The surprising conclusion is that Americans do not really overcome the tyranny of the majority. Its effects, however, are mitigated so as to render it less despotic and less enervating than it might be. He explains that Americans connect democratic equality and local autonomy through a chain that has several links. For them, democratic equality entails the idea of popular sovereignty. Popular sovereignty, in turn, involves the notion that government is legitimized by the free consent of individuals, and, therefore, the individual is sovereign outside the sphere of authority to which the people have given their consent. This concession to the limited autonomy of the individual within government is then extended so as to sanction a similar concession to the autonomy of local administrations in relation to the central government.

The energy and vigor of American democracy also stem from American adeptness at forming voluntary associations for all sorts of tasks. These voluntary associations as well as the local governmental jurisdictions are the mechanisms through which Americans overcome the individual impotence that democracy may produce. They function indirectly as schools through which Americans develop the habits of free people. Moreover, in a way that parallels what Tocqueville said about complex governmental administration, American reasoning connects vigorous voluntary associations with democratic equality. The link, in their minds, is "self-interest rightly understood." Tocqueville shows somewhat wryly how the crude doctrine of self-interest can be accepted almost beyond question by a democratic people like the Americans and how it can lead them to at least small acts of sacrifice such as are necessary for cooperative endeavor.

The more Tocqueville leads us to understand the attitudes that underlie the health and vigor of local government and voluntary associations in America, the more clearly we see that these things are in fact the results of democratic freedom rather than its fundamental causes. Assumptions about an easy compatibility between individual interests and any common good are highly questionable. Tocqueville merely observes—but does not defend the thought—that Americans share those assumptions. Ultimately, Americans believe what they do because it suits them. They have learned from their own practical experience the advantages of their complicated institutions. What they say in their defense is only the verbalization of what they feel, and what they feel is a result of lucky accidents—of America's geographical circumstances and its almost purely democratic tradition at all levels.

Mores and Religion in American Democracy

What, then, is the inference to be drawn by the democratic legislator? It is clear that in a democratic country unlike America, where the traditions of local freedom and voluntary association did not already exist, they would be difficult to implant. From the perspective of the nation, such localities and associations tend to appear as exceptions, even points of resistance, to the sovereign will of the nation. Put another way, if Tocqueville's argument is that local government and voluntary associations are preventive medicine against the grinding, atomizing effects of egalitarian jealousy, his argument seems to beg the question of why those institutions will not themselves be ground down by that very jealousy where it might already exist.

This much is certain: American political and social institutions would not have their beneficial effects for other democratic peoples. They can be of benefit to Americans because of peculiar American attitudes, or, in Tocqueville's broader word, *mores*. To understand completely why American democratic citizens are free, and what corollaries might be available in their own nations, democratic legislators need to consider the whole system of mores. Ultimately, as Tocqueville says explicitly, more than physical circumstances or even laws, it is mores that are responsible for maintaining republican freedom in America.

Tocqueville discusses mores in democracy, and in American democracy in particular, in both volumes of *Democracy in America*. This discussion is the richest and subtlest dimension of the work, with many features that are of interest to contemporary students of social psychology. The crown of the entire examination of mores, and thus the crown of Tocqueville's thought as a whole, is his discussion of religion. It turns out that the peculiar, marvelous combination of the spirit of religion with the spirit of freedom is just as fundamental to the health of American democracy as it was to that of the early Puritan New England towns—albeit not quite in the same way.

The religion of most of Tocqueville's Americans, that is, the preponderant religion, is Protestantism—of a sort that has made a full accommodation to this world. Protestantism includes the notion that humankind is on the road toward an indefinite perfection, and it interprets progress in material well-being as the sign of such perfectibility. This idea means that Americans are in fact animated to engage in industrial and commercial undertakings not simply from avarice or anxiety but from some satisfaction of grander emotions that they derive from their labors. They even seem to practice a kind of heroism in their commerce. They are sure that the wealth and power of their nation reflects the glory of God.

Not only is American religion worldly, but it is also in an intriguing way very conscious of itself as that. Americans are convinced that religion is indispensable to the maintenance of republican institutions. They take for granted that freedom depends upon a level of virtue among the citizens and, that to be relied on, such virtue needs the support of religion. In particular, virtue needs the support of the promise of reward and the threat of punishment in an afterlife. But Tocqueville confesses that it is very hard to tell whether Americans actually believe in such an afterlife. They say they do, but the secrets of the heart are hard to read. All that can be said for certain is that Americans believe that they ought to believe. Political freedom requires it. Tocqueville reports that this ironic attitude is held not only by the laity but even by ministers.

Tocqueville's analysis of religion in America continually leads to the question whether Americans are genuinely sincere in it. Is the faith they profess something devout, or rather is it politic? Ultimately, Tocqueville's teaching about American democracy revolves around his answer to this question: their faith is both. The best illustration of how this duality might be possible is what Tocqueville says about the separation of church and state in America. Tocqueville shares with Americans the conviction that separation of church and state is enormously valuable, not only to save the state from the ravages of sectarian conflict but also to preserve genuine religious feeling from unnecessary doctrinairism.

When liberated from politics, religion comes into its own, so to speak, as one lofty form of hope from which very few human beings are ever cut off. Sensing this, Americans are not professing the indifference of politics toward religion when they assert the advantages of separation of church and state. Rather, in a way, this separation is their religion. Their faith, at bottom, is something that might be called "natural." Their God is a humane one who loves an honest conscience (which they believe they have) more than doctrinal rectitude. Another way of putting it is to say that Americans make a sort of religion of tolerance; they blithely ignore the sources of such genuine diversity as would require much tolerance.

Tocqueville's showing that mores are the key to American democratic freedom—that they are the cause more than the effect of America's excellent political institutions—makes his reader aware of the artificiality that laces the American way of life. By this he does not intend an indictment. His broadest reflection is that all of human life is beset with artificiality, but that does not necessarily rob it of the prospects for genuine greatness.

What it does mean is that if democracy is to exhibit its own peculiar form of greatness, the artifices by which it lives must be guided by a legislator who sees through them and beyond them. Just who Tocqueville means by his legislator is hard to say. The word clearly does not refer to anyone who sits in Congress or in a state legislature. In the broad sense, Tocqueville's legislator may not even hold a political office but may exercise a natural authority by dint of a peculiar genius. Thus the equal birthright of all human beings to liberty does not cancel out the relevance of a fundamental inequality among human beings. It does, though, probably require more subtlety among the practitioners of the new science of politics.

See also Mill, John Stuart; Popular sovereignty; Religion, Civil; Rousseau, Jean-Jacques.

JOHN C. KORITANSKY

BIBLIOGRAPHY

Rousseau, Jean-Jacques. *The Social Contract*. Translated by Maurice Cranston. London: Penguin Books, 1968.

Tocqueville, Alexis de. *Democracy in America*. Translated by George Lawrence; edited by J. P. Mayer. New York: Harper and Row, 1966.

_____. *Journey to America*. Translated by George Lawrence. Edited by J. P. Mayer. New Haven: Yale University Press, 1960.

_____. *The Old Regime and the French Revolution*. Translated by Stuart Gilbert. Magnolia, Mass.: Peter Smith, 1978.

_____. *Recollections*. Translated by George Lawrence. Edited by A. P. Kerr. Garden City, N.Y.: Doubleday, 1970.

_____. *Writings on Empire and Slavery*. Edited by Jennifer Pitts. Baltimore: Johns Hopkins University Press, 2001.

Wolin, Sheldon S. *Between Two Worlds: Alexis de Tocqueville and the Making of a Political and Theoretical Life*. Princeton: Princeton University Press, 2001.

✦ Weber, Max

A founding thinker of sociology and an important German theorist of the connections between capitalism, bureaucracy, and democracy. Karl Emil Maximilian Weber (1864–1920), as he was christened, suffered from a nervous disorder that forced him to resign his professorship early in a budding academic career. He nevertheless became Germany's most important sociologist and contributed enormously to the rise of modern social science.

Weber is best remembered for his study of how early Protestantism helped generate the cultural basis for modern capitalism. His scholarship also encompassed pathbreaking work on the philosophy and methodology of social science, multifaceted conceptual and empirical studies, and sweeping comparative historical research on Eastern and Western societies from antiquity to modern times. He stressed in particular the role of the distinctively rational aspects of Western culture in the rise of modern capitalism, bureaucracy, and democracy. Weber influenced not only conservative and libertarian views of democracy but also the views of progressives and the radical left. His ambivalent vision of "mass democracy" continues to be debated and appropriated in divergent ways today.

Early in his career Weber argued that Germany should follow Britain's path of "liberal imperialism," but he later abandoned this stance. After supporting Germany's entry into World War I, he attacked its territorial annexations and aggressive submarine warfare. Against the prevalent garrison state mentality, he called for a strengthened parliament and a popularly elected chancellor.

Weber held that authoritarian rule had stunted the development of parliamentary institutions and democratic leadership in Germany. Following the war, he helped prepare the German reply to charges of war guilt made at Versailles during the Paris Peace Conference, helped found the German Democratic Party, and contributed to the drafting of the Weimar constitution. Prophetically, he warned that "a polar night of icy darkness and hardness" would emerge from Germany's national humiliation and social disintegration and from the despotic tendencies of romantic extremism of both the right and the left.

Weber's ideas about democracy are scattered throughout his scholarly works. In antiquity, he argued, all-encompassing state power throttled capitalism and democracy. Landowning elites amassed wealth through military expropriation and widespread slavery and dependency. They dominated the cities, from which they administered the hinterlands and extracted surpluses from rural producers. In medieval Europe, by contrast, craftsmen and merchants made revolutionary breaks from the landed aristocracy, turning towns into centers of production and commerce. The ascendant bourgeois class liberated slaves and serfs and created liberal institutions, such as equality before the law, rational trial procedures, individual rights, general citizenship, occupations open to talent, and representative politics.

The nation-state ended city autonomy in early modern Europe by the sixteenth or seventeenth century, but monarchs, competing with relatively equal neighbors and depending on urban resources, tolerated the independence of the bourgeoisie. Weber held that, although new central governments consolidated disparate European fiefdoms and cities, competition among the nation-states and bourgeois interests within them prevented the type of total power manifested in ancient empires and permitted the continued development of capitalism and liberal democracy.

Contradictory aspects of Western democratization are visible in Weber's treatment of the Reformation. Puritan values of tolerance, ethical community, and principled dissent, combined with the sovereignty of a congregation composed exclusively of individuals who had demonstrated their qualification for full membership, prepared the way for democratic civil society and voluntary association. Moreover, the Puritan ethic of "duty in a calling" gave rise to secular values of commitment and responsibility in professional vocations.

But Weber also linked Puritanism to ruthless capitalistic acquisition, pessimistic individualism, and pure utilitarianism. In his view, Puritan culture contributed indirectly to the class polarization, cultural homogenization, and authoritarian statism characteristic of mass democracy, while also providing the resources to resist these same forces.

The Power of Bureaucracy

Modern bureaucracy, according to Weber, is the unparalleled means for coordinating large numbers of functionally specialized workers. Its rational discipline, technical knowledge, precision, and "objective discharge of business" are all essential to capitalism and continue to shape contemporary culture. Like all modern bureaucracies, governments require small numbers and secrecy for fast, decisive, and efficient action. Thus heads of state and appointed officials make many important decisions away from public view.

Professional staffs in political parties do the same. Citizens are targets of every cheap demagogic means of persuasion at election time and are otherwise treated as inert objects of administration. Weber implied that political legitimacy depends mainly on suffrage and legal equality and on a minimum of material support and security, but he recognized that these offer the masses neither participation nor social justice. Rather, mass democracy produces relative powerlessness below the bureaucratically based elites.

Genuine revolutionary transformation, in Weber's view, becomes increasingly improbable with the growth of bureaucracy. Victors and vanquished alike depend upon quick restoration of administrative machinery. Weber's point that bureaucracies function smoothly even under enemy occupation showed a chilling prescience about France a few decades later.

While thinkers of both the right and the left promised harmonious futures, Weber saw conflict among values, interests, and groups as modernity's most precious resource. Peaceful struggles, alliances, and compromises produce cultural dynamism and create space for minority opinions and individuality. Weber feared, however, that competing organizations would someday be fashioned into a singular bureaucracy, destroying the countervailing forces upon which pluralism depends. In the name of nationalism or social justice, a new total state would forge an inescapable, top-to-bottom system of mass surveillance and control, with no independent unions, no professional associations, no parties, and no news. Weber predicted that communist regimes like the Soviet Union's would be thoroughly bureaucratic and repressive and that similar authoritarian systems could arise from the right.

Yet Weber believed that efforts to increase social justice and democracy do not inevitably expand the state. They also produce tensions, struggles, and changes that enhance diversity and prevent inflexible orthodoxy.

Even bureaucracy has some democratizing tendencies. Unclear jurisdictions, lack of consistently applied rules, and broad official prerogative made premodern states opaque, rigid, and immune to reconstruction. By contrast, modern bureaucracy's small number of ultimate decision makers, clear hierarchy, and rational legalism fix responsibility with specific individuals and open organizations to critique, challenge, and reform. Functional specialization, moreover, raises the costs of authoritarian rule. Arbitrary, rigid micromanagement unduly restricts specialized knowledge and skill and generates technical failures, malingering, and even outright resistance.

Overall, Weber implied that multicentered bureaucratic societies, although resistant to revolution, are open to substantial democratic change. Reforms, however, will not free the working class from authoritarian work settings or from compulsion "by the whip of hunger." Thus Weber saw German constitutionalism as legitimating capitalist inequality, and he considered participatory democracy to be a pipe dream.

The Power of Politics

A vibrant political sphere is the countervailing force against bureaucracy, Weber believed, with politics and administration being fundamentally different domains. In contrast to the hierarchical rule in state and party officialdom, politics is a struggle between different values and voices, originating in divergent sociocultural interests and different locations in socioeconomic hierarchies. Whereas officials are expected to be obedient, loyal, and technically competent, politicians must be able to articulate convictions, calculate consequences, make autonomous decisions, and, above all, lead. Such skills are honed in electoral and parliamentary battles, not in administrative offices.

Although he viewed the politics of plebiscites as inherently demagogic, Weber saw value in subjecting potential leaders to public scrutiny and choice. Even the Caesarist tendencies of such politics break the ruts of administrative and economic control. Critics fault Weber on this point for exaggerating the threats of bureaucracy and understating the dangers of charismatic demagogues.

Weber held that the long authoritarian rule of Otto von Bismarck (1815–1898) as chancellor left Germany with a tyranny of officials, a toothless parliament, deformed politics, and an obsequious intelligentsia. Although cultural pessimism and an aversion to political prophecy discouraged Weber from theorizing about an alternative, more strongly democratic regime, he argued that two core ethics of Puritan culture—conviction and cool reserve—had the power to revitalize democratic politics. He called for a new breed of politicians, who would combine passionate vision with an ethic of responsibility about the consequences of their normative and electoral postures. They would be able to face bitter realities without illusions, to tame demagogic aspects of mass culture, and to control the vanity inherent in creative leadership.

In the wreckage of the Treaty of Versailles after World War I, however, Weber thought that Germany's lethal mixture of political demagoguery, leaderless bureaucracy, and dispirited masses pointed directly toward the total state. His premature death in 1920 spared him from seeing his nightmare realized in Nazi Germany.

See also Bureaucracy.

ROBERT J. ANTONIO

BIBLIOGRAPHY

Beetham, David. *Max Weber and the Theory of Modern Politics.* 2d ed. Cambridge: Polity Press; New York: Blackwell, 1985.

The Cambridge Companion to Weber. Edited by Stephen Turner. Cambridge and New York: Cambridge University Press, 2000.

Eden, Robert. *Political Leadership and Nihilism: A Study of Weber and Nietzsche.* Tampa: University Presses of Florida, 1983.

Käsler, Dirk. *Max Weber: An Introduction to His Life and Work.* Translated by Philippa Hurd. Cambridge: Polity Press; Chicago: University of Chicago Press, 1988.

Mommsen, Wolfgang J. *Max Weber and German Politics 1890–1920.* 2d ed. Translated by Michael S. Steinberg. Chicago: University of Chicago Press, 1984.

Scaff, Lawrence A. *Fleeing the Iron Cage: Culture, Politics, and Modernity in the Thought of Max Weber.* Berkeley and Los Angeles: University of California Press, 1989.

Swedberg, Richard. *Max Weber and the Idea of Economic Sociology.* Princeton: Princeton University Press, 2000.

Weber, Marianne. *Max Weber: A Biography.* Translated and edited by Harry Zohn. New York: Wiley, 1975.

Weber, Max. *Economy and Society: An Outline of Interpretive Sociology.* 2 vols. Edited by Guenther Roth and Claus Wittich. Translated by Ephraim Fischoff et al. Berkeley and Los Angeles: University of California Press, 1978.

_____. *From Max Weber: Essays in Sociology.* Translated and edited by Hans H. Gerth and C. Wright Mills. New York: Oxford University Press, 1958; London: Routledge, 1991.

✦ Wollstonecraft, Mary

Pioneering English writer and political theorist who challenged the virtual exclusion of women from contemporary thinking about freedom and equality. Determined to be economically independent, Wollstonecraft (1759–1797) supported herself first by teaching and then by writing. She married William Godwin after the father of her first child abandoned her. She died shortly after giving birth to a second child, Mary, who was to become the wife of the poet Percy Bysshe Shelley and the author of *Frankenstein*.

Wollstonecraft lived through a turbulent and politically unstable period. She was influenced by the experience of the French Revolution and by the writings of its political theorists, in particular Jean-Jacques Rousseau, as well as by William Blake, Thomas Paine, William Godwin, and Henry Fuseli in England. All these writers believed in the rights of man, but they generally understood those rights to apply differently, if at all, to women. Wollstonecraft accepted the view, developed by Enlightenment thinkers in the eighteenth century and later applied to nineteenth-century theories of sexual difference, that men and women have different duties within the "separate spheres" of the public world of civil society and the private world of the family. However, she did not interpret that idea to mean that women could not become full citizens.

According to liberal theory, citizens were to be governed by reason. Because women were thought to be governed by feeling—not least because they were closer to nature than men—citizenship was restricted to men. Wollstonecraft challenged the view that only men were capable of reason. Provided women were treated with the same dignity and shared the same privileges as men, they too could become rational beings and, at the same time, would honor their duties as wives and mothers more fully. As she wrote in *A*

Vindication of the Rights of Woman (1792), "Why do they expect virtue from a slave, from a being whom the constitution of civil society has rendered weak, if not vicious?"

If women were not treated equally in the private sphere, Wollstonecraft believed, morality in the public sphere would be undermined, because "the virtue of men will be worm eaten by the insect whom he keeps under his feet." Her writings point to the limitations of liberalism, which posits a separation and an opposition between the public and private spheres of life and naturalizes women's subordinate place within the family.

See also Feminism; Democracy, Women and.

HILARY LAND

BIBLIOGRAPHY

Todd, Janet. *Mary Wollstonecraft: A Revolutionary Life.* New York: Columbia University Press, 2000.

III. Philosophical Concepts and Issues

✦ Anarchy

A political ideology whose central tenet is that the state must be abolished and society organized by voluntary means without resort to force or coercive authority. Whereas conservatives, liberals, and socialists all assign the state an essential role in their contrasting visions of the good society, anarchists seek its outright destruction.

In support of this position they make two general claims. First, those who staff the various branches of the state—politicians, civil servants, judges, the police, and the military—together form a ruling class that pursues its own interests and exploits the rest of society, especially the working class. Second, insofar as the state does attempt to promote general social interests, the means that it has at its disposal—laws and other directives emanating from the center and coercively enforced—are ineffective for this purpose. Societies, anarchists believe, are highly complex entities, and they should be organized from the bottom up, with full attention paid to the varying needs of individuals and localities.

Anarchists therefore look to voluntary associations to maintain social order, to organize production and exchange, to protect the environment, and to perform other necessary social functions. But different anarchists hold different views of how a society organized by voluntary means might function. Individualists, such as the American anarchist Benjamin Tucker (1854–1939), envisaged a market-based system of free exchange and contract, with private protective associations acting to safeguard the rights of each individual who has bought their services. In contrast, collectivists such as Mikhail Bakunin (1814–1876) and communists such as Pyotr Kropotkin (1842–1921) sought to transcend the market and believed that social needs could be met through voluntary cooperation in workplaces and local communes. These bodies might federate for specific purposes (such as organizing a transport system), but the federal body would not have the right to compel its constituent parts if they dissented from its decisions. These socialist forms of anarchism have had the greatest political influence, helping to radicalize the workers' movements of late nineteenth and early twentieth century Europe, especially in France, Italy, and Spain. Anarchism had its greatest practical success at the outset of the Spanish civil war in the 1930s, when many areas came for a time under anarchist control, but subsequently its influence has waned. Anarchists today are effective chiefly through their participation in the peace and ecology movements.

Anarchists have been harsh critics of representative democracy on the Western model.

Their critique can be boiled down to three essential points. First, a democratic state is still a state: its way of operating shows the same insensitivity to social needs as do other, more overtly authoritarian political institutions. Second, democrats often claim that what is represented in representative democracy is the will of the people, which informs and controls government policy. But, according to anarchists, the idea of a single, consistent popular will is a myth. People are divided in their opinions, their ideas are shifting, some are better informed than others. It is absurd to suppose that a majority view, expressed in a ballot at one moment in time, constitutes the will of the people. Third, anarchists attack the idea of popular representation in legislative assemblies. They argue that people, when called upon to choose their representatives, are very likely to vote for those who appear well educated and articulate—in other words, aspiring members of the middle class. But even if members of the working class were willing to select representatives from their own number, these would soon be corrupted by their new position as servants of the state.

In a famous passage, Bakunin argued that workers elected to form a government would be transformed almost at once from democrats into a new authoritarian aristocracy. Pierre-Joseph Proudhon (1809–1865), the most influential of the French anarchists, confirmed this principle for himself when he was elected to the Constituent Assembly in 1848. Absorption in the business of government, he found, quickly distanced him from the needs and desires of his constituents.

Except in very special circumstances, therefore, anarchists have favored a policy of political abstention and have sought to encourage a revolutionary transformation of society through a variety of extraparliamentary means, including propaganda, direct action, syndicalism, and finally insurrection. But does democracy play any part in their ideal society of the future? For anarchists of an individualist persuasion there is little room, if any, for collective decision making in such a society. Each person would make his or her own contractual arrangements with others according to tastes and preferences. Agreeing to decide certain matters by democratic vote would not be excluded, but neither would it be required.

For other anarchists the issue is a little more complicated. Inevitably questions will arise within workplaces and local communities that require collective decision. Ideally, these would be resolved unanimously, but if unanimous consent proved to be impossible the majority would have to decide. The minority would then face a choice: either to go along with the decision reached or else to withdraw and allow the majority to proceed. No anarchist would allow the minority to be forced to comply with the majority decision. To force compliance would be to reintroduce coercive authority, the hallmark of the state.

Direct democracy would, then, have some place in the ideal visions of most anarchists, but it would be subordinate to the principles of free agreement and noncompulsion. Even this arrangement would be going too far for some: the English philosopher William Godwin (1756–1836), the first systematic exponent of an anarchist political philosophy, argued against popular assemblies on the ground that the consensus they tended to produce resulted from irrational forms of persuasion, corrupting the independent judgment of each participant. Anarchist suspicion of democracy in any of its forms runs very deep.

See also Communitarianism.

DAVID MILLER

BIBLIOGRAPHY

Bakunin, Mikhail. *Bakunin on Anarchy: Selected Works by the Activist-Founder of World Anarchism*. Edited,

translated, and with an introduction by Sam Dol-
goff. New York: Vintage Books, 1972.

Crowder, George. *Classical Anarchism: The Political
Thought of Godwin, Proudhon, Bakunin, and Kropotkin.*
Oxford: Clarendon Press, 1991; New York: Oxford
University Press, 1992.

Krimerman, Leonard I., and Lewis Perry, eds. *Patterns
of Anarchy: A Collection of Writings on the Anarchist
Tradition.* New York: Anchor Books, 1966.

Kropotkin, Pyotr. *Kropotkin's Revolutionary Pamphlets: A
Collection of Writings by Peter Kropotkin.* Edited by
Roger N. Baldwin. New York: Dover, 1970.

Miller, David. *Anarchism.* London: Dent, 1984.

Ritter, Alan. *Anarchism: A Theoretical Analysis.* Cambridge: Cambridge University Press, 1980.

Woodcock, George. *Anarchism.* Harmondsworth: Penguin Books, 1963.

✦ Autonomy

Literally, self-rule or self-government. Autonomy has often been thought to bear a particularly
close relation to democracy. Only in a democracy,
it is sometimes said, can an individual or a people
be truly autonomous. Spelling out why this should
be so, however, takes some care.

In its ancient meaning, autonomy was taken to
be a property of states, rather than of individuals.
An autonomous people was one that was self-sufficient and self-governing, rather than being ruled
by an outside force. In the modern world, we have
not lost this understanding of the term: the "puppet" regimes of the former Eastern bloc, for
example, were commonly contrasted with the
apparently more autonomous regimes elsewhere
around the globe. To have autonomy in this sense,
no doubt, is part of what is required for a nation
to be a democracy, but we should remember that
in the ancient world even tyrannical states were
often regarded as fully autonomous.

The modern understanding of the term attributes autonomy, or the lack of it, to individuals. In
the philosophical literature, personal autonomy
has been identified with a great variety of other
notions, including self-government, freedom,
responsibility, morality, dignity, independence,
and self-knowledge. Yet the core concept seems to
be simply that an autonomous person is one who
makes, and acts upon, his or her own decisions.

The relationship between autonomy and
democracy was perhaps most fruitfully worked
out by the eighteenth-century French philosopher Jean-Jacques Rousseau, whose views were to
inspire the moral and political works of the great
German philosopher Immanuel Kant (with whom
the term *autonomy* is most often associated).
Rousseau's ideas were also to influence G. W. F.
Hegel and Karl Marx in different ways.

Rousseau makes a powerful attempt to bring
together the ancient and modern understandings
of *autonomy*. The idea of individual autonomy
is given perhaps its classic formulation by
Rousseau in *The Social Contract* (1762). According
to Rousseau, freedom is obedience to a law that
we prescribe to ourselves. The problem of social
order, then, becomes the problem of reconciling
the individual's right to autonomy with the existence of the state, and in particular with the state's
right to create and enforce laws. In Book 1, chapter 6, of *The Social Contract*, Rousseau sets out this
problem as the need to find a kind of association
"in which each, while uniting himself with all,
may still obey himself alone, and remain as free as
before."

Rousseau's solution is simple and elegant: all
must equally play a part in the creation of laws to
which all will equally be subject. In other words,
individual autonomy is reconciled with the
authority of the state by a form of direct, participatory democracy. At the same time, group autonomy is preserved: Rousseau's ideal state is self-
governing.

That this solution works has often been doubted. Some critics have questioned whether we can identify "self-rule" with "rule by a corporate body which includes oneself." If an individual is outvoted, he or she may be made subject to disagreeable restrictions that normally would be thought to be a limit on autonomy. Thus some have even argued that the only form of government consistent with due respect for autonomy is a direct democracy in which laws are passed only if they are accepted unanimously. Because, in practice, such a state would be impossible to achieve, the contemporary American political philosopher Robert Paul Wolff, in *In Defense of Anarchism* (1973), has argued that giving autonomy its full due requires anarchism. According to this view, no autonomous person can obey the law simply because it is the law: for the autonomous person, there is no such thing as a command.

One response to this argument suggests that the claims made on behalf of autonomy are greatly exaggerated. On the contrary, an autonomous person can accept the advantages of government as a way of pursuing his or her own ends. This response, however, ignores the problem of those who are regularly outvoted. A more promising strategy is to concede that a concern for individual autonomy may well create a pressure toward anarchism but to insist that other values can be called on to provide a more powerful counterargument for the state. The state offers individual and collective security, together with a level of prosperity that could not be achieved without it. As the nineteenth-century English philosopher John Stuart Mill argued, in *On Liberty* (1859), all that makes anyone's life worth living depends on the existence of enforceable restraints on the behavior of others. In this view, life without the law would be worthless.

In sum, by combining respect for autonomy with recognition of the importance of security and prosperity, it is possible to provide a more robust and convincing defense of majoritarian democracy. Once we have accepted the necessity of government, concern for individual autonomy provides strong reason for favoring democracy over other forms of government. Even if it is wrong to say that the individual retains complete autonomy in majoritarian democracies, nevertheless democracy is the closest we can feasibly approach to the idea of individual self-government in a political context.

But are modern liberal democracies autonomous in the ancient sense of autonomy? The growing influence of the global market, of multinational companies and international banking and political organizations, has led to a decline in the ability of nations to control their own destinies, particularly with respect to economic policy. States in the contemporary world are becoming less autonomous than they were formerly. To the extent, then, that we see group autonomy as a condition of national democracy, we must conclude that increasing globalization has undermined the possibility of genuine local democracy.

See also Anarchy; Consent; Democracy, Justifications for; Democracy, Participatory; Hegel, Georg Wilhelm Friedrich; Kant, Immanuel; Majority rule, minority rights; Mill, John Stuart; Rousseau, Jean-Jacques.

JONATHAN WOLFF

BIBLIOGRAPHY

Autonomy and Order: A Communitarian Anthology. Edited by Edward W. Lehman. Lanham, Md.: Rowman and Littlefield, 2000.

Berlin, Isaiah. *Four Essays on Liberty.* Oxford: Oxford University Press, 1969.

Dworkin, Gerald. *The Theory and Practice of Autonomy.* Cambridge: Cambridge University Press, 1988.

Held, David. "Democracy, the Nation-State and the Global System." In *Political Theory Today*, edited by David Held. Cambridge: Polity Press, 1991.

Mill, John Stuart. "On Liberty." In *Utilitarianism*. Edited by Mary Warnock. Glasgow: Collins, 1962.

Rousseau, Jean-Jacques. "The Social Contract." In *The Social Contract and Discourses*. Edited by G. D. H. Cole, J. H. Brumfitt, and John C. Hall. London: Dent, 1973.

Wolff, Robert Paul. *In Defense of Anarchism*. New York: Harper, 1973.

✦ Bureaucracy

A form of organization for administration that is marked by a concern for rules and procedures, a chain of command defining superiors and subordinates, and precision in job descriptions and division of labor. The word *bureaucracy* comes from the French *bureau* and *cratie*. *Bureau* is derived from the cloth that covered the desks of the king's finance clerks; *cratie* comes from the Greek word for "rule." Bureaucracy literally means "rule by desks," or the rules and records stored in those desks. In modern liberal democracies bureaucracy is the primary organization for carrying out the administration of government at all levels in society. Management and reform of bureaucracy have become a principal focus of modern government.

Bureaucracy is not new. It existed in ancient Egypt and Sumer. But bureaucracy emerged as the principal form of organization for administration as society became technologically sophisticated.

Advances in science and technology facilitated organizing for complex and difficult tasks, and bureaucracy became the primary organizing principle in both government and private industry. Virtually every form of government relies upon bureaucracy.

Weber and Bureaucratic Theory

Modern bureaucracy is the product of the philosophical movement known as German idealism. Perhaps the foremost theorist on the influence of bureaucracy in society was the German social scientist Max Weber (1864–1920). Weber published his theory of bureaucracy in the early twentieth century. According to Weber, in order to function effectively in a complex, democratic, and industrial society, organizations must be based on law and a rational arrangement of power and authority. The highly developed bureaucracy, he wrote in *The Theory of Social and Economic Organization*, should adhere to certain fundamental principles of organization. The bureaucracy rests on a body of law, which establishes the legitimate authority of the organization and defines the organization's purpose and responsibilities. The organization has established rules and procedures to govern how it will carry out its responsibilities. These rules and procedures are highly specialized and specific, governing the day-to-day operations of the personnel within the organization. They provide direction for the organization and limit the possibility of arbitrary action by individuals within the organization as well as arbitrary action by the organization itself.

Employees within a bureaucracy are appointed solely on the basis of their competence to perform specific tasks, and their competence is determined through testing and experience. All personnel decisions regarding hiring, promotion, and tenure are to be based on competence and achievement, as determined by superiors, and on seniority. Employees' salaries are determined by their rank within the organization. Within a bureaucracy, all positions are arranged hierarchically, with each position under a higher, or superior, one. Individuals supervise employees who occupy positions below them.

The highest ranking person within the bureaucracy is accountable to someone outside the organization. In democracies this is usually an elected official or office. All decisions and actions of the bureaucracy are written. This profusion of written records and files serves to guide future actions by the bureaucracy and helps to ensure that it remains accountable to outside authority.

The Rational Approach

The single most important organizing principle behind bureaucracy is procedural rationality. Procedural rationality is the belief that it should be possible to design an organization in such a way as to ensure that it accomplishes its goal in an efficient and effective manner. Advocates of procedural rationality argue that by establishing rules and procedures to direct the actions of the bureaucracy it is possible to construct an organization that will respond efficiently to instructions issued to it. The focus is on how to structure rules and procedures so as to minimize the amount of discretion left to individuals within the organization, thereby ensuring that the organization will act with precision in regard to whatever instructions it receives.

In the United States this approach to organization and administration was espoused by Woodrow Wilson (1856–1924), who was a professor of political science before he entered politics and was elected president. Wilson's essay "The Study of Administration" argued for a science of administration that could improve upon government by developing rational theories of administration. Wilson argued that it should be possible to determine the best way to organize the agencies of government in order to accomplish the purposes of government within a democratic society. He urged the study of the organization and administration of governments around the world in order to determine what works and why and to apply these lessons to the American system. According to Wilson, there is a dichotomy between politics and administration: politics is about making decisions and administration is about implementing those decisions. Bureaucracy is organization for administration.

The modern bureaucracy reflects the attention to procedural rationality and concern with a politics-administration dichotomy espoused by scholars such as Weber and Wilson. Modern bureaucracy is highly organized, and its personnel constitute a professional civil service who have been trained especially for careers within the bureaucracy. The political and legal authority of the bureaucracy is well established in most states. In highly developed democracies the bureaucracy constitutes a major portion of the government; it exists somewhat removed from the processes of partisan elections. Bureaucracy rests upon notions of political neutrality and merit, principles at odds with the overriding concern with public opinion that tends to drive elected officials in legislative and executive institutions. The makeup of the legislative and executive institutions may change frequently, but the responsibilities, authority, and character of the bureaucracy and the civil service are resistant to change. Bureaucracy therefore exerts something of a conservative force upon government and is oriented toward the status quo.

The influence of bureaucracy in modern government and industry originates from the expertise it possesses. Bureaucracies bring together in a highly organized and concentrated way highly trained technical experts, and this expertise is then harnessed to accomplish the tasks set before the organization. In government, political leaders are responsible for defining those tasks. But the bureaucracy itself wields great influence in defining the tasks.

institutions and processes of government, bureaucracy increases. This increase is true for virtually every form of government, not only for democracies. Moreover, as a society moves away from an agricultural economy toward an industrial economy, bureaucracy increases. Again, this is true regardless of the political system in place. When the Soviet Union was at the peak of its power, it possessed a vast bureaucracy that controlled virtually every aspect of the economy and the state.

A well-developed, functioning bureaucracy is the prime attribute of a modern, advanced state. It has evolved as the means by which government responds to the demands of the society as those demands are reflected in the political decisions reached by elected officials. Bureaucracy will, in all likelihood, be very influential in shaping the future of liberal democracy.

See also Democracy, Participatory; Weber, Max.

EUGENE W. HICKOK

BIBLIOGRAPHY

Democracy, Bureaucracy, and the Study of Administration. Edited by Camilla Stivers. Boulder, Colo.: Westview Press, 2000.

Downs, Anthony. *Inside Bureaucracy.* Boston: Little, Brown, 1967.

Mosher, Frederick C. *Democracy and the Public Service.* 2d ed. New York: Oxford University Press, 1982.

Redford, Emmette S. *Democracy in the Administrative State.* New York: Oxford University Press, 1969.

Simon, Herbert A. *Administrative Behavior.* 3d ed. New York: Free Press, 1976.

Weber, Max. *The Theory of Social and Economic Organization.* New York: Free Press, 1964.

Wilson, James Q. *Bureaucracy.* New York: Basic Books, 1989.

Wilson, Woodrow. "The Study of Administration." *Political Science Quarterly* (June 1887).

✦ Citizenship

The condition of being a citizen and the responsibilities and rights this status entails. Citizenship is a key notion in democratic thought and practice. Citizens are full and equal members of a democratic political community; their identity is shaped by the rights and obligations that define that community. There are many different interpretations of the nature of citizenship, and disputes over those interpretations have played an important part in the evolution of democracy.

Ancient and Classical Citizenship

Emerging jointly with the democracy of the Greek city-states, the notion of citizenship derives from the classical Greco-Roman concept of the self-governing political community. Ancient citizenship implied equality in rights and obligations before the law and active political participation. To be a citizen was to be capable of governing and being governed. In the Greek democratic city-states, however, citizenship was restricted to free, native-born men, which meant that citizens constituted a minority of the population, even in Athens. Their participation in public life was made possible by the existence of slaves, who were responsible for performing the principal economic functions.

During the Roman Empire the extension of citizenship first to lower classes and then to conquered foreigners produced a much more heterogeneous group of citizens. The term began to refer more to equal protection under the law than to active participation in the making and implementing of laws. Initially, the assertion of a political identity indicating allegiance to and active participation in a political community, citizenship came to signify a particular legal and juridical status. At the height of the Roman Empire the emperor Caracalla issued an edict (A.D. 212)

Challenges to Democracy

Bureaucracy and the bureaucratic state present special challenges to democratic government. The essence of democracy is self-government: citizens governing themselves through a system of elections and representation. It is a form of government that emphasizes the relationship between the individual and the government, the participation of citizens in politics, and popular accountability of government officials. Bureaucracy, however, emphasizes expertise, procedures, rules, and records. Those individuals employed by a bureaucracy are hired because of their fitness to fulfill specific tasks. The link between the bureaucracy and the people therefore is indirect. Citizens are served by the bureaucracy, but, as an organization, the bureaucracy is removed from popular accountability.

It is the responsibility of elected officials to provide the link between the citizens and the bureaucracy. In modern liberal democracies, much of the responsibility of elected officials is related to oversight of the bureaucracy in an attempt to keep it accountable. But the very nature of the well-established bureaucracy presents serious challenges to accountability.

In most democracies bureaucracy is accountable to elected officials within the government or to those who have been appointed by elected officials to oversee the operations of the bureaucracy. But the vast size and complexity of modern bureaucracy limit the degree to which the bureaucracy can be held accountable for much of what it does. In theory, a bureaucracy modeled after the image provided by Weber might respond efficiently to instructions issued to it by elected officials and might easily be held accountable for its actions. But because personnel within the bureaucracy respond to their superiors within the organization and to specific job responsibilities and procedures, bureaucracies tend to be resistant to changes introduced from outside by public officials responding to calls for change issued by the citizens. Moreover, any change in the responsibilities of the bureaucracy must be accompanied by the necessary changes in bureaucratic procedure, routine, and policy. Change, when it does occur within the bureaucracy, is usually slow.

The bureaucracy also represents a challenge to democratic government because of the expertise it possesses. Elected officials often come to rely on the bureaucracy for information and data on issues they confront. The bureaucracy often is the primary source of information for citizens as well. This reliance on the bureaucracy can undermine the independent political authority of elected officials in a democracy. Political leaders often find themselves reacting and responding to changes in the political environment that have been created by the bureaucracy. In addition, they become dependent on the bureaucracy to accomplish the purposes of legislation. And as citizens make more and more demands on government, bureaucracy increases. The size and expense of modern bureaucracy are such that it constitutes the major costs associated with government.

In light of all these considerations, the reform of bureaucracy is an ongoing concern in most developed democracies around the world. But bureaucracy has proved difficult to reform, resistant to change, and resilient to attack.

Endurance of the Bureaucratic State

The growth of the modern bureaucracy is considered by many to be an inevitable by-product of political development. The advent of the advanced bureaucratic state is a twentieth-century phenomenon associated with centralization of government and an industry-based economy. Highly decentralized states do not characteristically have large bureaucracies, nor do agricultural societies. As the state centralizes the granting citizenship to the great majority of Rome's male subjects; only the very lowest classes were excluded.

After a long eclipse during the Middle Ages, Greek and Roman notions of republicanism and citizenship were revived in the city-states of the Italian Renaissance. In the sixteenth century Niccolò Machiavelli, especially in his *Discourses on Livy*, championed a concept of politics generally referred to as "civic republicanism" or "civic humanism," the main tenet of which is that human potential can be realized only if one is a citizen of a free and self-governing political community. Machiavelli's ideas acquired an English pedigree when they were reformulated and reasserted by John Milton and others during the constitutional revolution of the seventeenth century. By synthesizing Aristotelian and Machiavellian elements, the English version of civic republicanism provided a political language organized around the notions of the common good, civic virtue, and corruption.

That language later traveled to the New World, where it played an important role in the revolutions in North America and Latin America. Several historians have contested the idea that the American Revolution represented a rupture with the old world inspired principally by the ideas of the English philosopher John Locke. These historians stress the centrality of the idea of "corruption" in the vocabulary of the American patriots, an idea profoundly influenced by the culture and theory of civic humanism.

The ideal of citizenship, however, found its culmination in the French Revolution with the Declaration of the Rights of Man and the Citizen (1789). In *The Social Contract* (1762), Jean-Jacques Rousseau established the basis for the modern concept of the role of citizen by connecting it to the theory of consent. The citizen, in Rousseau's view, is a free and autonomous individual entitled to participate in making decisions that all are required to obey. This concept of citizenship draws both on the classical tradition and on modern contractualism by linking the republican concept of the political community with the premises of individualism. Writing in the context of an emerging commercial society, Rousseau was aware of the tension between the common good and private interests and considered that tension to be the main threat to the well-being of the body politic. To be a true republican citizen, Rousseau believed, was to place the common good before one's individual self-interest.

Modern Citizenship

With the development of market relations and the growing influence of liberalism during the nineteenth century, the republican concept of the active citizen was gradually displaced by another view expressed in the language of natural rights. The classical concept of politics, in which individuals participate actively in the *res publica*, was replaced by a new paradigm in which people were no longer thought to be connected by their common identity as citizens but were regarded as individuals with conflicting interests. The insistence on public virtue and the common good disappeared. As direct democracy was rejected in favor of representative democracy, liberal writers came to view the idea of political participation in a community of equals as a relic of the past. They argued that in order to defend the "liberties of the moderns" it was necessary to renounce the "liberties of the ancients."

Although it took time to overcome many forms of discrimination, liberalism undeniably contributed to the idea of universal citizenship based on the argument that all individuals are born formally free and equal. However, it also reduced this condition to a mere legal status, based on the possession of individual rights against arbitrary actions by the state. How those rights are exercised is irrelevant as long as citizens do not break the law or interfere with the rights of others. In such a view, cooperation is justified to the extent that it promotes individual prosperity, not by its contribution to the common good.

Citizenship and Rights

The notion of citizenship that became prevalent in the nineteenth century should be understood as the set of rights and obligations that defines the relationship between nation-states and their individual members. Its origins are clearly Western, but its principles have now been adopted by many other societies.

According to T. H. Marshall's celebrated model of citizenship, civil rights developed first in the eighteenth century. The rights in question were freedom of speech, right to a fair trial, and equal access to the legal system. At the time, many people were refused those rights on grounds of class, gender, race, and other factors. During the nineteenth century, as an outcome of working-class struggles for political equality, important advances in political rights provided wider access to the electoral process. In the twentieth century the idea of "social rights" emerged. These involved access to an expanding set of public benefits provided by the state in such fields as health, education, insurance, and retirement benefits. With the creation of the welfare state following World War II, citizens became "entitled" to social security payments in periods of unemployment, sickness, and distress. In Marshall's view, the expansion of citizenship served to contain the socially divisive effects of class conflict and to limit the social and economic inequalities generated by capitalism. He considered that a necessary tension existed between capitalism and its class system, on the one hand, and citizenship as a status involving a fundamental equality of rights, on the other.

Although influential in the work of American sociologists such as Talcott Parsons, Reinhard Bendix, and Seymour Martin Lipset, Marshall's account of citizenship has been criticized for its ethnocentric assumptions and evolutionary bias. Michael Mann has argued that Marshall's argument applies only to Great Britain and is inappropriate for other societies. Bryan Turner faults Marshall's failure to recognize the extent to which the growth of social citizenship had been the outcome of struggles that brought the state into the social arena as a stabilizer of the social system. Turner also stresses the shortcomings of approaching citizenship exclusively in terms of class relations. An adequate theory of citizenship, he argues, should not overlook the violent "modernization" of aboriginal communities that has accompanied the development of citizenship in countries like the United States, Canada, and Australia.

Liberal Versus Communitarian Citizenship

Thinkers have also debated the question of what type of democracy best corresponds to the exercise of citizenship. A school of "communitarians" emerged in the 1970s to denounce the individualistic bias of the liberal understanding of citizenship dominant in Western democracies. In their view, liberal individualism has eroded social cohesion in those societies; the rejection of notions like the common good and civic virtue in liberal thought has destroyed feelings of common purpose and obligation as well as community values.

Whether individual rights can exist independently, without reference to the community, is a question that lies at the heart of the controversy between communitarians and liberals. John Rawls, in *A Theory of Justice* (1971), describes the citizen in terms of equal rights. Once citizens see themselves as free and equal persons, they should recognize that if they are to pursue their different concepts of the good, they will need the same primary goods—that is, the same basic rights, liberties, and opportunities, the same means (wealth), and the same social bases of self-respect. According to that liberal view, citizenship is the capacity of persons to form, revise, and rationally pursue their personal definition of the good. Citizens use their rights to promote their self-interest within certain constraints, notably respect for the rights of others.

Communitarians object that Rawls's formulation precludes the notion that it is natural for the citizen to join in common action with others to pursue the common good. The communitarian alternative, which rests on the revival of civic republicanism, strongly emphasizes the notion of a public good that exists prior to and independent of individual desires and interests. Advocating a more participatory form of democracy, communitarians define democratic citizenship as active participation in a political community unified by shared values and respect for the common good.

Liberals retort that communitarianism is incompatible with the pluralism of modern democracy. To them, assumptions about the common good have totalitarian implications. It is not possible to combine modern democratic institutions with the same sense of singular purpose that premodern societies enjoyed. Citizenship as active political participation is antithetical to the contemporary idea of liberty understood as the absence of coercion.

Quentin Skinner, a leading British political theorist, denies that there is a basic incompatibility between the classical republican concept of citizenship and modern democracy. Several forms of republican thought—for instance, that of Machiavelli—conceived of liberty in terms of the absence of coercion or oppression but also included political participation and civic virtue. In such thought, liberty is seen as the absence of impediments to the realization of chosen ends.

But individual liberty can be guaranteed only in a "free state," a community whose members participate actively in government and pursue the common good. The idea of a common good transcending private interests becomes a necessary condition for enjoying individual liberty in this concept of citizenship.

Citizenship and Recognition of Differences

Just as there are serious problems with the liberal concept of citizenship, the civic republican solution has shortcomings. Some of its advocates would renounce pluralism in the name of a fabricated vision of the common good. Although the ideas of shared purpose and active participation play an important role in political thought, a modern democratic community cannot be organized around a single idea of the common good. The emergence of the individual, the development of civil society, and the separation of the public and the private are valuable and unavoidable components of modern democracy. The recovery of a more participatory notion of citizenship must acknowledge the tension that necessarily exists between the identity of persons as citizens and as individuals.

A revised concept of citizenship should also take account of feminist critiques. Several feminists have argued that ancient and modern concepts of citizenship have been inimical to women. Carole Pateman has shown that the ideal of the universal citizen was based on the exclusion of women. Women were confined to the private sphere because they were seen as lacking the qualities of independence required for responsible citizenship. Centuries later, after bitter struggles, women were finally awarded their formal rights of citizenship, but the conditions for their full exercise are still far from being attained. Feminists declare that as long as women are not equal to men in all respects, they cannot be complete citizens. Full incorporation of women would require a radical transformation of the public-private distinction. Difference, diversity, and plurality ought not to be relegated to the private sphere. The idea of a homogeneous public sphere where universality reigns in opposition to the particular should be abandoned.

This feminist debunking of "abstract universalism" echoes demands from many other quarters to reformulate the concept of citizenship so as to take in account the significance of differences. Whatever crucial role the universalistic idea of citizenship might have played in the emergence of modern democracy, it has become an obstacle to the expansion of democracy. Many of the new rights being claimed by women, ethnic groups, and sociocultural minorities cannot be universalized and extended equally to all. As expressions of specific needs, such rights apply only to particular groups or constituencies. Only such a pluralistic concept can accommodate the specificity and diversity of contemporary demands and take into consideration the proliferation of political identities.

Such a revised concept of citizenship might draw inspiration from both the civic republican and the liberal approaches, but it would have to go beyond them and tackle the problem of how to make belonging to different communities of values, language, culture, and interests compatible with membership in a single political community whose overarching rules must be accepted.

Contemporary Problems of Citizenship

Although it has become increasingly controversial in Western democracies, the liberal model has gained new momentum in postcommunist countries, where the main task is to establish the basic conditions for civil society and pluralistic democracy. This effort has raised serious questions concerning the relationship between citizenship and nationality. With the upsurge of competing nationalisms, the very conditions of membership in a political community are strongly contested in many places. The growth of ethnic nationalism constitutes a serious threat to modern ideas of democratic citizenship.

Many of the Western democracies are facing similar problems because of the increasingly multiethnic and multicultural character of their populations. In both East and West, the question of how to maintain the political community as a space for creating unity without denying specificity is hotly contested. Several solutions have been proposed that suggest separating nationality from citizenship and establishing criteria for granting citizenship rights that do not depend on nationality. The ideal of "European citizenship" is one step in that direction: nationals of the member states of the European Union will have certain, albeit limited, rights in all other member states.

The notion of "constitutional patriotism" defended by Jürgen Habermas is another attempt to break the connection between ethnicity and citizen identity by linking the granting of citizenship to allegiance to certain universalistic principles. The danger in approaches of this sort is that, in postulating the availability of so-called postconventional identities, theorists tend to ignore the important emotions and passions that are roused by existing symbols of nationhood. Their incapacity to understand the strength of these sources of identification leaves them unable to offer a real alternative to the forces of ethnic nationalism. It would be more promising to counter such forces by fostering a form of "civic nationalism," one that would not only acknowledge the need for belonging and for acquiring a national identity but would also try to satisfy that need by mobilizing the common values of a shared democratic tradition.

With the collapse of the communist model, many movements aiming at a radicalization of democracy are increasingly trying to formulate their goals within the framework of pluralism.

Instead of challenging the basic institutions of the political regime, they struggle for an increased democratization of both the state and the civil society within that regime. The idea of democratic citizenship is at the center of this effort by the left to extend democracy. Long used to challenge the antidemocratic practices of neoliberalism or to revive a more participatory form of political community, the theme of citizenship is becoming central to the task of promoting awareness of individual and collective rights.

One interesting proposal would involve a "universal grant" to every adult male or female to cover basic needs. The idea is to shift the meaning of welfare benefits from the domain of assistance to that of the rights of citizens. To be sure, in many Western countries several such rights are already granted in practice, but they have never been adequately theorized and justified. That omission has left them exposed to the neoliberal campaign to restrict them.

Another set of questions is linked to the increasing globalization of socioeconomic relations and the limits of nation-states in coping with this phenomenon. The present territorial model of citizenship creates difficulties that are not easy to overcome. Some argue that in a world subject to globalization, the idea of citizenship should be shaped by a new discourse on human rights. But the practical implementation and enforcement of such rights remain unresolved and extremely intricate issues.

Linked as it is to the idea of democracy, the notion of citizenship is inevitably complex. Different concepts of democracy construct the role of the citizen and the rights and obligations of citizenship in quite diverse ways. The nature of democratic citizenship will remain as contested as the idea of democracy itself.

See also City-states, communes, and republics; Civil society; Classical Greece and Rome; Communitarianism; Liberalism; Machiavelli, Níccolò; Democracy, Multiethnic; Republicanism; Rousseau, Jean-Jacques; Virtue, Civic.

CHANTAL MOUFFE

BIBLIOGRAPHY

Bendix, Reinhard. *Nation-Building and Citizenship: Studies of Our Changing Social Order.* New York: Wiley, 1964.

The Demands of Citizenship. Edited by Catriona McKinnon and Iain Hampsher-Monk. New York: Continuum, 2000.

Finley, M. I. *Politics in the Ancient World.* Cambridge: Cambridge University Press, 1983.

Habermas, Jürgen. "Citizenship and National Identity: Some Reflections on the Future of Europe." *Praxis International* 12 (1992): 1–19.

Mann, Michael. "Ruling Class Strategies and Citizenship." *Sociology* 21 (August 1987): 339–354.

Marshall, T. H. *Citizenship and Social Class.* Cambridge: Cambridge University Press, 1950.

Mulhall, Stephen, and Adam Swift. *Liberals and Communitarians.* Oxford: Blackwell, 1992.

Pateman, Carole. *The Sexual Social Contract.* Cambridge: Polity Press, 1988.

Skinner, Quentin. "On Justice, the Common Good and the Priority of Liberty." In *Dimensions of Radical Democracy: Pluralism, Citizenship, Community*, edited by Chantal Mouffe. London: Verso, 1992.

Turner, Bryan S. *Citizenship and Capitalism: The Debate over Reformism.* London: Allen and Unwin, 1986.

✦ City-states, communes, and republics

Forms of government in medieval and early modern Europe, from the eleventh through the seventeenth centuries, that played an important role in the development of modern democratic theory and institutions. Notable among these were the city-states of northern Italy, particularly Florence and Venice; the Swiss Confederation; and the Dutch republic. These communal and republican regimes applied doctrines of popular sovereignty and created representative systems of government that have been fundamental to modern democracy. But few of them can be called democratic by modern standards. They were oligarchies (systems of rule by the few) controlled by the landed aristocracy or prosperous merchants.

Beginning in the eleventh century the towns and cities of Europe assumed increasing economic and political importance. Some became centers of regional trade, while others took a leading role in international commerce. In relatively strong kingdoms, such as England and France, towns were incorporated as privileged members of the commonwealth, with certain fiscal responsibilities and a limited ability to regulate themselves internally. In other parts of Europe, especially where political authority was not very stable, as in northern Italy, the Rhineland, and the Low Countries (Belgium, Luxembourg, and the Netherlands), towns and cities became much more independent, treating neighboring principalities and lordships as their political equals. Especially in northern Italy, where a strong tradition of Roman law survived, towns refined a series of legal and theoretical justifications of their independence.

Italian City-states and Communes

The word that towns used to describe themselves was *commune*. The commune was "the thing held in common" by the citizens of a town. Governments known as communes were formed in various Italian urban centers in the late eleventh and twelfth centuries, for instance at Pisa (1081–1085), Arezzo (1098), Genoa (1099), Pistoia (1105), and Bologna (1123). Although all residents of a city were subject to the commune, participa-

tion in government was initially restricted to a fairly limited number of citizens defined principally by property qualifications.

To ensure impartial administration of justice and to curb factionalism, an officer known as the *podestà* was invited from another city for what was generally a six-month term as judge and chief magistrate. In the thirteenth century guild-based movements arose in the Italian communes and sought to place control in the hands of the merchant and artisan classes, who were together known as the *popolo*. The *popolo* generally seized power by force. It created executive officers known as "captains of the people," who served alongside the *podestà* and were charged with protecting the interests of the *popolo*.

The success of the Italian popular regimes even resulted in a few rare instances in which the word *democracy* was used in a positive sense, rather than to signify the debased, tyrannical regime of Aristotelian political theory. The German scholar Albertus Magnus (1206–1280) inverted traditional expectations when he criticized timocracy, the rule of the honorable, as a corrupt regime and praised democracy as "not a deviant constitution but a polity." On the whole, however, the weight of the Aristotelian tradition was such that writers avoided the negative implications of the word *democracy*, preferring to use *polity* and *republic* even when describing the most democratic of contemporary regimes. Not until the Enlightenment in the eighteenth century would political theorists offer general endorsements of regimes they dared to call *democratic*.

The idea of popular sovereignty that would prove so important in the free republics of Europe actually had its origin not in republican but in imperial practice. Various Roman emperors had asserted that their absolute power rested on a cession of sovereignty by the Roman people. In the Middle Ages, during the conflicts between the popes and the emperors of the Holy Roman Empire, jurists in Roman civil law argued that the sovereignty of the Holy Roman Empire was independent of the papacy since it was derived from this original popular cession of sovereignty. With the decline of the empire as a political force, princes and city-state governments looked for ways to justify the establishment of their own laws and statutes. The civil lawyer Bartolus of Sassoferrato (1314–1357) was the most important of the legal theorists who established the principle that sovereignty did not belong to the emperor alone, but that it might be possessed by a particular association of people acting as the government of a city-state.

The percentage of the population that actually was able to participate in the affairs of these governments was quite small. In Venice, with a population of roughly 120,000 at the beginning of the fourteenth century and 115,000 in 1509, office holding from 1297 on was limited to the members of the roughly 200 patrician families that belonged to the Great Council. When the Florentine republic was at its most democratic (during the period 1494–1512), it had an officeholding class of about 3,500 male citizens in a total population of about 60,000.

Electoral procedures in the Italian city-states were generally devised with the aim of preventing domination by any single group or faction. A list of persons eligible to hold office, periodically revised and presided over by an electoral commission, served in each commune as the basis for an often complicated process involving nomination, majority approval, and selection by lot. In Florence, beginning in 1291, election took place through a procedure called *imbursation*. Small parchment strips bearing the names of eligible candidates were placed in leather purses. Those whose names were drawn at random from the purses would become officeholders. Much polit-

ical struggle surrounded the composition of electoral commissions, since they decided which names would be placed in the purses. Only at the final electoral stage, when names were drawn from the bags, did a strong element of chance exist. By controlling appointments to electoral commissions, the Medici family was able to exercise unofficial control over Florentine politics for much of the fifteenth century.

In the course of the fourteenth century many independent communes were taken over by more powerful neighbors; others came under the control of princes or tyrants. The Florentine republic became increasingly oligarchical, notwithstanding two episodes of renewed popular government, in the years 1494–1512 and 1527–1530. In 1530 the city became a principate ruled by the Medici family. Free republics such as Venice, Genoa, and Lucca, which maintained their independence down to Napoleonic times in the early nineteenth century, survived as fairly rigid patrician oligarchies.

The Swiss Confederation

Switzerland—whose republicanism fascinated intellectuals from Niccolò Machiavelli, the sixteenth-century Florentine political theorist, to Jean-Jacques Rousseau, the eighteenth-century Geneva-born philosopher—also owed its independence to an inability of greater European states to assert their sovereignty successfully. The earliest documentary evidence for the existence of a Swiss Confederation dates from 1291, when the cantons (or states) of Uri, Schwyz, and Unterwalden allied to protect their independence from the Hapsburg monarchs. The treaty of 1291 governed relations among the cantons until 1798.

In contrast with the urban world of the Italian communes, the Swiss cantons comprised many small rural communities along with a few cities.

Peasants and city dwellers were considered citizens of equal status. During the fifteenth and early sixteenth centuries, when (thanks to their infantry) the Swiss were one of the most important and successful military powers in Europe, cantonal institutions seem to have been especially democratic, both in practice and in spirit. Not without reason does Switzerland consider itself the world's oldest continuous democracy.

But the "democracy" of Switzerland in the medieval and early modern period was fundamentally local. Legislative powers rested with each canton, each of which was governed according to its own customs and statutes. The confederation was a largely ineffectual body, unable to impose its decisions on recalcitrant cantons. Moreover, from the sixteenth century on, the Swiss were riven by religious disputes. In the sixteenth and seventeenth centuries an awareness that disagreements over foreign policy could sunder the confederation led Switzerland to develop its stance of defensive neutrality toward all foreign powers. By the mid-sixteenth century, as the cantons turned increasingly inward, provincial aristocracies of wealth and blood asserted themselves, dominating local elections. Reform was impeded at both the national and cantonal levels down to the time of the French Revolution.

The Dutch Republic

The Dutch republic, established in 1579, was born of the resistance of the northern provinces of the Low Countries to Spanish rule. Although writers such as the Dutch scholar and jurist Hugo Grotius (1583–1645) attempted to present the Dutch political system as largely unchanged since Roman times, and the myth of Dutch traditionalism would act as a powerful deterrent to further social and institutional change, the republic that emerged from the Dutch revolt was novel in many respects.

Once the Dutch were rid of the Spanish, the republic that they structured around several fiercely defended tiers of autonomy maintained a remarkably durable equilibrium. Sovereignty resided in the seven United Provinces, which met in an assembly known as the States General. The States General was supposed to act "as one province," so most decisions regarding war, peace, and taxation were made unanimously. Because Holland was by far the wealthiest and most populous of the provinces, it tended to control the decisions of this assembly.

Often opposed to the States General—and thus to the province of Holland—was the princely House of Orange. Each province appointed an officer known as a *stadhouder*, who was responsible for commanding local troops and preserving public order. Beginning with William the Silent, prince of Orange (1572–1584), it became common for the prince of Orange to be joint *stadhouder* of most of the provinces. This arrangement provided the republic with effective leaders during military crises, but members of the House of Orange were ambitious to establish themselves as monarchs. A rivalry between Orangists and republicans lasted until 1702, when William III of Orange died without direct heirs, and republican forces remained in control.

There was little that was democratic about the Dutch republic. Office holding was available only to a relatively small noble or propertied elite. A few writers, such as Pieter de la Court (1618–1685), argued for increasing political participation among the propertied classes, but their aim was to restrain the unpredictable masses. What later English and American theorists found most interesting in the Dutch model was its largely successful accommodation of competing power interests—including the *stadhouder* as a kind of "tamed prince."

The eighteenth-century writers and statesmen who established the modern democracies of

America and Europe spent much time studying the histories of medieval and early modern republics, but they were not just seeking lines of evolutionary descent. As John Adams, second president of the United States, once noted, the imperfections of these regimes are "full of excellent warning for the people of America."

WILLIAM J. CONNELL

BIBLIOGRAPHY

Barber, Benjamin R. *The Death of Communal Liberty: A History of Freedom in a Swiss Mountain Canton.* Princeton: Princeton University Press, 1973.

Bertelli, Sergio. *Il potere oligarchico nello stato-città medievale.* Florence: La Nuova Italia, 1978.

Black, Antony. *Political Thought in Europe, 1250–1450.* Cambridge and New York: Cambridge University Press, 1992.

Handbuch der Schweizer Geschichte. 2 vols. Zürich: Verlag Berichthaus, 1972.

Price, John Leslie. *Holland and the Dutch Republic in the Seventeenth Century: The Politics of Particularism.* Oxford and New York: Oxford University Press, 1994.

Riesenberg, Peter. *Citizenship in the Western Tradition: Plato to Rousseau.* Chapel Hill: University of North Carolina Press, 1992.

Skinner, Quentin. "The Italian City-Republics." In *Democracy: The Unfinished Journey,* edited by John Dunn. Oxford and New York: Oxford University Press, 1992.

✦ Civil society

A specific mode of relations between the state and social groups such as families, business firms, associations, and movements that exist independent of the state. This mode of relations developed above all in modern societies, although its seeds can be found in earlier periods. Several components of civil society are necessary for the persistence of modern democracies and are helpful for the transition from an authoritarian or totalitarian regime to a democratic one.

Components of Civil Society

The first, most obvious, and indispensable component is autonomy from the state. The second involves the access of different sectors of society to the agencies of the state and their acceptance of a certain commitment to the political community and the rules of the state. The third aspect rests on the development of a multiplicity of autonomous public arenas within which various associations regulate their own activities and govern their own members, thereby preventing society from becoming a shapeless mass. Fourth, these arenas must be accessible to citizens and open to public deliberation—not embedded in exclusive, secretive, or corporate settings.

Thus one necessary, but not sufficient, condition for a viable democracy is the existence of many private arenas of social life that are independent of the arena of public authority or private coercion. At the same time, these self-organized groups must offer access to the major political arena and have a relatively high degree of acceptance of the basic rules of the political game.

No social group or institution should effectively monopolize the society's bases of power and resources so as to deny other groups access to power. Such monopolization has occurred at various historical periods in many oligarchic societies that have formally adopted democratic constitutions but in which access to power has been limited to very narrow groups.

It is not just the existence of multiple autonomous social sectors, then, that is of crucial importance for the foundation and continuous functioning of democracies. Rather, it is the existence of institutional and ideological links between these sectors and the state. The most important among these links have been the major institutionalized networks of political representation (legislatures and political parties), the major judicial institutions, and the multiple channels of public discourse that collectively determine how politically relevant information is communicated and who has access to these communications. The extent to which these links are not controlled by the public authorities, or monopolized by any dominant class or sector, and the extent to which they foster the accountability of the rulers, are of crucial importance for democracy.

The structure of civil society—and above all of public arenas and the paths of access of various sectors of society to the political arena—varies greatly between different countries and within them at different periods in their history. That structure is affected by social and economic forces, such as the extent of division of labor and the type of political economy in a society. It is also affected by cultural and institutional factors. Among them are the major symbols of collective identity, especially the relative importance of primordial (tribal, ethnic, national), religious, and ideological components among those symbols; the prevailing conceptions of the arena of political action, the scope of the state, the nature of statehood, and the desirable relationship between state and society; the conceptions of public authority and accountability prevailing in the principal sectors of society; the place of law in political discourse and activity; the concept and practice of citizenship; the pattern of interaction between central and peripheral institutions and sectors; the structure of social hierarchies and classes, the level of their collective consciousness, and their modes of political expression; and, finally, the basic characteristics of protest movements and other challenges to political authority.

The way in which these cultural and institutional factors are promulgated and implemented by a society's elites—in interaction with broad sectors of the society—greatly influences the way in which various components of civil society come together, the way in which different social groups relate to each other, and whether they share a vision of the common good for the society.

Early Forms of Civil Society

The first full-fledged civil society emerged in Europe in the seventeenth and eighteenth centuries. It was built on several basic institutional characteristics and cultural premises of European civilization. The most important of these were the presence of several competing centers of society (for example, state, church, and cities) and a pattern of interdependence, as well as competition, between the centers and their respective peripheries. Class, sectoral, ethnic, religious, professional, and ideological groups were largely separated—from each other and from the state. Often, they changed their structure while maintaining their autonomy and their ease of access to the centers of society. Various elites (cultural and economic or professional) were so closely related that they often overlapped and frequently engaged in political activity on a nationwide basis. Finally, the legal system was highly autonomous, as were many cities, which served as centers of social and cultural creativity and as sources of collective identity—for example, with respect to the group's ideas of the meaning of citizenship. A good example is provided by the Italian cities of the Renaissance.

These cultural and institutional features greatly influenced the development of civil society in modern Europe. In particular, they influenced the processes of competition and confrontation between rival national, regional, and local centers and between various groups and elites with regard to access to the centers and influence over their policies.

The same cultural and institutional features have also greatly influenced the major movements of protest that developed in Europe, especially those that demanded the transformation of the centers in the name of an ideology such as socialism or nationalism. This confrontational style was to no small extent rooted in the heritage of the great revolutions of the seventeenth and eighteenth centuries, especially the French Revolution of 1789.

In western and central Europe during this period there developed some very important variations in the structure of civil society and in the links between civil society and the state. These differences were influenced by a variety of historical and structural conditions as well as by cultural factors. Among these were the relative emphasis on equality or hierarchy, differing conceptions of the political arena, and the relative importance of ideological and civil components in the construction of collective identities. They also were influenced by the prior existence of a common political community or, conversely, the extent to which the struggle for access to the political center was interwoven with struggles over collective boundaries—especially territorial boundaries—and identities.

In England, for example, a common political community developed early, and the confrontation between state and society was relatively muted. In Germany and Italy a common political community did not develop until the middle of the eighteenth century. Its very construction was a focus of protest, and the resulting society was greatly fragmented. Constant confrontations, which occurred between the state and those fragmented societies, contributed to the breakdown of constitutional democratic regimes in the 1920s and 1930s.

The crystallization of a distinct American civilization with its strong emphasis on equality, its weak conception of the state, its collective identity based on ideological (more than historical) components, and its strong moralistic principle of the accountability of rulers gave rise to yet another distinct type of civil society. Society generally was seen as relatively more important than the political and administrative center. Earlier movements of protest had been oriented to the ideological reconstruction of the center, as in Europe, or to the construction of distinctive collective political identity. Protest movements in the United States were much more oriented toward moral purification or the enhancement of the national social community.

The Expansion of the Western Model

The expansion of modern European civilization beyond the Western world has transplanted modern political institutions and ideologies, including democratic ones, to civilizations that did not share the basic premises and institutional characteristics that shaped the first modern constitutional regimes and the initial forms of civil society. Non-Western countries have been able to adopt or adapt these institutions and ideologies in many cases. Some components of non-Western traditions—such as the accountability of rulers to a higher law or order, the existence of groups and professions autonomous from the state, and even the caste system of India—have aided democratization, or at least the operation of constitutional systems. In addition, international pressures for democratization have been felt in many countries. The combinations of these factors in different countries has generated far-reaching developments in the structure of civil society and has influenced the ways in which modern political institutions have been incorporated into non-Western civilizations.

The various formats of civil society—European, American, Latin American, and Asian alike—have changed continuously in response to structural changes and new cultural and ideological ideas. A major example of this kind of change is the institutionalization of welfare-state programs.

All societies have redefined the boundaries of the political arena. They have modified conceptions of the appropriate range of activities of the state, the degree of access that different sectors of society should have to political power, the nature of the links between the sectors, and the kinds of benefits that different sectors of society should receive. Whether a country moves from a nondemocratic to a democratic regime, or whether it evolves within a consistent constitutional framework, changes in civil society have involved struggles over competing conceptions of good social order. During transitions, civil society may develop in one of several directions. Some sectors may become more autonomous from the state or more politically active than they have been before. New sectors may emerge and assert their independence.

There is always the danger that changes may undermine those characteristics of civil society that are most conducive to the development and continuity of democratic regimes. First of all, social and economic transformations may cause a redistribution of power within the social sectors and erode existing centers of power. Often policies initially intended to weaken existing centers of power (for instance, policies connected with the welfare state) can increase the power of the state to such an extent that they obliterate independent bases of power.

Furthermore, during periods of transition, existing groups within civil society may fight the changes. There may develop within them tendencies to represent narrow interests based on race, class, ethnicity, or economic status at the expense of acceptance of a common social framework of rules and distribution of power. Thus they can become impediments to the restructuring of the relations between civil society and the state, even to the extent of jeopardizing the continuity of constitutional-democratic regimes.

Finally, the emergence of new sectors within civil society may give rise to the formation of volatile mass movements that define themselves in opposition to other sectors or to the center of political and administrative authority.

In many cases—for example, in Germany and Italy in Europe and even more so in Asian and African societies—these problems have been aggravated by becoming closely entwined with the processes of constructing new national and ethnic communities.

See also Authoritarianism; Autonomy; Liberalism; Majority rule, minority rights.

S. N. EISENSTADT

BIBLIOGRAPHY

Bobbio, Norberto, ed. *Democracy and Dictatorship*. Minneapolis: University of Minnesota Press, 1988; London: Polity Press, 1989.

Calhoun, Craig, ed. *Habermas and the Public Sphere*. Cambridge, Mass.: MIT Press, 1992.

Ferguson, Adam. *An Essay on the History of Civil Society*. With a new introduction by Louis Schneider. New Brunswick, N.J.: Transaction Books, 1980.

Hegel, G. W. F. *Hegel's Philosophy of Rights*. Translated by T. M. Knox. London: Oxford University Press, 1967.

Keane, John, ed. *Civil Society and the State: New European Perspectives*. New York and London: Verso Books, 1988.

Maser, Charles S., ed. *Changing Boundaries of the Political: Essays on the Evolving Balance between State and Society, Public and Private, in Europe.* Cambridge and New York: Cambridge University Press, 1987.

Perez-Diaz, Victor M. *The Return of Civil Society: The Emergence of Democratic Spain.* Cambridge, Mass., and London: Harvard University Press, 1993.

✦ Class

A grouping or positioning within a social hierarchy in which divisions are derived from a society's economic relations. Although people often refer to classes as rich or poor, class divisions, in precise usage, stem from differences in types of economic ownership, not simply in amounts of wealth. Karl Marx, the nineteenth-century founder of contemporary work on class, proposed that with industrialization, two main classes would emerge: the bourgeoisie, or capitalists, who employ individuals and own economic profits, and the proletariat, or propertyless workers.

Debate about class often revolves around three core issues: social opportunities, identities, and politics. First, do members of different classes face unequal opportunities to advance in society (for example, in educational institutions or in the job world), or do they confront unequal, discriminatory treatment in day-to-day social encounters? Second, do class members share common personal identities (for example, common self-conceptions, cultural outlooks, leisure interests, or communication styles)? And, third, do class members share common political interests, and do they act together to work for political change?

Marx answered all three questions in the affirmative. He believed that the everyday work experiences of those in the same class generate in them a wide range of common personal and political identities. A society's dominant class—for example, the capitalists in industrialized societies—attempts to suppress the rise of common identities among subordinate class members by using ideological coercion; an example is using schools to instruct the young of subordinate classes to accept ideas favorable to dominant class interests. Marx, however, maintained that subordinate classes would eventually attain a consciousness of their oppressed status (class consciousness) and would then initiate open conflict.

At the turn of the century the German social scientist Max Weber offered three influential objections to Marx's ideas. First, Weber disagreed that capitalists and workers alone are the main classes in industrialized societies. In addition to the labor market or job world, which divides capitalists from workers, important economic relations could also exist in the credit market, which divides lenders from borrowers, or in the commodity market, which divides sellers from consumers. Second, Weber disputed Marx's position that the objective fact of class divisions in regard to socioeconomic opportunities always spawns the formation of subjective class identities and political movements. Weber countered that status groups, defined solely by a shared cultural style of life (for example, among members of an ethnic enclave or hereditary social elite) could sometimes exert a stronger influence than classes over subjective affiliations. Third, Weber included the state—its administrators and the political parties that fight for power within it—as an active social force. For Marx, the state was a neutral site where class conflict plays out.

Twentieth-century developments have compelled further revisions of these views. For instance, the rise of finance, computer, and related high-technology industries in the private sector, and the increase of administrative offices in the public sector, have caused a better paid, mental-laboring "middle class" to grow, while the classic, manual-laboring working class (to which Marx typically referred) has diminished. Aristotle in the fourth century B.C. observed that a large middle class can buffer the competition and conflict that otherwise develop between upper and lower classes. This role of the middle class is especially important in ensuring the political stability of a democracy. Its rise has contributed to the decline of class conflict during the twentieth century.

In addition to the classic division of capitalist and working classes, several intermediate classes, such as professionals, middle managers, and small-business owners, are now commonly identified. Members of these intermediate classes have distinct labor market experiences and locations in the economy, but the differences are not as encompassing of social existence as the differences between capitalists and workers. Consequently, it is now less plausible for the members of any one class to share a fundamentally distinct personal or political identity or, without forming a cross-class alliance, to engage in meaningful political action.

In democracies the effect of class on politics can be seen by the extent to which members of a particular class vote for the same political parties. Most contemporary parties were formed to appeal to particular classes. Recent research, however, shows that in some democracies, class voting has declined since World War II. Blue-collar workers, for example, vote for left-leaning parties less often than they did formerly.

Broadening the focus beyond class, some researchers propose that ideological and political domination along intersecting hierarchies of class, race, and gender combine to affect social opportunities, personal identities, and politics. Therefore, reference to just one of these three hierarchies is inadequate to explain the true complexity of modern social and political life. For example, some American researchers on urban poverty identify a predominantly African American and Latino "underclass," characterized by the severe conditions of social isolation and institutional abandonment now prevalent in the urban ghettos of the United States. Although this view focuses on class-based social isolation in the present, those proposing it typically emphasize the factors of race or ethnicity as having a major subordinating influence historically.

Other researchers suggest abandoning the use of class terminology altogether. The contemporary sociologist Bryan Turner, for instance, suggests that conflict now exists among several single-issue status blocs, ranging from consumer advocates to gay rights activists to welfare recipients. These groups more often are concerned with consumption or lifestyle issues than with traditional class issues, such as working conditions or unemployment. Furthermore, Turner maintains, instead of competing with each other directly, these status blocs approach the state with their demands, affirming Weber's point that the state plays a vital adjudicating role in social conflict.

Although Turner freely uses Weberian terminology, his status blocs are more confined groups, which come together around specific issues, than are Weber's status groups, whose ideological bonds subsume entire cultural styles of life. Moving further in Turner's direction, we might conclude that the greatest challenge to class—and the combined hierarchies of race, class, and gender—and modern status-based concepts is the radical position that we live in a postmodern world, characterized by a fragmented hodgepodge of competing values, identities, and political groupings. If this position is valid—which remains heavily debated—class and status distinctions may have declined irrevocably in social and political significance.

See also Democracy, Critiques of; Marxism; Weber, Max.

MICHAEL REMPEL AND
TERRY NICHOLS CLARK

BIBLIOGRAPHY

Clark, Terry Nichols, Seymour Martin Lipset, and Michael Rempel. "The Declining Political Significance of Social Class." *International Sociology* 8 (December 1993): 293–316.

Lipset, Seymour Martin, and Stein Rokkan. "Cleavage Structures, Party Systems, and Voter Alignments: An Introduction." In *Party Systems and Voter Alignments*, edited by Seymour Martin Lipset and Stein Rokkan. New York: Free Press, 1967.

Marx, Karl. *Karl Marx: Selected Writings*. Edited by David McLellan. Oxford and New York: Oxford University Press, 1977.

Turner, Bryan S. *Status*. Minneapolis: University of Minnesota Press; Ballmoor, Bucks.: Open University Press, 1988.

Weber, Max. *From Max Weber: Essays in Sociology*. Edited by Hans H. Gerth and C. Wright Mills. New York: Oxford University Press, 1946; London: Routledge, 1991.

Wilson, William Julius. *The Truly Disadvantaged: Inner City, the Underclass, and Public Policy*. Chicago: University of Chicago Press, 1987.

Wright, Erik Olin. *Classes*. New York and London: Verso, 1985.

✦ Classical Greece and Rome

The sites of the earliest democratic institutions. The first theoretical reflections on democracy and democratic institutions are found in the Greek city-states and the Roman Republic. Classical Greece and Rome were also models for later political regimes.

Niccolò Machiavelli, the Florentine political practitioner and theorist of the early sixteenth century, in his *Discourses on Livy* urges his readers to learn from and imitate the political regimes and noble actions of antiquity. In particular, he turns back to the regime of republican Rome, a sharp contrast to the Rome of his own time. Although he recognizes that republican Rome can never be re-created in the modern world, Machiavelli praises the political institutions and heroic values of a pre-Christian era, when men sought public glory for themselves and for the city in which they lived. The lessons of Machiavelli's *Prince* earned him ignominy, but his exhortations to imitate the republicanism of ancient Rome spawned interest among political theorists in the institutions of the Roman Republic.

From the sixteenth century on, Roman republicanism enjoyed a renaissance in the writings of political theorists and in political movements toward more popular participation, but it was not until the nineteenth century that the institutions and principles of Athenian democracy won favor among political theorists and practitioners. Until then Athenian democracy symbolized a regime to be avoided; it showed the dangers of allowing the many to rule, a practice that would lead to chaos. Nineteenth- and twentieth-century authors reversed this focus by finding in Athenian democracy, whether accurately or not, freedom for the individual and a model of participatory government for the modern world to admire, if not to emulate.

Athenian Democracy

Discussions of ancient democracy today usually refer to the institutions of Athens from 508/507 B.C. to 338 B.C. Athens was the largest of the classical Greek city-states, the most powerful of the democratic cities, and the only one to leave a sufficient written record by which we can understand how it functioned and how its citizens viewed it. From Thucydides, the fifth-century B.C. historian of the Peloponnesian War between Sparta and Athens, we first learn of the dominant categories for the governments of the ancient Greek world: oligarchy and democracy. Both oligarchies and democracies might have assemblies at which major decisions concerning the public life of the community would be made, but oligarchies opened political participation to a fraction of their populations, usually the wealthy. Democracies gave power to the *demos*, the people, allowing large numbers of their populations (though certainly not all, since women and slaves were excluded) to be citizens and engage in political self-rule.

Sparta led the oligarchies and Athens the democracies. Thucydides' history presents a conflict between democracy and oligarchy, the disorder but vitality of the former and the order and immobility of the other. From Aristotle's *Politics* we learn that there were many different forms of democracy, depending on who "the people" were (farmers, fishermen, merchants), what limits laws set on the decisions of the assembly, and what offices were filled by lot or by election. Despite the great variety of regimes Aristotle describes, Athens remains the one we know best and the one to which subsequent generations have turned for their vision of ancient democracy.

The political transformation of Athens from a landed aristocracy to a democracy began in the early sixth century B.C., with the reforms of Solon, the elected leader of Athens in 594 B.C. Faced with social unrest, Solon tried to balance the conflicts between the rich and poor by enacting laws controlling consumption and display, freeing those men who had sold themselves into bondage, and

opening political offices to a wider portion of the population. In poems describing his reforms he emphasized that all members of the city, not the gods, are responsible for saving the city and maintaining the principles of justice. Although Solon did not institutionalize democracy in Athens, and his reforms were almost immediately replaced by the tyranny of Peisistratus, he articulated the principles of community action and responsibility central to the emergence of a democratic regime.

Cleisthenes, who lived at the end of the sixth century, is credited with creating the institutions associated with Athenian democracy. In the early years, at least, the Athenians referred to their regime as an *isonomia* (equality before the law) rather than a *demokratia* (power of the people). In an appeal for political power to the people, Cleisthenes "founded" democracy by reorganizing the city. He replaced the four ancient patrilineal tribes with ten artificially created tribes, composed of locally based administrative units, or *demes*, which were themselves divided into three subunits. Each of the tribes contained demes from three distinct geographic areas, thus ensuring that tribes had an administrative, but not political, role in Athens.

Following Cleisthenes' reorganization, Athens in the fifth century B.C. developed its major democratic institutions. The Assembly replaced the aristocratically dominated Areopagus as the center of the city's decision making. Participation was open to all citizens. Citizenship at first required an Athenian father, with confirmation of parentage and age at a local inscription ceremony. In the middle of the century, citizenship required that the mother as well as the father be Athenian (though women did not participate as citizens in the political life of the city). An executive council determined the agenda for each meeting of the assembly and formulated draft proposals. The assembly met about forty times each year. Membership on the executive council, which was determined by lot, changed each month, while the chair, also chosen by lot, changed each day. The courts were also open to all citizens, and service was determined by lot. All offices in the city, from port authority officials to market and treasury supervisors, were likewise assigned by lot. It is estimated that close to 1,000 positions were filled this way each year.

At the end of a year of service, all public officers were subjected to scrutiny to ensure that no untoward actions, particularly embezzlements, marred their service. Toward the end of the fifth century, officers received modest remuneration for their service, as did those attending the assembly. The major elected officials were ten military commanders. Pericles (c. 495–429 B.C.), the renowned leader of Athenian democracy, derived his political power from his repeated yearly election as commander for almost twenty years. While Pericles was in power Athens asserted its dominion over the islands of the Aegean Sea, forcing them to become revenue-paying subjects and bringing great wealth to Athens.

Scholars debate the degree to which Athenians participated in the processes of self-government and the different levels of participation during the 170 years of Athenian democracy. There can be no doubt that the system depended on the engagement of large numbers of citizens. Recent archaeological work suggests that the site where the assembly met had space for only 6,000 individuals, and, though that number is large, it is a fraction of the 20,000–30,000 Athenian citizens eligible to attend. Participation in the life of the city, however, did not depend only on the assembly. There were many offices to be filled at the city and deme levels. Calculations of the number of citizens and of offices to be filled suggest that few citizens could have avoided serving in an office during their lifetimes.

Athenian democracy, and with it Greek democracy, disappeared with the Battle of Chaeronea in 338 B.C. when Philip of Macedon conquered Greece and subjected the Greek city-states to Macedonian rule.

Theoretical assessments of Athenian democracy suffer because there are no authors who we might consider democratic theorists. The Sophist Protagoras, appearing in Plato's dialogue of the same name, is the most promising spokesman of democratic principles. He claims that all participate in self-government because Zeus, the supreme divinity, has given all a sense of justice and a sense of shame. It is not an argument of equality but of shared qualities that enable humans to survive because they can live together and rule themselves. Characters in the tragedies of the fifth century often indicate pride in the self-rule of the Athenian regime. Aeschylus, the tragedian of the early fifth century, has a character in his *Persians* describe the Athenians as "slaves of no man, not listening to any one person." In his *Suppliant Women* he portrays the Athenian rulers as making no decisions without consulting the people, but he offers little analysis of the structure and virtues of the democracy. Herodotus, the historian writing in the mid-fifth century of the conflict between the Greeks and Persians, portrays the Greek city-states under the leadership of the Athenians as autonomous in contrast to the despotically ruled Persians. Herodotus attributes Athenian success in battle to self-government and an independent spirit. In Thucydides' history, Pericles in his funeral oration for the first Athenian soldiers killed in the Peloponnesian War, vividly expresses the Athenians' pride in a regime that favors the many rather than the few, affords equal justice, and attends to individual qualities rather than family or economic background. Although one may debate whether the funeral oration idealizes the regime, Pericles articulates the principles on which the Athenians built their democracy.

From most other authors there is criticism of the democracy. In a work attributed to an unidentified "Old Oligarch," the author, while critical of the rule of the "worse" over the "better," describes Athenian success at institutionalizing through their assemblies, courts, and the rotation of offices a system that enables the poor to control the wealthy. Plato's criticisms are more serious. He focuses on the incapacity of the many to have a true science of politics and says that rhetoric, based on the manipulation of opinion, controls the many and corrupts the young men who might have the capacity for philosophy. Aristotle's analysis of politics draws heavily on the experiences of Athens. His definition of the citizen as one who participates in the offices and judgments of the city derives from Athenian practice, but he worries about democracy's potential for turning the people into a tyrant and for limiting the role of the truly good man.

Until the nineteenth century Athenian democracy was considered a regime to be avoided. The political turbulence in Athens supposedly illustrated the dangers of allowing the people—especially the poor—excessive power. The *Federalist Papers*, written to support the adoption of the U.S. Constitution, warned against adopting the political institutions of the Greek city-states and instead urged adoption of those institutions that would restrain the excessive effects of a popular democracy. In the nineteenth century this attitude changed. In the 1830s, with Andrew Jackson in the White House, Jacksonian democracy emerged as a potent political force, Hellenism swept America, and in England such authors as George Grote, the historian of Greece, rejected earlier histories that condemned Athenian political life and turned to Athenian democracy as the true source of greatness—political, moral, and cultural.

This exaltation of the democratic political life of the ancient world continues in the thought of recent political theorists such as Hannah Arendt, who harks back to the Athenian citizen engaged in debate, seeking an immortality of action rather than involvement in the daily necessities of economic life that engage the modern citizen. Arendt is one of many writers who find in the ancient democracy a model of political participation that reveals the inadequacies of the individualistic liberal democracies of today.

The Roman Republic

The Roman Republic grew from a small city by the Tiber River to a massive empire controlling much of the known world for almost 500 years. During that time numerous changes took place in its political organization as a series of concessions were made to the poorer classes and to newly conquered cities of the Italian peninsula.

Polybius, a Greek who came to Rome in the middle of the second century B.C. as a political exile, wrote an extensive history of Rome in which he commented favorably on the Roman constitution. He described the regime as successfully mixing the elements of kingship, aristocracy, and democracy to ensure a permanence impossible for any of the pure regimes. Although the accuracy of the details of Polybius's description may be doubted and his assurance of Rome's imperviousness to change was shortly shown to be false, his classification captured the central elements of the Roman Republic.

Once the kings were overthrown, about 509 B.C., the Roman Senate became the primary locus of political power. Elected magistrates became lifelong members of the Senate, thus giving the Senate a flavor of popular or democratic origins. But membership in the Senate was confined to a small number of wealthy families with the funds to secure the magisterial election. Until the first century B.C. the Senate predominated, despite the creation and increasing influence of the more popularly constituted assemblies of the people and the institution of tribunes as the official defenders of the people.

All the officers of the state, including the consuls and the tribunes, were elected for one-year terms in one of the assemblies of the *plebs*, or common people. The consuls, whom Polybius identified as the monarchical element of the Roman constitution, had primary authority as the conveners of the Senate and representatives of the state to foreign powers, but they did not control the decisions taken in the Senate. At times of extreme danger the consuls could recommend that all power be turned over to a dictator for a period of six months. The tribunes had the power to veto laws decreed by other magistrates that they judged harmful to the people. At first the tribunes had no authority for positive actions. They could call the assemblies and ask for views, leading to the advisory, but not binding, *plebi scita* (resolved by the people). After the Lex Hortensia of 287 B.C. such *plebi scita* could become binding laws without approval of the Senate.

There was a division of responsibility between the popular assemblies. The *comitia centuriata*, whose complicated structure was originally based in part on what sort of armor a citizen was able to provide, thereby ensuring the continued influence of the wealthier sections of the society, elected the magistrates, authorized declarations of war, and voted on proposals submitted by the consuls. No opportunity was provided for discussion, and voting was so structured that the wealthy groups voted first, with voting ceasing once a majority was attained. Progressively the *comitia tributa* became the more significant assembly. It could pass laws and elected a number of officials. Its voting structure was not nearly so complicated as that of the *comitia centuriata*, and with the expansion of

citizenship to the Italians perhaps close to one million people had the right to vote by tribes in the *comitia tributa*. The structure of these assemblies, however, made them susceptible to bribery. Bribery became more of a problem as the institutions of the republic deteriorated at the end of the second century B.C. with the emergence of opposing political parties, the senatorial Optimates and the more popularly focused Populares. Attempts at economic reforms by Tiberius and Gaius Gracchus led to divisions among the traditional senatorial leadership and diminished the Senate's unified control over the activities of the state.

In the first century B.C. the conflicts escalated, and individual leaders acquired armies of men loyal to them. The result was open battles on the street, conspiracies against the republic, and individual leaders such as Sulla and Marius gaining dictatorial power for brief periods. Julius Caesar, the successful military leader, was assassinated in 44 B.C. for fear that he would diminish further the power of the Senate and establish an autocracy. After the battle of Actium in 31 B.C., in which Octavian, the adopted son of Caesar, defeated Mark Antony, the republic with its powerful Senate and assemblies of the people was replaced with a principate, rule by one man. Octavian, now called Augustus, was the prince.

Unlike Athens, Rome did not produce a large number of authors who reflected on the political life of the city. Polybius (who was Greek) wrote the most serious analysis of the political experiences of the Roman Republic before Cicero. The writings of Cicero, while drawing inspiration from Plato, praise Rome of the second century B.C. before the decline of senatorial authority. Sallust, a historian writing in the first century B.C., found much to criticize as he looked at contemporary signs of corruption and much to long for from the early days of the republic when, according to report, men loved their country and were virtuous by instinct rather than because of law. Writers focused on an idealized vision of patriotic heroes who devoted themselves to the state's welfare rather than to their private interests. They did not focus on the participation of the many in the political regime.

The word used to describe the Roman state captures the difference between the participatory democracy of the Athenian city-state and the aristocratic governance of Rome: *res publica* means the "public thing." The state belonged to the public, and those who served Rome could protect that which belonged to the whole. Care for the public thing did not mean that all needed to participate in public life. Responsibility for care fell on those who had positions of authority. This concept of responsibility for those who needed protection characterized Roman thought within the state and served as a justification for the wide expansion of the empire while republican institutions developed at home. The state, however, was continuously shaken by challenges to this vision of aristocratic benevolence as the people demanded more control over the political agenda.

Rediscovery of Ancient Models

During the Renaissance, Roman republicanism and Cicero's activity as a major participant in that republic enchanted those rediscovering ancient models. Machiavelli looked to the glory of the Roman Republic for his presentation of how political men behaved before they were corrupted by Christianity. The conflicts between the patricians and plebeians represented for him the engagement of a people in their public life and a commitment to a glory that was worldly rather than otherworldly. J. G. A. Pocock has traced the influence of Machiavelli's thought through a tradition of republicanism in Europe and America. In the *Federalist Papers* the early defenders of the American Constitution recalled the nobility of Roman statesmen as the model for their own behavior. The structure of the Roman state offered a paradigm for their radically new political system. They turned to the language of the Roman state to name the central body of the American political system, the Senate. Jean-Jacques Rousseau, the first great modern democratic theorist, arguing for the feasibility of combining freedom and equality in his *Social Contract* (1762), suggested studying the Roman popular assemblies to see how this approach might be possible. And the leaders of the French Revolution, following Rousseau's suggestion, looked to the Roman Republic for their inspiration as they, like the Romans, instituted a republic upon the overthrow of a monarchy.

Today we often find a conflation of the republican model of Rome and the participatory model of Athens as theorists hark back to a classical age for earlier examples of democratically constituted regimes; the two, however, are distinct in their underlying principles and structure.

See also Aristotle; Cicero; Communitarianism; Democracy, Participatory; Dictatorship; Machiavelli, Niccolò; Plato; Popular sovereignty; Rousseau, Jean-Jacques; Theory, Ancient; Virtue, Civic.

ARLENE W. SAXONHOUSE

BIBLIOGRAPHY

Arendt, Hannah. *The Human Condition*. Chicago: University of Chicago Press, 1958.

Cowell, F. R. *Cicero and the Roman Republic*. Baltimore: Penguin Books, 1967.

Finley, M. I. *Democracy: Ancient and Modern*. Rev. ed. New Brunswick, N.J.: Rutgers University Press, 1985.

Grote, George A. *A History of Greece*. 12 vols. London: J. Murray, 1851–1856.

Hansen, Mogens Herman. *The Athenian Democracy in the Age of Demosthenes: Structures, Principles and Ideology*. Oxford and Cambridge, Mass.: Blackwell, 1991.

Nicolet, Claude. *The World of the Citizen in Republican Rome*. Translated by P. S. Falla. Berkeley: University of California Press, 1980.

Ober, Josiah. *Mass and Elite in Democratic Athens: Rhetoric, Ideology, and the Power of the People*. Princeton: Princeton University Press, 1989.

Pocock, J. G. A. *The Machiavellian Moment: Florentine Political Thought and the Atlantic Republican Tradition*. Princeton: Princeton University Press, 1975.

Stockton, David. *The Classical Athenian Democracy*. Oxford and New York: Oxford University Press, 1990.

Taylor, Lily Ross. *Party Politics in the Age of Caesar*. Berkeley: University of California Press, 1971.

✦ Consent

One of the central justifying concepts in democratic political theory. Defenders of democracy commonly argue that democracy's superior moral legitimacy derives from the fact that democratic governments act with the consent or authorization of their citizens. Sometimes the claim is that popular consent is necessary for just or legitimate government. The American Declaration of Independence, for example, asserts that governments derive "their just powers from the consent of the governed." But even when the claim is that consent is only one possible source of political legitimacy, democratic political society is still thought to be especially suitable for realizing consensual legitimacy.

Justification by appeal to consent is understandably central to the philosophical structure of liberal thought. Liberals generally conceive of individuals as self-conscious choosers, whose plans and choices are morally valuable and hence merit respect. Free consent is regarded as the primary mechanism through which individual liberty may justifiably be limited, for consent is a clear source of created obligations that is nonetheless plainly consistent with respect for individual liberty and choice. Consensual undertaking of obligations is one among many possible uses of individual liberty, a use that can morally justify the increased restrictions necessary for beneficial social interaction. Within liberal societies a showing of free, informed consent by one party is normally taken to justify or remove liability for the actions of another. Thus the maxim *Volenti non fit injuria* (The willing person is not wronged.) governs transactions as diverse as business dealings, medical treatment, and sexual relations.

Consent may be defined as a kind of act by which one attempts to alter the existing structure of rights and duties, normally by freely assuming new obligations and authorizing others to act with respect to one in ways that would otherwise be impermissible for them. Consent is often taken (as in John Locke's political philosophy) to include all sources of self-assumed obligations, including not only what we might normally call consenting but also promising, contracting, and entrusting. But whatever the specific definition, we must distinguish consent in this active sense (as a ground of special obligations and rights) from weaker notions of consent as an attitude of approval or of consent as mere passivity or acquiescence.

In democratic theory, discussions of consent usually involve debates over and developments of the consent theory of political obligation and authority. In its simplest form this theory maintains that the consent of each person to political membership is the only possible source of the person's obligations to obey the law and support the state and of the state's authority over or right to command the person. But political obligation and authority have also been alleged to rest not on direct, personal consent but on tacit (or indirect) personal consent, on consent given by others (such as one's ancestors or the majority of one's fellow subjects), or on hypothetical consent (usually understood as the consent that would be given by rational contractors).

Appeals to tacit consent have always been important within consent theory, for little in the behavior of most citizens resembles the giving of express or direct consent to the authority of their governments. Appeals to the consent of others to justify an individual's obligations have been found unpersuasive by most modern theorists. And appeals to hypothetical consent (following the lead of Immanuel Kant) have again become popular in this century, in an effort to focus attention not on what persons actually agree to but on what they ought to agree to. Here, as in the case of appeals to tacit consent, the motive is partly to show that reasonable political institutions can still be justified in terms of consent, despite the seeming absence of actual consent to these institutions by those subject to them.

Proponents of traditional, nonhypothetical consent theory have argued in three ways for a strong connection between legitimizing consent and democratic government. First, some have argued (following John Locke) that the choice to continue residing in a country that one is free to leave counts as giving one's personal (tacit) consent to the authority of that country's government. Because democracies typically grant their citizens the right of free exit, citizens of democracies will, according to this argument, typically be consenters. Second, others have maintained that possessing or exercising the right to vote in democratic elections constitutes consent to the authority of elected governments and free acceptance of the obligation to obey. Finally, some have claimed that full and direct participation in the processes that determine the requirements of political life is the only way to give meaningful political consent and that only in a democracy is such participation possible.

Against the last of these claims, it can be argued that democratic societies today permit few citizens, if any, to pursue full, direct participation. Against the second claim, skeptics maintain that mere possession of a right to vote is not an act that one performs and so can hardly count as an act of consent. Moreover, far too few citizens in democracies either vote regularly or fully understand the political processes for many of them to be characterized fairly as giving free, informed consent to their governments with their votes. Against the first claim, critics argue (following David Hume) that the choice to continue residing in one's country of birth cannot for many be understood as a free choice, given the high cost of emigration. Furthermore, few people understand their continued residence to involve any morally significant choice at all.

In an effort to answer these objections, proponents of consent theory continue to refine their positions. Those who are persuaded by the objections, however, tend to fall into one of three camps. Some—for example, the contemporary philosopher John Rawls—turn from actual consent to hypothetical consent as their primary justifying concept. Others abandon altogether the ideal of government by consent and attempt to justify democratic government in other terms (such as procedural fairness). And the most radical skeptics embrace philosophical anarchism, which contends that no political societies, democracies included, are morally legitimate.

See also Contractarianism; Hobbes, Thomas; Democracy, Justifications for; Liberalism; Locke, John; Obligation.

A. JOHN SIMMONS

BIBLIOGRAPHY

Beran, Harry. *The Consent Theory of Political Obligation.* London: Croom Helm, 1987.

Hume, David. "Of the Original Contract." In *Hume's Moral and Political Philosophy*, edited by Henry D. Aiken. New York: Hafner, 1975.

Kleinig, John. "The Ethics of Consent." *Canadian Journal of Philosophy*. Supp. vol. 8 (1982): 91–118.

Locke, John. *Two Treatises of Government.* Edited by Peter Laslett. Cambridge: Cambridge University Press, 1960.

Rawls, John. *A Theory of Justice.* Cambridge: Harvard University Press, Belknap Press, 1971; Oxford: Oxford University Press, 1973.

Simmons, A. John. *Moral Principles and Political Obligations.* Princeton: Princeton University Press, 1979.

———. *On the Edge of Anarchy: Locke, Consent, and the Limits of Society.* Princeton: Princeton University Press, 1993.

Singer, Peter. *Democracy and Disobedience.* New York: Oxford University Press, 1974.

✦ Consolidation

A process of transforming the accidental arrangements, prudential norms, and contingent solutions that have emerged during the uncertain struggles of a political transition into institutions that are reliably known, regularly practiced, and normatively accepted by the participants, citizens, and subjects of such institutions. Democracies are not supposed to be fully consolidated. Unique among political types, they possess the potential for continuous change and even self-transformation. By a process of deliberation and collective choice among the citizenry, democracies can not only peacefully remove governments from power but also alter their basic structures and practices.

This abstract reflection clashes, however, with the everyday experience of well-established democracies. Not only do their patterns and norms become structured in highly predictable and persistent ways, but considerable effort is expended to make it quite difficult to change these structures. So-called founding generations write constitutions that attempt to bind subsequent ones to a specific institutional format and set of rights. They also draft statutes and codes that render certain kinds of political behavior punishable, create specific constituencies and reward particular clienteles, make difficult (or even exclude) the entry of new parties into the electoral arena, confer monopolistic recognition on certain associations, and even try to make these constitutions and laws almost impossible to amend. Although constitutions can be ignored, policies can be reversed, and laws can be changed in response to public pressures, it can be difficult and costly to do so even in the most loosely structured and recently consolidated of democracies.

It has been said that uncertainty of persons and policies is the central characteristic of a democracy. If so in theory, this uncertainty is heavily conditioned in democratic practice by relative certainties. For citizens to tolerate the possibility that opponents might occupy or influence positions of government and even pursue different and possibly damaging courses of action requires a great deal of mutual trust—backed by a great deal of structural reassurance. The consolidation of democracy can be seen as the process that makes such trust and reassurance possible and that therefore also makes possible regular, uncertain, and yet circumscribed competition for office and influence.

Embodying Consent and Invoking Assent

How does democracy accomplish and legitimate such a delicate task? What is the underlying operative principle that provides the necessary elements of trust and reassurance? The simple answer is the consent of the people; the more complex answer is that it all depends on the contingent consent of politicians and the eventual assent of citizens—all acting under conditions of bounded uncertainty.

The challenge for democratic consolidators is to find a set of institutions that embody contingent consent among politicians, that are capable of invoking the eventual assent of citizens, and that can therefore limit the abnormally high degree of uncertainty that is characteristic of most transitions from autocracy. They do not necessarily have to agree on a set of goals or substantive policies that generate widespread consensus. Disagreements on goals and policies will furnish much of the content for subsequent democratic competition. This "democratic bargain" can vary a good deal from one society to another, depending on inequalities and cleavage patterns within the citizenry, as well as such subjective factors as the degree of mutual trust, the standard of fairness, the willingness to compromise, and the legitimacy of different decision rules.

When a society changes from one political regime to another, it initially passes through a period of considerable uncertainty in which it is unclear where its efforts are leading. During this period, regression to the previous status quo is possible. The transition period can vary in length, depending in large measure on the mode of regime change that has been adopted, but it must end eventually. The psychic and material costs are simply too great for those active in politics to endure indefinitely. Although there will always be some for whom the exhilaration of participating in a continuous "war of movement" remains an end in itself, most of these actors look forward to settling into a "war of positions" with known allies, established lines of cleavage, and predictable opponents, or to resuming their other careers or pursuits.

Specifying the Type of Democracy

When some form of autocracy is changed to a democracy, rather than the reverse, the problem of consolidation takes on special characteristics. For one thing the number and variety of people who are potentially capable of proposing new rules and practices increases greatly. Moreover, these empowered citizens (and the groups they form) have much more autonomy in deciding whether they will accept the rules and practices being offered to them. This is not to suggest that modern political democracies are anarchies in which individuals are free to choose their own norms and to act without regard for the norms of others. But the problem of reducing uncertainty and ensuring the orderly governance of the political unit as a whole is likely to be more acute in a new democracy than, say, in the aftermath of implanting an autocracy.

Democracy does not, however, seek to remove all sources of uncertainty. A polity in which there was no uncertainty about which candidates would win elections, what policies the winners would adopt, or which groups would be likely to influence their choice of those policies could hardly be termed democratic. But the uncertainty that is embedded in all democracies is bounded. Not just any actor can enter the competitive struggle, practice any tactic, raise any issue, cooperate with others in any way, and expect to hold office or exercise influence. Not just any policy can be decided by any procedure—even by the overwhelming majority—and then be imposed on any segment of the population—even if that minority was represented in the decision-making process. What the exercise of democracy begins to do during the transitional period is to reduce "abnormal" uncertainty to "normal" uncertainty, and it does this through the generation of formal rules and informal practices. Sets of these rules and practices that manage to acquire some autonomy and to reproduce themselves successfully over time become institutions.

All successful democratizations have involved four processes of institutional choice: the formation of a party system, the formation of an interest associational system, the drafting and approval of a constitution, and the submission of the military to civilian control. Unless all four of these processes take place, there is very little likelihood of an eventual consolidation. Their timing, however, is variable, and these differences in sequence contribute much to differences in outcome. *When* something is accomplished may be as important as *what* has been accomplished. For example, in some fortunate cases, civilian control over the military may have been accomplished largely by the previous authoritarian regime. In others, the newly incumbent rulers may be able to agree quickly on reinstituting some ancient or recent constitution and thereby save themselves possible conflicts over the definition of key rules and institutions.

As a process, democratic consolidation involves choosing these institutions. Much of this process takes place in an open, deliberative fashion and manifests itself in formal public acts: the drafting and ratifying of a constitution, the passing of laws by the parliament, the issuance of executive decrees and administrative regulations. Some elements of consolidation, however, emerge more incidentally and unself-consciously from the ongoing "private" arrangements within and between the organizations of civil society and from the often informal interactions between these organizations and various agencies of the state.

One major implication of the preceding discussion is that no single institution or rule defines consolidated democracy. Not even such prominent candidates as majority rule, territorial representation, competitive elections, parliamentary sovereignty, a popularly elected executive, or a "responsible" party system can be taken as its distinctive hallmark. It may be easier to agree on what has been called the procedural minimum without which no type of democracy could exist: secret balloting, universal adult suffrage, regular elections, partisan competition, associational freedom, and executive accountability. But underlying these accomplishments and flowing from them are much more subtle and complex relations that define both the substance and the form of nascent democratic regimes.

Forming a Professional Stratum and Coping with a Dilemma

The consolidation of modern democracy involves both the choice of institutions and the formation of a political stratum. Although this group may vary a great deal in its origins, openness, diversity, interests, coherence, and longevity, most of its members will be representatives of organizations (with differing degrees of authenticity). They are also increasingly likely to be professionals (of differing degrees of dedication to the job). Most members of this small group live not "for politics" but "from politics." Depending on the mode of transition, they may include various proportions of actors from the former autocracy and those recruited from the ranks of the previously excluded. Most important for the long-run future of democracy, they have every reason to develop a loyalty to the existing rules of the game—since these are the rules by which they entered the profession and that may eventually enable them to enter government.

This emphasis on the likely emergence of a distinctive political stratum during the transition and its professionalization during consolidation has important implications for the choice of institutions. It establishes a major dilemma within its core: representatives will have to design a set of rules and practices that they, as politicians, can agree on and live with and that their members and followers, as citizens, can assent to and are willing to support.

A stable solution to these demands may be difficult to find, especially in the climate of exaggerated expectations that tends to characterize the transition to democracy. The choices are intrinsically conflictual: politicians, grouped into different parties, prefer rules that will best ensure their own reelection or eventual access to office; citizens, assembled into different social groups, want rules that will best ensure the accountability of their representatives. The choices are also extrinsically consequential. Once they are translated, through the uncertainties of elections and influence processes, into governments that begin to produce public policies, the rules and practices applied will affect rates of economic growth, willingness to invest, variation in the value of currency, competitiveness in foreign markets, access to education, perceptions of cultural deprivation, racial balance, and even national identity. To a certain extent, these substantive matters are anticipated by the actors involved and incorporated in the compromises they make with regard to procedures. But there is nonetheless considerable room for error and unintended consequence.

Exploring the Conditions of Consolidation

To paraphrase Karl Marx, those who would consolidate democracy may be making their own history but not under conditions or at moments of their own choosing. The list of factors that could possibly influence—even determine, some would say—the choices they make is virtually endless. The literature on existing, stable democracies tends to stress "prerequisites," such as the level of

development, the rate of economic growth, the distribution of wealth, the size of the middle class, the dynamism of the bourgeoisie, the existence of private property rights, the level of literacy and mass education, the existence of stable borders and national identities, the supportiveness of the international system, the extent of linguistic or ethnic homogeneity, and the presence of proper civic attitudes or of a "Western" (in particular, Protestant) culture. Even such relatively idiosyncratic features as having been colonized by the British or having been defeated and occupied by the armed forces of a foreign democracy have been associated with successful democratization.

No one is likely to contest that these conditions have contributed to consolidation in the past and probably can facilitate it in the present. What is less clear is whether those countries that do not score so well on them are irrevocably condemned to failure. Unfortunately, all the changes in regime since 1974 have occurred in socioeconomic settings that lack several of these properties; some have virtually none of them.

Consolidators must also confront one of the major paradoxes of modern democracy. Most citizens support this form of political domination and accord it legitimacy because they expect it to change their living conditions for the better. More concretely, as the French political observer Alexis de Tocqueville recognized in the 1830s, many will expect to use public power to redistribute material goods and symbolic satisfactions more equally throughout the population. No democracy that wishes to reproduce itself over the long run can afford to ignore this passion for equality.

To consolidate themselves in the short to medium run, however, the institutions of democracy must reflect existing conditions—conditions that are often highly unequally distributed. If this were not already enough of a challenge, these institutions cannot be based exclusively on the principle of one citizen, one vote. They must somehow recognize that social groups, even minorities that stand no chance of winning an election or referendum, have varying intensities of interest and passion concerning different issues. It is prudent, as well as ethical, to ensure that such voices be somehow "weighed" and not just "counted" in the policy process. It may even be desirable to protect these economic, social, ethnic, or cultural minorities by enshrining their rights in formal institutions, not just by making informal arrangements.

Coping with Cleavages and Capacities

Democracy requires cleavages in the society and the dispersion of political capacity among the citizenry. A polity without predictable and significant sources of differentiation would find it very difficult to organize stable patterns of electoral competition or associational bargaining.

Political sociology offers two major orienting hypotheses concerning these patterns. First, whatever cleavages exist in a society should be distributed in such a way that their impact is not cumulative. Ideally, each source of differentiation—class, sector, age, gender, race, language, and religion, for example—should cut across all the others so that no group is permanently and simultaneously disadvantaged on more than one ground. Because this is virtually impossible to accomplish, even in the most "pluralist" of societies, the effect of cumulative discrimination can be mitigated if individuals have a substantial possibility of mobility across categories during their lifetime.

Second, whatever the level of resources in a given society, no group—private or public—should have a monopoly or even concentrated control over any of them. If this condition proves impossible for reasons of economic efficiency, social prejudice, or historical accident, it is better that there be as many levels of political aggregation

as possible, that there be as many resource bases as possible, and that the process of converting them into political power at any given level should be as variable and difficult to calculate as possible.

These are general and abstract conditions, not specific prerequisites. Three views are currently held regarding the conditions that must be satisfied before democracy has any chance of consolidating. First, Dankwart Rustow argues that there must be a prior consensus, rooted in obscure historical events and memories, on national boundaries and identity. Second, according to Barrington Moore, Jr., there should be no dominant class of large, precapitalist landowners who do not produce primarily for the market and who require the use of coercion to sustain their labor forces. Finally, Guillermo O'Donnell maintains that there should not be such substantial urban inequalities in income, wealth, and decent living standards that privileged groups cannot conceive of the underprivileged as "fellow citizens."

Presumably, if any of these conditions were not satisfied, it would be impossible to consolidate any type of democracy. All the prerequisites for consolidation can be met through the choice of appropriate rules and practices.

Finding and Valuing Rules

Regime consolidation, then, involves converting patterns into institutions and endowing what are initially fortuitous interactions, episodic arrangements, and ad hoc solutions with sufficient autonomy and value that they stand some chance of persisting. Citizens and politicians respond by adjusting their expectations to the likelihood of persistence and come to regard these emergent rules as given and even desirable.

When democracy is being consolidated, the predominant rules will address competition for office or influence, cooperation in the formation of governments or oppositions, and contingency in the mobilization of consent and assent. The predominant resource should be citizenship, although under the conditions of modern, indirect, and liberal democracy, citizens usually act through representatives and are free to mobilize other, much less equally distributed, resources such as money, property, status, expertise, and "connections" in their efforts to capture office or influence policy.

The mere existence of these rules is, however, insufficient to ensure consolidation. To become institutions, these rules must be successfully legitimated. They must come to be valued in and by themselves, not just for the instrumental and momentary benefits they bring. The normative expectations must not be set too high, however. In most established democracies, high levels of positive identification, ethical approval, and participatory enthusiasm are rarely the norm. Indeed, their authorities and representatives are typically regarded with some skepticism, if not scorn. Although intensely democratic values may be very much present and very important during the transition, what seem to suffice in the longer run are diffuse feelings among the citizens of the "naturalness" or "adequateness" of their regime. As long as there is a consensus that the new rules and emerging institutions conform better to prevailing standards than conceivable alternatives, or that normatively "superior" forms of governance are too difficult or costly to attain, regime legitimation is likely to settle in—along with a certain amount of disenchantment among the citizenry with what has been accomplished.

But politicians will not always agree on the rules of competition and cooperation, and, even if they do, citizens will not always give their assent. Few countries have been successful in their first effort at consolidating democracy. The reason is that it is difficult to find a set of institutions that are both appropriate for existing socioeconomic conditions and capable of satisfying future expectations.

This difficulty does not mean that most of the countries in which new democracies have emerged since 1974 will regress to their previous autocratic forms of government. Many of these fifty or so countries seem destined to remain unconsolidatedly democratic for the foreseeable future, if only because no feasible alternative mode of domination is available. Democracy in its most generic sense will likely persist, but it will less frequently be consolidated into a specific and reliable set of rules or practices.

See also Democratization.

PHILIPPE C. SCHMITTER

BIBLIOGRAPHY

Dahl, Robert. *After the Revolution: Authority in a Good Society*. New Haven and London: Yale University Press, 1970.

———. *Dilemmas of Pluralist Democracy*. New Haven and London: Yale University Press, 1982.

Moore, Barrington, Jr. *Social Origins of Dictatorship and Democracy*. Boston: Beacon Press, 1966; Harmondsworth: Penguin Books, 1991.

O'Donnell, Guillermo. "On the State: Democratization and Some Conceptual Problems: A Latin American View with Glances at Some Postcommunist Countries." *World Development* 21 (August 1993): 1355–1370.

Przeworski, Adam. "Some Problems in the Study of the Transition to Democracy." In *Transitions from Authoritarian Rule: Prospects for Democracy*. Vol. 3. Edited by Guillermo O'Donnell and Philippe C. Schmitter. Baltimore: Johns Hopkins University Press, 1986.

Rustow, Dankwart. "Transitions to Democracy: Toward a Dynamic Model." *Comparative Politics* 2 (April 1970): 337–363.

Schmitter, Philippe C., and Terry Lynn Karl. "What Democracy Is . . . and Is Not." *Journal of Democracy* 3 (summer 1991): 75–88.

✦ Democracy, Critiques of

Critiques of democracy, questioning the basis and goals of democratic political thought, are as old as democracy itself. Inevitably they are influenced by the changes in the concept and practice of democracy over time. In the history of Western political theory, the critics of democracy have usually far outnumbered its advocates. Only relatively recently, beginning with the French Revolution in 1789 and gathering momentum after the revolutions of 1848, has democracy come to be regarded as the goal of every society solicitous of human dignity.

The most dramatic change in the theory and practice of democracy occurred during the transition from direct democracy, as embodied in the institutions of Periclean Athens, to what is described today as liberal or representative or constitutional democracy. Modern scholars vigorously debate how much Athenian direct democracy, instituted by Cleisthenes in the reforms of 508–507 B.C., and modern representative democracy have in common. There is a profound difference between a regime based on the direct participation of all citizens in the popular assembly, like in Athens, or one based on the indirect participation of the people through representation in a legislature, in which political parties play a role. The two concepts overlap somewhat, however, and elements of direct democracy (town meetings, referendums, recall elections, and so forth) are present in most modern liberal democratic regimes. Furthermore, the ancient Athenian democratic ideals of freedom of expression, rotation of office,

and equality before the law are also goals of modern representative democracies.

The earliest preserved criticism of democracy is found in the Greek historian Herodotus (485–425 B.C.). Although not an Athenian, Herodotus had spent time in Athens, where presumably he learned much of what he knew both about democracy and its critics. In his *Histories*, he includes a debate over the best form of government. Democracy loses the debate to monarchy; the *demos*, or the common people, are judged to be arrogant and selfish. In addition, they are said to need the protection of the monarch against the few who are rich.

One of the earliest surviving critiques of Athenian democracy by an Athenian is the composition by an unknown author referred to as the "Old Oligarch," probably written between 431 and 424 B.C. Its form is that of a fictitious speech by a cynical and worldly-wise member of the Athenian upper class who detests democracy in principle but who concedes that, because in Athens it has proved to be militarily successful, democracy must be accommodated. The Old Oligarch shudders at what he perceives to be the moral emptiness of democracy, even as he marvels at its economic and military vitality. Democratic Athens, he complains, favors the vulgar and unscrupulous mob at the expense of those who are best in character.

Thucydides (c. 471–400 B.C.), in his *History of the Peloponnesian War*, includes many examples of how Athenian democracy could degenerate into mob rule. In one case he recounts how the greed of the common people led them to demand the invasion of Sicily. During the debate in the assembly, the wiser heads remained silent out of fear of the aroused populace. The invasion, in clear defiance of Pericles' policy of caution, resulted in one of Athens's worst defeats. Thucydides implies that a democracy such as that established in Athens is not stable enough to conduct a prudent long-term foreign policy.

Democracy in the "Canon" of Political Theory

Most authors in the traditional canon of Western political theory have either ignored democracy or criticized it. Plato, who held the democratic regime in Athens responsible for the trial and death of Socrates in 399 B.C., condemned democracy in the *Republic* as the rule of the many trapped in the cave who mistake the shadows for reality. For Plato, democracy meant the rule of license in which all the passions of the soul indiscriminately have their way. Democratic chaos was the prelude to tyranny.

In Plato's *Gorgias*, Socrates criticizes not only the Athenian people but their most famous democratic leaders as well. Pericles and Themistocles are said to have neglected the education of the people in the virtues of justice and moderation. Instead, they built docks and harbors and expanded commerce with outsiders. Plato's dialogues contain many speeches by Socrates denouncing the practice of choosing members of the Council of 500 (or senate) by lot. In these speeches, also summarized by Aristotle in his *Rhetoric*, Socrates asks whether anyone would choose a surgeon or a ship navigator by lot. When the negative reply inevitably follows, Socrates scornfully concludes that it makes as little sense to select political leaders by lot. To Plato's Socrates (and apparently to the historical Socrates as well), political knowledge is a craft analogous to medicine or navigation. The statesman is the physician of the soul.

Particularly in the *Gorgias*, Plato has Socrates criticize democracy on yet another ground: it corrupts public speech or rhetoric. Democratic rhetoric, as perfected by the Sophists, tells the people what they want to hear rather than what they need to hear. Socrates is said to have paid with his life because he refused to go along with this corruption.

Plato may have softened his view later. In the *Statesman*, democracy is described as the worst of the lawful regimes and the best of the lawless ones; in the *Laws*, it is considered one of two "mother constitutions" for the "mixed regime" (the other one being monarchy). Both Plato and Aristotle enumerated six "simple" regimes: the rule of one (monarchy) and its corruption (tyranny); the rule of the few (aristocracy) and its corruption (oligarchy); and the rule of the many (moderate democracy) and its corruption (extreme democracy). The mixed regime resulted from a blending of elements from two or more of the simple regimes, with the requirement that the mixture must contain elements of different numerical categories. That is, it would not do to mix monarchy and tyranny, aristocracy and oligarchy, or the two versions of democracy because they would not adequately restrain their excessive tendencies to favor the one, the few, or the many. Thus Plato's "second best" regime in the *Laws* has some democratic features, including the limited use of the lottery to choose some public officials. Finally, however, it is Plato who is the source of law, although he provides lengthy preambles to the laws designed to win the people's consent. The preambles, which elucidate the theoretical rationale for the laws, were designed to elicit consent rather than blind obedience.

Aristotle's view of democracy seems somewhat more affirmative than Plato's. Still, in both the *Ethics* and the *Politics* he favors polity—a mixture of democracy and oligarchy—as the best practicable regime because polity checks the tendency of the few rich to exploit the many poor as well as the tendency of the many poor to exploit the few who are rich. Aristotle expresses an aversion to rule by many people concentrated in small urban

areas, preferring landowners in rural areas as more moderate and less likely to be swayed by demagogues. Both Plato and Aristotle held philosophy to be the highest kind of life, a life that could be led only by those few possessing leisure and virtue. Philosophers are by right the judges of the priorities to be pursued in the city-state because they excel in prudence or practical reason. In the *Politics*, Aristotle proclaims the best regime to be a society in which citizenship is limited to the best persons—in other words, an aristocracy based on character rather than on heredity or wealth.

The Roman statesman Cicero (106–43 B.C.) thought undiluted democracy a disaster and put forward a theory of the mixed constitution (with monarchical, aristocratic, and democratic elements) as the absolutely best regime. In *De republica*, Cicero insists that the Senate, which represents the nobility, is essential to the proper operation of the government, although he grants that the popular assembly, organized into tribes and represented by the ten tribunes of the people, rightly holds veto power in certain areas. Cicero, who had served a term as one of the two consuls, or chief executives, of the Roman Republic, thought the wealthy should control the consulate as well. He also thought it necessary that in emergencies a constitutional dictatorship of six months' duration could be invoked.

Medieval Christian political thought was greatly influenced by the passage in Paul's letter to the Romans enjoining Christians to be subject to the higher powers as ordained by God. Authority descended from God to the rulers and nobility; the common people were conceived of as passive—to be acted upon. Democracy in the early Christian Middle Ages was not explicitly criticized, in part because of the loss of the Greek classical sources. This situation changed in the thirteenth century with the recovery of Aristotle's *Politics*. Thomas Aquinas, Aristotle's major medieval Christian interpreter, rejected democracy in favor of limited monarchy. In *On Kingship*, he extols rule by one: just as God rules the universe and the queen bee rules the hive, so the monarch must rule the multitude. Democracy is against the natural order. Dante Alighieri drew on this analogy even more emphatically in his *On World Monarchy* (1321).

Marsilius of Padua is often mistakenly credited with being a medieval precursor of modern democracy. In his *Defender of Peace* (1324), Marsilius declares that the "weightier part" of the people is the source of law; however, he significantly adds the phrase "in quantity and quality." Marsilius actually deserves to be ranked among the critics of democracy. Withering criticisms of the people's poor judgment and susceptibility to demagogic appeals are scattered throughout his work. It seems more probable, as Leo Strauss has suggested, that his occasional "populism" was camouflage for his support of a new antipapal elite.

Beginnings of Modern Political Theory

Despite his reputation for being an apologist for tyranny, the early sixteenth-century political philosopher Niccolò Machiavelli expressed considerable sympathy for the common people. He even wrote in the *Prince* that there is some truth in the proverb "the voice of the people is the voice of God." The people, however, he wrote in the *Discourses*, constitute only one of the two "humors" in the body politic; the powerful few are the other indispensable force. Machiavelli was also emphatic about the necessity for a single leader to found "new modes and orders." In the *Discourses*, he treated democracy as an unstable form of government and espoused a doctrine often described as civic republicanism rather than democracy. In the *Prince*, he appears to express contempt for the vulgar majority who are easily taken in by appearances. He may, however, have been uncovering

the manipulation of public opinion for the many to see.

Thomas Hobbes, in the *Leviathan* (1651), held democracy to be one of the three forms of government, monarchy and aristocracy being the other two. Democracy is a regime in which the sovereign power is lodged in an assembly of all the citizens. Despite his formal neutrality on the question of whether one, few, or many should exercise the sovereign power, Hobbes clearly favored monarchy as the form most likely to produce peace and security. Democracy (direct rule by all the people) is so patently impracticable as to be out of the question. In his *Behemoth*, a history of the English Civil War of the 1640s, Hobbes denounces those democrats who wanted to govern themselves. In Hobbes's view, the common people think only of their selfish interests. They are inclined to be swayed by religious demagogues. Their only proper role is to consent to the rule of the sovereign. Hobbes detested what are today known as interest groups, declaring them to be so many worms in the body politic.

One is tempted to say that John Locke reversed Hobbes, but this assertion is only partially true. Locke did reject absolute monarchy. Because he grounded government on the original and continuous consent of the property-owning males in the population, Locke is today often hailed as the foremost democratic thinker. To the extent that safeguarding minority rights is thought crucial to democracy, however, Locke is vulnerable to the charge of promoting the "tyranny of the majority." Significantly, in the *Second Treatise*, Locke referred to democracy only twice; he described the political system he advocated as civil government rather than democracy. It seems clear from his emphasis on property and its inevitably unequal possession because of the lack of reason and industry in the mass of men that Locke would have been averse to egalitarian, participatory, and populist versions of democracy. He thought that only those with a stake in the system should decide whether a revolution is justified.

Although widely hailed as the father of modern democracy, Jean-Jacques Rousseau rejected democracy, in the literal sense of government by all or even a majority of the people, as impracticable. In the *Social Contract* (1762), he wrote that a true democracy has never existed and never will exist because it is unthinkable that the people will remain perpetually assembled to discuss and administer public affairs. Indeed, it is a violation of the natural order for the many to govern the few. Only a "people of gods" could govern themselves democratically. It is important, however, to bear in mind Rousseau's sharp distinction between government and legislating. Although the people cannot govern, they should declare the basic legislative principles or constitutional framework within which the magistrates do their daily work.

Even if one were to excise Rousseau's commentary on government from the *Social Contract*, he can be shown to have been more preoccupied with the problem of leadership than with day-to-day rule by the people, collectively considered. He emphasizes the role of the (unelected) founder-legislator in creating the conditions from which a community bound together by a "general will" could emerge. Rousseau's distinction between the general will and the "will of all" has given rise to endless debate as to his meaning. It would appear that to Rousseau we vote properly only when we follow the inner voice of our own idealized selves and vote for the public interest regardless of how it affects us individually. If we selfishly decide issues of public policy on the basis of what we think will be to the advantage of our particular interest group, we will produce a corrupt result. The will of all stands for the mere sum of particular (selfish) wills. Thus a majority—or even a

unanimous—vote is only procedurally democratic. A decision that is substantively democratic results only when all or most of the people declare the general will. Rousseau rejected the idea of representative government. The only true legislators are the people; a parliament of representatives (as in England) deprives the people of their right to declare the general will and returns them to slavery after each election.

John Stuart Mill, whose *On Liberty* (1859) is hailed as a classic of liberal democratic thought, was highly suspicious of unqualified majority rule. He feared that newly emerging electoral majorities might themselves become tyrannical and ride roughshod over the privacy of individuals and the legitimate claims of minorities. He also feared the extension of the lowest common denominator of taste to all areas of life in a democracy.

In *Reflections on the Revolution in France* (1790), Edmund Burke, the father of conservatism, refers to undiluted democracy as the most "shameless" thing in the world. A mass democracy is shameless because it acknowledges no standard higher than itself. Such a democracy destroys morality as traditionally understood—that is, as an objective standard discoverable by reason and beyond the reach of majorities. Earlier, in his famous *Speech to the Electors of Bristol*, he declares it to be the duty of the parliamentary representative to be guided by conscience and explicitly rejects any idea that constituents could command him to follow any course of action. Burke's preference for a "natural aristocracy" is reminiscent of Aristotle. Horrified by the violence of the French Revolution, he roundly condemns the notion that will is the source of law, no matter whether it be the will of the many or of the few. Reason and tradition should hold in check the will of both majorities and minorities, of both peoples and kings. Burke's notion of the independent representative is directly opposed to Rousseau's rejection of representative government.

G. W. F. Hegel also opposed the ideas of the French Revolution, such as popular sovereignty and the mandate theory of representation. In his *Philosophy of Right* (1821), Hegel rejects any notion of the people conceived of as a collection of atomistic individuals whose opinion should be binding on those who govern. "The people" is an abstraction and as such has no will to be followed.

In his *Critique of Hegel's Philosophy of the State* (1843), Karl Marx contrasts what he calls true democracy with the false democracy of bourgeois liberal representative government. For Marx, true democracy is not a political system but a condition he later calls "final communism"; it represents the transcending of all political constitutions and the negation of the multiple tyrannies—economic, social, religious, cultural, political—that hitherto have ruled over humans. In *The Communist Manifesto* (1848), Marx and Friedrich Engels state that the first step in the coming working-class revolution is to bring the working class up to the level of the ruling class and achieve democracy. By democracy, Marx does not mean the practices or aspirations of liberalism then current, such as universal suffrage, regular elections, competition of two or more political parties, freedom of the press, and the rule of law. These practices are merely façades for the oppression of the proletariat by the bourgeois ruling class. At best they may be used by the proletariat as part of its strategy to overthrow the liberal order. The *Manifesto* discusses liberal or representative democracy as a "democracy of unfreedom." True freedom involves the end of alienation in all its forms, and the precondition for abolishing alienation is the overthrow of capitalism. (Engels later contended on the basis of the electoral success of the German Social Democratic Party that universal suffrage might hasten the revolution.)

Although critiques of democracy are generally perceived to come from the right, Marx and Engels show that there also exists a left-wing critique. Left-wing critics attack liberal democracy for not being democratic enough. Left-wing critics tend to make a distinction between the people's declared will as distorted and manipulated by its current oppressors and the people's authentic will. The people's true will can express itself only after the class society is transformed into a condition of equality. As the Italian Marxist Antonio Gramsci put it, until now societies have been divided into "those who know" and "those who do not know." The elite, those who know, condition the great majority of people to accept inequality as natural and inevitable. Only through a thoroughgoing revolution in popular culture can those in the majority become aware that they need not remain inert. As democratic citizens they can transform the sociopolitical world and abolish the division between those who know and those who do not.

A controversy exists in contemporary political science over whether the very notion of the people's true will inevitably leads to totalitarianism. J. L. Talmon, who coined the term "totalitarian democracy," argues that this current of thought, originating with Rousseau's concept of the general will and running through Marx to Vladimir Ilich Lenin and Joseph Stalin, uses democratic rhetoric to subvert democracy. According to Talmon, totalitarian democrats have an arbitrary, restricted notion of who qualifies as the people.

Few scholars today go as far as Talmon, and some thinkers who attempt to combine the insights of Marx and Sigmund Freud reject his thesis. In fact, they argue that an authentically radical critique of democracy such as that offered by Marx and Gramsci leads to the opposite of totalitarianism—that is, to a true democracy. Herbert Marcuse is one example of such a radical democratic thinker. Robert Paul Wolff is another.

One could cite many more criticisms of democracy from the classics of political theory. James Madison in *Federalist* No. 10 (1787) wrote that a pure democracy cannot cure discord caused by factions. In his epoch-making work *The Spirit of the Laws* (1748), Montesquieu harbored grave suspicions about democratic republics and clearly preferred aristocratic republics. Montesquieu rejects the idea of popular sovereignty in his famous doctrine of the separation of powers. For Immanuel Kant the only choice is between a republican and a despotic form of government. In a republic the executive and legislative powers are separate; in a despotism they are united. Democracy, which Kant understands as resting on the union of the legislative and executive powers, is inherently despotic, even though the will of the majority rules rather than the will of a single person.

The Elite School

Having set forth the major critiques of democracy in Western political theory, we are now in a position to examine the arguments of the so-called elite school of political theorists in the twentieth century. In common parlance the term "elitist" today has a uniformly derogatory connotation. The assumption is that theorists who emphasize the inevitable rule of elites in any society are antidemocratic and perhaps even profascist. Closer inspection, however, will reveal that increasingly theorists of democracy have come to adopt some version of elite theory, although this tendency is not universally shared. Joseph Schumpeter, Carl J. Friedrich, Robert Dahl, and Seymour Martin Lipset are representative of "realistic" democratic thinking in postwar social science in the United States.

The elite school of thought began about the turn of the twentieth century with Gaetano Mosca, Vilfredo Pareto, and Robert Michels.

Mosca is the author of such terms as "the ruling class" and "the political class." Pareto wrote about the "circulation of elites." Michels, in his study of the German Democratic Socialist Party, coined the term "the iron law of oligarchy."

Mosca, who began as early as 1883 to write about the role of elites, or organized minorities, in every society, proclaimed that whether a society labels itself a democracy, an aristocracy, or a monarchy, it will be governed by a minority. Every society is divided into a ruling class (the minority) and a ruled class (the majority). The ruled class does not share in government but only submits to it. Mosca insisted that it is a lie to assert that the masses of the people choose their representatives in representative democracies. On the contrary, their representatives are nominated and elected by organized minorities that force their will on the disorganized majority.

Given Mosca's conclusion that elections are nothing but unequal contests between organized minorities and the disorganized majority, it is somewhat surprising to find him expressing strong opposition to expanding the suffrage. Nonetheless, he declared in 1933 in the final version of his ruling-class theory that universal suffrage is the chief threat to liberal democracy because the masses are more volatile and subject to manipulation by demagogues than are the elites. The experience of the Italian fascist dictatorship appears to have caused Mosca to revise his ideas of the passivity of the masses, who, he thought, had been mobilized by Benito Mussolini in a way that would have been unlikely before universal suffrage and the encouragement of democratic participation.

Writing at the height of the fascist dictatorship, Mosca observed that autocratic regimes have greater staying power than liberal regimes. He thought liberal regimes could flourish only under conditions of economic prosperity and intellectual flowering. Ironically, Mosca alone in the Senate defended liberal parliamentary government when, in 1925, Mussolini pushed through a law declaring the head of the government (himself) no longer responsible to parliament.

Mosca's true successor in the elite school was Guido Dorso, who today is virtually unknown outside Italy. Like Mosca, Dorso, who died in 1947, was from the south of Italy. Dorso divested Mosca's theory of its aversion to the masses by insisting that the strength of liberal democracy rests in the rapid and continuous movement of the most able elements from the rank and file into the ruling class. Dorso also diluted Mosca's notion of the organized minority to the point that any hint of conspiracy disappeared. By stressing continuous competition between sections of the ruling class and the political class through political parties, Dorso gave strong support to liberal democratic institutions. He played a leading role in the resistance movement against the fascist dictatorship, and after the war he supported the left-of-center Action Party.

The French sociologist Maurice Duverger, in *Political Parties* (1951), provided the foundation for a "realistic" theory of democracy in the spirit of Mosca, as revised by Dorso, when he wrote that Abraham Lincoln's famous formula "government of the people, by the people, and for the people" needed to be rewritten as government for the people by an elite derived from the people. Then this maxim could serve as the only definition of democracy compatible with reality.

Ortega on the Triumph of Hyperdemocracy

If the elitist school inaugurated by Mosca, Pareto, and Michels declared the inevitability of minority rule, the Spanish man of letters José Ortega y Gasset argued in *The Revolt of the Masses* (1930) that just the opposite had happened in the

West. Writing in a vein somewhat reminiscent of Friedrich Nietzsche (although much more sympathetic to liberalism and socialism than Nietzsche was), Ortega lamented that, while liberal democracy had formerly been animated by devotion to the rule of law, now a kind of hyperdemocracy prevailed, corrupting common people and elites alike. In all areas of life, including art and literature, the "revolt of the masses" had ruined the quality of human existence.

For Ortega, as for Nietzsche, mass democracy is less a governmental form than a cultural disaster. The term "mass man" is not synonymous with the poor or the working classes but is the representative psychological type of current society regardless of income level and education. Education has been destroyed; humanistic learning has been replaced by technical training.

Ortega claimed that democracy, conceived of as the rule of the common people from below, is contrary to the proper ordering of public affairs. It is the destiny of persons of ordinary talents and taste to take direction from cultural elites. By definition, he wrote, the mass of humanity exists only to be raised up by selected minorities who impose standards of morality and taste on them.

Like Mosca, however, Ortega refrained from attacking liberal parliamentary government and specifically endorsed parliamentary institutions. Like Mosca, he rejected Mussolini's fascism. In effect, he declared the fascist police state to be nothing but hyperdemocracy with a brutal face.

Gentile and Fascism

Italian fascism's aversion to representative democracy was best expressed by the philosopher Giovanni Gentile (1875–1944). Gentile, who held various offices under the Italian fascist dictatorship, wrote much of the article on fascist doctrine published in the *Italian Encyclopedia* in 1932, even though Mussolini had signed his name to it. The article declares fascism's opposition to democratic ideologies. Fascism rejects the possibility of rule by the majority and extols the inequality of human beings as beneficial. Democratic regimes give the illusion that the people are sovereign; in truth, sovereignty is exercised by special interests behind the scenes. In contrast to a regime openly ruled by a king, democracy is a regime with a number of hidden kings who exercise a collective tyranny far worse than that of any avowed tyrant.

The prestige of the word *democracy* was so great in the twentieth century that even fascism found it necessary to claim to be the true democracy. Thus the fascist doctrine declared that, although fascism is opposed to a democracy that reduces the nation to the lowest common denominator of the majority, it is nonetheless the purest form of democracy if the nation is properly organized into a structure of corporate groups, thereby allegedly allowing the best talents in the mass of people to rise to the top. The implication is that the nation's true will is expressed by the one leader, *Il Duce*, Mussolini himself.

In his last work, *Genesis and Structure of Society*, published posthumously in 1946, Gentile expanded on his paradoxical claim that fascism is the true democracy by arguing that authentic democracy rejects privacy and individualism in the name of a complete merger of the individual with the state. Far from the state swallowing up the individual, the reverse occurs in fascist democracy, for the fascist state is the will of the individual in its universality. To justify this centralized and authoritarian view of democracy, Gentile claimed the ancient Greek city-state as his source.

Fascist Intellectual Opponents of Democracy

It is important to recall that critiques of democracy vary widely in substance and intent, and that it is quite possible to have theoretical reservations about democracy while in practice preferring it to alternatives. Conversely, as the discussion of Gentile shows, some prominent intellectuals critical of democracy in varying degrees actively supported the Nazi and fascist dictatorships. Among the most prominent were the philosopher Martin Heidegger, the jurist Carl Schmitt, and the playwright Luigi Pirandello.

Heidegger (1889–1976), author of *Being and Time* (1927) and the leading existentialist philosopher of the twentieth century, joined the Nazi Party shortly after Hitler's accession to power in 1933 and served as rector of the University of Freiburg for ten months. Even after leaving this position, during which he made a number of speeches supportive of Hitler's "national revolution," he clearly remained convinced that National Socialism (Nazism), in principle or at least initially, had the potential of saving Europe from bourgeois democratic nihilism.

In his inaugural address as university rector, Heidegger attacked democracy on numerous grounds. He seemed to endorse an idealized version of Hitler's leadership principle. Modern society, he proclaimed, must be reorganized to combat the corrupting influences of urbanization and runaway technology. A hierarchy of estates must replace mass society. Society must be organized around discipline, work, and "manly service." Multiparty systems have no right to exist; in their place is one party serving a united people with one will and one führer.

In a posthumously published interview with the editors of *Der Spiegel*, conducted in 1966, Heidegger, though repudiating what he euphemistically called the rougher manifestations of National Socialism, remained skeptical of democracy, declaring that he was not convinced that democracy could react creatively to the technological ethos permeating the modern world. Democracy, Heidegger continued, is at best only half true, in part because it operates under the illusion that global technology is something that can easily be controlled or mastered.

Carl Schmitt, a famous legal scholar during the period before Hitler seized power, shared with Heidegger an initial enthusiasm for the Nazi dictatorship, but later his attitude was more reserved. Both Schmitt and Heidegger extolled the sacrifice of the individual to the state in war, which for Schmitt was the essence of politics. In *The Concept of the Political* (1927), Schmitt defined politics in terms of the relationship between friendly states and enemy states. He repudiated cooperative and humanitarian ideas designed to support democracy. During the Nazi regime he authored justifications of Hitler's lawlessness in the name of a decisionist theory of law.

Luigi Pirandello (1867–1936), winner of the Nobel Prize for literature in 1934 and best known for his plays *Six Characters in Search of an Author* and *Henry IV*, became an active supporter of Italian fascism in 1924 when, in a much publicized event, he joined the Fascist Party at the regime's greatest moment of crisis following the murder of the Socialist deputy Giacomo Matteoti. Long before the advent of fascism in the March on Rome of October 28, 1922, Pirandello had become disillusioned with Italian parliamentary democracy. Italian democracy, he made clear in his novel *The Old and the Young* (1909), had betrayed the spirit of the nineteenth-century liberation movement embodied in Giuseppe Garibaldi's military expedition to unify Italy. Pirandello was outraged over what he perceived to be the corruption prevalent in the new national government in Rome after unification in 1870. In the novel he described Italian liberal democracy as a regime covered in mud. He bitterly resented the exploitation of southern Italy by successive liberal governments in Rome. During and after World War I he turned furiously against the

Italian Socialist and Communist Parties and called for a rebirth of nationalism. Like Heidegger in Germany with reference to the cruder currents of Nazism, Pirandello gradually distanced himself from the Fascist Party as it set about promoting a rigid social conformity. He never wavered in his public support of Mussolini, however, whom he hailed as the consummate actor imposing his sense of perpetually changing life on the contemporary political scene.

Voegelin and Strauss: Emigré Critics

Eric Voegelin (1901–1985) and Leo Strauss (1899–1973) were the two leading political theorists who emigrated to the United States as refugees from Nazi Germany and Nazi-occupied Austria, respectively. Both thinkers were highly critical of the modern liberal democratic tradition, which neither thought possessed the intellectual and spiritual resources to defend the dignity of the individual against the unprecedented assaults of totalitarian mass movements in the twentieth century. Each sought in different ways to recover the classical (Platonic and Aristotelian) foundations of political science. Unlike Heidegger and Schmitt, Voegelin and Strauss were fiercely antitotalitarian; they resisted Nazism rather than collaborating with it.

Voegelin was especially critical of the Lockean elements in Anglo-American social science. Locke, to Voegelin, was a destroyer of traditions who put nothing in their place. Strauss inveighed against American political science, with its mélange of positivism, behaviorism, and historicism (a euphemism for Heidegger's philosophy). Both Voegelin and Strauss thought it was vital for the liberal democracies to reconstitute elites capable of shaping the issues to be discussed in elections. They agreed that knowledge of the premodern classics of political theory is essential to understanding the modern crisis of constitu-tional democracy, which has been called upon to weather the storms of apocalyptic mass movements desirous of transforming politics into a process of inner-worldly salvation through utopian magic.

Conclusion

As the examples of Gentile, Heidegger, Schmitt, and Pirandello show, some twentieth-century critics of democracy promoted fascism and Nazism in varying degrees. Most of the other critics discussed here, however, can scarcely be labeled enemies of the open society or fascist precursors. Indeed, it may well be the case that, to be true to itself, democracy needs thoughtful critics.

See also Authoritarianism; Classical Greece and Rome; Conservatism; Constitutionalism; Theory, elite; Elites, Political; Fascism; Democracy, Justifications for; Liberalism; Majority rule, minority rights; Marxism; Theory, Twentieth Century European.

DANTE GERMINO

BIBLIOGRAPHY

Dahl, Robert A. *Democracy and Its Critics.* New Haven and London: Yale University Press, 1989.

Gentile, Giovanni. *Genesis and Structure of Society.* Translated by H. S. Harris. Urbana: University of Illinois Press, 1960.

Germino, Dante. *Beyond Ideology: The Revival of Political Theory.* New York: Harper and Row, 1968.

Klosko, George. *The Development of Plato's Political Theory.* New York and London: Methuen, 1986.

Machiavelli, Niccolò. *The Prince* and *The Discourses on Livy.* Vol. 1 of *Machiavelli: The Chief Works.* Edited and translated by A. Gilbert. Durham, N.C.: Duke University Press, 1965.

Marcuse, Herbert. "Repressive Tolerance." In *A Critique of Pure Tolerance.* Boston: Beacon Press, 1969.

Meisel, James H. *The Myth of the Ruling Class.* Ann Arbor: University of Michigan Press, 1958.

Sartori, Giovanni. *The Theory of Democracy Revisited.* 2 vols. Chatham, N.J.: Chatham House, 1987.

Schmitt, Carl. *The Concept of the Political.* Translated by G. Schwab. Rutgers, N.J.: Rutgers University Press, 1976.

Strauss, Leo. *On Tyranny.* Edited and translated by V. Gourevitch and M. Roth. New York: Free Press, 1991.

Talmon, J. L. *The Origins of Totalitarian Democracy.* New York: Praeger, 1961.

Voegelin, Eric. *The New Science of Politics.* 2d ed. Chicago: University of Chicago Press, 1987.

_____. *The World of the Polis.* Baton Rouge: Louisiana State University Press, 1957.

Wolin, Richard, ed. *The Heidegger Controversy.* New York: Columbia University Press, 1991.

✦ Democracy, Justifications for

Justifications for democracy are part of the democratic enterprise; that is to say, to practice democracy is in part to argue for its legitimacy, while to debate the meaning and justifying grounds of democracy is much of what democracy is about. To a considerable degree, political thought has been a continuing debate about whether democracy can be justified and, if so, how. All the major texts of the Western tradition bear on the question of whether the people need to be ruled or whether they have the right and the capacity to rule themselves. Democracy is one way of justifying political authority itself, and thus it engenders a debate about legitimacy.

From the time of the ancient Greeks there have been two rather distinctive ways of asking whether a people is justified in governing itself.

The first is concerned with issues of capacity; the second, with issues of right. In the first case, the question is, Who rules best? This question, in turn, requires some clear conception of the ends and objects of government: Who rules best to which ends? In the second case, the question is, Who has the right to rule? This entails a discussion of the nature of rulership and the relationship between rulers and the ruled.

Although there are democratic and antidemocratic arguments associated with both of these questions, arguments from capacity have tended toward aristocratic or meritocratic answers (the wisest should rule, the best should rule, the most able should rule, the experts should rule), whereas arguments from right have tended toward democratic answers (those who suffer the consequences of rulership should rule, those born with rights should rule, or simply the ruled have the right to participate in ruling themselves).

The Classical Debate

The quarrel between Plato and the Athenian *demes*, or residential tribes of ancient Athens, was not simply over who was most fit to rule but over who had the right. For Plato, the object of government was justice: a well-ordered commonwealth. Only those blessed with the capacity to discern the true and just forms that undergird all order could govern well. Thus, Plato concluded, until philosophers (students of true knowledge and hence of justice) become kings or kings become philosophers, human society is doomed to disorder and injustice.

The democratic response to Plato has not been that ordinary people can discern the just as clearly as philosophers can—although some theorists, such as Niccolò Machiavelli in the sixteenth century, have claimed that the people generally know their interests and ends better than do individual rulers, whether philosophical or not. Rather, the democratic response has been to argue that government is not about what we know but about what we have to do, not about truth but about interests. It is a practical rather than a speculative science and requires debate, political interaction, and deliberation—all of which are offered by a democracy. Aristotle understood politics to be a practical science and was more hospitable to democracy, at least as one element in a mixed constitution, than his philosophical predecessors had been.

The trial of Socrates in 399 B.C. embodied the essence of the quarrel between philosophical aristocrats and practical democrats in ancient Athens. To the democrats, Socrates used an appeal to truth to disguise the base interests represented by Athenians of status and wealth who detested democracy (even philosophers have interests). To the friends of Socrates, the democrats were trying to impose their prejudices on a noble and just man by brute force, inverting the natural order between reason and passion. The party of philosophy understood government as the rule of reason, which suggested that the most reasonable should rule. To the party of the people, the government could never be more than the rule of interests and hence of the interested: because each interest was the equal of the next, the interested (the people themselves) had every right to govern.

The quarrel in Athens also points to the intimate connection between equality and democracy, for equality finds its way into nearly every justification of democracy. Plato made hierarchical assumptions about human nature: the soul came in several versions—some base, some noble—and the noble were suited by nature to govern the base.

Aristotle believed that Greeks were superior to barbarians as men were superior to women. This belief meant that some men were natural slaves who needed to be ruled by others. If one begins with such assumptions, it is hard to arrive at a position that justifies universal democracy (although equality within a ruling caste—say, white propertied males—might ground a partial democracy of the kind established in the new United States in 1789).

Yet if the premise is that human nature is defined by equality, which was the basis for Stoic and then for Christian philosophy, a different style of argument emerges. If human beings are born free and equal, or if they are equal by virtue of common birth from a common parent, they would appear to have an equal right to governance. Among equals, the only suitable form of preeminence is numbers: fifty-one outweighs forty-nine. Majority rule thus becomes associated with an egalitarian account of human nature.

Specific Arguments for Democracy

With this underlying complex of arguments on the table, it is easier to scrutinize a representative sampling of specific justifications that have been advanced on behalf of democracy. These arguments overlap and reinforce one another and in practice are found mixed together. The controversies explored here reappear in one form or another in many of them.

The argument from skepticism. In the nineteenth century, John Stuart Mill captured an important skeptical element in justifications for democracy in his insistence that knowledge, being in part a product of social interaction, was secured if at all primarily through deliberation—hammered out on the anvil of debate. Because neither truth nor right can be known absolutely or agreed upon universally, uncertainty is the human condition and democracy the only prudent system of government. It is, Mill observed, as likely that one individual will be right and the whole world wrong as it is that one will be wrong and the whole world right. Twentieth-century philosophers such as Bertrand Russell and Karl Popper have offered similar fallibilist arguments (that it is impossible to know anything with absolute certainty and that the closest to knowledge we can come is "not yet falsified"). These arguments are rooted in the idea that what knowledge we have derives from our capacity to falsify rather than to know with certainty and depends on collective consensus rather than on individual discernment.

The argument from comparison. A version of the skeptical claim for democracy bordering on cynicism can be extracted from Winston Churchill's quip that democracy is the worst form of government in the world except for all the other forms. For all its failings, democracy can be shown to be far less pernicious than other forms of government and thus is good government in the default mode. The argument is connected with Thomas Jefferson's observation that if men are not equipped to govern themselves (as critics of democracy insist they are not) surely they cannot be equipped to govern others; therefore self-rule is always more prudent than rule by others.

The argument from divine will (vox populi, vox dei). An early democratic argument bent a traditional argument for the divine rule of kings to popular purposes. As Christian monarchists once claimed that God spoke to his human subjects through popes and kings, Deist democrats such as the English philosopher William Godwin (1756–1836) could argue that God spoke through the people themselves: *vox populi, vox dei* (the voice of the people is the voice of God). The people were in effect God's deputies in things political. The ultimate legitimacy of the people was thus made out to be a matter of divine will rather than human will. Often, the argument that humans were fit by nature to rule themselves concealed the premise that God (as nature's maker) lay behind natural right.

The argument from natural equality and consent. If, as Jean-Jacques Rousseau and Thomas Jefferson argued, human beings are born free and equal, they have an equal right to participate in government. Endowed with liberty by nature (or by their creator, according to the argument from divine will), they have the right of consent whenever they are asked to comply with or surrender to political authority. The tradition of social contract reasoning, which evolved from Thomas Hobbes and John Locke in the seventeenth century through Rousseau and the American Founders, relies on this instrumental logic: equality and freedom entail right; right entails consent; consent entails a social contract legitimating the exercise of political authority; the social contract entails democracy—the sovereignty (original authority) of the people in government.

The argument from natural liberty and consent. Although the argument from liberty and consent is to a degree built into the argument from equality, it takes a unique form in Rousseau's notion of the general will. Rousseau suggests that democracy is the only solution to a natural paradox: how can humans (born free) obey government and belong to a community yet still be as free (by nature) as they were before? The answer lies in participatory democracy, in which people participate in making the laws to which they owe their obedience. In obeying laws they give to themselves, they are merely obeying themselves and thus are not compromising their liberty. They are willing what they hold in common with others—the general will—and thus are at once expressing their liberty and living under a community of laws they create for themselves. Although this solution does not quite leave people as free as they were before, it endows them with a higher civil and moral freedom. To Rousseau, democracy is the sole form of government that is legitimate—uniting the individual and the community, the will of one and the general will, liberty and legislation. Rousseau not only provides a justification for democracy but argues that democracy is the only justifiable form of government that is compatible with human liberty.

The argument from utility. Utilitarianism offers a contractarian justification for democracy that shares the instrumentalism of the social contract but emphasizes the moral worth of the majority. If all humans have comparable needs and desires, and experience commensurate pains and commensurate joys, the satisfaction of the needs of one can never be privileged over the satisfaction of the needs of another. Each must count for one. For a community to make decisions in common, counting heads is all that counts—a principle that dictates that the greater number, representing the greater happiness, must prevail over the lesser number. Jeremy Bentham and James Mill offered the classic version of this position, while John Stuart Mill offered a classic critique (though it is made in the name of utility).

The argument from interest. If government is understood as the pursuit of the common interest, it can be argued that only the interested are fit to govern. Who knows better what the people need or want than the people themselves? Modern social science and pluralist theory have relied on this justification. Because political scientists regard politics as (in Harold Lasswell's definition) a question of who gets what, when, and how, it is necessarily a competition for power by the interested. Joseph Schumpeter's neoelitist conception of democracy as a competition among elites for the votes of the interested is one version of this argument. David Truman and Robert Dahl offer another that focuses on the plurality of interests and on voting as a just system of arbitration.

Property as a particularly salient interest has played a special role in this justification. It suggests that to hold property (defined in Locke as the property men hold in those parts of the nat-

ural world with which they mix their own labor, which in turn embodies their identity) is to possess a natural right to participate in governance as well as to determine questions of how property is defined, taxed, and transferred. It also suggests that those without property do not have such a right. Some have attributed this position to John Locke, and it has been used to exclude nonproperty owners from suffrage, as did many early American states imitating English law.

The argument from peace and stability. Proponents of peace and an international order have argued that democracies are far less likely to engage in warfare with one another than are nondemocratic states and that democracy therefore offers a recipe for global peace. Others have suggested that democracy produces greater stability over the long run than do other forms of government. Both claims are historically contestable, and some critics have even insisted that democracy is a particularly unpredictable and uncertain form of government, especially in its early developmental phase. Nonetheless, for many the propensity of democracies to breed peace and concord, at least among themselves, has served as an important justification.

The argument from capitalism and markets. Historically, democracy has had a close association with the growth of industrial society and the emergence of market economies. Democracy and capitalism have in common a focus on liberty. Because of this close link, democracy has often been regarded as an ally of, and thus a justification for, capitalism. Friedrich von Hayek, Milton Friedman, and more recently Robert Nozick have all argued that democracy and capitalism are reciprocal entailments of one another: democratic government is justified by the service it offers to capitalism and the virtues and liberties capitalism supposedly secures. This argument, rooted in a concern with liberty, has had to contend with arguments concerned with equality that contend that democracy has a closer kinship to socialism and economic egalitarianism than to capitalism and is naturally at odds with the market. But in recent times the connection to markets has been one of the most widely used justifications for democracy and currently is a vital part of the theory and practice of democratization in the former Soviet empire.

The argument from spontaneous revolutionary will. Thomas Jefferson, Hannah Arendt, and others have argued that democracy is justified because it maximizes spontaneity, revolutionary change, and participation—goods in themselves. Jefferson embraced the democratic formula in ward politics because it permitted ongoing participation and the revisiting and revisioning of all dogmas, including constitutional dogmas. Calling for a little revolution every nineteen years, Jefferson associated democracy with an activist expression of personal liberty. More recently participatory and strong democrats have suggested that democracy serves common deliberation and common action and that this attribute is itself an argument on democracy's behalf.

The Role of Justification

These foregoing justifications are by no means the only ones that have been deployed to establish the grounds of democratic rule, but they are a representative sample. Nor do they represent wholly discrete arguments; they overlap with one another, and they are all informed by the logic sketched in the introduction to this essay. Moreover, two important caveats attend the justificatory enterprise itself. The first is a historical point about the secondary role of justification in the founding of democracies; the second is a conceptual point about the essentially antifoundational and thus antijustificatory character of democracy itself.

Historically, justifications for democracy have often been made after the fact. They are efforts by lawyers and political theorists to legitimize the popular seizing of government through revolution. That is to say, democracy as a regime has most often been established by protest and force; the rights of the people have not been granted by elites yielding to sound justificatory arguments but have been seized or established by rebels for whom theory comes afterward. The battle to define democracy is carried on democratically, but the battle to establish it takes place on the turf of revolution and force. This is not a justification for violent revolution but simply an observation about the secondary role that justification plays in the founding of democratic regimes.

The second caveat grows out of the first: the search for a justification for democracy tends to be foundational, aimed at grounding democracy in some prepolitical philosophical or natural or legal or religious footing. But as democracy embraces spontaneity and autonomy, it abhors fixed antecedents. It can be justified externally but derives its most convincing justification not from its genealogy but from its reflexivity: its self-critical, self-scrutinizing practices that continually put its provisional principles to the test of deliberation. It processes itself and produces its own procedural conventions; that is the virtue of its participatory, representative, deliberative, and interactional practices. In this sense, paradoxical as it may seem, democracy is its own justification.

See also Democracy, Critiques of; Legitimacy; Locke, John; Democracy, Participatory; Plato; Rousseau, Jean-Jacques.

BENJAMIN R. BARBER

BIBLIOGRAPHY

Arendt, Hannah. *On Revolution.* New York: Viking, 1963.

Barber, Benjamin R. *Strong Democracy: Participatory Politics for a New Age.* Berkeley: University of California Press, 1984.

Bentham, Jeremy. *An Introduction to the Principles of Morals and Legislation.* Edited by J. H. Burns and H. L. A. Hart. London: Athlone Press; New York: Free Press, 1970.

Dahl, Robert A. *Who Governs? Democracy and Power in an American City.* New Haven: Yale University Press, 1961.

Friedman, Milton. *Capitalism and Freedom.* Chicago: University of Chicago Press, 1962.

Locke, John. *Second Treatise on Government.* Cambridge: Cambridge University Press, 1960.

Mill, John Stuart. *Utilitarianism.* Edited by George Sher. Indianapolis: Hackett, 1979.

Nozick, Robert. *Anarchy, State, and Utopia.* New York: Basic Books, 1974; London: Blackwell, 1978.

Rousseau, Jean-Jacques. *The Social Contract.* Harmondsworth, England: Penguin Books, 1968.

Schumpeter, Joseph. *Capitalism, Socialism, and Democracy.* 3d ed. New York: Harper, 1950.

✦ Democracy, Measures of

Attempts to gauge the political democracy of nations. It is nearly impossible to determine the first attempt at measuring democracy, though efforts date back at least to ancient Greece. Aristotle in the fourth century B.C. distinguished five varieties of democracy, which he ranked in a descending scale. Debate has always surrounded the measurement of democracy. Part of the disagreement consists of disputes over definitions. Thus a first step in examining how democracy is measured is to clarify the type of democracy in question.

This article examines some measures of political democracy—that is, the extent to which democratic rule and political liberties exist in a country. *Democratic rule* refers to the accountability of the governing elites and the openness of participation in the political system. *Political liberties* concern the freedom of expression and the freedom of association. The definition precludes some traits. For instance, the performance of democracies is separated from the meaning of democracy. Similarly, economic or social inequality have links to, but are distinct concepts from, political democracy. A political democracy can give rise to citizen satisfaction or discontent, apathy or involvement, but these are not defining components of the definition.

Any attempt to measure political democracy involves several major issues. Among them are categorical versus continuous measurement, objective versus subjective indicators, individual judge versus panel of judges, and single-time versus multiple-time measures.

Categorical vs. Continuous Measurement

In the earliest twentieth-century efforts at measuring political democracy, a country was either democratic or not. James Bryce's survey of democracy in the 1920s, for instance, listed only Argentina, Belgium, Chile, Denmark, France, Greece, Holland, Italy, Norway, Portugal, Sweden, the United States, the United Kingdom (and its self-governing dominions), and Uruguay as democracies. In 1959 Seymour Martin Lipset used one dichotomous classification of democracy for European and English-speaking countries and another for Latin American countries. Phillips Cutright, an early critic of this approach, proposed a continuous measure that would better reflect the gradations in democracy.

The issue of dichotomous versus continuous measures continues in contemporary research, though the difference between views may be less than it first appears. Analysts who use dichotomous measures often acknowledge that some cases fall between categories. For instance, where should Colombia, Malaysia, Mexico, Russia,

Thailand, and Zimbabwe be placed (as of the early 1990s)? The acknowledged difficulty of placing countries into one of two categories supports the idea that political democracy is present in varying degrees. The treatment of democracy as a dichotomy seems to be based largely on the convenience and simplicity of such a measure. In addition, there is the belief that countries tend to cluster around the high end or low end of a continuum of democracy. Thus treating democracy as a dichotomy is a practical device for analysis.

Analysts who argue for continuous indicators suggest that measurement should correspond to the nature of the construct; a continuous construct should be measured on a continuous scale. The advocates of continuous measurement argue that categorical measures incorrectly treat countries within a category as homogeneous with respect to democracy. Broad categories also may lead analysts to miss real changes and trends in democracy within a country if the changes are not sufficient to shift the nation into a different category. Over a region, dichotomous measures of democracy might give the impression that the regional level of democracy is relatively homogeneous when in fact it varies widely. Africa and Asia in the early 1990s are cases in point. Using dichotomous measures would hide the diverse levels of democracy present in these regions. In addition, continuous measures often are more suitable for quantitative analysis because most quantitative techniques assume that continuous concepts are measured on continuous scales.

Thus the controversy seems to be less about whether democracy is present or absent than about whether it makes any practical difference to measure it as a dichotomy or as a continuous variable.

Objective vs. Subjective Indicators

To measure democracy, researchers have used either objective or subjective measures. In the twentieth century the earliest efforts used subjective indicators. For example, in the 1920s James Bryce, author of the two-volume work *Modern Democracies*, was the sole judge of which countries were classified as democracies. In the 1940s Russell H. Fitzgibbon organized a panel of judges to assess more than a dozen indicators of democracy for Latin American countries. From the late 1950s onward these pioneering studies stimulated the generation of expert ratings by other analysts. The measures derived from these studies were all formed from the judgment of one or more experts, so they are all considered to be subjective indicators.

In 1958 Daniel Lerner produced one of the earliest objective measures of democracy, using voter turnout statistics as an indicator. A few years later Phillips Cutright used party composition of the legislative body as an alternative. In his system, countries dominated by a single party were scored lower than countries with a greater mix of parties. Analysts have continued to rely on objective measures of political democracy. For instance, Tatu Vanhanen has measured democracy as a function of percentage of the population that votes and the percentage of the legislative seats held by the largest party in a nation's legislature.

Other indices of political democracy include both objective and subjective indicators. In 1973 Robert Jackman included an objective measure (voting turnout statistics) along with three other, largely subjective indicators. Kenneth Bollen's Political Democracy Index also combines objective indicators, such as whether the chief executive is elected, and subjective indicators, such as how free the press is and the effectiveness of the legislative body. A later version of the Political Democracy Index contains three subjective indicators (freedom of group opposition, political rights, and legislative effectiveness) and one objective indicator (legislature elected or not).

The objective indicators seem more likely than the subjective ones to be replicable across investigators. In addition, some allow finer gradations than do subjective indicators and therefore are more likely to allow continuous measurement. But objective measures have disadvantages as well. For example, the agencies reporting voter turnout may falsify statistics or may not record them accurately. And given the value placed on high turnout as a sign of government legitimacy, governments may be tempted to overreport voting. Countries that have political systems dominated by a single party or dictator are more likely to engage in such practices. In most countries, the national legislature is a public institution, so it is difficult for a state to hide the percentages of seats held by various political parties.

A key problem of the validity of many objective indicators is that they fall short of measuring political democracy as defined at the beginning of this article. Voter turnout, for instance, may reflect voter apathy or voter satisfaction, the existence of a law requiring citizens to vote, or even the weather on election day. An objective measure of whether the chief executive of a country comes to office by election only partly reveals the extent of the executive's democratic accountability. If the indicator is the party composition of the legislative body of a country, it is difficult to know what proportion of majority or minority parties best reflects the degree of democracy. A problem with indicators such as voter turnout, whether the chief executive is elected, and party composition is that the indicators do not always reflect the openness or fairness of the elections to which they correspond. For instance, the elections might be ridden with fraud, restrictions might inhibit candidates' ability to campaign, and limitations might be imposed on candidates for office. These factors all diminish the political democracy of a country, but they would not necessarily be revealed in statistics based on objective indicators.

The subjective indicators also have both advantages and disadvantages. On the positive side, subjective measures can gauge some of the key traits of political democracy that otherwise would escape detection. Freedom of expression, freedom of association, and fairness of national elections are important traits for which subjective ratings are available, while objective measures are lacking. In addition, judges are capable of incorporating many factors within a country when making their assessments. For instance, repressive practices often are not publicly recorded, though they may be widely known. These could be missed by objective indicators, yet they can be taken into account by expert judgments.

The main disadvantage of subjective measures is that they may reflect the judge's idiosyncrasies, which would lead to random or systematic errors in measurement. If these errors are large enough, they can render the subjective measures useless. On the other hand, provided the measurement errors are small, researchers are less likely to be misled in analyses that incorporate some subjective indicators.

Empirical evidence on the relative merits of subjective and objective indicators is limited. Voter turnout appears to have a weak (sometimes inverse) correlation with other subjective indicators of political democracy. Vanhanen found that his composite of objective measures was highly correlated with the subjective indicators developed by Raymond D. Gastil. Analyzing a mixture of subjective and objective indicators, Bollen found that subjective variables outperform the objective measure of whether the chief executive is elected.

Another strategy is to combine objective and subjective indicators. For example, the objective indicator of elected legislative body in the Political Democracy Index was multiplied by the subjective indicator of the effectiveness of the legislature. This helped give less weight to "puppet" elected legislatures that have essentially no power. Other such combinations of objective and subjective indicators are possible.

Individual Judge vs. Panel of Judges

An important issue concerning subjective indicators is whether an individual or a panel of experts should create the measure. Two of the earliest efforts at measuring democracy exemplify the problem. Bryce was the only judge developing his ratings, while Fitzgibbon's subjective democracy ratings came from a panel of experts on Latin America. The ratings now published by Freedom House, a nonprofit organization based in New York, offer another example of ratings that derive from a panel of judges. Single-judge ratings, however, also are still common.

A panel of judges has several positive features. One is that the pool of expertise is greater than when relying on a single judge. It is extremely difficult for an individual to be sufficiently familiar with all the countries that are to be rated; the task is more feasible if a group of judges are employed. Second, individual idiosyncrasies are less obtrusive when a study employs the weighted average of a pool of judges.

A single judge, however, is likely to be more consistent in the application of rating criteria. Individual members of a panel may have different standards for making their ratings. This raises the issue of how to weight the opinions of the different judges. This problem does not arise for a single judge.

Not much empirical evidence is available concerning the relative performance of panels versus individual judges. Fitzgibbon found considerable variance in the ratings of Latin American countries by his panel of experts. In the 1960s Ray-mond B. Nixon's panel of experts on freedom of the press also showed some divergence of ratings. Nonetheless, the Fitzgibbon measure correlates closely with the Political Democracy Index already mentioned, and Nixon's free press rating shows very high reliability.

Instead of a panel of judges, some analysts use multiple indicators from different sources to form a single measure of democracy. Thus freedom of the media might be rated by one judge, while the effectiveness of an elected legislative body is assessed by another. Each measure comes from a single source, either an individual or a panel of judges. Both measures then are incorporated into a democracy index. Collectively, this multiple indicator–multiple source measurement approach leads to a panel of judges even if each rating comes from a single judge.

Other Validity Issues

An indicator consists of three parts: validity, systematic error, and random error. Validity is the component of an indicator that truly measures the construct. Systematic errors are nonrandom and consistent errors that do not match the construct. Random error includes nonsystematic and unstable departures from the true variable. Few studies have estimated the relative contribution of these components, but those few suggest that some indicators of political democracy have large errors, whether systematic or random. For instance, the indicators in the Political Democracy Index generally have high validity. Considered individually, however, they show some evidence of systematic measurement error because of data source. In this case it was possible to combine the indicators into an index that minimized the systematic error and maximized validity.

Nearly all definitions of political democracy, including the one given at the beginning of this article, imply that democracy involves the largest possible proportion of the adult population of a country. But scholars often ignore the inclusiveness of the definition when constructing a measure. This omission may introduce systematic error into their measurements. For example, universal male suffrage is often used as a criterion for classifying countries as democratic, even though the definition of democracy implies that both males and females are included. Similarly, obstacles to voting or political participation of ethnic minorities often do not affect the ranking of countries.

Analysts who have collected information on suffrage have found that, except for a few countries, this indicator does not discriminate well between countries; most countries formally have universal suffrage. The problem is even more serious for studies that examine democracy in past years or those that focus on the few post–World War II countries that have had considerable periods with a restrictive franchise (such as Kuwait, South Africa, and Switzerland).

Another source of systematic error is found in indices that incorporate aspects of the political system that are related to, but conceptually distinct from, democracy. One common practice is to develop measures of political democracy that incorporate political stability. Lipset, for instance, looked for stable democracies in his classification of countries. In forming his measure, Cutright examined the party composition of legislative bodies and the nature of the executive-selection process over a twenty-one-year period.

Systematic error can also arise from confounding democracy with some of its possible causes and consequences. For example, Fitzgibbon included standard of living, national cohesion, and civil supremacy over the military among his measures of democracy. When a relation is found between one such indicator and another variable, it is difficult to know whether the association is due to democracy or to the other confounding variables contained within the democracy index. For instance, one study showed that a measure that incorporates stability tends to support the hypothesis that the timing of development influences the chances for democracy, while a measure that excludes stability does not support this hypothesis.

Virtually all studies treat measures of political democracy as if they were error-free. It is not known how far this approach has led to biased assessments of the causes and consequences of political democracy.

Single-time vs. Multiple-time Measurement

The temporal dimension is another way to classify measures of democracy. Single-time measures may cover a single year or a period of years. Cutright's measure, for instance, covers a single twenty-one-year period. J. S. Coleman's competitiveness measure is for a single time point (around 1959). Multiple-time measures range from two-time measures to annual measures for many years. Generally, analysts used single-time measures for one of two reasons: lack of data or the attempt to gauge democracy over a period of years. Most contemporary researchers prefer multiple-time measures because these measures allow more flexibility in analyzing trends and studying the dynamics of democratic development. In addition, analysts can group annual measures to produce period measures, while period measures often do not allow a return to the annual measures that went into them.

Conclusions

The measurement of political democracy is still at an early stage in its development. It has advanced further than the measurement of some other social-science constructs, such as national cohesion, openness of markets, or economic dependency. It is less developed, however, than the measurement of others, such as energy consumption or gross domestic product.

To agree on the measurement of political democracy, analysts will have to arrive at a consensus on the meaning of the term. Then they will have to resolve the issues outlined here. Some of the important tasks include (1) finding objective indicators to replace subjective measures, such as the fairness of elections and effectiveness of legislative bodies; (2) developing more precise measures than those currently available; (3) finding ways to incorporate aspects of inclusiveness into indices; and (4) gaining more knowledge of the validity and error in existing measures. Although perfect measures of political democracy will remain elusive, substantial improvements in measurement are feasible.

KENNETH A. BOLLEN

BIBLIOGRAPHY

Anderson, Lisa. *Transitions to Democracy*. New York: Columbia University Press, 1999.

Bollen, Kenneth A. "Issues in the Comparative Measurement of Political Democracy." *American Sociological Review* 45 (1980): 370–390.

_____. "Liberal Democracy: Validity and Method Factors in Cross-National Measures." *American Journal of Political Science* 37 (November 1993): 1207–1230.

Bryce, James. *Modern Democracies*. 2 vols. New York: Macmillan, 1921.

Coleman, J. S. "Conclusion: The Political Systems of the Developing Areas." In *The Politics of Developing Areas*, edited by G. A. Almond and J. S. Coleman. Princeton: Princeton University Press, 1960.

Cutright, Phillips. "National Political Development: Its Measures and Analysis." *American Sociological Review* 28 (1963): 253–264.

Fitzgibbon, Russell H. "Measurement of Latin-American Political Phenomena: A Statistical Experiment." *American Political Science Review* 45 (1951): 517–523.

Gastil, Raymond D., and Freedom House. *Freedom in the World*. New York: Freedom House, annual.

Inkeles, Alex. *On Measuring Democracy*. New Brunswick, N.J.: Transaction, 1991.

Jackman, Robert. "On the Relation of Economic Development to Democratic Performance." *American Journal of Political Science* 17 (1973): 11–21.

Lerner, Daniel. *The Passing of Traditional Society*. Glencoe, Ill.: Free Press, 1958.

Lipset, Seymour Martin. "Some Social Requisites of Democracy." *American Political Science Review* 53 (1959): 69–105.

Nixon, Raymond B. "Freedom in the World's Press: A Fresh Appraisal with New Data." *Journalism Quarterly* 42 (1965): 3–5, 118–119.

Przeworski, Adam, and Susan C. Stokes. *Democracy, Accountability, and Representation*. Cambridge and New York: Cambridge University Press, 1999.

Vanhanen, Tatu. *The Process of Democratization*. New York: Crane Russak, 1990.

✦ Democracy, Multiethnic

An independent, sovereign political system that is characterized both by democratic decision-making institutions and by the presence of two or more ethnic groups. An ethnic group can be defined as a group of people who see themselves as a distinct cultural community; who often share a common language, religion, kinship, and/or physical characteristics (such as skin color); and who tend to harbor negative and hostile feelings toward members of other ethnic groups.

Ethnic group used to be defined more narrowly, since the possession of a common language used to be considered almost a necessary criterion. Nowadays, however, the term has become virtually synonymous with *communal group*. For instance, the major groups in the former Yugoslavia—Serbs, Croats, and Bosnian Muslims—as well as the Christian and Muslim sects in Lebanon are commonly referred to as ethnic groups. They differ from each other in religion but not (or only barely) in language.

Since the middle of the nineteenth century there has been broad agreement among social scientists that the division of a society into different ethnic groups constitutes a formidable obstacle to stable and viable democracy. For instance, political theorist John Stuart Mill argued that democracy was next to impossible in multiethnic societies, especially if the ethnic groups were linguistically differentiated from each other. (This argument was made in his *Considerations on Representative Government*, first published in 1861, one of the first book-length studies of the operation of democratic institutions.)

Later thinkers have generally supported both Mill's conclusion and the basic argument that underlies it. Democratic decision making, according to Mill, can work well only if the differences to be resolved with regard to preferred public policies are not too great. Therefore, although democracy does not require a completely homogeneous society, it does require a minimum of social and political unity and consensus. The degree of unity and consensus in multiethnic societies is generally below this necessary minimum.

The most extreme interpretation of Mill's proposition—that multiethnic democracy is impossible—leads to the conclusion that the only way for people in a multiethnic society to enjoy democracy is to eliminate their ethnic differences. Logically, there are four possibilities for doing so: genocide, expulsion, partition, and assimilation. Social scientists who have regarded multiethnic

democracy as a difficult, but not impossible, objective have identified four principal models of democracy that may be able to manage ethnic differences and conflict: power sharing, cross-cutting cleavages, vote pooling, and majority control.

Eliminating Ethnic Differences

Of the four possibilities of eliminating ethnic differences, genocide and expulsion are not without historical precedent, but they are morally unacceptable policies. Partition and assimilation can be regarded, at least in principle, as acceptable solutions.

Partition entails the geographical division of a multiethnic society into two or more sovereign states, each of which is ethnically homogeneous—and each of which can therefore more easily sustain a democratic system. The major problem with partition is that ethnic groups are almost never perfectly concentrated in particular geographical areas. The usual intermixture of ethnic groups makes it impossible to divide a multiethnic society in such a way that perfectly homogeneous separate states are created. The breakup of the Soviet Union and Yugoslavia into a large number of independent states in the early 1990s provides telling examples. Although the successor states are often thought of as ethnic states, and although most of them carry ethnic names (such as Russia, Armenia, and Croatia), all harbor large minority ethnic groups within their borders.

Thus, to reach the objective of creating homogeneous states, partition must be accompanied by population transfers. Even if such transfers are voluntary and take place under peaceful circumstances, they involve painful changes for the individuals who must leave their residences and resettle in different areas. And if they are involuntary and take place under conditions of widespread violence and civil war, they are tantamount to morally unacceptable "ethnic cleansing."

Many states have opposed partition out of fear that it may have a domino effect. Because so many countries are multiethnic in character, allowing one state to divide into two or more separate monoethnic, or at least ethnically more homogeneous, states may encourage ethnic minorities in other states to seek the same goal. The trend has the potential to trigger conflict and instability within states as well as the fragmentation of the international system of states.

Although international opposition to partition and secession has been far from unanimous in the post–World War II era, attempts at partition and secession have rarely been successful. The primary examples before 1990 are the creation of Bangladesh in 1971 and Singapore in 1965. The hostility toward partition may have softened in the 1990s, however, as evidenced by the international acceptance of the partition of the former Soviet Union and Yugoslavia, as well as the breakup of Czechoslovakia and the secession of Eritrea from Ethiopia.

The fourth method of eliminating ethnic differences is cultural assimilation—that is, the blending of different ethnic groups into one ethnically homogeneous group. This approach has been widely used under the rubric "nation building" in developing countries after decolonization. It has sometimes involved the encouragement or requirement that ethnic minorities adopt the ways and customs, and especially the language, of another ethnic group, usually the majority or dominant ethnic group. But it also sometimes involves the imposition of a lingua franca that is not the native language of any ethnic group, such as Malay in Indonesia and Swahili in East African states.

Primordialism vs. Instrumentalism

Nation-building policies are based on the premise that ethnicity is flexible, adaptable, and manipulable. Whether this view is correct is the subject of much controversy in the social sciences between the so-called primordialists and their critics, who espouse what is variously called the instrumental or situational approach to ethnicity.

Primordialist theory assumes that ethnic identity is an inherited characteristic and, if not permanently fixed, at least very difficult to change. The opposite perspective is that ethnicity is fluid and manipulable, and that it does not become politically salient unless and until politicians use it to mobilize political support. In contrast with a primordial "given," it is an instrumental "made" or "taken" created by political leaders.

A third approach, which can be thought of as steering a middle course between the primordialists and the instrumentalists, is that of the constructivists. Constructivists share with the instrumentalists the assumption that ethnicity is made rather than given, but they emphasize the imaginative creation of ethnicity to satisfy the social needs of groups in the process of profound political, social, and economic change. In this view the constructors of ethnicity are social-cultural brokers rather than political entrepreneurs.

Both the primordial and the instrumental approaches can be criticized. There is much empirical evidence, especially in Africa, of the fluidity of ethnic boundaries. Yet it is unrealistic to assume that politicians can make successful ethnic appeals where such appeals do not resonate with basic cultural differences among people. Moreover, where such differences do exist, it is equally unrealistic to think of politicians as completely free agents who can decide either to use or to ignore these divisions. On the contrary, they often have a strong incentive to mobilize support on the basis of ethnic divisions and can ignore them only at their own peril. Most important for the purpose of this article, efforts at manipulating ethnic identities in order to build culturally unified nations have had very limited success, and attempts to discourage or suppress ethnic differences have often backfired, strengthening ethnic feelings and exacerbating ethnic conflict.

Modernization Theory

The 1950s and 1960s were characterized by an exaggerated faith in the possibilities of nation building. One reason is the popularity of modernization theory, which held that the various processes of modernization—industrialization, urbanization, increases in transportation, improvements in communication, the growth of mass education, and so on—would inevitably undermine the "premodern" forces of ethnicity and lead to national and even worldwide integration. The industrialized Western world was seen as already largely devoid of ethnic conflicts, and the developing countries were seen as moving to the same end.

From the 1970s on, however, it has become clear that modernization and ethnic assimilation do not necessarily develop in tandem. There has been a remarkable resurgence of ethnic demands and conflict in the most modern parts of the world. Outstanding examples are English-French tensions in Canada, racial conflict in the United States, the linguistic struggle in Belgium, the Jura separatist problem in Switzerland, and Catalan and Basque nationalism in Spain. Furthermore, ethnic loyalties in most developing countries have persisted in spite of strong nation-building efforts. Similarly, ethnic divisions have survived in the former Soviet Union and other communist countries through the years of communist efforts to "solve" the nationality problem.

The other reason for the confidence in nation building in the 1950s and early 1960s was the prominence of the U.S. "melting pot" model of ethnic and cultural assimilation and the worldwide prominence of American political and social scientists. Since then, however, the melting-pot model has come under attack as an idealized depiction of only partially successful assimilation. Correspondingly, public policy in the United States has shifted to the recognition of cultural diversity and the introduction of programs of affirmative action for the benefit of explicitly defined ethnic and racial groups. Another weakness of the melting-pot model was the failure to recognize the difference in the strength of ethnic loyalties in immigrant and nonimmigrant societies. Immigrants, having voluntarily uprooted and resettled themselves, have shown a greater willingness and aptitude to assimilate culturally than have nonimmigrants, although even here there are the major exceptions of the French speakers in Canada and the Afrikaners in South Africa.

If ethnic differences cannot be eliminated, can they be successfully managed and accommodated in multiethnic democracies? Three of the four models of democracy that answer this question in the affirmative (cross-cutting cleavages, vote pooling, and majority control) can be grouped together in the broad category of majoritarian models, and they stand in sharp contrast to the fourth model of power sharing.

Joint Decision Making in Power Sharing

Power-sharing democracy—often called consociational democracy—can be defined in terms of four characteristics. The two primary characteristics are the participation of the representatives of all significant ethnic groups in political decision making and a high degree of autonomy for these groups to run their own internal affairs. The secondary characteristics are proportionality and the minority veto. The major aim of these four devices is to increase each group's sense of security by maximizing its control of its own destiny, without increasing the insecurity of other groups.

The joint exercise of governmental, especially executive, decision-making power may take a variety of institutional forms. The most straightforward and common form is that of a grand coalition cabinet in a parliamentary system, as in Belgium and Malaysia. The Swiss seven-member executive provides another example: the seven members are selected in such a way that all major religious and linguistic groups as well as the four largest political parties are given representation.

In presidential systems of government, a grand coalition is more difficult, but not impossible, to arrange. In the Lebanese presidential system (with a powerful although not popularly elected president), power sharing is organized by distributing the presidency and other high offices to the different groups: the presidency is reserved for a Maronite Christian, the prime ministership for a Sunni Muslim, the speakership of the legislature for a Shi'ite Muslim, and so on. In addition, the Lebanese cabinet is a broadly representative power-sharing body. In both parliamentary and presidential systems, power sharing may be strengthened by broadly representative councils or committees with important advisory or coordinating functions.

Nevertheless, a presidential form of government is not optimal for power sharing in multiethnic societies. Presidentialism usually entails the concentration of executive power in the hands of one person, who, in an ethnically divided country, is almost inevitably a member of one of the major ethnic groups. Power sharing requires joint decision making by the representatives of the different ethnic groups; the best vehicle for this is a multimember collegial body. The Lebanese power-sharing arrangement alleviated this problem but did not solve it completely because, until the constitutional changes of 1989, the presidency

was by far the most powerful of the offices distributed among the ethnic groups.

Group Autonomy in Power Sharing

The second characteristic of power-sharing democracy is group autonomy. On all issues of common concern, decisions are made jointly by the representatives of the different ethnic groups; on all other matters, decision-making power is delegated to the separate ethnic groups to be exercised by and for each group. If the ethnic groups are geographically concentrated, group autonomy can take the form of a federal system in which federal boundaries coincide with ethnic boundaries so as to create ethnically homogeneous or largely homogeneous territorial units. Examples are multilingual Switzerland, in which most of the cantons are monolingual, and Canada, where the majority of French speakers are concentrated in the province of Quebec.

If the ethnic groups are geographically intermixed, autonomy must assume a nonterritorial form. For instance, the 1960 constitution of Cyprus set up separate Greek Cypriot and Turkish Cypriot communal chambers with exclusive legislative powers over religious, cultural, and educational matters. These chambers were separately elected by Greek and Turkish Cypriot voters, respectively, regardless of where on the island they lived. In addition, the constitution prescribed similar separately elected municipal councils in the five largest towns in the island.

Another example of power sharing without regard to geography is the Law of Cultural Autonomy adopted by Estonia in 1925, which gave each minority ethnic group with more than 3,000 formally registered members the right to establish autonomous institutions under the authority of a cultural council elected by the members of the ethnic group. The council could organize and administer minority schools and other cultural institutions such as libraries and theaters. The German and Jewish minorities took advantage of this law to establish their own autonomous institutions.

Territorial and nonterritorial autonomy may be used in the same system, as in the case of Belgium, which has experimented with the delegation of political authority both to geographically defined areas that are ethnically homogeneous (Dutch-speaking Flanders and French-speaking Wallonia) and to communities defined in nonterritorial terms (French speakers and Dutch speakers in bilingual Brussels).

Proportionality and Minority Veto

Proportionality, the third characteristic of power-sharing democracy, serves as the basic standard of political representation, civil service appointments, and the allocation of public funds. Proportionality is especially important as a guarantee for the fair representation of minority groups. The most common and straightforward method for achieving proportionality of political representation is to use a proportional representation electoral system, as in Belgium and Switzerland. Reasonable proportionality can also be achieved by other partly proportional methods that guarantee minority representation (as in Lebanon), or by single-member district electoral systems when the ethnic groups are geographically concentrated (as in Canada), and when, in addition, the ethnic groups make informal agreements about the distribution of seats (as in Malaysia).

Two extensions of the proportionality rule entail even greater minority protection: overrepresentation of small groups and parity of representation. An example of the former is the allotment in Cyprus's 1960 constitution of 30 percent of the seats in the national legislature to the Turkish Cypriot minority, which made up less than 20 percent of the total population. The Belgian constitution prescribes parity of representation in the national cabinet for the Dutch-speaking majority and the French-speaking minority.

The fourth characteristic of power-sharing democracy is the minority veto. This device is usually restricted to the most vital and fundamental matters, and it is usually based on informal understandings rather than formal legal or constitutional rules. Examples of the latter, however, are the requirements of concurrent majorities (that is, a majority not only of the total legislature but also majorities within each of the ethnic groups represented in the legislature) for the passage of legislation with regard to taxes, the municipalities, and the electoral system in the 1960 constitution of Cyprus and for the adoption of laws on cultural and educational matters in the Belgian constitution.

Power Sharing vs. Majority Rule

All four characteristics of power-sharing democracy contrast sharply with the basic features of majority-rule or majoritarian democracy, exemplified most clearly by the British Westminster model of parliamentary government. The essence of majoritarianism is the concentration of political power in the hands of the majority. Instead of concentrating power, the power-sharing model's basic approach is to share power, to diffuse and decentralize power, to divide power proportionally, and to limit power.

First, the grand coalitions and joint decision making characteristic of power sharing contrast with the concentration of power in a one-party, bare-majority, noncoalition cabinet typical of the Westminster model. Second, group autonomy on a territorial or nonterritorial basis contrasts with the unitary and centralized nature of the Westminster model, which does not allow for geographical or functional areas from which the parliamentary majority at the center is barred. Third, the Westminster model's basic election rule is plurality, or winner-take-all: the candidate with the most votes wins, and all other candidates lose. In proportional systems both majorities and minorities can be winners in the sense of being able to elect their candidates in proportion to each group's electoral support. In practice, the plurality rule tends to exaggerate the representation and power of the majority and therefore entails disproportional representation. The two extensions of proportionality—minority overrepresentation and parity—are also methods of disproportional representation but in this case the disproportionality works in favor of minorities and small groups. And, fourth, the minority veto on constitutional or other vital matters contrasts sharply with the unwritten constitution in the Westminster model of democracy, which gives the majority the right to change even the most fundamental rules of government, limited only by morality and common sense.

Examples of Power Sharing

Power-sharing democracies can be found in all parts of the world. The Netherlands in 1917 accommodated the conflicts between the country's religious-communal groups by instituting proportional representation elections, granting far-reaching autonomy in the field of education, and cementing informal agreements to pursue government by broad coalitions and to accord minorities veto rights on the most sensitive political issues.

Switzerland's arrangement, worked out in 1943, stipulated a permanent grand coalition of the four largest parties, representing more than 80 percent of the Swiss voters, as well as a grand coalition of the major religious and linguistic groups. These were added to existing proportional representation and a decentralized federation that provided strong linguistic autonomy.

In Lebanon, also in 1943, the several Christian and Muslim sects agreed to govern the country, which had declared its independence from France, according to a complex system of the distribution of the top political offices to the different sects. They guaranteed representation in the parliament for each sect according to a predetermined, roughly proportional, ratio. They set up separate and autonomous sectarian schools as well as autonomous sectarian courts to administer the personal status laws (concerning such matters as marriage, divorce, and inheritance) that tend to differ from sect to sect. And, finally, they established an informal veto power.

Austria had experienced a civil war in the early 1930s between Catholics and Socialists. In 1945, at the end of World War II, the groups decided to govern together rather than to compete. Their agreement was complemented by strict adherence to proportionality, respect for each other's autonomy, and an informal but firm agreement on a mutual veto power.

In 1955 a broad and inclusive coalition of ethnic (Malay, Chinese, and Indian) political parties was formed in Malaya. The arrangement continued after independence in 1957 and also after the addition of the Bornean states of Sabah and Sarawak (and, briefly, Singapore) to the federation, renamed Malaysia, in 1963. This coalition was originally called the Alliance and later, when additional parties joined the coalition, the National Front. The coalition partners negotiate the nomination of joint candidates in the single-member districts used for parliamentary elections, thereby achieving a rough proportionality of representation for each ethnic party.

A 1958 accord ended a long and bloody civil war in Colombia, in which the formerly feuding Conservative and Liberal Parties, representing the country's main communal groups, agreed to collaborate according to the rules of parity and coparticipation and to take turns in occupying the country's powerful presidency. The Cyprus constitution of 1960 has been mentioned. It provided for a Greek Cypriot president and a Turkish Cypriot vice president with virtually coequal powers, far-reaching educational and cultural autonomy for the two groups, a strong veto power for the Turkish Cypriot minority, and overrepresentation of this minority in the legislature and the cabinet. Another previously discussed example is Belgium. The 1970 amendments to the constitution required equal representation of Dutch speakers and French speakers in the cabinet, established a veto power for the French-speaking minority over proposed legislation concerning culture and education, and granted regional decentralization and autonomy for the linguistic communities.

All of these power-sharing democracies are characterized by both thorough power sharing and full democracy. In addition, many instances can be cited of predemocratic power sharing (such as the United Province of Canada from 1840 to 1867 and Belgium during the first decades of its independence after 1831) and of partial power sharing (especially the use of federal or highly decentralized systems to give autonomy to minority linguistic groups, as in India, Canada, and Spain).

The first modern scholar to identify the power-sharing model of democracy was the economist and Nobel laureate W. Arthur Lewis. In *Politics in West Africa* (1965), he proposed broad interethnic coalitions, proportional representation elections, and ethnic group autonomy by means of federalism for the ethnically divided countries of West Africa. Although Lewis did not attach a comprehensive label to these proposals, they clearly add up to power sharing. He developed his proposals as a solution to the failures of majoritarian democracies in the West African countries, which, as an economic adviser to several of their governments, he observed and deplored.

Criticisms of Power Sharing

Power-sharing theory has been criticized on a variety of grounds. Because it recommends power sharing as a model of stable and effective democracy that multiethnic countries ought to follow, these criticisms deserve careful examination. The most serious charge is that power sharing cannot work well because of its inherent problems of immobilism and deadlock and its tendency to encourage rather than to discourage political mobilization along ethnic lines. Critics have also placed great emphasis on the failure of power-sharing democracy in two of its major examples—Cyprus and Lebanon—as well as the British government's lack of success in its efforts to solve the Northern Ireland problem by power sharing.

Power-sharing theorists respond that the theory does not claim that power sharing will be successful in every case. In fact, they have tried to refine and strengthen power-sharing theory by defining the conditions in which power sharing is more or less likely to be instituted and maintained. The two most important favorable conditions are the absence of a majority group—majority groups understandably prefer majoritarian to power-sharing solutions—and the absence of large socioeconomic inequalities among the groups. Both of these factors have been major obstacles to power sharing in Cyprus and Northern Ireland, particularly the presence of strong and uncompromising majorities—an almost 80 percent Greek Cypriot majority and a two-thirds Irish Protestant majority, respectively. Other favorable conditions are as follows: the groups do not differ greatly in size, the country has a relatively small population, internal unity is strengthened by external dangers, countrywide loyalties counteract ethnic loyalties, and traditions of compromise and consensus already exist when power sharing is instituted.

The collapse of the Lebanese power-sharing system in 1975 presents a special problem for power-sharing theory because most of the favorable conditions were present in this case. It should be pointed out, first, however, that several of the background conditions were not favorable in Lebanon: foreign threats reinforced rather than weakened internal divisions, there were substantial socioeconomic inequalities among the Christian and Muslim sects, and the country was fragmented into a relatively large number of sects. Second, the outbreak of the civil war in 1975 should not obscure the fact that power sharing worked quite well in this severely divided country from 1943 to 1975. Third, a major part of the blame for the collapse of power sharing belongs not to internal problems caused by the power-sharing system itself but to Lebanon's precarious position in the international arena of the Middle East and, in particular, to repeated Palestinian, Syrian, and Israeli interventions. In this sense, the civil war that broke out in 1975 was not an ordinary civil war but an international conflict fought on Lebanese soil. Finally, it must be admitted that Lebanon's power-sharing system had some weak spots. The fixed 6:5 ratio for parliamentary elections continued to give the Christian sects the majority of the seats despite the fact that the Muslims gradually had become the majority of the population. Furthermore, the most powerful political office, the presidency, was permanently assigned to the Maronite Christians. But the Lebanese themselves have recognized these problems and have tried to solve them. The 1989 Taif Accord changed the 6:5 ratio to equal parliamentary representation for Christians and Muslims, and it also roughly equalized the powers of the Maronite president and the Sunni Muslim prime minister.

The most important lesson of the Lebanese case is that power sharing needed to be repaired and improved rather than replaced. In the eyes of most Lebanese and knowledgeable foreign observers, a switch to a majoritarian form of democracy has not been regarded as a realistic option. It is even more significant that the same conclusion applies to Cyprus, where, admittedly, power sharing never worked well. Instituted in 1960, it was ended by the 1963 civil war, and it appeared to be permanently doomed by the Turkish invasion in 1974 and the subsequent de facto partition of the island into a Greek Cypriot southern state and a Turkish Cypriot northern state. Nevertheless, since 1985 Javier Pérez de Cuéllar, then UN secretary general, and his successor, Boutros Boutros-Ghali, have made several proposals for a unified Cyprus that strikingly resemble the basic power-sharing features of the 1960 constitution. Their efforts demonstrate their recognition of the fact that power sharing, although it may not succeed, represents the optimal chance for a successful solution. Similarly, the British government's failure to have its power-sharing proposals accepted in Northern Ireland has not budged it from its basic conviction that power sharing is the only possible and acceptable solution there.

One weakness the critics of power sharing have focused on is its alleged tendency to immobilism and deadlock. In particular, executive power sharing and the minority veto are seen as threats to effective decision making; majority rule appears to be much more decisive and efficient. Short-term efficiency under majority rule, however, is likely to cause antagonism and frustration on the part of the losing groups. In the long run, tensions and instability result. Conversely, the slower operation of power sharing in the short run is more likely to be effective over time.

The other characteristics of power sharing also appear to have negative consequences. If proportionality, in addition to individual merit, is a standard for appointment to the civil service, some administrative inefficiency may result. And group autonomy may require an increase in the number of governmental units and the duplication of schools and other facilities to serve the different groups, both of which may entail additional costs. These, however, are relatively minor problems rather than system-threatening ones. They are offset by other aspects of the same rules: proportionality is a valuable time-saving formula for allocating resources and appointments, and group autonomy distributes the total decision-making load among several bodies and hence alleviates the burdens on each of them.

Ethnic Group Cohesion
Under Power Sharing

Another alleged weakness of power sharing is that it strengthens rather than weakens the cohesion and distinctiveness of ethnic groups. By explicitly recognizing the legitimacy of these groups, by giving group organizations a vital function in the political system, by subsidizing them on a proportional basis, and by encouraging ethnic parties through the use of proportional representation, power-sharing democracy undoubtedly increases the organizational strength of ethnic groups. The existence of strong and autonomous ethnic groups, however, does not necessarily translate into serious conflict among them. Under power sharing, the strengthened ethnic groups are designed to play a constructive role in conflict resolution.

A variant of this criticism is that power sharing, by recognizing particular groups as the constituent units of the political system, rigidifies ethnic differences that may be fluid and changing and discriminates against groups that otherwise might have formed by splits and mergers. This criticism is to some extent valid. Many power-

sharing systems, notably those of Belgium, Lebanon, and Cyprus, have been based on formally predetermined groups. For instance, the Belgian constitution explicitly names Dutch speakers and French speakers (and, for some purposes, the small group of German speakers) as the officially recognized communities that make up the Belgian political system. On the other hand, power-sharing systems based on broad coalitions of communal parties, as in Malaysia, Colombia, Austria, and the Netherlands, have been much more flexible.

Power sharing does not require the predetermination of specific groups. In fact, for any group that wishes to make use of it, there are major advantages to allowing the groups to be self-determined by such means as proportional representation (which does not rigidify ethnic groups or discriminate in favor of or against any groups) and Estonian-style cultural autonomy.

Because power sharing has been studied more extensively in the European cases and by European scholars, it is sometimes alleged to be a European or Western model that is foreign and unsuitable for multiethnic societies in other parts of the world. This criticism is clearly erroneous because it ignores such major examples as Lebanon, Malaysia, and Colombia, where power sharing was developed by indigenous leaders without external influence or assistance. It is also worth pointing out that Lewis, the first power-sharing theorist, was not a European or a student of European politics but a native of the Caribbean island of St. Lucia, a black scholar whose interest was in African politics. Finally, Lewis and numerous other non-Western scholars and political leaders have emphasized that majority rule violates their native traditions of trying to arrive at consensus through lengthy deliberations—traditions that correspond closely to the power-sharing idea.

The Democratic Nature of Power Sharing

As serious as the criticism that power sharing cannot work well is the charge that it is not sufficiently democratic. This charge is based on the importance of compromises negotiated, often behind closed doors, by the leaders of the various groups in power-sharing systems. Moreover, power-sharing systems often use list forms of proportional representation, in which party leaders have a great deal of influence on the composition of the lists and hence on who can get elected. These observations are not wrong, but it is wrong to imply a stark contrast with majority-rule democracy.

For instance, in the United Kingdom, the flagship of majoritarian democracy, all important decisions are typically prepared by bureaucrats, adopted in the cabinet in complete secrecy, and, after being announced, hardly ever changed under parliamentary or public pressure. And, in spite of Britain's plurality electoral system, party leaders have usually been able to reserve safe seats for themselves and to oppose the nomination of undesirable candidates by constituency organizations. Elite domination does not vary a great deal among democracies. The difference between majority rule and power sharing is not whether leaders do or do not predominate but whether they tend to be competitive or cooperative.

Opponents of proportional representation concentrate their criticism on its tendency to encourage multiparty systems and multiparty coalition governments, which allegedly make government less decisive and effective. Friends and foes of proportional representation largely agree that, purely in terms of the quality of democratic representation, proportional representation is superior to majoritarian election systems. Finally, the criticism of insufficient democracy is difficult to maintain when one looks at actual cases. Switzerland, Belgium, and the Netherlands, for instance, are usually and correctly considered to be not just unambiguously democratic but among the most decent and humane of the world's democracies.

The three theories that argue that majoritarian democracy can deal more effectively with the problem of ethnic divisions than power sharing are the theories of cross-cutting cleavages, vote pooling, and majority control.

Cross-Cutting Cleavages

The theory of cross-cutting cleavages is the leading interpretation of how democracy in the multiethnic United States works. It has found its clearest articulation in the work of Seymour Martin Lipset, especially in his classic 1960 volume, *Political Man.*

Lipset's theoretical point of departure is the notion that in any society, but especially in divided societies, political moderation and tolerance, and hence the chances for stable democracy, are enhanced if individuals have cross-cutting affiliations to a variety of groups that pull them in different directions. If, on the other hand, a person's affiliations are to groups with the same outlook and/or within the same ethnic or cultural community, they are mutually reinforcing and are likely to lead to intolerance and hostility.

If cross-cutting loyalties moderate voters' politics, as voting behavior studies imply, two-party systems, majoritarian elections in single-member districts, and federalism may be preferable to, respectively, multiparty systems, proportional representation, and unitary government. Both parties in a two-party system will seek to win majorities of the voters; this objective forces them to try to appeal to a variety of groups, which in turn forces them to be moderate. On the other hand, the many smaller parties in multiparty systems have a stronger incentive to seek support from a limited base and to target their appeals narrowly to this base; this aim rewards immoderate rather than moderate positions and promises. Consequently, in a multiethnic society with a large number of ethnic minorities, a two-party system entails moderate competition between two large multiethnic parties, whereas a multiparty system is likely to be characterized by more extreme confrontation among many ethnically exclusive parties.

Lipset's preference for majoritarian electoral systems rests on their discrimination against small parties and their consequent tendency to encourage two-party systems, in contrast with the tendency of proportional representation to allow and encourage a multiparty system. Federalism has the advantage of enhancing the cross-cutting of cleavages by adding regional divisions to ethnic and other divisions. But Lipset adds the crucial qualification that such beneficial cross-cutting occurs only when federal boundaries cut across ethnic boundaries. When federal and ethnic boundaries tend to coincide, federalism becomes a disadvantage, as in the cases of India and Canada.

Criticisms of Cross-Cutting Theory

Just as power-sharing theory has been criticized mainly by majoritarians, the cross-cutting cleavage approach has been criticized by power-sharing theorists. The latter have argued that, although plurality elections entail strong pressures toward a two-party system, these pressures work only imperfectly in multiethnic societies. The reason is that ethnic loyalties are usually strong and that ethnically motivated voters will often vote for small ethnic parties despite the low probability that these parties will be elected or, if elected, will be able to exert much influence. Plurality elections have usually yielded a three-party or four-party system in Canada, a multiparty system (with one dominant party) in India, and a multiparty system in Nigeria (except in the 1993 elections, when the military government imposed a strict

two-party system). Even in the mainly two-party British Parliament elected by plurality, Scottish, Welsh, and various Northern Irish ethnic parties have almost always been represented, albeit in small numbers.

A more serious criticism of the cross-cutting approach, forcefully articulated by Lewis, is that even when plurality elections do lead to two-party systems, or at least to limited multiparty or dominant-party systems in which one party is likely to win election victories, such an outcome is undesirable. Again because of the rigidity of voters' loyalties in ethnically divided societies, such a system lacks the floating vote that makes alternation in exercising governmental power possible. Winning parties are likely to be permanent winners—which, Lewis argues, is both undemocratic and destabilizing.

Dominant-party systems are undemocratic because the primary meaning of democracy is participation in decision making, either directly or through elected representatives, and the permanent exclusion of the losing minority or minorities violates this fundamental principle. Moreover, permanent majorities are dangerous because minorities that are permanently excluded from power feel discriminated against and tend to lose their allegiance to the regime. This danger is especially serious when the winning party represents not a coalition of ethnic groups but one ethnic group, as was the case in Northern Ireland for many decades. Of course, proportional representation cannot reduce a popular majority to a parliamentary minority either—this is one reason why the power-sharing approach does not rely exclusively on proportional representation—but it gives at least some encouragement for a majority ethnic party to split into two or more parties along intraethnic dividing lines.

A further criticism of the cross-cutting approach is that it favors incentives toward political moderation at the expense of allowing voters to elect representatives belonging to their own ethnic group. More important, this approach ignores the potential for moderation that multiparty systems consisting of several ethnic parties can have for a different reason: having its own representative in government can give a group a sense of security that limits antagonism between ethnic factions.

The historical evidence concerning the adoption of proportional representation in Western Europe about 1900 and in the early decades of the twentieth century shows that one of the main motivations for this change was to ameliorate linguistic and religious tensions. The previous majoritarian systems had proved unable to foster the kind of moderation that the theory of crosscutting cleavages credits them with.

The evidence of the use of federalism in multiethnic countries demonstrates that the goal of creating autonomy for ethnic groups by drawing federal boundaries that coincide with ethnic dividing lines has won out over the idea of fostering moderation by designing cross-cutting federal arrangements. In addition to the examples of India and Canada, the Nigerian case is instructive. The government started out in 1960 as a three-unit federation with heterogeneous units, but it has gradually increased this number to about thirty states that have a much higher degree of ethnic homogeneity. Belgium has found its unitary system of government, established upon independence in 1831, incapable of managing interethnic tensions. It moved via a strongly decentralized but still formally unitary system in 1970 to a fully federal system in 1993—maximizing autonomy for the ethnic groups and minimizing the cross-cutting of federal and ethnic boundaries. And in the universally admired Swiss federal system, most of the cantons are monolingual and cross-cutting is limited to a handful of linguistically more heterogeneous cantons.

Vote Pooling

The vote-pooling approach was launched by Donald L. Horowitz in his influential book *Ethnic Groups in Conflict* (1985). It was elaborated further in his 1991 book on South Africa, which contained detailed proposals for the structure of a democratic system there. Horowitz uses the term *vote pooling* specifically for the kind of electoral system he advocates, but the expression can be used aptly and conveniently for his entire set of proposals. Although he agrees with Lewis's critique of plurality elections in multiethnic societies, he disagrees with Lewis's preferred alternative of proportional representation and broad power-sharing cabinets. Horowitz argues that the formation of a power-sharing coalition by seat pooling (the pooling of parliamentary seats in order to build majority, or larger than majority, support for a cabinet) does not necessarily produce compromise. If compromise is to be achieved, there must be additional incentives for it; without such incentives, coalitions will quickly fall apart. Incentives for vote pooling can be interpreted as refinements of the cross-cutting cleavage approach.

The two major examples of electoral systems that can foster moderation by vote pooling are the special vote distribution requirement used in the Second Nigerian Republic (1979–1983) for presidential elections and the alternative vote used in Sri Lanka and a few other countries. The Nigerian system required the winning candidate to obtain not only the largest number of votes nationwide but also at least 25 percent of the vote in no less than two-thirds of the nineteen states. The second requirement made it impossible for a candidate to be elected by the ethnic groups of one major area of the country. All candidates were forced to appeal widely to different ethnic groups and different parts of the country.

In alternative vote systems, voters are asked to rank order the candidates. If a candidate receives an absolute majority of first preferences, he or she is elected; if not, the weakest candidate is eliminated, and the ballots with that candidate as first preference are redistributed according to second preferences. This process continues until one of the candidates has reached a majority of the votes. For instance, if there are three candidates who receive 45, 40, and 15 percent of the first preferences, the third candidate is eliminated and the 15 percent of the ballots with the third candidate as first preference will be redistributed according to second preferences. In this hypothetical situation, the two major candidates will have to bid for the second preferences of the third candidate's supporters in order to win—which, according to Horowitz, has the major advantage of rewarding moderation.

Horowitz advocates a presidential system of government with the proviso that the president be elected by the alternative vote. The main reason for this proposal is that it provides another chance for vote pooling to be applied. In contrast, power-sharing theory sees presidentialism as inherently majoritarian and prefers the collegial executives that cabinets in parliamentary systems can provide. Moreover, while the alternative vote is an unusual voting system, it is clearly a majoritarian system; in fact, any method for the election of one top officeholder must logically be a majoritarian method.

Like the cross-cutting cleavage advocates, Horowitz favors heterogeneous federal units. But the federal boundaries must be drawn in such a way that large ethnic groups are divided over several states in order to reduce their political power compared with that of smaller ethnic groups. He therefore approvingly cites the Nigerian example of creating a large number of states. Increasing the number of states also entails increasing the homogeneity of these states.

Criticisms of Vote-Pooling Theory

Vote-pooling theory can be criticized, first, for disregarding the incentives for compromise that are inherent in the process of coalition building. There are indeed many examples of multiethnic coalitions that have fallen apart, but also there are many contrary examples of broad coalitions that have worked effectively, as in most of the major cases of power sharing. Coalescence and compromise are analytically distinct, but the desire to coalesce implies a need to compromise: if parties are interested in gaining power (which is a basic assumption in political science), they will, in multiparty situations, want to enter and remain in coalition cabinets. To do so, they must reach compromises with their coalition partners.

A problem with the distribution rule is that it may fail to produce any winner. The very first application of the method, in the 1979 presidential election in Nigeria, provides a telling example: the nationwide plurality winner gained a minimum of 25 percent support in twelve of the nineteen states—falling just short of the two-thirds of the states needed. (However, the electoral commission expediently decided that he had come close enough to be declared duly elected.)

The weakness of the alternative vote as a moderation-inducing mechanism is that bidding for the second preferences of other ethnic groups is likely to decrease the number of first preferences from the candidate's own group. The only two examples of the use of the alternative vote in an ethnically divided society—in Sri Lanka's 1982 and 1988 presidential elections—yielded victories on the basis of first preferences, and therefore they do not lend empirical support to Horowitz's proposal.

There is also some doubt that the incentives for moderation inherent in the alternative vote are much greater than incentives in other majoritarian systems. For instance, if the plurality method were used in the hypothetical situation of three candidates with 45, 40, and 15 percent support, respectively, many of the weakest candidate's supporters would not want to waste their votes on a hopeless candidacy, or the candidate might decide to drop out of the race. The two major candidates would have to appeal to the third candidate's supporters in order to win. If there is a difference between plurality and the alternative vote with regard to the inducement of moderation, it is a difference only of degree.

The alternative vote resembles the third principal majoritarian electoral method, the majority runoff, even more closely. As in plurality, the voters cast their ballots for one candidate only. If no candidate wins an absolute majority of the votes, a runoff election is held between the top two candidates. In the hypothetical example mentioned above, the third candidate is eliminated in the first round, and the two major candidates have to compete for the votes of the third candidate's supporters in the runoff. The alternative vote merely accomplishes in one round of voting what requires two ballots in the majority-runoff system. The incentives for moderation do not differ much. The introduction of proportional representation in Western Europe gives rise to doubt about the merits of the alternative vote: most of the failed majoritarian election systems were majority-runoff systems.

Control Theory

Ian Lustick formulated his control model as an alternative to the power-sharing model. His main point is that power sharing is not the only method for achieving civil peace and political stability in ethnically divided societies. Control entails an asymmetrical relationship in which the superior power of one group is used to impose stability by constraining other groups. Lustick concedes that control is not an attractive alternative to power sharing, but it is preferable to civil war, extermination, and deportation. Control usually entails a political system that is not democratic and hence cannot be a model for multiethnic democracy.

The only exception is the case of a majority group that controls one or more minority groups in a majoritarian democracy. A clear example is Northern Ireland, where Protestant majority control was relatively successful in preserving both peace and democratic institutions from the 1920s to the 1960s. This example also shows the two major drawbacks of majority control: the "peace" and "democracy" that it can achieve are both questionable. Majority control in Northern Ireland meant the permanent exclusion from power of Roman Catholics and widespread discrimination against them. Majority control therefore spells majority dictatorship rather than majoritarian democracy. Moreover, while majority control may endure in the short and medium run, in the long run it tends to cause much frustration on the part of the excluded minority. Northern Ireland's four decades of civil peace turned into civil war in the late 1960s.

Lustick's control model, however, can serve as a useful refinement of the power-sharing model. Perfect power sharing means completely equal influence (when the groups are equal in size) or proportional influence (when the groups are unequal) in decision making. In practice, the groups' relative powers are usually not perfectly equal or proportional.

Perfect power sharing and perfect majority control can therefore be seen as opposite ends of a continuum. For instance, Malaysian multiethnic democracy—which is based on broad interethnic power sharing but with a predominant and disproportionately strong Malay share of power—can be placed on this continuum at a spot that is some distance removed from perfect power sharing but still considerably closer to the power-sharing end than to the majority-control end of the continuum.

Abstract Models and Concrete Cases

The example of Malaysia shows that concrete cases do not always fit perfectly with abstract models. In fact, Malaysia can also be used to exemplify vote pooling since the nomination by the National Front of one joint candidate in each single-member district means that this candidate must seek voter support across ethnic divisions. The same can be said of just about all the cases mentioned in this article. Even the United States does not fit the cross-cutting model perfectly: the drawing of election districts in such a way as to virtually to guarantee the election of ethnic and racial minority representatives, as well as affirmative action in civil appointments and college admissions, clearly follows the power-sharing principle of proportionality.

Similar mixes of cross-cutting and power sharing may be used in the design of democratic constitutions for multiethnic countries. For countries with relatively shallow and fluid ethnic cleavages, such as the immigrant multiethnic society of the United States, the mixture may be weighted toward cross-cutting. For the most deeply divided societies, however, power sharing must be the main component of the democratic prescription.

See also Federalism; Majority rule, minority rights; Mill, John Stuart; Pragmatism; Theory, Postwar Anglo-American.

AREND LIJPHART

BIBLIOGRAPHY

Daalder, Hans. "The Consociational Democracy Theme." *World Politics* 26 (July 1974): 604–621.

Dix, Robert H. "Consociational Democracy: The Case of Colombia." *Comparative Politics* 12 (April 1980): 303–321.

Hanf, Theodor, Heribert Weiland, and Gerda Vierdag. *South Africa: The Prospects of Peaceful Change.* London: Rex Collings, 1981.

Horowitz, Donald L. *A Democratic South Africa? Constitutional Engineering in a Divided Society.* Berkeley: University of California Press, 1991.

_____. *Ethnic Groups in Conflict.* Berkeley: University of California Press, 1985.

Lehmbruch, Gerhard. *Proporzdemokratie: Politisches System und politische Kultur in der Schweiz und in Österreich.* Tübingen: Mohr, 1967.

Lewis, W. Arthur. *Politics in West Africa.* London: Allen and Unwin, 1965.

Lijphart, Arend. *Democracy in Plural Societies: A Comparative Exploration.* New Haven and London: Yale University Press, 1977.

Lipset, Seymour Martin. *Political Man: The Social Bases of Politics.* Expanded and updated ed. Baltimore: Johns Hopkins University Press, 1981; Aldershot: Gower, 1983.

Lustick, Ian. "Stability in Deeply Divided Societies: Consociationalism versus Control." *World Politics* 31 (April 1979): 325–344.

McRae, Kenneth D., ed. *Consociational Democracy: Political Accommodation in Segmented Societies.* Toronto: McClelland and Stewart, 1974.

Messarra, Antoine Nasri. *Le modèle politique libanais et sa survie: Essai sur la classification et l'aménagement d'un système consociatif.* Beirut: Librairie Orientale, 1983.

Montville, Joseph V., ed. *Conflict and Peacemaking in Multiethnic Societies.* Lexington, Mass.: Lexington Books, 1990.

Orenstein, Mitchell A. *Out of the Red: Building Capitalism and Democracy in Postcommunist Europe.* Ann Arbor: University of Michigan, 2001.

Steiner, Jürg. *Amicable Agreement versus Majority Rule: Conflict Resolution in Switzerland.* Chapel Hill: University of North Carolina Press, 1974.

Von Vorys, Karl. *Democracy without Consensus: Communalism and Political Stability in Malaysia.* Princeton: Princeton University Press, 1975.

✦ Democracy, Participatory

Participatory democracy has also been called direct or pure or strong democracy. It can be understood in two ways: as a variation on the democratic form of regime or as the essential form. Democracy, which means government by the people (the *demos* in classical Athens), refers to popular rule (or popular sovereignty) in a broad and general sense. Participatory democracy, however, denotes the form in which the people literally rule themselves, directly and participatorily, day in and day out, in all matters that affect them in their common lives.

All democracy is of course to some degree participatory. Even minimally democratic governments are rooted in an act of original consent—a popularly ratified social contract or constitution, for example—and in periodic popular elections. To its advocates, however, participatory democracy involves extensive and active engagement of citizens in the self-governing process; it means government not just for but by and of the people. From this perspective, direct or participatory democracy is democracy itself, properly understood.

Representative Versus Participatory Democracy

The distinctiveness of participatory democracy can be seen clearly in the contrast with representative democracy. In representative systems, popular sovereignty—once it has been manifested in a founding document, a constitution, and a set of working political institutions—is delegated to chosen representatives who do the actual work of government. These representatives remain accountable to the people through elections; the people retain their sovereignty only in a passive or potential sense. Representative democracy thus relegates citizens to the role of watchdogs, and democracy comes to mean periodic legitimation of representative governors through elections. From the point of view of participatory democrats, representative democracy is weak or thin democracy. In the words of Robert Michels, the German sociologist and economist, liberty disappears with the ballot into the polling box.

Historically, the earliest forms of democracy—in ancient Athens or the town republics of early modern Europe or the Alpine communes of the Helvetic confederation (Switzerland), for example—were participatory. Representation came later, as the scale of society increased. In Athens in the fifth century B.C. the entire body of citizens met every seven to ten days in assembly to deliberate and pass laws, regulate trade, and make war and peace. Citizens sat on large juries of 500 to 1,000 or more to adjudicate legal and policy disputes. Citizens, selected by lot, also occupied nearly one-half of the public magistracies on a regular basis. In the classical scheme of classifying regimes (in the manner of Polybius, Aristotle, and Cicero, for example), democracy meant participatory democracy, rule by the many in contrast with aristocracy (literally "rule by the best") and monarchy (the rule of one). In the same way that monarchy's corrupt form was tyranny and aristocracy's corrupt form was oligarchy (rule by the few), so democracy's corrupt form was ochlocracy, or rule by the mob. Aristocratic critics of democracy argued that democracy was always likely to be corrupt—that democracy and mob rule were identical.

In the ancient world, participatory democracy required the participation of every citizen, but not everyone was a citizen. In Athens only those qualified by birth and talent (civic virtue or excellence) could participate: only Athenian-born males—who made up approximately one-fifth of the total population of men, women, resident foreigners, and slaves—qualified as citizens. Aristotle regarded women and non-Greeks ("barbarians") as unfit for self-rule and suggested that, slaves by nature, they were perpetually unfit to be citizens. Many later participatory democracies, including the Swiss Confederation and the American Republic in its first century and a half, limited citizenship to males. One of the great ironies of Western political history is that as democracies became more inclusive they became less participatory. The ancients permitted only a few to be citizens but asked much of them, while the moderns extend citizenship to everyone but ask almost nothing of them.

This irony arises in part from the fact that robust participation is possible only in small states with limited, but virtuous, citizen bodies of the kind found in the town governments and rustic republics of the Swiss, the Dutch, the Italians, and the Germans. In the eighteenth century the French philosopher Montesquieu believed that democracy was appropriate only to very small political entities, while empire was appropriate for large ones. This belief was widely shared throughout the eighteenth century. Indeed, the American Founders understood their challenge to be how to devise a form of democracy that could function in a compound and extended republic of potentially continental proportions. The device of representation was introduced in part to salvage the idea of democracy in polities too large to afford regular participation by all citizens and too diversified, heterogeneous, and commercial to support classical civic virtue in the entire citizen body. Popular accountability was maintained through elections nominally open to all (in reality, only to propertied males). But the actual tasks of government were delegated to elected officials who were (in John Locke's term) fiduciary representatives, entrusted to rule on behalf of the sovereign people.

Representative government was in part intended to preserve the spirit of democracy in large-scale societies where the cumbersome institutions of participatory democracy could no longer function. But it also reflected a certain anti-democratic impulse in that it provided a remedy to the excesses of popular government, which many eighteenth-century constitution makers distrusted. In the new American Republic there were those, especially among the Federalists, who disdained ancient democratic republics as sources of contention and petty jealousy. American Founders such as James Madison and Alexander Hamilton believed that representation was a filter by which prudent government might be screened from popular prejudices and demagogic individuals. Civic virtue was not a property of everyman and everywoman, but elections, especially indirect elections, might put those who were virtuous in office. To a considerable extent, this distrust of direct, or pure, democracy has been retained by modern social scientists who express suspicion of too much direct democracy. Samuel Huntington, for example, has suggested that an overactive populace can create a democratic overload that paralyzes a representative democracy.

Modern Accommodations

Given the larger scale of modern societies, participatory democracy as a political reality has in any case been reserved mostly to local and municipal government. The Swiss-born philosopher Jean-Jacques Rousseau observed in the eighteenth century that for a people to discover or forge a common will (the general will) they had to share common customs, simple beliefs, and local institutions. Participatory democracy worked best on a modest scale where institutions like the town meeting or the cantonal or state initiative and referendum could facilitate consensus and common willing in a face-to-face society.

Arguments about scale, however, have been challenged in recent decades. In many Western democracies, cynicism about the professional ruling classes has given a new appeal to referendums and to such antigovernmental devices as term limits for elected officials and recall mechanisms for corrupt representatives. Moreover, new telecommunications technologies have offered the possibility of interaction among widely dispersed citizens across space and time in a fashion that encourages new experiments with participation. Aristotle had argued that the ideal republic was small enough that a man could walk across it in a single day, thus ensuring regular participation in the assembly by all citizens. Interactive telecommunications technologies, which in effect permit the hundreds of millions of citizens of a mass society to be in touch without leaving their television screens, raise the possibility of "teledemocracy" and "virtual communities." These new forms look far more participatory (if also potentially more demagogic) than older representative models. Experiments in deliberative teledemocracy currently are under way in which citizens participate in debates and vote on several readings of a bill before reaching a final decision.

At the same time that technology has enhanced the feasibility of new forms of participation, communitarian political theory emphasizing obligation and responsibility rather than personal liberty and rights has asserted the desirability of more participatory forms of democracy. Communitarians use both the language of civic virtue of the ancients and the new rhetoric of community and national service to argue for a more vigorous form of democracy. Critics of communitarianism fear that too much emphasis on participation and community, especially when reinforced by new interactive technologies, increases democratic overload and imperils individual liberty. From Alexis de Tocqueville to Robert Nozick, liberals have worried that excessive participation will lower the level of rationality in politics and nurture majoritarian tyranny and a disregard for the rights of private persons and private property. Now, as in ancient times, critics of pure democracy see in it merely a rationalization of demagoguery and mob rule: the government of opinion and prejudice.

Education for Deliberative Government

Proponents of participatory democracy sometimes dismiss their liberal critics as privileged defenders of property who attack democracy because it undermines their hegemony. Yet they also acknowledge the powerful liberal line of criticism that worries about majority tyranny. Their response is to defend not mob rule but the distinction between it and deliberative democracy. Direct democracy requires not simply participation but the civic skills and civic virtues necessary for effective participatory deliberation and decision making. Participatory democracy is thus understood as direct government by a well-educated citizenry. Citizens are not simply private individuals operating in the civil sphere but informed public citizens as distanced from their wholly private selves as the public is from the private sphere. Democracy is less the government of the people or the masses than the government of educated citizens.

From Thomas Jefferson's time in the early days of the American Republic to our own, an enthusiasm for participatory democracy has thus been coupled with a zeal for public and civic education: the training of competent and responsible citizens. With Jefferson, participatory democrats enjoin those anxious about the indiscriminate public abuse of power not to take away the public's power but to inform the public's discretion. Democracy demands a public well educated in the liberal arts, which also are the arts of liberty. Jefferson, like his Massachusetts colleague John Adams, saw education as indispensable to democracy and showed more pride in his role as father of the University of Virginia than in his role as the two-term third president of the United States—having the former office but not the latter inscribed on his tombstone.

The argument today for participatory, or strong, democracy, consistent with Jefferson, is thus an argument for civic education as well as for participation, for the cultivation of civic virtue as well as for the nurturing of popular sovereignty, and for an emphasis on community responsibility as well as for a focus on individual engagement. The debate among advocates and critics continues to be about the nature of the deliberative process (can average men and women be educated to be as prudent and deliberative as experienced representatives?), the character of civic education (will civics courses, community and national service, or direct political engagement successfully train individuals for responsible citizenship?), and the attributes required by diligent citizens (should public citizens merely give public expression to their private interests, or do they need to develop new public ways of thinking about policy—"we" thinking rather than "me" thinking?).

Theoretical Bases

The political philosophy of participatory democracy has roots in the early modern theorists who extrapolated a defense of democracy from the practices of the ancient Greeks. Rousseau is perhaps the authoritative source, although elements of his theory can be found in the writings of the sixteenth-century Florentine political philosopher Niccolò Machiavelli and in Montesquieu. In his *Social Contract* (1762), Rousseau argues that a communal authority can be legitimate only when it leaves individuals who obey it as free as they were before. Direct democracy affords individuals the opportunity to participate in making the laws they must obey, thus guaranteeing that in obeying the law they will obey only themselves. Freedom to do anything at all is a kind of license, Rousseau concludes, while obedience to a law we prescribe to ourselves is true freedom.

Immanuel Kant, the eighteenth-century German philosopher, and other modern advocates of positive liberty concur with Rousseau in seeing in liberty a positive power for action rather than a negative liberty from interference. Negative liberty turns out to be incompatible with active government and underlies liberal political philosophies that distrust all government. Positive liberty is in harmony with democratically enacted laws and thus is compatible with a more forceful understanding of a democratic welfare state or a democratic socialist society. While negative liberty is associated with theories of limited government and representative democracy, positive liberty is associated with participatory democracy. Only laws we make for ourselves leave us with freedom. Democracy requires self-legislation: for Rousseau, it must be participatory.

Although Jefferson was not a theorist, the author of the Declaration of Independence and the Virginia Statute on Religious Freedom (as well as president of the United States) was in many ways America's founding participatory democrat. He argued on behalf of the involvement of citizens in every aspect of their local affairs and suggested that ward government in which all citizens might participate regularly could alone secure American democracy. Not among those who feared the people (as he boasted), he insisted that only popular participation could prevent government from becoming tyrannical. To critics who preferred to insulate the people from government through representative institutions, Jefferson replied that it was absurd to think that citizens who could not even be trusted to govern themselves might somehow be trusted to govern others.

In the late nineteenth and early twentieth centuries American Progressive and Populist politicians and pragmatic philosophers argued the virtues of participatory democracy. John Dewey, the American philosopher and educator, saw in democracy not merely a form of government but a way of life; he was convinced that only participating citizens could make free government function. The debate continues today, with many social scientists and professional politicians still distrustful of what they think of as too much democracy. Participatory and strong democrats prefer to think that real democracy has never been tried and that the demagogic excesses visible in today's political arena are precisely the consequence of the professionalization of politics and the exclusion of an alienated public from any real civic responsibility.

As in ancient Greece, the real question remains whether a regime that is not genuinely participatory can be regarded as a democracy at all, or whether democracy, to be safe, must be coupled with limited government and the indirect popular accountability of representative government. Because democracy is in part the debate about what democracy is, this argument can be expected to continue as long as citizens argue about how they best can rule themselves.

See also Communitarianism; Popular sovereignty; Representation; Theory, Ancient; Democracy, Types of; Virtue, Civic.

BENJAMIN R. BARBER

BIBLIOGRAPHY

Arendt, Hannah. *The Human Condition.* Chicago: University of Chicago Press, 1958.

Barber, Benjamin R. *Strong Democracy: Participatory Politics for a New Age.* Berkeley: University of California Press, 1984.

Cronin, Thomas E. *Direct Democracy: The Politics of Initiative, Referendum, and Recall.* Cambridge, Mass., and London: Harvard University Press, 1989.

Dewey, John. *The Public and Its Problems.* Chicago: Swallow Press, 1954.

Fishkin, James S. *Democracy and Deliberation: New Directions for Democratic Reform.* New Haven and London: Yale University Press, 1991.

Mansbridge, Jane J. *Beyond Adversary Democracy.* New York: Basic Books, 1980.

Matthews, Richard K. *The Radical Politics of Thomas Jefferson: A Revisionist View.* Lawrence: University Press of Kansas, 1984.

Pateman, Carole. *Participation and Democratic Theory.* Cambridge: Cambridge University Press, 1970.

Rousseau, Jean-Jacques. *The Social Contract.* Harmondsworth, England: Penguin Books, 1968.

Tocqueville, Alexis de. *Democracy in America.* Edited by J. P. Mayer. Translated by George Lawrence. Garden City, N.Y.: Anchor, 1969.

Warren, Mark E. *Democracy and Association.* Princeton: Princeton University Press, 2000

✦ Democracy, Social

An egalitarian politics that includes a strong commitment to the modern welfare state and to the redistributive function of the state. Social democrats affirm the classic liberal principles associated with representative democracy and the mixed economy, embrace political reformism (as opposed to the revolutionary tradition stemming from Karl Marx), and give allegiance to the moral ideal of social justice. Although it is impossible to situate social democracy on the liberal-socialist continuum with any precision, it is located roughly to the left of liberalism and to the right of socialism.

It is considerably easier, however, to define social democracy in relation to more extreme political alternatives—for example, libertarian liberalism and Marxist socialism. Whereas libertarians uphold an uncompromising vision of the rights of individuals to resist the welfare state in its aspirations to redistribute wealth, social democrats emphasize notions of social responsibility and the duty of the state to aid less privileged members of the community. Social democrats see the power of the state as a legitimate agent of these collective responsibilities.

On the other side of the spectrum, Marxists hold that capitalism must be overthrown, whereas social democrats look to find the solution to social ills within the free market economy (suitably modified). One might say that Marxism seeks to "economize" the idea of social justice, that is, to identify the moral claims of disadvantaged social classes with the advance of a fully rational (post-capitalist) economy. Social democracy, on the other hand, seeks to "remoralize" political economy, that is, to phrase the question of social justice as a problem of morality rather than one of economics.

Evolution of the Movement

Social democracy arose at the beginning of the twentieth century, when Eduard Bernstein, a German Marxist, presented his version of socialism. Bernstein acknowledged that Marx's predictions—presumed to be scientific—of the demise of capitalism and the consequent triumph of working-class revolutionism were little more than false prophecies. This acknowledgement of Marxism's spurious promise gave rise to Bernstein's revisionist socialism, which emphasized a parliamentary and reformist pursuit of socialist aims. A comparable political development, begetting

social democracy as a middle position between socialism and liberalism, took place in Britain in the late nineteenth and early twentieth centuries through the vehicle of the Fabian movement. (Beatrice and Sidney Webb, Graham Wallas, George Bernard Shaw, and H. G. Wells were notable Fabians.) This Fabian revisionist-socialist tradition in Britain extends to C. A. R. Crosland's book *The Future of Socialism* (1956).

Viewing social democracy historically as a process of political accommodation with capitalism, or with the quasi-capitalist mixed economy, an unchastened Marxist no doubt would object that socialism is watered-down Marxism and social democracy is watered-down socialism—a double dilution. To address such a challenge, with its implicit charge that social democracy retains no theoretical integrity of its own, but simply defines itself by its half-heartedness in relation to the social ideals from which it borrows its real substance, it might be helpful to put aside the question of the historical genesis of the social democratic movement and of its century-long course of development (a development that in practice shades off into welfarist liberalism). Let us inquire instead at the level of principles, asking whether social democracy does indeed name a coherent set of ideas possessing a moral core with its own distinctive identity.

Justifications

The basic rationale underlying any version of socialism or social democracy is that it is offensive for certain members of society to earn incomes that are grossly out of relation to their real contribution to the welfare of society. (Such disparities in earnings arise because of arbitrary aspects of the social system.) When one reflects on the wealth accumulated today by sports stars, celebrities in the entertainment industry, and opportunistic speculators, this perception seems well founded. And if one considers the social power commanded by wealth and ownership in an even moderately or benignly capitalist society, the case mounts for social democratic redistribution, that is, for direct state intervention in the web of economic relationships to promote moral purposes.

A variety of arguments can be made to justify social democratic policies. One strategy is to argue that all individuals in a liberal society should receive an equitable share of social resources in order to explore and give play to each individual's unique visions of his or her life purpose or plan of life (whatever it happens to be). Moreover, there should be no lack of moral and material encouragement for individuals to make of their lives something that confers self-respect and wins the respect of others and to grasp the opportunities for self-development that a liberal regime puts in their hands. This argument is, roughly speaking, the form of social theory associated with welfarist liberals such as John Rawls and Ronald Dworkin. The authoritative statement of this liberal-individualist version of social democracy is Rawls's towering work *A Theory of Justice* (1971).

It may be helpful to contrast the idea of distributive justice, which defines this kind of theory, with the libertarian doctrines formulated by Robert Nozick and Friedrich von Hayek. Nozick and Hayek allow no legitimate place for state economic intervention or redistributive social policies. An egalitarian liberal like Rawls believes that a just society must engage its citizens in an agreement, at least hypothetically, as to a fair distribution of all the goods and benefits that the society makes available for consumption. That is, social justice requires, and social theory attempts to clarify, what Nozick labels, in order to reject it, a "patterned principle" of distributive justice.

A libertarian thinker like Hayek, by contrast, does not allow some kind of supercontract somehow negotiated by the society as a whole. Rather, he maintains, procedural justice extends no further than the imperative that the multiplicity of discrete contracts entered into by consenting individuals must be honored by those who have promised to do so. For Hayek, Rawls promises something that is necessarily out of reach—namely, the vision of an overarching social order that legislates specific distributive outcomes. As Hayek sees it, Rawls's appeal to substantive principles of macrojustice cannot help but coercively invade and overturn acts of microconsent, and therefore one would be better off abandoning altogether the search for a general theory of distributive justice.

Another argument to justify social democratic policies has a collectivist orientation. Michael Walzer, for instance, defends a robustly egalitarian liberal regime. In *Spheres of Justice* (1983), he argues that the standard for judging questions of distributive justice is not based on individuals' rights to design for themselves an autonomous plan of life but rather is a communal standard, arising from the shared experiences and collective self-understanding of a given society. Walzer wants to show that sometimes a society is implicitly committed, according to the logic of its shared practices and self-conception, to ideals that are insufficiently realized in its existing institutions and policies. Such an account, he believes, applies in particular to the American welfare state. If Americans had a clear grasp of their own identity, of the underlying commitment to provide for reciprocal needs implicit in their historical community, they would embrace more expansive collective provision for health care than their social and political system currently offers. They would empower less privileged groups in the society to seize greater control over their own social and economic destiny (for instance, by encouraging the formation of workers' cooperatives). And they would strive to lessen the domination of money and market power in shaping power and opportunities across the whole fabric of social and political life—or so Walzer argues. In any case, the comparison of Rawls and Walzer shows that one can argue from either individualist or collectivist premises in the direction of more or less convergent policy commitments.

Characteristics

Social democracy, then, admits of alternative routes to a common destination. Yet there is an irony in appealing to American theorists to defend social democratic conclusions, whether one prefers the more liberal or more socialist version, for in an important sense, social democracy is the outgrowth of an authentically European social consciousness (and, in this sense, is remote from the categories of thought of American liberalism). The social democratic idea is sometimes conceived in terms of social rights, characteristic of twentieth-century liberal democracies, which are thought to offer a supplement to the nineteenth-century political rights and eighteenth-century civil rights associated with earlier incarnations of liberalism. (The original, and still most famous and influential, source of this conception is T. H. Marshall's work on citizenship and social class.)

The problem with this formulation is that it favors the notion of rights held by individuals at the expense of notions of social duty and obligation. In this regard it seems alien to the collectivist traditions upon which European social democracy historically draws. According to the definition of socialism that Mikhail Gorbachev, then leader of the Soviet Union, offered in his address to the Twenty-seventh Communist Party Congress in 1986, citizens' rights must be tied to their duties. Moreover, as Morris Janowitz has pointed out, it may well be that Marshall himself meant to affirm a reciprocity of rights and duties, rather than intending any one-sided primacy of individual

rights and entitlements. For these reasons, a more promising idiom to express the idea of social democracy is offered by the vocabulary of citizenship (where citizenship is not taken to be exhausted by a rights-based concept).

The idea here is that social democracy specifies a certain concept of citizenship, of the social conditions that must be met in order for individuals to consider themselves full members of the political community. Social democracy, on this understanding, presupposes at least a minimal core of social membership: no one starves, no one goes homeless, no one lacks for essential medical needs; the elderly are cared for; and no child is denied the opportunities necessary for eventual full participation in the life of the society. It seems reasonable to draw from the logic of the social democratic idea a further corollary: all people should have the opportunity for employment and the sense of dignity that goes with the knowledge that they are making a productive contribution to the needs of society.

Admittedly, this last requirement looks impossibly ambitious, given the onerous public debts and the huge structural unemployment being suffered at present by most liberal-capitalist countries (even those ruled by nominally socialist or social democratic governments). For that matter, the other items on our list defining social democratic citizenship are also far from being realized in contemporary liberal democracies. Of this social democratic vision, some intimations can be detected in the muted idealism expressed by U.S. president Bill Clinton in his inaugural address in 1993. Clinton voiced the conviction that the nation, conceived as a moral community, cannot be indifferent to whether its members, as individuals and as whole classes, thrive or are crushed in the marketplace of everyday life. He said the state must ensure that the perils of life in civil society are not so overwhelming that certain members of the society are effectively denied the conditions of meaningful citizenship.

The Meaning of Social Democracy

What does it mean, then, to embrace social democratic commitments? Typical of the social democrat is a sympathy for the underdogs in society, whether workers, women, or cultural minorities or the elderly, sick, or disabled. Social democracy implies a principled commitment to the welfare state, as opposed to a merely instrumental acceptance of it. Social democrats tend to be the ones who mobilize political support for progressive social legislation—welfare and unemployment benefits, labor legislation favorable to trade unions, expanded educational opportunities, provisions for health care and child care, guaranteed pension plans, public housing, and so on—prodding the rest of the population to adopt creative means to ameliorate the social condition. In this respect, the cause of social democracy has made notable advances with the postwar achievements of the welfare state in most Western democracies.

As a species of democratic theory, social democracy may be construed as an ambitious interpretation of what full democracy requires. Defining the social democratic synthesis in relation to its two components—socialism and democracy—we might say that social democracy is more than democracy but less than socialism. A social democrat believes that a set of fair and reasonable mechanisms for electoral representation does not sufficiently qualify a society as a genuine democracy. Real democracy depends on shaping a more robustly egalitarian web of social relationships. As the Canadian political theorist C. B. Macpherson has argued, democratic theory falls short of its mandate if it limits itself to the question of how to democratize government; rather, democratic theory in its fullest sense must concern itself with how to democratize society. That is, it must address the problem of how to institute a more egalitarian government throughout economic and social life. This challenge to the standard liberal understanding of democracy has been given a sharp formulation in the claim by Gorbachev (in *Perestroika*, 1987, 127–128) that the democratic claims of Western societies would be more credible if workers and office employees started electing the owners of factories and plants, bank presidents, and so on.

Accordingly, efforts by various democratic theorists such as Carole Pateman and Robert Dahl to investigate possibilities of democratizing the workplace are entirely in the spirit of social democratic ideals. In this sense, social democracy means more democracy; but it means less socialism insofar as social democrats do not necessarily share a faith, or perhaps have shed their faith, in the economic prescriptions of classic socialism (as regards, for example, the nationalization of industry). When one has given up on any magic solutions supposedly forthcoming from the economic doctrines of socialism, what remains is a demanding egalitarian morality that is common to social democrats and old-style socialists.

In the 1980s the energies of Marxism expired in the debacle of Eastern European command economies. At the same time, the attack on the welfare state during the administrations of President Ronald Reagan in the United States and Prime Minister Margaret Thatcher in Great Britain revealed itself to many as another, and opposing, false promise, exposing the social and moral bankruptcy of libertarian ideals. As the extremes come to be discredited, social democratic morality and politics gain a renewed legitimacy.

Social democracy, one is tempted to say, is the moral residue that is left when socialists lose their confidence about how to organize a modern economy. But even if this definition of social democracy seems ungenerous, the power of this moral residue should not be underestimated. Indeed, in the 1990s social democratic ideas may be winning back a bit of their former luster (to the extent that we have not yet reached the stage where all social doctrines and ideologies yield to universal cynicism).

See also Marxism; Socialism.

RONALD BEINER

BIBLIOGRAPHY

Bauer, Otto. *The Question of Nationalities and Social Democracy.* Edited by Ephraim J. Nimni. Translated by Joseph O'Donnell. Minneapolis: University of Minnesota Press, 2000.

Beiner, Ronald. *What's the Matter with Liberalism?* Berkeley: University of California Press, 1992, chap. 6.

Dahl, Robert A. *A Preface to Economic Democracy.* Berkeley: University of California Press; Oxford: Polity Press, 1985.

Macpherson, C. B. *Democratic Theory: Essays in Retrieval.* Oxford and New York: Oxford University Press, 1973.

Marshall, T. H. *Class, Citizenship, and Social Development.* Garden City, N.Y.: Anchor Books, 1965.

Pateman, Carole. *Participation and Democratic Theory.* Cambridge and New York: Cambridge University Press, 1970.

Plant, Raymond. *Citizenship, Rights, and Socialism.* Fabian Tract 531. London: Fabian Society, 1988.

_____. "Social democracy." In *The Blackwell Encyclopaedia of Political Thought,* edited by David Miller. Oxford: Blackwell, 1987.

Rawls, John. *A Theory of Justice.* Cambridge: Harvard University Press, Belknap Press, 1971; Oxford; Oxford University Press, 1973.

Walzer, Michael. *Spheres of Justice: A Defense of Pluralism and Equality.* New York: Basic Books, 1983; Oxford: Blackwell, 1985.

✦ Democracy, Types of

Various types of democracy other than the forms of liberal representative government that constitute the prevailing democratic systems in the contemporary world have been found in practice or have been advocated by various political thinkers. Some of these types of democracy have not been based on principles of representation. Others are based on methods of representation that differ markedly from those found in most liberal democracies. Nevertheless, many of these alternatives to conventional representative government have strong claims to be considered democratic.

Definitions of Democracy

The core definition of democracy is "the rule of the people." The word derives from the ancient Greek *demokratia*, which was composed from the word for the people *(demos)* and the word for power *(kratos)*. This apparently straightforward definition, however, conceals considerable problems of political theory and practice since the meaning of neither *the people* nor *rule* is self-evident.

The reference to the people implies that in a democracy all those within a country are equally entitled to participate in ruling. The composition of the people, however, has been a matter of dispute throughout the history of democracy. In ancient Athens, for example, slaves were a majority of the population but did not have the rights of citizens and were not part of the people. Nevertheless, the word *demos* also connoted the masses, and democracy was sometimes regarded as the rule of the poor. Other states have termed themselves democracies while denying political rights to persons of a particular color or race. Only in this century have women gained the vote. In most countries those below the age of eighteen cannot vote and, in some sense, are not part of the people who rule.

The people may also be considered either as a unified body with a single will or as composed of numerous individuals, a majority of whom rules on the basis of counting votes. Democracy has therefore sometimes been defined as government in which the will of the majority of qualified citizens prevails. This definition, however, raises the question how far the preferences of the minority may be ignored in a democracy. It is also necessary to consider what constitutes a majority (whether policy can be made according to the vote of the largest group—a plurality—or whether it is necessary to have the support of more than half the voters—the majority) and whether the consent of a majority can be obtained for every proposal.

The concept of *rule* is no less problematic. The original type of democracy entailed direct decisions by the people, meeting in an assembly. In modern democracies, decisions are made by representatives elected at intervals; hence, the rule of the people is indirect and is exercised through the accountability of the representatives to the electorate.

For these reasons, no single definition of democracy is entirely satisfactory. A broad definition might be as follows: democracy is a system of government in which all adult persons within the unit of rule are entitled to participate equally in making general laws and policy. Each of the elements within this and most other definitions will require further specification. In the course of such elaboration most theories go beyond description and definition to some statement of democratic ideals.

Direct Democracy

Direct democracy refers to political systems in which the citizens make the laws themselves rather than choose representatives to make the laws on their behalf. The ancient Greek democracies about which evidence survives were all direct democracies. In this sense, direct rather than liberal representative democracy is the original type of democratic government. The most celebrated example is ancient Athens, where direct democracy was the form of government with brief interruptions from 507 B.C. to 322 B.C.

In ancient Athens the entire citizen population was entitled to sit in the Assembly, which was the supreme governing body of the state. At the height of Athenian democracy, in the fifth century B.C., the Assembly was responsible for passing laws. It made decisions on matters of foreign policy, such as the signing of treaties with other states or the declaration of war. The Assembly elected some of the chief executive officers and magistrates. It could also make decisions about taxation.

The Assembly of the people could be described as sovereign. Although some of its powers were curtailed in the fourth century B.C., it remained the determining body within the state. The Assembly met about forty days a year. Within it every citizen had an equal right to speak and to initiate a proposal for debate. Decisions were made on the basis of majority rule.

In Athens the principles of direct democracy applied not merely to the legislative process but also to the executive aspect of government. Most administrative offices were performed by the ordinary citizens themselves. Thus the Council of Five Hundred, which handled the agenda of the Assembly, was filled by lot. In addition, many offices were rotated. A few offices, particularly those concerned with the military, were recognized as requiring more than average technical competence. These were elected annually by the Assembly, and the officeholders were permitted to stand for reelection repeatedly. Some, notably Pericles, gained positions of great influence.

Direct democracy in Athens also extended to the judicial process. There were no appointed judges or professional lawyers. The courts dealt with a wide range of matters, including criminal cases, civil disputes, the award of state contracts, and allegations of administrative incompetence or political corruption. The court was presided over by private citizens. For major political cases the verdicts were reached by mass juries of up to 2,501 citizens. The juries were chosen by lot from those who put themselves forward.

The combination of these direct democratic devices made for an intense level of citizen participation in politics. It has been calculated that a third of the citizens had served on one occasion as members of the council and a quarter had been its president (in a sense, the leader of Athens) for one day in their lives.

Nevertheless, by modern standards of democracy Athens fell far short. The citizens who held democratic rights were only a minority of the adult population. Only a man born of Athenian parents counted as a citizen. Women had no rights of citizenship. The large number of foreigners living in Athens (like resident aliens and "guest" workers in modern states) did not enjoy the full rights of citizens. Finally, Athens was a slave society. Slaves labored in mines, on farms, and as domestics. The numbers are not known, but estimates range up to five times the number of citizens—perhaps 150,000 in the fourth century, when the citizen population was probably 30,000. Accordingly, it has always been a controversial question whether the direct democracy of Athens was made possible by the existence of slavery, which enabled the male citizens to spend time in the Assembly, the council, the juries, and the administration and on active duty in the army and navy.

Scholars usually have argued that such direct democratic systems can exist only in small states.

Among the city-states of ancient Greece, Athens was unusually large. Yet its territory was only 1,000 square miles. The total population in the fourth century, including male citizens, women and children, foreigners and slaves, might have been 400,000. Some other city-states had populations of about 10,000.

Athens was at the limits of the size of a "face to face" society, the type of society that many believe to be a precondition for direct democracy. In such a society, citizens could possess a personal knowledge of the characters and abilities of the leading political activists. They would be aware of the domestic and external social, economic, and political circumstances of the country. Their lives would be immediately affected by policy decisions. Advocates of direct, participatory democracy have argued that such conditions stimulate civic virtue. The system depends on participation and encourages political awareness and involvement. Civic activity is itself educational and creates a politically mature citizenry. By contrast, advocates of direct democracy allege that indirect, representative democracy discourages citizen involvement and favors professional political elites.

Criticisms of direct democracy have, however, persisted since ancient times. Some conservative writers of the time pointed out that not everyone lived up to the ideals of participation. Although all 30,000 citizens could in principle attend and vote in the Assembly, the quorum was 6,000, which is all the meeting place could hold. Even the daily payment for attendance might be interpreted as reliance on an economic incentive rather than civic virtue to obtain participation.

The most influential critic was the philosopher Plato. He argued that decisions, rather than being made by persons who were expert in political matters, were in the hands of an Assembly composed of people from all walks of life who had no special understanding of government. Consequently, direct democracy was in reality mob rule. The decisions were rash and inconsistent. The voters were swayed by rabble-rousing demagogues who appealed to emotion and prejudice rather than to reason. In his comedies the Greek dramatist Aristophanes indulged in satire at the expense of members of the Assembly who were barely literate, were politically ignorant, and could be persuaded to follow any political leader.

The importance of the Athenian instance of direct democracy is that it defined the meaning of the term *democracy* for more than 2,000 years. Until the advent of ideas of representative democracy about the time of the American Revolution, the term referred to direct democracy on the Athenian model. For most thinkers, democracy was not a viable form of government, carrying the connotations of mob rule and confined to small states. Most strikingly, there was no further example of a democracy in Western history after the fall of the Athenian system in 322 B.C.

Modern Direct Democracy

Direct democracy has never died out as an ideal in the modern era. Moreover, local examples of direct democracy have been put into practice. Political thinkers have regularly revived its central ideas within the theory of participatory democracy. A major attempt can be found in the work of Jean-Jacques Rousseau in the eighteenth century. Rousseau advocated a system of popular sovereignty in which, as in Athens, all male citizens would vote on the laws in an assembly. He did not, however, favor direct citizen participation in the executive process. He recognized that such a system of popular rule could occur only within a very small city-state.

An attempt to reconcile direct democracy with the complexities of large states can be found in the writings of Karl Marx in the nineteenth century.

While Marx's views on democracy have to be pieced together from several sources and are a matter of some controversy, it is clear that he believed that elements of direct popular rule were essential to the achievement of the goal of freedom as he understood it. Liberal, representative, constitutional democracy was merely a competition between bourgeois parties to sustain class repression. Instead, the people should determine their own affairs. At the smallest community level they would deliberate and vote directly on issues. Beyond this there would be a pyramid structure in which the community would elect delegates to a district assembly to deal with wider issues. The district would itself elect delegates to a national assembly. To keep these delegates under popular control, they were to be given strict instructions on how to vote and were subject to "recall"—that is, they would be required to go back to the electors for new instructions and possibly face the forfeit of their authority.

Marx also aimed to introduce direct democracy into the executive process. Administrators and judges would be subject to frequent election. The army would be replaced by a citizen militia. Ultimately, Marx believed, in a communist society in which the abolition of property had removed the prime source of conflict, even these aspects of direct democratic government would become superfluous. In place of the state there would be a system of self-regulation. The actual practices of regimes that have claimed to be inspired by Marxism have diverged markedly from Marx's democratic proposals.

Participatory Democracy

Participatory democracy is a term applied to theories of democracy that seek to involve the ordinary citizen more fully in the decision-making processes than is normal within representative democracy. Participatory democrats usually seek both to reform representative systems and to combine them with certain elements of direct democracy. Reforms to representative government might include holding more frequent elections or opening up a wider range of offices to election. In this sense, the United States is already more participatory than most European democracies, where fewer offices are open to election. In addition, participatory democracy would entail more active involvement by citizens in community affairs, social movements, and interest groups. Advocates of participation often support greater democracy in the workplace, sometimes termed *industrial democracy*. Supporters of participatory democracy usually look to civic education to encourage a more politically interested and active citizenry.

Direct democratic devices that might be incorporated within participatory democracy include direct popular rule at the local neighborhood level, combined, somewhat in the manner of Marx, with delegation to higher bodies dealing with district issues. Participatory theorists also usually favor the more extensive employment of recall (used in some states of the United States), as well as referendum and initiative (familiar in many liberal democracies, such as Switzerland and the United States, but rarely used in others, such as the United Kingdom).

The most notable surviving examples of direct democracy in practice are the town meeting in the United States (especially in New England) and the commune assemblies *(Landsgemeinde)* in Switzerland. Both are examples of local democracy and therefore differ significantly from the politically autonomous city-states of ancient Greece.

In the purest form of New England town meeting the citizens assemble from one to several times a year to determine policy for the community. They can determine school budgets, zoning regulations, levels of road repair, approaches to local policing, and appropriate taxation. They also elect the town's executive officers. In some towns the procedure is to delegate powers of action to executives for a determinate period. The town meeting has been widely praised by commentators at earlier periods of American history, such as Thomas Jefferson and Alexis de Tocqueville, as an instrument of civic education. Although the powers of the town meeting remain quite extensive, however, even by the standards set for local self-government by some participatory democrats, it has much less autonomy today than in earlier periods. The town must exercise its control within the context of policies laid down by the state and the federal governments, not to mention the international economic and political environment. It would be harsh to say that the town meeting has great power but only over small issues, since many of these matters affect peoples' lives closely. Nevertheless, the degree of direct democratic self-government that a town can exercise in the modern world is restricted.

The Swiss *Landsgemeinde* is an assembly of citizens meeting as a direct democracy in a small local community. The first such assemblies met in the fourteenth century. At their height there were hundreds of these assemblies, which determined all matters affecting their villages. They survive in only five cantons and half-cantons, but the practice of direct democracy in Switzerland is sustained by the exceptionally extensive resort to the referendum and citizen initiative at local (cantonal) and national (federal) levels. Switzerland also retains the direct democratic concept of the citizen army.

Direct democracy has in the past been confined to small states or local governments, but in recent years it has been argued that modern communications technology has made it possible to arrange for direct mass participation in the affairs of the largest states. The term *teledemocracy* has been used to describe this new political phenomenon, of which there are many potential variants. In its most radical form the new direct democracy would involve equipping every citizen's home with a voting device so that every citizen could vote on legislative propositions for the whole nation, for the locality, or for a group such as a labor union. The votes would be registered by computer; so a popular vote could be taken instantaneously, as in ancient Athens. The ease and simplicity of home voting might increase levels of participation.

Objections to teledemocracy echo objections to earlier direct democracy. First, as in any form of referendum, it would be important to determine how questions to be voted on are phrased and who is to ask them. These procedures are notoriously susceptible to manipulation.

Second, critics since Plato have charged that voters would not possess the level of education and knowledge necessary to enable them to make informed choices on legislative propositions. This is a general objection to the referendum and similar devices. Accordingly, it is said that the electorate is equipped to choose who is to decide rather than to decide itself. Some advocates of teledemocracy respond by claiming that interactive communication technology enables citizens to call up large quantities of information and data on the television screen to facilitate their choice. Arguments for and against various propositions could be listed more fully than with current referendums. The charge of citizen incompetence, however, remains at the core of critiques of direct democracy and of all types of democracy.

Third, it is argued that teledemocracy does not permit the debate between the voters that is feasible in a direct democratic assembly. The technology is limited in this respect. Yet modern means of communications such as electronic mail can permit voters to exchange views or to put questions to those who have brought the proposi-

tions forward. Call-in shows and teleconferences can also, to a degree, help to re-create in the modern world certain features of the direct democratic assembly.

It is, however, more likely in the short run that interactive communications technology will be employed to supplement the established procedures of indirect, representative democracy than to replace them. The technology would facilitate greater use of the referendum and the initiative and is already being used extensively in polling public opinion. Although the size of modern states and the complexity of society have previously rendered direct democracy a largely outmoded system, it is possible that direct democracy is due for a partial revival as a result of technological advances.

Whether direct democracy—or, more generally, participatory democracy—is considered desirable depends on views about the political knowledge, judgment, and interest of the mass of citizens. It is wrong to suppose that direct democratic votes are clear and unambiguous expressions of the will of the people. The work of Kenneth Arrow and other social choice theorists has demonstrated that even in systems that seek fully to consult individual preferences, it is impossible to ensure that the outcome of votes is consistent and procedurally fair. Direct democracy lies at the origin of all democracy but is not a panacea.

Direct democracy is not the only alternative to liberal representative democracy. Many other forms of democracy based on representation have been proposed, and some have been used in government systems. Most suggest that interests rather than persons should be the basis of representation.

Statistical Representation
The idea of statistical representation derives from the notion that representatives should be a

microcosm of the electorate and proposes that such representatives be selected by statistical sampling methods. A probability sample of the country could generate a government of representatives that would be a more accurate microcosm of the society than any electoral system yet devised. The process is analogous to the ancient Greek direct democratic procedure of selection by lot, and also to the selection of juries in American and British courts, so as to be a cross section of the public. A variant of this proposal is that issues that affect a particular segment of the population, for example, hearing-impaired people, would be decided by a commission composed of a probability sample from that segment who wished to stand for the office. Rather than having all citizens participate in choosing decision makers across the whole range of matters facing a nation, this system would have representatives of the affected interests determine special issues.

The democratic nature of the idea of statistical representation relies on its claim to be entirely representative. Although the method supposedly would give each person an equal chance to be selected, its basis is the representation of the interests or functions that comprise a society rather than of persons, in contrast to traditional forms of democratic representation. As a realistic proposal, statistical representation faces difficulties in coordinating policies favored by the various interests and in identifying those who are affected by a given policy issue, even if only indirectly as taxpayers.

Functional Representation

Proponents of functional theories of representation argue that the major functions or interests in modern society should be represented in the processes of decision making. According to these arguments, society is composed of a number of associations and organizations that have specific purposes. Each of these purposes can be represented by elective bodies. Such associations or organizations might range from industries to educational institutions.

Among the most elaborate versions of functional representation is that of the Guild Socialists, a group of British antistate socialists writing in the first two decades of the twentieth century. The most notable theorist was George Douglas Howard Cole (1889–1959). Cole argued that the representation of one person by another person was impossible because each individual has a variety of different purposes. Functions such as industry could be represented, however. Consequently, representative bodies for each industry and for industry as a whole should be established alongside the traditional political representative legislature; the legislature's tasks would be confined to matters of common concern to all persons and functions. Within each function there would be a hierarchy of representative bodies from the local to the national. Persons would have votes in every functional body in which they were involved. The objective was a participatory and pluralist democracy in which the sovereignty of the state would be restricted.

As a theory, functional representation faces difficulties in specifying which functions constitute the distinct interests to be incorporated into the representative process. There are also problems in balancing the autonomy of the functions with the need for coordination of functions and with more transcendent considerations of equality and justice. As a movement, Guild Socialism declined after the 1920s. Nevertheless, in practice functional representation is widespread in modern democracies where associations representing major industrial, commercial, labor, agricultural, and professional interests have established consultative positions in the policy-making process.

Corporatist Democracy

Corporatist democracy can be defined as a system in which associations, or "corporations," representing a restricted number of major interests in society are formally recognized by the state and are involved in the consultative stages of policy making and in their implementation. Corporatism is a form of functional representation. Conventionally, it is divided into state corporatism and liberal corporatism. These have different implications for democracy.

State corporatism theories developed in the second half of the nineteenth century in a number of European countries in opposition to both liberal and socialist thought. In contrast to liberal emphases on the individual and the market, and to socialist ideas of structural class conflict, corporatism advanced the idea that society constituted an organic whole to which the major interests of society, especially industry and labor, contributed. Hence the term *organic democracy* has also been applied to such theories. These ideas were influenced by Roman Catholic teaching, which perceived the various sectors of society as serving the greater divine order. This type of corporatism also appealed to nationalists, who regarded the state as the unit within which all elements in society found their common interests.

The democratic credentials of state corporatism were often seen as tenuous in both theory and practice. State corporatism explicitly rejected the ideas of individualism and equality associated with liberal democracy. Proponents of state corporatism also opposed conventional ideas of majority rule, based on one person, one vote, as divisive and atomized. The democratic aspect, to the extent that it was acknowledged, consisted of the state's recognition of the major corporations as representative of essential functions and as possessing formal consultative status. In turn, the theory proposed that the corporations had powers of self-regulation and responsibilities for implementing policies. These responsibilities included influence over prices, production levels, industrial relations, wages, and welfare. The overall objective was a solidarist, consensual community that would avoid the class conflict and the economic crises generally found in capitalist economies.

In practice, state corporatism was associated with authoritarianism rather than democracy. It came nearest to implementation in Italy in the fascist era (1922–1943) and in Portugal under the dictator António de Oliveira Salazar (premier, 1932–1968). Corporatist institutions were also to be found in certain Latin American countries. The European instances were marked by strong state control, and the corporations did not play the representative role intended by corporatist theory.

Liberal corporatism, also termed *neocorporatism*, developed after World War II within a number of liberal democracies in Europe. The "peak associations" representing major interests in a country, such as employers, professions, agricultural producers, and labor, are given a privileged position by the state in negotiations over policy making. In return, the associations deliver support from their members for the resultant policies. Liberal corporatist arrangements provide a form of functionalist representation alongside orthodox parliamentary institutions. Liberal corporatist democracy differs from pluralist democracy in that certain interest groups are privileged over others and in that the distinction between public and private authorities is less sharp.

The prime examples of liberal corporatist democracies are Austria and Sweden; corporatist processes also occur in the Netherlands and in Germany. The United States is usually regarded as the least corporatist of major nations in its politics. In many countries, however, there are middle-level corporatist arrangements. In these, interest groups within specific sectors of society and the economy are granted privileged positions in the consultative and regulatory processes. Frequent examples are found in agriculture. Defenders of liberal corporatism often claim that it promotes consensus and legitimacy for policies with beneficial effects for the economy and society. Critics are concerned about the privileged access to influence that powerful interests may gain at the expense of other groups in society.

Consociational Democracy

Consociational democracy is a type of representative government in which, in contrast to majoritarian systems, power sharing is institutionalized. Consociational practices typically have developed in countries that are deeply divided by clear-cut religious, ethnic, or linguistic differences. The aim of consociationalism is to ensure that all the major cleavages or segments in society are represented in the government in proportion to their size in the society. Power sharing implies that the government is a coalition of the representatives of the major segments, rather than composed of the single winning party, as in a majoritarian system such as the United Kingdom. Policy is produced as a result of negotiations between the leaders of the segments in a process known as "elite accommodation." The system of power sharing may also extend to the allocation of senior civil service posts or positions in significant public authorities.

The organizations representing each social segment are guaranteed considerable autonomy in determining which issues affect that particular grouping. Each segment may also possess rights of veto over matters that affect their vital interests, such as religious or linguistic schooling. Advocates of consociationalism argue that such power-sharing devices enable deeply divided societies to hold together. Countries that have had well-developed consociational democracies for considerable periods include Belgium, Switzerland, the Netherlands, Malaysia, and, in some views, Lebanon.

People's Democracy

People's democracy is a term used by those who wish to claim that the one-party states of the former Soviet Union, its former Eastern European satellites, and the People's Republic of China constitute a type of democracy. The claim rests on a number of arguments within Marxist-Leninist doctrine. Although *democracy* means the rule of the people, Marxist-Leninist theory argues that conventional liberal democracies do not provide genuine government by the people. The equal political rights and constitutional guarantees amount only to a "formal" democracy, since they are not reinforced by substantive economic and social equality. Liberal democracy is a shell that protects capitalism and the bourgeois ruling class.

The genuine rule of the people would imply control of government and the economy by the proletariat, or working class. The proletariat is identified with the people on the ground that within the Marxist scheme of history the proletariat constitutes variously the majority, the poor masses, and also the emancipatory, revolutionary class that represents the interests of humanity. The rule of the proletariat, and hence of the people, is not necessarily exercised directly. It may be exercised through the agency of the Communist Party, the vanguard of the proletariat. The party possesses a knowledge of the line of march to the realization of the proletariat's interests. The proletariat may fail to understand its true interests as a consequence of oppression and manipulation in the bourgeois era. Rule by the vanguard Communist Party is government for the people and, if only indirectly, by the people. Ultimately, in a true communist society in which the sources of class repression have been abolished, this rule will be superfluous and will wither away to a form of self-regulation.

One-party states in a number of African countries have justified their claims to being democracies by similar kinds of argument to those advanced in people's democracies. The dominant party in those instances claims to be leading the nation, formerly oppressed by colonialism, to a condition of economic development.

Plebiscitarian Democracy

Plebiscitarian democracy refers to political systems in which constitutional amendments are put to the people in a plebiscite or in which the head of state derives authority from being directly elected. A plebiscite (derived from the Latin term for a vote of the people, *plebs*, in ancient Rome) is a vote by the electorate on a proposed change in some aspect of the constitutional arrangements. As such it is a form of referendum, and the two terms are not always strictly differentiated. The French Fifth Republic (which began in 1958) is an example of a democracy that allows for plebiscites. A system in which the head of state is directly elected is also termed plebiscitarian, in that the person elected gains a legitimacy from the people distinct from that acquired by the representatives in the legislature. The powerful presidency of the French Fifth Republic is an instance. By extension, it is sometimes argued that modern representative democracies are becoming more plebiscitarian in that general elections increasingly are perceived as competitions between rival leaders who appeal directly to the people rather than as competitions between the political parties.

See also Classical Greece and Rome; Corporatism; Democracy, Participatory; Democracy, Social; Federalism; Rousseau, Jean-Jacques; Theory, African; Theory, Ancient.

GERAINT PARRY

BIBLIOGRAPHY

Arterton, F. Christopher. *Teledemocracy: Can Technology Protect Democracy?* Newbury Park, Calif.: Sage Publications, 1987.

Barber, Benjamin. *Strong Democracy: Participatory Politics for a New Age.* Berkeley: University of California Press, 1984.

Birch, Anthony H. *The Concepts and Theories of Modern Democracy.* 2d ed. New York: Routledge, 2000.

Burnheim, John. *Is Democracy Possible?* Cambridge: Polity Press, 1985.

Finley, Moses I. *Democracy Ancient and Modern.* London: Chatto and Windus, 1973.

Hansen, Mogens H. *The Athenian Democracy in the Age of Demosthenes: Structure, Principles, and Ideology.* Oxford and Cambridge, Mass.: Blackwell, 1991.

Held, David. *Models of Democracy.* Cambridge: Polity Press, 1987.

Hirst, Paul Q., ed. *The Pluralist Theory of the State: Selected Writings of G. D. H. Cole, J. N. Figgis, and H. J. Laski.* London and New York: Routledge, 1989.

Holden, Barry. *Understanding Liberal Democracy.* Oxford and Atlantic Highlands, N.J.: Philip Allan, 1988.

Lijphart, Arend. *Democracy in Plural Societies: A Comparative Exploration.* New Haven: Yale University Press, 1977.

Lively, Jack. *Democracy.* Oxford: Blackwell, 1975.

Mansbridge, Jane J. *Beyond Adversary Democracy.* New York: Basic Books, 1980.

Pennock, J. Roland. *Democratic Political Theory.* Princeton: Princeton University Press, 1979.

Sartori, Giovanni. *The Theory of Democracy Revisited.* Chatham, N.J.: Chatham House, 1987.

Stockton, David. *The Classical Athenian Democracy.* Oxford and New York: Oxford University Press, 1990.

Williamson, Peter J. *Varieties of Corporatism: A Conceptual Discussion.* Cambridge: Cambridge University Press, 1985.

✦ Democracy, Women and

Women and democracy concerns the roles, especially the political roles, of women in democratic societies. Through the nineteenth century, even as democracy began to flourish in the world, most women were excluded from meaningful participation in the political processes of the nations in which they lived. Legal restraints, as well as societal norms and customs, kept women from exercising the rights that were accorded to men. Only in the twentieth century were women granted the right (and society's permission) to vote and run for office in democracies.

In most nations of the world at the end of the twentieth century, women have the same rights of citizenship as men. Like men, their participation in the democratic process is typically characterized by voting, serving in parliamentary bodies, and acquiring political leadership roles. In many nations, despite the removal of legal constraints on women's involvement in the democratic process, limitations on their ability to participate as full political beings remain. In fact, in all nations of the world, women are vastly underrepresented at the elite levels of power.

During most of the history of the world, political activism was viewed as an inappropriate role for women. Support for women's participation in the democratic institutions of government is a very recent phenomenon, and in many countries the commitment remains largely rhetorical. Article 21 of the Universal Declaration of Human Rights, ratified by members of the United Nations in 1948, proclaims everyone's right of participation in government. The struggle for women to achieve that goal has taken many forms, including the existence of active women's (and in many cases, feminist) movements, which also address other legal and social interests of women.

Women's Rights in the Industrial Democracies

Concern with women's rights can be traced back to the Enlightenment in eighteenth-century France. By the onset of the French Revolution in 1789, the lists of grievances submitted to the king contained demands for legal equality between men and women, including the reform of marriage laws. Olympe de Gouges's *Declaration of the Rights of Women*, which argued for economic and political equality between the sexes, was published in 1791 in the midst of revolution. Yet in 1793 the revolutionary leader Maximilien Robespierre reversed the progress that seemed possible when he banned all women's organizations and barred gatherings of more than five women.

After the revolution, with the enactment of the Napoleonic Code in 1804, women's rights were set back. The code firmly established women's subordination to their husbands in the home and denied women's equality outside the home. As part of this framework, women were considered legally incompetent in France until 1938, when the restrictions on women were removed.

Despite the setback in France, concern with women's equality grew with the spread of liberal democracy and the Enlightenment to other nations of the world. Soon after the onset of the French Revolution came advocacy of the rights of women in England, when Mary Wollstonecraft's *Vindication of the Rights of Woman* (1792) was published.

In the nineteenth century the women's movements in Great Britain and the United States increasingly worked toward extending the vote to women. In Great Britain, prostitution laws and the working conditions of women were early targets of the women's movement, and the Liberal Party was an ally of the women's groups for a time. John Stuart Mill, the philosopher and member of Parliament, published an essay called *The*

Subjection of Women (1869). In Mill the suffrage movement had an influential advocate.

The movement became increasingly radicalized when one of its leaders, Emmeline Pankhurst, affiliated the movement with the Independent Labour Party and then formed the Women's Social and Political Union in 1903. The Women's Social and Political Union undertook a campaign of "direct action" that was characterized by attacks on property, followed by mass arrests of the women. In prison, Pankhurst's followers went on hunger strikes and were force fed by prison authorities. Women's suffrage in Great Britain was won in two stages: in 1918 women aged thirty and over were allowed to vote, and in 1928 women were enfranchised on the same terms as men (at the age of twenty-one).

Women's suffrage activity in the United States arose from the antislavery movement of the 1830s. Elizabeth Cady Stanton and Lucretia Mott, barred—like all women—from attendance at the 1840 World Antislavery Convention in London, convened the Seneca Falls Convention in 1848 to demand women's rights. At this convention, delegates adopted the first formal statement of the women's rights movement. Women remained committed to the abolition of slavery, but they were also beginning to express concern for the political, economic, and social status of women in society.

After the Civil War ended in 1865, women joined in support of a constitutional amendment to enfranchise the former slaves, hoping that it would include a provision granting women the right to vote as well. When the Fourteenth Amendment, ratified in 1868, extended suffrage only to male former slaves, women, including newly freed slaves such as Sojourner Truth, were divided over whether to support it.

Two rival suffrage organizations arose at this time, based in part on the split over support of the Fourteenth Amendment; they eventually combined in 1890 to form the National American Woman Suffrage Association. After a long struggle, the women's suffrage movement, led by Susan B. Anthony, Elizabeth Cady Stanton, Lucy Stone, Carrie Chapman Catt, and, later, Alice Paul, succeeded in securing the vote for women in national elections when the Nineteenth Amendment to the Constitution was ratified in 1920.

On the European continent, as in Great Britain and the United States, women in the nineteenth century organized on their own behalf. In several countries women's groups formed, but their progress was slow; few gains were made anywhere until the twentieth century. Aside from those of Great Britain, the most successful European women's movements emerged in the Scandinavian countries. Women won the right to vote in Norway and Finland before World War I.

Eventually, when women were well established as participants in the political system, they ventured into more and more arenas. By the 1960s a second wave of women's movement activity had emerged in North America, Great Britain, France, Germany, Italy, Denmark, the Netherlands, and even in Spain (after the death of Spanish dictator Francisco Franco in 1975). The most active of the women's organizations were, to varying degrees, influenced by radical philosophies, drawing heavily on Marxist and socialist thought. Many "women's liberation" and feminist groups were committed to reform of abortion laws so as to make abortion more accessible as well as reform of marriage and divorce laws. They also sought to expand women's social and economic opportunities.

Women's Rights in Other Parts of the World

The Soviet Union and its successor states present a different picture. With the success of the

Russian Revolution in 1917, the constitution of the newly formed Soviet Union declared men and women equal. A byproduct of the formal declaration of equality was the subordination of women's issues to the problem of the class struggle. For ideological reasons, no independent concern for women was allowed to surface in the new revolutionary society. Despite obvious inequities in society—for example, women were expected to assume responsibility for all housework and child care as well as to participate in the labor force—it was not until the 1980s and Soviet leader Mikhail Gorbachev's *perestroika* that a women's movement was born.

Amidst the tremendous changes taking place in the nations formed through the breakup of the Soviet Union in 1991, women are struggling to bring the question of the status of women to the political agenda. As before, it is possible that matters of special concern to women, such as economic discrimination, domestic violence, and reform of marriage and divorce laws, will become lost in the larger political debate.

In the less industrial countries, women became involved in many of the national liberation movements. Political unrest in colonial possessions provided opportunities for women to challenge men's domination in the political realm while contributing to the overthrow of the colonial regime. Women in Algeria, Cuba, and Vietnam succeeded to some extent in altering the status of women in the new regimes that sprang up with the victory of the revolutionary forces. With the victory of the Communist Party and the establishment of the People's Republic of China in 1949, women made major strides in improving their economic and social status. Even under the authoritarian regime, women's conditions with respect to marriage, education, and work improved. Nonetheless, women have generally been unable to overcome the patriarchal structure that dominates Chinese cultural and economic life.

In many of the nations of Latin America and Asia, women are hindered by authoritarian regimes and social and religious norms that militate against their participation in the democratic process. Women's movements have been unable to bring about effective political changes and have concentrated instead on revising sexual norms related to prostitution, abortion laws, and male violence against women. Women in India, Mexico, Pakistan, and Thailand have had some success, although quite limited for the most part, in these areas.

In most of precolonial Africa, women were legally subordinate to men. In traditional African societies, women had some autonomy because of their role in agricultural production. During the colonial period, African women's autonomy was diminished as men, aided by the colonial powers, increasingly began to control agricultural development. Reinforcing traditional views of the proper distribution of power within the family, the colonial powers helped strengthen male authority. The emerging colonial state created a distinction between public and private sectors in which women were relegated to a subordinate private role, and men became the dominant public actors. The modernization process thus undermined African women's economic base and forced them into subservient positions within the household and within the polity. By the time most Subsaharan African nations achieved independence, in the 1950s and 1960s, women had little economic or political power.

Although women played important roles in the liberation movements of the post–World War II era in Africa, for the most part they were unable to organize effectively when independence was won. Women are often considered outside the political process because many of their concerns are only marginally related to the larger picture of economic development and modernization.

The diversity among African nations makes generalization difficult, but many problems are common across the continent. Although African men are subject to many of these hardships, women suffer disproportionately from problems of illiteracy, unemployment, malnutrition, low life expectancy, and physical abuse. Women have achieved some success in protecting property rights in Zambia, instituting divorce law reform in Zimbabwe, and creating limited equality in marriage in Senegal, but social and political change to advance women's rights has often been sacrificed to competing economic and cultural interests.

Patterns of Enfranchisement

In the early twentieth century, after long decades of struggle, women were finally granted the vote in more and more of the democracies. Women in New Zealand could vote by 1893, and Australian women of European descent had won the vote by 1901. (Aborigines of both sexes in Australia were not allowed to vote until 1967.) Women had been allowed to vote for school committees in Norway as early as 1889. By 1910 women had secured the right to vote in local elections, and in 1913 Norwegian women were enfranchised in parliamentary elections. Finnish women got the vote in 1906. In Canada, non-Indian women won the right to vote in federal elections in 1918, the same year as many women in Great Britain—although women's enfranchisement at the local and provincial levels in Canada came later. With limitations, Canadian Indians were permitted to vote in 1950; all Canadian adults were eligible to vote by 1960.

Most of the remaining countries of Western Europe granted women the right to vote between 1915 and 1919: Denmark and Iceland in 1915; Austria, Germany, Ireland, and Sweden in 1918;

Luxembourg and the Netherlands in 1919. In Belgium, women connected to the military through their husbands or sons were granted the vote in 1919; all others, in 1948. Unable to overcome restrictive laws, French women were not permitted to vote until 1944. Swiss women were not able to vote in national elections until 1971. Women in Liechtenstein were finally allowed to vote in 1984.

Although the right to vote does not always signify the existence of real democratic institutions, many Eastern European women were eligible to vote in the post–World War I period: in Poland and the Soviet Union (1918) and in Czechoslovakia (1920). Not until the end of World War II were women permitted to vote in Albania and Hungary (1945) and in Yugoslavia (1949).

Women in some countries of Asia and the Middle East had been able to vote relatively early for those parts of the world: Lebanon (1926, far earlier than women in the colonial power, France, that administered the country), Sri Lanka (1931), Thailand (1932), and the Philippines (1937). Most other women in Asia and the Middle East were unable to vote until World War II had ended. In some cases, enfranchisement was simultaneous with the expiration of colonial rule. Indonesian women were thus able to vote in 1945, Vietnamese women in 1946, women in the Republic of Korea in 1948, Syrian women in 1949, Indian women in 1950, Egyptian women in 1956, and Algerian women in 1962. The People's Republic of China was engaged in civil war after World War II; women were granted the right to vote in 1949 with the final success of the Communist revolution.

Women's political emancipation in Japan was begun during the 1870s, when women were becoming a more visible part of the work force and began to agitate for better working conditions. Women's political activity was sharply curtailed by the Meiji constitution of 1889, which prohibited women from voting, joining political parties, or even attending political meetings. Although that constitution was later revoked, women were still banned from party activity until 1930, when they were allowed to join parties and vote in local elections. Japanese women attained suffrage in 1945 with the end of World War II.

The vote had come earlier to women in Latin America, where many had been enfranchised in the 1930s: in Chile (for local elections in 1931), Uruguay (1932), and Brazil (1934). In other Latin American countries, women were not allowed to vote until the 1940s and 1950s. These countries include Argentina and Mexico (1947), Chile (national elections, 1949), Peru (1950), and Colombia (1957).

In most African nations, women won the right to vote only after World War II. Enfranchisement often accompanied a nation's independence. The earliest votes for women came in Gabon in 1944 and Djibouti and Senegal in 1946. Postcolonial suffrage was granted to women in Tanzania in 1959, in Uganda in 1962, in Kenya in 1963, in Angola in 1975, and in the Central African Republic in 1986. Because voting rights in South Africa were based on race, nonwhite women were not permitted to vote until the nation's first democratic elections in 1994. As in many other nations of the world, having the right to vote, for either sex, does not guarantee access to other democratic rights. Few African countries are democracies.

Women today in most of the world have the same formal voting rights as men; indeed, according to a 1991 survey by the Inter-Parliamentary Union, the only exceptions to the worldwide enfranchisement of women are Kuwait and Bahrain. (As an absolute monarchy, Bahrain has no representative institutions—that is, no one can vote.) Having the right to vote, however, does not necessarily mean that women are deeply engaged in democratic governmental processes.

Women in Legislatures

One important indicator of women's participation in democratic society is the degree to which they seek and gain public office. In most nations the right to vote and the right to hold office were granted to women at the same time. In a significant number of countries, however—namely Mexico, New Zealand, Peru, Syria, Rwanda, Zaire, Zimbabwe, Belgium, Canada, Djibouti, the Netherlands, and the United States—the right to vote was not granted with the right to be elected to office. In the Netherlands and the United States, women were able to hold office before they were permitted to vote.

In many countries, women were elected to the national parliament soon after being allowed to run for office. In other nations, it took years for the first women to be elected after they became eligible to seek office. The gap was significant in Senegal (ten years), Uruguay (ten years), and New Zealand (fourteen years). In Singapore women had the right to run for office thirty-six years before the first women were elected; in Australia women of European descent were first elected forty-two years after becoming eligible. In 1992 there were still some countries, including Lebanon, Morocco, Tonga, the United Arab Emirates, and Djibouti, where no woman had ever been elected to national office.

The removal of legal constraints against women officeholders does not change the fact that they continue to hold only a small proportion of legislative seats. Although women make up more than half the population in most nations of the world, according to an Inter-Parliamentary Union survey, as of June 30, 1993, they constituted a little over 10 percent of the membership of the 170 national parliaments. This figure is slightly lower than the 13 percent tallied in June 1989.

The 1993 survey indicates that the parliament with the most parity between men and women representatives, the People's Assembly of Seychelles, had twenty-four members, eleven of whom were women (45.8 percent). The Scandinavian countries had the next highest percentage of women parliamentarians—39 percent in Finland, 35.8 percent in Norway, 33.5 percent in Sweden, and 33 percent in Denmark—followed by the Netherlands with 29.3 percent. Women made up 18 percent of the Canadian House of Commons. Most legislatures, though, from the British House of Commons to the French National Assembly to the Indian Lok Sabha to the Zambian National Assembly and the Greek Chamber of Deputies, had between 5 and 10 percent women members. After the general election of 1992, women made up 9 percent of the House of Commons in the United Kingdom. In the United States the proportion of women in the 103d Congress (1993–1995) was 10 percent, up from 6 percent in the previous Congress.

In some nondemocratic nations, where parliamentary power was not commensurate with political power, such as the People's Republic of China, Cuba, or the Democratic People's Republic of Korea, women representatives held more than 20 percent of the parliamentary seats. In the Soviet Union women had almost 15 percent of the seats in the Council of the Union. Seats had been reserved for women in some of the parliaments of East Central Europe; the demise of these communist states led to the eradication of this system. Consequently, the number of women parliamentarians in this part of the world has dropped since the advent of greater political competition in national parliamentary elections.

In the 1980s women on average held only 6 percent of national legislative seats in Subsaharan

Africa, although they reached the 10 percent mark in Rwanda, Cameroon, Malawi, and Senegal. According to statistics compiled by the United Nations in 1986, women have never made up more than 25 percent of the membership in any African legislative body.

Women as Political Leaders

Despite some gains in legislative office holding, women are underrepresented in positions of political leadership in the nations of the world. A few women have held the highest posts (prime minister or president) in their countries: in Europe, Margaret Thatcher of Great Britain, Vigdís Finnbogadóttir of Iceland, Gro Harlem Brundtland of Norway, and Milka Planinc of Yugoslavia; in the Americas, Eva Perón of Argentina, Kim Campbell of Canada, and Violeta Chamorro of Nicaragua; and across the Middle East and Asia, Indira Gandhi of India, Golda Meir of Israel, Benazir Bhutto of Pakistan, Corazon Aquino of the Philippines, Sirimavo Bandaranaike of Sri Lanka, and Tansu Çiller of Turkey. The small number of women in top leadership posts is testimony to the difficulty women face in gaining power as government leaders or heads of state in the nations of the world.

Women have been infrequent occupants of lower ministerial positions as well. The United States has typically had only one or two women cabinet members since the 1930s. President Bill Clinton in the 1990s appointed four women to cabinet-level posts and others to high positions in the executive branch. Women have never held the key posts of secretary of defense, secretary of state, or secretary of the treasury. Despite their own positions as leaders, neither Indira Gandhi nor Margaret Thatcher appointed women to their cabinets. Women have most often served in the national cabinets of the Scandinavian countries and the Netherlands, and, when François Mitterrand was president in the 1980s and 1990s, in France. The record for the highest number of women in office goes to Norway, where almost half (40 percent) of Brundtland's Labour government from 1986 to 1989 were women.

Overall, women have fared less well in achieving cabinet-level positions in Eastern European and less industrialized nations. Although women may have held high-sounding titles, they fulfilled largely ceremonial roles. The number of women with positions of real power was very small. In 1982 Planinc of Yugoslavia became the first woman to be appointed prime minister in an Eastern European nation. And Alexandra Biryukova was appointed to a Central Committee post (as secretary) in the Soviet Union in 1986. (In the Soviet Union, most women who held government positions were restricted to local or regional offices.)

Women have been absent from cabinet positions in most of the Latin American nations. Costa Rica has been an exception. In 1979, 25 percent of the government positions there were held by women. In Asia, with the exception of a few women in national ministerial posts in Sri Lanka and India during the 1980s, the governments were almost entirely male. In Africa women held only 2 percent of the national ministerial posts, and half the states had no women cabinet officials.

The statistics on women in high positions do not by themselves reveal the type of positions women hold. For the most part, women are appointed as ministers of education, the family, or social development, not the "important" policy-making positions in which men still predominate. Despite their success in attaining positions of national office in the Scandinavian countries, most women even in these countries occupy positions that conform to stereotypical gender roles in society.

Promoting Women's Participation

Within the last century, virtually all of the formal limitations on women's political participation have been revoked. Yet women remain underrepresented in positions of political power. In recent decades the participation of women in the political life of their nations has attracted a good deal of national and international attention. The activities associated with the United Nations Decade for Women (1975–1985) have raised awareness of the issues. In addition, national and international feminist organizations, political parties, and other nongovernmental actors have pressured governments to integrate women more fully into political life.

Political parties and nongovernmental actors can often play a significant role in empowering women. For example, the Canadian Committee for '94 was created in 1984 with the goal of attaining gender equity in the Canadian House of Commons by 1994. Although this and other groups have lobbied for equal representation of women in Parliament, they have not achieved their goal for the Canadian House. The National Council of Women in Denmark, founded in 1899, has almost one million members; this organization plays an active role in encouraging women's political participation in Danish politics. The National Council on Women in the Philippines works to bring women's problems to the forefront of the national agenda. In the United States organizations such as the League of Women Voters and the American Association of University Women also promote civic awareness and participation among women.

Aside from their roles in the established political parties of their nations, women have also been instrumental in creating political parties, some devoted to women members and women's issues. Examples of such parties are the Feminist Party of Canada, the Chilean Women's Party, and the

Nationalist Party of Korean Women in the Republic of Korea. Similarly, most national parties have women's branches that are designed to promote the participation of women in the political system as well as to foster adherence to the aims of the party among women.

Government action has often taken the form of establishing a ministry or cabinet office, or legislative committee, dedicated to improving the status of women. The 1991 Inter-Parliamentary Union survey indicates that twenty-four countries have created ministry-level governmental bodies. Fifty-seven nations have lower-level governmental agencies devoted to the status of women, such as the Department for Emancipation of Women in the Ministry of Social Affairs and Employment in the Netherlands and the General Directorate on the Status of Women in the Ministry of Labour and Social Security in Turkey. Of course, the numerical results of the survey do not indicate the effectiveness of nations' efforts and the commitment to change within each nation. Undoubtedly, many governments attempt to give the impression of concern about the roles and status of women without any hope or intention of accomplishing their stated goals.

Most national constitutions and laws prohibit discrimination against women in political participation. The United Nations has highlighted the problem of discrimination against women's political participation in a number of conventions and resolutions. The Convention on the Elimination of All Forms of Discrimination against Women was adopted by the UN General Assembly in 1979. Earlier, in 1967, the General Assembly had approved the Declaration on the Elimination of Discrimination against Women.

Women in most of the world remain underrepresented in the political arena, although legal barriers are few. Some states employ special measures designed to improve women's political status. Various mechanisms have been devised to increase the number of women in office: for example, a certain number of candidates for office must be women; the political party structure designates a certain number of women members; seats are reserved for women; or women are appointed by the head of the government. Quota systems for elective and appointive office are not common; affirmative action for women, like other forms of affirmative action in politics and business, is controversial.

In the twentieth century, women of the world have made significant progress in the political arena. In democratic societies, voting is now an established right for almost all women; most women have also won the right to seek election, or be appointed, to public office. In many democratic nations, however, women's political activity is constrained by cultural and economic restrictions. Until these obstacles are overcome, women's ability to participate fully in the democratic processes of their nations will continue to lag behind men's.

See also Feminism; Mill, John Stuart; Wollstonecraft, Mary.

SUSAN GLUCK MEZEY

BIBLIOGRAPHY

Bredbenner, Candice Lewis. *A Nationality of Her Own: Women, Marriage, and the Law of Citizenship*. Berkeley: University of California Press, 1998.

Bystydzienski, Jill, ed. *Women Transforming Politics: Worldwide Strategies for Empowerment*. Bloomington: Indiana University Press, 1992.

Duverger, Maurice. *The Political Role of Women*. Paris: UNESCO, 1955.

Epstein, Cynthia Fuchs, and Rose Laub Coser, eds. *Access to Power: Cross-National Studies of Women and Elites*. London: Allen and Unwin, 1981.

Iglitzin, Lynne B., and Ruth Ross, eds. *Women in the World: A Comparative Study*. Santa Barbara, Calif.: Clio Books, 1976.

Kerber, Linda K. *No Constitutional Right to Be Ladies: Women and Obligations of Citizenship*. New York: Hill and Wang, 1998.

Kohn, Walter S. G. *Women in National Legislatures: A Comparative Study of Six Countries*. New York: Praeger, 1980.

Lovenduski, Joni. *Women and European Politics: Contemporary Feminism and Public Policy*. Amherst: University of Massachusetts Press, 1986.

———, and Jill Hills, eds. *The Politics of the Second Electorate: Women and Public Participation*. London: Routledge and Kegan Paul, 1981.

Norris, Pippa. "Women's Legislative Participation in Western Europe." *West European Politics* 8 (October 1985): 90–101.

Parpart, Jane L., and Kathleen A. Staudt, eds. *Women and the State in Africa*. Boulder, Colo.: Lynne Rienner, 1989.

Penna, David, et al. "Africa Rights Monitor: A Woman's Right to Political Participation in Africa." *Africa Today* 37 (1990): 49–64.

Rai, Shirin, Hilary Pilkington, and Annie Phizacklea, eds. *Women in the Face of Change: The Soviet Union, Eastern Europe, and China*. London and New York: Routledge, 1992.

Randall, Vicky. *Women and Politics: An International Perspective*. 2d ed. Chicago: University of Chicago Press, 1987.

Rowbotham, Sheila. *Women in Movement: Feminism and Social Action*. New York and London: Routledge, 1992.

Staudt, Kathleen. "Women's Politics, the State, and Capitalist Transformation in Africa." In *Studies in Power and Class in Africa*, edited by I. L. Markovitz. New York: Oxford University Press, 1987.

Wolchik, Sharon L., and Alfred G. Meyer, eds. *Women, State, and Party in Eastern Europe*. Durham, N.C.: Duke University Press, 1985.

✦ Democratization

A wave of democratization occurs when a set of changes in regime occur within a short time span and over a geographically circumscribed group of countries—all in the direction of greater democracy and all caused by the same events or processes. Eventually, the direction of change becomes less unidirectional and the wave recedes, leaving behind some cases of consolidated democracy.

Any attempt to plot the dates when democracies have been founded or have significantly expanded their practice of citizenship or degree of accountability will reveal a strong tendency toward "clustering" in time and space. Except for a few countries that followed idiosyncratic paths and timed their changes in regime in seeming disregard for what was happening to their neighbors, most contemporary democracies emerged in a series of waves—in close physical and temporal proximity to other democracies.

Defining the Waves

Beyond these general observations, however, analysts tend to disagree on when and how many of these waves have occurred. Samuel P. Huntington, for example, maintains that there have been three waves of democratization. He argues that the first wave flowed uninterruptedly for almost one hundred years—from 1828 to 1926. The impetus for his second wave was World War II; his third corresponds to the period since the mid-1970s.

By my reckoning, there have been four, more compact, waves. The first (the so-called Springtime of Freedom), which began in 1848, was spectacular but ephemeral. All of the countries affected were European, and most had reverted to their previous form of governance or to an even more autocratic regime by 1852. France, the German confederation, and Austria were the most prominent reversals.

The second major "outbreak" of democracy corresponded to World War I (1914–1918) and its aftermath. During this wave, new countries were carved out of the defunct Austro-Hungarian Empire, which had ruled over much of East Central Europe and the Balkans, and the czarist Russian Empire, which was overwhelmed by the Bolshevik Revolution in 1917. All these states initially turned to democracy. In Germany the Weimar Republic replaced the imperial Reich. Moreover, important extensions of the franchise and inclusions of new parties into government occurred in those Western European countries that already were partially democratic, such as Belgium, Italy, the Netherlands, and the Scandinavian countries.

The third wave came in the aftermath of World War II. Numerous countries that had been democratic before the war were liberated to return to their previous status, and new democracies were established in Western Germany and in Italy after the defeat of Nazism and fascism. This time the process of change spread far beyond Europe, through decolonization in Asia and Africa, reaching Ghana, Guinea, Nigeria, Ceylon, Burma, India, Malaysia, Indonesia, and others. Japan and South Korea were both given democratic institutions by a withdrawing occupying power. In Latin America numerous dictators frozen in power by the war were overthrown.

The fourth wave of democratization began quite unexpectedly in Portugal on April 25, 1974, with a virtually bloodless military coup. This was followed shortly by similar changes in Greece and subsequently in Latin America. It does not yet seem to have receded. Needless to say, those who participated in these first experiments with changes of regime could not have known that they would be instrumental in initiating a wave that would eventually cover almost the entire surface of the earth. Each subsequent case of regime change was linked to the previous ones through processes of diffusion and imitation. Each success (or failure) in one country tended to create a model for others to follow (or to avoid).

Characteristics of the Fourth Wave

Compared with previous waves, the fourth wave has some peculiar characteristics. First of all, it has been much more global in its reach than the earlier ones. The fourth wave began in southern Europe in the mid-1970s, then spread to Latin America and affected some Asian countries in the 1980s, and literally swept through Eastern Europe after 1989. Moreover, from Mongolia to Mali, Madagascar to Mexico, important changes were still in the offing in the mid-1990s. Only the Middle East seemed immune, although even there some change was occurring in Tunisia, Jordan, and Kuwait. In Algeria in 1992, however, the experiment was abruptly called off when the first competitive elections held out the prospect of a victory by Islamic fundamentalists.

Furthermore, as a consequence of its global nature, the fourth wave affected far more countries and was more thorough in its regional impact than previous waves. Some parts of the world that had been almost uniformly autocratic became almost equally uniformly democratic—the changes in Latin America and Eastern Europe being the most dramatic. Cuba and Serbia stand out in their respective regions for their unwillingness to change their regimes.

Finally, countries affected by the fourth wave so far have suffered far fewer regressions to autocracy than did countries in the past. The only clear reversal was Haiti, whose first democratically elected president, Jean-Bertrand Aristide, was forced out by a military coup in 1991. Aristide, however, was restored through outside intervention in 1994. Thailand and Nigeria are special cases that seem to oscillate persistently in type of regime. The former seems to have broken the cycle in the 1990s; the latter remains mired in a repressive military dictatorship. In Peru it remains to be seen whether President Alberto Fujimori's *autogolpe*, or "self-coup," of April 1992 will produce a permanent reversal. With the country under siege by drug traffickers and a guerrilla group known as the Shining Path, Fujimori declared a state of emergency, arrogated to himself special powers, and dissolved the legislature. He was reelected president in 1995, in large part because of his success in ending guerrilla terrorism and moving the country's economy forward. In Burma and China strong pressures for democratization surfaced in the 1980s and 1990s, but they were suppressed before change could take place.

Merely pointing out this temporal and spatial clustering of experiences does not explain its occurrence. The most obvious hypothesis is that waves of democratization are produced by processes of diffusion. Contagion is the most plausible explanation, especially when no simultaneous external event is present. The successful example of one country's transition establishes it as a model for other countries to imitate; once a region is sufficiently saturated with democratic political regimes, pressure will mount, compelling the remaining autocracies to conform to the newly established norm.

The hypothesis of diffusion is particularly appealing to explain the post-1974 wave for two reasons. On the one hand, the countries affected have not suffered any common external event such as a world war or an economic depression. And, on the other, the development of transnational communications systems has provided greater assurance that the mechanisms of diffusion are working. Until the advent of sophisticated communications devices, the main empiri-

cal evidence for diffusion hinged on geographical propinquity: an innovation was supposed to reach nearby countries before it got to ones farther away. Hence the observation that democratization in the fourth wave began in southern Europe and then "leap-frogged" to Latin America in the late 1970s and early 1980s without first affecting countries in North Africa or Eastern Europe, which were closer at hand, would have contradicted the diffusion hypothesis. However, contemporary systems of communication are complex and instantaneous. They are not spatially bound and may not even be culturally confined. Given the extraordinary capabilities of such systems, it should come as no surprise that the messages and models of democracy could be received and responded to in Mongolia before Mali or Mexico.

The Momentum Effect

The notion of waves suggests that with each successive instance of democratization the influence of international events will tend to increase in the same direction. Those countries that come later in the wave will be increasingly influenced by those that preceded them. Whether they can be expected to learn from the mistakes made earlier is perhaps less predictable, but there may be advantages to "delayed democratization"—just as it has been argued that late economic development has advantages. Latecomers can adopt the practices and values of their forerunners without having to pay the same discovery and start-up costs.

One of the reasons for this momentum effect is that each successive case of democratization has contributed to the development of more and more formal nongovernmental organizations and informal networks of activists devoted to measures intended to further democratization. Among them are groups that promote human rights, work to protect minorities, monitor elections, provide economic advice, and foster exchanges among academics and intellectuals. When the first democratizations in the fourth wave occurred in Portugal, Greece, and Spain, this international infrastructure hardly existed. But by the mid-1990s an extraordinary variety of international parties, associations, foundations, movements, networks, and public interest firms were ready to intervene to promote or to protect democracy.

The existence of these groups suggests that the international context surrounding democratization has shifted from a primary reliance on public, intergovernmental channels of influence toward an increased involvement of private, nongovernmental organizations. The activity of these agents, rather than the abstract processes of diffusion, accounts for the "global reach" of contemporary democratization and the fact that so few regressions to autocracy have occurred.

Moreover, close empirical observation rarely confirms the sustained importance of diffusion alone. Take, for example, the cases of Portugal and Spain. Despite their geographical and cultural proximity and the temporal coincidence of their transitions, it is implausible to assert that Spain embarked upon its change of regime in 1975 because of the events of April 1974 in Portugal. In fact, the Spaniards had long been waiting for the death of Francisco Franco, whose dictatorial rule had lasted since the 1930s. His death—not the Portuguese revolution—was the triggering event for democratization. In many ways the Spanish were much better prepared for democratization than were their Portuguese neighbors precisely because they had begun preparing for it much earlier. At most, it could be claimed that Spain learned some negative lessons about what to avoid during the transition and therefore had a relatively easier time of it than might otherwise have been the case.

Irrefutable proof of effective diffusion from southern Europe to Latin America or to Asia or the countries of Eastern Europe would also be difficult to provide. Spain (and, more recently, Chile in the late 1980s and early 1990s) seemed to have offered latecomers a model of successful transition that may have encouraged them to venture into uncertain terrain. But this speculation is a long way from claiming that Spain actually caused the others to change their type of regime.

The argument for waves of democratization based on contagion is more persuasive within specific regional contexts. The unexpected (and highly controlled) transition in Paraguay seems to have been influenced by prior changes in its neighborhood. The removal of Gen. Alfredo Stroessner in 1989 by a clique of military officers came not long after the country was literally surrounded by nascent democracies. Stroessner had maintained dictatorial rule in Paraguay for thirty-five years.

Chile under Gen. Augusto Pinochet held out successfully against such pressures during the 1980s. In 1988 Pinochet even dared to use the poor economic performance of the country's recently democratized neighbors as an argument for citizens to vote "sí" in a plebiscite that would have perpetuated his rule for another eight years. His defeat in that plebiscite suggests (but does not prove) that Chilean citizens were influenced not just by their own democratic tradition but also by the wave of democratization that had already engulfed their neighbors.

Eastern Europe may provide the best possible case for contagion, even though the initial impetus for changes of regime in the countries of this region came from an external event: the shift in Soviet foreign and defense policy in regard to its satellites. No one can question the accelerating flow of messages and images that traveled from Poland to Hungary, to the German Democratic Republic and Czechoslovakia, to Romania and Bulgaria, and eventually to Albania, or the impact that their declarations of national independence had upon the republics that made up the Soviet Union.

The Impact of Multilateralism

The situation in Eastern Europe suggests that the most effective international context for influencing the course of democratization has increasingly become regional and multilateral, not bilateral or global. Both the lessons of contagion and the mechanisms of consent seem to function better within geographical and cultural confines.

The very existence of this embryonic transnational civil society—whether at the regional or the global level—seems also to have influenced the diplomatic behavior of national governments. Those countries whose citizens have most strongly supported the efforts of nongovernmental organizations working for democratization have found themselves increasingly obligated to support efforts at democratization officially and resolutely, in ways that go beyond normal calculations of national self-interest. Traditional protestations against interference in other nations' domestic affairs have become less and less compelling; the distinction between the realms of national and international politics has been eroded.

Even more significant in the long run may be the increased reliance on multilateral diplomacy and international organizations to bring pressures to bear on remaining autocracies or democracies that relapse into autocratic government. "Political conditionality" has taken its place alongside the "economic conditionality" so long practiced by the International Monetary Fund and the International Bank for Reconstruction and Development. Global and regional organizations explicitly link the concession of credits, the negotiation of commercial agreements, and the granting of membership in their ranks to specific demands. Receiving governments must take measures to reform political institutions, hold honest elections, respect human rights, and protect the physical safety and culture of ethnic or religious minorities.

In extreme cases—and Eastern Europe seems to be one of them—various bilateral and multilateral conditions combine in such a fashion as to place considerable restrictions on the maneuvering space of new democratic leaders. Remarkably, these leaders have literally demanded to be subjected to international conditions so that they can tell their populations that they have no choice but to take certain unpopular decisions.

The European Union, with its multiple levels and diverse incentives, has been of primary importance in the successful consolidation of democracy in southern Europe. Its role is also likely to be significant in Eastern Europe, despite the growing evidence that its members are unwilling to make similar concessions and commitments in that area. The European Union's inability to act collectively and decisively in preventing war between the nationalist groups that sprang from the former Yugoslavia, however, is a sobering reminder of the limits of providing multilateral security to nascent democracies.

No other region of the world has an institutional infrastructure as complex and resourceful as that of Western Europe. The Organization of American States and the Organization of African Unity have both taken some steps toward providing collective security for new democracies and relaxing their traditional inhibitions against interfering in the domestic affairs of their members. The Arab League and the Association of Southeast Asian Nations have been conspicuously silent on the issue.

When a region such as Latin America becomes almost saturated with democracy, pressures are likely to increase on the few autocracies that remain, and the countries that have relapsed to autocracy will find themselves cast out of the fold.

But such pressures seem incapable of guaranteeing democratization—as demonstrated by the case of Cuba. In Haiti outside intervention by armed force eventually restored the country to its (delayed) place in the fourth wave, but it took the unilateral action of the United States to do so. Collective protests and embargoes by the Organization of American States and the United Nations were manifestly insufficient.

The Crest of the Wave

A wave of democratization has crested when it becomes equally likely that a change in regime will occur in a democratic or an autocratic direction. It has reversed its direction when regression to some form of autocracy is the most likely response to crisis. The wave of democratization that began in Portugal on April 25, 1974, may have lost some of its energy—and it seems increasingly possible that certain cultural areas such as the Islamic Middle East and Southeast Asia will be protected from its full force—but it has lasted longer and has been more extensive than any of its predecessors. Moreover, it has already left several of its "victims" high and dry on the beach as consolidated democracies and has not yet dragged any of them back to autocracy.

See also Consolidation.

PHILIPPE C. SCHMITTER

BIBLIOGRAPHY

Gill, Graeme J. *The Dynamics of Democratization: Elites, Civil Society, and the Transition Process.* New York: St. Martin's Press, 2000.

Huntington, Samuel P. *The Third Wave: Democratization in the Twentieth Century.* Norman: University of Oklahoma Press, 1991.

The International Dimensions of Democratization: Europe and the Americas. Edited by Laurence Whitehead. New York: Oxford University Press, 2001.

The Internet, Democracy, and Democratization. Edited by Peter Ferdinand. Frank Cass, 2000.

The Politics of Memory and Democratization. Edited by Alexandra Barahona de Brito, Enriquez Carmen Gonzalez, and Paloma Aguilar. New York: Oxford University Press, 2001.

Pridham, Geoffrey, ed. *Encouraging Democracy: The International Context of Regime Change in Southern Europe.* Leicester: Leicester University Press, 1991.

Schmitter, Philippe C. "The International Context for Contemporary Democratization." *Stanford Journal of International Affairs* 2 (fall/winter 1993): 1-34.

Tetreault, Mary Ann. *Stories of Democracy.* New York: Columbia University Press, 2000.

✦ Elites, Political

Political elites make up a somewhat elastic category that includes a country's most senior politicians and also the most politically influential leaders of governmental, economic, military, professional, communications, religious, and cultural organizations and movements. They are distinguished by their proximity to political decision making and their ability to influence political outcomes regularly and significantly.

There are two main types of political elites: established elites, which initiate and implement policies, and counterelites, which mainly oppose and try to block policies, sometimes by overthrowing the elites that are responsible for them.

Analyzing political elites involves several important and controversial issues. These include how to identify political elites, the significance of their social makeup, their modes of behavior and degrees of integration with each other, and their relationship to the mass public, especially in democracies.

Who Are Political Elites?

No clear line can be drawn between political elites and everyone else. Popular references to them imply that they include a large assortment of policymakers, leaders of organizations, and opinion leaders, plus numerous advisers and experts, at both the national and the local levels. This implication makes political elites equivalent to a political class, and the two terms tend to be used interchangeably. For example, the million or so persons cleared to hold important party-state (*nomenklatura*) positions in the Soviet Union were long regarded as its political elite or political class.

Scholars, however, usually construe the term more narrowly as applied to a single nation. It is used to refer to a few hundred or a few thousand holders of top-level positions in the largest or otherwise most resource-rich institutions, organizations, voluntary associations, and political movements. Thus one systematic study of political elites in the United States during the early 1980s identified some 6,000 individuals who held roughly 7,000 top positions in institutions that together controlled more than half of the country's resources.

Political elites can be identified by methods other than strictly positional identification. One method asks well-chosen political insiders to name the most influential persons in key sectors of society. Those receiving the most nominations clearly have the widest reputations for influence, no matter what their formal positions may be, and they are regarded as political elites. Another method studies who actually participates in political decision making in specific policy domains and uses this information to identify the most powerful and influential persons. A third method charts the decision-making and influence networks that enmesh and cut across policy domains; network members are classified as political elites.

No method of identifying political elites is foolproof. Political decision making is complex and often is shrouded in secrecy. In addition, agreements not to treat some issues (nondecisions) may be as important as actual decisions, yet they are much more difficult to discern. Studies of political elites increasingly combine methods, hoping that the advantages of each will make the list comprehensive.

Analysts scrutinize the social background and demographic profiles of political elites: their age and gender, family and class origins, education, and career, as well as their religious, ethnic, regional, and other affiliations. In authoritarian political regimes, detailed investigations of elite attitudes and actions are difficult to conduct. In such cases, public biographical data about political elites may be the only information available about them.

Elite Recruitment and Representation

One aim of scholars is to assess the open or closed character of elite recruitment. This undertaking is based on the assumption that a steady flow of persons from mass to elite positions and vice versa is essential for political equality and thus political stability. A second aim is to uncover biases in elite decisions and actions favoring the groups and population categories from which elites are drawn. In a famous study of the American "power elite," for example, the sociologist C. Wright Mills showed that business, political, and military leaders in American society during the nineteenth and twentieth centuries were recruited overwhelmingly from a small, privileged social stratum. He argued that their policies and decisions systematically favored that stratum.

Studies like Mills's have been conducted in many countries and have usually found a similarly skewed pattern of elite recruitment. Such results have led exponents of greater democracy to demand that the social composition of political elites more accurately reflect the diversity of mass electorates. The issue is not a simple one, however. It is possible that effective representation of ethnic minorities suffering serious discrimination or of women long consigned to subordinate places in society can be achieved only by elites who themselves have experienced such disadvantages. On the other hand, people who watch the maneuvers of elites often observe that their policy choices and other actions result most directly from current political and organizational needs and dilemmas. In short, elites do what they must in order to survive. If this is so, then the social profiles of political elites reveal more about magnitudes of political and social inequalities in societies than about how effectively elites represent different categories of citizens.

In any event, over the long term, democratic politics does seem to make the social profiles of political elites, especially those in politics and government, more similar to those of the mass public. The necessity to appeal for popular support, to placate emerging discontents, and to incorporate leaders of movements organizing those discontents, plus routine electoral turnover, gradually narrows the obvious differences between political elites and everyone else. The presence that women have achieved in representative and executive political bodies, as well as some other elite arenas, in virtually all democracies is the most obvious illustration of this long-term trend. It seems that a robust democracy inexorably erodes the closed and privileged character of the political elites that tend to dominate its early life.

Elite Decision Making and Interaction

Because of the roles that political elites play in making and influencing decisions, their attitudes on policy issues are regarded as principal determinants of political outcomes. Consequently, much journalistic and scholarly effort goes into tracking elite policy preferences. Compared with public opinion, the attitudes of elite groups have been found to be in more conflict over a greater range of issues, while the attitudes of each group are more coherent and logically consistent, more intensively held and stable over time, and more shaped by party attachments and the policy positions parties take. A difficulty, however, is that organizational and popular pressures often force political elites to say one thing but do another. Aware of this, political elites tend either to express their views ambiguously or to parrot the stated policies of the governments and parties with which they are affiliated. Their real thoughts and goals remain elusive. Thus it is always risky to predict elite actions on the basis of their recorded attitudes.

Different modes of interaction among political elites may help or hinder democracy. In particular, stable democracy appears to depend in part on institutionalizing a mode of elite interaction characterized by restrained partisanship and by a view of politics as "bargaining" rather than "war." This involves elite consensus about democratic procedures and values, together with a tacit but widely shared code of political conduct that prizes accommodation and cooperation. Day-to-day policy disputes and power competitions, however, inevitably blur or conceal this mode of interaction. In addition, the procedures, values, and codes on which elites agree are always being modified. Observing and investigating the basic mode of interaction among political elites in stable democracies is therefore difficult. Usually, analysts must infer the mode of interaction from the comparative restraint that elites display in their conflicts, from their collaborations aimed at avoiding or defusing explosive issues, and from internal policing actions that penalize or expel persons who flagrantly violate the "rules of the game." Dramatic scandals and exposés—such as the Watergate affair that terminated the presidency of Richard M. Nixon in the United States in 1974 or the revelations and prosecutions that toppled a sizable part of Italy's political elites during the early 1990s—are perhaps best seen as policing actions by elites and subelites, aimed at reaffirming and strengthening the rules by which democratic politics is played.

Degrees of Integration

Closely related to the mode of interaction is the extent of integration of political elites in stable democracies. Several models have been advanced. A pluralist model depicts loose integration, with each elite group being distinct and narrowly based and having its power and influence confined to the issues most relevant to its supporters or constituents. The power elite model highlights a coincidence of interests among economic, political, and military institutions; similar social origins and outlooks among the persons who command those institutions; and the social intermingling that helps them to dominate other more dispersed elites. A class model stresses the recruitment of elites from propertied backgrounds, their extensive family and other social connections, and their use of power in service to ruling class interests in capitalist societies.

Studies of networks among political elites in democracies, such as the United States, Australia, and West Germany, have suggested a fusion of these models. Elites operate through overlapping, informal, flexible, but still cohesive circles of influence that form around and across issues and institutions. Within these circles people engage in repeated, often indirect, interactions on common policy issues and purposes. This system provides a significant amount of integration without any group or set of leaders predominating. Instead, there is a central influence circle that consists of several hundred holders of the uppermost positions in the most important institutions and organizations. This circle overarches and integrates the many smaller, issue-specific circles. Political elites in stable democracies thus appear to be tightly integrated, as they do in the power

elite and class models. The fluidity of their relations, the diversity of their social profiles, and the conflicts indicated by their opinions and actions on issues are more in accord with the pluralist model.

The several models of integration of political elites lead to different interpretations of the relationship between elites and the mass public in democracies. The power elite and class models downplay the extent of elite consensus in order to emphasize the manipulative and coercive ways in which a few core elite groups perpetuate their supremacy and that of the class from which they come. The trappings of democracy are thus largely a façade for power elite or class dominance. The pluralist model highlights the existence of elite consensus and peaceful accommodations, but it regards these patterns as stemming from a rough balance of power among elite groups and from elite adherence to the democratic values and beliefs of the wider political culture. The network model focuses on shared elite access to decision making and implies that shared access keeps most or all elites motivated to sustain and even extend the democratic procedures and values in which their decision-making access is embedded.

To the extent that accommodation and sharing of power among elites are a principal feature of all stable democracies, it seems that democracies have an inescapably "elitist" character.

See also Theory, elite.

JOHN HIGLEY

BIBLIOGRAPHY

Domhoff, G. William. *The Power Elite and the State.* New York: Aldine De Gruyter, 1990.
Dye, Thomas R. *Who's Running America? The Reagan Years.* Englewood Cliffs, N.J.: Prentice-Hall, 1983.

Etzioni-Halevy, Eva. *The Elite Connection: Problems and Potential of Western Democracy.* Cambridge: Polity Press, 1993.

Gill, Graeme J. *The Dynamics of Democratization: Elites, Civil Society, and the Transition Process.* New York: St. Martin's Press, 2000.

Higley, John, Ursula Hoffmann-Lange, Charles Kadushin, and Gwen Moore. "Elite Integration in Stable Democracies: A Reconsideration." *European Sociological Review* 7 (1991): 35-53.

The International Dimensions of Democratization: Europe and the Americas. Edited by Laurence Whitehead. New York: Oxford University Press, 2001.

The Internet, Democracy, and Democratization. Edited by Peter Ferdinand. Frank Cass, 2000.

Mills, C. Wright. *The Power Elite.* New York: Oxford University Press, 1956.

Moyser, George, and Margaret Wagstaffe, eds. *Research Methods for Elite Studies.* London: Allen and Unwin, 1987.

Parry, Geraint. *Political Elites.* London: Allen and Unwin, 1969.

The Politics of Memory and Democratization. Edited by Alexandra Barahona de Brito, Enriquez Carmen Gonzalez, and Paloma Aguilar. New York: Oxford University Press, 2001

Putnam, Robert D. *The Comparative Study of Political Elites.* Englewood Cliffs, N.J.: Prentice-Hall, 1976.

Tetreault, Mary Ann. *Stories of Democracy.* New York: Columbia University Press, 2000.

✦ Human rights

Human rights are the claims that all human beings are justly entitled to make merely by virtue of their being human. When this concept was introduced in the seventeenth century, these claims were described as natural rights and were said to be derived from the essential nature of every human individual. Over the centuries the more common term became first *the rights of man* and then *human rights.* This change reflected in part a broadening of the range of such rights to include claims that cannot easily be regarded as natural and that in some cases can be fulfilled only in a prosperous society.

The concept of human rights is intimately bound up with the development of modern democracy. *Democracy,* as the term is most often used today, comprises two essential elements: rule by the majority and the protection of individual human rights. Political rule by the majority of the citizens flourished in classical Greece; the notion of human rights, however, is a modern innovation. All previous moral and political teachings emphasized duties or obligations rather than rights. To the extent that rights were acknowledged at all, they were regarded as dependent on the political order to which one belonged, not as natural or universal rights.

Hobbes and Locke

Although some would trace the origin of the concept of human rights back to the Dutch jurist Hugo Grotius (1583–1645) or even to earlier thinkers, the first fully elaborated doctrine of natural rights appeared in the work of Thomas Hobbes (1588–1679). The key to Hobbes's political philosophy is his doctrine of the *state of nature,* the term he uses to describe the prepolitical situation that he regards as the natural human condition. According to Hobbes, all men are by nature equal, and each is dominated by the desire for self-preservation. As a result, where they are not governed by a sovereign power, they are in a perpetual state of war with one another. In this situation, there is no law, and no actions can be considered unjust. Although human beings thus have no natural duties, they do possess the "right of nature": all individuals are free to do whatever they deem necessary for their own self-preservation.

Despite—indeed, because of—this unbounded liberty, human life in the state of nature is, in Hobbes's most famous phrase, "solitary, poor, nasty, brutish, and short." But reason suggests to human beings a way in which they may escape from the misery of their natural condition: they can mutually agree to transfer their natural right to all things to a sovereign power that will seek to preserve peace among them and defend them against external enemies. Thus the basis of all political orders is this covenant, or social contract, entered into voluntarily (though largely out of fear) by free and equal individuals in order to improve their own security.

Hobbes himself favored monarchy over republicanism and was a notorious champion of absolutism. Believing that the horrors occasioned by civil war were the greatest calamity that could befall human beings, he maintained that the rights of the sovereign should be unchecked and indivisible and that subjects have no right to withdraw their consent to obey the sovereign once it is given. (Even Hobbes, however, held that certain rights, such as that of resisting assaults upon one's life, are inalienable and cannot be transferred or renounced; in the same spirit, he opposed self-incrimination and the admissibility of evidence obtained through torture.) Yet the principles that he put forth were to become the basic framework of the liberal tradition: that human beings are naturally free, equal, and independent and that only their own consent can provide a sound and legitimate foundation for political rule. Unlike previous political thinkers, Hobbes taught that by nature the solitary individual and individual rights precede the political or social community and the duties owed to it.

One of those who adapted the Hobbesian framework to produce a teaching more favorable to the rights of subjects was Benedict de Spinoza (1632–1677), who proclaimed democracy to be the most natural form of government and the one most compatible with individual liberty. The most influential exponent of a more liberal version of the doctrine of natural rights, however, was John Locke (1632–1704).

Locke's teaching differs from that of Hobbes in some important ways. Although Locke follows Hobbes in characterizing humans in the state of nature as being perfectly free and equal and preeminently concerned with their own self-preservation, he also presents the state of nature as differing from the state of war. Locke claims that the state of nature is governed by a "law of nature" that teaches people not to harm one another. Yet he also asserts that in the state of nature individuals have the right to punish transgressions against the law of nature, including the right to destroy those who threaten them with destruction. Thus, however one finally interprets Locke's puzzling account of the law of nature, it is not surprising that he concludes that the rights of the individual in the state of nature are precarious and subject to repeated violation by others. And, like Hobbes, he prescribes as the remedy for the constant fears and dangers of the state of nature a voluntary agreement among individuals to form a political society.

According to Locke's account, however, individuals do not unreservedly transfer their natural rights to the sovereign when they establish a commonwealth. Because their very purpose in entering into political society is to secure the rights that they enjoy in the state of nature, it would be foolish and counterproductive for them to endow the sovereign with absolute, arbitrary power. Thus legitimate political power must be strictly confined to the pursuit of the public good of the society, which is understood as the preservation of the lives and possessions of those who compose it. Moreover, such power should be divided between a supreme legislative authority (preferably entrusted to an assembly whose members will themselves be subject to the laws they have made) and a subordinate executive. Even the legislative power, should it betray its trust, may be removed or altered by the people. Although Locke's teaching is not incompatible with limited monarchy, he clearly advocates the sovereignty of the people.

Locke formulated what became the classic trinity of natural rights—life, liberty, and property. For Hobbes, property did not exist in the state of nature. Locke, by contrast, tries to show that human labor can give a right to property outside the bounds of political society. Indeed, Locke sometimes seems to give property pride of place among the natural rights, asserting that the preservation of property is the goal of political society and stressing that government does not have the right to confiscate or even to tax the property of the people without their consent. Labor, Locke suggests, is essential not just for the bare preservation of human beings but for their comfort and security; hence they must be guaranteed secure property rights that will enable them to enjoy the fruits of their labor.

The American and French Revolutions

The doctrine of natural rights, chiefly in its Lockean formulation, was to become the theoretical inspiration of both the American and French Revolutions, as reflected in the most famous documents of those revolutions. The American Declaration of Independence states: "We hold these truths to be self-evident, that all men are created equal, that they are endowed by their Creator with certain unalienable Rights, that among these are Life, Liberty and the pursuit of Happiness. That to secure these rights, Governments are instituted among Men, deriving their just powers from the consent of the governed. That whenever any Form of Government becomes destructive of

these ends, it is the Right of the People to alter or to abolish it." And the Declaration of the Rights of Man and of the Citizen, issued by France's National Assembly in 1789, asserts: "The end of all political associations is the preservation of the natural and imprescriptible rights of man; and these rights are liberty, property, security, and resistance of oppression."

The French declaration also enumerates a variety of civil or political rights that citizens can expect their government to uphold as a way of fulfilling their basic natural rights. Similar guarantees of civil and political rights can be found in the U.S. Constitution and in the Bill of Rights, with which it was amended. These include the rule of law; various protections regarding the administration of criminal justice; freedom of religion, of speech, and of the press; protection of property rights; the institution of a separation of powers within the government; and the right of citizens to participate in choosing their representatives in the legislature.

Although theorists belonging to the Lockean tradition of natural rights strongly favor representative government, and thus a certain measure of majority rule, they often are highly critical of "democracy," particularly as it was practiced in the ancient republics. This viewpoint is evident in *Federalist* No. 10, in which James Madison asserts that the great flaw of popular government is its tendency toward oppression by a majority faction. Thus Madison argues that "pure," or direct, democracies, like those of antiquity, have always been incompatible with personal security and the rights of property. The goal of the "new science of politics" elaborated in *The Federalist*, whose chief principles are constitutionalism, representative government, and the separation of powers, is to combine popular sovereignty with the protection of every citizen's rights to life, liberty, and property. The success of this project has been so great that today the defense of individual rights is generally regarded as a constitutive element of democracy.

The Influence of Kant

The doctrine of natural rights—grounded in rights that belong equally to all human beings—clearly is universalist in character. At the same time, however, this doctrine holds that political orders derive their being and their legitimacy only from the consent of those who are party to the social contract. The social contract embraces not the whole of humanity but only the members of a particular society, whose government is obliged to protect the life, liberty, and property of its own citizens. Moreover, the various political societies remain in a "state of nature" with one another, subject to no binding law or common power. Thus the citizens of one political order would appear to have no compelling interest in how another sovereign power treats its own citizens or in securing the protection of human rights internationally.

The turn toward internationalizing the concept of human rights is associated with the thought of Immanuel Kant, who in his *Perpetual Peace* (1795) elaborates the idea of a federation of nations composed of states that have representative (or republican) governments. According to Kant, republican government is the only kind appropriate to the rights of man, and it is also the most conducive to peace among nations. By establishing international concord, Kant's proposed federation would render more secure the rights to life, liberty, and property of individual citizens by protecting them against the danger of war, thus completing humanity's escape from the state of nature to a state of peace.

Kant also effects a far-reaching transformation in the qualitative understanding of human rights. In Kant's thought, human freedom is no longer understood primarily as a means for achieving the ends of self-preservation or the pursuit of happi-

ness. Building upon the distinction, introduced by Jean-Jacques Rousseau, between natural liberty (which consists in following one's own inclinations) and civil, or moral, liberty (which consists in self-imposed obedience to law), Kant identifies freedom with self-legislation. But he extends Rousseau's notion of the "general will," which constitutes the self-legislation of a particular political community, into a principle of universal human morality.

The central principle of that morality—the "categorical imperative"—commands that human beings act only in accordance with maxims that they can also will to be universal laws. Kant also offers a second formulation of the categorical imperative, which commands that we treat human beings always as ends and never only as means. By this standard, to violate the rights of others is to treat them as mere means and hence is morally impermissible. The rights of individuals must be respected not because they are naturally impelled to seek their self-preservation but because they are rational beings capable of obeying the moral law. According to Kant, it is because human beings are capable of morality that they alone have dignity.

The influence of Kant is immediately apparent when one turns to the most prominent human rights document of the twentieth century, the Universal Declaration of Human Rights proclaimed by the United Nations (UN) in 1948. Its preamble begins: "Whereas recognition of the inherent dignity and of the equal and inalienable rights of all members of the human family is the foundation of freedom, justice, and peace in the world." The first sentence of Article 1 ("All human beings are born free and equal in dignity and rights") also adds the Kantian emphasis on human dignity to the older language of inalienable rights.

Economic and Social Rights

The first twenty-one of the thirty articles of the Universal Declaration generally speak of the kinds of rights that are familiar from the eighteenth-century French Declaration of the Rights of Man and of the Citizen. Article 22, however, begins the enumeration of a new kind of rights: "Everyone, as a member of society, has the right to social security and is entitled to realization, through national effort and international cooperation and in accordance with the organization and resources of each State, of the economic, social and cultural rights indispensable for his dignity and the free development of his personality." The succeeding articles not only affirm the right to work and to join trade unions but also promote such entitlements as the right to leisure, including paid holidays; the right to an "adequate" standard of living and to financial security in the event of unemployment, sickness, and old age; the right to free compulsory elementary education; and the right to enjoy the arts. This section concludes with Article 28, which states that all are entitled to "a social and international order" in which the rights outlined in the declaration can be fulfilled.

The inclusion of this new class of rights seems to reflect a kind of universalization of the goals of welfare-state liberalism, as embodied in Franklin D. Roosevelt's New Deal in the United States. Indeed, the preamble to the Universal Declaration explicitly cites the aspiration toward a world in which all will enjoy Roosevelt's famous "four freedoms"; these include not just freedom of speech and belief but also freedom from fear and want. Most governments, however, are not as capable of ensuring their citizens freedom from want as they are of guaranteeing freedom of speech or belief. The degree to which a government can honor these social and economic rights must depend on its own "resources" or on "international cooperation."

The question of whether such economic and social aspirations can properly be considered human rights remains a subject of both political and intellectual controversy. The United Nations has given equal status to economic, social, and cultural rights, on the one hand, and to political and civil rights, on the other. Twin International Covenants on these two classes of rights were adopted in 1966. Subsequent UN documents affirm not only that human rights are "indivisible" but that attainment of civil and political rights requires the enjoyment of economic and social rights and hence demands "effective" national and international development policies. More recent UN declarations have proclaimed a universal "right to development."

The cause of economic and social rights has been championed at the United Nations by representatives of developing countries and of communist countries. Critics of the UN doctrine on economic and social rights, however, charge that it allows authoritarian governments in poor countries to justify their failure to comply with political and civil rights by claiming that such noncompliance is the fault of richer countries that have inadequately provided them with international development assistance. The eminent Soviet dissident Andrei Sakharov (1929–1989) argued that, contrary to the official state propaganda of communist countries emphasizing economic and social rights, it is really civil and political rights that guarantee individual liberty and give life to social and economic rights.

In any case, it seems clear that the concept of economic and social rights reflected in UN documents represents a departure from the orientation that informed the natural rights tradition. The very notion of equal and inalienable rights traditionally extended only to those goods that individuals were naturally entitled (one might even say compelled) to seek, prior to and apart from their membership in any political society. In forming or joining themselves to a social contract, individuals transferred some portion of their natural rights to the community. In return, they became better able to achieve the ends they sought in the state of nature because of the security granted by the new rights they obtained as citizens. These civil and political rights offered them a protected sphere in which each could engage in the pursuit of happiness. The role of government was not to provide individuals with goods but to enable them to pursue their own goods.

This older tradition was by no means silent about economic rights. Indeed, it gave a central role to the right of property, founded on the natural right of individuals to enjoy the fruits of their own labor. It thus emphasized economic freedom (appropriately regulated by the political community) as opposed to economic entitlements. The UN Universal Declaration still includes the right of individuals to own property and not to be deprived of it arbitrarily (Article 17), but there is no longer any mention of property rights in the two International Covenants or in most subsequent UN declarations. Nonetheless, in the 1990s, with the fall of Soviet communism and the worldwide trend toward privatization, signs have appeared that the notion of a human right to property is coming back into favor. In fact, the draft Russian constitution proposed by President Boris Yeltsin in April 1993 proclaimed the inviolability of private property and even called it a natural right.

Human Rights and International Politics

The issue of human rights moved to the forefront of international politics in the 1970s. During that decade the activities of the dissident human rights movement in the Soviet Union and Eastern Europe captured the attention and the imagination of the world. In the 1975 Helsinki Agreement of the Conference on Security and Cooperation in Europe (CSCE), the Soviet Union and its allies, in exchange for gains they sought regarding economic and security issues, agreed to a series of Western-inspired human rights provisions. This public commitment on the part of their governments further energized the dissidents, and unofficial Helsinki Watch committees sprang up in both East and West to monitor compliance. Periodic CSCE review meetings provided a regular opportunity to call the communist countries to account and to bring worldwide attention to the plight of the dissidents. Many observers believe that the human rights movement made a crucial contribution to the subsequent collapse of European communism.

Human rights was brought to new prominence in U.S. foreign policy during the administration (1977–1981) of Jimmy Carter, who made the promotion of international human rights a central focus of his presidency. A bureau of human rights and humanitarian affairs was established in the State Department, and it was charged with compiling an annual report to Congress on the human rights performance of countries throughout the world. The brutal violations of human rights (including torture and "disappearances") in a number of Latin American countries during this period brought enhanced world attention to the issue. Several nongovernmental organizations dedicated to the worldwide struggle for human rights also rose to prominence, most notably Amnesty International, which was awarded the Nobel Peace Prize in 1977.

Human Rights and Democracy

As the promotion of human rights was a central theme of U.S. foreign policy during the 1970s, so the promotion of democracy became a central theme during the 1980s. In part, this focus on democracy emerged because many dictatorial regimes, including some of the most flagrant abusers of human rights, weakened or fell, making transition to democracy seem a more feasible goal than it had been before. It also reflected, however, the view of Ronald Reagan's and George Bush's administrations that the negative side of human rights policy embodied in opposition to human rights abuses should be accompanied by a positive, long-term effort to foster democracy as the best safeguard of human rights. In 1993 Bill Clinton's administration, which designated support for democracy as one of the three pillars of its foreign policy, appeared to aim at a synthesis of the Carter and Reagan-Bush approaches. Nonetheless, some political controversy continued in the United States, perhaps partly fueled by old partisan divisions, regarding the relationship between human rights and democracy.

How one understands the relationship between human rights and democracy depends largely upon how one defines democracy. As noted at the outset of this article, today the term is generally reserved for regimes that are characterized by both majority rule and the protection of human rights—that is, for what often are called liberal or constitutional democracies. The relationship between democracy thus understood and human rights cannot by definition be anything but harmonious, in that failings in the protection of human rights would reduce a regime's claims to democracy. Another argument for the congruence between human rights and democracy lies in the fact that the Universal Declaration recognizes as a human right the right to take part in the government of one's country through voting in "periodic and genuine elections." Not only does democracy require the observance of human rights, but the observance of human rights requires democracy.

At the same time, it cannot be denied that an inevitable tension exists between what we have identified as the two essential aspects of democracy—rule by representatives of the majority and protection of the rights of individuals. As James Madison pointed out, majority rule in itself is no guarantee against oppression of the rights of unpopular minorities or individuals. There is no shortage of examples of democratically elected governments that, once in power, have trampled upon human rights. The tension between majority rule and human rights is acutely visible in Islamic countries with strong fundamentalist movements. To honor the results of free and fair elections in such countries, many observers claim, would be to bring to power governments that would harshly restrict human rights.

Just as it is possible for democratically elected rulers to violate human rights, in principle it would be possible for monarchs or other unelected rulers to honor individual rights. Yet autocrats would have to be extraordinarily benevolent indeed to tolerate expressions of freedom of speech, press, and assembly explicitly directed against their own right to rule. More generally, rulers who are not regularly accountable to an electorate and who do not expect to be bound themselves by the laws they make have little personal incentive to protect individual rights. Although not all democratically elected governments scrupulously respect human rights, a glance at the contemporary world reveals that the only regimes that scrupulously respect human rights are democracies.

Nondemocratic governments vary greatly in the extent to which they violate human rights, and sometimes they may even marginally improve their conduct in response to external pressure. Democratic governments and nongovernmental organizations have had some success in inducing autocratic regimes to release individual political prisoners. Yet in no case has this kind of pressure ever produced a thoroughgoing change in a government's general stance toward human rights.

Human rights activists living within a nondemocratic regime may well couch their efforts, for reasons of prudence, in terms of getting their existing government to comply with its own laws or otherwise improve its own human rights performance. Yet those who take human rights seriously are almost invariably led to favor a democratic regime for their country as soon as circumstances permit. This position has certainly been adopted by such renowned human rights activists as Sakharov, Burmese democratic leader Aung San Suu Kyi, and exiled Chinese dissident Fang Lizhi. They have recognized that democracy—a regime based on majority rule through free elections, tempered by the separation of powers, the rule of law, and constitutional protections for individual liberties—provides countries with the only secure institutional framework for guaranteeing human rights in the contemporary world.

See also Contractarianism; Hobbes, Thomas; Kant, Immanuel; Locke, John; Madison, James; Majority rule, minority rights; Natural law; Obligation; Spinoza, Benedict de.

MARC F. PLATTNER

BIBLIOGRAPHY

The Federalist Papers. Edited by Clinton Rossiter. New York: New American Library, 1961.

Hobbes, Thomas. *Leviathan.* Edited by Herbert W. Schneider. Indianapolis: Bobbs-Merrill, 1958.

Human Rights: A Compilation of International Instruments. New York: United Nations, 1983. Rev. ed. London: HMSO Books, 1988.

Kant, Immanuel. *Foundations of the Metaphysics of Morals.* Edited and translated by Lewis White Beck. Indianapolis: Bobbs-Merrill, 1959.

———. "Perpetual Peace." In *Kant on History.* Edited and translated by Lewis White Beck. Indianapolis: Bobbs-Merrill, 1963.

Locke, John. *The Second Treatise of Government.* Edited by Thomas P. Peardon. Indianapolis: Bobbs-Merrill, 1952.

Plattner, Marc F., ed. *Human Rights in Our Time: Essays in Memory of Victor Baras.* Boulder, Colo.: Westview Press, 1984.

The Power of Human Rights: International Norms and Domestic Change. Edited by Thomas Risse, Stephen C. Ropp, and Kathryn Sikkink. Cambridge and New York: Cambridge University Press, 1999.

Spinoza, Benedict de. "Theologico-Political Treatise." Vol. 1 of *Works of Spinoza.* Translated by R. H. M. Elwes. New York: Dover, 1951.

Strauss, Leo. *Natural Right and History.* Chicago: University of Chicago Press, 1953.

U.S. Dept. of State. *Country Reports on Human Rights Practices.* Washington, D.C.: U.S. Government Printing Office, annual.

✦ Interest groups

Organizations that try to influence the decisions of government. The most common types of interest groups represent business, labor, people in a profession, or citizens who advocate a particular cause or issue. An organization does not have to exist for the sole purpose of influencing government to be considered an interest group. In the United States, for instance, a corporation like General Motors (GM) is organized primarily for the purpose of manufacturing and selling automobiles. Nevertheless it has an office in Washington, D.C., staffed by government relations specialists, or "lobbyists," whose job is to advocate GM's policy preferences. Accordingly, GM is an interest group as well as a manufacturing firm.

Interest groups are of central concern to the study of government because, on the one hand, they are an embodiment of democracy and, on the other hand, they are a threat to democracy.

Roles

Interest groups are a manifestation of a free and open society. They play a vital role in democracies because they are vehicles by which people express their political views. In a democracy people are free to organize to pursue their political views even if most other people find those views objectionable. In the United States people's right to organize into interest groups is guaranteed by the First Amendment to the Constitution, which says that Congress may not pass laws to prohibit the right of citizens "to petition the government for a redress of grievances." When antiabortion marchers protest in front of the Capitol in Washington, they are asking for a redress of their grievance. An environmental group going to court in an effort to stop offshore oil drilling is also exercising the First Amendment rights of its members. Few people would want to live in a society in which they did not have the right to join an organization that could speak on their behalf before government.

People are empowered by joining advocacy organizations because policymakers understandably are more interested in what groups of people think than in what any one individual thinks. People also are empowered by interest groups because the lobbyists who represent an organization are experts in dealing with government. A small-business owner may feel overburdened by the governmental regulations that affect his or her company. Yet, unlike a business lobbyist, the same small-business owner may have no idea of what specific regulations may be open to challenge, who in government is responsible for them, or what strategies should be pursued in trying to get them changed.

Interest groups also enhance their members' ability to influence government by communicating to them vital information, such as the introduction of relevant legislation. Members of the group can then express their opinion of the proposed law to their representatives. By activating members to work on an issue, interest groups facilitate the participation of individuals in the governmental process.

For all the positive contributions that interest groups make to the functioning of democracy, there is still reason to be concerned about the role they play in the political process. The reason for unease is that lobbying groups are organized to pursue the interests of their members, and those interests may not coincide with what is best for the nation as a whole. For instance, American steel manufacturers who want tariffs placed on foreign steel to reduce the price advantage of imports are working for the benefit of their managers, shareholders, and employees. All other Americans would be better off with the free importation of lower-cost foreign steel, which would reduce the price of consumer products and keep inflation low. In the United States, however, the steel lobbies are free to pursue their own narrow interest at the expense of the broader interest of consumers.

No interest group would admit that it is working for its own interests. The steel companies working for tariffs would argue that the country benefits from a strong manufacturing base and that they are also fighting to protect U.S. jobs. More dispassionate observers would argue that laudable as those goals might be, steel companies should achieve them through gains in efficiency and through the development of new products rather than through a political solution that effectively raises prices for everyone.

Some organizations are not tied to economic or professional endeavors and claim to represent the "public interest." Environmental groups, for example, assert that they should not be judged in the same light as corporations because the policy objectives they pursue offer them no private gain. If, for example, these organizations persuade the federal government to take action to protect a threatened species, they have done nothing to protect the jobs or investments of their members. Their gain is purely ideological in nature. Yet others might argue that the environmentalists' work is not in the best interests of the country. If the environmentalists preserve an endangered species by winning approval for a policy that makes a forest habitat off limits to loggers, jobs for blue-collar workers are lost.

In short, a democratic political system gives people the freedom to organize for the purpose of pursuing interests that benefit them or support their beliefs but that may be harmful to others. Writing in *The Federalist* (1787–1788), James Madison recognized that the pursuit of self-interest would be part of the U.S. political system. He said that in any free society it is inevitable that people will divide into groups—what he called factions—and that each group will try to achieve policy goals that come at the expense of other groups. Nevertheless Madison emphatically rejected restrictions on liberty as a way of restraining the selfish advocacy of interest groups. Such a remedy, he wrote, would be "worse than the disease."

Over the years Americans have followed Madison's advice and have done little to restrict the freedom of interest groups. Indeed, in the U.S. political system, interest groups play an integral role in policy making. Interest groups represent their constituents before government, making sure that their voices are heard as governmental decisions are made about the distribution of goods and services. But how do interest groups in a democracy affect the allocation of governmental benefits (such as tax breaks) and the assignment of costs (such as taxes) to pay for those benefits?

Questions of Equality

The question of who gets what from government is a question about equality. Critics charge that interest groups work to maintain or exacerbate inequality. In this sense, equality is tied to the level and effectiveness of interest group representation. Not all the different constituencies (or "interests") are represented equally before their government. Single mothers, for example, are poorly represented in the policy-making process in Washington. A few organizations do work on behalf of single mothers and their children, but given the large size of this constituency and the problems single mothers face, the interest group representation they receive is clearly inadequate. In contrast, hospitals, insurance companies, professional associations, pharmaceutical manufacturers, medical equipment suppliers, and other health-related concerns are well represented. These various lobbies are not a united front—they disagree on a great deal—but each provides effective representation for its members.

Democracies in free market countries have no requirement for all groups of citizens to receive equal benefits from government or to pay equal taxes. Political equality is an important principle in democracies, but most people accept the reality that market economies generate economic inequality. Economic equality could be achieved only within a different economic and political structure.

Still, interest groups foster inequality in a way that is undesirable in free market democracies: they reduce opportunities for companies and economic interests to compete with each other, and a primary tenet of a free market system is that such competition is most likely to produce the best products at the lowest prices. People assume that they will be best served economically by ensuring a "level playing field." That is, inequality of results is justified if the rules of economic competition are the same for all. Most interest groups, however, work to make the playing field uneven, to shape the rules for their own advantage. For instance, when AT&T fought to keep other companies from selling long-distance telephone services, it was working for a monopoly rather than for equal competition among all those who might want to enter the telephone business. After the company was forced to divest itself of many of its business activities, regional phone companies were created. They constantly lobby the government to protect and expand their turf against AT&T, other long-distance carriers, foreign companies, and a wide variety of telecommunications firms. All these competitors in the telecommunications field want government to fix the rules of competition through regulatory decisions that will favor them at the expense of other companies.

Although uneven playing fields in the business world reduce economic efficiency and economic growth, the greatest source of concern about interest groups and inequality is the persistent lack of organization among low-income constituencies. Membership in political organizations is strongly correlated with social class. High-income citizens are likely to belong to a number of organizations that engage in political advocacy. Poor people are likely to belong to few, if any, lobbying organizations. Thus a primary reason that single mothers are inadequately represented in government is that most of them are poor. Even single mothers who work full time may not be able to afford the membership dues of an advocacy group.

Broad constituencies in which people have little in common other than their political interests are also inadequately represented. Consumers—which includes just about everybody—could be a powerful political force if most of them joined a lobbying organization to work for their interests in such areas as product safety, truth in advertising, and anticompetitive business practices. Consumers are poorly organized, however, because consumers' lobbying groups have little to offer

any individual member. If a consumers' lobby is able to persuade the government to adopt a safety standard for toys, all consumers benefit regardless of whether they pay dues to the organization. The toys will be safe for all children, not just for those whose parents are dues-paying members of the lobby. Consequently citizens who do not join the group can be "free riders" on the backs of those who pay the dues.

Many groups that engage in lobbying successfully overcome the free-rider problem because they are organized primarily for nonpolitical purposes. Doctors belong to a medical association because that organization provides them with information and opportunities for professional interaction that allow them to do their jobs better. A portion of the doctors' membership dues, however, is spent on lobbyists who work vigorously on behalf of their interests.

Not all lobbying organizations have dues-paying members. Corporations are organized to provide some product or service, but they can use their organizational structure to pursue political goals as well. Instead of having to collect dues, corporations can simply use some of the profits from their business activities. This structure gives them an enormous advantage in the interest group arena: they do not have to struggle to get organized for lobbying because they are already organized for other purposes.

When voluntary memberships are the principal basis of financial support, two factors seem to be of particular importance in determining whether a group can be successfully organized. The first is the skills and resources of the potential members. The second is the benefits the organization offers to members. The higher the level of political knowledge and resources possessed by a constituency and the more valuable the benefits offered by the group, the more likely an organization will be to succeed in getting established.

These factors, in turn, produce enormous inequality in a political system like that of the United States. It is not merely that some constituencies have more lobbyists speaking on their behalf in Washington or in the state capitals. Organization and resources facilitate other forms of political influence. For example, interest groups can use money from their members to fund political action committees (PACs), which can then donate money to political campaigns and thereby earn the gratitude of the candidates who win. Furthermore, information sent by interest groups to members helps members communicate directly with their government. Such grassroots lobbying is a powerful complement to the work of Washington lobbyists.

In broad terms, interest groups are both a reflection of the inequality that already exists in society and a principal reason that it is difficult to overcome that inequality. Is it possible to maintain society's freedoms while reducing the undesirable effects of interest group politics?

Majoritarianism Versus Pluralism

Madison's own solution to the dilemma he posed was to try to control the "effects" of faction. By this he meant that the national government should be structured to prevent one or more factions from amassing too much power. He hoped that in the United States the representative form of government, diverse population, and large size would mitigate the power of any particular faction. Few today are convinced that Madison's solution has worked satisfactorily to control the adverse effects of faction.

Many reforms to restrain interest groups in some ways have been proposed—for example, more stringent registration rules for lobbyists and changes in the campaign finance laws. In light of the democratic commitment to individual freedoms, it is hard to imagine that any law could be enacted that would fundamentally change interest group politics.

Another proposal for controlling the effects of faction is to focus on strengthening political parties. The goal of such reform would be to enhance the political power of the majority by giving it greater control over public policy through elections. In the United States political parties could be more effective counterweights to interest groups if they were more unified and more clearly committed to specific policies that were spelled out during the election campaign. Great Britain and many other democracies have party systems structured according to majoritarian principles. In a majoritarian democracy the party (or coalition of parties) that controls the legislature carries out the platform on which it campaigned in the previous election.

A majoritarian political system in the United States would require that voters cast their ballots for members of Congress based primarily on the policy stands of the national parties. Once elected, members of Congress would be expected to vote for the policies backed by their parties. By contrast, in the current U.S. system, members of Congress are independent of the national parties. National parties do not control the nomination of candidates for Congress, and they supply only a small fraction of the money that candidates must raise for their campaigns.

The political system of the United States is characterized more by pluralism than by majoritarianism. In a pluralistic system, policy making derives largely from the interaction of interest groups with government. The virtue of pluralism is that, ideally, those who are most affected by an issue have the greatest say about its resolution. This would be the case if all those directly affected by prospective policy changes were represented by interest groups, and all interest groups were included in the bargaining and negotiating that lead to new legislation or regulatory action. As noted earlier, however, the interest groups that come to the bargaining table may not represent all the constituencies affected by the policies being debated.

JEFFREY M. BERRY

BIBLIOGRAPHY

Berry, Jeffrey M. *The Interest Group Society.* 2d ed. Glenview, Ill.: Scott, Foresman, 1989.
_____. *Lobbying for the People.* Princeton: Princeton University Press, 1977.
Cigler, Allan J., and Burdett A. Loomis, eds. *Interest Group Politics.* 4th ed. Washington, D.C.: CQ Press, 1994.
Costain, Anne N. *Inviting Women's Rebellion.* Baltimore: Johns Hopkins University Press, 1992.
Heinz, John P., Edward O. Laumann, Robert L. Nelson, and Robert H. Salisbury. *The Hollow Core.* Cambridge, Mass., and London: Harvard University Press, 1993.
Olson, Mancur. *The Logic of Collective Action.* New York: Schocken, 1968.
Petracca, Mark P., ed. *The Politics of Interests.* Boulder, Colo.: Westview Press, 1992.
Schlozman, Kay Lehman, and John T. Tierney. *Organized Interests and American Democracy.* New York: Harper and Row, 1986.
Walker, Jack L. *Mobilizing Interest Groups in America.* Ann Arbor: University of Michigan Press, 1991.

✦ Justice, Theories of

Theories of justice examine the philosophical question of what constitutes justice. The concept of justice provides much of the ethical basis of democratic theory. Specifically, social (or distributive) justice defines the appropriate means for distributing the benefits and burdens of social cooperation within democratic systems.

The close affinity between the concepts of democracy and justice arises from their shared attachment to the principle of equality. Ever since Aristotle wrote about justice in his *Politics* in the fourth century B.C., it has generally been accepted that the quest for a theory of justice involves the definition and interpretation of some notion of equality. Similarly, recognition of equality is a basic condition for democracy. As the French political theorist Alexis de Tocqueville pointed out in *Democracy in America* in the mid-nineteenth century, the ruling passion of people in democratic ages is the love of equality.

The concept of justice has enjoyed unrivaled prominence in moral and political philosophy from the Socrates of Plato's *Republic* in the fourth century B.C. to the contemporary American philosopher John Rawls. Socrates argued that justice is fundamental to any concept of living well and that living according to justice is intrinsically good. Rawls claims that justice is the first virtue of social institutions.

Defining Justice

Many philosophers, including Aristotle, have treated justice as the most important part of morality; yet they have also recognized that the sphere of morality is wider than the sphere of justice. Both Plato and Aristotle saw justice as a specific virtue to be distinguished from virtue in general, a distinction that still holds today. For example, we may want to say that certain acts—such as murder—are wrong, although we would not say that murder is unfair or unjust. More specifically, a system of morality should provide a framework for dealing with situations in which interests conflict, but it does not have to provide a definite answer to every question of who should get what, which is the domain of justice. The concept of justice becomes more useful the more precisely it is defined. Two fundamental distinctions concerning justice help restrict the scope of this concept.

The first is Aristotle's distinction in Book V of his *Nicomachean Ethics* between distributive justice and commutative justice. *Distributive justice* refers to the distribution of assets among members of a community. Taking as a basis the idea that like beings should be treated alike, Aristotle argues that the distribution of goods should be in proportion to merit or desert; those who merit equal shares should get equal shares, whereas those who merit unjust shares should get unequal shares in proportion to their unequal merits or deserts. *Commutative justice* concerns issues that arise from transactions between people, including market or other forms of reciprocal exchange, and all civil and criminal disputes. Commutative justice aims to equalize the consequences of just as well as unjust acts. Gratitude and equal return of good for good are important aspects of commutative justice.

The second distinction concerns the subject matter of justice. Justice can apply either to individuals or to social institutions. As an individual virtue, the emphasis of justice rests on individuals and their actions. At the institutional level, justice applies to the basic structure of society, in particular to its social, economic and political institutions.

The distributive-institutional approach to the question of justice has dominated recent debate. According to this approach, the aim of a theory of justice is to prescribe principles whereby each person receives what is due to him or her. Although this approach has intuitive validity, the insurmountable problem remains the indeterminancy of what is to count as a person's due. To overcome this obstacle, philosophers have agreed on the necessity of investigating the philosophical question of what constitutes the nature of justice.

Historically, two competing approaches have been used to answer this question. One approach looks for an answer in the natural law tradition. The other approach takes as its starting point David Hume's idea of the circumstances of justice. These two approaches have shaped the contemporary debate on justice.

Natural Law

In its most general form, natural law states that the ultimate measure of right and wrong is to be determined in accordance with nature. The simplicity of this doctrine is misleading, however, and different interpretations have developed over the centuries, usually because of the ambiguity of the meaning of *nature*. According to the medieval notion, natural law emerged from the hierarchic order of humankind's natural ends. From the assumption that human nature is essentially rational, St. Thomas Aquinas (1225–1274) argues in the *Summa Theologica* that natural law is the foundation of morality and the paramount standard by which social and political institutions ought to be judged. The modern notion of natural law, following the seventeenth-century English philosophers Thomas Hobbes and John Locke, takes as its starting point the idea of the natural right to self-preservation.

In contemporary debates on social justice, the marriage between justice and natural law has been reasserted by John Finnis and Robert Nozick. Finnis (in *Natural Law and Natural Rights*, 1980) appeals to the premodern notion of natural law by defending a traditional Thomist perspective that identifies justice with a willingness to favor and foster the common good of the community. Nozick revived the modern notion of natural law and its corresponding idea of natural rights. Its starting point in his influential book *Anarchy, State and Utopia* (1974) is the belief, associated with John Locke, that all humans enjoy a set of natural rights, including a right to life, liberty, and property. Furthermore, Nozick believes that all patterned theories of justice (the idea that justice entails sustaining a particular pattern of distribution) are intrinsically unfair. On the basis of these premises, Nozick argues that a just distribution is simply whatever distribution results from people's voluntary exchanges.

In terms of democratic theory the underlying assumption in Nozick's argument is that any form of political organization, to be legitimate, must be reducible to the voluntary action of every individual. It follows that only a minimal state can be justified. The state uses resources raised through taxation to enforce law (free contracts) and order (protection). Any state that pursues the redistribution of resources for reasons other than its minimal functions violates the rights of those from whom resources are taken and hence is intrinsically immoral.

Although popular among libertarian circles, Nozick's theory has faced two recurring criticisms. The first is that unlike Locke, who grounded his theory of rights on the existence of God, Nozick simply assumes the existence of a set of inalienable basic rights. The second criticism is that Nozick fails to consider the threat to democracy when individuals are in a position to translate their superior material well-being into political power. In particular, Nozick fails to consider the effect on third parties of distributions of resources based on fully voluntary transactions. For example, future generations will find that the value of their own share of resources is affected by what others have inherited and how this inheritance is distributed.

The Circumstances of Justice

Alternatives to the natural rights approach start from the "circumstances of justice"—the conditions that must exist for questions of justice to have meaning. David Hume (1711–1776), the

Scottish philosopher who coined the phrase, argued that moderate scarcity of resources and restricted benevolence are two basic circumstances of justice. If there were unlimited resources, or if people were normally generous, questions of justice would not arise.

John Rawls in *A Theory of Justice* (1971) openly endorses Hume's account of the circumstances of justice, putting forward two principles of justice that he believes a constitutional democracy should satisfy. These principles provide much of the normative dimension of democratic theory. The principles of justice defended by Rawls are produced from the contractarian construction known as the "original position." People are asked to choose principles of justice on the basis of their best interest but from behind a "veil of ignorance," where all knowledge of their individual attributes (both natural and social) is concealed. Rawls believes that this hypothetical construction is capable of reproducing the moral conditions of impartiality and fairness, since from behind the veil of ignorance we are incapable of advocating narrow or sectional interests. Further, it enables us to perceive more clearly our moral intuitions that people should be regarded as free and equal.

Rawls's first principle concerns political goods, particularly the distribution of basic rights and liberties. It states that each person should have an equal right to the most extensive total system of basic liberties that can provide equal liberty for all. Rawls's second principle concerns social and economic goods, particularly the distribution of income, wealth, and opportunities. It states that social and economic inequalities should be arranged so that they are both to the greatest benefit of the least advantaged (the "difference principle") and are attached to offices and positions open to all under conditions of equality of opportunity.

These two principles of justice reflect the two ways in which the concept of justice provides a normative dimension to the idea of democracy. First, justice is seen as a protection of equal rights or basic liberties, a characteristic feature of any democratic order. Indeed, it is essential to democracy that democratically elected majorities not have the power to deprive minorities of their political rights. It is not a coincidence that Rawls's list of basic liberties corresponds to the constitutional guarantees provided by any liberal democracy: freedom of thought, speech, press, association, and religion; the right to hold personal property; freedom to vote and hold public office; and freedom from arbitrary arrest and seizure as defined by the rule of law.

The other way in which justice is linked to the normative dimension of democracy concerns the democratic ideal's attachment to autonomy and reasoned public deliberation. The emphasis here is that in a democracy all individuals ought to be free and equal in determining the conditions of their own association. The extent to which individuals are free and equal defines their autonomy. The distribution of resources plays a vital role in determining degrees of individual autonomy. As Joshua Cohen and Joel Rogers argue in *On Democracy* (1983), the belief that individuals ought to be free and equal goes a long way toward justifying a fair distribution of resources among people in a society. If the absence of material deprivation is a precondition for free and unconstrained deliberation and a capacity for political action, then a basic level of material well-being for all becomes a requirement for a full-fledged democracy.

A New Generation of Scholars

The theories of justice that were championed by Rawls and Nozick have inspired a new generation of scholars. David Gauthier, an exuberant defender of Nozick's libertarian philosophy, advocates in *Morals by Agreement* (1986) a form of distributive justice that is the result of voluntary agreements. Gauthier believes that everyone who benefits from the goods that arise from a cooperative venture must share in the burden of contributing to it. The level of benefits received should reflect the level of contribution made—even to the extent that no contribution implies no benefit. According to Gauthier, questions of social justice must be based on the idea of mutual advantage; the amount one is able to contribute must be respected in the distribution of cooperative benefits.

Although Gauthier's theory is presented in terms of a social contract, it differs markedly from Rawls's contractualism. For Gauthier, the motive for justice is the pursuit of individual advantages, whereas for Rawls it is the pursuit of impartiality. Further, in Gauthier's theory the agreement reflects the different bargaining powers that people bring to the table; in Rawls's theory all bargaining advantages are eliminated.

These two key features of Gauthier's theory of justice—the idea of self-interested motivation and the recognition of bargaining advantages—have drawn much criticism. For example, Brian Barry in *Theories of Justice* (1989) argues that theories of justice as mutual advantage cannot be the sole foundations of a moral system, since (in Gauthier's words) all those without bargaining powers will fall beyond the pale of morality. Hence some individuals will fall outside the system of rights entirely. It is not clear how Gauthier's theory of justice reflects the spirit of democracy when not all individuals share the same rights.

Nozick's libertarian philosophy is also the starting point of Hillel Steiner's theory of justice, although the conclusions Steiner reaches are substantially different from those of Nozick or Gauthier. In *An Essay on Rights* (1994), Steiner defends a libertarian theory of justice with relatively strong redistributive implications.

While Nozick has inspired a new generation of libertarians, Rawls has inspired further research on the view of justice as impartiality. In recent years the moral intuition of defining justice in terms of impartiality has been criticized on different fronts by both feminists and communitarians. By introducing the important distinction between the "ethics of justice" and the "ethics of care," Carol Gilligan in *In a Different Voice* (1982) argues that the concept of impartiality is not gender neutral.

Alternatively, communitarian philosophers have criticized the metaphysical abstraction of liberal theories of justice, especially for transcending social and cultural contexts. Michael Walzer argues in *Spheres of Justice* (1983) that questions of justice must be articulated within the contingencies of particular cultures. According to Walzer, democracy is not about universal truths and right decisions but about decisions that embody the will of a citizenry.

Notwithstanding such criticisms, the view of justice as impartiality has become increasingly influential in recent years. Brian Barry champions it in *Justice as Impartiality* (1995). This view of justice as impartiality is an attempt to defend the basic egalitarian intuitions in Rawls's theory of justice while correcting some of its weakest aspects. For example, this approach faults Rawls's original position—the model of rational choice under uncertainty—for failing to capture our basic moral commitments to fairness and impartiality. According to Barry, an effort should be made to identify principles of justice that everyone finds reasonably acceptable.

The criterion of reasonable acceptability can be established with the help of a hypothetical contract that differs from Rawls's original position in important ways. For example, in efforts to reach agreement the dominant motivation ought to be a desire to find principles of justice that others similarly motivated could not reasonably reject. It follows that a theory of justice as impartiality finds bargaining advantages morally unacceptable, since these are grounded on inadequate moral motivations (self-interest). Furthermore, bargaining advantages would be deemed unacceptable by those negatively affected by them.

It is the criterion of reasonable acceptability that does most of the work in a theory of justice as impartiality. In fact, this criterion sheds some light on the idea of fundamental equality and—subsequently—of democracy. Reasonable acceptability implies taking equal account of the interests of all the parties in the agreement, especially those who would benefit less than others from the institutional endorsement of certain principles. According to the view of justice as impartiality, the essence of democracy is whether the set of rules and principles that determine the basic organization of society is justified to each person affected by those rules and principles.

Equality and Freedom

Although theories of justice differ in the ways in which they attempt to reconcile the twin claims of equality and freedom, it is their very concentration on this problem that forms the major link between the ideas of justice and democracy. In the final analysis, theories of justice and theories of democracy can be considered two sides of the same coin, since both stem from the moral assumption that societies should view people as free and equal.

See also Autonomy; Communitarianism; Egalitarianism; Liberalism; Natural law.

Vittorio Bufacchi

BIBLIOGRAPHY

Barry, Brian. *Justice as Impartiality.* Oxford: Oxford University Press, 1995.

_____. *Theories of Justice.* Berkeley: University of California Press, 1989.

Cohen, Joshua, and Joel Rogers. *On Democracy: Toward a Transformation of American Society.* Harmondsworth, England: Penguin Books, 1983.

Finnis, John. *Natural Law and Natural Rights.* Oxford: Clarendon Press, 1980.

Gauthier, David. *Morals by Agreement.* Oxford: Oxford University Press, 1986.

Gilligan, Carol. *In a Different Voice.* Cambridge: Harvard University Press, 1982.

Kymlicka, Will. *Contemporary Political Philosophy.* Oxford: Clarendon Press, 1990.

Mulhall, Stephen, and Adam Swift. *Liberals and Communitarians.* Oxford and Cambridge, Mass.: Blackwell, 1992.

Nozick, Robert. *Anarchy, State and Utopia.* Oxford: Blackwell, 1974.

Rawls, John. *A Theory of Justice.* Cambridge: Harvard University Press, Belknap Press; Oxford: Oxford University Press, 1971.

Steiner, Hillel. *An Essay on Rights.* Oxford and Cambridge, Mass.: Blackwell, 1994.

Walzer, Michael. *Spheres of Justice.* New York: Basic Books, 1983.

✦ Leadership

The guidance of a group, party, or political entity, typically undertaken by an individual. Although styles of leadership vary in scope and manner, it is expected that leaders will avoid merely representing (as would a clerk) the tallied demands of followers, on the one hand, or engaging in violence or duplicity against them, on the other. The term can refer either to leading a part of a polity in need of defense against the whole or to acting and thinking on behalf of a whole people or nation whose parts (or parties or interest groups) would, in its absence, be deadlocked or too shortsighted for prudent action.

Leadership is counted on not only to advance interests but also to overcome the warring of clashing interests and even to undertake the education and elevation of those interests to broader and deeper views. At the same time, leadership is expected to cut through the deliberation—and, if Niccolò Machiavelli (1469–1527) is to be believed, the morality—of political partisans, supplying the morally suspect, though politically necessary, qualities of decisiveness, secrecy, and dispatch. The leader must combine something of the diverse qualities of the partisan political infighter, the farseeing nation-building founder or legislator, and the inspiring and daring general.

Democracy's Ambivalence Toward Leadership

The relationship of democracy to leadership is complex and controversial. Historically democracies have taken pride in being schools for statesmen but have also suspected and even ostracized them. Theoretically, democracy has been understood both to require particularly virtuous and astute leadership and to require the rejection of all leadership as such. In the contemporary United States there is, at the popular or journalistic level, a continuous (and, it seems, an increasingly desperate) admission of a "need for leadership." This call receives two quite disparate responses from political scientists. Those engaged in leadership studies generally are sympathetic to the demand and try to encourage the phenomenon through a proper understanding of it. Increasing numbers of democratic theorists, on the other hand, ignore or condemn this demand, maintaining that democracy requires first and foremost a vigorous and self-directing citizenry, confident enough in its ability to exercise political judgment that it can dispense with leaders. Although this latter group claims to be invoking Jeffersonian democracy, it should be noted that Jefferson expected citizens to become competent only in selecting what he called the "natural aristoi" to lead them.

In some sense, leadership constitutes democracy's (or, at any rate, liberal democracy's) greatest embarrassment. Democracy, of course, means "rule by the people." And liberal democracy is premised on the view that all are born free by nature and so no one has a right by nature to rule another. Accordingly, in a liberal democracy, there are no leaders by divine right or tradition or family background: citizens must choose or consent to their leaders. If we believed that anyone could do the job, we would adopt what Aristotle refers to as the purely democratic mode of selecting leaders—namely, lot. In electing our leaders, we implicitly concede that some are better than others for this important job. (Thus Aristotle refers to election as an aristocratic mode of selection.) And this admission, in turn, is tantamount to conceding that democracy requires some supplemental principle by which to govern itself. A democracy's attitude toward leadership, then, reveals whether it seeks a form of radical or direct democracy, which would consist wholly of citizens directing themselves, or a moderate democracy (as conceived by the Framers of the U.S. Constitution and most older democratic theorists), which would accept the need for a mixture of some nondemocratic elements in a regime.

Democracy's attitude toward leaders thus is related to its attitude toward greatness or superiority generally. The most abiding criticism made of democracy is that it is leveling—that is, it comes to be irritated by any distinction, however legitimate. This irritation, strangely enough, is today more frequently voiced by "elite" spokesmen for democracy (for example, democratic theorists) than by citizens of democracies. Thus we see the spectacle of (some) democratic theorists

condemning the admiration for the great man as an undemocratic tendency. This criticism of ruling appears to have had an effect, though not perhaps the one expected. Citizens of democratic states still long for strong leadership, but the potential leaders who might answer that call seem increasingly hesitant to lead. Some students of leadership have suggested that reluctance to exert power is more a problem today than is the reluctance to follow. Leaders still exert power, but they do so in spite of, not with the guidance and blessing of, the predominant political sentiment. Condemned to lead with a bad conscience, they lead less well than they might.

Despite these objections, some argue that democracies are particularly in need of leadership. Put simply, democratic equality is strong on gaining wide-ranging and diverse input but weak on taking decisions or on ranking alternatives. Moreover, liberal democracies invite citizens to take their private lives seriously, leaving the tiller of the ship of state unattended. Leaders then must decide while others are satisfied with deliberating; they must concern themselves with politics or the public good while others concern themselves with private life; and they must break to some degree with the prevailing democratic ethos even as they seek to serve it.

Democratic Theory and Leadership

In some sense our understanding of leadership derives from the social contract theories of Thomas Hobbes (1588–1679) and John Locke (1632–1704), which—in spite of the continued and increasing theoretical criticism to which they are exposed—lie at the root of our political system. Such theories aim at avoiding the bad, not at achieving the good. Yet, according to the same theories, an executive—perhaps even an energetic executive—is necessary to ensure the execution of laws (the chief means by which the bad is avoided).

The appropriate status of that executive thus becomes a major problem in liberal democratic theory. Some, chiefly Hobbes, have asserted the need for an absolute sovereign who would constrain citizens through fear so as to secure them. Others, specifically Locke, have accepted Hobbes's premises but condemned Hobbes's politics.

Locke, however, did not deny the inescapable need for an executive, and one, moreover, armed with the prerogative of acting in the absence of the law, and sometimes even against it. Leadership could never simply be reduced to the rule of law. For the law sometimes cannot be sovereign, as in the managing of foreign affairs, and sometimes is dormant, silent, self-contradictory, or simply too weak to accomplish much good. Hence leaders or executives are needed to supply the wisdom or prudence—or merely the brute strength—sometimes lacking in law. Contemporary liberals often have been unwilling to concede the necessary inadequacy of law. Emphasizing one strand of liberal thought, such liberal democrats, for all their talk of the need for leadership, ultimately seem more concerned with limiting the potential of bad or dangerous leaders than with guaranteeing the potential of good or helpful ones. Often only a serious crisis—a depression or a war—will reconcile some democrats to leadership.

Modern political theory has consisted, in large measure, of the liberation of political leadership from the cumbersome restraints of ancient and Christian morality, followed by a series of subsequent efforts to "tame" or domesticate such ferocious princes. Machiavelli, the first political philosopher to side with the people, nevertheless argued that a people can attain nothing without leaders. But, as modern democracy took root and flourished, it became increasingly ambivalent about leadership as such. (The ambivalence sometimes seemed to grow in proportion to the flourishing.) Machiavelli's followers focused on limiting government rather than on strengthening it. They invented the separation and balancing of powers, which turned leadership against itself, and promoted a politics of commerce, which, according to Montesquieu (1689–1755), would render authoritative leadership increasingly clumsy and unnecessary. Yet Montesquieu also defended the need for an executive and eloquently described the compatibility of democracy and leadership, warning against the potential egalitarian hostility toward all leaders.

The case of the United States reveals the democratic ambivalence about leadership at its origin. On the one hand, Alexander Hamilton called for an "energetic" executive and pointed to the Roman use of the dictator as evidence of the compatibility of republicanism (and, by extension, of democracy) and leadership. On the other hand, James Madison spoke disparagingly of leaders apt to quarrel amongst themselves for private purposes and proudly defended the American regime for not relying on the presence of "enlightened statesmen" (*Federalist* Nos. 10 and 70). The remarkable innovations of modern political science—separation of powers, checks and balances, extended sphere, representation, and so forth—seemed to hold out the hope that rightly constructed institutions could do away with the need for any further reliance on leadership, a hardly dependable commodity in any event.

As these suspicions of leaders hardened into opposition, a certain counterrevolution occurred. Inclined to the view that democratic envy or herd mentality (or simply an excessive reliance on institutions and laws) rather than sound political or moral judgment lay at the root of this opposition to leadership, supporters and practitioners of the idea of leadership began to enter the debate. In the nineteenth century, Alexis de Tocqueville warned that, just as aristocracies tended to overestimate the capacity of one man to change the course of history, so democracies tend to under-estimate it. And this latter error is more damaging than the former because it reinforces an already debilitating materialism and determinism that is fatal to self-government. At the practical level, Abraham Lincoln's rise to prominence with his criticism of Stephen Douglas's thesis of popular sovereignty in the 1850s implies that a leader will always be needed, at least in the hard cases, to remind people of their principles lest they succumb to a base, narrow self-interest or a lazy compliance with circumstance.

Responsibilities of Leadership

The fundamental responsibility of leadership might best be understood as the need to navigate between the two major tensions present in modern, liberal democratic politics: between the good (or utility or security) and justice (or rights) and between wisdom and consent. If one element of either of these pairs comes to dominate the other, liberal politics, and hence individual happiness, will be at risk. Seeking the good (healthy souls or efficiency, for example) without respecting rights is illiberal (and, according to liberalism's founders, conducive to civil war), while defending rights without a concern for the consequences will likely prove damaging to such things as community, family, church, and moral fiber. Similarly, granting wisdom unrestricted sway smacks of an elitist contempt for people's preferences and sensibilities, while an unlimited deference to consent likely will lead either to confusion (as when various incompatible policies are simultaneously consented to) or to majority tyranny. Leadership then must balance competing ends (the good and justice) as well as competing means (reason and consent). A genuine or effective leader must be both flexible (without being vacillating or merely reactive) and principled (without being obstinate or absolutist).

Although the securing of rights is said by the American Declaration of Independence to be the purpose of government, rights cannot be secured except by an existing and relatively stable government, able as well as inclined to secure them. Hence there arise occasions, so troubling to principled defenders of liberal democracy, on which civil rights must apparently give way to such concerns as the common good, civic order, and national security. President Lincoln, in defending as constitutional his suspension of the constitutionally mandated writ of habeas corpus during the Civil War, has supplied the necessary justification for such actions in asking whether we must sacrifice the workings or existence of the government as a whole to the sanctity of each and every law. Vigilant defenders of liberty nevertheless are right to warn against the danger of the slippery slope.

The other difficulty that leadership must confront is the tension between what wisdom or sound administration or expertise demands and what the people have actually or presumptively consented to. The German philosopher Johann Fichte (1762–1814), embracing one horn of the dilemma, argued that whoever possesses reason has the right to compel everyone else to follow his views. This sort of leadership presents obvious difficulties for societies premised on the notion of consent, as societies do not always consent to what is rational. On the other hand, people can be presumed to have consented to that government and those policies which can reasonably be expected to secure their rights. Again Lincoln points to the most tenable solution to this problem when he suggests that public sentiment is decisive: whoever molds public sentiment makes it either possible or impossible to have a law-abiding polity. Simply stated, the chief responsibility of liberal democratic leadership is to educate public sentiment, through the use of rhetoric, so as to enable the people to consent to what is reasonable.

Leadership styles can be broadly related to two preferred manners of setting goals—either allowing goals to percolate up from a slowly building national consensus (the leader as agent) or having them devolve from the top down, that is, from an active executive branch (the leader as independent actor). But this dichotomy is in some ways misleading, as Lincoln's observation implies. For leadership is constrained by public opinion even as it seeks to educate or change it. Liberal democratic leadership neither dictates nor simply submits to public opinion. This "dialectic" does not exist in a political vacuum, however, but rather—in the case of the United States—within the context and boundaries of the Constitution, which sets the goals of American politics. A leader thus defends the constitutional interests of the people against the whims, fancies, and even settled but improper tendencies of the people.

Leadership and Statesmanship

Finally let us consider leadership as a variant of—or replacement for—statesmanship. Behind these terms lie two fundamentally different understandings of what the relationship between ruler and ruled should be. There are, in turn, two views of leadership itself. In one, leaders, by virtue of inspiration or charisma, supply their followers with a vision that functions as a map to new and uncharted regions. Such leaders, according to the German sociologist Max Weber (1864–1920), the discoverer of charisma, owe their authority neither to tradition (in the sense of being elders steeped in the tried and true ways of the community) nor to rationalism (in the sense of bureaucratic legalism and its putative standards of merit) but, rather, to their divine inspiration and mission. Such leadership is vindicated by nothing so formal as consent or election or representativeness but solely by the attainment of its initially mysterious end: no miracle accomplished, no more charis-

matic authority. As to the followers, they cannot know what they are in for until they get it.

In the second view, the leader discerns, through a peculiar talent for deft and sensitive listening, from the followers' discordant debating, or even from their pregnant silences, the vision implicit in what they are or desire. Woodrow Wilson, impatient with formalistic constraints (here, those of the Constitution), made the soundest argument for this type of leader. According to Wilson an almost biological imperative for societies to develop and progress exists, but it has been thwarted by unsound political structures (chiefly a division of powers that divides leadership against itself) and by the absence of leaders genuinely ready to listen sympathetically (and perhaps a bit creatively) to the spirit of their times. Wilson sensed and denounced the dangers of demagoguery inherent in the charismatic alternative, though his condemnation seems to have arisen despite, rather than because of, his theories. Here we have leadership of opinion, an effort to give voice to the people as against the people's representatives, with their secretive and conservative interests. In either case, the relevant metaphor for leadership is that of the journey, designed to broaden us by opening us up to new possibilities and showing us new horizons.

Statesmanship, on the other hand, implies neither the creativity of the former view nor the docility of the latter. (Wilson, it must be noted, spoke of the ultimate need for leaders to submit to what the public wants, if they are unable to convince it otherwise.) It involves turning one's gaze from the implicit and unformed yearnings of the citizens to the state or, better, to the political regime in which the statesman and the citizens find themselves. The statesman confronts the twin challenges of maintaining both the regime's existence and its character. In the view of a democratic people, the latter enhances the former: a democracy is made more secure by being made more democratic. Where a leader would tend, perhaps after some foot dragging, to comply with such a popular demand, a statesman would look to the regime, taking as his responsibility the occasional need to limit, rather than extend, the principle of the regime. Accordingly, the statesman's primary goal is not to propose something altogether new but to defend or improve the political regime by deepening its attachment to the political and moral principles already undergirding it. The relevant metaphor here then is the gymnastic trainer, who challenges us to be more fully what we already are.

It should be apparent by now that, to those bemoaning the "need for leadership," the statesman will often appear to be unimaginative, sluggish, lacking in daring, and unaccountably ready to side with the security-minded and even conservative citizens against their justice-loving and progressive fellows. The great African American abolitionist Frederick Douglass conceded that such was his initial view of Lincoln, the "white man's president." But when he came to recognize the harsh demands of the events under which Lincoln was laboring, he began to appreciate Lincoln as a veritable radical from the point of view of his people, a genuine statesman who sought and achieved a considerable measure of liberty and progress.

See also Aristotle; Theory, elite; Elites, Political; Hobbes, Thomas; Locke, John; Machiavelli, Niccolò; Madison, James; Montesquieu; Tocqueville, Alexis de; Weber, Max.

RICHARD S. RUDERMAN

BIBLIOGRAPHY

Burke, Edmund. "Speech to the Electors of Bristol." In *Burke's Politics*, edited by Ross J. S. Hoffman and Paul Levack. New York: Knopf, 1949.

Burns, James MacGregor. *Leadership*. New York: Harper and Row, 1978.

Charnwood, Lord. *Abraham Lincoln*. London: Constable, 1919.

Jones, Bryan D., ed. *Leadership and Politics*. Lawrence: University Press of Kansas, 1989.

Mansfield, Harvey C., Jr. *Taming the Prince*. New York: Free Press, 1989.

Tulis, Jeffrey. *The Rhetorical Presidency*. Princeton: Princeton University Press, 1987.

Weber, Max. "Politics as a Vocation" and "The Sociology of Charismatic Authority." In *From Max Weber*. Translated by Hans H. Gerth and C. Wright Mills. New York: Oxford University Press, 1946.

✦ Legislatures and parliaments

Assemblies of elected representatives from geographically defined constituencies, with lawmaking and other functions in the governmental process. Legislatures, called parliaments in most countries, exist in nearly all contemporary political systems, although they are particularly associated with democracies.

The size of legislatures is related imperfectly to the size of the populations of their countries. Most are composed of 100–300 members. Countries with small populations may have parliaments as small as the 15-member Diet of Liechtenstein. Large countries may have congresses of more than 1,000 members, as Russia did between 1990 and 1993. The U.S. Senate, with 100 members, is at the low end of the range of major legislatures. The U.S. House of Representatives has 435 members, and some of the oldest parliaments of European countries have more than 600 members.

Members of legislatures base their authority on the claim that they represent the citizens. Since each member is equally a representative, each is equal to every other in formal authority and status. To transform the strong and often contentious views of such a large number of individuals into collective decisions requires distinctive procedures. These have developed through centuries of experience and have been passed from older to newer parliaments.

At minimum, all legislatures are public forums for the discussion of major issues, an important function in democracies. In some cases, notably in the United States, legislatures are important lawmaking and budget-making bodies. In most countries, however, their role in lawmaking and in the formulation and enactment of the budget is subordinate to that of the executive branch. The executive drafts most bills, proposes the budget, and manages the passage of items through the legislature. In parliamentary systems of government the legislature participates in selecting the chief executives of government. They are generally chosen from among leaders of the dominant party or parties in the legislature. In most systems, legislatures supervise the executive branch in various ways, exercising what is known as oversight. As the capacity of legislatures to make laws and budgets has become more limited everywhere, this oversight has gained in political importance.

Legislatures exercise different functions from time to time and from place to place, but they have a characteristic structure that determines how they work and that distinguishes them from the executive branch of government. Members of a legislature do not stand in a relationship of authority and subordination to each other but are formally equal. They base their authority on their claim to represent others, rather than on a claim of their own subject expertise. Legislatures conduct their business at least partly in the public view. The decisions of legislatures are made collectively rather than by the command of superiors.

The capacity of several hundred men and women to reach collective decisions depends on the complicated patterns of influence that develop among these nominally equal individuals when they become members of the legislature. These patterns are a product of (1) the legislature's institutional history; (2) the relationship of representation between members and the outside world; (3) the legislature's distinctive organization; and (4) its distinctive procedure.

Predemocratic History

Parliaments predate the advent of democracy. They arose in medieval Europe as early as the twelfth century. Many of the procedures of modern legislatures have evolved from their long historical experience. These procedures have been preserved by successive generations of parliamentarians in the form of parliamentary precedents. The parliamentarians of the British House of Commons were particularly adept at recording and maintaining these precedents. The concept of representation, on which the authority and the composition of legislatures rests, also has medieval origins. Thus the legislature is a product of medieval European civilization, transformed in the age of democracy to suit the needs of a great variety of contemporary political systems, including some systems in which the legislature serves largely to legitimate nondemocratic authority.

In the five centuries preceding the American Revolution, the normal form of government in Europe was monarchy. Monarchs reigned over societies in which the Catholic Church, the landowning nobility, and trading organizations in the towns claimed rights and privileges from the crown. These varied groups—called orders, corporations, colleges, or, more generally, estates—composed a society of status groups. The state that was built on the distribution of power among these groups was appropriately called a *Stän-*

destaat, a state of estates. The privileges that these estates claimed were based on custom, contract, or civil and church law.

To come to terms with these centers of power, monarchs found it prudent to assemble leading members of these groups from time to time to consult them concerning important questions of war and peace, of taxation, and of the administration of justice. In some countries monarchs met separately with the nobility; this pattern led to bicameralism, or parliaments composed of two houses. These assemblies, which usually met irregularly, existed in most of the countries of Europe west of Russia. They were variously called *Cortes* (Spanish), *Etats-Généraux* (France), *Landtag* (German), *Parlemento* (Italian), or *Riksdag* (Swedish). Such names denoted the place or day of meeting or the group's composition or activity. The name *legislature* came much later, during the seventeenth-century revolution in England, when the House of Commons claimed to be the lawmaking body, a claim that the institution did not finally achieve in Great Britain. The claim, however, was heard and remembered by the British settlers in North America, who used it successfully to gain autonomy from the king by insisting on the lawmaking powers of their own assemblies. Thus the institution has been called the legislature in the United States, while almost everywhere else its name does not connote a lawmaking function.

To the extent that these assemblies, by whatever name, developed a sense of their collective power, that power was justified by the idea that they were a representation of society: when they met it was the meeting of the country in the presence of the monarch. These early assemblies exercised influence on government at the provincial and national levels throughout Europe for five centuries before the advent of democracy. They were therefore familiar political institutions at the dawn of democracy in the late eighteenth and early nineteenth centuries. Furthermore, because their influence was based on their capacity to speak for and make commitments for the most powerful groups in society, these assemblies could be adapted to the requirements of democracy when participation in politics expanded to new groups of the population.

Indeed, democratic movements in Europe regarded a parliament as an instrument for imposing the will of the people on the monarch. Parliaments therefore arose out of the needs of a predemocratic but pluralistic society and out of efforts to restrain executive power. Although they were not the invention of democracies, they proved to be the most suitable instruments of democracy among the traditional institutions of European government.

Some medieval European parliaments, like the Estates General of France, fell victim to the democratic revolutions of the late eighteenth and early nineteenth centuries because they were too strongly associated with the privileges of the medieval estates, communities, or corporations. Their composition could not withstand the democratic claim that the nation was composed of individuals deserving representation as equals. Others, like the British Parliament and the provincial German Landtage, were reformed and became instruments of democracy. Whether the democratic parliaments were new creations or modifications of traditional parliaments, their composition continued to rest on the principle of representation, and their organization and procedures were based on those of the medieval assemblies. Without the centuries-old traditions accumulated by the medieval European parliaments, the modern institution is unimaginable.

Representation

A legislature whose members claim to be representative of a democratic society must have its members elected by the people at regular intervals. Some democracies may tolerate appointed second chambers as vestiges of a class-based society, like the House of Lords in the United Kingdom. All democracies, however, insist that the dominant parliamentary chamber be elected by a broad franchise. The idea of "virtual" representation—that constituents who have not voted are nevertheless represented in Parliament—may have been credible to defenders of the unreformed House of Commons in Great Britain in the nineteenth century. The concept is inconsistent with democratic thought, however, except as it may pertain to children and others who are incapable of exercising the franchise. Consequently, the democratization of legislatures has consisted of defining and expanding the electorate, organizing the massive electorates characteristic of modern states, and broadening eligibility for membership in Parliament.

One-third of the world's parliaments consist of two houses. The members of half of these second chambers are directly elected, while those of the other half are either elected indirectly or appointed. In the twenty-five years after World War II, three countries replaced a bicameral legislature with a one-house, or unicameral, legislature: Denmark, New Zealand, and Sweden. When parliaments were democratized in Central and Eastern Europe following the withdrawal of the Soviet Union from support for communist regimes, Poland added a second chamber to its parliament. Still other countries contemplate the establishment of a second house. There is no clear trend away from bicameralism, despite its predemocratic roots. Indeed, a house to represent constituencies not based on equal populations continues to be attractive, particularly in federal states where one house, like the U.S. Senate or the German Bundesrat, is used to represent the component states.

Nevertheless, the effort to democratize parliaments principally has consisted of extending the right to choose members. Thus a franchise limited to property holders was expanded to "universal" manhood suffrage and then to suffrage without regard to gender, race, or ethnicity and finally to eighteen-year-olds. This development began in the United States early in the nineteenth century, in Great Britain with the first reform of parliamentary representation in 1832, and on the continent of Europe after the revolutions of 1848. It was completed in most countries in the second half of the twentieth century and had profound consequences for the composition and internal organization of parliaments.

The democratic franchise created mass electorates that needed to be organized in order to be able to act at all. To that end modern legislatures retained the medieval notions that the country consists of geographic communities and that the representative assembly should be a house representing these communities, or *commons*, as the British called them. Thus the British elected chamber is the House of Commons. By comparison, the notion that the country consisted of estates or orders was generally abandoned. Also abandoned were attempts to give a modern, functional form to the medieval corporations by establishing a chamber representing professions, occupations, and interest groups. The electoral process by which members of legislatures are chosen is therefore organized territorially, with geographically defined constituencies electing single or multiple representatives.

The mass electorate is also organized by political parties, successors to the factions that existed within predemocratic parliaments. Unlike factions, parties work outside parliaments as well as within them, linking groups of like-minded members with their voters. Parties nominate candidates for parliament, mobilize the voters, formulate electoral programs, and attempt to hold the elected members accountable to their voters. Democratic legislatures are distinguished from legislatures in dictatorships by the fact that their members are selected in competition between candidates of two or more political parties. The organization of democratic electorates has therefore taken two forms: territorial and partisan. There is considerable variation from one country to another in how territorial constituencies are drawn and how party competition is regulated.

In the United States, as in most federal states, constituencies are divided first among the component states by a formula that reflects their relative populations. The state legislatures then draw congressional constituency boundaries, under supervision by the courts to make certain that two basic criteria of fairness are followed. First, constituencies must have strictly equal populations. Second, racial and ethnic minorities must have a chance to win their proportional share of seats. The votes of minorities may not be "diluted" by the way constituency borders are drawn. In Great Britain, Germany, and many other democratic countries, boundaries are drawn by nonpartisan, quasi-judicial commissions, and expectations of fairness are different. In most countries the principle of population equality is not as strictly enforced as in the United States, and regard for the representation of minorities varies greatly. The populations of British parliamentary constituencies can deviate by more than 20 percent from the national average. Especially in countries having multiparty systems, the expectation that the partisan preferences of the electorate should be fairly represented in parliament is more highly developed than in the United States.

In about half of all democratic countries, each parliamentary constituency is represented by several members. This makes it possible to have proportional representation, or the election of candidates of the various political parties in proportion to their relative number of votes. The precision of this proportionality depends on the number of representatives elected for each constituency. Partisan proportionality avoids the dominance of a single party over time, like Democratic Party dominance in the U.S. House of Representatives. It results, however, in an increase in the number of political parties that win seats in parliament.

The preference for proportional representation developed in Europe after World War I, expressing a democratic sense of fairness toward the whole spectrum of political parties. As a result, political parties proliferated, causing an early form of gridlock in parliaments. After World War II many countries limited proportional representation by requiring parties to obtain at least 5 percent of the vote in the entire country before they could claim their proportional share of seats in parliament. This "threshold" provision was also adopted by most of the newly democratic legislatures that were established in Central and Eastern Europe after 1989. The structure of representation therefore has direct consequences for the party composition of legislatures and for the process of decision making in the legislatures, in which parties play an important role.

In addition to the expansion of the electorate, democracy required the expansion of eligibility for membership in parliament. Most countries impose criteria for election of members that are more exacting than the criteria for voting. They do this not from an antidemocratic impulse but to increase the probability that members of legislatures will be qualified to carry out their responsibilities. Most countries require members to be at least twenty-one years of age, even if voters need only be eighteen. In the United States members of the House of Representatives must be at least twenty-five, and members of the Senate must be thirty years old. Most countries also require members to have been citizens and residents of their country for a specified number of years, and many bar candidates who have serious criminal records or other legal incapacities. To avoid conflicts of interest, many countries establish the ineligibility for parliament of holders of certain public offices or even members of certain occupations.

Broadening the right of the population to participate in the selection of members of parliament and broadening eligibility for membership do not ensure that the composition of the legislature will appear to be representative of the population. A few hundred representatives cannot fully mirror a large population, but democratic publics do expect representative institutions to resemble them in salient respects. All countries expect that the membership of the legislature should reflect the geographic diversity of the population, and most expect that the party composition of the legislature should bear a reasonably close relationship to the distribution of the vote by party in the electorate.

On the continent of Europe there have long been expectations that parliaments should be composed of members from a wide range of professions and occupations. Many countries are sensitive to balance within parliament among members belonging to the principal religious, ethnic, or tribal groups. The nomination of candidates by the political parties is the mechanism by which the composition of the legislature is made to correspond to public expectations, but that mechanism is imperfect. The sensitivity of the parties may lag behind voter expectations, and election outcomes may in any case be governed by the accidents of the distribution of votes across constituencies. The very slow increase in the number of women in legislatures exemplifies many of the imperfections in the mechanism by which changing cultural expectations are translated into changes in the composition of legislatures. Over time, however, legislatures do tend to mirror the expectations of the electorates regarding what constitutes "representativeness." Failing this, their authority is impaired.

The "electoral connection" between members of the legislature and the population is a critical aspect of democratic representation. It provides the incentive for members to be responsive to their voters. The influence of the electoral connection on responsiveness is in part determined by the frequency of elections. Only the U.S. House of Representatives has a term of office as short as two years. In other countries the normal term is four or five years, but in parliamentary systems the term may end abruptly if parliament has voted its lack of confidence in the executive branch and the prime minister responds by dissolving parliament and calling new elections.

The advantage enjoyed by incumbents in seeking reelection—notably greater in U.S. elections than in the more party-oriented legislative elections of most other countries—raises the question of the desirability of limiting the number of terms that a legislator may serve. The purpose would be to maintain the competitiveness of elections. Only nondemocratic parliaments limit members to single terms, because inexperience in members contributes to a legislature's weakness. In the United States, several states have imposed term limits on their own legislators and have attempted to impose them on their representatives in Congress as well. In other democratic countries, where the advantages of incumbency have not been so conspicuous, no term limits exist.

An idealized image of responsiveness would measure its achievement by the extent of congruence between the views of constituents and those of their representatives. Such an idealized image would overlook two very important political realities. First, there is usually no unanimity of views within single constituencies and certainly no unanimity across the constituencies of a nation. Second, political issues are of peripheral concern to most citizens, who therefore have no views at all, or no stable views, on most issues.

As a result of these realities, representatives cannot be delegates of their constituents or merely mirror their views. By their engagement in parliamentary politics, organization, and procedure, they develop information and views about politics that their constituents lack. They are bound to have views that differ from those of their constituents. Thus representatives often act as trustees of the interests of their voters. This in itself does not violate their obligations as representatives. Rather, their role as representatives includes that of formulating the political agenda, proposing alternative solutions, seeking public support for these solutions, and responding to public wishes when these are clearly expressed. Edmund Burke, a member of the British Parliament at the time of the American Revolution, gave classic expression to the view that a member is not a mere delegate of a constituency in the medieval sense but a trustee of constituents, owing them his "unbiased opinion, his mature judgment, his enlightened conscience."

Experienced legislators recognize that their constituents are not attentive to most issues. They rely on their similarity to their constituents to avoid conflict between their own judgment and what their voters would accept. They act as agents of their constituents, however, when constituents press their individual needs or requests. Indeed, constituency service in this sense is a universal function of members of legislatures and parliaments. Members characteristically hold office hours in their constituencies, intervene with government agencies on behalf of their constituents, answer mail, and issue newsletters. With their large personal staffs, members of the U.S. Congress develop and attend to a much larger volume of constituency "casework" than do members of other legislatures. The activity itself is universal among members of legislatures and parliaments in all countries.

The "electoral connection" is an important bond between the individual member and his or her voters, but the sum of these bonds of the individual members to their individual constituencies does not necessarily serve the interest of the entire population. Achieving that ideal requires methods for identifying the interests of the population of each constituency. These interests, and the incentives that each member has to advocate the plurality of these constituency interests, then have to be transformed into collective decisions that will serve the common interest. Parliamentary organization and procedure are the means for achieving that transformation. These turn an assembly of equals into a structure in which a division of labor and an implicit hierarchy of influence make it possible for the members to be true representatives of the people.

Organization

The complexity of modern society makes it particularly difficult to identify the general interest of the represented. Many aspects of the organization of legislatures help members identify interests, however, and then induce them to reconcile the sum of these interests with the general interest. The method of selecting the members of a legislature leads them to identify and advocate the multiple geographic interests in a society. The dependence of the members on regular reelection causes them to be particularly attentive to interest groups in their constituencies that provide them with valuable information on issues, organizational skills, and possibly campaign contributions. Although members of these groups may be included in the membership of the legislature, this occurrence is less common in the United States than in Europe. To the extent that interest group members do not sit directly in the legislature, their external organizations contact legislators, an activity called *lobbying*.

In addition to the external pressure of interest groups, legislatures have a special propensity to respond to the plurality of interests because they organize themselves into committees specializing in particular subject areas. The U.S. Senate has 16 specialized standing committees as well as 86 subcommittees, and the U.S. House of Representatives has 22 standing committees with 115 subcommittees. Committee specialization in the U.S. Congress exceeds that in other national legislatures. The number of committees ranges from just 6 in each house of the French parliament to 29 in the directly elected house of the Dutch parliament. The usual number is 10 to 20 committees, and subcommittees are seldom used.

In the British Parliament most committees are organized on an ad hoc basis, appointed anew for each bill. This limited specialization among members reflects the limited lawmaking function of the House of Commons and places members at a great disadvantage in relationship to party leaders in the executive branch and their civil servants in the bureaucracy. To offset this liability, and to improve the ability of members of Parliament to supervise the executive branch, a system of what are now 14 specialized select committees was established in 1979. The British approach to committee organization reveals the subordination of the British Parliament to party leaders and the bureaucracy. Elsewhere legislatures have long relied on specialized committees to develop their own specialized knowledge.

To the extent that legislatures adopt a specialized committee system, they emulate the executive branch. This is true especially because the subject jurisdiction of legislative committees tends to reflect the specialization among cabinet departments. This is in part the result of the committees' role in exercising oversight over executive departments, a role as important as lawmaking and appropriations even in the United States.

Legislators naturally prefer assignment to committees whose subject areas are familiar to them and whose subjects serve their constituents. This means that committee members start out with specialized knowledge and interest in the area of their committees, and they gradually develop further expertise. Their specialization is aided by professional committee staffs, which are very extensive in the United States and have now been established in most democratic legislatures. The U.S. Congress employs more than 3,000 committee staff members. No other national legislature has a staff even one-tenth as large. Still, many U.S. state legislatures have developed good-sized staffs, as have the parliaments of Western Europe and Japan. Through the specialization of their members and staffs, these committees produce a range of expertise on the major issues of politics. In most legislative bodies, that expertise does not approach what is available to the executive branch; however, it comes closer in the U.S. Congress than anywhere else.

Geographically defined constituencies and committee specialization clearly help legislators to identify the special interests of their constituents and to serve them. This emphasis on particular interests, however, presents obstacles to the formation of legislative majorities. One way members overcome these obstacles is by trading votes with each other. Relying on differences in the intensity of their various preferences, legislators exchange support on matters of indifference to them for support on matters they regard as extremely important to their constituents. This is the basis of "pork barrel" legislation, in which appropriations measures provide individual benefits for every member's constituency at a cost greater than what would be economically efficient for the entire nation. This pattern is called *distributive politics*, in which everyone appears to win but the collectivity is ill served.

Two major countervailing pressures limit the effect of distributive politics. One limit is imposed by political parties, which combine the interests of individual legislators into general policies attractive to their electorates nationally. Parties are organized within legislatures into what are called *caucuses* in the United States and *parliamentary parties* in Great Britain. These groupings of legislators belonging to the same party organize to choose their floor leaders and whips, as well as the presiding officer of each chamber, called the *speaker* in the English-speaking world or *president* elsewhere. They may allocate committee chairmanships to the extent that these are not automatically assigned by a seniority system, as in the United States, or by a system of proportional representation among the parties. These groupings also endeavor to negotiate committee assignments among their members. They attempt to formulate party policy on issues before the legislature, often employing their own specialized party committees for the purpose. They try to persuade members to maintain a common position on important issues. If more than five or six parties are represented in parliament, their contribution to the aggregation of interests and to the organization of work is obviously limited.

As a result of party organization within the legislature, and of the capacity of parties to influence the nomination of candidates and election campaigns, the voting behavior of members of legislatures exhibits considerable party cohesion. This is the case particularly in European parliaments that have long-established party systems in which the electorate is strongly influenced by party labels in choosing representatives. Even in the United States, where members of Congress contest their seats far more as individuals than as party members, half the votes on the floor of the two houses are party votes in the sense that a majority of Democrats vote together against a majority of Republicans. Furthermore, members have shown a growing tendency to vote with the majority of members of their party. By the early 1990s the proportion doing so reached 80 percent among House Democrats and was even higher on crucial issues, such as the budget.

Party discipline exceeds 90 percent in most democratic parliaments outside the United States, except on matters of individual conscience. In the 1980s and 1990s Democrats and Republicans in the U.S. Congress also attained this level of cohesion on important issues. In parliamentary systems, when the prime minister and the cabinet consist of leaders of the party or parties holding a majority in the assembly, party discipline adds to the authority of the executive. In the U.S. presidential system, where the presidency and Congress are often in the hands of different parties, party discipline may make for divided government. In that case the presidential veto becomes an important source of executive influence over the legislature, limited only by the capacity of the Congress to override the veto by a two-thirds vote.

A second countervailing influence on the propensity of members to engage in distributive politics is their uncertainty about the consequences of particular policies. In a complex modern society the outcomes of legislative actions are often so unclear that legislators cannot make reliable calculations about the political consequences of their votes. Outside the areas of their own expertise, legislators are often uncertain about the policy implications of a particular vote, about probable voter reaction, and about possible policy alternatives. Such uncertainty leads members to defer to the experts among them. They thus have a tendency to trade specialized information as well as votes based on their specialized interests.

The effect of information trading on the collective decisions of the legislature is different from the effect of vote trading. Expert information is likely to reflect a large variety of considerations, technical expertise supplied by committee staffs and executive departments, nationwide party interests, and calculations about the eventual outcomes of a particular policy decision. To the extent that members defer to it, their decisions are likely to serve the general interest rather than narrow interests. The committee, party, and interest group structure of legislatures thus enables members to identify both the multiple interests of the represented and the general interest—at least to the extent that deliberation among the best informed leaders of government and politics can determine it.

Procedure

The patterns of influence that committees and parties have on the decisions of the entire legislature are determined by its procedure. Procedure governs three very important aspects of parliamentary activity: the lawmaking and budgetary process, the resolution of differences between the two houses in bicameral systems, and the conduct of public debate. Procedure is set out partly in written regulations, partly in interpretations and precedents based on the written rules, and partly in informal norms of conduct. Although legislatures generally have the authority to make their rules of procedure, in practice most newly elected legislatures readopt the procedures of their predecessors. Newly established legislatures generally borrow the procedures of long-established parliaments in other countries. Although rules of procedure vary from one legislature to another, many contemporary versions of parliamentary rules can be traced back to the procedures of the British Parliament in the predemocratic era.

The uninterrupted 500-year history of British parliamentary procedure was carefully recorded in its journals and in compilations of precedents. This history was transmitted to the colonial legislatures of North America and later to the legislatures of the British Commonwealth. The diffusion of British parliamentary experience sometimes took the form of direct imitation, as in the manual based on the procedure of the British House of Commons that Thomas Jefferson prepared when he presided over the U.S. Senate. Sometimes it occurred through the writings of political theorists, such as Jeremy Bentham, whose *Essay on Political Tactics* (1816) influenced Belgian, French, and later German legislative practice. When parliaments were established in newly independent states in Asia and Africa after World War II, the British Parliament provided technical assistance to parliamentarians in those countries. The U.S. Congress provided similar assistance to the newly democratic parliaments of Central and Eastern Europe after 1989.

Legislatures take a traditional approach to their own procedures because they recognize the difficulty of designing ways to reconcile the wills of the members of a large assembly. In most legislatures members develop great respect for the historical experience of the institution and the parliamentarians who interpret that experience. Legislative procedure tends to evolve over time, deriving its authority more from tradition, precedent, and custom than from explicitly enacted rules.

Even such a deceptively simple proposition as "decisions must be taken by a majority" is by itself quite inadequate for reaching conclusions in legislatures. Unlike voters in general elections, legislators vote on a constant stream of related issues. As they do so, they interact with each other, taking a variety of interests into account and negotiating compromises. As soon as there are more than two alternatives on which legislators must vote, each successive pairing of alternatives may have a different result, leading to an endless cycle of majority votes with different outcomes. The varied preferences of a group of legislators choosing among many alternative solutions to an issue will not naturally lead to a single majority decision. Subsidiary rules must determine the sequence in which alternatives are considered and the point at which a vote becomes final.

Outsiders often mistakenly disparage legislatures that wrangle over "mere procedural questions." Rules have an effect on decisions, so they are potentially extremely controversial. They allocate authority among committees, between committees and the whole house, between majorities and minorities, between decisions made at different points in time, and, in parliamentary systems, between the leaders of parliament in the cabinet and their "back bench" followers. The rules determine the sequence of actions—for example, the order of consideration of bills and amendments. They can themselves arouse intense conflict even as they seek to structure conflict over substantive issues.

The lawmaking process begins with the introduction of bills. Bills are introduced in one of several ways: by individual members, as in the U.S. Congress; by the cabinet, in parliamentary systems of government where the cabinet consists of leaders of parliament; by the component states in a federal system, as in Germany; by voters in the form of an initiative, as in Switzerland and many of the states of the United States; or by committees, as in half the world's legislatures. Bills are nearly everywhere referred to committees, which may revise them substantially before reporting them back to the full chamber. In the United States a committee often fails to report a bill back

at all. This is because each member of the U.S. Congress may propose unlimited numbers of bills, a procedure that results in 10,000 bills in each biennial Congress, far more than in any other legislature.

Procedure determines the sequence by which bills are reported back and the restrictions, if any, on their further amendment on the floor. In the U.S. House of Representatives, the Rules Committee proposes a special rule for each important bill, to govern the particular circumstances under which it will be considered by the whole chamber. Special restrictive rules thus determine the influence of the committee version on the final outcome. In the U.S. Senate the sequence of business must be negotiated among the party leaders to achieve the "unanimous consent" of all 100 members, for senators are unwilling to delegate this important matter to a committee on rules.

A special process generally governs the appropriation of public funds, in recognition of the technical expertise required to formulate a national budget and of the temptation of legislators to appropriate funds in excess of what they are willing to vote in taxes. Despite the conviction rooted in U.S. history that the appropriation of funds should be the province of the legislature—and the special province of the House of Representatives—the executive branch has the obligation to present an annual budget even in the United States. In Great Britain the House of Commons abdicated its right to introduce money bills nearly three centuries ago.

Most countries place limits on the right of legislatures to raise the level of appropriations recommended by the executive branch. The U.S. Congress long insisted on full power to raise and cut expenditures. It, however, passed a series of laws, beginning with the Congressional Budget Act of 1974, by which it developed special procedures that compel it to set budgetary priorities and provide the staff to match the expertise available to the executive.

The collective decision of a legislature takes the form of a vote of its members. Procedure determines whether the decision is by a simple majority of voting members, by an absolute majority of all members whether voting or not, or by a qualified majority of three-fifths, two-thirds, or three-quarters of the members. Procedure also determines how the vote is taken: orally by calling for "ayes" and "nays"; visually by show of hands or by asking members to stand; by a secret ballot (provided for the election of leaders or prime ministers in some parliaments); or by a call of the roll of members. The traditional "roll call vote," by which members' decisions are readily reported to their constituents, has been replaced in the U.S. Congress and many other legislatures by electronic voting, which allows members to cast instantly recorded votes from their seats by pushing buttons. The method of voting affects the public visibility of the members' votes and the opportunities for last-minute bargaining during the conduct of a vote. In the British Parliament the substitute for roll calls or electronic voting is an efficient procedure called a *division*. In a division, members leave their seats and reenter the House through opposite doors, one for the "ayes" and one for the "nays," while tellers record their vote.

At least as important as the form of the vote is the sequence by which amendments are considered, for this directly affects the final outcome. The importance of this sequence has always been understood by experienced legislators, who often become skilled in exploiting particular sequences to their own advantage. Informed observers can distinguish between "tactical" and "sincere" voting. Legislators vote tactically, for example, if they support an amendment that they dislike because they calculate that this amendment would increase the prospects for passage of a bill that they favor.

Sophisticated research employing mathematical models has demonstrated the calculations involved in such a voting sequence.

The existence of two chambers in a legislature, as in France, Germany, Great Britain, and the United States, adds to the complexity of the legislative process. Special procedures govern the ways in which the separate decisions of the two houses can be reconciled. In the United States a joint conference committee attempts to formulate a compromise that can be adopted in identical form by each house. The joint committee may consist of more than 100 members of the two houses and is sometimes divided into subcommittees. Its role late in the legislative process gives subject specialists who dominate conference committees important influence on the final text of legislation. In other countries, such as Australia, Canada, and France, bills shuttle back and forth between the chambers until an identical text is adopted by both. Some parliaments use a combination of these procedures. Some, such as France, Germany, and the United Kingdom, grant the directly elected house the last word, giving it power in relation to the number of shuttle trips permitted.

Public debate in parliament is important for its effect on particular decisions within the chamber, as in the case of debate over a piece of legislation. It also has an effect on the policies of the executive branch and on the public. Procedures governing debate determine the opportunities for public deliberation and the allocation of time among speakers. Debate on legislation generally takes place in three stages, called *readings*. Debating time is limited, both by general rules and by rules specific to a particular item of business. An exception is the U.S. Senate, which allows members to speak without time limit unless "cloture" of debate is adopted by a three-fifths vote. The Senate's unlimited debate is an extreme example of a procedure to protect minorities against majority rule. In most legislative bodies debating time is allocated to individual members by the leaders of their parties, after the parties agree on an allocation of time among themselves. The presiding officer may have influence in recognizing individual members, but above all he or she has the duty to maintain orderly debate and to stop inflammatory remarks. The British House of Commons has a fully developed set of precedents regarding what constitutes unparliamentary language; most other parliaments follow its example in ways consistent with their own national cultures.

Debate for the purpose of influencing the executive branch or the public takes a variety of special forms, most of them originally developed in Great Britain. A regular hour for questioning the prime minister and members of the cabinet has become a favorite vehicle for the parliamentary interrogation of executives, in part because it offers an opportunity to air ministerial actions publicly. It is equivalent in some respects to presidential press conferences in the United States or to committee hearings. These procedures all tend to attract television coverage, which enhances their intended effect on the public. Most parliaments also afford their members an opportunity to debate government policies generally, without attaching the debate to a particular item of business. The purpose may be to persuade the electorate rather than other members of the legislature or the executive.

Together, parliamentary organization and procedure produce the informal hierarchies and asymmetries by which assemblies of equal members are turned into working bodies capable of decision making. The subtle, implicit codes of courtesy and good conduct among members—often called *informal norms*—contribute to members' ability to work together. In most effective parliaments there is reciprocity in interpersonal relations. This consists of showing courtesy even when sharp substantive differences exist, of keeping promises even during intense tactical maneuvering, and of cooperating even in the face of competition. Members learn that they must work with each other and respect each other's burden of work. They learn that even the fiercest political differences are best acted out when they are depersonalized. These informal norms contribute to the transformation of a collection of individuals into a corporate body.

Legislatures in Democracies

Parliament seemed so ideally suited to be the central institution of democracy that liberal democrats regarded government based on it as a perfect form of government. It permitted the people to exercise controlling power through their representatives. Exaggerated expectations led to exaggerated disillusionment when proponents were faced with the uneven quality of members, their partisanship, and the inattention of the public. Much of the criticism reflected predemocratic conceptions of a representative assembly composed of "elites," coupled with unrealistic expectations of public interest in government.

Unrealistic expectations of parliaments were expressed again with regard to the newly independent states of Africa and Asia after World War II and the newly democratic states of East Central Europe after 1989. Experience in both the old and the new democracies indicates that parliaments do not necessarily produce politically enlightened publics or responsive governments. They do, however, perform indispensable functions in modern political systems. They attract public attention to politics. They recruit and train political leaders. They provide governments with crucial information about what the public wants and what it will accept, and this affects the formulation of public policies and budgets. Finally, a parliament helps define a nation.

The last of these functions proved especially important in the second half of the twentieth century in the newly independent nation-states of Africa and Asia, and in Central and Eastern Europe after the dissolution of the Soviet Union. In many of these places populations seriously divided by tribal and ethnic loyalties had no commitment to being governed together as members of a single political community. At best they had been tied together by a common hostility to their former colonial or Soviet masters. When they gained independence they faced the challenge of agreeing on institutions of government and on solutions to their most urgent social and economic problems, even though they lacked a sense of their common political identity. In these circumstances legislatures played a nation-building function, defining the constituencies of the nation, linking these constituencies to the central government, training a political leadership as well as an opposition, and providing a symbol of the new state. Parliaments had earlier performed this function in the nation-building stages of European history.

Although legislatures and parliaments supposedly represent the public and are second only to presidents and prime ministers in their public importance, they are surprisingly unpopular. Public opinion in all countries generally takes a dim view of their work. Two characteristics of the institution help to explain this paradox. First, the internal organization of legislatures is complicated and relatively inscrutable, and the private sector has nothing that resembles it closely. Second, members of legislatures emphasize how they serve their own constituencies, whether geographic units, political parties, or interests. Yet to be effective these same members must reach compromises, which they find difficult to explain, let alone defend, to their own constituents. Legislators therefore are tempted to blame their colleagues publicly for what they have arranged with them quietly, and this fuels public criticism of the institution. They practice one style of politics at home and another style in the legislature, and their failure to reconcile the two leads to public distrust. Individually, members of legislatures are able to champion the causes of their constituents and thereby to personalize government. Collectively, however, legislatures and parliaments appear destined to be the target of much of the criticism that government policies in a democracy attract.

The evaluation of parliaments by the general public depends largely on public satisfaction with government policy, and it fluctuates accordingly. In new states facing exceptionally severe and urgent problems, legislatures have few opportunities to act in ways that produce public satisfaction. Yet attentive citizens and political leaders have a strong commitment to the institution. The number of cases in which legislatures have been abolished by political elites is much smaller than the number of cases in which legislatures have been created or re-created. In most countries political leaders are the products of legislatures. Political careers begin with service in local or provincial legislatures, and positions of leadership in the executive branch are achieved in parliamentary systems primarily by leaders of parliament.

Regardless of the ups and downs of public attitudes toward the legislature, political leaders in democratic states are committed to it. Their challenge is to employ the institution in such a way as to maintain political stability. Working in their favor is the absence of attractive alternatives. In the last decades of the twentieth century nonparliamentary political elites abdicated in many states—in southern European and Latin American states, where the elites had seized power from democratic predecessors and in the former communist states that had depended on the support of the Soviet Union.

The principal challenges to parliaments continue to be identifying the interest of the represented and responding to that interest in the formulation and adoption of public policies and budgets. The organization and procedure of legislatures are designed to provide members with the capacity to gather information on political issues from the greatest variety of sources, to combine that information, to exchange interpretations of it, eventually to reach conclusions based on it, and then to seek the endorsement of their constituents. Viewed from this perspective, legislatures and parliaments make distinctive informational contributions to the governmental process. When bureaucratic executive institutions dominate political systems—as they did during communist rule in Central and Eastern Europe between 1945 and 1990, and at various times in newly independent, developing countries—governments are deprived of both the information and the public support that effective parliaments can provide. The distinctive role of legislatures in modern democracies is to help identify the public policies that a nation's ablest experts are able to devise and to reconcile them with the expectations of the nation's citizens.

See also Federalism; Interest groups; Parliamentarism and presidentialism; Representation.

GERHARD LOEWENBERG

BIBLIOGRAPHY

Converse, Philip E., and Roy Pierce. *Political Representation in France*. Cambridge: Harvard University Press, 1986.

Dodd, Lawrence C., and Bruce I. Oppenheimer, eds. *Congress Reconsidered*. 5th ed. Washington, D.C.: CQ Press, 1993.

Fenno, Richard F., Jr. *Home Style: House Members in Their Districts*. Boston: Little, Brown, 1978.

Goldsworthy, Jeffrey Denys. *The Sovereignty of Parliament: History and Philosophy*. New York: Clarendon Press, 1999.

Inter-Parliamentary Union. *Parliaments of the World*. 2d ed. New York: Facts on File, 1986.

Jennings, W. Ivor. *Parliament*. 2d ed. Cambridge: Cambridge University Press, 1957.

Keefe, William J., and Morris S. Ogul. *The American Legislative Process: Congress and the States*. 8th ed. Englewood Cliffs, N.J.: Prentice Hall, 1993.

Kim, Chong Lim, Joel D. Barkan, Ilter Turan, and Malcolm E. Jewell. *The Legislative Connection: The Politics of Representation in Kenya, Korea, and Turkey*. Durham, N.C.: Duke University Press, 1984.

Krehbiel, Keith. *Information and Legislative Organization*. Ann Arbor: University of Michigan Press, 1992.

Loewenberg, Gerhard, and Samuel C. Patterson. *Comparing Legislatures*. Boston: Little, Brown, 1979. Reprint, Lanham, Md.: University Press of America, 1988.

Loewenberg, Gerhard, and Malcolm E. Jewell, eds. *Handbook of Legislative Research*. Cambridge: Harvard University Press, 1985.

Matthews, Donald R. *U.S. Senators and Their World*. Chapel Hill: University of North Carolina Press, 1960.

Mayhew, David R. *Congress: The Electoral Connection*. New Haven: Yale University Press, 1974.

Norton, Philip, ed. *Legislatures*. New York: Oxford University Press, 1990.

Pitkin, Hanna Fenichel. *The Concept of Representation*. Berkeley: University of California Press, 1967.

Taagepera, Rein, and Matthew S. Shugart. *Seats and Votes*. New Haven: Yale University Press, 1989.

✦ Legitimacy

An accepted entitlement or sanction to rule. All governments depend on some combination of coercion and consent for survival. Democracies, however, differ from autocracies in the degree to which their stability rests on the consent of the majority of those governed. Too great a reliance on coercion to keep order would stifle the political competition and liberty that constitute much of the essence of democracy.

Almost as a given, theories of democracy stress that democratic stability requires legitimacy. Elites and the masses must share the belief that the system—that is, the set of constitutional arrangements, not the particular administration— is the best form of government (or the least evil). Hence elected officeholders are morally entitled to demand loyalty and obedience—to tax and draft and regulate, to make laws and enforce them—even from those who voted against them or are strongly opposed to their policies.

Legitimacy of any kind is derived from shared beliefs; such consensus develops slowly. That is not to say that everyone in a society must share basic beliefs about governance. In any population some people do not care at all, or do not feel deeply, about the polity. In any given society many who believe that democracy is a desirable form of government are not ready to fight for it or to make any effort to defend it from danger. In every democracy some who consider freedom desirable in principle do not believe that political freedoms are appropriate in the particular circumstances of their country. Some people (and at some historical moments, perhaps many) who value democracy may consider certain other objectives more important or believe that different ways of organizing political life are more efficient for attaining their goals.

The attitudes of a society's members toward democracy as a political system should not be confused with their evaluation of the performance of specific institutions or with their judgments about particular officeholders. Certainly a negative

opinion over a long period of time about democratic outcomes, about chronic failures or corruption among democratically selected leaders, as in Italy in the 1980s and 1990s, will erode legitimacy. But opinions about the legitimacy of democracy and the effectiveness of democracy have to be distinguished and analyzed separately.

Democratic legitimacy derives, when it is most stable and secure, from a commitment to democracy as an end in itself, as the best form of government, even in very difficult circumstances. Although no regime is entirely immune to breakdown, highly legitimate democratic systems can survive serious crises and challenges. Generally, the deeper the legitimacy of a regime, the more likely it will be able to endure intense stress.

Democratic stability is supported by the interplay of legitimacy and effectiveness. Regimes that are both legitimate and effective generally enjoy high levels of voluntary compliance. Systems with neither legitimacy nor effectiveness by definition will have to deal with insubordinate citizens and may even break down, unless they are dictatorships that can maintain themselves by force and guile. Thus democratic regimes with strong legitimacy have tended to survive failures of effectiveness, as did the Netherlands, the United Kingdom, and the United States during the Great Depression of the 1930s. Those in which support for democracy is based only on effectiveness are likely to break down, as did the German Weimar Republic in 1933, where the government's legitimacy was never accepted by the many who favored the monarchy, or the post–World War I regimes of Eastern Europe, which lacked any historic claim to govern.

The Role of Elites
Despite the presumably strong linkage between democracy and popular participation and support, the legitimacy of popularly based systems

depends first on backing from political elites—mainstream political leaders, military officers, civil servants, business and labor officials, and religious and other opinion leaders. Considerable research indicates that the impetus for the transition to democracy (and to a considerable extent for democratic consolidation as well) comes from the political choices, actions, and skills of contending political elites in both government and opposition.

If important minorities (not to mention majorities) among the elites question the value of democracy (either for their society or in principle), or even if they are indifferent about the desirable type of regime, democracy is in danger. This situation occurred in the early 1920s in Italy, and more recently in much of Eastern Europe and in the successor states to the Soviet Union. Such elites tend to have the resources, the mobilizing capacity, and the strategic position to produce a crisis in the regime if they are not committed to the system. Masses, even where they are organized, typically have a much less forceful and rapid impact, in part because their major resource—numbers—makes it difficult for them to act decisively on their own.

If elites do not harbor democratic sentiments, even if democracy in principle has wide popular support, the chances of preserving a free system are slim. On the other hand, elites may establish a majoritarian regime even in the absence of significant democratic loyalties on the part of the citizenry, as in Portugal after António Salazar died in 1970 and in Spain after Francisco Franco died in 1975. The construction of democracy, like its overthrow, is largely engineered by elites.

Nevertheless, popular attitudes can influence elite choices. The more widespread the democratic commitment and the more deeply it is rooted throughout society, the more likely it is that systems will be able to handle crises. The pro-gressive erosion of democratic legitimacy, or the crystallization of doubts as to its effectiveness, emerges with stunning regularity as a critical factor in many cases of regime breakdown. Weak and eroded democratic legitimacy has permitted weak civilian rulers or military elites in many countries to constrict or shut down democracy, as in France on at least ten occasions since 1789, in Russia in the October 1917 Bolshevik revolution (which overthrew an eight-month-old democracy), in Argentina from the 1930s on, or in Haiti repeatedly. By contrast, intrinsic legitimacy is associated with the persistence of democratic regimes even through very stressful times, as in Costa Rica in the late 1940s and in the United States during the Watergate crisis in the 1970s. How legitimacy is produced and lost, and how it contributes to democratic stability, are among the most important issues in understanding the persistence, failure, and renewal of democracy.

Global Trends

How do elites (and the larger society) become convinced that democracy is the best form of government? Since the 1980s a diffuse climate of opinion has played a central role in creating these democratic convictions. This pro-democracy climate has become increasingly global and has been supported by international institutions such as the European Community (now the European Union), the World Bank, and the International Monetary Fund.

Legitimacy is inherently relative. To judge that a political system is not merely satisfactory or efficacious but the best type of government for a country involves a weighing (explicitly or implicitly) of alternatives. And people judge not only the comparative experience of other countries but also their own historical record. The legitimacy (still weak) of the new democratic regimes that emerged in South America in the 1980s derived from a renewed appraisal of democracy in the light of the preceding authoritarian regimes. Repressive systems, like those in Argentina, Spain, or the former totalitarian states, may "inoculate" their citizens to reject antidemocratic appeals.

To say that legitimacy is relative, then, implies that people may come to view democracy as preferable by default—because there is no other appealing or plausible model, because it is the "least bad" alternative. This is often the judgment (especially among elites) by which democracy gains a purchase in unstable and conflict-ridden political circumstances. Although its relative merit can serve perfectly well to initiate democracy, being the least bad form of government is not a promising foundation for intrinsic legitimacy. Ultimately, democracy will be most stable when it is viewed as a positively good form of government.

Historical Traditions and Charisma

As the German sociologist Max Weber (1864–1920) recognized in his classic writings on the subject, historical traditions can provide a natural source of legitimacy. This source may be particularly important for societies in the early stages of political liberalization and democratization. If previously entrenched social forces feel threatened by democratic change, they may work to undermine democracy by playing on the conflict between tradition and modernity.

Some legitimate traditional institutions, such as monarchy, have facilitated democratic change. It remains one of the enduring ironies of comparative politics that most of the world's longest-standing democracies are monarchies. In these (predominantly northern European) countries, democracy emerged through a gradual process in which monarchs first shared their right to rule and later surrendered it to democratically accountable governments, while remaining in place as the head of state and source of authority, distinct from the temporary elected agents of authority.

The most successful nonmonarchic polity, the United States, attributes legitimacy to what has become a hallowed authority, the U.S. Constitution. But it took well over a century for the nation to acquire legitimacy. During its first seventy-five years of existence, it faced at least five threats of secession, from the New England states during the War of 1812 to the South in 1860–1861, and national authority was clearly not legitimate south of the Mason-Dixon line for many decades after the Civil War. The post–Civil War United States acquired legitimacy as it became the most productive economy with the highest standard of living in the world. Postrevolutionary France, in contrast, was unable to form a legitimate democratic polity until very recently. It had seven regimes between 1789 and 1871, and then gave birth to three republics under distinct constitutions from 1871 to 1958.

Given the inherent lack of legitimacy in new systems, rulers who wish to reduce the need for force to maintain control often resort to a cult of personality. As Weber emphasized, legitimation through charisma—the imputation of extraordinary qualities to the leader—appears frequently where traditional authority is weak. Marxist theory deprecates the role of leaders in making history. Yet most communist countries have violated this tenet and have imputed charismatic qualities to their heads: V. I. Lenin and Joseph Stalin in the former Soviet Union, Mao Zedong and Deng Xiaoping in China, Ho Chi Minh in Vietnam, Josip Tito in Yugoslavia, Enver Hoxha in Albania, Nicolae Ceausescu in Romania, and others. Similar developments have occurred in many Asian and African new states.

Charismatic leadership, moreover, because it is so dependent on the actions of one person, is extremely unstable. The source of authority is not distinct from the actions and agencies of authority, so particular dissatisfaction can easily become generalized disaffection. Therefore, the charismatic leader must either make open criticism impermissible or must transcend partisan conflict by playing the role of a constitutional monarch. Even where opposition to specific policies on an individual basis—or informal factional basis—may be tolerated, no opposition party with its own leader can be formed. Hence charisma has rarely laid the ground for legitimate democracy.

The Role of Success

Entrenched legitimacy often evolves from prolonged success, that is, from efficacious results. Comparative work on democratic transitions has shown that, initially, elites often choose or settle on democracy because it is the best, or the safest, institutional means for managing their current divisions and achieving their other goals—not from any intrinsic value commitment to it as the best possible system in all conditions. As they practice democracy over a long period of time, however, its values and habits can become embedded in a political elite and (eventually) in a broad societal consensus. Historically, the longer and more successfully a regime has provided what its citizens (especially the elites) want, the greater and more deeply rooted its legitimacy becomes. A long record of achievement tends to build a large reservoir of legitimacy, enabling the system better to endure crises and challenges.

New democratic regimes are particularly dependent on current achievements for legitimacy. They lack a tradition of democratic loyalty and a record of past accomplishments to which they may point as proof of the regime's efficacy in the face of presumably temporary failures. The link between immediate performance and regime legitimacy is also intensified when there is inadequate separation between the source of democratic authority (the constitution or constitutional monarch) and the elected agent, the temporary incumbent of that authority.

Political leaders, movements, and parties that have brought about the transition to democracy often become identified with the new regime itself. Their failures, instead of being attributed to individual or partisan flaws, may be attributed to democracy as a system. This was true for most of the postcolonial new states of Africa, and has been one of the most acute challenges facing the new democratic regimes of Eastern Europe as the euphoria of overthrowing communism quickly gives way to the pain and dislocation of the economic transition from state socialism to a market system.

The capacity to find solutions to the pressing problems of society is necessary for the stability of all polities, authoritarian as well as democratic. Apart from their need for legitimacy to survive, democratic regimes also depend more on effective performance than do nondemocracies. This is so because failures in performance of democratic regimes are transparent to a unique degree. Being open societies, democracies provide much more complete and accurate information on how they are doing, and they allow specialists, the mass media, and the general public to criticize, publicize, and protest their failures.

The simple passage of time is an element in legitimating democracy. To the extent that a system works well enough to endure across generations, successive age cohorts become socialized into a fully functioning democratic polity so that elites and citizens seem to become "habituated" (to use Walt Rostow's term) to democracy. Reviewing fifty-two cases of internal breakdown of democracy between 1900 and 1985, Robert Dahl found that only in one case, Uruguay, did democratic breakdown occur in a country that had experienced at least twenty years of continuous democracy.

When democracy is institutionalized in nontraditional systems, its legitimation generally follows a pattern that Weber described as rational-legal. That is, prolonged effectiveness has led to the widespread and deep acceptance of the basic system of rules that determine minority rights and the ways in which the opposition may compete to win office. But that basic law, if accepted as the source of legitimacy, takes on an exceptional character, as with the U.S. Constitution.

Political Performance

It is often said that modern governments live and die on their economic records. This is often true, not only in industrialized countries but also in developing ones. However, withdrawal of support for a particular government (a temporary agent of authority) by no means implies loss of faith in the democratic regime. Moreover, even as a legitimating factor, performance does not encompass economic matters alone. No doubt growth in individual income and material improvement in the conditions of daily life are among the most universal personal aspirations and expectations of government. But there are others as well.

Regime performance encompasses a number of political dimensions. Everywhere, to a greater or lesser degree, people want government to maintain order, to resolve conflicts peacefully, to provide a climate of peace and security in which people can go about their daily lives unfettered and without fear of harm to themselves or their families. Citizens expect their government to be able to formulate policies to respond to the basic problems facing their society; in other words, they expect a certain minimum level of political efficacy in the conduct of governmental affairs. Especially in democracies, citizens desire fair and equal treatment by government authorities, and they trust that those officials will use public resources for the defined purposes of government and not for their own advantage and enrichment.

Finally, there is a special expectation of democratic regimes: citizens of free societies believe that, if nothing else, their polities should excel at being democratic, at safeguarding civil and political liberties, honoring the provisions of the constitution or basic laws, ensuring a rule of law and free and fair elections, and being responsive and accountable to the citizenry. To the extent that elected, putatively democratic governments behave in an authoritarian fashion, their citizens are likely to see little point in putting up with them unless they can point to other great accomplishments.

There is substantial evidence of the danger posed by economic crisis and decline to new, fragile, and embattled democracies. This point raises a pertinent question: Why, in spite of low legitimacy, have so many of the newly restored democracies of Latin America and the formerly communist countries of Eastern Europe survived since being formed in the 1980s? How could they have lasted in economic circumstances far worse than those that accompanied most of the breakdowns of the 1960s and 1970s? These countries have seen high inflation rates; decreasing standards of living; drastic increases since 1985 of the numbers of people living below the poverty line; deteriorating health, education, and other public services; widespread unemployment and underemployment; and severe reductions in real wages. These economic circumstances have had profound social and political effects, producing a drastic loss of confidence in major institutions.

But why have these developments not undermined the fragile legitimacy of the new democracies?

There are several reasons why some of the new democracies have survived. First, most of their economic crises predate the new regimes, and their citizens still hold the preceding dictatorships responsible for many of the problems. (With time, however, the new governments' freedom from responsibility will progressively erode.) Second, many influential people understand that the circumstances, including heavy foreign debt and weak commodity prices, lie outside the immediate control of their own governments and that there may simply be no alternative to painful economic restructuring. The military, in particular, may not try to take over governments because the problems would come along with power. Third, because of the unprecedented repressiveness of the preceding regimes, and because the alternatives may not be viable or attractive, the new democracies of the 1980s and 1990s have had considerably greater initial acceptance—legitimacy by default—than have earlier constitutional regimes. This fragile legitimacy enables them to stagger on, painfully, for a while.

Beyond Economics

Three points bear emphasis beyond the linkage between economic achievement and democratic legitimacy. First, people value other dimensions of regime performance, particularly freedom, order, and personal security. Clearly freedom, participation, and lawfulness were of high salience in post-Franco Spain after several decades of authoritarian rule, as they are in Latin America. Most new democracies have done much better in satisfying these popular expectations than the economic ones.

Second, the impact of economic downturns (or other performance declines) on legitimacy will be moderated by considerations of whether any other type of regime could govern more effectively. It has been argued that the key to avoiding democratic breakdown is the ability of leaders to form new coalitions or reaffirm old ones in order to give direction to the national economy. The degree to which political leaders are adept at managing adversity determines whether economic crisis will be blamed on the regime.

Although good performance can serve as a foundation of legitimacy, some level of legitimacy is a precondition for efficient governance. As noted, regimes that cannot command the voluntary compliance of citizens must rely on extensive force to ensure order and govern effectively. Democracies cannot govern primarily on the basis of force and remain democracies.

Because regimes begin with little legitimacy, it is difficult for new democracies to make the necessary tough policy decisions. Key economic and military actors may challenge the government's authority with impunity, leaving it little effective power to meet popular expectations. It is easy to understand why in such systems, those who come into power can squeeze personal profit from the system, setting in motion a dynamic of intense corruption and violence that leads to the breakdown of democracy. Not surprisingly, most efforts to institutionalize democracy in postrevolutionary and postcoup systems or in newly independent states have failed. The success of the American Revolution is truly exceptional.

For the long-run success of democracy, there is no alternative to economic stability and progress. Unless today's new regimes implement the kinds of market-oriented changes that stimulate economic growth, they will be doomed at best to limp along indefinitely with fragile legitimacy. To succeed, new systems often require a political pact and coalition among several parties. They may also need broad social and economic agreement among business, labor, and political groups to share the sacrifices needed for growth and stability. To make such changes has often been impossible.

See also Elites, Political; Monarchy, Constitutional; Weber, Max.

LARRY DIAMOND AND
SEYMOUR MARTIN LIPSET

BIBLIOGRAPHY

Bendix, Reinhard. *Max Weber: An Intellectual Portrait.* Garden City, N.Y.: Doubleday, 1962.

Dahl, Robert A. *Polyarchy: Participation and Opposition.* New Haven and London: Yale University Press, 1971.

Dogan, Mattei. "The Pendulum between Theory and Substance: Testing the Concepts of Legitimacy and Trust." In *Comparing Nations: Concepts, Strategies, Substance*, edited by Mattei Dogan and Ali Kazancigil. Oxford: Blackwell, 1994.

Linz, Juan. *Breakdown of Democratic Regimes: Crisis, Breakdown, and Reequilibration.* Baltimore and Northampton: Johns Hopkins University Press, 1978.

_____. "Legitimacy of Democracy and the Socioeconomic System." In *Comparing Pluralist Democracies: Strains in Legitimacy*, edited by Mattei Dogan. Boulder, Colo.: Westview Press, 1988.

Lipset, Seymour Martin. *Political Man: The Social Bases of Politics.* Expanded and updated ed. Baltimore: Johns Hopkins University Press, 1981; Aldershot: Gower, 1983.

Powell, B. Bingham. *Contemporary Democracies.* Cambridge, Mass., and London: Harvard University Press, 1992.

Sternberger, Dolf. "Legitimacy." In *International Encyclopedia of the Social Sciences*, edited by David L. Sills. New York: Macmillan and Free Press, 1968.

Weber, Max. *From Max Weber: Essays in Sociology.* Translated by Hans H. Gerth and and C. Wright Mills. New York: Oxford University Press, 1946.

✦ Majority rule, minority rights

Majority rule and *minority rights* are terms that incorporate the essential tension in democracy between the need for collective decision making and respect for equality and individual choice. As an abstract idea, democracy requires that the governed decide matters of public importance. There is no higher authority than the citizenry. As a practical matter, political issues of importance are rarely resolved by unanimous decision. In virtually every instance, some people will win in the public deliberations and some will lose. The best justification for majority rule therefore is that it provides a legitimate and realistic way to make collective decisions while requiring the smallest number of citizens to accept the decisions of others as their own. Although it minimizes the number of citizens who must obey laws to which they did not consent, majority rule is nevertheless in tension with the democratic principle that individuals are most free when they are obligated by laws of their own making.

Majority Rule and Democracy

Majority rule is implicit in the concept of democracy, but it also logically follows from two other principles: equality and respect for the autonomy of individuals. Majority rule treats all individuals as equals. The decision of a numerical majority thus carries the most weight; in contrast, accepting the decision of the minority would mean a relative devaluation of the vote of each member of the majority. Because majority rule respects the individual choices made by the majority of the citizenry, it implies a utilitarian theory of justice. If people vote according to their own perceived best interest, majority rule will result in policies that are perceived to benefit the most people. Majority rule presumes that all individuals are capable of understanding their own interests and that no single group has a monopoly on truth or political wisdom. Majority rule therefore is not compatible with claims to possess and enforce the singular truth about human nature, the good life, or the just society.

Although majority rule is a pragmatic solution to the problem of who shall rule, it does not fully capture the essence of democracy. Constitutional democracies attempt to balance majority rule with the equally important principle of minority rights. Minority rights serve as a counterbalance to majority rule by preserving such liberal democratic principles as liberty, equality, and respect for individual choice.

If the principle of equality is to be upheld, for example, minorities cannot be excluded entirely from access to institutions of power. Such exclusions compromise the principle of equality, which is the ultimate justification for majority rule itself. If members of a minority cannot participate fully in democratic decision making, there is no rational reason for them to consider government legitimate. Similarly, when the state singles out a group for adverse treatment under its laws, that group has less to gain by upholding those laws. When such abuses target a single group, the state not only exceeds its legitimate power; it also violates the principle of equality.

Actions by the state that are overly broad and unjustified violate the liberal theory of limited government, which is itself based on a respect for individual choice and personal liberty. In constitutional democracies, the government may be prohibited from making decisions that are properly made by other social institutions, such as families or religious organizations, or that are matters of personal conscience. The state may be prohibited from taking certain actions if those actions deprive individuals or groups of something to which they have a protected right, such as prop-erty, or if an action is arbitrary and harms an individual or group without furthering the state's legitimate purposes.

Constitutionalism

The balance between rule by majorities and the rights of minorities is at the core of constitutionalism, which may be defined as the principle that governments should follow their own laws regarding the exercise of state authority. A nation's constitution (which is not limited to the idea of a written constitution) can refer both to the composition of its citizenry and to relationships among its political institutions. The idea that a constitution was the sum total of all relationships between the state and society, and among social classes, was particularly strong in ancient and medieval republics, in which the different social classes were given offices and institutions to represent their interests. Although such republican constitutions allowed for the representation of all interests, they were not democratic because they treated individuals of different classes unequally, providing them with different mechanisms by which to influence political decisions. Majoritarian institutions require first that all citizens are at least formally equal in their legal and political rights and in their ability to influence decisions on matters of public policy.

The antimajoritarian institutions of early republics originated in the wealthy minority's fear that the poor majority might expropriate their riches. The danger that the majority might be uncontrollable was particularly strong when there were great differences between rich and poor, slave and free. What Aristotle referred to as a "mixed" constitution was an established mechanism for balancing the interests of all recognized factions: all constituent classes were represented through their own institutions, and each class would check the ambitions and interests of the others. Many modern liberal democracies, especially constitutional monarchies such as Great Britain, evolved out of mixed constitutions through which the monarch shared power with both nobles and representatives of the Commons.

The liberal democracies of Australia, Canada, New Zealand, and the United States are distinctive because they have no history of feudal institutions. In these societies, class and status are more fluid and less easily identifiable with specific political and economic interests than in the European democracies. Majority rule in these states has been based on aggregations of individuals, without resort to the representation of different social estates based on a feudal past. These nations, however, have been troubled with the task of accommodating the rights of cultural and racial minorities. Indigenous peoples were not extended full rights until late in each nation's history. The United States has had the distinctive problem of extending full rights to African Americans, who were first enslaved and later discriminated against and systematically excluded from the nation's political and legal institutions.

Although liberal states have faced constitutional struggles in protecting racial and cultural minorities against discrimination by the majority, the protection of the propertied minority against the aspirations of the laboring majority evolved gradually, notwithstanding the expansion of the electoral franchise during the nineteenth and twentieth centuries. Rather than basing the protection of private property on the ability of the propertied to reject unfavorable legislation, liberal democracy has instead understood expropriation by the state to be unacceptable because it exceeded the legitimate power of the state. Guarantees of personal liberty and private property limited the state's ability to regulate private decisions and transactions between individuals.

The development of the welfare state in industrial democracies, beginning in the late nineteenth century, required some modification of this understanding. In the United States, where the judiciary had zealously protected property rights from governmental regulation, special constitutional protections for the wealthy left a legacy of suspicion of minority rights and a belief that unelected institutions such as the Supreme Court should not obstruct implementation of the will of the majority in economic matters. When the Supreme Court rejected special constitutional protections for wealth, however, it articulated a new role of protecting the fundamental personal rights of very different kinds of minorities—those without power or privilege.

Defining Majorities and Minorities

The rights of minorities are not reducible solely to individual rights. Minorities are not merely smaller aggregates of individuals than majorities. Both majorities and minorities may be groups composed of individuals with similar interests, attributes, or beliefs. Often, however, they are not. Majorities may be unstable, composed of shifting combinations of minorities who bargain and cooperate to further their own particular interests. James Madison believed that such a system of competing and countervailing "factions" would, along with proper constitutional constraints, prevent majority tyranny by making such majorities rare and fragmented. Members of the current majority may be induced to behave more conscientiously, knowing that they might in the future be in the minority themselves.

The seriousness of the threat that majority rule may result in tyranny or intolerance thus depends on whether there is a stable and well-organized majority. In many countries, political parties represent well-defined social, economic, or cultural interests on a variety of issues.

Although popular support may shift between parties, even in strong party systems, political parties contribute to the identification of minority and majority political agendas. The danger of a strong party system is that the majority can more easily transform its own agenda into policies unacceptable to the minority. In countries that lack strong party systems, and where politics is characterized by the particular concerns of interest groups (as factions have become known), it is more difficult to form and preserve majorities to implement new governmental policy. Minorities in a fragmented political system may benefit from their ability to negotiate and trade votes on particular issues, building temporary majority coalitions to pass or block those policies about which they feel strongly. In a fragmented system, however, it may be especially difficult to build majorities that are sensitive to minority rights.

Minorities thus may play an important part in forming and preserving majorities. The protection of minority rights is not justified merely by the existence of a minority; to extend such protection would completely undermine the principle of majority rule by automatically conceding a veto power to those who lose in the political process. Minority rights, however, can be extended to groups who lose regularly because of social or political practices that violate the equality principle. In the United States, the Supreme Court, as a nonmajoritarian institution, has been particularly instrumental since the New Deal of the 1930s in protecting the rights of minorities against abuses by the majority. The Canadian Charter of Rights and Freedoms (1982) has also provided the Canadian judicial system with the authority to enforce the rights of cultural minorities in that country. Many civil law countries have separate constitutional courts that may hear challenges to discriminatory treatment.

A matter of constant dispute is whether the legislature or the judiciary should assume primary responsibility for protecting minority rights. Although some nations may protect cultural or racial minorities through special legislation, judicial protection of minorities may also be required to sustain democratic ideals of equality. Where such protections are not specifically provided for through the legislative process, the difficult task of defining which groups qualify as protected minorities may fall to the judiciary. The requirement that a protected minority be easily identifiable and bounded prevents confusion between those groups that have merely lost in the political process and those that have been unfairly denied the opportunity to participate in it. Because not all minorities can be protected equally (except in theory), there is often intense competition for protected status. Although conditions change, and some minorities do achieve vindication of their constitutional rights, few are willing to give up the advantages of identification as an oppressed minority.

In the United States groups that desire protected status must demonstrate that the state or private organizations have previously enforced policies that disproportionately burdened members of that group for no legitimate reason. Thus groups that desire enhanced protection of their voting rights must demonstrate that states employed seemingly legitimate tests or qualifications with the effect of depriving their members of the right to vote, and those seeking affirmative action requirements in employment or education must demonstrate that the organizations they have targeted have previously imposed requirements that benefited members of the majority group at their expense.

There is also considerable debate about whether, and when, rights attach to members of minority groups because of that membership and when rights are extended only to individuals who may, or may not, be minority group members. The basic theory of American constitutional law is that rights are individual even though deprivation of rights may be attributed to group membership; thus rights cannot be reserved for minority group members. Whites as well as blacks, for example, may invoke the protection of civil rights laws. In limited instances such as affirmative action in employment, school admissions, and electoral representation, however, special remedial rights and protections may be afforded to individuals solely because of their race, ethnicity, or gender.

Minority Representation

Because most political decisions in a democracy are made directly or indirectly through representative institutions, the rules governing how citizens will be represented have an important effect on the balance between majority and minority interests. The liberal tradition of representative democracy has grouped individuals by geographic area or political subunit and has been unsympathetic to claims to representation on the basis of cultural or racial affiliation. Democratic representation includes decisions about how social or political minorities may be made more or less efficacious. In particular, governments may act to protect a group's right to political participation when that right has been arbitrarily abridged. In the United States, for example, special protections have been devised for minorities who have been stable over time, whose members act or vote in concert, whose rights have been perpetually denied, and whose political efforts to achieve redress have been consistently frustrated by an identifiable majority that also acts or votes cohesively.

Different systems of representation may increase or decrease the prospects for majority rule or may even exclude minorities from political power. Single-member electoral districts, which are prevalent in the United States, perpetuate majority rule; candidates must focus on gaining at least a plurality of votes to win. Where minorities are residentially segregated and comprise a substantial portion of the population, at-large elections for multimember districts may dilute their voting strength and favor majority candidates. Proportional representation allows for greater minority representation by including legislative seats for groups that can muster a significant level of support, even if they are not a plurality. However, when a limited number of seats are distributed among many competing and qualifying groups within a proportional system, as in Israel, minorities may be overrepresented. The structural representation of small minorities may reduce the incentives for stable majority rule, although it may also promote the formation of semipermanent coalitions.

Conflict over representation centers on two issues: the apportionment of legislative seats and equal treatment in the political process. Conflict arises when the apportionment of legislative representatives does not reflect the principles of majority rule. Legislative districts may be based on geography, types of economic development, or political subunit, thus providing smaller populations with the same amount of representation as larger ones. Or legislative districts initially drawn on the basis of equal representation may not be revised periodically to reflect changes in population, resulting in severe malapportionment.

In the United States the Supreme Court has chosen to reaffirm the principle of majority rule based primarily on population ("one person, one vote"). The Court held in 1964 that the equal protection clause of the Fourteenth Amendment required that all voters have an equal voice in the election of state legislatures and other elected

5

government bodies. A similar principle was applied to elections for the U.S. House of Representatives.

In the United States, where representation is based primarily on population, designing systems of representation that protect the interests of disadvantaged minorities is particularly problematic. Until the 1990s the Supreme Court interpreted the Voting Rights Act of 1965 to mean that states shown to have discriminated against African Americans in the past should devise electoral districts in such a way as to maximize the number of majority African American districts so long as the geographic boundaries of those districts were not drawn solely on the basis of the districts' racial characteristics. In the 1990s the Court began to challenge the validity of this view, ruling that race may be more important than many other criteria, but it is not exclusive of other interests in representation. The claims of other underenfranchised minorities have not been considered to the same extent, although in theory the principle of affirmative action should also apply to large concentrations of other minorities.

Another strategy, useful in systems that use multimember districts, is to provide voters with several votes that they can allocate as they choose among several candidates. Instead of casting one vote per vacant seat, minority voters can choose to use all their votes to support one or two candidates ("bullet voting"). Of course, majority voters would not use this strategy since their goal is to maximize the number of seats their preferred candidates would receive. Such a form of representation might better reflect actual public opinion, and it would account for intensity of interest in a way that single-member-district voting cannot. Because most electoral systems in the United States involve single-member districts, however, balancing the interests of majority and minority groups in representation must be accomplished

through manipulation of the districts' geographic boundaries. Apart from the Voting Rights Act requirements, the Supreme Court has approved a modest amount of "political" gerrymandering while maintaining, somewhat inconsistently, that racial gerrymandering is unconstitutional except as required under the act.

Voting rights law also responds to the second problem in political participation by minorities: unequal treatment. Exclusion from political participation is an especially damaging form of infringement of rights. Denying minorities a fair opportunity to change the policies that disadvantage them invites destabilizing protest strategies. Majority groups, although they are favored by majority rule, may nonetheless attempt to deny minorities access to political power. Their fear is that minorities will become a political force by allying themselves with factions of the majority or by cooperating with other minority groups to form a new majority or displace a powerful plurality. More commonly, however, the denial or obstruction of political participation is based on racial animosity, cultural disagreements, or other conflicts external to the structure of the political process.

Special majorities are needed for certain types of decisions, such as amending constitutions. Constitutional change requires extraordinary majority support to ensure legitimacy. Neither mere bargaining nor a slight preference on the part of the majority is adequate for fundamental structural change. Requirements for ratification of amendments by a substantial majority of regional or administrative subunits (such as ratification of an amendment to the U.S. Constitution by three-quarters of the states) help to keep regional coalitions from forcing an unpalatable decision on other regions. Similarly, in many U.S. states, changes in state constitutions require two legislative votes separated in time by an intervening election. Such requirements ensure that the majority that authorized the change is stable and cohesive and give the electorate a chance to express an opinion.

Minority Rights in Civil Society

Many minority rights are protections against unequal treatment or abuse by political majorities; others are both created and curtailed by the liberal concept of the limited state. The liberal distinction between the state and civil society requires that the state not interfere with the internal decisions of the institutions of civil society unless they adversely affect the larger society. At the same time, those institutions—economic, social, and cultural—may be actively hostile toward or intolerant of minority groups, so that the state must intervene to preserve the democratic principles of equality of access and, sometimes, equality of outcome.

Majority rule is not unrelated to rule by popular opinion. Nineteenth-century liberal theorists such as John Stuart Mill and Alexis de Tocqueville wrote of the dangers of tyranny arising through popular opinion in a democratic society. They argued that the need for vigilance against social pressure becomes greater as people become more equal and less likely to tolerate differences. Minority rights are often asserted in an atmosphere of hostility and social pressure. Therefore, to obtain their rights, minorities may need to call on governmental institutions to enforce constitutional norms. Government protection may thus provide symbols of minorities' right to assert their rights. Government action on behalf of minority rights is evidence that majorities accept this general principle.

The awareness of being a marginalized or excluded group pervades the assertion of rights by minority communities, particularly cultural minorities who feel pressured by what they view

as the assimilationist institutions of the majority. Such minorities may demand special cultural or social exemptions in order to protect their identity or heritage. Cultural minorities may seek to protect and preserve their language, for example. French-speaking Canadians' claim of cultural autonomy in Quebec underlies much of their conflict with English-speaking Canadians over the language used in public education, in broadcasting, and even on the signs used by private stores. French Canadians claim that their identity as a distinct group is threatened by the dominance of the language and culture of English-speaking Canada. They therefore demand—and have largely received—the special right to promote their own heritage and to prohibit the majority culture from intruding into those social practices that they view as integral to the maintenance of their identity. In the United States, similarly, assertions about the need for bilingual education have been made by Hispanic groups; and some African Americans have called for tolerance of, if not education in, "black English." The former has been incorporated into the Voting Rights Act; the latter remains very much in dispute.

As in many of the countries where there are strong cultural differences, the Canadian compromise on language has focused on federalism. Establishing provinces and autonomous zones has allowed many countries, such as India and Russia, to incorporate majority rule on matters of economics or foreign policy while accommodating indigenous minorities' desire to control their own internal affairs. Such solutions are always controversial. The strict laws that have been passed in Quebec, for instance, have led many English-speaking residents to claim that *they* have been discriminated against as a minority. More dramatically, the disintegration of the Soviet Union and the dismemberment of Yugoslavia have instilled the fear among many ethnic groups that the creation of a smaller state might leave them as a minority under the domination of another, possibly hostile, ethnic group. The violent conflict among Serbs, Croats, and Muslims in the former Yugoslavia attests to the difficulty of holding together such a volatile mixture. The Commonwealth of Independent States faces a similarly difficult challenge in establishing working relationships among the states that once constituted the Soviet Union.

Finding the Balance

The ultimate justification for minority rights is that majorities are not always right, fair, or just. Indeed, majorities are not always majorities. Representative institutions do not always directly reflect public opinion. Perhaps necessarily, representation in two-party states compels citizens to condense their positions on many different issues into a single vote or to vote on one or another side of an issue about which they are ambivalent, have only a slight preference, or would prefer a third alternative. Thus a common condition in democracies is "minorities rule" in the name of the majority.

A powerful justification for majority rule, whatever its imperfections, lies in the need for governmental legitimacy and public respect for the government and the law. The greater the agreement with a law, the more likely it is to be obeyed. When a law is systematically ignored or flouted, its legitimacy is threatened. Requiring majority approval of a law or other governmental policy ensures that governments retain their legitimacy by promulgating only policies that people will comply with and that will need minimal coercive enforcement. Such a consent theory of majority rule may more accurately reflect reality than theories that merely assume that majority rule reflects the will of the people. Minorities may be able to secure the passage of legislation that favors them if there is minimal opposition by the majority, and majorities may be indifferent at times to the measures passed in their name. Majorities, however, must be wary of measures that will be strongly opposed by others.

Securing a balance between majority rule and minority rights is critically important, therefore, because it provides both majorities and minorities with a stake in the democratic process. Although the principle of majority rule means that the majority generally will be victorious in political disputes, the principle of minority rights means that those victories will have limits. Minorities may be defeated at times, even often, but they must always have a chance to participate and some confidence that their very existence and identity are secure.

A democratic state may accomplish these tasks through constitutional mechanisms that feature countermajoritarian institutions, such as courts, or forms of representation that serve both majority and minority interests. Nations may legislate special treatment for certain minority groups while reserving other rights for the majority. But for all of these different institutions and procedures, the goal remains to tolerate the choices of the few while expressing the will of the many.

See also Aristotle; Consent; Constitutionalism; Democracy, Justifications for; Democracy, Multiethnic; Federalism; Interest groups; Madison, James; Popular sovereignty; Representation.

Joel B. Grossman and
Daniel M. Levin

BIBLIOGRAPHY

Chapman, John W., and Alan Wertheimer, eds. *Majorities and Minorities.* New York: New York University Press, 1990.

Commager, Henry Steele. *Majority Rule and Minority Rights*. New York: Oxford University Press, 1943.

Dahl, Robert A. *A Preface to Democratic Theory*. Chicago: University of Chicago Press, 1956.

Mayo, Henry B. *An Introduction to Democratic Theory*. New York: Oxford University Press, 1960.

Mill, John Stuart. *Utilitarianism, On Liberty, and Representative Government*. New York: Dutton, 1912.

Spitz, Elaine. *Majority Rule*. Chatham, N.J.: Chatham House, 1984.

✦ Monarchy, Constitutional

Constitutional monarchy is government under a constitutional monarch, a hereditary head of state with ceremonial responsibility and sometimes with a few political functions limited by law. Until the twentieth century the great majority of modern states were monarchies but not democracies. By the early 1990s the majority of modern states were democracies and republics headed by a ceremonial president politically subordinate to the prime minister and the parliament.

Origins of Constitutional Monarchy

The idea of kingship is as old as recorded history; its origins are lost in myths. Early kings were often heroic leaders in battle, inspiring confidence as well as fear in their subjects. They could claim office by popular acclaim, by choice of elders, or by force. The role of heredity in determining who was to be king came much later. This practice was adopted to end disputes and intrigues about leadership. In many countries only a male could inherit the monarchy, and the throne would pass to a more distant relative if a king had only daughters or was childless. In England, however, a woman could inherit the throne, and several did: Elizabeth I (ruled 1558–1603), Victoria (reigned 1837–1901), and Elizabeth II.

The development of constitutional monarchy followed from the creation of the modern state—that is, a central authority governing a well-defined territory by the rule of law. The feudal systems of the Middle Ages did not meet this standard because much power was in the hands of barons and other territorial lords. The first modern states centralized authority in an absolute monarchy. France under Louis XIV (ruled 1643–1715) is an early example of an absolute monarchy. Frederick the Great of Prussia (ruled 1740–1786) developed the central institutions of an absolute monarchy. Absolute monarchies were intended to maintain order and build up the military strength and wealth of the state. They were also designed to defend the state against the "excesses" of democracy, which since the time of Athens in the fifth century B.C. had been regarded as equivalent to mob rule.

By the nineteenth century the idea of constitutional monarchy was so taken for granted in Europe that when a new country was established it would import a king if it did not have a ruling family at hand. For example, when Italy achieved unification in 1861, the house of Savoy provided the royal family. Norway adopted a Danish prince as its first king on becoming fully independent in 1905. The Greeks declared independence from rule by the Ottoman Turks in 1821, and independence was guaranteed by their allies. In 1833 a new "Greek" king was imported from Bavaria; he was succeeded in 1862 by a Danish prince.

At the outbreak of World War I in 1914 the great majority of European states were monarchies; only France, Portugal, and Switzerland were republics. Furthermore, leading monarchies were usually not nation-states but multinational empires created by intermarriage and inheritance among royal families and sometimes by conquest. For example, England and Scotland were joined in 1603, when Elizabeth I of England died unmarried and childless and the nearest relative to inherit the crown was the king of Scotland. He reigned as James VI in Scotland and as James I in England until his death in 1625. The two kingdoms, however, were governed as separate countries until 1707, when an act of union created a single Parliament of Great Britain in London. The Austro-Hungarian Empire consisted of territories of the Hapsburgs, a royal family based in Vienna. The subjects of this empire had no common language or shared national identity; the only thing they had in common was their status as subjects of the same monarch.

Response to the Challenge of Democracy

Because constitutional monarchy originated in absolutism, nineteenth-century democrats usually regarded royalty as enemies. They also regarded as enemies the aristocrats, court servants, and state officials who advised or depended upon royalty. The French Revolution of 1789 took as its motto "liberty, equality, and fraternity." Its leaders deposed Louis XVI and proclaimed a republic. In 1793 the king was executed. Monarchs willing to grant popular demands, however, could do much to facilitate the introduction of democracy. They could endorse change and influence potential opponents, such as aristocrats, the church, and civil servants, to do the same. In practice, monarchies were altered in three very different ways: through evolution, revolution, and the dissolution of empire.

Seven European states preserved their monarchies through an evolutionary process in which royalty withdrew from politics: the United Kingdom, Sweden, Norway, Denmark, Belgium, the Netherlands, and Luxembourg. The withdrawal typically occurred as the result of pressures from aristocrats and notables to place restraints on an absolute monarch.

This was the case in seventeenth-century England when Parliament, then elected by only a small percentage of English males, successfully revolted against the Crown and beheaded Charles I. A king was restored later but with weaker powers than before. By the end of the eighteenth century Parliament had established its domination of the king, who now had to act on the advice of ministers. Parliament could vote confidence (or lack of confidence) in the ministers and also had the power to refuse the annual appropriation of money to run the government if the monarch refused to act as it advised. The movement for democracy in Great Britain that took place in the nineteenth century was thus a struggle between representatives of people seeking the right to vote and protectors of a Parliament elected by a small minority of the population. It was not a struggle between the monarch and the people, and Queen Victoria thus avoided being caught up in the politics of democratization.

As the example of Great Britain shows, a monarch who was not an absolute ruler was better able to negotiate a withdrawal from politics. In the nineteenth century such monarchs shared power with the nobility, landed interests, the church, and related groups in predemocratic parliaments. They also shared power with expert advisers and civil servants who had technical knowledge and interests that they lacked. The claims of democrats often involved a loss of power by notables, while the monarch could choose to remain above the conflict.

Sweden also preserved its monarchy through an evolutionary process. Here the process involved claims to power from popular representatives and also from estates of the realm whose authority rested on preindustrial and predemocratic practices. The Swedish king did not resist change and did not allow opponents of change to use the monarchy as a symbol of resistance. Instead, he endorsed compromises negotiated between conservative and democratic leaders; these agreements effectively turned the monarch into a symbolic head of state.

Japan is a distinctive case. The Japanese emperor maintained his position without interruption during an abrupt shift from a military dictatorship to democracy following Japan's defeat in World War II. Emperor Hirohito ascended the throne in 1926 as a monarch with very limited influence on government, although the office had great symbolic value. The country's involvement in war was the responsibility of a military government. Therefore, the emperor was allowed to remain as a symbol of national unity. Allied occupation forces ensured, however, that the 1947 Japanese constitution was democratic in form and that free and competitive elections then institutionalized democracy in practice.

Another distinctive case is that of Thailand. The institution of a traditional and absolute monarchy played a critical role in keeping Thailand free from Western colonial domination. It was the only country in South Asia and Southeast Asia that remained independent. In 1937, however, a military coup, inspired in part by students who had returned from Great Britain, forced the king to become a constitutional monarch. Since then the Thai kings have played a positive role in liberalizing Thai politics and in encouraging democratic tendencies.

In Europe the abrupt removal of the monarchy by revolution or military defeat did not guarantee the introduction of democracy. Most East European states created in the aftermath of World War I were republics. Of these, only Czechoslovakia remained a democracy until it was occupied by the armies of Adolf Hitler in 1939. The process of creating republics in Eastern Europe was completed by Soviet occupation at the end of World War II. The Soviets turned undemocratic monarchies, such as Bulgaria, Romania, and Yugoslavia, into republics. In most postcommunist societies of the early 1990s there was no royal family that could claim to inherit the throne and no significant popular demand for the creation of a monarchy.

An individual monarch can momentarily gain influence through involvement in politics, but political involvement creates opponents as well as allies. By taking sides in a major political conflict, a reigning monarch puts the future of monarchy at risk. When political fortunes change, an individual monarch may be forced to abdicate by the new government, or the monarchy itself may be abolished. Leopold III of Belgium chose to remain in the country when it was conquered by Hitler's army in 1940. His decision had important political consequences. In 1950 a referendum on the king resulted in 58 percent in favor of his remaining on the throne and 42 percent against. The country was so divided in its views of the king's wartime behavior that he was forced to abdicate in favor of his son, Baudouin. In Italy, Victor Emmanuel III was head of state for two decades of the fascist regime of Benito Mussolini. In 1946 a referendum in Italy voted to abolish the monarchy and create a democratic republic. Of the last six Greek sovereigns, one was assassinated and three were exiled because of their involvement in national politics. Greece became a republic in 1974.

The example of France demonstrates that republican revolutions can fail, leading to the return of a dictator or monarch. After the revolution of 1789 the country was ruled successively by a first consul (Napoleon Bonaparte), an emperor (Napoleon, crowned in 1804), a king, a republican head of state, and another Napoleon as president and emperor (Napoleon III). France has been a republic since 1871.

Spain is unique among contemporary European states in promoting democracy through the restoration of a monarchy in 1975. The circumstances were exceptional. The Spanish civil war of 1936 was begun by a military revolt under General Francisco Franco against the government of a republic. Franco's side won, and he became chief of state in a regime that was nominally a monarchy but lacked a king. The grandson of the last Spanish king was groomed to become a symbolic head of state and did so after Franco's death in 1975. This step was meant to calm conservative antidemocrats, who feared that democracy would lead to communism. Former republicans accepted the monarchy as a bulwark against the return of civil war. When colonels attempted a military coup in the name of the king in 1981, their efforts collapsed after being publicly repudiated by King Juan Carlos.

The breakup of empires in the wake of World War I brought an end to many monarchies. The empire of the Russian czar was replaced by a republican state, the Union of Soviet Socialist Republics. The Communist Party controlled the state, using the doctrines of Marxism-Leninism as the unifying force. The Austro-Hungarian Empire was replaced by a series of nation-states that were mostly republican in form. At the moment of military defeat in 1918 the German kaiser resigned the throne, and Germany became a republic based on a constitution prepared at Weimar. The Ottoman Empire was ruled by a sultan. The Young Turks, who sought to create an independent and modern Turkish nation-state, succeeded in abolishing the sultanate in 1922.

The breakup of empires outside Europe commenced in the Western Hemisphere with the revolt of colonies against the British, Spanish, and Portuguese crowns. Article I of the U.S. Constitution contains an explicit prohibition against the grant of titles of nobility. In the nineteenth century a few Latin American countries briefly had kings imported from or imposed by Europe, but they were soon deposed. Latin American countries have consistently been republics, whether democratic or nondemocratic.

The British Empire continued until after World War II, with the British monarch as its nominal head. The colonies were governed under constitutions subject to the rule of law as determined by the British Parliament. Successive kings and queens of England were also emperors of India and heads of state in old dominions, such as Australia and Canada. Anticolonial movements after 1945 demanded and received independence, with the result that the former British Empire became a commonwealth—a free association of independent states, many of them republics. The titular head of the commonwealth is Elizabeth II of England, but she holds this symbolic post by decision of the commonwealth and not by heredity.

A comparative analysis of the role of monarchies by Richard Rose and Dennis Kavanagh supports two major conclusions. First, the survival of a monarchy depends upon the readiness of the reigning family to withdraw from a politically active role. Second, the repudiation of a monarchy results from the involvement of the monarchy in politics.

Monarchy in Contemporary Democracy

In democratic political systems with a hereditary monarch, the primary role of the head of state is nonpolitical. Formally, a monarch may be asked to choose the head of government, and in Britain the government is technically referred to as Her Majesty's government. Elected politicians, however, have taken pains to specify procedures that reduce the discretion of the head of state, whether a monarch or a figurehead president. These procedures also maximize the room for the maneuvering of party leaders after a general election. In

Britain, one party normally wins a majority of seats in the House of Commons and thus gains the right to form a government. In many European countries no party wins a majority of seats, and a coalition is necessary. In the Netherlands the monarch appoints an elder politician to identify which politician is to be given the first opportunity to form a coalition government. In republican Greece the law prescribes an automatic procedure in which the leader of the party with the largest number of seats in the parliament is the first choice to form a coalition.

By virtue of many years in office, a monarch can claim to be experienced in the ways of government. Elizabeth II has been in office far longer than any of the cabinet ministers now governing Great Britain, and she has seen the occupant of the prime minister's office change nine times since her coronation. The queen is kept informed of major public business, especially foreign affairs, and normally meets with the prime minister once a week to discuss affairs of state. This is an opportunity for the prime minister to think aloud in the presence of a person who is not a competitor for that office. A monarch may focus attention on a problem through comments or questions. In Great Britain any attempt by a queen or king to give unwanted counsel can be rejected by a popularly elected prime minister, and any public hint of royal influence would risk the political neutrality of the monarchy.

The primary function of a monarchy in a democracy is symbolic: the monarch represents the unity of the country. This is an easy task in Scandinavian countries, where societies are extremely homogeneous. In Northern Ireland, however, there is a longstanding conflict about whether the country should be united with Great Britain or with the Republic of Ireland. In Northern Ireland the British crown represents one party to a conflict between nationalists, just as the Irish flag represents another party. The existence of a president of the Republic of Ireland symbolizes that country's rejection of everything British, including its monarch.

Members of a royal family have celebrity status. In earlier times they were treated respectfully, even reverently, by the press, whatever their behavior in private life. That situation changed with the advent of television. The increase in celebrity can make some members more popular, but it also creates far more embarrassment when members of a royal family lose their temper, become involved in extramarital affairs, or associate with people of dubious habits or morals.

Traditional royal pomp, financed by public funds, is under challenge in an era in which very few people inherit a job or enough wealth to live on all their lives. This is the case especially when the royal income is deemed to come from public funds. Scandinavian monarchs responded to the rise in egalitarianism by abandoning many of the ancient symbols of authority and wealth. They have frequently been described as "bicycling" monarchs, because they do not go everywhere in a limousine. By contrast, the British queen retains a lifestyle from an earlier, aristocratic era, which has attracted criticism from members of Parliament and the media.

As long as the monarch remains above party politics, his or her position is normally unchallenged. Still, the decision whether to make the monarchy controversial rests with the parties. A republican pressure group can stir up controversy about the monarchy. This has occurred in Australia, where Labor leaders decry having an English queen as their nominal head of state.

Any effort to abolish a monarchy faces problems, for every country requires a head of state. France and the United States are unique among democracies in having a head of state who is also the effective head of government. Everywhere else the role of the head of state is symbolic, whether it is filled by a hereditary monarch or by an elder politician holding the ceremonial office of president. The fact that a monarch holds office by virtue of birth may be inconsistent with democratic norms, but it offers one consolation to the country's prime minister: the head of state is in no position to challenge decisions taken by a national leader who can claim the legitimacy of popular election.

See also Leadership.

RICHARD ROSE

BIBLIOGRAPHY

Bogdanor, Vernon, ed. *Coalition Government in Western Europe.* London: Heinemann, 1983.

_____. *Constitutions in Democratic Politics.* Aldershot: Gower, 1988.

da Graca, John V. *Heads of State and Government.* London: Macmillan, 1985.

Lipset, Seymour Martin. *Political Man: The Social Bases of Politics.* Expanded and updated ed. Baltimore: Johns Hopkins University Press, 1981; Aldershot: Gower, 1983.

Rose, Richard, and Dennis Kavanagh. "The Monarchy in Contemporary Political Culture." *Comparative Politics* 8 (1976): 548–576.

✦ Obligation

The sense of moral responsibility that enjoins individuals to give others their due. In discussing the nature and problems of obligation, we shall seek to clarify such questions as, What are obligations and why do people fulfill them? Why do people shirk them? What is the connection between personal and political obligations? Why do individuals subordinate and even sacrifice themselves to the common good by obeying the laws and injunctions of political society? And how does American liberal democracy resolve the problems of political obligation?

Human beings in all societies generally admit that they have obligations and tend to act accordingly. Growing from our affections and associations, our sense of obligation helps bind us to our families, friends, communities, and countries even when we would rather not be bound. Parents accept the burdens of rearing their children; friends stand by friends and patriots stand by their country even in the face of danger. Obligation thus implies that individuals know what should be done and requires that they voluntarily subordinate their own immediate desire or good to that end. Responsible persons fulfill obligations.

Obligation rests upon justice. In saying that people should fulfill their obligations, we imply that doing so is just and that justice, being a greater end than personal satisfaction, requires and justifies sacrifice. Obligations entail justice in two reinforcing senses: First, they enjoin particular just acts, such as doing good to family and friends, and, second, they assume that the act of fulfilling obligations, such as keeping promises, in itself is just. Obligations help to order and unite our associations into a political society that aims at justice. The vitality of our sense of obligation demonstrates the authority of justice over human affairs.

The problems of obligation are inherent in its nature. People in all societies shirk their obligations. This avoidance stems from the voluntary nature of obligations. We should do our duty, but we can choose not to. Injustice in this sense is done knowingly. We shirk our obligations when some apparent good outweighs them. Parents might choose independence rather than support their children; soldiers might save themselves at the expense of their friends and country. Because those who make such choices must justify their actions, if only to themselves, they see some justice in choosing the apparent good. Obligation thus entails tensions in our sense of what is good and just that manifest themselves in the ongoing struggle between our own apparent good and the call of the common good. We can summarize the nature and problem of obligation as follows: Most people act justly because they are constrained by their obligations, and they can be so constrained because they respect justice. Constraint is required, however, because most people can and sometimes will choose injustice. The order imposed by obligations is fragile.

Political societies everywhere subordinate and sacrifice their members to the common good as expressed by laws and injunctions. Why do governments have such power and authority? Why, as the call to arms and its attendant loss of blood and treasure demonstrate, do individuals customarily obey? Ordinary associations most often depend upon political power and laws for definition, promotion, and preservation. This dependence bonds our own good and personal obligations to the common political good in a way that gives political obligations force. For example, if our family structure is generated and enforced by laws, the common good of parents and children is bound to the laws of our country. Our families and ourselves are political beings with the particular status of being members of one nation. We are Athenian or Japanese. Political society traditionally is seen as an organic whole that precedes and produces its members, and its laws and injunctions authoritatively preside over all internal affairs: law is justice, religion guards law, freedom is noble and worth dying for, and freedom entails allegiance to the nation's laws. Absorbing individuals into a corporate polity, which they feel obliged to defend as their own, greatly eases and arrests tensions between individual interests and the common good.

This traditional account of political obligation raises questions. All societies may require and often secure their members' obedience, but are all societies equally just? During World War II the soldiers of Nazi Germany and those of liberal democratic America may have done their duty, but were these opposing regimes both worthy of obedience? Can we be content to answer that the psychology and phenomenon of obligation is universal, but justice is relative to the laws of particular historical regimes? If not, by what standard can all regimes be judged?

Liberal democracy as expressed by the Declaration of Independence and the U.S. Constitution stands upon its claim to justice. The laws of nature evince the self-evident truth that all human beings have equal and inalienable rights to life, liberty, and the pursuit of happiness. Individuals consent to form a people and institute government to secure those ends. Government is obliged to serve the people's safety and happiness, and the people's consent obliges them to obey its laws as their own. But the people reserve the right to alter and abolish their government and to decide upon what principles their new government will stand. When government oppresses, it is the people's right, indeed their duty, forcefully to resist. Liberal democracy eases the tensions between individual interests and the public good by liberating the individual and by showing that liberty itself obliges dedication to the public good.

Liberal principles and political practices constitute a radical departure from traditional experiences and conceptions of political obligations. To understand liberal principles, one must turn to the writings of Thomas Hobbes and John Locke. The relation between liberal principles and democratic government is clarified in the writings and acts of the American Founders, who saw the American Republic as the first to be founded on the basis of liberal principles.

Liberal democracy may justify political obligation but not without presenting problems. Can the aggregate of private rights amount to a compelling common good? Because democracy entails majority rule, are opposed minorities obliged to obey? If government serves private ends, is anyone really obliged to obey? Liberal democrats are justly devoted to their regime, but they must always confront the paradox of being obligated to sacrifice for their own good.

See also Consent; Hobbes, Thomas; Locke, John; Majority rule, minority rights.

MICHAEL ROSANO

BIBLIOGRAPHY

The Federalist Papers. Edited by Clinton Rossiter. New York: New American Library, 1961.

Hobbes, Thomas. *Leviathan.* Edited by C. B. Macpherson. New York: Viking Penguin, 1982.

Locke, John. *Two Treatises of Government.* Edited by Peter Laslett. Cambridge: Cambridge University Press, 1967.

Pangle, Thomas L. *The Ennobling of Democracy.* Baltimore: Johns Hopkins University Press, 1991.

Plato. *The Apology of Socrates* and *Crito.* In *Four Texts on Socrates.* Translated with notes by Thomas G. West and Grace Starry West. Ithaca, N.Y.: Cornell University Press, 1984.

Rawls, John. *A Theory of Justice.* Cambridge: Harvard University Press, Belknap Press, 1971; Oxford: Oxford University Press, 1973.

✦ Popular sovereignty

The principle that government must be authorized by the people. The concept of popular sovereignty is fundamental to any conception of democratic government and to the history of American democracy in particular. The formula of the American Declaration of Independence (1776)—that governments derive power from the consent of the governed and that the people can alter or abolish their government for cause—heralded the coming of democracy in the American colonies and eventually throughout the contemporary world. For example, in the 1850s popular sovereignty was the central issue in the debates between Stephen A. Douglas and Abraham Lincoln over the extension of slavery to new states of the union. More recently appeals to popular sovereignty played a major role in populist movements in the German Democratic Republic in 1989, when demonstrators—chanting "we are the people"—challenged their communist government.

Although popular sovereignty clearly assigns the ultimate authority to the people, the concept is inconclusive as to exactly how this government by the people is to be realized. Douglas argued, for example, that it should be left to the people of a territory on the verge of statehood to decide whether they wanted their state to be slaveholding or free. Lincoln, however, declared that spreading slavery to new territories was a matter of concern to the whole nation. Aside from their obvious differences on the moral issues of introducing slavery to Nebraska, Douglas wanted to leave the decision to the consent of Nebraska voters, while Lincoln preferred that the issue be decided by the consent of all Americans of the Union, presumably through their representatives in the Congress.

Questions Raised by Popular Sovereignty

Just as popular sovereignty does not specify whether to seek the consent of local or regional people, or of the nation, or even of the whole world, it is vague or silent on all the other instrumentalities of modern popular government. It does not even answer the question clearly whether the people should determine only the basic form and mission of government—for example by ratifying a written constitution—or whether their consent is also required for the government's policies or the appointments of its leaders. Some early advocates of popular sovereignty, for example, the twelfth-century English cleric and scholar John of Salisbury, believed that the power of a medieval monarch was conferred fundamentally by the people and that kings were somehow kept in line by the people and the clergy. But these advocates shied away from granting the people the right to rebel against a tyrannical king or queen, to dismiss high government officials, or to change the old monarchic order itself.

The principle of popular sovereignty also leaves open to conflicting interpretations the question of whether an elected president or a British-style parliamentary government is more likely to ensure government by consent. The American-style system separates the powers between an elected president and an elected congress. Many knowledgeable observers view these competing popular mandates as an invitation to irresponsibility or gridlock. Parliamentary government, on the other hand, clearly removes the selection of executive officers and governmental policies a notable degree from the direct influence of the people and leaves it to the elected legislators. The choice between the two also raises questions about the usefulness to popular government of strong parties and a bipolar party system (preferable to a multi-party system) that may empower the voters by presenting distinctive alternatives in leaders and policies rather than the almost indistinguishable choices of the U.S. party system.

Popular control in the era of complex modern industrial societies obviously requires heavy reliance on intermediary organizations such as political parties, interest groups, and the media. However, none of these have yet been subdued reliably, if at all, to serving the popular will and not just their own purposes. Although there is almost universal agreement that the popular will must be delegated to representatives rather than exercised directly, the principle of popular sovereignty is mute as to exactly how these representatives are to be chosen, by what type of electoral law, for what offices, and for how long. Most significantly, the popular principle by itself does not resolve the question of how far even popularly legitimated rule should be permitted to intervene into the rights and interests of individuals.

Evolution of Popular Government

The idea of popular government has evolved through a long historical process of secularization and differentiation. For the peoples of European antiquity and even the Middle Ages, functions of politics and government were rarely as clearly discernible and separate from social and spiritual life as they have become in the past two centuries. Consequently, even though one can find many quotations of thinkers and writers relating to the people as an important source of legitimate authority, these statements were either largely descriptive of a rather undifferentiated and unreflected social reality enshrouded in tradition and religious beliefs, or they were detached from any practical consideration of how one might enable the people to rule.

Greek historians and medieval writers often described settings of apparent power sharing in which hereditary elites, and sometimes religious establishments, habitually deferred to the popular sentiments without giving the people any formal leverage, except perhaps in major crises or breakdowns of authority. In the sixth through fourth centuries B.C., Greek city-state democracy—such as it was, with its small scale and the presence of large slave and foreign resident populations—had notions of popular sovereignty, even though the Greek concept of citizenship was vague and undeveloped. Aristotle's *Politics*, for example, defines democratic freedom only as the right to rule and be ruled in turn. Aristotle did not advocate democracy, though he distinguished it from other kinds of regimes, such as monarchy and oligarchy (rule by the few). A rapidly changing setting of economic transformation and political crisis in his day marked Greek democracy as the least stable form of government unless it was "mixed" with strong elements of oligarchic or monarchic rule. In the midst of what Plato described as the tensions between the poor and the rich, popular government was bound to be associated with unruly and anarchic mob rule rather than with an institutionalized process of constitutional democracy.

Roman civilization in the republican era, which lasted from about 500 B.C. until 44 B.C., was much closer to the institutional and legal formulas that might give practical significance to notions of popular sovereignty, but there seemed to be little interest in popular rule. Instead, a strong tradition of law and shared governance between the aristocratic Senate and the popular tribunes evolved. With the arrival of imperial absolutism, under Julius Caesar and his successors, popularly legitimated law became an empty shell, its authority usurped by senatorial and imperial decrees without popular sanction. The rise of the absolute authority of emperors and of the rapidly expanding empire swallowed up the republican concern, for example, of the Roman orator Cicero (106–43 B.C.) with creating a well-ordered republic and with its common virtues. Cicero's references to popular sovereignty, like the Athenian leader Pericles' praise of democracy in his funeral oration (431 B.C.) on the first soldiers killed in the Peloponnesian War (reported by Thucydides), were expressions of nostalgia rather than prescriptions for practical political action.

The revival and reinterpretation of important Roman legal concepts in the Middle Ages, nevertheless, helped the idea of popular sovereignty to an unexpected renaissance amid the restraints of religious faith, customary law, and feudalism. The Roman Catholic Church, with its great councils that represented the priesthood, contributed by its example the most distinctive instrument of the secular popular governments of the future—namely, representative government and clear notions of who was being represented and against whom. Feudalism and custom further sharpened ideas of rights and privileges, at first only of lords and corporate bodies, but this precedent provided a basis for future development of all individual rights. Some city republics of the Italian Renaissance experimented with forms of government that would give the ultimate power of lawmaking to "weightier" members of the citizenry of the town. Marsilius of Padua, in his *Defender of Peace* (1324), supplied the theory behind this principle. Thus many of the conceptual prerequisites for the practical realization of popular sovereignty were beginning to emerge from the Middle Ages and the Renaissance, even though their practice was limited to feudal parliaments, courts, and occasional French or Italian examples of municipal self-government or the ancient town meetings of some Swiss cantons.

The Victory of the British Parliament

What was still missing for popular government to come into its own was a widespread sense of the emancipation of the individual from the fetters of religion and traditional social bonds. Massive social and political upheavals in the sixteenth, seventeenth, and eighteenth centuries accomplished this liberation. Thus self-governing individuals, now many in number, granted popular consent to a government that itself had become a secular state, differentiated from religious authority and social control and increasingly abstract in its own authority. One of the harbingers of this great change was the emergence of a democratic political theory espoused by agrarian defenders of the English village commons against the wave of enclosures of common land in the seventeenth century. The Diggers and Levellers not only argued for the birthright of the lower classes against greedy landowners but they struggled for a kind of constitutional convention and solemn enactment that would keep kings and parliaments from taking away the rights of the people. Their protests were to little avail in the midst of the civil wars between king and Parliament but, along with the other political theories generated by that turbulent century, they set the stage for the American and French Revolutions of the eighteenth century.

The great struggle between the kings of England (James I and Charles I) and Parliament was fought in the battlefields and resulted in the establishment of a kingless commonwealth under a supreme, elected Parliament. The latter, consisting of nobles and the merchant classes, was not elected by all the people. Nevertheless it clearly derived its authority from this fact of "popular election," and a number of the most distinguished political philosophers of that age drew their conclusions from the signal defeat of the divine-rights claims of the king.

Among these was John Locke who, in his *First Treatise of Government* (1689), attacked arguments by Thomas Hobbes and Robert Filmer in the defense of the absolute, divine right of kings, the very opposite of popular sovereignty. As Hobbes had done with a very different outcome, Locke in his two treatises resorted to the fiction of individuals "in a state of nature." He used this device to state both their "natural" rights and their deliber-

ate consent to a social contract that brought them together in a society and under the political obligations of an organized state. To Locke and the English Whigs (the party of the nobility who wanted to limit the power of the Crown), the social contract enabled them to spell out the civil liberties and property rights they wished to protect—not only from a monarch but even from the people whose ultimate, residual authority they readily acknowledged. Monarchy in England eventually made a comeback in spite of republican arguments, such as those of James Harrington and John Milton, who believed in popular sovereignty. But it did so only at the pleasure of Parliament, which derived its authority from popular election—from "the consent of the majority," according to Locke.

The Revolutionary Spirit

On the European continent the new individualistic thinking had flourished in the Low Countries. Benedict de Spinoza, in his *Theologico-Political Treatise* (1670), argued that only democracy gives individuals some say in their own government. But most of Europe was still under strong absolutist governments. In France the political side of the Enlightenment came to the fore only with the advancing eighteenth century—and nowhere as radically as in the writings of Jean-Jacques Rousseau in his *Social Contract* (1762).

Rousseau believed that popular sovereignty was inalienably vested in the people, and, unlike the English Whigs, he believed it could not be delegated to a legislature because the legislature likely would act only in its own interest or in the interests of a select group. No true law can be made without the consent of the people. Rousseau described the process by which a community makes law as the emergence of the general will, which is intrinsically moral and suffers no dissenting minorities. A mystifying mélange of determined dedication to the public interest and of the civic virtue of republicans (from Rome to the soon-to-be-born American Republic), this doctrine of the general will has been called totalitarian by some and blamed for the fanaticism of the French Revolution by others. Some of the Jacobins, the most radical wing of the French revolutionaries, who were responsible for the Reign of Terror, such as Maximilien Robespierre, were disciples of Rousseau.

In the meantime, however, the American Revolution and Constitution had developed along a rather different path. The successful War of Independence and establishment of popular sovereignty, it seems, led the Framers of the Philadelphia convention to follow the counsel of Locke and of the French political philosopher Montesquieu rather than that of Rousseau. Their celebrated Constitution, which fell far short of establishing democratic government, went to great lengths to curb the power of the elected people's representatives in the House of Representatives. The Constitution established checks and balances by the other bodies, which were not directly elected: senators, the president (elected by the electoral college), and the federal judiciary. A prime example of an attempt at mixed government along lines suggested by Aristotle and Montesquieu, the U.S. Constitution heralded a new trend of moderate liberal thought and constitutional government. After centuries in which the practice of popular government had lagged far behind its theories, theories were devised to rein in its practice.

The French Revolution and its Terror drew many critics who, like Edmund Burke and David Hume, challenged the philosophical foundations of individualism and popular rebellion on which they were founded. The most important of the postrevolutionary political thinkers were moderate liberals, such as Benjamin Constant de Rebecque and Alexis de Tocqueville. They defended popular sovereignty but preferred to hem in its exercise. Like many nineteenth-century writers, Constant preferred a constitutional monarchy on the British model, but he favored one that protected civil liberties against arbitrary government action. Tocqueville's astute observations about American mass democracy in the days of Andrew Jackson revealed his fear of a tyranny of the majority despite his support for the coming of democracy. John Stuart Mill perhaps expressed the moderate liberal perspective best when he warned in *On Liberty* (1859) that the true tyrant is the collective mass of individuals composing society itself.

Each of these nineteenth-century thinkers wanted institutional safeguards for individuals and minorities against an oppressive majority of the sovereign people. Tocqueville also praised the power of voluntary associations to protect the rights of minorities and nonconforming individuals. Unlimited popular sovereignty, along the lines of Rousseau and the French Revolution, according to Lord Acton, one of Tocqueville's best-known disciples, was to be avoided at all costs.

Twentieth-Century Questions

At the end of the twentieth century a return to seeking the ultimate political authority in tradition or religion seems remote. Nevertheless religious fundamentalists of many stripes are pursuing a revival of theocracy, subordinating their political system to their God and religious revelations. Moreover, vast popular mobilizations behind ideologies such as communism, fascism, and revolutionary nationalism have invoked the authority of "the people," if in dubious ways and without any legal or constitutional safeguards. On the other hand, the concept of popular sovereignty continues to play a major role in the making of modern constitutions, whether they are radically democratic or hedged with checks upon the exercise of popular authority.

Religious fundamentalists differ from each other not only in their respective religions but also in the extent of their otherworldliness, which leads most of their sects to abstain or withdraw from politics. In some cases, however, the intent was indeed to create a theocracy. For example, Allah and Islamic law were to be the ultimate source of all authority in the Shi'ite Muslim revivalist movement of the Ayatollah Ruhollah Khomeini that began in Iran in 1979. Khomeini's Iran was to be a "theodemocracy" of "limited popular sovereignty under a paramount God," who remained the true sovereign. The ideal Islamic community was conceived as a community of believers in the Word, as interpreted by *imams*, or spiritual leaders, such as Khomeini.

Although shared beliefs and community values created a strong bond between the rulers and their subjects, dissension among rival Muslim interpretations and groups inevitably drew the transmission of theocratic authority into question. Who would decide which *imam* was the right one and whether the community consensus was true or false if such questions could not be resolved by a majority vote of the people? Other politically interested, religious fundamentalists, including some in the United States, have faced similar problems: How shall we know the true messenger of God and his message in case of a challenge? It would be blasphemous to subject the truth of religion to a majority vote of the people. Theocracy and democracy do not mix.

The vast mobilizations of communism and interwar fascism brought countless revolutions and immensely destructive wars on the twentieth century, much of it in the name of the people or, by implication, of popular sovereignty. Communist parties everywhere fought and ruled by the authority of the historical advance and eventual triumph of the downtrodden, international industrial proletariat, or so they said. Once established in power, the parties proceeded to manufacture majority consent by a mixture of ceaseless agitation and propaganda, with iron-fisted repression against those who challenged or resisted them. European fascist and revolutionary nationalist movements after World War I similarly claimed to represent the defeated peoples against their victors, or the allegedly downtrodden ethnic communities against other ethnics who presumably rose to power over them in Eastern Europe. They also learned the techniques of mass mobilization and the manufacture of consent, not to mention of massive repression, from the communists and from each other.

After World War II revolutionary nationalist movements worldwide made similar appeals to the popular sovereignty of their colonial or otherwise oppressed peoples against the domination of colonial empires or of ethnic majorities in their countries. In all these cases, the invoking of popular sovereignty was linked to a community of shared values—proletarian, ethnic, or racialist—and always promoted with massive propaganda. In nearly all these cases, this process of legitimation fell short of any real democratic affirmation and of constitutional protections for minorities and individuals. Even the communists who shared some of the legacy of Rousseau and of the French Revolution, and of populism in various settings, would not hear of submitting to genuine procedures of popular consent or to the constitutional controls on arbitrary governmental power that have long been the hallmark of the contemporary practice of popular sovereignty.

Aside from these dubious alternative applications, then, is the concept of popular sovereignty still relevant to the political life of today's constitutional democracies? The answer undoubtedly is "yes," even though the great battles over the theory and practice of popular government have long been won and popular sovereignty, in one form or another, reigns supreme almost everywhere. The concept is so fundamental to today's democratic practice that we can hardly expect it to be an issue of ordinary electoral campaigns or of parliamentary debates anymore. Even when populist appeals of various sorts tax political elites for ignoring the interests of the people, those elites are unlikely to challenge the ultimate authority of the people to give themselves a particular political order in harmony with their beliefs and values and to intervene when their "general will" is thwarted.

In the sixteenth century, when the Protestant French Huguenots had to defend themselves against an oppressive Catholic king, they presented their argument of a "right of revolution" as the last resort of a community of believers against religious and political repression. As with the Calvinists of Scotland, their right of revolution inevitably became the fundamental right of a God-fearing people to resist and rebel against their tyrannical government, an assertion of popular sovereignty with religious justification. It did not take long, given the rise of differentiated modern state organization with rational administrative and legal structures, for this claim to become secularized. The upheavals of the seventeenth and eighteenth centuries, and the political theories reviewed earlier, revived and refined older traditions of thinking in terms of a rational constitutional order in which the place of popular sovereignty was spelled out. The rise of constitutional enactments couched the concept, in legal language, as the constituent power, the fundamental right of the people to sanction their basic political order with their consent.

In terms of constitutional law, this right meant and still signifies three things. First, the people have the right to make or influence the making of a new constitution. To be sure, some constitu-tional systems, for example, Great Britain, still operate without a written constitution, and in other countries constitutional drafts are often worked out by a committee of constitutional experts rather than by a popularly elected constitutional assembly.

Second, the sovereign people have the right to ratify their constitution, after extensive public debate and possibly some modification of the original draft. Again, there are exceptions, such as the Federal Republic of Germany's Basic Law of 1949 (and now the Constitution of unified Germany), which was not sanctioned by popular ratification in 1949. It was not ratified because the Federal Republic was still occupied by the three Western powers, and the German leaders wanted to emphasize the provisional character of their Western rump state until reunification. When unification occurred in 1990, the leaders once more avoided popular sanction for reasons of expediency.

Third, the people have the right to be consulted about constitutional changes and amendments. The people's constituent power is usually enshrined in the carefully prescribed process by which constitutional amendments have to be solemnly ratified. Again there are exceptions and various methods of amendment, such as by two-thirds majorities of parliament or, in federal systems, with the states (provinces, cantons) having a constituent power of their own—derived from each state's people—with regard to the federal constitution. The biggest exception, perhaps, is found in major constitutional changes that occur over long periods of time and without a particular act of popular consent. An example is the dominance of the twentieth-century American presidency over Congress and the rise of federal preeminence over the states. Before 1900 Congress was more important than the president, and the states mattered more than the federal government. These changes were not decreed by constitutional amendments but came about through long-range social and economic changes.

Gross abuses of this constituent power have also occurred in the form of system-changing plebiscites (direct votes of the people). For example, plebisicites were used to legitimate the dictatorial powers of Napoleon Bonaparte and Napoleon III and later of Adolf Hitler, who clearly intended to destroy the constitutional order. Such plebiscitary democracy does not fairly represent popular sovereignty because its effect usually depends on the personal popularity of a man on horseback—and often on fraud and coercion as well. Ordinary initiatives and referendums may also trivialize the constituent power of the sovereign people where these devices are used with excessive frequency to add minor technical or policy prescriptions to a constitution (as in California and other western states in the United States).

The final major aspect of popular sovereignty today lies in the use of popular elections to determine the government's officers, party strengths in legislatures, and major policy programs. Although elections do not involve the constituent power in the same sense, they are capable of changing existing regimes in fundamental ways, not only by "throwing the rascals out" but also by instituting major reforms and major new policies, at least for the duration of the legislators' terms of office. For the day-to-day assertion of the popular will short of constitutional change today, elections provide the powerful control leverage so that "the government of the people," to quote Abraham Lincoln, "shall not perish from the earth."

See also Consent; Fundamentalism; Legitimacy; Locke, John; Montesquieu; Populism; Virtue, Civic.

PETER H. MERKL

BIBLIOGRAPHY

Barker, Ernest. *Principles of Social and Political Theory.* London: Oxford University Press, 1965.

_____. *Social Contract: Essays by Locke, Hume, and Rousseau.* With an introduction by Sir Ernest Barker. New York and London: Oxford University Press, 1960.

Friedrich, Carl J. *Constitutional Government and Democracy.* 4th ed. Waltham, Mass.: Blaisdell, 1968.

Hansen, Mogens Herman. *The Athenian Democracy in the Age of Demosthenes.* Oxford: Blackwell, 1991.

McIlwain, Charles H. *Constitutionalism, Ancient and Modern.* Rev. ed. Ithaca, N.Y.: Great Seal Books, 1958.

Sabine, George H. *A History of Political Theory.* 3d ed. New York: Holt, Rinehart and Winston, 1961.

✦ Representation

The mechanism by which the people participate indirectly in government through representatives. Modern democracies, or republics as they also are called, are based on elective representation. Not all public officers are elected by the people in such governments, but those who are not elected must be chosen by those who are so elected.

In the United States, for example, the people elect members of the House of Representatives and the Senate—the two branches of the federal legislature—and the electors who choose the president. In effect, the people may be said to elect the president, inasmuch as presidential electors almost always act as rubber stamps for the preferences of those who elected them. All other officers in the federal government are chosen by elected officials, the most important of them by the president with the Senate's consent. In modern representative government, all officers must be responsible to the people. In the United States and most other democracies, all elective and some appointed officers serve for limited terms or at the pleasure of those who appointed them or, in the case of judges, as long as they demonstrate good behavior. Put another way, democratic or republican government, as it is commonly understood today, excludes hereditary offices and offices held for life.

It is possible to combine hereditary and life offices with elective ones, but such a government would not be wholly republican. The British government, for example, includes an elective House of Commons, a cabinet drawn mainly from the Commons, a hereditary monarchy, and a House of Lords based in part on heredity and in part on life appointments. Strictly speaking, the British have a mixed form of government, though in view of the predominance of its elective elements, it is commonly described as democratic. The French philosopher Montesquieu, writing in the mid-eighteenth century, was so impressed with the importance of the House of Commons that he called Great Britain a republic under the cover of a monarchy. We may say the same of countries like Denmark and the Netherlands whose public business is conducted almost entirely by elective legislatures and cabinets drawn from one or both legislative chambers, and whose monarchs play mainly ceremonial parts.

It is also possible for an elective or representative government to serve as a cover for one that is independent of the people. Such a government ruled the former Soviet Union and the "people's democracies" of Eastern Europe. They are still found in some countries today, not limited to those of a communist cast. For example, in Indonesia the same person, backed by the power of the military, has been easily reelected at five-year intervals since he and the army seized power

in 1965; and this military government dominates legislative proceedings.

Origins of the Popular Assembly

The citizens of the ancient republics of Greece and Rome governed themselves directly, in the assembly. Direct representation limited the size of the city-state, or *polis*, as it was called in Greece, to the distance that citizens could travel to meet together. In the assembly they made laws; decided questions of war and peace; chose ambassadors, generals, and magistrates; and reviewed these officials' performance of duties. Some offices in the city-state were filled by lot on a rotating basis. This method of rotating offices was especially prevalent in the democratic city-states, which believed that every citizen should have an equal chance to hold office.

Modern governments' experience with "direct democracy" is pretty much limited to the use of juries drawn more or less randomly from the population, but only the British government and those influenced by British legal practice go this far. Most nations (for example, Italy and France) do not go this far and rely solely on the decisions of judges, sometimes acting in conjunction with "lay judges," as in Sweden. Modern juries, moreover, are small in number and are under the direction of government attorneys (in places where grand juries are used) or judges (in the case of trial juries). By contrast, ancient juries were large in number, and their members acted in effect as judges as well as jurors. The Athenian jury that convicted Socrates of impiety and corrupting the youth in 399 B.C. numbered more than a thousand.

Some writers have said that the existence of elections and selection by lot in the ancient city-states is evidence that the ancients understood the concept of representation. Why, then, it has been asked, did the Greeks not use representation to expand their states beyond the narrow compass imposed by the need to assemble all the citizens for the conduct of government? Had they formed a single national government, it has been said, they would have been more secure against powerful monarchies such as Persia. Instead, they had to rely on leagues and loose confederations, which were liable to disunity among their members. Furthermore, it has been suggested, an extensive republic would have made citizens more secure against domestic factions and the danger of anarchy or tyranny posed by such factions. In short, why did the ancient Greeks not do what Americans did in 1787? The newly independent American states formed a large republic, rather than continuing under the Articles of Confederation, forming several smaller confederations, or allowing the thirteen existing states to go their separate ways.

It is not at all clear that the Greeks understood elections, whether conducted by citizens or by lot, as a means for representing the people in government. They seem to have employed these devices for participatory, not representative, purposes, to ensure that all or almost all citizens would have a chance to rule as well as to be ruled. Moreover, they considered the city-state to constitute a natural society. Citizens knew each other directly or through immediate acquaintances and therefore were connected by trust.

The modern counterpart of the ancient assembly is the lower house of the legislature. It is everywhere elected by the people, whereas the upper chamber is often chosen by local governing bodies. It is primarily this lower house that represents the people in government. Thus the American Founders sometimes referred to the House of Representatives as "an assembly" or "a popular assembly," and the French and Pakistanis have formally designated their lower house as the National Assembly. Lower chambers usually are entrusted with preponderant legislative power.

The British House of Lords, for example, may delay legislation enacted by the House of Commons for only a year (thirty days in the case of financial bills); the Japanese House of Representatives may overcome the opposition of the upper House of Councillors by repassing legislation by a two-thirds majority (or by its original simple majority for financial legislation). The American Senate is rather exceptional in this respect: its powers are roughly coequal to those of the House of Representatives.

Early Americans generally considered the institutions of government to be more or less representative as they measured up to the assemblies of the ancient republics. The Senate was a representative body, in the eyes of early Americans, but less so than the House of Representatives, for it represented the states directly and the people indirectly. Furthermore, the Senate's small size (two members from each state) and long term of office (six years) distanced it from the people. In the early years of the American Republic the president was not often viewed as a popular representative. Never, apparently, was the term *representative* applied to judges. Judges operated in that part of the government most removed from the people, and (unlike the president, who had the veto) they were given no share in the legislative power.

Hobbes and Representation

The doctrine of representation was the invention of the English philosopher Thomas Hobbes, who used the term in his *Leviathan* (1651). For Hobbes, representative government was a government authorized by the people. It could be hereditary as well as popular, entrusted to one person or to an assembly, so long as power was not shared. Hobbes preferred a sovereign individual to a sovereign assembly because he believed that a monarch would be better able to achieve the purpose of government, to protect the people from threats to each other and from foreign nations. Thus Hobbes has been associated with the defense of absolute monarchy. What made government representative for Hobbes was that the people had empowered it to act in their behalf.

Hobbes's doctrine of representation was developed further by John Locke, later in the seventeenth century. Locke agreed that a people could place the supreme power of society, which he identified as the legislative power, in whatever hands they wished, but he indicated that it was best entrusted to an elective body. Representative government for Locke was also directed toward security, but Locke emphasized the security of individual rights. The American Declaration of Independence (1776) incorporates Locke's improvement upon Hobbes. It proclaims the right of a people to base the foundations of government on such principles and to organize governmental powers in such a form as they think will provide for their safety and happiness.

Thomas Jefferson, the Declaration's author, later said that he would not question a people's choice even when it was reposed in a Napoleon Bonaparte or an Alexander the Great. The Declaration, however, does unobtrusively provide guidance. How many kinds of government, after all, profess a belief in the equality of birth and inalienable rights to life, liberty, and the pursuit of happiness? And if legitimate government must derive its powers from popular consent in the first place, would it not likely occur to a people to insist on a government that required their consent on a continuing basis? In any event, toward the end of his life Jefferson stated that the issue had been settled, for modern experience had demonstrated that only government chosen by the people could secure equal rights.

And yet Hobbes's notion of the representative ruler, as contrasted with the representative assembly, has had its influence. Locke stated in his *Sec-ond Treatise of Government* (1689) that when the executive consists of a single person possessed with the power of veto, it is as if the executive reflected the polity as a whole. If this executive is made elective and accountable to the people, we have a sketch of the American presidency. Indeed, instilled with "energy," the president was intended by the Framers to fulfill Hobbesian and Lockean ends; he was to be essential not only in executing the laws but in providing security against external and internal dangers.

Andrew Jackson, U.S. president from 1829 to 1837, held the view that, as president, he was as much the representative of the people as was Congress. Jackson was the first president openly to press his positions on the legislative body and to carry his quarrels with it to the people. Today it is widely accepted that the president represents the national interests of the people, while Congress represents their local and particular interests.

So, too, the executives of other modern democracies who are elected directly by the people are generally regarded as representatives of their nations. Elected presidents have achieved such ascendancy in relation to the legislature in governments that contain this office that these governments frequently are called "presidential" governments, to distinguish them from the parliamentary kind, with their plural executives responsible to the lower house of parliament.

Such are the governments of nations influenced by the American political example. Most of these are in Latin America, but they also include, since World War II, the governments of the Philippines, the Republic of Korea, and Nigeria. Most nations copied the British model or (in the case of European countries) had it implanted on their soil. A few governments (for example, France and Russia) combine a popularly elected executive with an executive chosen by parliament. Purely parliamentary governments themselves have felt the impulse toward a strong popular executive: they are sometimes referred to as "cabinet" or even "prime ministerial" governments.

Most democracies other than the United States have displayed more confidence in their lower legislative chambers. As we have noted, they have entrusted them with greater power than they have their second chambers, which typically are less directly under popular control. Also, most of these democracies have been unwilling to give their judges the power to strike down legislative enactments, and the small number that do hedge the exercise of that power much more than is done in the United States.

It might be said that representative government today features the interplay of two models: Hobbes's single ruler and the ancient assembly, both made accountable to the people through elections, can be seen in modern representative governments.

Trends

Representative government, then, replaces the people with persons who act for them. Some early Americans explained representation as a necessity, required by the size of the nation. And yet nearly all Americans at the founding regarded representation as an improvement upon direct rule by the people. They would have preferred a representative republic even if America had been the size of the Athenian city-state. *The Federalist*, a series of essays written to support the ratification of the Constitution in 1787 and 1788, maintains that representation improves the public debate by causing ideas to be refined through a select body of citizens (*Federalist* No. 10). The people are competent to choose their governors and to judge how well they have been served by them, but not to govern themselves.

Representation by itself, however, was not sufficient to produce good government, for what it produced was the House of Representatives, a large and changeable body that in the view of the Framers contained many of the defects of the ancient popular assembly. To make their government more stable, the Founders made the Senate, executive, and judiciary somewhat more distant from the people, and they added energy to stability by placing the executive power in the hands of a single person. The Senate, president, and judiciary were given the task of restraining the people when they needed moderation by restraining the House of Representatives.

All representative government places some distance between the people and their representatives. This distance seems inevitable, however short the terms of office and however few the checks on legislative bodies. The heart of the matter perhaps lies in representation itself. We need no philosopher to tell us that our representatives are not ourselves, as the eighteenth-century French philosopher Jean-Jacques Rousseau, a critic of representative government, pointed out. Their opinions, ambitions, and interests cannot be identical to those of the electorate, no matter how they are chosen. And, as we have noted, the American Founders thought that representative popular government conducted by popularly elected representatives was superior to government directly by the people.

Attempts are being made today to allow the people to act in place of their elected representatives or, at least, to become active participants in making government policy. Nowhere has this effort been carried further than in the United States. Some American reformers have suggested having members of Congress chosen by lot or allowing citizens to vote on legislative issues electronically after watching them debated on television. More moderate changes, actually in operation, allow citizens to communicate their views to government on a continuing basis, not just at times of election, through public opinion surveys, radio and television talk shows, informal telephone voting on issues presented on television, and demonstrations covered by the media. Government officials use these sources of information in framing their policies and conduct their own televised "meetings" with the people. A striking trend in American politics is the extent to which government officials, including some members of the Supreme Court, "go public," that is, seek popular support for themselves and their views. And self-appointed representatives of the people mediate between the people and government, explaining government to the people and instructing government as to what the people want. Members of the media play a crucial role in this activity, mediating among the contending parties and making their own contributions.

To state the current situation in a somewhat exaggerated way, America has become a new Athens. Its citizens are informed about each other by the media and carry on public deliberations in a vast assembly whose proceedings have been made possible by television. Interested parties vie for attention in this assembly, government officials along with private citizens, and they stage "media events" to attract attention. Officials, including members of Congress, thus are not representatives of the people, chosen to deliberate in their stead, but magistrates, chosen, like those in the ancient city-states, to carry out the popular will.

See also Classical Greece and Rome; Hobbes, Thomas; Locke, John; Mill, John Stuart; Montesquieu; Democracy, Participatory.

ROBERT SCIGLIANO

BIBLIOGRAPHY

Barber, Benjamin R. *Strong Democracy: Participatory Politics for a New Age.* Berkeley: University of California Press, 1984.
Fustel de Coulanges, Numa D. *The Ancient City: A Classic Study of the Religious and Civil Laws of Ancient Greece and Rome.* Baltimore: Johns Hopkins University Press, 1980.
Hamilton, Alexander, James Madison, and John Jay. *The Federalist.* New York: Modern Library, 1937.
Mansfield, Harvey C., Jr. *The Spirit of Liberalism.* Cambridge: Harvard University Press, 1978.
Mill, John Stuart. *Considerations on Representative Government.* London: Longmans, Green, 1873.
Pitkin, Hanna F. *Representation.* New York: Atherton Press, 1969.

✦ State growth and intervention

The expansion of state organization and personnel and the imposition of state interests and activities upon society. The state's performance of social and group-specific functions and its extraction of revenues, conscripts, and other resources from society are important features in the development of human history. The first interventions of the state into society accompanied the emergence of the state as a distinct institution.

As Charles Tilly wrote in his *Formation of Nation States in Western Europe* (1975), intervention began with the emergence of states as organizations that were able to control the population of definite territories, were distinct from other organizations, were sovereign entities, were centralized, and were composed of formally coordinated parts. Later extensions of the state into the lives of its subjects and citizens came with its modernization in the age of industrial, national, and democratic revolutions. The functions of the state proliferated in the twentieth century.

Premodern States

Before the great revolutions in communications, nationalism, democracy, and industry that marked the modern era, the high costs of territorial control relative to available resources limited the state's intervention in people's lives. Both social and technological means of control and subduing popular resistance to control were costly. A self-equipped army could maintain itself for only three days in the times of Alexander the Great and Julius Caesar. Beyond the third day, ancient armies had to turn to foraging and pillaging local lands and populations or to establishing long and extremely costly supply lines. Foraging and pillaging carried on within a state's territory risked the ruination and alienation of the state's subjects, while supply lines strained the surplus production capacity of societies in which most people lived close to subsistence. Sustained intimidation by distant armed forces might extract periodic tributes and command allegiance for future wars; however, it also decentralized power, saving semi-independent tributaries from becoming fully subject to the state. In most empires the activities of the state were essentially limited to the metropolitan core.

Despite the serious obstacles to state expansion, the ancient world did produce states that intervened in the lives of their populations. Such states emerged in the extraordinarily fertile river valleys of Egypt, the Levant, India, and China. In those places agriculture depended on irrigation, and centralized, coercive control of the necessary infrastructure both enhanced the power of the state and subsidized its operation.

In Greece and Rome unprecedented extensions of slavery released new wealth for financing state rule. At the same time, innovations in mass mobilization and military organization cut the costs of territorial control. The new institutions of political participation and legally encoded citizenship extended the reach of military conscription deep into domestic populations in republican Greece and Rome. In the Roman Empire, with its elaborate rule of law, extensive conscription per-

sisted for a time, until it was largely replaced by reliance upon German mercenaries.

Extraordinary plunder could also sustain a state for a time. This was the case in sixteenth-century Spain, which reaped the wealth of its newfound colonies. State revenue extraction from plunder, tribute, customs duties, labor obligations, tax farming, rentals of public lands, and the like, however, seldom made up as much as 10 percent of the value of production within a given territory during the premodern era. The scarcity of surplus production beyond the subsistence needs of populations and inefficient premodern techniques of revenue extraction made any larger share for state coffers impracticable. Indeed, intrusions by invading foreign states may have had more of an effect on everyday life than state interventions did, at least until the modern era.

Modern States

Merchant, financial, and industrial capitalism emerged in the late Middle Ages and the Renaissance. In that era, monarchs and their allied "war parties" built up state administrations for financing and managing armed forces. These official structures were closely linked to the new class of capitalists. Aided by resources supplied by capitalists, monarchs were able to subordinate ethnic and linguistic minority groups, as well as less aggressive groups of nobles. The growing states were absolutist where their capitalist allies were duly subordinated; constitutionalist states developed where capitalists voiced their views by means of "estates" and parliamentary assemblies. In all cases, the growing states of the sixteenth through eighteenth centuries pursued both military and mercantile expansion.

The case of Great Britain provides an early and well-documented instance of state growth. The revenues of the British state tripled in about a century, between the reigns of Elizabeth I (1558–

1607) and James II (1685–1688). Its expenditures then doubled from the reign of William and Mary (1689–1702) to the outbreak of the French Revolution (1789). In their pursuit of international military advantage, states nurtured productive enterprises by means of purchases of military goods, investment in the infrastructures of military manufacturers, and policing of colonial markets. Thus the British state's domestic and colonial spending, as well as military spending, rose throughout the period 1500–1785.

Revolutionary and Napoleonic France infused new ideals of nationalism and citizenship into this dynamic by fueling warfare with huge numbers of volunteers and conscripts. French mobilization for total war under the young Napoleon Bonaparte raised the levels of mobilization throughout Europe as various European nations instituted conscription and other institutions copied from the French. For example, passage of income and wealth taxes in France in 1793 and in the early Napoleonic era appears to have stimulated the Dutch, English, and Austrians to pass similar taxes in the last years of the eighteenth century. But the rise in military expenditures was the most direct and pronounced effect of the French model. From 1790 to 1815 British military expenditures grew by 700 percent, while total British state spending increased by 300 percent.

In the nineteenth and twentieth centuries similar dramatic expansions in state revenue extraction and spending followed each major escalation of warfare by newly industrialized and nationalistic states and peoples. With World War I, state expenditures for the first time began to exceed 10 percent of the national production of large nations. Between 1913 and 1917 spending as a percentage of gross national product (GNP) jumped from roughly 10 percent to 34 percent in France, from 7 percent to 57 percent in Great Britain, and from 2 percent to 24 percent in the United States.

These increases in national spending, buoyed by increases in nations' domestic incentives and compensation for war mobilization (in forms as varied as soldiers' compensation and general public pensions), did not return to prewar levels. By 1924 spending had settled at about 20 percent of GNP in France and at 16 percent in Great Britain, although it fell back to 4 percent in the United States.

Military spending as a percentage of national spending grew explosively during World War II, hitting peaks of 42 percent, 61 percent, and 64 percent of GNP, respectively, in the United States, Germany, and Great Britain. Moreover, domestic spending once more grew in tandem with military spending, and total postwar spending remained (once again) at levels well above those of the prewar period: at 25 percent of GNP in the United States and at more than 35 percent in Germany and Great Britain. U.S. spending had increased by 600 percent from comparable 1930 levels, while spending in Germany and Great Britain had increased 300 percent. Much of the growth in spending from 1930 to 1950 represented increased social spending, for such purposes as social insurance payments, education, job training, public works, and buoying up of consumer demand. The increase in social spending was a result of the rise of the welfare state.

The Multifunctional State

From their first appearance, states were involved in managing their relations with other states and regulating the relations of their subjects or citizens with other nations and their peoples. These activities included diplomatic relations, migration, war, war preparations, and deterrence of war. Early states also had to undertake the financing and administration of these international activities. By the early modern era some states were extensively involved in regulating their citizens' roles in property ownership, commerce, and so forth. They also made expenditures to improve the national infrastructure, building roads, schools, port facilities, and courts. They undertook other activities thought to be crucial to economic prosperity and military capability.

In the late nineteenth and early twentieth centuries the functions of the state proliferated. States began to address risks to health, income, and general welfare posed by the new industrial order. For example, early factories posed grave threats to life and limb; marketplace employers fired workers more freely than feudal patrons; and a slow shredding of the extended family tore up a traditional safety net. Fortunately, democratic movements and institutions opened up new avenues for the newly at-risk populations.

Varied philosophical and political orientations guided policy responses to the new risks: patriarchal and progressive-liberal, social Christian and communist, social democratic and Christian democratic. As diverse as they were, however, these orientations shared certain themes relating to the communitarian redirection, or revision, of the liberal-capitalist order. They also tended to focus on similar kinds of programs, such as child-labor laws, industrial accident insurance, and old-age and unemployment insurance, if not necessarily health insurance or child allowances. There was more divergence on other measures, such as those for fiscal and monetarist macroeconomic stabilization. Only some governments pursued full-employment goals and offered job-training assistance.

Capitalist economic development and democracy appear to have been important preconditions for the proliferation of government functions, especially social security measures. By the end of World War I, almost all substantially industrialized nations (except for a few marginal cases like Spain) had adopted a social insurance policy covering work accidents. In addition, the ten sovereign nations that adopted three out of four major types of social insurance programs—old age and disability insurance, sickness insurance, work accident insurance, and unemployment compensation insurance—were among the twenty most economically developed nations in the world. Moreover, nearly all the nations that underwent economic development early on (c. 1918) were political democracies. The exceptions were a few monarchies (Austria, Germany, and Spain) that could claim active and influential, though circumscribed, parliamentary and party politics.

Within the developed democratic nations, differences in particular aspects of democratic politics remained important for the adoption of social insurance measures and the development of social insurance policy. Partisan differences in governmental leadership became the driving force behind social reforms during the first half of the twentieth century. Before the Great Depression began in 1929, liberal parties, pressured and aided by labor unions and parties (the so-called lib-lab coalitions), led the way in countries where liberal parties were strong. In Belgium and the Netherlands, where liberals were weak, Catholic parties with ample labor constituencies pioneered reforms. During the 1930s social democratic governments took the lead in the Scandinavian nations and in Australia and New Zealand. These were paralleled by the reform-oriented governments of Franklin Delano Roosevelt in the United States and Mackenzie King in Canada. During and after World War II, social democratic governments, complemented by Christian democratic governments, enacted virtually all social insurance and related income and job security reforms.

The social insurance reforms of the capitalist democracies in the 1930s and 1940s were accompanied and followed by state interventions aimed at recovering or sustaining high levels of employment by means of public works, labor market training and job search policies, and, most important, fiscal stimulation of consumer demand and thus of production and employment. The stimulative fiscal policy was pursued under the influence of the macroeconomic theories of John Maynard Keynes. Indeed, the whole array of employment and social security policies that emerged after World War II was encouraged by Keynes's ideas, which reversed policymakers' attitude toward government spending. Earlier, policymakers' approach to relieving hard times had been to balance the budget; now their approach was to spend, even to engage in deficit spending.

During the Keynesian era from 1950 to 1980, government spending and taxation as a percentage of gross domestic product (GDP) in the most affluent capitalist democracies rose from an average of 25 percent to about 50 percent. The goals of the Keynesian welfare state with regard to employment, stabilization, and growth appear to have complemented the reduction of risks and inequalities sought by these policies. Between the 1930s and the 1960s average rates of unemployment in the sixteen most affluent capitalist democracies fell from more than 15 percent to less than 5 percent. The percentage of normal income that could be reclaimed from state social insurance programs everywhere increased dramatically. In many of the small democracies of western Europe, income-replacement levels approached 100 percent. In combination with effective "high employment" policies, this strategy virtually eliminated poverty in Scandinavia, the Netherlands, and Austria.

Among less developed nations, the rates of adoption and financing of social insurance programs have lagged behind those in affluent democracies. Yet adoption of such programs has spread widely, through a process of diffusion characterized by demonstration in developed countries and imitation in developing countries.

In communist countries, state command economies were put in place by midcentury. In such economies the state produced and distributed most of the goods and services and even consumed much of what was produced during the period 1950–1990. In these countries, even without considering intrusions of party agents and state police into private life, state penetration into the lives of subjects reached unprecedented levels. These countries lacked the aid of political democracy (that is, competitive election of government leaders by a wide franchise of citizens) to subject state intervention to a measure of institutionalized citizen control. Nonetheless, communist concepts of citizens' socioeconomic, if not civil or representative, rights were often lofty, encompassing rights to free medical care and gainful work. Before the economic and political exhaustion and unraveling of the communist system in the late 1980s, communist delivery of the material goods promised to the average citizen was substantial, though it never rivaled that of social democratic, capitalist nations.

Crisis and Reconsideration

Between 1973 and 1983 the long postwar economic expansion of the West and its high levels of consumer, entrepreneurial, and state economic confidence were severely shaken by events. In the early 1970s the system of fixed exchange rates that had prevailed since the late 1940s collapsed, undoing the ability of the massive U.S. economy (with its costly arsenal) to finance itself without risk to the value of the dollar and without increases in U.S. interest rates. The price of oil increased more than 300 percent, and the prices of wheat and other agricultural commodities doubled or tripled, driving up producer and consumer costs worldwide. Stagflation (simultaneous recession and inflation) handcuffed Keynesian policy instruments, such as governmental deficit spending to stimulate demand when productive resources were underutilized. Keynesian techniques could not arrange trade-offs between inflation and unemployment once the two had exchanged their age-old negative correlation (more inflation, less unemployment, and vice versa) for the positive one (more inflation, more unemployment) of the stagflationary period. Keynesian policy making came under assault, and policymakers' favorable predisposition toward spending eroded, cutting off the expansion of programs and budgets. Moreover, increased U.S. military spending triggered a huge explosion in the U.S. public debt, and the increase in the long-term interest rates needed to finance the debt raised international interest rates, placing a high rent on the operations of an already sluggish international economy.

The events that undercut Keynesian rationales and material resources for state expansion in the affluent democracies hit the developing nations with a massive transfer of international loans and then with demands for debt repayment. Thus the economic strength and state expansion of these nations suffered especially severely.

The communist countries (in particular, those dominated by the Soviet Union) were by no means insulated from these events. Indeed, the transfer of international loans and, later, the burden of their repayment posed special difficulty for them. Moreover, the accelerating U.S. military spending posed a direct competitive challenge to the Soviet-dominated countries that sorely strained their adaptive capacities. The breakup of Soviet domination and of the Soviet Union itself in the late 1980s and early 1990s meant that the fullest state retrenchment occurred outside the Western sphere of initial economic (stagflation-ary) and ideological (Keynesian) crisis. The command economies disintegrated, while in Western democracies the expansion of the welfare state merely slowed, and developing states mainly retrenched their economic and welfare functions and outlays.

Although such leading welfare states as Sweden and the Netherlands were also retrenching in the early 1990s, the interventionist state still found supporters. The public industrial policies of Japan and Germany were still admired. As of the early 1990s the direction of movement in the public-private mix was unclear for the affluent democracies taken as a whole.

In the developing world, a resurgence of democracy has been accompanied by an inexorable debt burden and the continuing spread of laissez-faire, anti-Keynesian, and anti-welfare ideas. Yet democracy typically enhanced state intervention in social security during the twentieth century, although preferences for a substantially market-oriented, public-private mix remained influential. The late twentieth-century debt crisis strengthened the control of the International Monetary Fund (IMF), a transnational bank with great power over international credit. It reinforced IMF calls for international economic openness and domestic "restructuring." This meant a decided tilt toward the free market (for example, lowered tariff barriers and private purchase of formerly nationalized firms). Nonetheless, the sum of the forces acting on the public-private mix remains difficult to tally. Whether or to what extent an overall reversal in trends toward increased state intervention has taken place is an open question.

A decisive reversal of modern trends toward increased state intervention can be clearly seen in the emergent market-oriented economies of East Central Europe. Even in those countries, however, it is impossible to predict what type of transformation of Western political economic precedents will carry the day.

See also Capitalism; Laissez-faire.

ALEXANDER M. HICKS

BIBLIOGRAPHY

Bunce, Valerie, and Alexander Hicks. "Capitalisms, Socialisms and Democracy." *Political Power and Social Theory* 6 (1987): 89–132.

Collier, David, and Richard E. Messick. "Prerequisites versus Diffusion: Testing Alternative Explanations of Social Security Adoption." *American Political Science Review* 69 (1975): 1299–1315.

Kolberg, Jon Eivind. *The Study of Welfare State Regimes.* Armonk, N.Y.: M. E. Sharpe, 1992.

Maddison, Angus. *Dynamic Forces in Capitalist Development: A Long-run Comparative View.* Oxford and New York: Oxford University Press, 1991.

Mann, Michael. *The Sources of Social Power: A History of Power from the Beginning to A.D. 1760.* Vol. 1. Cambridge and New York: Cambridge University Press, 1986.

Poggi, Gianfranco. *The State: Its Nature, Development, and Prospects.* Stanford, Calif.: Stanford University Press; Oxford: Polity, 1990.

Przworski, Adam. *Capitalism and Social Democracy.* Cambridge and New York: Cambridge University Press, 1985.

Scharpf, Fritz. *Crisis and Choice in European Social Democracy.* Ithaca, N.Y.: Cornell University Press, 1987.

Tilly, Charles, ed. *The Formation of Nation States in Western Europe.* Princeton: Princeton University Press, 1975.

Webber, Caroline, and Aaron Wildavsky. *A History of Taxation and Expenditures in the Western World.* New York: Simon and Schuster, 1986.

✦ Virtue, Civic

Civic virtue is the public spirit required of citizens if a republic is to survive and flourish. It requires a readiness to set the public good above one's private interests. In the classical republican tradition, virtue is the opposite of corruption. In recent republican thought public spirit is contrasted with the self-interested individualism taken to be characteristic of liberal societies.

The Classical Concept of Virtue

Reflections on civic virtue are at the heart of traditional republican thinking. In the ancient world, republics in which power was shared among the citizens were vulnerable to conquest from without and to civil war and tyranny from within. Their autonomy, insofar as they managed to remain independent and stable, was attributed largely to the solidarity and courage of the citizens, and particularly to the citizens' willingness to sacrifice their lives and private interests for the city. Sparta's warrior-citizens, often regarded as models of civic virtue, were formed by means of a harsh and intensive discipline designed to make them hardy, brave, and totally identified with their comrades. The long stability and military success of Sparta were widely attributed to this ethos.

Virtue in the classical context was the characteristic of a male citizen (Latin, *vir*), and its connotations are overwhelmingly military. It denotes the qualities that make good soldiers and good armies: courage, toughness, loyalty, and solidarity. It was strongly associated in the classical mind with simplicity of life (epitomized by the notoriously unsavory black broth eaten at Sparta's communal meals), and it was contrasted with the "corruption" induced by wealth. From Aristotle onward it was agreed that citizens needed some property (preferably in the form of land) if they were to have the leisure and independence to be virtuous citizens.

The point of economic activity, however, was to serve politics, rather than vice versa, and the ideal citizen possessed property without seeking or enjoying wealth. Where a modern observer might see a rise in the standard of living, ancient moralists saw luxury, which threatened civic virtue in a number of ways. For one thing, softer living made citizens less able to face the physical rigors of military campaigns. For another, it sowed dissension among citizens by increasing divisions between rich and poor and undermining justice. Above all, if citizens were attending to their private wealth and material possessions, their energies were diverted from the public good. An ideal example of the priorities befitting a virtuous citizen was provided by the Roman hero Cincinnatus, summoned from the plow in 458 B.C. to take charge as dictator in a military crisis. After leading the Romans to victory, he rode in triumph with the army but did not seek personal profit and went straight back to his frugal agricultural life.

Aristotle's claim that life as a citizen is necessary for human fulfillment may seem to imply that the welfare of the individual and that of the city are ultimately compatible. Republican moralists in the ancient world, however, more often assumed that the public good requires the sacrifice of private interests and attachments. Rome's early historians underlined this point with their stories of citizens whose heroic dedication to the republic had made Roman freedom and greatness possible, such as Lucius Junius Brutus, the founder of the republic, who executed his own sons for conspiring to restore the monarchy. Another example held up before the eyes of budding citizens was that of the Roman general Regulus, who was captured by the Carthaginians in 255 B.C. and sent to Rome bearing peace terms, under oath to return to execution in Carthage if the terms were rejected. Concentrating selflessly on the public interest, he persuaded the Senate to reject peace and returned to certain death in fulfillment of his oath.

Certainly no republican supposed that civic virtue came naturally. Virtuous citizens had to be molded by education and by the general ethos of the city. It followed that attitudes, habits, and the conduct of what a liberal might regard as private life were matters of political importance because laxity here might undermine the city's defenses. Classical republicanism had a strong puritanical streak that gave rise to laws controlling consumption and display. In their anxiety to preserve civic virtue, the censors of the Roman Republic prohibited women from wearing colored robes, limited the number of guests at banquets, and even controlled the details of menus. In the second century B.C. Cato the Elder acquired a reputation for virtue in part because of his rigor as a censor in taxing such items as jewels.

The conundrum faced by moralists of the later Roman Republic was (as the historian Livy explained) that the virtues that had made Rome great thereby undermined themselves. As a united band of tough, frugal, hardy soldiers the Romans had conquered much wealthier societies than theirs. Once left to enjoy their conquests in peace, however, they succumbed to the temptations of luxury and avarice and began to lose their military virtues and public spirit. When Rome yielded to imperial rule, the first-century writers Juvenal and Sallust attributed this submission to the effeminacy and self-centered avarice into which former citizens had sunk.

The classical concept of civic virtue was profoundly conservative, with a deeply pessimistic attitude toward time. Change tended to be equated with decay, and virtue was located in the past, in the days of the heroic founders of the republic. The efforts of those concerned with virtue were therefore directed toward preservation rather than toward improvement. One of the main reasons for Sparta's exalted reputation was that it had stayed the same and resisted corruption for an exceptionally long time.

The Renaissance and Enlightenment

From late antiquity until the Renaissance these classical views became overshadowed by a different concept of virtue. Although the Roman moralists continued to exert an influence, moral thinking was dominated by the Christian Church. Puritanism and ideals of self-sacrifice were common to both traditions, but Christianity redirected attention away from secular glory to individual salvation in the next world. When efforts were made during the Italian Renaissance to recover ancient civilization, including classical republicanism, Niccolò Machiavelli openly complained that Christianity was incompatible with civic virtue. His concept of *virtù* was from a Christian point of view an amoral resolution to confront fortune and to strive by all necessary means for glory in this world, instead of submitting humbly to the decrees of Providence. In his republican *Discourses on Livy*, Machiavelli contrasted Christianity with ancient Roman religion, which had been a civic religion wholly supportive of the state and its interests. Christianity, Machiavelli complained, glorified "humble and contemplative men," thereby offering no resistance to the wicked. The ancient Roman religion, by contrast, glorified victorious generals and engaged in bloody sacrifices that reinforced the ferocity of the soldiers.

As this example makes clear, the classical concept of civic virtue reaffirmed by Machiavelli in the early sixteenth century was incompatible not only with Christianity but also with the liberal values that began to emerge in Western Europe a little later. By the end of the seventeenth century educated Europeans had available to them not only the classical concept of freedom as the collective achievement of an armed band of virtuous citizens but also a new concept of freedom as the private possession of peaceful individuals living their own lives within the order established by a modern state. The challenge to militarist values included a new stress on happiness that legitimized material comfort and a new humanism that condemned violence and cruelty instead of regarding them as reassuring signs of military prowess.

As the commercial wealth of Western Europe grew rapidly in the eighteenth century, opinion was divided between those who hailed a new age of improvement and progress and the more classically minded who saw ominous similarities with the luxury and corruption that had destroyed republican Rome. These debates were particularly common in Britain and its American colonies because the parliamentary monarchy that had emerged from the constitutional struggles of the seventeenth century was widely interpreted (in language derived from classical sources through Machiavelli and James Harrington) as a kind of classical republic. If this interpretation was accurate, Britain's freedom must lie in the virtue of her citizen-soldiers, the freeholders of the shires, who were (in the guise of a civil militia) the proper defenders of the realm. From the republican point of view, threats to liberty could be seen just as clearly in the country's ever increasing commercial wealth as in the king's standing army and the systematic corruption of Parliament by the king's ministers. Britain's impending ruin was presaged by luxurious practices such as tea drinking and material comforts such as warm, draft-free houses. From a liberal point of view, by contrast, material wealth could be seen as evidence of progress.

Although it is possible in retrospect to discern a conflict between radically different systems of political values, most eighteenth-century political thinkers and actors oscillated uneasily between republican and liberal attitudes. For example, in his enormously influential *Spirit of the Laws* (1748), Montesquieu reiterated the importance of classical virtue in republics, but he also proclaimed that political liberty was to be found under the shelter of the balanced constitution of England, in spite of that country's commercial society and lack of ancient virtue. Among the thinkers of the Scottish Enlightenment, including Adam Smith, notions of the benefits of economic growth and of a natural development of human society from barbarism to civilization were worked out in an intellectual context still deeply suspicious of the moral and political implications of commercial activity. Bernard Mandeville's satirical poem, *The Fable of the Bees: or Private Vices, Public Benefits* (1714), which foreshadowed Smith's account of how the "invisible hand" of the free market transforms material self-interest into general welfare, depended for its effect on the lingering conviction that concern for wealth and material consumption were vices.

Rousseau and the Age of Revolution

In America the debates surrounding the Revolution and the adoption of the Constitution were complicated by the difficulty of adapting a discourse derived from the militaristic republics of antiquity to fit a modern commercial society. Classical echoes can be found in the Jeffersonian assumption that armed citizen-farmers leading frugal lives are the bastions of republican liberty as well as in more unexpected quarters. For example, Thomas Paine, in most respects a thoroughly modernist liberal, observed that commerce threatens patriotism and military valor, while John Adams remarked as a matter of course that in a republic "Virtue and Simplicity of Manners" are indispensable. The extent to which Antifederalist opposition to the Constitution can be understood in terms of classical republican values is a matter much disputed among historians.

The most influential exponent of the idea of civic virtue among eighteenth century political thinkers was Jean-Jacques Rousseau, in whose ambiguous writings classical themes underwent some interesting transformations. Rousseau was one of the chief progenitors of the modern concept of "positive liberty," according to which true freedom is enjoyed not by the freestanding individuals of liberal theory but by participants in civic life. Characteristically, Rousseau's thought contains two incompatible versions of this notion—one democratic, the other romantic and potentially fascist.

One of the strands in Rousseau's *Social Contract* (1762) is an ideal of participatory democracy, that is, popular sovereignty in the most literal and direct form, with lawmaking carried out in a face-to-face assembly of all the citizens of a small city-state. Civic virtue in this context consists in putting the general will one shares with one's fellow citizens above the private will for the satisfaction of one's selfish interests. Rousseau implies that such conduct is not only virtuous but also rational and satisfying. Modern sympathizers with classical republican thinking usually follow this democratic strand in Rousseau's thought. A different and more disquieting theme, however, takes up the classical emphasis on the importance of a republic's ethos. Building on Machiavelli's criticisms of Christianity, Rousseau argues that a republic needs a civil religion; he also maintains that it needs a lawgiver who will lick the citizens into shape as the legendary Lycurgus had formed the Spartans in the ninth century B.C.

Classical republican theory had always recognized the importance of socialization in molding citizens and inspiring them to virtue. Most thinkers had assumed that civic virtue does not come naturally but demands the suppression of natural human inclinations, from fear and love of pleasure to family loyalties. In a famous passage in *Emile*, his book on education (1762), Rousseau sharpened this point, contrasting education for humanity with education for citizenship and arguing that the latter demands complete loss of self and immersion in the life of the community. In stating this, Rousseau was doing more than reiterating classical clichés. For ancient republicans the point of self-abnegation on the battlefield was simply that without that kind of commitment a republic could not remain free. With Rousseau, however, loss of self in identification with an intense community became part of the romantic quest for wholeness in opposition to the fragmentation of modern life. In the subsequent thinking about civic virtue and the nature of citizenship, hard-headed analysis of the ethos necessary for the survival of free states has often been overlaid by romantic rejections of modern individualism and yearnings for community and wholeness.

Tocqueville and the Modern Age

Alexis de Tocqueville, pondering the nature and prospects of American democracy (in *Democracy in America*, 1835–1840), did not indulge in romantic nostalgia for ancient community. It seemed to him, however, that although freedom appeared to be firmly established in the United States, it could not be taken for granted in modern societies. Republican thinking, up to and including that of Rousseau, had always assumed that although a particular republic might be "democratic" in the sense that its citizens had equal political rights, citizenship itself was a privilege restricted to a small part of the population. The United States, by contrast, was not only an

exceptionally large republic but also an unprecedentedly inclusive one in which citizenship was diluted by extension. Tocqueville feared that the advance of democracy (by which he meant a society without hereditary ranks) would tend to give rise to "individualism," an atomization of society into a mass of separate and impotent individuals, each immersed in private concerns. By undermining public spirit, this fragmentation could make possible a new kind of despotism.

Tocqueville considered that in America this tendency was counterbalanced by the high rate of participation in political and voluntary organizations, which drew people out of their narrow private concerns and involved them in efforts to advance the welfare of the republic. He also observed that the strength of religion in America restrained its citizens from the worst excesses of selfish materialism. A century and a half later, with political participation down, religion weakened, consumption vastly increased, and the atomization of society proceeding apace, recent commentators have been less sanguine than Tocqueville and have drawn upon the republican tradition of thinking about civic virtue in criticizing the excesses of liberal individualism. Communitarian critics of liberalism tend to maintain that liberalism is incompatible with civic virtue.

If civic virtue is understood in the classical sense, with all its overtones of aggressive militarism, puritanical censorship of private life, and rigid hostility to change, any form of liberalism must be opposed to it. No modern republican, however, wishes to resurrect the tradition of civic virtue in its original inhumane, exclusively male, deeply illiberal form. Those who have recently borrowed from the tradition have tended to play down its puritanism and to emphasize the Aristotelian idea of fulfillment through participation in ruling and being ruled rather than the Spartan ideal of patriotic self-sacrifice. In response, defenders of liberalism have pointed out that many notable liberal thinkers, such as John Stuart Mill, enthusiastically supported political participation and public spirit while at the same time celebrating individual diversity.

One battleground for struggle between liberals and classically minded communitarians concerns education for citizenship. The republican tradition is antimaterialistic in two senses: it condemns material consumption, and it stresses the importance in politics of nonmaterial elements such as the ethos of the republic. If republics depend on the virtue of their citizens to maintain their freedom, common attitudes must be matters of public interest, and the moral formation of future citizens becomes particularly important. This concern conflicts with the recent liberal tendency, most famously expressed in John Rawls's *Theory of Justice* (1971), to negotiate the problems of modern pluralistic societies by claiming that citizens can be united in accepting principles of justice without sharing any substantive moral commitments at all.

One of the points at issue here is a question of historical sociology. Does the process of economic development naturally lead to free and democratic societies, or are free republics always rare and fragile exceptions in a world where tyranny is the norm? If the former is the case, more citizen participation and public spirit may be desirable, but neither is crucial; if the latter, civic virtue may be a matter of life and death for the republic. One of the first neorepublican thinkers, Hannah Arendt, was driven back to classical thinking by the experience of Nazi and Soviet totalitarianism, which she analyzed as subordination of human interests to material forces, made possible by a lack of public-spirited citizens prepared to take responsibility for defending freedom. Although she argued, like her successors, that political action is intrinsically satisfying, the ultimate point of active citizenship, for her as for Machiavelli and the ancients, was that without it freedom cannot last.

Since World War II attempts have been made in a great many states to establish republican and democratic institutions, in most cases without success. Although many complex reasons may be given for such failures, political scientists agree that one important problem is corruption in the sense of diversion of public funds to private purposes and that some level of public spirit is indeed a necessary condition for the flourishing and perhaps the survival of free states.

See also Aristotle; Classical Greece and Rome; Communitarianism; Liberalism; Machiavelli, Niccolò; Mill, John Stuart; Montesquieu; Democracy, Participatory; Popular sovereignty; Republicanism; Rousseau, Jean-Jacques; Theory, Ancient; Tocqueville, Alexis de.

MARGARET CANOVAN

BIBLIOGRAPHY

Arendt, Hannah. *The Human Condition*. Chicago: University of Chicago Press, 1958.

Aristotle. *The Politics*. Edited by Stephen Everson. Cambridge: Cambridge University Press, 1988.

Machiavelli, Niccolò. *The Discourses*. Edited by Bernard Crick. Harmondsworth: Penguin Books, 1970.

Montesquieu, Charles-Louis de Secondat, Baron de. *The Spirit of the Laws*. Edited by A. M. Cohler, B. C. Miller, and H. S. Stone. Cambridge: Cambridge University Press, 1989.

Oldfield, Adrian. *Citizenship and Community: Civic Republicanism and the Modern World*. London and New York: Routledge, 1990.

Pocock, J. G. A. *The Machiavellian Moment: Florentine Political Thought and the Atlantic Republican Tradition*. Princeton: Princeton University Press, 1975.

Rahe, Paul A. *Republics Ancient and Modern: Classical Republicanism and the American Revolution*. Chapel

Hill and London: University of North Carolina Press, 1992.

Rousseau, Jean-Jacques. *The Social Contract, with Geneva Manuscript and Political Economy.* Edited by R. D. Masters. New York: St. Martin's, 1978.

Sinopoli, Richard C. *The Foundations of American Citizenship: Liberalism, the Constitution, and Civic Virtue.* Oxford: Oxford University Press, 1992.

Tocqueville, Alexis de. *Democracy in America.* Translated by G. Lawrence. Edited by J. P. Mayer and M. Lerner. New York: Harper, 1966; London: Fontana, 1968.

✦ War and civil conflict

War and civil conflict have figured prominently in the history of democracy. Violent conflicts between states and between domestic groups have been causes of, reasons for, and consequences of democracy. However, war and civil conflict are qualitatively different phenomena. Their significance in the history of democracy has not been the same. Moreover, in the long, discontinuous history of democracy, from ancient Greece to the present day, the relationship between war and civil conflict on the one hand and democracy on the other has shifted.

Historically, states have been above all military organizations, organizations designed for war. Democracy refers to the distribution of power within a state. Inevitably, the form of war and its organization have influenced and have been affected by the pattern of internal political power and political rights.

Arms and Classical Democracy

In premodern times the control of territories and populations was the source of power and wealth. The competition for power and wealth was largely an armed zero-sum game, in which one state's victory was another's defeat. In this context the power of the people—that is, the extent of democracy—depended heavily on the distribution of arms and the mode of waging war.

The relatively broad political participation in classical Greece was based in large part on the infantry, pioneered by Sparta and sustained by relatively affluent propertied farmers. The wider Athenian democracy rested militarily on a navy in addition to the infantry. The Athenian navy, which was the main force of the empire, was staffed by the poorer elements of the citizenry.

The democracy of the Nordic Viking age—most typically in its kingless Icelandic form with a national annual *Althing* (parliament) of adult, male freehold farmers, but common to all Viking-ruled territories—was based on an egalitarian distribution of the means of violence: the sword and the spear. The participants in Nordic assemblies were usually armed, and the clashing of weapons was a frequent means of expressing opinion.

Ancient Greek and, in particular, Athenian warfare depended on the collective contribution of the citizenry. The ancient Nordic organization of violence, on the other hand, was built on individual freeborn men and their personal arms. The Nordic system was prone to armed civil conflict and feuding, and eventually led to the breakdown of Icelandic democracy in the thirteenth century. In Athens, civil strife and conflict generally took nonarmed forms.

Because European armies—in contrast to military organizations in China and other Asian empires—generally tended to be self-equipped, the soldiers, whether farmers or knights, and their commanders had a certain autonomy with regard to the central ruler. Cities usually developed as combinations of fortresses and marketplaces. The unique feature of the European city was its legal and political autonomy from the local ruler. This trait derived largely from the military organization of the West, together with the relative weakness of kinship ties, which also favored territorially based self-organization. This classical tradition, which links a widespread distribution of property, arms, and political participation, has been carried into modernity in some of the former British colonies, notably the United States and Australia.

Gradually, the people in arms of the ancient democracies were replaced by imperial armies, imported mercenaries, and, for a time in medieval Europe, wealthy, mounted knights. Patriarchal democracies across Europe gave way to monarchical empires, to feudalism, and to absolutist rule. Among the old European democracies, Switzerland has been the only enduring exception to the pattern, keeping both its militia and its autonomous assemblies while exporting formidable soldiers of fortune to France, Italy, and other places.

External War and Modern Democracy

The modern concept of the nation provides a crucial link between external war and modern democracy. Broadly defined, a nation is a population of a territory, actual or desired, defining itself as a political community. Democracy is a political system in which political power within the territory is vested in the whole adult population of the territory. External wars in a system of nations become wars of nations and of whole populations. The modern era has, therefore, returned to the classical notion of democratic peoples in arms, a tendency recently reversed with the substitution of professionals for conscripts.

In premodern times a nation's only means of increasing its power was through expansion—the acquisition of additional territory and populations. That fact has given way in modern times to the improvement of a nation's existing territory, including its resources and infrastructure, and of its existing population, through education and motivation. Conquest is no longer the major road to power and wealth, but in the event of war the quality of the population matters significantly.

The first major steps toward a genuinely national army were taken during the French Revolution (1789–1791), when France promulgated a constitution guaranteeing universal male suffrage and an army based on national mass mobilization. Neither succeeded very well by later standards. Ninety percent of eligible voters abstained from the elections of 1792. Because of the war, the civil terror, and the subsequent coup d'état against Maximilien Robespierre, the virtual dictator, in July 1794, the June 1793 constitution was never applied. The revolution's call to arms got a massive response, and revolutionary-nationalist reforms brought about a formidable war machine, but the principle of voluntary participation was not upheld in practice, nor was universal military service instituted. (Universal military service was established in France only in 1872.)

For all its limitations the French Revolution witnessed the first connection between popular rights and modern warfare. Far more than the original revolutionary message of freedom, equality, and fraternity, it was the military success of a politically motivated mass army, the consciousness of the nation, and the realization of the dependence of that nation on armed power that forged the new link between war and democracy. Nations emerged in the wake of the French Revolution; wars were perceived as deciding the fate of nations, not only of kings; and victory in war seemed to be decided by the strength of nations. The health and the living standards of the national population came to be perceived as important resources for war.

National warfare did not supplant or override civil class conflict over the issue of democracy. The dissolution of feudalism—which in Europe was also largely an effect, direct or indirect, of the French Revolution—and the ascendancy of capitalism gave rise to large numbers of independent farmers and of free workers, with increased capacities for organizing themselves and for demanding political rights. War—preparation for it, waging it, and the outcome of it—intervened, often decisively, between the forces for and against democracy.

War has brought many democracies into being. The two world wars of the twentieth century (1914–1918 and 1939–1945) were critical to the democratization of the world's most socioeconomically developed nations. The actual conduct of war, however, is usually detrimental to democracy and to popular political rights. War calls for the discipline of command and the conformity of unquestioned loyalty. It fosters suspicion, surveillance, incarceration, and deportation. But war has been conducive to democracy or to an extension of popular political rights in two major ways.

First, the promise of democracy or of widened citizens' rights can be a means to mobilize for war and to smooth over civil conflict during wartime mobilization. This course could be called "democratization by national mobilization." Second, democracy can emerge as a consequence of the military defeat of an authoritarian regime. This might be called "democratization by defeat."

Means and Effects of War Mobilization

Among the most clear-cut Western examples of democratization by national mobilization were the Italian franchise reform of 1912, which was instituted to legitimate Italy's colonial war in Libya, and the Canadian War Times Election Act of 1917, which was intended to pave the way for that country's entry into World War I. Granting the right to vote was intended to bring the people closer to the state and its war policy. In the Canadian case, it was also intended to weaken the resistance to conscription.

Democratization can also be used as a stratagem during war. In 1866 the German nationalist chancellor Otto von Bismarck of Prussia proposed equal and universal male suffrage for a new constitution of the German Confederation in a calculated move to undercut support for Austria. The ploy contributed to Prussian victory in the Austro-Prussian War in the battle of Königgrätz. After another successful Prussian war, this one against France in 1870–1871, the German Reich was proclaimed under a Prussian emperor. The Reich had universal male suffrage and a legislature with severely limited powers.

In a number of non-Western states that were threatened but never colonized by European and North American powers, political rights were granted to the populations by local rulers as means of national mobilization in preparation for defensive war. The menace and superior strength of the Western powers was acknowledged, and their institutions of popular participation were associated with this strength. Such institutions were therefore imported as a means to mobilize for resistance.

The first example of such democratization under threat of colonization was the Tanzimat ("reorganization") reforms of the Ottoman Empire in 1840. The 1881 Imperial Rescript of Meiji Japan, issued under similar circumstances, promised (and delivered in 1889) a constitution with significant popular rights, although it fell short of establishing democracy. In 1908 the Chinese imperial court announced a similar, gradual introduction of parliamentary government, which was begun in 1909 but was cut short by the republican revolution in 1911 and the subsequent civil conflict.

Examples of the democratic effects of consensual wartime mobilization include the Danish conservatives' acceptance of democracy in 1915, the institution of universal male suffrage in the Netherlands and Belgium in 1917–1918, the enlarged suffrage of the British Reform Act of 1918, the institution of female suffrage in the United States in 1920, and its acceptance in Belgium, France, and Italy in 1944–1946.

Democratization by Defeat

The first modern democracy to arise from a nondemocratic regime's defeat in an external war was France after 1871. Defeat in the Franco-Prussian War finished off the French Second Empire, although the issue of universal male suffrage was left until the late 1870s.

The end of World War I led to a number of new democratic states, which broke off from the defeated empires, and to the temporary democratization of the defeated states themselves—Austria and Germany. The most renowned manifestation of this democratization by defeat was the Weimar constitution of Germany, written by the distinguished scholar-politician Hugo Preuss, who before the war was a constitutional monarchist and not a democrat.

Defeat can affect democratization indirectly as well. The Swedish right wing, for example, was adamantly opposed to parliamentary democracy in the early part of the twentieth century, and its resistance had been strengthened by the rising might of the German Reich. After the Reich's defeat and fall in 1918, however, a constitutional transition to democracy became possible in Sweden.

The democratic outcomes of World War I were contested by antidemocratic forces, often successfully for a while. A number of new dictatorships arose in southern and central Europe. Yet another wave of democratization by defeat took place after World War II, when democracy returned to Austria, Finland, and Germany and, for the first time, prevailed in Italy and Japan. In Germany and, particularly, in Japan, the victorious Allied army was the crucial midwife of democratization.

Defeat in external war has been important in later processes of democratization as well. Examples include Pakistan in 1971, after the loss of East Pakistan, which became Bangladesh; Greece in 1974, after its disastrous attempt to capture Cyprus in the face of an acute Turkish threat; Portugal in the same year, after protracted losses in colonial wars; and Argentina in 1982, after its catastrophic attempt to wrest the Falklands/Malvinas Islands from the British.

The Legacy of Civil Wars

Whereas external wars have had an overall positive effect on modern democratization, the legacy of civil wars has generally been negative. It is true that ancient Athenian democracy was established in 508 B.C. after a brief civil war and lasted for a century, until it was overthrown by a short-lived oligarchy in 411 B.C. It would seem that the outcome of modern civil wars, however, has been restrictive in terms of citizens' rights, regardless of which side has won. A civil war implies an enemy within, with which a reconciliation is very difficult.

The enemy in a civil war is typically regarded as a traitor and is likely to be treated as such after its defeat. The outcome of the American Civil War (1861–1865) is a good example. In spite of President Abraham Lincoln's efforts at national reconciliation, the effective postwar alternatives were either reconciliation with the Southern whites at the expense of the blacks or emancipation of the blacks at the expense of the white racists. In any case, full democracy did not ensue from the American Civil War.

In the postrevolutionary civil war in Russia (1917–1921), neither side stood for democracy—neither the Bolsheviks nor their counterrevolutionary enemies, the so-called Whites. The effect of the civil war was a general devastation of the country and a brutalization of all the forces involved. Similarly, in the 1940s the protracted civil war in China between the Communists and the Nationalists (Kuomintang) strengthened authoritarian tendencies on both sides and led to nondemocratic regimes in Nationalist-ruled Taiwan and in Communist-ruled mainland China.

In the Finnish civil war of 1918, both communists and noncommunists were originally open to democratic ideas. But the German-aided victory of the noncommunists ushered in severe repression. Moreover, there is no indication that the effect on elementary human rights would have been different with another outcome.

The Spanish civil war (1936–1939) was won by the anti-democratic forces of Gen. Francisco Franco, and almost three decades of dictatorship ensued. A victory by the republican forces would most probably have led to democracy in Spain much earlier, but hardly without an initial wave of repression.

Civil Conflict: Property and Poverty

The socioeconomic issues involved in democracy were very clear to the ancient Greeks 2,500 years ago. Democracy was from the very beginning an assertion of the rights of the common people against the rich and against the aristocracy. Class conflict is a thread running throughout the history of democracy: ancient, medieval, and modern. Demands for democracy have been raised by the middle classes, especially by those strong and self-confident enough to demand their rights—that is, small farmers, artisans, skilled workers, and industrial workers.

In modern times the labor movement has been the most consistent pro-democratic force across nations. The modern labor movement began in the 1830s with the British Chartists, supporters of the "People's Charter," which demanded universal male suffrage, use of the secret ballot, elimination of property qualifications for members of Parliament, and other reforms. The movement was carried on by the international organization

of Social Democratic labor parties and trade unions, which comprised the Second International of 1889–1914.

Fear of democracy, or more precisely fear of the nonpropertied mass of the population, is a recurrent theme in political theory, which until the end of the nineteenth century was written by people from or associated with the privileged classes. Classical Athenian democracy had in fact not involved any redistribution of land or other property, but Greek philosophers remained hostile to democracy nonetheless. The Founders of the United States were also fearful of democracy, but they retained a republican commitment to accountability to a broad citizenry.

The most principled battles for and against democracy were fought in Europe. The battles were developed in the aftermath of the English civil war in the mid-seventeenth century but gathered momentum only with the French Revolution. The issue of popular political rights took on a new character after Napoleon III showed, in the 1850s, that it was possible to run a propertied empire with universal male suffrage. Until the 1888 presidential election in the United States, the largest electorate in world history was that of the French Second Empire. Prime Minister Benjamin Disraeli in England and Bismarck in Prussia soon learned as well that universal suffrage did not mean an abdication of the prerogatives of the executive and of the aristocracy. The dynamics and outcomes of war, therefore, had great importance for the achievement of democracy.

The Legitimacy of Debate and Channeling Conflict

The legitimacy of conflict and debate within democracy was questioned for a long time. In classical Greece, *stasis* (meaning "faction," "discord," "dissent," or "sedition") was held to be the great evil to which democracies were prone. Faction was also singled out for severe criticism in the *Federalist*, written by James Madison, Alexander Hamilton, and John Jay in support of ratification of the U.S. Constitution. One of the first principled defenders of parties was the English Whig Edmund Burke, in 1770, but party conflict and party government became legitimate only in the nineteenth century, and then only in some countries. The replacement of partisan conflict—whether based on ideology, class differences, or ethnic cleavages—by national unity has been a recurrent theme of modern dictatorial regimes.

The extent to which democracy presupposes or promotes certain forms of social conflict is still open to debate. Elitist theories of modern democracy see democracy as primarily an institution for selecting political leaders by competition. In this view a certain insulation of the polity from the population and from society's strife is necessary if elites are not to become "overloaded" by popular demands. In pluralist conceptions of democracy the polity is the arena of conflict between a large number of dispersed and competing interests of various sorts. Democracy is in danger, the purveyors of pluralist theory argue, when interests coalesce and cumulate into polarized social blocs.

Other theories of democracy and civil conflict have started from a perception that modern democracies often contain socioeconomic and sociocultural interests that coalesce in stable, even polarized, constellations. To account for the compatibility of democracy and such patterns of social conflict, two theories have evolved: consociationalism, which is based on cooperation between the elites representing the major segments of a divided population, and corporatism, which is based on an institutionalized regulation of socioeconomic conflict by interest associations. The importance of negotiations and transactions between different interests and forces has also been stressed in studies of democratization and democratic consolidation.

Democracy can affect the forms of civil conflict. Modern democracy provides outlets for civil conflict in the form of elections for political office. Thereby, conflicts may be channeled into institutionalized patterns. Recurrent elections with uncertain outcomes tend to reduce the pain of defeat and to restrain the enjoyment of the fruits of victory in conflict.

Competitive elections have also proved to be compatible with persistent violence and social oppression. In such situations, certain parts of society are sealed off from the democratic process. This oppression is most likely to be directed against impoverished ethnic-minority groups and those in outlying parts of the state who contest central authority. The worst example of this kind of persistent and violent mass repression coexisting with formally democratic central institutions is probably Guatemala, since the military coup of 1954. The combination of repression with formal democracy has been widespread in the developing world generally as well as in such places as Sicily and the Kurdish areas of southeastern Turkey.

War and Peace

The modern developmental paths to power and wealth, which by and large coincided with democratization, have tended to diminish the frequency of wars. There is little evidence, however, that democracy must be peaceful. Many wars, notably World War I, have been popular, at least at the outset.

Democratic great powers seem to be no less inclined to armed intervention in other countries than nondemocratic ones, though the reasons may differ. After World War II the Soviet Union intervened militarily four times in other countries: in East Germany in 1953, in Hungary in 1956, in

Czechoslovakia in 1968, and in Afghanistan in 1979. The United States intervened directly five times in the same period: in Korea, Vietnam, Grenada, Panama, and Iraq. After the collapse of the Soviet Union in 1991, the United States intervened militarily in a sixth country—Somalia—not to mention conducting covert war operations elsewhere. France fought wars in Vietnam, Madagascar, Algeria, Egypt, and Chad.

It appears that there is no straightforward relationship between peace and democracy but that universal socioeconomic developments promote both peace and democracy. Military dictatorships and military coups are related more to domestic situations and to weaknesses of internal civil society than to external war. The long series of military putsches and regimes characterizing some Latin American countries, such as Bolivia and Haiti, are being repeated in many African countries. They are manifestations of unbuilt nations, of populations never fully nationally mobilized for war or for any other purpose.

The two world wars demonstrated that democracies can wage war very well, even protracted wars in which they suffer initial defeats. But the French war in Algeria and the American war in Vietnam also showed the possible strength of domestic antiwar opposition and the sensitivity of conscripted armies to that opposition. The current tendency toward professional armies, protected and backed by immense technological power, renders the leaders and commanders of democratic states less dependent on national mobilization, and even on popular legitimacy, than they have been in the past. On the other hand, television has made the violence of war more visible. A new relationship between war and democracy is just beginning.

See also Burke, Edmund; Classical Greece and Rome.

GÖRAN THERBORN

BIBLIOGRAPHY

Eckstein, Harry, ed. *Internal War: Problems and Approaches.* Glencoe, Ill.: Free Press, 1963.

Finer, S. E. *The Man on Horseback: The Role of the Military in Politics.* Harmondsworth, England: Penguin Books, 1976.

Finley, M. I. *Democracy Ancient and Modern.* Rev. ed. New Brunswick, N.J.: Rutgers University Press, 1985.

Hintze, Otto. "Military Organization and State Organization." In *The Historical Essays of Otto Hintze,* edited by Felix Gilbert. New York: Oxford University Press, 1975.

Huntington, Samuel P. *The Third Wave.* Norman, Okla., and London: University of Oklahoma Press, 1991.

Líndal, S. "Early Democratic Traditions in the Nordic Countries." In *Nordic Democracy,* edited by Erik Allardt et al. Copenhagen: Det Danske Selskab, 1981.

Therborn, Göran. "The Right to Vote and the Four Routes to/through Modernity." In *State Theory and State History,* edited by Rolf Torstendahl. London and Newbury Park, Calif.: Sage Publications, 1992.

———. "The Rule of Capital and the Rise of Democracy." *New Left Review* 103 (May–June 1977): 3–41.

Tilly, Charles. *Coercion, Capital, and European States.* Rev. ed. Cambridge, Mass., and Oxford: Blackwell, 1992.

Index